CW00740060

The Modern Philosophical Revolution

The Luminosity of Existence

The Modern Philosophical Revolution breaks new ground by demonstrating the continuity of European philosophy from Kant to Derrida. Much of the literature on European philosophy has emphasized the breaks that have occurred in the course of two centuries of thinking. But as David Walsh argues, such a reading overlooks the extent to which Kant, Hegel, and Schelling were already engaged in the turn toward existence as the only viable mode of philosophizing. While many similar studies summarize individual thinkers, this book provides a framework for understanding the relationships between them. Walsh thus dispels much of the confusion that assails readers when they are only exposed to the bewildering range of positions taken by the philosophers he examines. His book serves as an indispensable guide to a philosophical tradition that continues to resonate in the postmodern world.

David Walsh is professor of politics at The Catholic University of America. The editor of three volumes of *The Collected Works of Eric Voegelin,* he has published numerous articles in political science and philosophy journals, as well as essays in anthologies. This is the third volume in a trilogy concerning the modern world that includes *After Ideology: Recovering the Spiritual Foundations of Freedom* and *The Growth of the Liberal Soul.*

The Modern Philosophical Revolution

The Luminosity of Existence

DAVID WALSH

The Catholic University of America

CAMBRIDGE UNIVERSITY PRESS

CAMBRIDGE UNIVERSITY PRESS

Cambridge, New York, Melbourne, Madrid, Cape Town, Singapore, São Paulo, Delhi

Cambridge University Press

32 Avenue of the Americas, New York, NY 10013-2473, USA

www.cambridge.org

Information on this title: www.cambridge.org/9780521727631

First published 2008

Printed in the United States of America

A catalog record for this publication is available from the British Library.

Library of Congress Cataloging in Publication Data

Walsh, David, 1950–
The modern philosophical revolution : the luminosity of existence / David Walsh.
p. cm.
Includes bibliographical references and index.
ISBN 978-0-521-89895-9 (hardback) – ISBN 978-0-521-72763-1 (pbk.)
1. Philosophy, Modern – History.   I. Title.
B791.W25   2008
190 – dc22   2007051565

ISBN   978-0-521-89895-9 hardback
ISBN   978-0-521-72763-1 paperback

To Brendan, Emma, David, and Talia,
as well as Austyn and Tyler

Contents

Preface

Contemporary literary theory has induced enough skepticism about the notion of a preface that one is inclined to abandon the attempt to write one. Yet the urge to communicate prevails over inevitable reservations. If anything has been learned, it is perhaps that all books are in the manner of a preface, an insight that Kierkegaard alone carried through in a book composed wholly of prefaces. One remains always in the mode of a pre-face, wanting to say what must be said before one faces the reader but never actually managing to say it. Indeed, the entire book is an ample demonstration of that failure, for if communication were as simple as saying what is on our minds, there would hardly arise the need to elaborate our thought in books. In that sense the operative assumption of all book writing is that the task can never reach its end. The book goes on, and all that is produced is merely a preface to what remains to come. Books, too, partake of the "between" character of existence, and although we impose a limit on them, they immediately overflow the boundaries in every direction. We are back in the end at the acknowledgment that we have not reached the end. We have only a preface, which must be offered in the knowledge that we have fortunately not been able to say what we sought to say. The saying can go on.

But it can also go backward, and that is the main justification for beginning with a preface. This is especially the case with a volume that is offered as the third in a series hitherto unannounced. A retrospective identification of the unity of a work has at least the merit of permitting inspection of its claim without delay. Readers can, with the author, judge the extent to which unity has or has not been achieved. No attempt has been made to prejudge the outcome by imposing even the constancy of volume numbering in advance. Yet there has been a consciousness of the unity of subject matter from the start. *The Modern Philosophical*

Revolution is the final volume of a trilogy that includes *After Ideology* and *The Growth of the Liberal Soul*. The goal of the latter two books was to deal comprehensively with the character of the modern world in which we find ourselves. The problem of "modernity," of that world that remains a question to itself, was the guiding thread. But in contrast to the intention of much of the literature that addresses the "crisis of modernity," the purpose was to avoid being captivated by the most captivating elements. The idea was to understand our world as profoundly as possible, recognizing that it is capable of erupting into orgiastic homicide just as it is capable of maintaining civilized societies of impressive durability. We live in a complicated historical epoch. There is no way to do justice to the modern world by selectively focusing on particular features of it. Only an approach that enables us to dwell with the contradictions, to wait for their inner vitality to reveal itself, holds any promise of enlarging the understanding of who we are. It is that aspiration to undertake a fair and capacious reading of the world in which we live that is the main attribute, if not the achievement, of the volumes here presented by their culminating member. They have been guided by an approach to modernity that has aimed at weighing truly and truly weighing its bewildering range of manifestations.

Even the formulation of the project as a study of modernity is only now reticently broached because it suggests that an entry into the modern world can be found outside of it. The guiding intuition of *After Ideology*, a book that was initially named "Ascent from the Depths," was that the truth of the modern world could be pronounced only from within it. Only those individuals who had confronted its most harrowing manifestations and found at that point the meaning of existence could speak with the requisite moral authority. That is why *After Ideology* is a study of the catharsis evoked by the totalitarian crisis. It is not a study of totalitarianism, a genre of writing whose objectivity of tone often masks the very abyss of subjectivity that made totalitarianism possible. As a spiritual deformation, there can be no account of totalitarianism that absents itself from the struggle against it. Perfunctory condemnation is not adequate to the task of contemplating the possibility of evil that lay within the heart of modern civilization. Nothing less was required than a confrontation with the manner in which the very meaning of philosophy and Christianity could yield such distortion. But the struggle for understanding was worth it. The result was an understanding not only of the possibility of evil, but also of the force of goodness capable of overcoming it. If the ideological madness of the twentieth century was the fruit of the misapplication of philosophy and Christianity, only their true application could assuage the longing that had been so sadly misdirected. *After Ideology* was therefore a study of the innermost truth of the modern world that emerges only in the moment of its calamitous contemplation of the abyss. Far from being merely "values" or "ideas," good and evil were discovered as the imprescriptible boundaries of our existence.

That insight into the priority of existence over all formulations of it became the thread for exploring the impressive achievement of political order that also characterizes our world. Totalitarianism did not simply disappear, nor was it demolished by the heroic witness of individuals opposing it. Totalitarianism was defeated militarily and politically. That meant that there were resources of spiritual strength that were sufficient to the task of resisting evil, appearances to the contrary notwithstanding. Indeed, it has remained a puzzle even to the liberal democratic societies themselves as to how they mounted such formidable efforts. The whole thrust of liberal democracy had long seemed to privilege the realm of private satisfactions over any demand of civic virtue. It was in order to address this mystery of inexplicable success that *The Growth of the Liberal Soul* examined both the historical sources and the contemporary articulations of the liberal political tradition. It found that nothing in the arguments adduced could adequately account for the durability evinced by liberal polities. Nor were the achievements simply attributable to the spiritual capital accumulated throughout Western history. That explanation merely begged the question of how such capital functioned in the present. What needed to be explained was how the seemingly fragmentary invocations of liberal principles, of natural and human rights, sustained an enduring consensus in the absence of any sustaining whole. The answer lay in liberal political practice, which recurrently called forth an actualization of the virtues indispensable to sustaining it. By relying on a maximum of individual freedom, a way had been found to promote a freedom that was more than individual. This is why, despite all appearances, liberal polities have proved to be the most formidable powers on the world scene. To a remarkable degree they rely far less than any other regime on the necessity of coercion. The abbreviated language of rights, it turns out, contained within it the possibility of the growth of the soul by which responsibilities are eventually served. A surface incoherence conceals an inward coherence that is nowhere revealed except through existence itself.

Now *The Modern Philosophical Revolution* examines the philosophical logic of the prioritizing of existence that has been the implicitly unfolding direction of the modern world. The subtitle, *The Luminosity of Existence*, is intended to suggest the distinctive character of the shift. Philosophy is the way in which we become self-conscious. It is the language by which an age can, if at all, articulate what it is to itself. The growth of science and technology and of the global moral and political language of rights are two manifestations of the modern spirit. But it is arguable that the philosophical revolution that prioritizes existence is a third achievement that may eventually be seen to be as momentous as the other two. While the philosophical shift may be the last to come into focus, it is the one that enables us to understand the viability of both science and rights. How is it possible for science to resist the dehumanizing implications of reductionism and instrumentalization? How is a universal language of rights to avoid a collapse into incoherence in the absence of any overarching intellectual framework? In each case the crucial insight is that the thinker and practitioner always escape the products of thought and action. We no more live in a world of instrumentalized rationality than we live in a world of individualized chaos. Our lives are spent within the eschatological openness that is the indefinable mystery of the personal. What makes it possible for us to build cooperatively the world that is sustained by just such efforts is that we are not simply entities within that world. Over and above all that is done in history is the singular person that transcends it all. That insight is not by any means new, for it is present at the very inception of philosophy and Christianity. But its formulation within a language of appropriate transparence has been the achievement of the modern philosophical revolution.

This recognition of the uniqueness of modern philosophy became a major discovery as I worked on the present volume. Any project that extends over twenty years marks a learning curve for the author who begins with vague intuitions of the material into which his investigation must plunge. So just as *The Growth of the Liberal Soul* entailed a revision of the presentment of liberalism that had tangentially surfaced in *After Ideology*, the guiding assumption concerning the modern philosophical context throughout both volumes had also to undergo significant modification. When sustained attention is directed toward a body of thought, it turns out to be different from its peripheral apprehension. Liberal political thought on closer examination emerged as far more than an unstable compromise tilted toward a totalitarian collapse. Not only had liberal polities historically demonstrated their staying power, but their theoretical inconclusiveness evidenced the same irrepressible vitality. Now it is the larger philosophical tradition defining the modern world that turns out to bear a very different aspect than at first supposed, for while there had always been a willingness to concede significant advances in highlighting the importance of subjectivity, the modern philosophical achievement had been viewed in largely negative terms. At best philosophy had failed to find the means of countering the ideological madness; at worst it had been complicit in the very decline into irrationality it was powerless to overcome. The crisis of nihilism so traumatically announced by Nietzsche seemed to coincide with the fate of philosophy itself. Looking back, it seemed as though the course had already been set in the Kantian removal of the possibility of metaphysics, a vacuum that could only unfold into the endlessly proliferating incoherence synonymous with the very term "postmodern." It was no wonder that many looked for a fresh beginning before the fatal modern misstep had taken place, or simply retreated into the self-imposed boundaries within which the search for analytic coherence might be pursued.

The Modern Philosophical Revolution proposes a distinctly different narrative. Based on a conscientious rereading of eight major figures, from Kant to Derrida, it argues that there is a remarkably consistent unfolding within this philosophical development. Studies of individual figures or periods within this time frame have often gone a considerable distance in dispelling the fog of conventional misjudgments. But the achievements as a whole have not come into focus; indeed, the era of philosophy from Kant to the present has hardly been conceived of as a whole, because we have lacked an overarching interpretative hypothesis. That is what the present volume seeks to provide. It suggests that philosophy, beginning with Kant, has explicitly shifted from an account of entities and concepts to an existential meditation on the horizon within which it finds itself. So while metaphysics in the propositional sense may have become defunct, it is not by any means the case that our orientation within metaphysical openness has disappeared. The death of metaphysics in thought has meant the return of metaphysics in life. God, immortality, and freedom, as well as the unsurpassable exigency of goodness in its unending struggle with evil, not only remain real but have acquired an existential force that is all the more powerful for our inability to contain them within discursive limits. No surprise is prompted by the return of religion or the echoes of Greek philosophy in contemporary thought. But if we are to make sense of these strange reverberations in a context that has understood itself apart from all theological and metaphysical reference, we must be prepared to understand why the transcendent can surface only within this profoundly mysterious mode. It is not that we in the modern world have lost faith, but that philosophy has come to understand the meaning of faith in a very different way.

Now whether that way of faith is continuous with the tradition of faith that has descended to us is for the reader to judge. All that the present study can offer is a way of reading the development of modern philosophy as an opening to the possibility of faith. Of course, it is more than the opening of sheer possibility that Kant announced. It is more like the practice of faith that his own philosophical odyssey evidenced, even while he sought to assimilate his project to the authority of science. A revolutionary shift is, in other words, not always fully visible even to those who carry it out. So it is by no means surprising that it should remain invisible to those in whose midst it occurs. Only in looking backward do the contours begin to emerge, and then we realize that a revolution has occurred when, as the term suggests, everything has changed and yet nothing has changed. We are back where we started. If that realization occurs, the quest of modern philosophy will have been vindicated, for not only will its convergence with rational and revelatory tradition have been demonstrated, but the necessity for its departure from the traditional modes of such discourse will also have been recognized. A guiding intuition can be confirmed only through the intuition toward which it guides. But there may be no harm in stating it forthrightly at the beginning. It is that the modern philosophical revolution has done no more than bring to light what has all along been the source of the very tradition against which it sought to distinguish itself. The practice of faith has ever and always been the only available source of faith. Now philosophy has found the means of conceding what had hitherto only been said silently. The achievement seems slight, but it is the slightness that clarifies more than we thought.

The debt of gratitude an author incurs can never be fully discharged, and certainly not in the customary acknowledgment of it. But this is all the more reason for undertaking the attempt. In the order of material assistance, I am deeply grateful for the support provided by a number of grants from the Earhart Foundation, as well as a sabbatical leave from Catholic University of America. For friendship and conversation over the years on the themes of this volume, I thank Brendan Purcell, Joe McCarroll, Cyril O'Regan, Steve Schneck, and Claes Ryn. It has been a pleasure to work with Beatrice Rehl of Cambridge University Press, and I am grateful for her supportive encouragement at every phase of the project. The external readers selected by the Press were all that one could hope for in terms of an insightful and helpful review. In addition, I much appreciate the dedicated professionalism of Janis Bolster, the production editor, and Mary Racine, the copy editor. As always, I thank my wife, Gail, for her constant support and share with her the distinct joy of dedicating this volume to our grandchildren.

Introduction

The dominant force of the modern world is instrumental reason. This is what dictates the flow of capital within an ever more integrated global economy, what compels our submission to the demands of the computerized manipulation of data, and what subjects us to the dehumanizing possibilities looming over the biotechnology horizon. The problem of modernity becomes conscious in the realization of modernity as a problem. We sense a fatal entrapment from which all avenues of escape have been foreclosed. Neither technology nor its benefits can be surrendered. We can no more live without electricity than we can live without water, as periodic breakdowns vividly remind us. But the costs of our access to electrical energy are measured not just by our monthly utility bills. They are also purchased by the dependence on which our independence has been built. Our putative mastery of light and heat and power is purchased at the cost of our entanglement in the vast network of grids by which we are held fast. Power and powerlessness seem coeval moments.

Normally the irony passes without remark. It is only when the realization of our predicament is propelled into consciousness that the contradiction becomes explicit. Then we cast a glance over the whole development in which we have become entangled and bemoan the loss of our freedom. We see that it has been an ever more comprehensive project of liberation that has paradoxically led to our ever greater confinement. Our subordination to the tools of our domination becomes transparent. But in that realization we simultaneously transcend the fatality of our situation. We can step outside of who we are and ensure that we are never just the sum of our constituents. The failure of our mechanical schemes of perfection gives way to a wry satisfaction. Like the prankster, the human spirit refuses to be captured by the rationality it has imposed on itself. It is this mood of detachment that ensures that the levels of ironic self-observation can finally not be fathomed. We are unlike the machines we have built because we are capable of delighting in their failure. The bounded rationality of the "iron cage" is continuously surpassed by the boundless rationality of the human spirit.

This is why a technological society is never simply what it appears to be. Its pervasive instrumentalization is haunted by the awareness of its noninstrumental source. Technological society becomes a problem to itself. All around us we see evidence of the refusal to submit to the demands of rigorous efficiency. Nostalgia for the old, monuments of spiritual aspiration, the worldwide revival of ancient religious forms, the power of orgiastic political movements of destruction, and the protest impulse that has driven artistic expression for more than a century all testify to the profound ambivalence with which the success of instrumental rationality has been greeted. The incoherence of the attitude is perhaps best captured by its defining aspiration that we rid ourselves of the dehumanizing consequences of a technological society while retaining all of its benefits. Fundamentalists with their technical expertise and their spiritual ignorance best embody this lethal conjunction. But it would be a mistake to regard them as unique. The underlying attitude is pervasive. It can be countered only by a direct confrontation of the challenge posed by the instrumentalization of reason in the modern world. Ghosts may spook, but they cannot illuminate our technological problematic. Only reason can grapple with the self-imposed limitation of reason. Instrumental rationality is primarily a challenge for philosophical reflection, and its engagement has given rise to the formidable modern philosophical development whose scope and coherence are still not fully understood.

The task of establishing a boundary to the reign of technology is generally taken to be so great that the efforts of resistance seem at best to be inconclusive. Pressures to bend every aspect of nature and of life to the demands of mastery seem relentless. Nothing is sacrosanct; nothing is immune to exploitation so long as it can be put to service. Yet this very critique is the fruit of modern philosophical reflection. Technology, which treats everything as a means and nothing as an end, cannot furnish its own purpose. Instead, it undermines all final goals, refusing to acknowledge anything as an end in itself. Everything is drawn into its imperious grasp, and nothing is allowed to stand in judgment over it. We are left with a technique of control that can direct everything except itself. The project of technological mastery, our philosophical reflection has shown, can remain rational only if it is subordinate to a noninstrumental finality beyond itself. Man himself cannot submit to the same instrumentality; otherwise the instrumentality ceases to have any purpose. The problem, however, is that we seem to have struck a Faustian bargain. We have been able to obtain this vast technical prowess only because we have been willing to override all presumptive limits. Neither nature nor tradition nor mystery has been allowed to hinder the enlargement of man's estate, which now threatens to include humanity too within its reach. The exigency of instrumental rationality has been well understood philosophically.

The crisis of meaning that has confronted modernity is inseparable from the technical drive. Not only can nature no longer provide a guide when we subject it to universal dominion, but even the coherence of nature as a concept begins to fall apart. Nature may be the means by which we dominate nature, but the boundary between the natural and the artificial can then scarcely be maintained. All becomes simply raw material for homogenization and manipulation. Nothing is simply given as fixed or permanent; everything is drawn into the process of trans-formation. The dream of universal mastery finds no limit except one. Mastery cannot master itself. In the end the vast expansion of power is itself unmastered because it is left without purpose or guide. Technology has no goal. But in this realization our philosophical reflection has at the same time illuminated the self-limitation of all instrumentality. Noth-ing can really be an instrument unless it somehow serves a goal that is not instrumental. Just as in each case the object pursued is regarded as a relative end, so the scheme of instrumentality as such can function only if it is embedded in an order of things that limits its expansion. The process cannot continue indefinitely. It is only because of the over-whelming power of technological development that we gain a sense of its omnivorousness. The reality is that the whole structure crumbles unless it is sustained by an order of limits that defines and guides it. Formal rationality may seem to exercise unchallenged dominance, but without a substance of ends it falls apart. The pursuit of means is always structured by ends.

Correlative with the great philosophical critique of instrumentaliza-tion is the growth of the alternative by which it is judged. The still incom-pletely acknowledged revolution in modern philosophy consists in the progressive articulation of substantive reason. Modern science may have succeeded by virtue of its restriction to the world of phenomena, but modern philosophy has correspondingly found itself within a substantive reality it knows from within. Technology, too, is ultimately known from the inner perspective of participation, and this in turn is what enables our philosophical reflection to escape the realm of technique. Unlike the superficial expectation that a technical solution will be found to all the problems of technology, our philosophical meditation unfolds at the heart of the technological project. Refusing to be limited to the realm of appearance, the philosophical penetration of the underlying reality is an opening toward being as such. It is a disclosure of reality from within, in contrast to the illusion of domination from without. In place of the subject standing over against a world of objects, we expand the meditative knowledge of our participation within existence. Illusory superiority is replaced by submission to truth. This is the shift of perspective that has been under way in modern philosophy against the subject–object model whose dominance has been so great that the countermovement has scarcely been noticed.

The pattern begins with Immanuel Kant. His so-called Copernican revolution in epistemology attracted so much attention that its setting within his own thought was often overlooked. By reversing the epistemological question from "How does the subject know reality?" to "How does reality conform to the categories of our understanding?" he seemed to have installed the priority of the subject on a permanent basis. Our minds no longer had to conform to reality; rather reality had to fit within our minds if it were to be known. This yielded, of course, not knowledge of things-in-themselves but only knowledge of appearances as the only form of knowledge available to us. What lies beyond the realm of phenomena cannot be known. This seemed to spell the death knell not only for any metaphysics but for any knowledge of transcendent reality. Kant himself famously remarked that he had limited knowledge in order to make room for faith. Not as well recognized, even by Kant himself, was that the assertion of knowledge as merely phenomenal implied a knowledge of what was more than phenomenal. The status of Kant's own knowledge claim concerning knowledge was more than phenomenal. This was a line of critique and development from Kant that went through the idealists to culminate in Heidegger's assertion that Kant, while appearing to prioritize epistemology over ontology, had in fact demonstrated that all epistemology is founded in ontology.

A more general version of the same non-transparence prevailed over the whole "death of metaphysics" and "death of God" preoccupation. The critique of objectivist metaphysics and of an externalist theology drew its energy from a deeper faith it could scarcely acknowledge to itself, for to assert that truth no longer lies in dogma is already to employ some sense of the real character of truth. Propositional metaphysics and theology are opaque on their own terms. Only when the experiential sources of truth can be touched do the symbols function as paths toward the truth of being. Cut off from the moving forces of their origin, dogmas of every kind must appear to be an alien imposition over against the isolated subject. Marx's declamation against all forms of fetishism arose from some prior sense of what a nonfetishistic relationship would contain. In place of an objective power over against the subject, there would unfold a structure of openness already present from the start. It is from that deeper level that Marx's critique drew its resonance, for it was fundamentally a cry of revolt against the perversion of truth when both God and man had been reduced to their functional parts within an instrumentalized whole. Dead matter had come to dominate living existence. This is why it is a great, though understandable, mistake to view Marx as a materialist. Far from enclosing humanity within the horizons of material satisfaction, he sought to drive us toward the most transcendent possibilities within our nature. If religion was the cry of an oppressed creature, surely Marx gave voice to the religion of the nonoppressed creature.

The tragedy was, of course, that it inaugurated a new kind of oppression. Revolt against the objectification of truth and the commodification of life was still not enough to prevent a possible relapse into the same patterns. Dreams of dominance still held too powerful a hold on the imagination. Opposition to one form of exploitation did not safeguard the revolutionary from the temptation to adopt other, even deadlier modes. In particular, there was the perennial inclination to leap over the historical struggle toward the truth of existence in order to establish its definitive attainment within time, even though this would signal the end of all human development. It is perhaps the greatest irony that it was the movements that struggled most vociferously against the objectifying factors of our world that carried the logic of objectification to its ultimate conclusion. Impatience at the failure and variability of the movement toward truth had finally abolished the process completely. The government of men had indeed been replaced by the administration of things when humanity had surpassed the very struggle that constituted it. When history is over, there is no further inquiry, conversation, disputation, or reflection. The instrumentalization of man has been carried to its limit when he has found his place within a totality that no longer requires him to think.

The one thing a revolutionary regime would have no place for is revolutionaries. No such challenge of epic proportions would any longer confront humanity, and heroes with the requisite greatness of soul would no longer be forthcoming. The betrayal of the revolutionary impulse, the self-defeat of an excess of idealism, is a powerful testament to the power of the totalizing tendencies as well. Even the highest motives provide no moral bulwark. They may even make us more vulnerable. Outrage at the injustice we behold becomes a substitute for doing anything about it. Having placed ourselves on the side of the revolutionary apocalypse, we conceal from ourselves the failure to mitigate the sum total of evil in existence. We have even given ourselves permission to perpetrate its extension. Justice is no longer the constant unsurpassable measure of our existence. It has become the future whose advent will abolish all need of morality. Revolutionary justice will become a total presence in the world rather than the abiding absence by which all presence is measured. By "dreaming of systems so perfect no one will need to be good," we finally provided a moral justification for the abolition of morality. What the objectifying lust of domination could accomplish only with a bad conscience now had been set upon the world with the most exalted sense of mission. The tyranny of virtue was far worse than the tyranny of power because it justified cruelty on a mass scale. It became possible only when justice itself had become an instrument of world domination.

Resistance against one form of oppression can all too readily justify a far more total strain of dehumanization. Spiritual perversion is, however, no reason to abandon the life of the spirit. It is rather a call for greater vigilance, more humility, and a deeper respect for the nature of the challenge before us. Almost since the moment the ground of things was differentiated from the cosmos that compactly contains it, there have been attempts to lay hold of being within the world of beings. The temptation to find the way toward the ground through victory over the cosmos itself proved to be perennial. It is a fascination that recurred despite the impossibility of the project, for no victory could be any more than a mundane achievement, and the aspiration ultimately betrayed the tension of existence from which it arose. Attainment of wisdom would abolish the love of wisdom. This remains the ineliminable paradox of modern science, just as it is of the drive for global expansion. The goal is the eradication of its own possibility. Power in pursuit of power does not, of course, continue unchecked. Reality repeatedly escapes the grasp of power that is ultimately not creative but only manipulative, just as science does not really know but only grasps relationships. Even the tenuous hold we have on reality is made possible only by our capacity to be held by reality. Our mastery is a mastered mastery, as our modern world has finally begun to realize. Having reached the end of the unlimited scientific self-confidence, we are now perhaps in a better position than ever to appreciate the conditioned possibility it represents.

The difficulty is that we lack the language to articulate a boundary to the authority of science. Philosophy has spent much of the past few centuries apologetically carving out a role for itself as the mere under-laborer to the great empirical investigation of reality. Even when philosophy has exerted a more ambitious claim, the notion that there might be a form of knowledge more authoritative than science has met little public response. If science holds a monopoly on truth, how do we validate the truth of this monopoly? Occasionally it has been possible to puncture the self-assurance of scientific authority by raising such awkward questions. It has even been possible to suggest that the claim to such a monopoly is not itself a scientific proposition, but the struggle to elaborate the consequences has found no readily identifiable form. A plethora of individual initiatives has yet to be seen as part of a coherent whole. The reason is not hard to discover, for it lies in the hold of the instrumental model of reasoning on our minds. If all grounds are themselves only intermediate grounds for something else, the notion of uncovering an ultimate ungrounded ground is difficult to imagine. Philosophy's struggle to unfold the groundless that can never be objectified is fraught with the difficulty of intimating the ephemeral. How can something so unsubstantial provide the foundation for the far more massive reality surrounding us? The challenge has seemed so daunting to many in the philosophical community that they have abandoned all talk of foundations as impossibly chimerical, although it may well be that they thereby draw closer to the inarticulable ground than they themselves admit. Either way, the problem is that we have not found our way toward a language of the unconditioned that can be rendered publicly coherent. The present work may be viewed as yet another within that line of nondefinitive "raids on the inarticulate."

One of the reasons for being somewhat more sanguine about the task is that I approach it not merely as a philosopher. My political science perspective confirms that what has perhaps never worked in theory turns out to work pretty well in practice. No society waits for philosophy to arrive before it enjoys a self-understanding, and the reason for this is obvious. A concrete society is constituted by the meaning that it bears in the lives of its members. It is therefore not surprising that the modern world, too, has articulated its own moral order that has endured despite the inability to provide it with compelling intellectual justification. The universally authoritative language of human rights has created the basis for our common world. Disagreements certainly arise about their meaning and application, but there are few efforts to call into question the underlying conceptions of human dignity and worth. Indeed, one would be looked upon as rather strange if one seriously asserted that human beings are not worth valuing as unlimited ends in themselves, or suggested that they have such a status for any reason other than their common humanity. Not only is this the language of international debate, but it has continuously demonstrated its power in the face of the most abusive political regimes of our history. It is noteworthy that this enormous practical authority of rights has been validated not only in the absence of philosophical support, but even in the face of the philosophical abandonment of all such claims to truth.

The vital sources of authority are, in other words, quite unlike the conclusions of syllogisms. We respond to the pull of obligation before we have even begun to think about it. Only afterward do we search for words that might explain our heart, which has "reasons of which reason does not know." This is why we are capable of sustaining convictions whose justifications are only dimly intuited, affirming them unshakably even in the face of our evident lack of intellectual ability to explain them. Not only is it demonstrable that our moral intimations do not await their philosophical defense, it is very good that our moral commitments do not have such notoriously unreliable origins. We are, rather, moral beings even before we reflect upon ourselves. There is no going back to a premoral self that might be able to engage other similarly situated selves in an original condition. Rawls's "veil of ignorance" is not a visualization of that pre-moral condominium but a powerful indication of our inability to arrive at a point in which the pull of justice has ceased to count. It is this irrevocable moral undertow that explains how it is possible for the most profound resonances to persist within a social setting in which the regime of quantification seems to have assigned every item its value in the universe. Each human being still stands as an inexhaustible center of meaning and worth in existence.

Given the rigorous demands for efficiency in our vast economic enterprises, it is astonishing that the individual ultimately escapes the maw. This has, after all, been the point of the great historical effort to subordinate the energy of the capitalist mode of production to the human beings who sustain it. Marx was correct in pointing out the dehumanizing logic of a capitalist economics, but he was wrong in assuming it could never be brought under political control. Rather than abolish the efficiency of markets, we have found it possible to restrain them for the sake of the human beings who stand outside of them. The struggle for control remains real, but the outcome has hardly been in doubt given the conviction that human beings outweigh all other values. Everything can be measured in the universe but the person who does the measuring. As soon as we submit ourselves to a yardstick, we are no longer what is being measured, for we have escaped in the flow of what Jacques Derrida has called *différance*. Every reality we attempt to affix by reference has already deferred away from us, but in the case of human beings we cannot even retain the semblance of controlling their presence. In fact, the ineluctability of reality is most manifest in connection with ourselves. The mystery of human beings is penetrated only in the awareness of inexhaustibility. Enumeration can never reach its end. The infinite mystery of each human being is not in this sense a principle from which we derive our language of rights; it is the language of rights that gives support to the notion that each individual is an inexpressible depth hidden even to himself. "Human beings trump all other goods" is more than a slogan. It is the abiding intimation of our existence.

The massive undertow of living moral truth, despite its conceptual inarticulateness, testifies to the existential character of modern philosophy. Deeper than the drive to dominate a world of objects is the existence in which such an enterprise becomes possible. This nonobjectifiable background for all objectification is the theme that becomes increasingly the focus of our philosophical development. Each of the thinkers we will review struggled mightily with this new mode of philosophizing in which the challenge is to deal nonobjectively with what is nonobjective. To yield to the temptation to objectify what is nonobjective is to lose the emerging luminosity. It is to fall back on the light one can shed from the isolated position of the subject, rather than to open to the revelatory movement that unfolds from being itself. What could be more tempting than to draw the whole within the mastery of the self? The glamour of the project can be broken only by the awareness of the falsity of the instrumentalization of all truth, for everything can be assigned a price only if there is that which is beyond all price. The urge to reach such definitive possession of truth that it renders all further quest for truth obsolete can often prove too powerful. Yet that is the task to which modern philosophy has repeatedly called us. It does nothing less than return us to the Greek beginnings in which philosophy was primarily a way of life, before it lost its way in becoming a set of ideas available for control and commodification. The modern revolution in philosophy consists in rediscovering not the concepts by which we might further dominate reality but the powers by which we are ourselves judged and saved. When we abandon the effort to stand apart from reality, we can behold the reality by which we are sustained.

The movement of "existentialism" is only a minor episode in this far deeper and longer existential shift in the history of modern philosophy. We might even consider the familiarity with "existentialists" to be one of the principal obstacles to the recognition of the radically existential character of the modern philosophical revolution. Some measure of the problem is indicated by the tendency of many of the best-known "existentialists" to reject that label. Heidegger is perhaps the most obvious case, but there are many others, including Kierkegaard, who predates the appellation. Their reluctance arises from the self-referential character of what is commonly understood by existentialism. Instead of enlarging the perspective of existence toward the order of being in which it is embraced, "existentialism" seems to place the subject in supreme isolation over the whole of reality. When "man is condemned to be free," he stands aloof from all by which he is challenged and sustained. From that closed self, no bridge can be found toward the other; there is only the endless circling within a universe of one's own making. Absurdity is the limit of this self-closure. Only by being more existential can existentialism reach the openness of being in which disclosure can ultimately take place. Rather than carrying to its extreme the logic of the subject dominating the whole, existentialism must reverse the direction by submitting to what is present as its own possibility from the start. The misdirection of existentialism indicates the difficulty of resisting the hold of objectification.

Nothing less than a revolution in thinking is required. It is not the work of a generation or of a handful of thinkers. The whole course of the modern world seems to culminate round this necessity. An unending sense of crisis has pervaded the progressive movement by which we are carried forward, so that we might characterize modernity as the age defined by its self-questioning. Modernity is a problem to itself. This is not an accidental disturbance, but a structure of uncertainty that goes all the way down without escape. "Crisis" seems to suggest the episodic, from which recovery may be made. The reality is that modernity cannot overcome the problematic that is the permanence of crisis within itself. In other words, there is no crisis. There is simply the insufficiently understood constitution of a world that periodically erupts into consciousness as a crisis to be addressed or solved. The obliqueness of such resolutions is best demonstrated by the discovery that solving the crisis would require the abolition of the modern world. The so-called crisis of the modern world is nothing less than the failure to recognize the inexorability of the process of objectification by which we have succeeded in dominating much of the world in which we live. Instrumental reason can no more provide its own purpose than the control over meaning can ground itself. The lure of the natural may be all the more powerful in our artificial environment, but for that reason we cannot attain it simply by extending our reign of technique. Only when we begin to recognize that our situation is inescapable does the sense of crisis begin to evaporate. Frustration arose from our inclination to attempt the impossible, but now that the impossibility is recognized, alternatives have begun to open. Impossibility does not mean absolute impossibility; it can also point toward the possibility of another mode. The struggle is always to break the pull of the prevailing. It is to see that the impossibility of meaning grounding itself points toward its groundedness beyond itself.

The burden of creating meaning has been replaced by the openness to its reception. Instead of lamenting the inability to make present what always escapes us in the movement of signification itself, we can now shift our attention toward the ever-present reality that makes our pursuit of presence possible. Just as the failure to bring about a culmination of history within time does not empty history of its value but preserves it, so the inability to arrive at absolute meaning makes possible the inexhaustible search for meaning. We realize that we not only are moving toward a goal, but also are already beginning from it. History is in this sense both a realm in which nothing happens and a realm in which everything happens. The problem is, as Derrida points out, we are trapped by our own metaphors. Using the objectifying language of space and time, we are incapable of contemplating space and time as such. Yet the failure of metaphor is not the failure of thought, as evidenced by our ability to take note of the deficiency. We are rather invited to shift our attention to what makes our thought possible and which must, therefore, be neither one of the things included within our thought nor one that is radically excluded from the awareness itself. Besides the intentionality toward a world of objects, there is the luminosity that discloses reality from within. Revelation in the latter sense does not come to us from beyond, but is there before it begins. In the words of Augustine, you were within me while I was outside myself; you were more inward than myself. The modern discovery of the abyss of the interminable deferral of the ground of meaning is not nihilism. It is the turning point of recognition that unfolds the luminosity of existence as participation.

The allusion to Augustine reminds us that awareness of the problem reaches back to the ancient world. Modernity may have made its confrontation unavoidable, but the issue of using immanent language to speak about what transcends the boundary of discourse begins with its first differentiation in Greek philosophy. It was the unsatisfactory state in which the classical thinkers bequeathed the problem that necessitated the modern struggle. Widespread proclamations of the death of God or of the death of metaphysics never meant what they said. The demise was really that of certain conceptions of God or of metaphysics that by their excessive reliance on objectivity had betrayed the meaning they sought to convey. It was the death of a certain kind of ontotheology, for God and metaphysics remained very much alive even, or especially, when their propositional form had become opaque. Taking up the challenge of speaking of "God without being" would involve, therefore, a revisitation of the beginning of philosophy in order to retrace the steps that had led to the impasse. The modern problem turned out to be of ancient derivation. Its engagement would involve the resumption of a struggle toward transparence that had been sidestepped when philosophy embarked on its self-transmission in discursive reason. A new way of doing philosophy could not be reached unless it could be found as one of the pathways untraveled since its inception.

The result has been nothing less than a profound rethinking of the hitherto permanent categories of our thought. Our modern experience of extending our control over nature had already taught us that the conception of "nature" had become problematic. How could we conceive of nature as fixed once it was subject to our domination? On the other hand, what was the basis for our control if not mastery of nature in some sense? But it is only recently that we have begun to suspect that the source of difficulty lies less in the modern abyss of instrumentalization than in the fixity of the categories we have inherited from the ancient thinkers. Having become accustomed to contemplating nature as a self-contained realm, we are surprised by the appearance of its emergence under our own forming power. We had forgotten that *physis* meant not only what had been formed but the very process of formation itself. Far from offering raw material for manipulation, nature was itself already the disclosure of its tension toward that from which form originates. Physis could not be understood without *ousia*, because it did not simply happen but emerged as a way of being. The reality of nature is contained not within itself, but within its tension toward being as such. This profound readjustment of our most convenient categories, a readjustment on which we still have a long way to go, begins to shed light on the impossibility of our technological control of nature. We see that the dominance cannot be limitless since technology, too, stands within the light of being. The claim to have overstepped all order turns out itself to live within an order too.

Such revisions of a concept like "nature" attempt to clarify many of the most puzzling conundrums that have bedeviled the whole tradition of philosophy. In particular, the discussion of human nature has remained in prolonged suspension. Does man have a nature or a history? If the former, how could we account for the changes that occur over time? If the latter, how could there be a history of what is no longer unified by the changes? The search for a moral criterion in nature from the classical "right by nature," through the medieval "natural law," to the modern "natural rights" has often fallen victim to the truncated conception of nature. It had become an idea so familiar that its limitations slipped our awareness. Only when nature is no longer taken as an ultimate point of reference do we confront what we sought to avoid by opting for such a more apparently manageable entity. Now we more readily admit that nature cannot furnish guidance, because nature itself is derived from what stands beyond it. We, too, can acquire the guidance of nature only if we are prepared to stand within the same light that emanates from being itself. Neither human beings nor nature simply exist as entities without any questions about themselves. We exist as questioners because our very being is in question; we never reach a point at which we cease to be a question to ourselves. Human being, in other words, is defined by questioning that is itself a mode of being, never by a nature that has closed the process through an answer.

To really comprehend the far-reaching implications of this philosophical revolution, a revolution that does indeed return us to our beginning, we must follow the many aspects of its unfolding. An introduction only announces the project while also attempting to do more. It seeks to actually introduce by drawing us into the lines of reflection by which it is engaged. In this way we follow the most fundamental shift toward an existential mode of inquiry. Philosophy cannot be talked about; it can only be discussed from within. Writing a nonphilosophical account of the movement of modern philosophy would be like discoursing about an event of which we had no experience. No doubt much useful information could be assembled by such a strictly historical approach, but it would miss the core that justifies attention to the whole periphery. We can understand philosophy only by participating in it. This is a principle that increasingly informs and identifies the philosophical revolution of the modern period as the accent shifts from discourse to its existential roots. Once we become self-conscious in our discourse, attention turns toward the conditions of philosophical reflection. Among the conditions that cannot be overleaped is the existence of the philosopher himself. It is in this way that philosophy returns to its classical conception of a way of life. But mere recognition of the indispensability of the existential perspective does not necessarily enable a thinker to fully recognize the implications of the shift. Indeed, one of the patterns we will discern is that the modern philosophical revolution is often characterized by the struggle, not always successful, to remain true to itself. If we are to uncover the full dimensions of this movement, we cannot remain at the level of intellectual formulations left by the respective thinkers. We must reach beyond what they said to the dynamic of questioning that in many cases yielded developments the thinkers themselves had never acknowledged and had sometimes even distorted. Given the inconclusive state of much contemporary philosophical discussion, the claim that a unifying pattern exists at all requires some justification. For now, all we can do is prepare the way by taking note of the fundamental condition for perceiving its plausibility. We must be prepared to exist within the mode of philosophy. To understand those who worked toward this new way of conceiving philosophy, we must place ourselves within the same dynamic. We must be prepared to philosophize about philosophy.

Our study cannot stand apart from the movement it seeks to understand, for there is no understanding outside of the movement toward it. To the extent that this is the great insight of modern philosophy, it spells the end of scholarly externality as the medium of discourse. Philosophy, it insists, lives only from within itself. No reduction to the common coinage of ideas is possible. The tension between philosophical and historical approaches to the history of philosophy has perhaps always existed; the difference is that now it has become the centerpiece of the self-understanding of philosophy. When reason has so consciously turned its gaze on itself, it is not surprising that the superiority of the historical account of reason should also come under suspicion. It is not just the objectivity of a science of nature that is shattered. Even the assurance that reason knows itself is exposed to withering scrutiny. There is no higher viewpoint from which science or scholarship might master the materials of investigation, for it is precisely the possibility of such mastery that is under investigation. The task that philosophy has taken up is nothing less than the inquiry into its own possibility of inquiry. Once philosophy has understood itself in this way, it has already broken with the unthinking self-assurance by which it has compelled every other reality to submit to its ordering. Unthinking mastery is no longer possible, and with it, of course, goes the possibility of asserting such mastery again. Modern philosophy, after passing through an initial phase of naive self-forgetfulness, now recognizes that its penetration can never reach the self from which the endeavor springs. Having reached this hard-won insight into the Socratic ignorance that must ultimately limit the imperative to "know thyself," it is not about to surrender its gains to the currency of conventional discussions about human nature, knowledge, or psychology. Even "ontology" has been made to relinquish its position of preeminence.

Much of what is baffling in the language of contemporary philosophy arises from this need to make language say what cannot be said. The revolution in philosophy is at the same time a revolution in its language. This feature has become so prominent that philosophy since Nietzsche seems to have become identical with the preoccupation with language. When indirection has become its central theme, philosophy must increasingly focus on the limits of language as the only available means of communicating what cannot be communicated. The irony is not merely gratuitous, but is embedded in the recognition of the full implication of the perspective of a participant within existence. No overstepping of the boundaries, no easy recourse to conceptual pseudo-clarity, is available. The very possibility of existence is rooted in the impossibility of leaping outside of existence. But how can language suggest that impossibility without pretending it has thereby overcome it? The answer that has tortuously emerged in contemporary reflection is that language, too, submits to the fate of self-limitation that defines everything that comes into existence. In that realization, however, philosophy and its language bear a luminosity they can never contain, for they are more properly understood to be borne by it. Language is no more our possession than being is; we are rather possessed by language just as we are by being. The mystery by which we are guarded cannot be pronounced by us. That is precisely how it saves us from ourselves and, at the same time, lifts the cloud of depression that has hung over our most vaunted claims to instrumental mastery.

Reason cannot annihilate itself, because it has never really possessed itself. This is the liberating insight toward which the modern philosophical revolution has strained. Rarely has the path been clearly illumined; often it has itself been mistaken for a new goal to be achieved, and perhaps just as often, the obscurity of the movement has deepened the despair of finding a direction. But slowly and inexorably, especially in the phase after Heidegger, contemporary philosophy has breathed more expansively as the burden of resolution has been lifted. Now inconclusiveness is no longer a disappointment to be borne ruefully; it has been embraced as the condition of our continuing movement toward conclusions. The air of foreboding that had crept even into the advancement of science by which the settling of questions might put an end to the pursuit of questions, the nightmare possibility glimpsed in the Hegelian evocation of the end of history, had now dissipated. Our existential demise, moreover, had not just been postponed. A philosophical turning point had been reached. Just as the opening of reason by the Greeks was effectively irreversible, so the modern realization of the nondefinitiveness of reason has something of the definitive about it. More than a vague intuition, this is an insight that we reached only by going more deeply into the existential impossibility by which all possibilities of reason are made possible. Where Aristotle had understood that reason is an activity, never to be confused with its mere potency, there remained the discovery of what it is that sustains reason within its activity. It is precisely because reason remains unknown to itself that it is prevented from lapsing into the satisfaction of knowledge that would spell the end of its activity. The impossibility of reaching the horizon toward which it moves is not just an incidental dimension of the unfolding of reason, but the essential safeguard of its dynamism. The horizon cannot be reached, because it is carried within. Every step closer is at the same time a step farther away from it. Doomed to perpetual postponement, reason is thereby liberated from all final enclosure. Socratic wisdom is indeed the deepest available to us, only now grasped as an existential condition rather than simply an attitude toward existence. It is because, we now recognize, that reason cannot contain itself that it possesses the possibility of openness toward being. Existence is the mode of that which exists because it is not confined to what is.

To catch this insight that philosophy itself catches only on the run, we must be prepared to enter into the movement animated by the end that is present from the beginning. When philosophy has become the movement by which it is constituted, there is no access to what is going on except through participation in it. Individual thinkers are no longer fixed quantities, capable of being assigned a static role in the overall drama. They are rather moments whose meaning is defined less by their intentions than by the larger conversation to which they contribute. The variability of the meaning of historic events is a well-known problem of historiography, for there is never just one context that defines the significance of what has happened. We are faced with an evolving succession of contexts that necessitate the revisions of historical interpretation as history continues to unfold. In the case of philosophy, the situation is both better and worse. It is worse in the sense that there are no contexts outside of the philosophical events themselves, but it is better in the sense that the contexts are wholly constituted by the philosophical events. The idea that philosophy might be reduced to its history makes nonsense of its striving against the reduction to merely historical existence. Philosophy is in that sense a nonhistorical event that appears within history. The relationship between philosophy and history is of necessity problematic, for strictly speaking, philosophy has no history. It is simply one continuous conversation. The participants are to be understood as they seek to understand themselves, in relation to the whole. But, of course, this means that they are ultimately partners in a conversation that has already occurred before any of them utters a word. No account of the history of philosophy, or of any phase of it, can therefore do justice to what it is about, for it is precisely the inability to do justice that constitutes the movement of philosophy as such. Nevertheless, we will gain a more accurate, or a less inaccurate, reading if we are prepared to see the movement as a whole. The conversation yields more than the voices in isolation.

Even for the participants it has not always been easy to locate their own significance. We might suggest that it is for the participants above all that the question of their significance has proved most difficult. The distortions, exaggerations, and misdirections to which contemporary thinkers have been prone have often made their contributions appear to be an incoherent series of lurches toward and away from one another. The conversation is reduced to a cacophony. But this is to place too much credence in their emphasis of the divisions between them and to overlook the degree to which they converge on the same underlying questions. It has, for example, been noted that Marx and Kierkegaard maintain a far more ambivalent relationship to Hegel than their oft-voiced rejections would seem to suggest. In some profound sense they still operate within the orbit established by Hegel. Their very critique is peculiarly indebted to a way of thinking that owes much to the target at whom it is directed. Yet apart from the noting of this ambivalence, there is little in the way of insight into the larger tensions within which they are held together. One suspects that the inquiry would lead us back to a rereading of Hegel under the suspicion that he has still not been read rightly. Certainly his significance has not been exhausted in being pictured as a mere prelude to the rejection of all systems. The fact that he has been subjected to withering critiques from the Left and the Right does not preclude the possibility that he also sustained lines of reflection capable of answering, perhaps even anticipating, the critiques. Something more than the caricatures that usually serve as the starting point for such debates is required. We are compelled to once again take Hegel seriously on his own terms without presuming we know in advance what they are. A great thinker is precisely one who forces us to begin again with him.

That, of course, means that we must go back to his beginnings, which means in turn that there is no real beginning absolutely. That is certainly as we would expect. Yet a good case can be made for making a beginning with Kant, not only because he and everyone else understood him in that way, but because he did indeed inaugurate a new way of doing philosophy, albeit a way that he himself acknowledged as present in his immediate predecessors. Kant's particular contribution was in that sense to make explicit a revolution that had been under way since Descartes but that really had its earliest intimations at the very beginning of philosophy itself. When man discovered reason as the instrument by which he opened toward being, there had all along been the implication that being opened toward him through reason. He did not possess reason, reason possessed him. Now it may seem unorthodox to suggest that Kant's "Copernican revolution," by which he turned the subject away from an externalized world toward a world that had become internalized within the subject, would only underline the dimension of subjectivity of the relationship. But this initial impression is increasingly dispelled in Kant's own development. By the time he wrote the *Critique of Judgment,* a text long appreciated as crucial to the overall direction of his thought, it was clear that knowledge is not rooted in the subject but is rather the subject's rootedness in regulative ideas to which it must submit if it wishes to know reality. Knowledge becomes, therefore, not an event within a subject but a way of being through which knowledge occurs. Heidegger formulated most clearly the insight that Kant was occupied not with epistemology but with the prior ontological conditions that knowledge itself reveals. It was this profound intuition that gave rise to the great flowering of German idealism, which took as its point of departure the insufficiently elaborated tensions within Kantian philosophy. Kant had broken with the subject in isolation from the universe, but he had not fully worked out how the continuity between them was to be understood.

The decisive step had, however, been taken in recognizing that knowledge is a mode of being, not a holding of being at a distance in the act of contemplation. There is no knowledge of being other than through the being that discloses itself as knowledge. Even Kant's own distinction between theoretical and practical reason had begun to break down when the former was understood to be ultimately a mode of the latter. It is through existence that being is disclosed. This was the momentous issue seized upon in a wide variety of ways by the idealists who followed. Their story is replete with complications, and it is only now being given the attention it deserves, but it certainly entailed the unity of theoretical and practical reason by which the turn toward existence became the defining feature of modern philosophy. The revolution inaugurated by Kant became explicit in the project of German idealism. That did not, of course, mean that its implications were fully recognized. Despite their best efforts, the idealists were hampered by the continuing language of subject–object relationships. It was not so easy to jettison the notion that they aspired to reach the perspective of an absolute subject whose grasp might be coextensive with the knowledge of God himself. The very terminology of "ideas" could not easily shake the suggestion that they remained within a subject. German idealism, we might say, sought to unfold an existential philosophy through conceptual language. This is what related it so closely to its successors and at the same time distanced it so profoundly from them. Nietzsche and Kierkegaard sound as if they broke so completely from this context that only with difficulty can we trace their affinities. But the relationship does become plainer if we begin from the side of the idealists, and in particular, if we follow the emergence of their constructions before the conceptual elaboration began to overwhelm it. It has, for example, long been known that Hegel went through an early "existential" phase, but how this was integrated into his mature philosophy has often remained something of a puzzle. The simplest assumption has been that he broke away from a philosophy of existence to become the creator of a system that encompasses it. But what if there were no break? What if the later, more "systematic" accounts are still existential to their core – or at least preserve enough of that living reality to resist containment within the system? Only an unpreconceived reading of the texts can begin to address such questions. Then it may well turn out that the much declaimed "system" has a profoundly different meaning, one far more in line with the organic continuity so often invoked by the idealists as a whole. Indeed, if one pays attention to the frequency with which the term "living" is attached to "system," one can begin to appreciate the nature of the aspiration. Hegel sought above all to turn philosophy into a living movement, a vitality that would overcome the deadness of mere propositions. Normally such an aspiration is eclipsed by the sheer comprehensiveness of the project that impresses with its capacity to contain all questions within it. No doubt this remained an element of Hegel's ambition, but to suggest that it defined it would be to fail to take cognizance of his stature as a philosophical mind of the first rank. How could a philosopher devote himself to the task of abolishing philosophy? Even a cursory reading of Hegel demonstrates the frequency with which the boundaries of the system are forever being breached. The most telling examples are surely the endless digressions of the lecture notes inserted in the three parts of the *Encyclopedia* that, far from being merely supplementary, really invert the relationship between text and subtext. The published parts of the *System of Philosophical Science* seem to provide merely the beginning for the life of philosophy within the living lecture.

That pattern of the life of philosophy overtaking the writing of it finds full expression in the case of Schelling, with significant consequences for his reception up to the present. His early academic celebrity has fixed his conventional assignment as a transitional figure between Fichte and Hegel, a convenient allocation that permits the neglect of his extensive lecture series that continued for a quarter of a century after the death of the latter. Yet Schelling is the true culmination of German idealism in the sense that he saw most clearly why a system of life could never contain its own limits. What had persisted in ambiguity within Hegel now reached a pivotal clarification. There could be no attainment of absolute knowledge, because the attainment would itself necessarily fall outside of it. Spirit as the inwardness of all that is living is such by never being reducible to what it is. Philosophy too, when it philosophizes out of its existence, can never coincide with that from which it springs. No matter how fleet it is, thought is always too late to arrive at its own beginning. It was because Schelling had made the crucial character of existential philosophy so unmistakably clear that he could avoid the ambiguity by which God seemed to have been absorbed into the system from which his self-consciousness arose. The recognition of God's unambiguous transcendence gave Schelling's thought a reassuring orthodoxy that had much to do with his return to Berlin, but it was also what freed him to focus so completely on philosophizing in a thoroughly existential mode. Despite the fact that his success in this regard was limited, as evidenced by the disappointment of his most existentially profound listener, Kierkegaard, Schelling nevertheless remains indispensable if we want to understand how the speculative thrust of idealism ultimately yields a meditative transformation. That reconsideration of Schelling is ongoing, but its importance cannot be overestimated, for it is only in him that we see the continuity of German idealism with the more explicitly existential philosophies that emphasized their separation from it.

Nietzsche's dramatic rupture with idealism was mediated by the other great exponent of the existential turn within it, Schopenhauer. After an initial infatuation, Nietzsche broke both with Schopenhauer and with the cultural romanticism of Wagner. The reason for his rejection was their failure to live out their philosophical convictions. Having advocated a philosophy of existence, they had retreated, Schopenhauer to a contemplative indifference and Wagner to mere theatrical spectacle. A philosophy of existence that refused to be what it claimed to be was bankrupt. It was Nietzsche's willingness to stake his life on the search for truth that was the powerful source of his authority. When philosophy had become existential, existence must become philosophical. The boundary between the theoretical and the practical had disappeared completely. But while Nietzsche, by dint of his living witness to truth, exercised an enormous appeal that extends all the way to the present, he had not yet discovered how to give voice to what always lies outside of the giving voice. It was a puzzle that afflicted him as much as his readers and has resulted in a wide attribution of explanations and motivations for the contradiction by which he was himself held captive. Truth, he insisted, is among our least well grounded prejudices, yet he declaimed against it with the same unwavering reliance on truth. He was in that sense the last metaphysician who must, nevertheless, use metaphysics as the instrument of its subversion. Grappling with this patent contradiction has given rise to an inexhaustible stream of commentary, largely because it is incapable of resolution within any literary formulation as such. Heidegger was virtually alone in recognizing that it reflected not a personal failing of Nietzsche but the transcendence of every position by that which does the positing of it. No truth can contain itself.

It was thus with Heidegger that the turn toward existence in modern philosophy could finally begin to talk about itself. The revolution had become explicit. This was marked by Heidegger's own deepening understanding of what such a turn must be, especially as unfolded in the prominence that *Kehre* occupied in his own unfolding. Existence in the "existential" sense of the subject alone in his utterly unguided self-determination was no longer enough. The subject as *Dasein* must be awakened not only to his freedom but to his own impossibility of containing it. A thoroughly existential philosophy would extend the impossibility of being what it is to philosophy itself. Just as the idealists had understood philosophy to be a movement, the next step must be taken to set aside any suggestion that its linguistic elaboration had in any sense arrested the movement. If spirit is always that which is not what it is in any particular instantiation, its articulation in language must partake of the same transparence toward non-transparence. What makes existence possible is always what lies beyond the boundary of existence as an event of being that for that very reason cannot become an event within existence. Nietzsche sought to live what he could never formulate; Heidegger understood why living could never be formulated. Perhaps it was because he understood the impossibility so well, indeed clothed it so alluringly in language, that Heidegger was so tempted to transcend the impossibility itself. As the flawed culmination of the modern philosophical revolution, Heidegger is a powerful testament to the difficulty of sustaining a philosophy of existence. The betrayal that had earlier been exemplified in the conceptual system now showed its seductive capacity even at the point of the erection of the maximum barrier against it. Once the impossibility of philosophy containing itself had been proclaimed, that very self-limitation became yet a spur for overcoming it. The fatality that moved Heidegger to embrace the apocalypse did not, of course, vitiate his achievement of a philosophical language by which his own errors could be even more forcefully resisted. He is thus uniquely important for his negative almost as much as for his positive significance.

The most authoritative countermovement is undoubtedly that provided by Emmanuel Levinas, who went considerably beyond the prevailing condemnations of the dalliance with evil. He understood that the critique could be effective only if it arose from within the revolution that Heidegger had indeed worked on the nature of philosophy. Admiration for Heidegger's capacity to see what everyone else had overlooked was mixed with disbelief at his appalling willingness to degrade his own philosophical insights. Attempts to explain the misdirection in terms of an absence of an ethics or a politics from his thought were merely convenient forms of begging the question. Only Levinas was really able to get behind such manifestations of the problem to the underlying failure of Heidegger to complete the revolution he had carried further than anyone else. Despite all of his efforts to break with the intentionality of a subject confronting a world of objects, Heidegger's project had remained at the level of an aspiration. It had not been carried out, because he stayed too close to the priority of the "I" from which his meditation unfolded. Without displacing the "I" from its centrality, it would always be impossible to resist the tendency to make reality ultimately serve its apocalyptic sense of fulfillment. All experience, despite Heidegger's substantial efforts, remained within the subject. He had not yet reached an experience that could not be an experience because it had already occurred before the subject arrived at it. The nonencounter with the other was notably absent from Heidegger's thought. To the extent that the other was included in Heidegger's reflection, it was assimilated to the self, and from there, Levinas realized, it could never return to the otherness of the other. As a consequence, Heidegger's fundamental insight into the nonattainability of being had not encountered nonattainable being. Levinas may have added an "ethics" to Heidegger's "ontology," but his crucial significance is that he completed the philosophical revolution that remained uncertain. It is not just that the subject cannot reach that by which it reaches, but that nonreachability is precisely what constitutes the person, spirit as such. Being is personal.

This great insight, which Levinas worked out largely in the mode of resistance to Heidegger and others, remained to be developed in its full philosophical significance. It was because responsibility before the other could too easily be taken as a call to attend to beings, albeit personal beings, that Jacques Derrida sought to locate it definitively within the luminosity of openness. Levinas had shown why the grasping of being that perpetually hovered over the horizon of Heidegger's opening toward it could not be accomplished. In its limiting case, it would be tantamount to the abolition, by the absorption, of the person. But he had not clearly voiced the nonrealizability of the apocalypse. Derrida was the one who most forcefully expressed the insight that apocalypse is precisely what cannot be accomplished. If it were to become immanent, it would not be the apocalypse. In this way Derrida brought theoretical clarity to centuries of ecclesiastical struggles with dreams of the millennium, for the church forever exists within the tension of the millennium that has not yet happened and the millennium that is already now. Initially his path into perennial postponement was by way of a reflection on the endless deferral and difference that is both the character and condition of writing. Derrida coined the neologism *différance* to suggest a semiological condition that, far from being a limitation, was what provided the possibility of all meaning. Gradually it became apparent that this was an insight into more than textuality, that it was a glimpse at the possibility of meaning because meaning is itself the possibility of existence. Where the modern philosophical revolution had sought to unfold the insight that existence could never contain that by which it is contained, now it finally shed the temptation that had reached an apogee in Heidegger's intimation of such a comprehension. Derrida marks the point of realization of the saving effect of the nonattainability of the transparence toward which all our striving has been directed. Far from a disappointment, différance is the very air we breathe so long as we exist. Luminosity is the mode within which we exist precisely because we can never make it our own illumination.

Derrida himself had noted the strange affinity between this diagnosis of différance and negative theology, but this still suggested something like propositional theology. What he really sought was not an account of God but the unfolding of existence within the unattainable horizon of God. It was not surprising, therefore, that he found himself returning to the thinker who had already made existence within faith the center of his reflection. Søren Kierkegaard was a thinker whom one might expect to have encountered in any narration of the existential turn of modern philosophy. He had indeed figured prominently in the "existentialist" phase of this movement, but that early association has remained one of the principal obstacles to a full appreciation of his thought. Kierkegaard has been as easily dismissed as the subjectivist irrationalism with which "existentialism" has been tarnished. Only more recently has a reconsideration become possible as his anticipation of the insights of his successors has become more apparent. It may well be that Kierkegaard's place in the modern philosophical revolution lies in the postdeconstruction phase rather than in the postidealist setting within which he labored. The conversation by which philosophy moves does not always take adequate account of its participants, and as a consequence, their placement must sometimes deviate from the chronological sequence of their emergence. This is not just the case when a thinker is neglected, but a virtual necessity when his originality has permitted him to overleap the developments emanating from his own time. The reason we are struck by Kierkegaard's amazing prescience is that he carried the philosophical revolution to its limit. He understood that the turn toward existence could not be halfhearted. Even philosophy must be subordinated to the life by which it is sustained. This is why Kierkegaard is both the least theoretically articulate and the most penetrating of all modern thinkers. With him the luminosity of existence has firmly supplanted any inclination toward intentional mastery of it. Before philosophy had itself reached this position, the reception of his thought was bound to be difficult, but now that the logic of the turn toward existence has been unfolded, we can recognize his singular achievement in having already arrived at it.

A large factor in Kierkegaard's radical depth was his revulsion against the idealist system that had eclipsed its creator. He understood, like Nietzsche and Dostoevsky, that the value of any philosophy was to be measured by life, not by its conceptualization. But for Kierkegaard this was more than an intuition; he elevated it into a principle. The reason philosophy could not contain the life by which it was sustained was not just that reflection is inherently limited but, more importantly, that life is made possible only by its noncontainability within its formulation. This was the insight into différance long before Derrida's coinage, and it led to a virtually comparable literary unfolding. For Kierkegaard the equivalence was pseudonymous authorship. Initially it began as a literary device of indirection that he judged to be necessary within his contemporary setting. Not wishing to be taken as a merely Christian author, and therefore mistaken, he used pseudonymous authorship to provide the distance he needed to say what could not be said directly. Gradually, however, Kierkegaard began to realize that all writing is pseudonymous as he failed to abandon it even after the initial purpose had been served. The clear line between authorship under his own and other names, which he had earlier practiced, gave way to a more uncertain pattern in which even his most explicitly religious works appeared pseudonymously. Writing, as he discovered also in his repeated announcements of the conclusion of his authorship, cannot be concluded and it is this impossibility that provides the very possibility of writing. Never able to say what he meant, he had to continue saying it. Kierkegaard could maintain a unique perspective on his works because he understood more clearly than anyone that he was not their author; they were the author of him.

For him this was a more than literary insight. Its literary application was only an extension of the nonreducibility of his existence to any of the invocations by which it was sustained. That was for Kierkegaard the meaning of faith, the category (or noncategory) that formed the center of his thought. Faith is always in what we cannot know. It is not merely a substitute for knowledge, but is of an utterly different order from knowledge. What is known is over or possessed; what is believed is lived. So it is precisely the nonpossibility of knowledge that constitutes faith and existence. Just as the ideas of philosophy had become the principal barrier to the life of philosophy, the historical doctrines of Christianity had become the main obstacle to the life of Christianity. Kierkegaard understood the significance of the revolution he advocated. It was nothing less than the displacement of the content of philosophy and Christianity with their existential transcendence. The means available to him was the dynamic of self-contradiction inexorably and irremediably at work within them. Neither philosophy nor Christianity can ever live up to itself, because no matter how such satisfaction is proposed its mere formulation exposes its mendacity. Existence prohibits us from setting any finite limits. Nietzsche would later note the same pattern but fail to appreciate the extent to which in railing against limits he merely bore witness to the uncontainable truth of philosophy and Christianity. The assignment of Kierkegaard to a culminating position within this philosophical-Christian revolution is not to suggest that he either concluded or contained all that could be said about it. It is simply to suggest that he had a uniquely powerful insight into the necessity by which existence is borne along. Contrary to the Hegelian suggestion that the necessity might be grasped and thereby overcome, Kierkegaard understood that the necessity was precisely the nongraspability of necessity. And Kierkegaard, who was thus even more inward than Heidegger and his strictures against the unconcealment of *being* (for it is the lighting by which all unconcealment takes place), allows us to understand this imperative from within. Being cannot become present to us because, if it did, we would no longer be able to exist in relation to it. It is by the mercy of being in its absence that we exist. Dispensing with all the vague mysticism of a relationship to God who reveals himself, Kierkegaard made clear why there is no revelation outside the movement of faith that holds onto the God who does not reveal himself. This is the paradox on which philosophy now must turn.

1

Kant's "Copernican Revolution" as Existential

There are many contenders for the starting point of the modern philosophical revolution. Descartes is surely worthy of consideration, as are Leibniz and Spinoza in their different ways. Nor should we underestimate the empiricism inaugurated philosophically by Locke. Hegel considered Francis Bacon and Jacob Boehme to be fitting representatives of the two components, experimental and speculative, of the modern mind. Intellectual historians have increasingly focused on the crisis of late medieval thought, especially as manifest in nominalism, as the turning point of the modern spirit of self-assertive investigation of nature. Others have identified the rise of Gnosticism and the irruption of esoteric religious movements within Christianity as the decisive events that formed the modern consciousness of epoch. This is, of course, to abstract entirely from the large pragmatic developments in science and technology, industry and commerce, society and politics that propelled the enormous engine of modernization. The omission of the latter can be justified, however, on grounds of relevance. We are not painting a comprehensive picture of the emergence of the modern world, but attempting to delineate the essential features of its self-understanding. Myriad factors make possible the world in which we live, but they do not constitute its meaning. To discover what our world is about, we must interrogate what we think. Among the many avenues of self-interpretation available to us, philosophy furnishes a uniquely articulate self-awareness, and among modern philosophers Immanuel Kant can lay claim to having inaugurated its most explicit self-examination.[1]

---

[1] A sample of recent works that take Kant as the turning point for the development of modern philosophy include Paul Guyer, ed., *The Cambridge Companion to Kant and Modern Philosophy* (Cambridge: Cambridge University Press, 2006); Frederick Beiser, *German Idealism: The Struggle Against Subjectivism, 1781–1801* (Cambridge, MA: Harvard University

Kant was not unaware of the position he occupied in the history of modern philosophy. He understood that a new phase had begun with his critical approach to philosophizing whereby he placed our capacity for knowledge, including metaphysical knowledge, under the microscope. Where other philosophers had been content simply to think, Kant insisted that reflection must become scientific by first subjecting its own capacity to scrutiny. This is the so-called critical phase of Kant's thought, marked by the publication of *The Critique of Pure Reason* (1781), which ever afterward imposed a new criterion of rigor on the modern enterprise of reflection. The excitement of the event is evident in the claims for critical philosophy made in the preface. It is nothing less than the assertion "that there is not a single metaphysical problem which has not been solved, or for the solution of which the key at least has not been supplied" (A, xiii). Kant is even aware that his exuberance may arouse the reader's suspicion of "pretensions seemingly so arrogant and vain-glorious," but he persists in the claims he makes on behalf of his account of pure reason. He is confident that at last he has hit on the essential question in asking not how we come to know the world but "what and how much can the understanding and reason know apart from all experience?" Reason itself has become the focus of reason.

By the time he came to write the preface to the second edition (1787), the immediate excitement had subsided, but the understanding of his role had become more expansive. He now located his philosophical breakthrough in the larger context of the modern movement of thought as a whole, especially within its most successful branch, physical science. Kant interpreted his own achievement as the philosophical equivalent of Copernicus's reversal of perspective from a geocentric to a heliocentric worldview. This was, moreover, the culmination of the scientific revolution itself. "They learned that reason has insight only into that which it produces after a plan of its own, and that it must not allow itself to be kept, as it were, in nature's leading-strings, but must itself show the way with principles of judgment based upon fixed laws, constraining nature to give answer to questions of reason's own determining" (B, xiii). Once philosophy had taken note of the success of mathematical physics, it could find a way out of its persistent failure to make our knowledge

Press, 2002); Karl Ameriks, *Kant and the Fate of Autonomy: Problems in the Appropriation of the Critical Philosophy* (Cambridge: Cambridge University Press, 2000); Jerome Schneewind, *The Invention of Autonomy: A History of Modern Moral Philosophy* (Cambridge: Cambridge University Press, 1998); and Terry Pinkard, *German Philosophy 1760–1860: The Legacy of Idealism* (Cambridge: Cambridge University Press, 2002).

conform to reality. "We must therefore make trial whether we may not have more success in the tasks of metaphysics, if we suppose that objects must conform to our knowledge" (B, xvi). Philosophy must become like experimental science, which seeks not to know reality as it is but to test its own conceptualizations of it. According to "our new method of thought," we abandon the attempt to know how things are in themselves and accept that "we can know *a priori* of things only what we ourselves put into them" (B, xviii).

The two prefaces constitute a rich set of reflections on the great work. Like all prefaces, they occupy an ambiguous relationship to the project they precede and proceed from simultaneously. We have been taught by a long line of commentators, who have followed Kant's self-critical injunction, to look with suspicion on the whole notion of a preface. In its very nature a preface is supplementary, attempting to include what the work for all of its voluminous reach has not quite succeeded in capturing. This is one last effort by the author to insert into the volume what has so far escaped his control. It is a poignant attempt to insert, without our noticing it, what the work itself has failed to accomplish. We are asked to take the program for the result, presumably because the author cannot conceal a sense of the deficiency of the work he has produced. This is why a thinker like Kant can be and has to be read on multiple levels of self-awareness. We cannot simply assume that the irony of the Copernican analogy escaped him. Within a universe in which there are no fixed points, a geocentric hypothesis makes as much sense as a heliocentric one. But there is the more immediate irony that Kant takes phenomenal science as the model for a philosophizing that aims at a more than phenomenal knowledge of reality.[2] It may be that, like many of his Enlightenment contemporaries, Kant was overimpressed by the success of the new scientific method, although he remained too great a philosopher to allow it to interfere with the actual structure of his thought. This is why the critique of Kant has consisted largely of an extension of his own self-critique.

---

[2] It was this break with experience that marked Kant's departure from Hume, as he explains in the *Prolegomena to Any Future Metaphysics*. "This complete (though to its originator unexpected) solution of Hume's problem rescues for the pure concepts of the understanding their *a priori* origin and for the universal laws of nature their validity as laws of the understanding, yet in such a way as to limit their use to experience, because their possibility depends solely on the reference of the understanding to experience, but with a completely reversed mode of connection which never occurred to Hume: they are not derived from experience, but experience is derived from them." *Gesammelte Schriften*, vol. 4, 313.

Primacy of the Practical

The distinction he sought to maintain between knowledge of appearances and the thing-in-itself could not be sustained once it was subjected to self-examination. To know appearance as appearance is already to go beyond mere appearance; it is already to know the thing-in-itself. Hegel, among others, laid hold of the dialectic inherent in the distinction between *noumenon* and *phenomenon* to disclose the extent to which reason is itself a part of the reality it investigates and therefore already "knows" before it even begins. Once we recognize this as the direction implicit in Kant's *Critique of Pure Reason,* we begin to understand why the pursuit of the *a priori* of reason held such profound fascination for him. Kant, for all his talk of making philosophy "scientific," was engaged in the original philosophical quest for truth as such, not merely its appearance, and the method he used was not experimental hypothesis, but the meditative unfolding of the knowledge of reality that reason already knows through its participation in it. What was revolutionary was that the conditions for philosophical knowledge had now become explicit. The dogmatism of uncritical assertions had been rejected in favor of a scrupulous adherence to what reason could know *a priori* because it constituted its own reality. The language of the *a priori* ambiguously suggests both logical and psychological *a priori*. It is properly understood only if we recognize, as Heidegger suggests, that it is ontological.[3] Kant's exercise in erecting the critical foundation for metaphysics is metaphysical from the start. Toward the end of the first critique, Kant concedes the difficulty of extending the reach of reason beyond the limits of experience that, as self-critical, it is duty bound to impose on itself. But then he insists that the dismantling of dogmatic philosophy does not remove the questions from which it springs. In an almost obsessive repetition, he insists on

---

[3] Heidegger's reading of Kant, like his reading of many thinkers, may initially strike us as eccentric, and it is this impression that accounts for the failure of much Kant literature to take it seriously. Yet there is a grudging acknowledgment that its obscurity may contain something profound. The problem is that its profundity cannot be separated from the profundity of Heidegger himself. However, the struggle is surely worth the effort if we concede that Kant revolutionized the meaning of knowledge. The obvious question is what the character of this knowledge of knowledge is. As "transcendental" it is not quite knowledge in the same way as our understanding of sensible intuitions. Perhaps Heidegger's emphasis on primordiality points us toward the irreducibility of this metaphysical openness. See Heidegger, *Kant and the Problem of Metaphysics* and *Phenomenological Interpretation of Kant's "Critique of Pure Reason."* As with Heidegger's reflections on other thinkers, there is an almost total neglect of the texts of practical philosophy, an omission of considerable consequence for the weaknesses of his own existential line of inquiry.

the rights of reason to take such further steps once the limits have been acknowledged. "For all the concepts, nay, all the questions, which pure reason presents to us, have their source not in experience, but exclusively in reason itself, and must therefore allow of solution and of being determined in regard to their validity or invalidity" (A, 763; B, 791).

This is the faith that animated Kant's own quest for a knowledge that transcended the boundaries of experience, despite its manifest impossibility. One might say that it is precisely the depth of his faith in what cannot be known experientially that stiffened his resolve to confine speculative reason within the limits of experience. It is a discipline reminiscent of the purification preparatory to the meditative ascent. "I have therefore," he announces in a remark that seems intended for quotation, "found it necessary to deny *knowledge* in order to make room for *faith*" (B, xxx). When it is taken as a single sentence from the paragraph in which it is embedded, the meaning of "*faith*" becomes difficult to establish, but in its setting there can be little doubt that it refers to the confidence that guides the self-exploration of reason within critical philosophy. Rather than take his demolition of metaphysics, of our knowledge of God, of freedom, and of the immortality of the soul for the purely negative result it seems to present on its face, Kant welcomes it as the removal of "an obstacle which stands in the way of the employment of practical reason, nay threatens to destroy it" (B, xxv). For Kant this "positive" result far outweighs the negative aspects once "we are convinced that there is an absolutely necessary *practical* employment of pure reason – the *moral* – in which it inevitably goes beyond the limits of sensibility" (B, xxv).[4] Removal of the false faith of dogmatism is the liberation of the true faith of reason itself. The implausibility of this practical reappropriation of metaphysics is a problem only for those who have not entered into the radical shift of perspective inaugurated by Kant.

[4] The notion that Kant's ultimate purpose in the first critique was practical or moral has not, despite his explicit statements to that effect, received the attention it deserves. An exception is Richard Velkley, *Freedom and the End of Reason: On the Moral Foundations of Kant's Critical Philosophy* (Chicago: University of Chicago Press, 1989). Kant himself makes his intention unmistakably clear in the *Prolegomena to any Future Metaphysics* (1783), a work he published immediately after the *Critique of Pure Reason* so that the larger scope of his project might become clear. The "transcendental ideas," he explains, "open to us a field containing mere objects for the pure understanding which no sensibility can reach, not indeed for the purpose of speculatively occupying ourselves with them (for there we can find no ground to stand on), but in order that practical principles might find some such scope for their necessary expectation and hope and might expand to the universality which reason unavoidably requires from a moral point of view." *Gesammelte Schriften*, vol. 4, 362–63.

We are still inclined to hold onto the prospect that knowledge of God, freedom, and immortality might be grounded in some objective mode of comprehension. The notion that they are disclosed nowhere other than in existence itself remains unsettling. To overcome the reservations we must begin to appreciate the extent to which Kant inaugurated a revolution by eliminating the role of theoretical knowledge within philosophy. This is what the *Critique of Pure Reason* sets out to do. To read it rightly we must keep in mind Kant's constant reminders that the goal of the work is to erect the ultimacy of practical reason. We might even say that Kant is primarily a moral philosopher, if we could be sure that this assertion would not be misunderstood, for he is not just or principally concerned with moral questions, nor does he subordinate all philosophy to ethics. His purpose is rather to assert the moral perspective as the most comprehensive one available to human beings. He could agree with Levinas that "ethics is prior to ontology," while insisting that the priority not be the basis for separation. Kant remains deeply tied to the questions that speculative reason can no longer answer and has shifted the focus of attention to the practical operation of reason in its full range. This includes the practice of theory, too, which can never establish its own principles but must presuppose them (see A, 736–37; B, 764–65). Self-legislating morality is only the most dramatic instance of the fundamental insight inaugurated by Kant whereby the luminosity of existence displaces the dominance of intentionality.

Continuity of Theoretical and Practical

The clearest recognition of this shift is contained in the last critique, *Critique of the Power of Judgment* (1790), which Kant saw as the work that revealed the convergence of theoretical and practical reason within an underlying unity. This was important not only from the perspective of the unity of Kant's thought, but also as defining the direction in which the history of philosophy would unfold. German idealism in particular took the question of the unity of theoretical and practical reason as its central problematic and *Critique of the Power of Judgment* as indicative of Kant's own intended development. Having shown how "the understanding legislates *a priori* for nature as object of the senses, for a theoretical cognition of it in a possible experience," and "reason legislates for freedom and its own causality, as the supersensible in the subject, for an unconditioned practical cognition," the question repeatedly arose as to the relationship between these two forms of cognition. They seemed to be one form of "the great chasm that separates the supersensible from appearances" (*Critique of the Power of Judgment, Gesammelte Schriften,* vol. 5, 195). All of the antinomies that defined Kant's thought seemed to revolve around this one. Could what was known through nature and theoretical reason have any bearing on what was known through freedom and practical reason, and vice versa? It was, of course, true that the exercise of freedom could be known to lead to real effects in the realm of nature, but was any understanding of this possibility possible? Was any development of the relationship conceivable or were they to remain strictly parallel? Could there be any movement within the dialectic that Kant had introduced? A good deal of the excitement that was generated by the last critique arises from the sense that Kant had here broken through what could be regarded as the fundamental barrier of his own thought. He now saw that beyond self-legislating reason in both modes lies some conception of purpose.

It is perhaps remarkable that Kant's reputation as the source of a "deontological," or purely formal, morality has persisted despite the major preoccupation with teleology he evinces in *Critique of the Power of Judgment*.[5] A similar neglect has attached to his extensive concern with virtue, which belies the impression that he has replaced virtue ethics with rule-based morality.[6] Instead, we might more accurately regard Kant as retrieving the meaning of teleology within the modern world. In line with a revolutionary return to the beginning, he shows how teleology can regain viability within the instrumentalized world of modern science. When

---

[5] In part the comparative neglect of the teleological reflections begins with Kant scholarship itself, which is unsure of how they are to be taken. Reductionist views of biology retain such a hold on our thinking that we are wary of treading into the minefield. No such reticence hinders Heidegger's forays into the phenomenology of life, which are in many respects among his most illuminating contributions. See Heidegger, *The Fundamental Concepts of Metaphysics.* Kant scholars, by contrast, have considered themselves to be on safer ground in exploring the esthetic dimensions of the third critique. See Paul Guyer, *Kant and the Claims of Taste,* 2nd ed. (Cambridge, MA: Harvard University Press, 1997), and *Kant and the Experience of Freedom* (Cambridge: Cambridge University Press, 1993). Guyer provides a more extensive account by means of a juxtaposition with Hume's skepticism concerning laws of nature in "Kant's Ambitions in the Third *Critique,*" in *Kant and Modern Philosophy,* 538–37.

[6] This, however, is one area in which the profusion of Kant scholarship has served us well. It is now increasingly difficult to maintain the position that has distorted the reception of his moral philosophy since the publication of the *Groundwork:* that he proposed a purely formalistic account. See, in particular, Guyer, *Kant on Freedom, Law, and Happiness* (Cambridge: Cambridge University Press, 2000); Allen Wood, *Kant's Ethical Thought* (Cambridge: Cambridge University Press, 1999); and Lara Denis, *Moral Self-Regard: Duties to Oneself in Kant's Moral Theory* (New York: Routledge, 2001).

efficient causality dominates the understanding of nature, final causality has been eliminated as a category of explanation. Kant's *Critique of Pure Reason* followed the logic of the mechanization of nature in which we are strictly confined to what sensible intuition makes available for construction. Finality always remains outside the realm of the phenomenal, since it is what accounts for the generation of the phenomena. Now, however, Kant finds a place for teleology that restores it to its central place in the science of nature by showing that its origin had all along been the human experience of purpose in action. By eliminating the objectivist elements that attached to the notion of final causes, he had regained for finality its central role in ordering our view of reality. He found in judgment the link between the groundlessness of human purpose and a nature that no longer supplied the missing telos. Judgment mediates between the two in its *a priori* assumption of purpose. Human freedom requires purpose, and nature cannot be understood without it. "That which presupposes this *a priori* and without regard to the practical, namely, the power of judgment, provides the mediating concept between the concepts of nature and the concept of freedom, which makes possible the transition from the purely theoretical to the purely practical, from lawfulness in accordance with the former to the final end in accordance with the latter, in the concept of a **purposiveness** of nature; for thereby is the possibility of a final end, which can become actual only in nature and in accord with its laws, cognized" (*Critique of the Power of Judgment, Gesammelte Schriften,* vol. 5, 196).

Kant had still not recognized the connection between the purposiveness within him and the purposiveness outside of him, which his focus on judgment had made palpable and which would become the theme of the idealists. All that it would take is the realization that he is himself part of the larger reality. What is disclosed as the finality of his own exercise of freedom is already an instantiation of finality within nature. There is no absolute distinction between inner and outer. Once it had been admitted that we have no access to ends other than our own enactment of purposes. there was little point fretting, as Kant appeared to do, over our inability to find empirical confirmation for finality. We must simply admit that ends can be known only from within their pursuit and accept that, if we wish to apply the notion of finality to the working of nature, we have no option other than to extend the structure of purpose we already know through our own practice of it. Kant's great contribution was to demonstrate that it is only on that basis that we can make nature intelligible. He took the crucial step of relieving us of the burden of finding empirical proof for the process of empirical proof by showing us the impossibility of the task. If we could provide empirical verification, that would in turn stand in need of the same verification. The very notion of evidence is such that its conditions must be accepted in advance. Kant's significance in the history of thought is that he laid bare the conditions for the possibility of knowledge in ways that have not been surpassed, although he did not lay to rest the deeper questions of reliability that can never ultimately be answered by knowledge itself.

Without actually admitting it, Kant disclosed the extent to which reason rests on faith. The central question of his philosophy – "How are synthetic *a priori* judgments possible?" – is never and can never be answered. It is simply a question to be contemplated in a variety of ways. One such way is to ask, as Kant does by way of introducing the notion of finality, how it is possible for us to make esthetic judgments of taste. "How is a judgment possible which, merely from **one's own** feeling of pleasure in an object, independent of its concept, judges this pleasure, as attached to the representation of the same object **in every other subject**, *a priori*, i.e., without having to wait for the assent of others?" (288). What is fascinating about this case is that the judgment rendered is neither objective nor subjective, but both. More than a feeling of pleasure or displeasure, a judgment of taste asserts "a rule of the higher faculty of cognition . . . which is thus legislative with regard to the conditions of reflection *a priori*, and demonstrates **autonomy**" ("First Introduction," *Gesammelte Schriften*, vol. 20, 225). This autonomy, unlike that of the understanding or of reason, is not "valid objectively, i.e., through concepts of things or possible actions, but is merely subjectively valid, for the judgment from feeling, which, if it can make a claim to universal validity, demonstrates its origin grounded in *a priori* principles. Strictly speaking, one must call this legislation **heautonomy**, since the power of judgment does not give the law to nature or freedom, but solely to itself, and it is not a concept for producing concepts of objects, but only for comparing present cases to others that have been given to it and thereby indicating the subjective conditions of the possibility of this combination *a priori*" (225).[7] A judgment of taste is therefore the clearest instance in which the subjective *a priori* has objective validity since this is all that it expresses. Intended to furnish a rule of judgment for the beautiful, criteria of taste can never be exhaustively represented, no matter how comprehensive the series of

---

[7] This is from the "First Introduction," which Kant decided not to include because of its length.

examples, nor can their content ever be fully explicated. This is what Kant means by the "transcendental."

The possibility of judgments of taste lies, therefore, in the extent to which man is himself transcendental. An older language talked of man as a microcosm, but this fails to capture the more "originary" meaning of Kant. How can a microcosm be contained within the cosmos? Somehow a microcosm would have to be like the cosmos, which is contained nowhere but in itself since terms like "in" and "contained" themselves imply a cosmos. The revolution in philosophy, especially in its language, initiated by Kant requires us to pay attention to the difficulty we have in discussing what lies beyond experience, even though this is the source of what is unfolded in experience. Esthetic judgments are thus possible because we bring to experience what cannot be derived from it. If we were to find the measure in experience, it would be empirical and express a purely personal response. Judgments of taste are not in this sense expressions of personal preference. They are first and foremost judgments of beauty independent of my desires, interests, and inclinations; they are rooted in a truth that is grasped apart from all exemplifications of it. This is what makes it possible for judgments of taste to assert the universality of subjects and objects, of the way in which all other human beings would respond, and of the way in which reality actually is. The faculty of judgment is like practical reason, free from the heteronomy of nature to follow its own autonomous law. But unlike the practical operation of reason, the esthetic power of judgment finds its own law confirmed within the world beyond itself. Kant is the one who opens up the enormous significance of the esthetic, and especially of art, that would be articulated by the idealist philosophers and realized within romanticism.[8] It is no accident that esthetics becomes a distinct branch of philosophy, from its Enlightenment coinage all the way to the present. Art becomes the privileged point of access to the transcendental constitution of our existence. The faculty of the power of judgment, according to Kant, "sees itself, both on account of this inner possibility in the subject as well as on account of the outer possibility of a nature that corresponds to it, as related to something in the subject itself and outside of it, which is

---

[8] Andrew Bowie, *Aesthetics and Subjectivity: From Kant to Nietzsche*, 2nd rev. ed. (Manchester: Manchester University Press, 2000), and his "German Idealism and the Arts," in Karl Ameriks, ed., *The Cambridge Companion to German Idealism* (Cambridge: Cambridge University Press, 2000), 239–57. For the parallel within the German "Counter-Enlightenment" see Daniel Dahlstrom, "The Aesthetic Holism of Hamman, Herder, and Schiller," in the same volume, 76–94.

neither nature nor freedom, but which is connected with the ground of the latter, namely the supersensible, in which the theoretical faculty is combined with the practical, in a mutual and unknown way, to form a unity" (353).

The mystery of who we are remains impenetrable, although it is never a complete blank. Awareness of mystery is in part a disclosure of it. The temptation is to mistake the part for the whole and to turn the self into an object again. Kant resisted any such attempts by insisting that knowing about the supersensible is never the same as knowing the supersensible. We cannot make what makes objects of experience experiencable an object of experience again without undermining the entire investigation. All that we have is the possibility of a sideways glance at the movement of experience itself. The status of such adumbrations along the way of immanent experience remained uncertain for Kant, but in the *Critique of the Power of Judgment* he came closer to acknowledging their reality than anywhere else. While the first critique had seemed to vacillate over the question of whether the transcendental categories were purely intellectual constructions or whether they had ontological reference, he now seemed to tilt decisively in favor of the latter. The affirmation was, however, based not on some new independent verification (the impossible dream of epistemology) but on a recognition of the connection of the part to the whole. Our esthetic and teleological judgments could be taken as trustworthy because they instantiated what they sought to find outside of them. Not only was it impossible to verify the conditions of experience within experience, there was also no need to find affirmation of their reality. Beauty and purpose already exist once we take them as the highest reality there is. Judgment is the assertion that the world outside of us is to be measured by the reality within. We cannot ask for a justification of justification itself.

Reason Knows Itself Through the Unfolding of Reality

The realization that reason knows itself through the unfolding of reality was the slender reed on which Kant's thought came to rest. It would later prove to be far stronger than he had suspected once the idealists began to take it as their foundation stone. For now what was important was that Kant had discovered the bridge between inner and outer that had largely eluded him in the first critique. Now the distinction between them had begun to dissolve in the recognition that they are both modes of being. The problem of knowing a world beyond appearances no longer obstructs us once we realize that we already have access to being from within. There is not a world "outside" of us, persisting as an alien mute presence. We are ourselves a part of the world whose most immediate access is available through our self-presence within it. Our capacity to know the world arises from the reality we already share with it. We do not have to be concerned that the categories we bring to bear have no relationship to what we seek to know. Their emergence within us makes them part of the same reality. We are already related to the world before we begin to undertake the relationship. Without this prior unity we would not be able to even begin the differentiation that moves us on the way to knowledge. If we did not stand in the same light of being, we would never have been able to behold the being of anything that exists. This is not just a mere presupposition but the deepest ground of possibility. Even to raise the question of appearance versus reality is to stand in a far more primordial relationship that is before both of them. We can know reality as appearance only because we first know reality. In contrast to the notion of appearance as the certainty from which we must build a bridge to reality, a more fundamental perspective emphasizes that appearance is already a reality. We cannot avoid judging in light of the reality in which we exist.

Some of the excitement of this breakthrough in the third critique is still discernible behind Kant's discovery of the extent to which reason finds itself reflected in the reality it judges. The key insight is the impossibility of a purely external mode of explanation. Mechanical causality is insufficient to account for the world of nature. We may not have any more verifiable access to the interaction of the parts within a living organism, but we know that the processes they entail are not simply mechanical. An internal purposiveness is indispensable to comprehending them. "An organized being is thus not a mere machine, for that has only a **motive** power, while the organized being possesses in itself a **formative** power, and indeed one that it communicates to the matter, which does not have it (it organizes the latter): thus it has a self-propagating formative power, which cannot be explained through the capacity for movement alone (that is, mechanism)" (374). One cannot even explain it by the analogy of an artifice, as if organisms were biological clocks. They in a sense make themselves. One can only come close "to this inscrutable property if one calls it an **analogue of life**." But this is not merely asserting the tautology that life must be understood on the basis of life. It is to accept that biological causality must be taken as *sui generis* without reduction to anything else. The beauty of nature, Kant explains, can be apprehended by the analogy with human art because the latter relates to the appearance of things. But when we wish to apprehend the inner being of things, it "is not thinkable and explicable in accordance with any analogy to any physical, i.e., natural capacity that is known to us; indeed since we ourselves belong to nature in the widest sense, it is not thinkable and explicable even through an exact analogy with human art" (375). We can know living things only because we are ourselves living.

The teleology we ascribe to nature cannot, strictly speaking, be found there but only within ourselves. Kant again formulates the limits of thinking in terms of an antinomy of judgment. "All generation of material things and their forms must be judged as possible in accordance with merely mechanical laws.... Some products of material nature cannot be judged as possible according to merely mechanical laws (judging them requires an entirely different law of causality, namely that of final causes)" (387). What makes the antinomy so arresting is the static quality of this formulation. It does not include the statement of the opposition itself within either of the alternatives. What Kant points toward, without fully acknowledging, is that the identification of the limits of thought is already a transcending of them. He shows, without really calling to our attention, the extent to which thinking must move outside of the fixed parameters of the thesis and antithesis. Kant himself refuses to be bound by either of the alternatives and recommends that we move within the tension between them, avoiding the extremes of mechanical "fantasy" and teleological "enthusiasm" (411).[9] It was because Kant's own thought moved within the more originary fluidity beyond the antinomies that he was able to provide a theoretical clarity to the idea of evolution. He was struck by the kinship between different species, which suggested the possibility of generation from a common source over a period of time. Mere emergence, however, is not an adequate basis of explanation, since it is precisely the element of purposiveness that marks the reality of living things. Ultimately, Kant insisted, we "must attribute to this universal mother an organization purposively aimed at all these creatures, for otherwise the possibility of the purposive form of the products of the animal and vegetable kingdoms cannot be conceived at all" (419). Evolution is

---

[9] "...but to exclude the teleological principle entirely, and always to stick with mere mechanism even where purposiveness, for the rational investigation of the possibility of natural forms by means of their causes, undeniably manifests itself as a relation to another kind of causality, must make reason fantastic and send it wandering about among figments of natural capacities that cannot even be conceived, just as a merely teleological mode of explanation which takes no regard of the mechanism of nature makes it into mere enthusiasm." *Gesammelte Schriften*, vol. 5, 411.

not an objective description of the emergence of the natural world, but the only way to make it intelligible in terms of final causality. Darwin simply ignored the problem by passing over the "intention" of survival of the fittest. Why nature aims at survival is what cannot be explained. Kant understood that intentionality is the condition for our understanding it.

Once purpose is admitted into nature, even if only from the perspective of our judgments, it is admitted into the whole. If the parts of nature exhibit purpose, nature as a whole must have a purposive source. "Thus teleology cannot find a complete answer for its inquiry except in a theology" (399). Kant was far too sophisticated to consider this a cosmological proof of the existence of God, since we cannot make divine purposiveness a condition for the understanding of nature and then use this conception of nature's purposiveness to demonstrate the existence of God (381). But he was far more concerned to avoid the circularity of arguing that we can understand the purposiveness of nature without any basis for its possibility other than our experience of it in the particular instances of nature. "There must therefore be a circle in the explanation if one would derive the purposiveness of nature in organized beings from the life of matter and in turn is not acquainted with this life otherwise than in organized beings, and thus cannot form any concept of its possibility without experience of them" (394–95). The concept of God is, for Kant, neither the conclusion we draw from the finality of nature nor the necessary source of that finality, but the condition for our understanding it. It is for this reason that he insists "there remains no other way of judging the generation of its products as natural ends than through a supreme understanding as the cause of the world. But that is only a ground for the reflecting, not the determining, power of judgment, and absolutely cannot justify any objective assertion" (395).

Teleology's Source in the Moral Life

Physical teleology may point toward a theology, but it does not supply one (440). Only the moral life of man discloses finality in the full sense because it is only morality that grasps the possibility of a final moral end. Physical teleology can lead us toward the concept of an intelligent world cause, but it can give us no insight into the moral purpose of a creator. We can know the latter only because we are moral beings. Knowledge of God, for Kant, derives not from our knowledge of the world (which essentially presupposes God) but from our knowledge of ourselves. We can know God as the final cause of creation because we occupy a similar position.

It is only of a rational being, as a moral being, that "it cannot be further asked why it exists" (435). Everything else exists conditionally; only moral beings possess the unconditioned ground of their own existence. They are capable of standing over against the whole of nature, free from all its determinations, because they determine themselves. This is why Kant regards human beings as capable of providing the final purpose of creation. But it is not their theoretical capacity to contemplate the world that furnishes this highest end, for "if this consideration of the world were to allow him to represent nothing but things without a final end, then no value would emerge from the fact that they are cognized; and a final end would already have to be assumed in relation to which the consideration of the world itself would have a value" (442). Nor is it the feeling of pleasure, whether corporeal or spiritual, that defines the ultimate end of human beings. Rather, Kant insists, "it is the value that he alone can give to himself, and which consists in what he does, in how and in accordance with which principles he acts, not as a link in nature but in the **freedom** of his faculty of desire; i.e., a good will is that alone by means of which his existence can have an absolute value and in relation to which the existence of the world can have a **final end**" (443).

The reason "there lies in us *a priori* an idea of a highest being" (438) is that we occupy a similar position. It is not merely that man must postulate God as the moral author of the world "in order to form a concept of at least the possibility of the final end that is prescribed to him by morality" (453). We also share the divine perspective in the unconditioned causality of our nature, for nothing can compel us but the requirement to act only out of a sense of duty. Our action partakes of the divine freedom of action as moved by nothing beyond itself. Kant refers to the feeling of the sublime evoked by this realization, but he is always careful not to confuse the two, for the feeling is the effect, not the cause. We are even capable of doing without the feeling, so strong is the drive to live within the light of what is. Like Spinoza, on Kant's reading of him, we might even maintain fidelity to the moral law when faith in its possibility has been lost (452–53). It is our capacity to do without God that discloses our closeness to divinity. Not even the desire for union with God can deflect us from the severe path of duty for its own sake. What is right takes precedence over all else. Kant never ceases to marvel at this greatness of the human being as he wonders at what can evoke such a transcendent sacrifice. "This question stirs up the entire soul through the astonishment over the greatness and sublimity of the inner disposition of humanity and at the same time the impenetrability of the secret that it conceals (for the answer – it is *freedom* – would be tautological, precisely because freedom constitutes the secret itself)."[10]

To refer to an explanation of any type is already to place it at a distance, diminishing its mystery and robbing it of its power. The best that can be done is to recognize, as Kant seems to do, that we are dealing with a reality, not an explanation. If we really want to understand, we must stick close to the reality and avoid concealing it in language. We must remain close to the moving forces of existence without reifying reductions. Only by adopting this more existential reading can we make sense of Kant's acceptance of God and the immortality of the soul as "matters of faith" within the moral life. Denoting them as "postulates" always suggested something optional, as an afterthought to the actual exercise of moral choice. And indeed, there is more than a hint of atheism in the radical aloofness of his sense of duty. But Kant repeatedly insists that the moral life would be impossible without the assurance of this faith in the totality of goodness. Not all of his readers have been so convinced of this necessity or even of Kant's own depth of conviction, and the reason is surely their failure to give full weight to the existential character of the postulates in his work. The inability of theoretical reason to ground the moral life will, in his view, leave it hopelessly incapable of sustaining the heroic commitment demanded by duty. Conversely, the enlargement of moral practice toward the affirmation of faith by which it is sustained will more than compensate for the theoretical shortcomings. "The reason that it succeeds in the moral route (that of the concept of freedom), by contrast, lies in the fact that in this case the supersensible that is the ground (freedom), by means of a determinate law of causality arising in it, not only provides matter for the cognition of the other supersensible things (the moral final purpose and the conditions of its realizability), but also demonstrates the fact of its reality in actions, although for that very reason it cannot yield a basis for any proof except one that is valid from a practical point of view (which is also the only one that religion needs)" (474).

Existence as Knowledge

The reason Kant marks the beginning of the modern philosophical revolution is that he sees existence, practical reason, as providing the deepest

---

[10] Ibid., vol. 8, 402–3; *Raising the Tone of Philosophy: Late Essays by Immanuel Kant, Transformative Critique by Jacques Derrida*, ed. Peter Fenves (Baltimore. MD: Johns Hopkins University Press, 1993), 68.

access to being. This interpretation is in contrast to the prevalent view that originates in considerable measure from his own estimate of the scientific character of his work. There is a tension between the existential Kant and the scientific-critical one, although he may not have considered it as such. Ultimately they cannot be reconciled, because the existential meditation reveals the extent to which the theoretical perspective cannot include itself. The process of objectification cannot include objectification. Kant reassured himself that he was thereby advancing a critical approach to philosophy, although he was rather opening philosophy to the unfathomable mystery of its own source. While holding onto the lifeline of the latter provided no theoretical knowledge, he nevertheless insisted that the existential enlargement furnished all the knowledge we need. Kant's greatness as a thinker lies in his realization that to be scientific we must step outside the boundary of science. The implications of this recognition were not fully absorbed by Kant, just as they have not yet been digested within the history of modern philosophy, but he is clearly the one who made the issue visible. His insistence on the primacy of practical reason is the recognition that existence discloses essence. What remained to be determined was the status of that existential knowledge. The authority of scientific knowledge remained so strong for Kant that it still monopolized the claim to knowledge, even though his own critical philosophy had already exposed its relativity. This is the issue with which he struggled in the *Critique of Practical Reason* (1788) as he sought to articulate how the moral imperative conveyed a certainty deeper than the empirical.

Even the title of the work contrasts with the *Critique of Pure Reason*. It is not called the "Critique of Pure Practical Reason," because there is no longer a question of pure reason overstepping its bounds. "For, if as pure reason it is really practical, it proves its reality and that of its concepts by what it does, and all subtle reasoning against the possibility of its being practical is futile" (3). It is a critique of the entire practical faculty which shows that freedom "constitutes the *keystone* of the whole structure of pure reason, even of speculative reason" (3–4). With that opening Kant has established the primacy of the practical over the theoretical, capable of grounding the concepts of God and immortality, which cannot be justified in the latter. In this second critique Kant allows himself the exuberance of asserting the "objective reality" of such concepts because now they are supported by the reality of the moral law. In the concept of freedom, which is "apodictically certain," all that it necessarily implies becomes equally sure. The *Critique of Pure Reason* could not establish the unconditioned causality of freedom, because it confined itself to what can be intuited through experience. Once we shift to the practical perspective, the unconditioned causality of freedom is apparent in the imperative of the moral law. This is why Kant asserts that "pure reason, once it is shown to exist, needs no critique" (*Critique of Practical Reason, Gesammelte Schriften*, vol. 5, 15–16).

The theme of existence becomes the center of Kant's metaphysics. Prior to this an existential appeal had already formed the basis for the revolution in moral philosophy announced in the *Groundwork of the Metaphysics of Morals* (1785). There Kant had swept aside the conception of morality as teleological. Both Greek and Christian traditions had evinced a long-standing commitment to the notion of the highest good as what ultimately made sense of the moral life. Nature in particular had functioned as the intermediate realm whose hierarchy of ends was structured toward the highest divine one. Kant took issue with the Aristotelian formulation of *eudaimonia* as well as the Christian equivalent of beatitude as capable of constituting moral goodness. No doubt he was prompted in part by the awareness of the dubiousness of such notions in a world dominated by the model of scientific reason. He saw that they could not survive the death of metaphysics marked by the elimination of all claims to knowledge beyond the realm of spatiotemporal experience. Nor could a teleological construction limit the expansive drive of man's progressive domination of nature. Like many of the philosophical minds of the preceding two centuries, Kant was intensely aware of the sense of crisis created by the modern world. Instrumental rationality had begun to devastate the moral landscape. Unlike so many of his contemporaries, however, Kant did not seek refuge in some primal innocence of nature or dream of a lost Arcadia. He remained with the classical and Christian traditions, glimpsing the possibility of carrying them to a higher level of moral truth. This is why his arguments have proved so powerful and so durable in the modern world. Far from departing from Western history, he carried it to a higher level by compelling it to confront its own inner logic.

His critique of the philosophical-Christian moral tradition is from within, calling it to account on its own terms, just as Nietzsche and others would later claim to do. It is thus a mode of argument that already exists within the tradition it questions and acquires its authority from that existential appeal.[11] Kant does not provide a foundation for morality, which

---

[11] A critique that arises from within the tradition it critiques is naturally difficult to categorize, and helps to explain why the influence of Protestantism and Pietism has frequently

is precisely the error of all teleological approaches. His "metaphysics" does not, therefore, play a grounding role but is rather itself grounded in moral existence. When we later encounter Levinas's formulation that ethics is prior to ontology, we might properly give the credit to Kant. The metaphysics of morals may have a groundwork, but morals do not. Morality is not a task we acquire once we exist; it is already the givenness of our existence. All of this originary sense of our moral existence resonates in Kant's evocation of the inescapable primacy of duty. Before any discussion of what we should do or why we should do it, there is the imperious demand of duty. We cannot get behind it. Nothing is more fundamental, because it is the constitutive boundary of our being. As such duty is not completely transparent. We can never fully understand it, but we apprehend it sufficiently as the source of luminosity in existence. Reflection on the majesty of duty must therefore take the form of aphorism, a sideways glance at the transcendent order that holds us through our responsive unfolding of it. Existence discloses what theory cannot comprehend. This is why Kant engages not in a rational justification of morality but in a moral justification of rationality. The *Groundwork*, which is closest to Kant's own moment of existential intensity, makes a primarily moral argument, not an intellectual one. Far from stepping outside of existence to contemplate it, Kant draws us into a deeper affirmation of its moral imperative.

We do not create the imperative but discover that it creates us. When we search out the supreme principle of morality, we find that it is already present within us in the awareness that the only unqualified good is a good will. "It is precisely in that that the worth of character begins to show – a moral worth and beyond all comparison the highest – namely, that he does good, not from inclination, but from duty" (*Groundwork of the Metaphysics of Morals, Gesammelte Schriften*, vol. 4, 398–99). Kant himself often refers to this as a formal principle of morality, as if the only thing that counted was consistency and the content of duty was irrelevant. This was a line of criticism that was well mined by Hegel, but it was an objection that was made possible only by the more substantive direction in which Kant himself pointed.[12] The imperative to act only out of a sense of duty surely includes the duty to take seriously the discovery of its content.

been discounted. See Allen Wood, *Kant's Moral Religion* (Ithaca, NY: Cornell University Press, 1970), and Manfred Kuehn, *Kant: A Biography* (Cambridge: Cambridge University Press, 2001).

[12] One of the principal contributions of recent literature has been to make this far richer character of Kant's moral theory abundantly clear, thereby rescuing it from the formalist

While breaking with any conception of an immanent telos that can moti-
vate the will, Kant requires us to weigh every action in relation to the
transcendent telos of that which is done for its own sake.[13] The goal
in all our actions is to make the unqualified good of the good will our
criterion. This is not to act without a purpose. It is to refuse any purpose
but that which is absolutely the highest from becoming the principle of
the will. The demand can be made of us because we already recognize
its authority over us before we begin. "Therefore nothing but the *idea of
the law* in itself, *which admittedly is present only in a rational being* – so far
as it, and not an expected result, is the ground determining the will –
can constitute that pre-eminent good which we call moral, a good which
is already present in the person acting on this idea and has not to be
awaited merely as a result" (401).

This evocation of autonomy as the highest moral principle may strike
us as a departure from any subordination to an authority beyond the
human. It is an impression easily transmitted by Kant's own ringing
endorsement of "the Idea of the *dignity* of a rational being who obeys
no law other than that which he at the same time enacts himself" (434).
Yet the intention seems to be the opposite of suggesting the kind of unfet-
tered individual freedom now associated with autonomy.[14] For Kant the
liberation of man from all heteronomous law derives from his submission to the autonomous source of law. Once again the argument is moral.
Good action is most purely good when it is done for its own sake, without
any element of self-interest. The action must be chosen because it is good
quite apart from any consideration of its consequences. That is, it must
be chosen as a law binding on all, irrespective of their individual differences. The individual must therefore enact universal law and act only
out of universal law. Kant has no concern about leaving the individual
adrift in the ocean of his self-chosen actions, because he can choose only

strictures that were attached to it from its inception. See, in particular, Wood, *Kant's
Ethical Thought,* and Ameriks, *Kant and the Fate of Autonomy.*

[13] "The ground of this principle is: *Rational nature exists as an end in itself.* . . . The practical
imperative will therefore be as follows: *Act in such a way that you always treat humanity,
whether in your own person or in the person of any other, never simply as a means, but always at
the same time as an end.*" *Groundwork of the Metaphysics of Morals, Gesammelte Schriften,* vol. 4,
429.

[14] Karl Ameriks has helped to rescue Kant from this more radical version of autonomy by
demonstrating that it really originated with Karl Reinhold's exposition of Kant, which was
in turn the basis for the even less successful evocations of autonomy by the idealists. I am
less convinced of the failure of the idealists, but the recovery of a more accurate understanding of Kant's moderate conception of autonomy is one of the signal achievements
of recent scholarship. Ameriks, *Kant and the Fate of Autonomy.*

as a universal legislator. Autonomy is, contrary to our impression, not an individual orientation but an affirmation of the unity of all rational beings similarly situated.[15] The core of Kant's morality, which defines its sense of constituting a moral advance, is the notion of choosing because it is law. This is hardly a departure from classical and Christian views of the moral life, but it is a crucial differentiation within it. Where the tradition had emphasized that good action must be chosen because it is good, as Aristotle delineates in his account of how virtue is to be emulated, Kant elevates choice into the pivotal moment in the moral life. Unless we choose out of duty, the mere performance of duty loses its moral worth. It is the difference, he explains, between saying, "I ought not to lie if I want to maintain my reputation" and "I ought not to lie even if so doing were to bring me not the slightest disgrace" (441).

Where Kant seems to depart from the preceding moral tradition is in making the exercise of autonomy the incentive of moral action. Of course, he has already ensured that incentive has been thoroughly evacuated from the realm of morality. This may be why the problem of incentive is heightened for him and why he makes the nonincentive of autonomy as such the principal such force. The dignity of rational beings whose autonomy consists in "the property which the will has of being a law to itself" is an endless source of fascination for him. He most often refers to it in the language of "reverence," for it raises man to the divine level. "Even the Holy One of the gospel must first be compared with our ideal of moral perfection before we can recognize him to be such. He also says of himself: 'Why callest thou me (whom thou seest) good? There is none good (the archetype of the good) but one, that is, God (whom thou seest not).' But where do we get the concept of God as the highest Good? Solely from the *Idea* of moral perfection, which reason traces *a priori* and conjoins inseparably with the concept of a free will" (408–9). We can know God because we share the same nature as moral beings and indeed derive our whole notion of divine perfection from that which is highest within ourselves (443). As moral beings we stand at the summit of our existence, sharing the transcendence of God himself. Nothing can compel our assent, because we are capable of disregarding all but what is right. Our own happiness and all the inclinations of nature mean nothing beside this capacity for duty. The elevation of our rational dignity is

---

[15] This is the point exhaustively developed by Allen Wood. "The Kantian ideals of *autonomy, equality*, and *community* can be grasped and pursued only as a unity." Wood, *Kant's Ethical Thought*, 335.

carried far in Kant's meditation, but it is never in danger of overstepping the boundary of existence. This is finally the mystery that remains inexhaustible for him. Kant can understand everything about the categorical imperative except why.

The *Groundwork* trails off in this abyssal question as he struggles with the existential limits of his theoretical penetration. Chapter Three takes up the central question with which the *Critique of Practical Reason* is preoccupied. It is the mystery of why we ought to follow the moral law at the expense of our own happiness. We can, Kant observes, "as yet have no insight into the principle that we ought to detach ourselves from such interest – that is, that we ought to regard ourselves as free in our actions and yet to hold ourselves bound by certain laws in order to find solely in our own person a worth which can compensate us for the loss of everything that makes our state valuable. We do not see how this is possible nor consequently *how the moral law can be binding*" (450). Kant's attempt to deal with the mystery of obligation, by way of distinguishing our membership in the sensible and intelligible worlds, serves only to heighten it. He readily concedes that when we think of ourselves as belonging to the sensible world, we can comprehend our actions under the categories of causality and necessity. But once we regard ourselves as part of the intelligible world of things-in-themselves, we cannot overstep the limits of understanding. We have no intuition of ourselves in the manner of objects. All we have is the immediate knowledge of the moral law that binds our freedom. We belong to the world of appearances and to the world of things-in-themselves at the same time, but the relationship between the two cannot be penetrated further. How the categorical imperative is possible can be answered by the idea of freedom, but how freedom is possible remains impenetrable. Reason cannot supply a condition to explain the unconditioned necessity of the moral law, for to furnish such an explanation would be to abolish freedom. "And thus, while we do not comprehend the practical unconditioned necessity of the moral imperative, we do comprehend its incomprehensibility" (463).

Kant had stated the central issue of modern philosophy but he had only begun the work of its appropriation. Comprehending that incomprehensibility would be the task of the next two centuries as the arc of the revolution he had begun by displacing theoretical with practical reason continued to unfold. What did it mean when philosophy abandoned the claim to theory and accepted the realization that the deepest access to being lay through practice? The limits to theoretical reflection are definitively set by the conditions of its own possibility. We cannot penetrate beyond the necessity of knowing the world through the categories of the understanding that organize our sensible intuitions. However, we can take note of the conditions as we are engaged in the process of understanding, and to that extent, we glimpse the perspective of the way things actually are quite apart from our relating to them. A far fuller access to being is provided when we are ourselves the reality that is in question. Then we are not looking at a phenomenon from the outside but are ourselves responsible for the realization of being. In the moral life, man is the source of his own being to the extent that he is the one who determines whether he moves toward what is true or falls away from it. We may still not be able to see how and why things are as they are and not different, but we are most deeply engaged in the quest for reality and participate most intensely in its dimensions. Our deepest access to being thus lies through the moral life. The implication, as Kant saw, is that practical reason illuminates more than theoretical. What he did not see quite so clearly is why this is necessarily the case and why theory can never adequately comprehend practice. The reason is that no matter how far ahead theoretical reason projects itself, the practice is always one step further; the most it leaves for conceptual apprehension is the last trace of itself and never its action. Like Till Eulenspiegel, life escapes every net set for it. Existence can be known only as essence, never as existence. This is why theoretical reason cannot fully know even itself, since it too remains a practice.

Freedom Requires Eternity

Kant's struggle to overcome the dominance of theory is testament to the difficulty of absorbing this insight into the primacy of existence. The model of intentionality remained so strong that he never completely defeated the urge to conceptualize. His best moments were when he resisted theoretization in the name of preserving the truth of the moral life. Kant saw that the attainment of a motivational account of duty would undermine its very nature, for then it would be neither free nor moral. The work in which the struggle is explored most extensively is the *Critique of Practical Reason*. Kant is clear that the autonomy of practical reason provides us with a knowledge of a causality, in unconditioned freedom, that is beyond the boundary of sensible causes to which theoretical reason limits us. Faced with a cognition beyond the speculative limits, we now must ask, "How, then, is the practical use of pure reason here to be united with its theoretical use with respect to determining the boundaries of its

competence?" (*Critique of Practical Reason, Gesammelte Schriften,* vol. 5, 50).
Kant struggles with the duality of the two worlds of the sensible and the
intelligible, dividing them into "categories of nature" and "categories
of freedom" (65), suggesting "that it makes *law of nature* the type of a
law of freedom" (70). Yet he ultimately abandons the effort to assimilate
the two perspectives, which would be tantamount to a supertheoretical
comprehension.[16] There is no unity, contrary to Hegel's suggestion. Kant
is more faithful to the disclosure of freedom in accepting that it cannot
be comprehended; it can only be acknowledged. As a free moral being
he eventually "views his existence *insofar as it does not stand under the
conditions of time*" (97). This is an astonishing statement that we come to
only after many pages of wrestling with the conundrum of how we can be
free and subject to necessity at the same time. A moral being who must
weigh action *sub specie eternitatis* is not just capable of adopting an eternal
perspective but somehow exists within it. Freedom requires eternity. In
recognizing "the ideality of time," Kant has shifted to an existential self-
reflection that can reach its mark only in the language of myth.

The postulates of freedom, God, and immortality are in the Platonic
sense a "true myth."[17] We do not possess any knowledge of them, but we
are sure of their reality. Theoretical reason can give us no information
about them but must accept them "as extensions of its use from another,
namely a practical perspective; and this is not in the least opposed to its
interest, which consists in the restriction of speculative mischief" (121).
The embracing horizon is constituted by our practical interest, since
theoretical reason must operate within it. This is why Kant insists that
the subordination of practice to theory would "reverse the order, since
all interest is ultimately practical and even that of speculative reason is
only conditional and is complete in practical use alone" (121). Now what
precisely the status of that statement itself is remains obscure in Kant. He
insists that the interest of speculative reason is confined to "the restriction
of speculative mischief," as if it serves only to open up the possibility of

---

[16] Henry Allison has dealt with the genesis of this problematic of freedom and determinism
in relation to the third antinomy of the *Critique of Pure Reason.* Like many Kant scholars
he is inclined to suspect the claims of the idealists that they have moved beyond the
mere statement of the antinomy toward a resolution. Instead, Kant's suspension of any
movement beyond the antinomy is taken for the limits of what is possible. See Allison,
Kant's Transcendental Idealism, rev. ed. (New Haven, CT: Yale University Press, 2004), and
Kant's Theory of Freedom (Cambridge: Cambridge University Press, 1990).

[17] "It is the same with the remaining ideas, the possibility of which no human understanding
will ever fathom although no sophistry will ever convince even the most common human
being that they are not true concepts." *Gesammelte Schriften,* vol. 5, 133–34.

"rational belief" within the moral life. But is not this affirmation of God as "morally necessary" a theoretical statement? It may well be that Kant's emphasis on the primacy of practical reason is not what it appears to be. He may be more accurately seen as insisting on the primacy of the practical source for speculation. All discussions of metaphysics, he seems to say, must be taken out of the pseudo-objective categories of space and time and referred to the transcendent dimension of our own moral existence. Kant could insist that he had made metaphysics critical by regaining its true source in self-transcending existence.

This is in marked contrast to the other term he often applies to his project, as "scientific." He remained enthralled by the success of modern science, which had hit upon the "method," not of conforming its understanding to the real world, but of organizing the phenomena within the patterns generated by the understanding. The *Critique of Practical Reason* even concludes with a chapter on the "method" it, too, has identified of removing all incentive to action but duty. Yet Kant does not consider how completely the two methods, the scientific and the moral, diverge. Where mathematical physics tests the extent to which the world can be contained within our conceptions, the moral imperative requires us to submit unconditionally to the demands of the law. In one case we do the conforming, in the other we are conformed. Science becomes possible once we abandon the quest for knowledge of how things are in themselves and remain content with understanding phenomenal relationships. Duty takes its imperious stand in relation to the truth of reality, resolutely eschewing any merely phenomenal satisfactions. Science cognizes representations of reality; moral representations generate reality. Despite the frequency with which Kant voices such contrasts, their implication is rarely addressed – that is, that the moral perspective is not only beyond the theoretical, but subtends the theoretical as a deeper mode of knowledge. It is a mode that is deeper than science.[18] Kant has therefore

---

[18] This preoccupation pervades Kant's polemical and occasional writings as represented by the selection in *Political Writings*, particularly "On the Common Saying: 'That May Be True in Theory, but It Does Not Apply in Practice," 61–92. As with the other essays, "Idea for a Universal History with a Cosmopolitan Purpose" and "Perpetual Peace," Kant prioritizes his insistence that it "is quite irrelevant whether any empirical evidence suggests that these plans, which are founded only on hope, may be successful," while also noting that "various evidence suggests that in our age, as compared with all previous ages, the human race has made considerable progress, and short-term hindrances prove nothing to the contrary." *Gesammelte Schriften*, vol. 8, 309–10. It is because the argument from freedom so thoroughly occupies the center of his thought that Kant can allow himself the luxury of ancillary historical observations.

not made philosophy scientific but has rather made science ultimately philosophical, that is, practical. The priority of the moral perspective is perhaps best seen in the reflections that conclude the main part of the *Critique of Practical Reason,* in which Kant wonders why we are so ill-equipped by speculative reason for our practical vocation. His response is rooted in moral necessity, for if our theoretical reason had provided a clear perspective on the necessity of fulfilling our duty, it would rob us of our strictly moral incentive. Human life would be reduced to mechanical good behavior, since it would be almost impossible to go against the moral law. Fortunately this is not the case, Kant observes, for "when the governor of the world allows us only to conjecture his existence and his grandeur, not to behold them or prove them clearly; when, on the other hand, the moral law within us, without promising or threatening anything with certainty, demands of us disinterested respect; and when, finally, this respect alone, become active and ruling, first allows us a view into the realm of the supersensible, though only with weak glances; then there can be a truly moral disposition, devoted immediately to the moral law, and a rational creature can become worthy of the highest good in conformity with the moral worth of his person and not merely with his actions" (147–48). What had been viewed as a limitation with respect to speculative reason is penetrated more deeply by the light of moral existence. It turns out, therefore, that contemplation arises not from the detachment from existence but only by participation within it. Metaphysics has again become scientific by becoming moral.

Yet metaphysics never becomes scientific as a system. It is noteworthy that Kant does not envisage a completed metaphysics. His writings consist of a "metaphysics of" that is always on the way, as befits their source in the unending moral struggle. This, too, prefigures the path of modern philosophy in which the "death of metaphysics" is paralleled by a lively effort to live within the questions of metaphysics. What does fidelity to being disclose about being? For Kant the question is most acute when he considers the possibility of revelation, a rupture of existence from the beyond. The necessity of confronting revelation arises not only from the historical impact of Christianity within his environment, but more intrinsically from the challenge that revelation presents to an autonomously constituted metaphysics. Can there be a knowledge of God that is given rather than surmised from within the boundary of the moral imperative? The possibility of revelation seems to have been foreclosed by the critique of speculative reason that keeps us firmly within the limits of spatiotemporal experience. Yet the critique of practical reason provides an opening toward supersensible reality that bursts the bounds of immanence. It is to clarify this confusion that Kant wrote *Religion Within the Boundaries of Mere Reason* (1792), a work whose title seems to suggest that he is retracing the path of deism as the only viable rational theology. Such a project would, however, hold little attraction for Kant, as he had long since left speculative theology behind in the interest of extending the reach of the moral imperative that now formed the center of his thought. The boundaries are thus no longer "mere reason" but reason that strains to live in accordance with what is most divine.

Reason Within the Limits of Religion

Religion Within the Boundaries of Mere Reason discloses the astonishing reach of Kant's ambition. Not only did he inaugurate a revolution in philosophy, he sought to extend it into the realm of religion. He understood that the revolution in philosophy would remain incomplete so long as it failed to take account of religion. Christianity, he understood, had differentiated a deeper and more comprehensive understanding of the human condition that philosophy could not afford to neglect. At the same time, Christianity as dogmatically constructed had rendered itself opaque in the modern world. It stood in need of the renovation under way within philosophy. We might thus read Kant as a Christian philosopher, despite the conventional preconception, because he ultimately aimed at a religious reform. This can explain both the boldness of his interpretation of Christianity and his willingness to test the limits of Prussian censorship. Kant could afford to be audacious because he was so thoroughly convinced of his religious mission. It was nothing less than the advent of true Christianity. We fail to comprehend his project if we assimilate it to some variant of secularization. His critique of Christianity sought not to abolish it but to renew it more profoundly. It is a line of critique that is all the more powerful, as we see in Kant's successors up to Nietzsche, because it originates from within Christianity itself. When we look back over his work, we can discern the practical purpose that animated him from the start. *Dreams of a Spirit-Seer Elucidated Through Dreams of Metaphysics* (1766), as its full title indicates, may seem to be a debunking of Swedenborgian spiritualism, but its real intention was to save it, although Kant still lacked the philosophical means.[19] It was only after the critical turn that he saw

---

[19] Kant's critique of Swedenborgian spiritualism was already the moral insistence that consideration of an afterlife can never furnish a source of virtue. He even announced his

clearly that the spiritual world, while it cannot be grounded objectively, does become luminous through our participation in it.[20]

Perhaps it was because Kant now understood the thoroughly existential character of the moral universe that he was able to tackle questions he had not confronted in his moral philosophy. It is striking that the *Religion* opens with a sustained meditation on the problem of evil, a dimension that previously seemed out of place in the Age of Reason. No doubt the debacle of the French Revolution, then in its early stages, played a role. The intractable reality of history had taken its toll on the idea of progress to such an extent that Kant was prepared to doubt as "a sheer fantasy" (*Religion Within the Boundaries of Mere Reason, Gesammelte Schriften,* vol. 6, 34) his own aspiration for perpetual peace. But he went considerably further than mere observation, to trace the roots of the problem to the inner propensity to evil that lies deep within the human heart. This was no temporary obstacle that might be remediated through education and reform. He understood that evil is evil precisely because it has no cause. We take pleasure in the misfortune of our friends for no good reason, not because depravity and cruelty serve a particular purpose. The search for an explanation of evil, Kant now understood, occurred only because we think it can be grasped theoretically, as if evil were something outside of which we ourselves exist. Such

"moral faith" as the realization that "there probably never was a righteous soul who could endure the thought that with death everything would end and whose noble disposition had not elevated itself to hope for the future. Therefore, it seems to be more in accord with human nature and the purity of morals to base the expectation of the future world upon the sentiment of a well constituted soul than, conversely, to base its good conduct upon the hope of anther world." Ibid., vol. 2, 373/ *"Dreams of a Spirit-Seer" and Other Writings,* 63.

[20] Frederick Beiser is one of the few commentators to recognize the necessity of a sympathetic reading if we are to glimpse the sources of *Religion Within the Boundaries of Mere Reason.* To understand the pivotal idea of the highest good around which the text turns, we must be prepared to give it its full eschatological weight. "It always meant for him, as he described it in *Religion,* 'the kingdom of God on earth.' But this did not imply, as modern scholars believe, that the earth will remain natural; it meant rather that the divine will come down to the earth, which will be completely transformed." Beiser, "Moral Faith and the Highest Good," in Guyer, ed., *The Cambridge Companion to Kant and Modern Philosophy,* 599. As a consequence, Beiser is able to clear up the confusion about the inconsistency of Kant's reflections here about happiness, which seem to undermine the demand that good action be undertaken without consideration of rewards. "Even this problem begins to disappear, however, once we fully understand why Kant demands incentives for moral actions. What Kant is looking for is not rewards for moral intentions and actions, but the motivation to persist in moral action at all. His ultimate worry is (for lack of a better word) *existential:* the despair that comes from believing that all our moral efforts and strivings in the world are in vain." Ibid., 616.

an approach cannot explain; it can only miss the reality. When we shift our perspective to the dynamics of the moral struggle, we behold the problem more clearly. Evil is possible because our actions are free in the sense that they are not determined by anything prior in time (39–40). In every moment we retain the possibility of inverting the maxims that ought to govern our actions, choosing self-love over duty. To adequately articulate the condition Kant reaches back to the mythic symbolizations of original sin, quoting Roman and Christian sources, only now they are shorn of all literal connotations. Myth extrapolates the boundaries of experience. It does not explain, but marks the limit of explanation. Yet myth, as Kant demonstrates, is indispensable for fully articulating the parameters of the moral life, which must confront the difficulty of eradicating evil that is the inexplicable failure of goodness. Without addressing its greatest threat, the force of the moral imperative would be vitiated.

The "ought," Kant recognizes, is finally not sufficient to resist the undertow of evil. To the extent that the propensity to wickedness is somehow innate in human beings, there are no natural barriers to its effects. The purification of our maxims of action "cannot be effected through gradual *reform* but must rather be effected through a *revolution* in the disposition of the human being (a transition to the maxim of holiness of disposition)" (47). Kant uses the language of *metanoia*, by which the soul is transformed in light of the idea of God. "Holiness" is the term he generally uses to identify the transcendent love that includes, sustains, and goes beyond duty. He understands that love is the secret, the greatness of Christianity, without which the moral life would be radically incomplete and defenseless in its contest with evil. Autonomous morality is not self-sufficient. It needs the all-absorbing movement of love, by which it is carried immediately toward the goal that it has yet to reach over the travail of a long distance. The mystery of love is what ultimately triumphs over the mystery of iniquity. Virtue, the formation of character, is the classical theme that looms large over Kant's late moral philosophy, but it is to Christianity that he looks for the deepest affirmation of the spiritual progress he seeks. Such a Christianity would, however, have to abandon the "religion of rogation" (*Gunstbewerbung*), with its emphasis on cult and the imputation of forgiveness, to become the "moral religion," in which the imperative of living a moral life had become the highest concern (51–52). While this may appear to be dismissive of the traditional dogmas of Christianity, it would be a mistake to overlook the extent to which it is a call for the inner deepening of the Christian life. Indeed,

Kant brings in most of the discarded theological structure as extrapolations from within Christian existence.

The most central such dogma concerns the divinity of Christ, and it is intriguing to follow the way Kant handles it. His first inclination is to flatly deny that the divinity of Christ makes any sense from a moral point of view, since then he could no longer function as the authoritative model of conduct for our emulation. It is not that Kant disputes the theoretical possibility that Christ is indeed the Son of God, descended from heaven, but that this stands "in the way of the practical adoption of the idea of such a being for our imitation" (64). In other words, he takes no position on the dogmatic question but focuses attention on what is relevant from the moral perspective, "since the prototype which we see embedded in this apparition [Christ] must be sought in us as well (though natural human beings)" (63–64). Kant is less interested in the historical Christ than in the idea of Christ we apprehend within ourselves. When we take up the full reach of our moral duty, we see that it is nothing less than to conform to the divine requirement of holiness, which is perfect moral goodness. It is, Kant explains, "precisely because we are not its authors but the idea has rather established itself in the human being without our comprehending how human nature could even have been receptive of it, it is better to say that that *prototype* has *come down* to us from heaven, that it has taken up humanity" (61). Kant is willing to suspend judgment on the historical Christ, but he insists on the divine origination of the idea of Christ within us. This inward Christianity still bears a resemblance to the gospel Christ, who declares, "Flesh and blood have not revealed it to you but my Father who is in heaven" (Mt 16: 17). Kant's formulation may be unorthodox, but the necessity of locating revelation as an inward event is surely understandable. Legitimate questions can be raised about the relation between inner and outer worlds, questions that Kant never adequately confronted, but the core of his "*practical faith in the Son of God*" remains clear. It is nothing less than the reality of holiness through abhorrence of the delusion of its mere representation (168).

All objectification of religion contains the possibility of idolatry, the worshiping of the false deity of our own imagination rather than the consummate moral perfection we behold within. "Thus divine blessedness is not a surrogate for virtue, a way of avoiding it, but its completion, for the sake of crowning it with the hope of the final success of all our good ends" (185). It is in *Religion* that we see what the postulates of morality really mean. They are not factors extraneous to the categorical imperative but its inner dimensions. So while God does not function as the guarantor of justice in the universe, and therefore as the ultimate motivator of our actions, he is present as the completion of the path of virtue on which we are engaged, and thus confirms the reality of justice in the whole. Kant no longer has to believe in a divine dispenser of justice, because he already knows him to be the truth of his own moral existence. In the extent to which our own attainment of virtue falls short of the perfection toward which we are drawn, we experience the presence of a divinity whose judgment we cannot escape and whose goodness we cannot resist. The account is thoroughly Christian in its correlative dimensions of guilt and redemption. We are aware of our fallenness by virtue of our proximity to God. But unlike traditional Christian theology, Kant has radically eliminated all objective reference, which does not so much deny the mysteries of dogma as prevent us from knowing anything beyond the limits of our own participation in them. Enlightenment railing against the superstitious misuse of religion is here displayed in its own deepest religious inspiration. Not even "God" can stand in the way of God disclosed in the immediate presence of virtue, for "there is in this something that so uplifts the soul, and so leads it to the very Deity, which is worthy of adoration only in virtue of his holiness and as the legislator of virtue, that the human being, when still far removed from allowing this concept the power of influencing his maxims, is yet not unwilling to be supported by it" (183).

Pure religion has become the means of restoring the core of Christianity. Kant is so convinced that he has discovered the real source of the Christian revelation that he is prepared for a radical reevaluation of its contents. It is in the movement toward moral holiness that we encounter the divinity of God, which he calls "a revelation (though not an empirical one) permanently taking place within all human beings" (122). On this basis he is willing to salvage the doctrine of the Trinity, as indicating the three irreducible aspects of the divine personality by which God is the creator, the benevolent redeemer, and the judge of human freedom. Other elements of traditional Christianity, such as the resurrection and ascension of Christ, are considered no longer relevant to the striving toward the highest virtue and may even distract us from the task. Yet it would be a mistake to interpret Kant's project as the reduction of Christianity to its moral teaching. He exhorts us not simply to live within the boundaries of practical reason but to recognize the latter as religious, as pointing toward a reality it cannot fully apprehend. Historical Christianity provides intimations of those not fully adumbrated dimensions, and Christianity is in turn tested in its capacity to evoke the highest moral perfection. Kant

thereby makes clear what had been known, yet never adequately articulated, throughout the millennial history of Christianity: eschatological
existence. This is not a doctrine about the end of time but the existential perspective that allows us to grasp it. Our actions, Kant repeatedly
reminds us, cannot be understood to originate in time, for they partake
of unconditioned eternity rather than the contingent necessity of time.
Now he is able to more fully reveal our eschatological existence and at
the same time show that Christianity is not just a phenomenon within
time. The relationship is conceived again as an "antinomy of reason" by
which he asks whether a historical faith must always remain or whether
"it will finally pass over . . . into pure religious faith" (116). Like the other
antinomies, there is no resolution of the question other than the recognition that it marks the limits of our capacity to penetrate the condition
in which we find ourselves.

Ultimately, Kant seems to be saying, we do not sit in judgment over
historical Christianity, because Christianity, to the extent that it differentiates the essential meaning of the moral imperative, sits in judgment
over us. The worth of any historically emergent symbolism is demonstrated by its ability to intimate the nonhistorical reality toward which
we reach. We have history because we do not simply live within history.
Like the prominence Kant accorded to esthetics, he similarly marked the
recognition of history as constitutive of philosophy, although it was left
to succeeding generations to undertake the study required for such an
integration in both fields. Philosophy had, however, confronted its own
limits and therefore could not neglect the other dimensions of existence
in which the same boundaries were approached. Once the luminosity of
moral existence had displaced any aspiration for mastery, art and revelation would no longer be regarded as phenomena of history but lines
of meaning that reach into our own present. In this sense the historical
trail of symbols ceases to be merely historical and becomes constitutive
of a moment that is outside the flow of history yet obviously still within
it. Kant was clearly aware of the self-defeating quality of language in
this area. We are still tied to metaphors of "within" and "outside" that
retain their spatiotemporal connotations, and we can escape them only
by a continual struggle against their entrapment. There is no solution
to the antinomies, for even to search for one is already to recede from
the realization Kant struggled to articulate – that is, that practical reason
represents the limit of our penetration of what is.[21]

---

[21] "What Is Orientation in Thinking?" *Political Writings*, 237–49. Explaining why practical
reason must supersede theoretical reason, Kant grounds his argument in moral neces-

It is through practical reason alone that we can "see" what remains opaque to our comprehension. Kant occupies a pivotal place in modern philosophy because he makes explicit what had only been sensed throughout both the history of philosophy and the human search for meaning as a whole. His position even misled him into thinking that no one before him had any such intimations of the primacy of the practical perspective. As a consequence he often seemed to consider his interpretations of Christianity to be entirely novel, and not merely explications of what the faithful had always held. Despite this element of Enlightenment superiority, however, the impact of his work is in deepening the understanding of what had hitherto been presented in largely dogmatic terms. Kant now found a way of making the dogma more transparent for its source when he located it in relation to the two dimensions of guilt and redemption within our moral consciousness. The moral evil of which we are culpable "brings with it an *infinity* of violations of the law and hence an *infinity* of guilt" because the evil is not a mere failure but a choice of a universal maxim (72). But after we have undergone a conversion, the infinite punishment we deserve cannot be seen as appropriate. The just punishment, which can neither be denied nor applied, must be thought, Kant explains, "as adequately executed in the situation of conversion itself" (73). As a morally other being, the penitent has already passed through the process that remains to be traversed in time. "And this disposition which he has incorporated in all its purity, like unto the purity of the Son of God – or (if we personify this idea) this very **Son of God** – bears as *vicarious substitute* the debt of sin for him, and also for all who believe (practically) in him: as *savior,* he satisfies the highest justice through suffering and death, and, as *advocate,* he makes it possible for them to hope that they will appear justified before their judge" (74). A divine atonement for human sinfulness remains ineluctable, but it must emerge from within the exigencies of our moral existence, for otherwise it threatens to invalidate the very disposition it seeks to sustain. This is why Kant reiterates at the close of the book the central principle "that the right way to advance is not from grace to virtue but rather from virtue to grace" (202).

sity. Thus, in contemplating God and happiness, practical reason does not present them in order to derive "the binding authority of the moral laws or the motive for obeying them (for they would have no moral value if the motive for obeying them were derived from anything other than the law alone, which is apodictically certain in itself), but only in order to give objective reality to the concept of the highest good – i.e., to prevent the latter, along with morality [*Sittlichkeit*] as a whole, from being regarded merely as an ideal, as would be the case if that [being] whose idea is an inseparable accompaniment to morality [*Moralität*] did not itself exist." *Gesammelte Schriften,* vol. 8, 139.

This seems to be a reversal of the historical Christian narrative, which places emphasis on the divine initiative, but Kant can argue that he has arrived at it through fidelity to Christian moral existence. Even though we can act only on the hope of divine assistance making up our deficiency in virtue, we cannot afford to regard the decision as anything but our own inescapable responsibility. "Hence we can admit an effect of grace as something incomprehensible but cannot incorporate it into our maxims for either theoretical or practical use" (53). Why, then, does Kant feel the need to discuss it so extensively? The reason is that while grace does not become a basis for our actions, it does illuminate the context in which such actions take place. Partaking of both time and eternity, we act always as if we implicate the whole of our existence in each moment and reach beyond ourselves into the divine relationship to all of creation. Kant emphasizes the absolute primacy of the practical imperative whose purity could be contaminated only by the introduction of a speculative dogma. Yet his insistence that the moral perspective has no theoretical significance is itself the adoption of a theoretical judgment. How can he know that the adumbrations of grace we gain within the moral life are not revelatory of the structure of reality as a whole? How can he know that the historical Christ was not in some way the means of the very fulfillment of grace in existence? Do not such demurrals mitigate the faith that he acknowledges is needed for the arduous devotion to duty? If morality requires faith for its completion, we must be prepared to take that faith seriously. Kant's own readiness to prejudge what can be known through the unfolding of practice is itself a retention of the primacy of the theoretical. While marking the shift from intentionality to luminosity, he had yet to grapple with all of its consequences.

Metaphysics of Practical Luminosity

It is perhaps for this reason that the work in which he is farthest away from such theoretical concerns often contains the deepest illuminations of his theoretical perspective. *The Metaphysics of Morals* (1797) was conceived of as the bridge from metaphysics to morals, but it can just as easily be traversed in the other direction. Kant's own emphasis on the primacy of practical reason would seem to support such a reading even if he retains the convention of metaphysics grounding morality. The work itself is the most convincing demonstration that morality grounds metaphysics. It is a model of what metaphysics must be when it becomes existential. Disclosure occurs not through contemplation but through action. We cannot step outside of ourselves or view reality from afar; we are immersed in a process that can be glimpsed only from within. This becomes clear when Kant engages the questions of right and of virtue, the problematic of politics. It is no accident that politics has been at the heart of philosophy, especially in periods of crisis, because the political presents us with questions that cannot be avoided. Responsibility is thrust upon us in ways that not only rob us of the leisure of contemplation but compel us to confront depths of existence we had scarcely even suspected. We cannot get outside of the political. It is the realm that enlarges our view of reality because its engagement makes us larger than we were. The connection was well understood in the ancient insistence on the public life as the only adequately human one. An equivalent modern rediscovery has been under way since Machiavelli, but as with so much else, it becomes self-transparent in Kant's recognition that it is through moral being that we arrive at being.

Despite this, the place of *The Metaphysics of Morals* in the history of modern political thought is still not sufficiently appreciated.[22] Indicative of its reception is the absence of any full-length English translation until 1991. This neglect is probably due in large part to the impression that Kant was mainly engaged in expounding a formal *Rechtslehre* that, while it paralleled the liberal unfolding of constitutional government, was not central to it.[23] What was missed was the extent to which Kant had taken the prevailing natural rights of the liberal tradition and identified their source. Nature and its attendant conceptions of a state of nature had already begun to unravel in Rousseau; the whole contractarian approach to political order was becoming increasingly unviable. Liberal theorizing was beginning its long search for alternative premises in the case of utilitarianism, the first of many implausible candidates. But Kant had catapulted over the next two centuries by understanding the extent to which the reference of liberal political language is internal. Instead of pointing toward some objectivist nature, the language of rights takes its bearings from its own practice.[24] The reason nature cannot provide a ground for law or rights is that we are incapable of stepping outside of

---

[22] The situation is changing in light of the prominence that Kant's philosophy as a whole now enjoys. For recent views on the text see Mark Timmons, ed., *Kant's Metaphysics of Morals: Interpretative Essays* (Oxford: Oxford University Press, 2002).

[23] The close interrelationships between Kant's arguments still encourage such a systematizing approach to his thought. See Leslie Mulholland, *Kant's System of Rights* (New York: Columbia University Press, 1990), and the alternative approach of Katrin Flikschuh, *Kant and Modern Political Philosophy* (Cambridge: Cambridge University Press, 2000).

[24] I have tried to develop this understanding of liberal politics as sustained through its practice rather than through its foundational articulations in *The Growth of the Liberal Soul* (Columbia: University of Missouri Press, 1997).

the nature that we are. Human nature is what is realized through our fidelity or infidelity to it. We may intend by our actions to enact natural law, but the possibility originates in our transcendence of nature. That is what Kant identifies, not by reference to the idea of right or of virtue, but to the idea of each within which we exist. His misreading as the creator of a formalistic political system may thus have originated with his idealistic formulations, but a more careful reading bears out the extent to which they aim at evoking the boundaries of our responsibility. The metaphysics of morals is what cannot be escaped.[25]

Aristotle expressed it in the language of nature, that man is a political animal. Kant articulates the same understanding in the form of a "metaphysics of right" (205), which defines the inescapable conditions of our existence together. Politics is never merely an option, for we are embedded in a network of obligations before we even begin. This was the weak point of all social contract explanations of civil society, with their inevitable implication of the arbitrariness of a state founded on individual choice. Kant reminds us of the extent to which the state provides the conditions for the exercise of free choice and is thus beyond the realm of choice. We are obliged to support the political constitution under whose order we exist, not because we derive benefits from it or because we have given our consent, but because it is part of the order of being.[26] An

[25] Robert Pippin has called attention to the development Kant signifies within liberal political thought. Agreement is no longer provisional but presupposed, so that "mine and thine, the basic boundaries of the private, are not treated as original starting points by Kant but as secondary and as some sort of socially mediated development. And this suggests that mine and thine are not properly descriptive terms but more like ascriptions of normative statuses, that they are not merely assured by a legal order but can finally only be said to exist within such a legal system of recognition, enforcement, and resolution of disagreement." Pippin, "Mine and Thine? The Kantian State," in Guyer, ed., *The Cambridge Companion to Kant and Modern Philosophy*, 438. Unfortunately Pippin does not take the next step to the recognition of metaphysics as the horizon of existence that would help to make sense of this "alternative form of liberalism, one in which rational individuality is not ultimate, but derivative and an achieved social status" (440). This is a chicken and egg suggestion whose circularity can be resolved only when it is recognized as contained by a more embracing order that, precisely because it constitutes experience, cannot be fully accessed.

[26] Kant's famous remark that "the problem of setting up a state can be solved even by a nation of devils (so long as they possess understanding)" (*Gesammelte Schriften*, vol. 8, 366) must be read within its context. It occurs in the essay "Perpetual Peace," in which having sketched the requirements that follow from the moral freedom of human beings he can then inquire as to how nature might have disposed things so as to overcome their resistance to an order of right. Kant is always clear that the achievement must be effected through the exercise of freedom and never simply follow from the external working of nature.

external system of right is indispensable to the exercise of our freedom and is therefore the first obligation imposed on that freedom. The formalistic style of Kant's exposition tends to convey the sense of a logical necessity, but the concept of right derives its authority from the moral imperative of our existence. It is in this way that he is able to render the contingent reality of the state transparent for an order of necessity. Support by its citizens may be variable, but their obligation is constant. The exercise of freedom contains a dimension of externality that cannot be abrogated. Freedom is civic responsibility. Yet that responsibility is finite, for it is not coextensive with the demand for moral perfection. Kant separates right and virtue along lines that recognize the intermediate reality of politics, where neither expectations nor authority can be unlimited. It is the rule of law, not of virtue.

This is an important theoretical clarification of constitutional practice that forbids the invasion of inner autonomy while avoiding legal positivism. Kant is able to explain how virtue can still be integral to an external order by recognizing externality as integral to virtue. There is thus no need to query the foundations of a legal system, since legality is precisely what an order of right is. We can ask about the difference between the legally right and the morally right because law exists within this distinction and can never escape its boundary. Law does not establish my right to what is mine; it merely recognizes it. To find the source of right we must go beyond the factual to what makes it normative. "Reason has then the task of showing how such a proposition, which goes beyond the concept of empirical possession, is possible a priori" (*The Metaphysics of Morals, Gesammelte Schriften,* vol. 6, 250). When he pursues the question in this way, Kant no longer employs the conceptual analysis of right but turns instead to the existence of practical reason. It is ultimately freedom as self-legislation that must underpin right and resolve the antinomy of the adequacy and the inadequacy of empirical possession, for "we cannot see how intelligible possession is possible and so how it is possible for something external to be mine or yours, but must infer it from the postulate of practical reason" (255). Beyond practical reason we cannot go, not because there is nothing further, but because the attempt to objectify freedom would nullify its exercise. From within the engagement of freedom we can apprehend only what becomes visible from within. Yet that is sufficient because freedom is precisely the obligation to stand in the light of what is, apart from all consideration of benefits and losses. What makes the external more than external is its representation of an order of right, an order that takes its bearings not from power and accident but from what is due in an eternal perspective. Law may be its content, but its force transcends our reach.

We may be the formulators of law, but we are not its authors. Right has its source in that reason that is the limiting horizon of our existence. It is perhaps because of this transcendental authorization of right that Kant has no compunction about dwelling on its coercive implication. "Right and the authorization to use external coercion therefore mean one and the same thing" (232). The creditor does not just have the right to remind the debtor of his obligation; he can compel him to repay his debts. This right of compulsion, while it derives from the law of reciprocal respect expressed in the idea of property, can be authorized only under the existence of a civil constitution. Political authority is the externality of right in the form of compulsion. Kant is even inclined to extend the exercise of compulsion back to the point of origination of the civil constitution, although he recognizes that its source ultimately lies in freedom. "Prior to a civil constitution (or in *abstraction* from it) external objects that are mine or yours must therefore be assumed to be possible, and with them a right to constrain everyone with whom we could have any dealings to enter with us into a constitution in which external objects can be secured as mine or yours" (256). The coercion of the civil constitution encompasses the civil constitution itself. It is a path along which Kant was prepared to travel a considerable distance, despite the risk of undermining the entire notion of right when the limits of coercion can no longer be defined. How are we to distinguish between legitimate and illegitimate coercion? Is all civil coercion per se legitimate? This was a question Kant was ill prepared to answer, especially in light of his anxiety about the revolutionary danger presented by resistance to authority.

Kant recognizes that the state is subjectively contingent but objectively necessary (264) in a way that often seems to elide the two. The categorical imperative of supporting the civil constitution seems to become identical with submitting to whoever controls its machinery. Surprisingly for an admirer of Rousseau, whose conception of the self-legislating general will had stimulated much of his political thought, Kant had been horrified by the terror of abstract freedom unleashed in the Revolution. Like many of his contemporaries, he was willing to resubscribe to the divine foundation of authority that would make it a crime "that cannot be forgiven" to execute a monarch (320). Kant saw the abyss of revolutionary action as "the complete overturning of all concepts of right" (320) from which it would be impossible to establish a new constitution. Yet it would be wrong to say that he was simply a blind supporter of the status quo. His position was that once political authority exists it must be the principal instrument of its own remediation. Revolutionary action was excluded, for "even if the organization of a state should be faulty by itself, no subordinate authority in it may actively resist its legislative supreme authority; the defects attached to it must instead be gradually removed by reforms the state itself carries out" (372). Such a conservative reform proposal was hardly unusual at the time, for many thinkers had concluded that responsibility for the debacle of the French Revolution had to be assigned to its rejection of all restraints. Kant, however, was providing more than a counsel of caution or registering pragmatic concerns. He had clarified the very idea of political change in the notion of right. This was not merely an abstract principle of critique, but the ineliminable boundary of political community from which the very possibility of critique arises and therefore the unsurpassable limit of the possibility of change. All discussion of right presupposes our membership in a civil constitution that it can never overthrow. Without that recognition the language of right has no reference.[27]

Historical reality, it will become clear in the philosophical development that follows Kant's lead, partakes of two worlds, time and eternity. "Every actual deed (fact) is an object in *appearance* (to the senses). On the other hand, what can be represented only by pure reason and must be counted among *Ideas*, to which no object given in experience can be adequate – and a perfectly *rightful constitution* among men is of this sort – is the-thing-in-itself" (371). The "city in speech" is not a wholly other reality from the historical city of Athens; even Plato probably never believed in Platonic forms. Now we are at the point where the history of philosophy begins to clarify this fundamental relationship at the heart of political thought. Despite the language of "Ideas," Kant was here on the verge of a revolutionary breakthrough that made sense of the whole historical turn that was taking place in his time. History was becoming thematic through the awareness that we live neither within history nor outside of it. Just as we cannot penetrate beyond appearances to the thing-in-itself, so we can

---

[27] Much has been made of Kant's insistence on the impossibility of making the maxim of revolutionary action public. "The injustice of rebellion is thus apparent from the fact that if the maxim upon which it would act *were publicly acknowledged*, it would defeat its own purpose. This maxim would therefore have to be kept secret." "Perpetual Peace" (ibid., 382). But this notion of publicity must be given its full weight, for it has nothing to do with the mere exposure of a plot. The impossibility is moral, not pragmatic, since Kant means that it is the existential impossibility of acting on such a principle that really counts.

have no knowledge of the latter without apprehending the former. We cannot know the idea of a civil constitution as it is in itself; we can know only the civil constitution in its appearances within history. The reason for this limitation is not that the idea of the civil constitution exists in some region remote from us, but that we live within it in an intimacy that cannot be severed. All that we can hold onto are the historically emergent appearances, but they are appearances of a reality that we know from within. The idea of a civil constitution is not one we possess when we approach historical reality but one that possesses us as historical beings. We live not within history but within that which can only present its appearance within history. Sovereignty is only a fact but its right is *a priori*.

What, then, does this mean that right derives its obligatory force from the priority of practical reason? It means that the understanding of right is realized in practice and that there is no right other than its historically emergent self-understanding. This is what occupies much of Kant's attention in *The Metaphysics of Morals* and accounts for the general perception of the work as Kant's "views" on concrete moral and civil issues. They are, of course, not his "opinions," but the self-articulation of the boundaries of right from the *a priori* of "metaphysics." "For all examples (which only illustrate but cannot prove anything) are treacherous, so that they certainly require a metaphysics" (355). The process of the metaphysics of morals is well illustrated by the way in which the interpretation of the principles is established through an internal meditation. Contrary to the conventional impression, Kant does not aim at a merely formal consistency. Right, he shows, requires us to wrestle with the conflicts generated by its own application. A particularly acute case arises when we confront opposing principles of right. We may have no problem with the logic of civil right that requires the imposition of death for the deliberate taking of life. But what of the killing that is mandated by honor? Kant grapples with the crimes authorized by considerations of the honor of one's sex and of military honor. A woman may kill the child who is born to her outside of marriage, and a junior officer may require satisfaction in a duel. The "quandary" for the penal law is that it must either set aside all consideration of honor or abrogate the demands of justice. Kant is sympathetic to the dilemma, recognizing that the illegitimate child is outside the law and can be ignored by it. "It has, as it were, stolen into the commonwealth (like contraband merchandise), so that the commonwealth can . . . ignore its annihilation" (336). Equally the young officer "has to prove his military courage, upon which the honor of his Estate essentially rests" (336). The categorical imperative of punishment is not suspended, but we recognize that the civil constitution itself is at fault to the extent that it "remains barbarous and undeveloped" in allowing the incentive of honor to exist outside of it. We still live within the inexorable unfolding of right even when we are not yet capable of acknowledging all of its demands.

We have no perspective for the understanding of right other than our own historical engagement in its realization. The excessive familiarity of the language of rights today is one of the principal obstacles to recognizing its existential status. Oblivious to the boundary-constituting role of rights, we are astonished when they refuse to serve our convenience. We have yet to follow the philosophical revolution opened up by Kant when he recognized that the language of rights refers not to the world of appearance but to the unsurpassable reality within which we exist. It was by making this shift in perspective that he was able to work out why a man's right to his reputation continues after his death. After all, he is no longer present in the spatiotemporal mode that is necessary to sustain an injury. How can it hurt him now? Normally we do regard a person's good name as an "external belonging" that he is entitled to defend and expect the law to protect. But why should we be concerned with a right to defend his reputation from the grave? Kant's answer goes to the heart of the matter. It has nothing to do with family or estate or abstract principles but everything to do with the only adequate context for treating human beings. Whether a person ceases or survives after death is not the issue. It is that we are required to treat him as transcending the limits of finitude "for in the context of his rights in relation to others, I actually regard every person simply in terms of his humanity, hence as *homo noumenon*" (295). It is because a person cannot be partitioned into appearances that marriage must entail a mutual commitment for life. Anything less would be tantamount to using a person as a thing. Kant's treatment of marriage as part of the externality of right is interesting for what it reveals about the existential character of right. While defined by externals, the right of "reciprocal use that one human being makes of the sexual organs and capacities of another" (277), marriage is in accordance with authoritative principles of right because it preserves the humanity of the partners. They may possess one another externally, but it is a complete giving by which they receive one another in turn. Both are given and received in their full humanity in the recognition that "acquiring a member of a human being is at the same time acquiring a whole person, since a person is an absolute unity" (278). Marriage is thus only the appearance of possessing as an object what cannot be possessed as an object. In the case of human beings, the part can stand for but cannot contain the whole.

The doctrine of right can only define the externals of the relationships that ought to hold between human beings. It cannot get at the reality from which the requirements spring. This is why the metaphysics of morals must go on to the doctrine of virtue, which should, in Kant's view, properly be called "ethics." Yet the fact that the doctrine of virtue is placed after the doctrine of right demonstrates that it is not simply an ethics of intention. External right constitutes the order in which we exist, and we cannot abrogate the universality of law on which it rests. The idea of the rule of law implies the equality of every human being under it. What it does not touch is the incentive that moves us to support the order of right. Contrary to the implication drawn from Kant of the priority of the right over the good, he seems to recognize precisely the deficiency of the right as such.[28] Law cannot exist without an ethics, for it cannot enforce itself. What is missing is the concern that has been at the heart of ethics since its classical beginnings, the reason I should make the priority of right my good. Kant has long been viewed as an advocate of duty who turns morality into the empty formalism of duty for duty's sake. Some support for this view derives from his formulations. Yet it cannot square with the intensity of conviction by which he makes duty an end in itself, nor can it be reconciled with the extensive discussion of virtue that forms the core of his metaphysics of morals. It is perhaps the most serious misreading of Kant, which arises from the tendency to overlook the extent to which he has made existence rather than objectivity the locus of his philosophical reflection. Conversely we should expect that his "Doctrine of Virtue" provides the most forceful confirmation of his existential stance.

---

[28] For Kant the priority of the right over the good is a moral priority, i.e., one that insists that it is not the consequences of an action but rather the principle by which it is intended that makes the action good. For John Rawls the priority is political, i.e., a means of reaching agreement on principles by individuals with pluralistic conceptions of the good. At the same time, the moral authority of Rawls's settlement draws heavily on the Kantian moral priority. We might conclude, therefore, that Kant provides a way of understanding the Rawlsian priority to be not so much a theory of justice as the existential predisposition to its actualization. A good example of the convergence is provided by Kant in rejecting a right of popular revolution. "I will only remark that such errors arise in part from the usual fallacy of allowing the principle of happiness to influence the judgment, wherever the principle of right is involved" (ibid., 301). Rawls, *A Theory of Justice* (Cambridge, MA: 1971), 27–33, and "Kantian Constructivism in Moral Theory," *Collected Papers*, ed. Samuel Freeman (Cambridge, MA: Harvard University Press, 1999), 303–58.

This expectation is not disappointed. Where the "Doctrine of Right" shows how freedom is possible, the "Doctrine of Virtue" tells us what we are to use it for. Virtue provides purpose to right. "The Doctrine of Right dealt only with the *formal* condition of outer freedom (the consistency of outer freedom with itself if its maxim were made universal law), that is, with right. But ethics goes beyond this and provides a *matter* (an object of free choice), and end of pure reason that it presents as an end which is also objectively necessary, that is, an end which, as far as men are concerned, it is a duty to have" (380). Virtue adds little to the categorical imperative, but that little is crucial. It is the recognition that the maxim of universal law, which is also at the source of right, should now be made the principle of *my* will (389), not just of will in general. Kant is aware of the contradiction contained in the suggestion that we ought to acquire certain dispositions, since it is only because of those dispositions that we can be expected to live up to them. "To have these predispositions cannot be considered a duty; rather, every man has them, and it is in virtue of them that he can be put under obligation" (399). A duty of virtue is a circular concept because it is nothing less than the duty of acquiring the duty of acquiring duty. We seem to be back at the empty formalism of morality that his ethics sought to avoid and, many readers seem to conclude, that he never escapes. But his solution is essentially the same as that of Aristotle in recognizing the same circularity of virtue. The obligation of making virtue an end is circular only from the perspective of logic; from the perspective of existence it is an endless progress. Dispositions to virtue are not fixed quantities available in advance of our efforts. They are more like movements that we actualize by participating in them. "Consciousness of them is not of empirical origin; it can instead only follow from consciousness of a moral law, as the effect this has on the mind" (399).

We begin to see in this remark the purpose of Kant's moral reflection, especially in the "Doctrine of Virtue." It is nothing less than the heightening of the existential movement by which we participate in what is highest and have access to it in no other way. The duty of virtue, or more properly of progress in virtue, is sustained "both by contemplating the dignity of the pure rational law in us (*contemplatione*) and by *practicing* virtue (*exercitio*)" (397). In each case it is the end of virtue as its own reward that emerges as the highest dignity of which we are capable. This is far beyond the grim admonition of duty for duty's sake. Kant's meditation now opens within the luminosity of being that is glimpsed insofar as we are drawn toward it. "Virtue so shines as an ideal that it seems, by human standards, to eclipse *holiness* itself, which is never tempted to break the law" (396–97). Kant, of course, goes on to suppress this exuberance as only an "illusion" derived from the subjective experience of self-transcendence. What is significant is not that the outburst occurs but that Kant refuses to allow it any role in the unfolding of virtue. Nothing extraneous to the process can be allowed to intervene because it would amount to the exchange of a substitute for the reality. Despite the closeness of his articulation to Aristotle's "*athanatizein* (immortalizing)" (*Nicomachean Ethics,* 1177b30), perhaps because of it, Kant is determined to retain the reality of participation in what is immortal in preference to the symbol of it. This is one of those important moments in the modern philosophical revolution in which the opening of an existential language secures the classical beginning against the dogmatization it underwent in the history of philosophy. It is unclear as to what extent this was Kant's intention, but there is considerable basis for regarding it as his achievement. Even while seeming to depart from Aristotle, he reaches a deeper affirmation.[29]

This is especially the case when he addresses the central contention of Aristotle's ethics that virtue aims at happiness. He seems, indeed, to take deliberate aim at Aristotle. "A eudaimonist's *etiology* involves him in a *circle;* that is to say, he can hope to be *happy* (or inwardly blessed) only if he is conscious of having fulfilled his duty, but he can be moved to fulfill his duty only if he foresees that he will be made happy by it" (377). Kant has drawn attention to what was on the verge of being lost in Aristotle: happiness is not external to virtue. There is no happiness apart from the happiness of virtue. Not only is virtue its own reward; virtue is the only reward. All other considerations are mere extrapolations beyond the boundaries of our moral existence. Justice is not an order that exists apart from our realization of it, as if it could be added as an afterthought to our existence. We literally have no choice but to be just or to destroy ourselves. Nothing is higher than the demand of fidelity to the call of what is right, for who can be happy without justice? Higher than happiness stands justice as its truth. Kant repeatedly emphasizes that it is justice that makes us worthy of happiness, but what he really means is that justice constitutes happiness. Worthiness is happiness. We stand in the light of being that must regard anything less than itself as mere counterfeit. By disdaining any form of eudaimonia other than the transcendent imperative of

---

[29] For a discussion of the relationship see Nancy Sherman, *Making a Necessity of Virtue: Aristotle and Kant on Virtue* (Cambridge: Cambridge University Press, 1997).

duty, Kant has secured eudaimonia against any possibility of its misplacement in substitutes. "If this distinction is not observed, if eudaemonism (the principle of happiness) is set up as the basic principle instead of *eleutheronomy* (the principle of the freedom of internal lawgiving), the result is the *euthanasia* (easy death) of all morals" (378).

The difficulty of maintaining this existential perspective as the highest is in many ways the centerpiece of Kant's philosophy. He knows that it is only by straining continually against the prevailing tendencies of theoretical dominance that we can recognize the authoritative truth within which theory itself has its place. The error of instrumentalizing morality arises easily in a context shaped by the expectations of the scientific assignment of causes. It is difficult to maintain the imperative of the categorical imperative. "Being unable to *explain* what lies entirely beyond that sphere (*freedom* of choice), however exalting is this very prerogative of man, his capacity for such an *Idea*, they are stirred by the proud claims of speculative reason, which makes its power so strongly felt in other fields, to band together in a general *call to arms*, as it were, to defend the omnipotence of theoretical reason" (378). It is difficult to judge the extent to which Kant understood the awareness of this problem in classical philosophy, but we can recognize that he marked out the distinction in a way that was not likely to be overlooked in the modern world. Meditation on the unsurpassable boundary of our participation in being had now become so clearly the task of philosophy that he could be permitted his sanguine conclusion. "And so now, and perhaps for a while longer, they assail the moral concept of freedom and, wherever possible, make it suspect; but in the end they must give way" (378).

It is this shift toward the existential perspective that accounts for the primacy of duty toward oneself. The duty of virtue, of becoming the kind of person who can fulfill his or her duty, is first owed to oneself. Then we become capable of carrying out our duties toward others. Kant even employs the term "practical wisdom" to denote the existential core of virtue in the same way as Aristotle (405). We may recall the ambiguity that exists in Aristotle's treatment as to whether practical wisdom is a moral or an intellectual virtue, which cannot be resolved because it is somehow the whole of virtue (*Nicomachean Ethics*, 1144b–45a). Kant recognizes the issue but has resolved it by avoiding completely the language of faculties that suggests that the virtues somehow preexist within us. Such theoretical denotations have no relevance within an articulation of the dynamics of moral responsiveness that has no reference beyond our fidelity or failure to participate. "Considered in its complete perfection, virtue is therefore represented not as if man possesses virtue but rather as if virtue possesses man; for in the former case it would look as if man still had a choice (for which he would need yet another virtue in order to choose virtue in preference to any other goods offered to him)" (406). Even the understanding of virtue as a habit, which Kant does not entirely reject, is still not quite adequate to the realization of virtue as the movement by which man transcends himself (409). The entire discourse of virtue, Kant has recognized, makes no sense given the understanding of man as a natural being in the manner of objects in the world. All talk of self-transcendence, of "being bound to bind myself" (417), is a contradiction in terms. It makes sense only in reference to a personality whose existence is contained nowhere but within the movement by which it actualizes itself (418).

Autonomy refers not to the movement of a whole but rather to our movement within a whole. This is why, as Kant goes on to explain in dealing with "elements of ethics," we are not free to commit suicide. Despite the example of the Stoic endorsement of it as the supreme expression of virtue, of autarky, Kant finds it a dereliction of the highest obligation imposed on us. Autonomy cannot be used to abandon autonomy. "To annihilate the subject of morality in one's own person is to root out the existence of morality itself from the world, as far as one can, even though morality is an end in itself" (422–23). Even to yield to the lewdness by which we turn our integral being into a mere means of sexual gratification is a dehumanization that "seems in terms of its form (the disposition it involves) to exceed even murdering oneself" (425). But the greatest violation of a man's duty to himself is the lie by which he demonstrates contempt for his own moral being. "By a lie a man throws away and, as it were, annihilates his dignity as a man" (429). Kant reserves his particular revulsion for the inner lie by which we deny to ourselves what we know to be true. Moral suicide is both a possibility for a being who can throw away his autonomy and yet an impossibility, since we can use only our autonomy in the process. Virtue consists in remaining faithful to what makes virtue possible. This is also what characterizes the sum total of our relationships to others. We preserve their autonomy not only by the love that ministers to their needs but also by the respect that maintains the distance required for their own attainment of virtue. Autonomy for Kant always includes the autonomy of others, as he demonstrates in a remarkable paean to friendship reminiscent again of the Aristotelian model.[30]

---

[30] "Hence friendship cannot be a union aimed at mutual advantage but must rather be a purely moral one, and the help that each may count on from the other in case of need

Serving humanity in ourselves and in others is always at the core of our exercise of autonomy. Self-government has no higher purpose than self-government. How we connect with what is below us or above us remains a mystery; we have duties toward each only to the extent that our humanity is engaged. We can see no further than our own existence, in the sense that our obligations toward other beings cannot become transparent. The only moral universe to which we have access is our own rational autonomy. We cannot really know what is owed to God or nature, but we can discern what our own autonomy requires. This is why Kant insists that all of man's duties are duties toward himself. What we owe toward animals may be directed toward them, but its source lies within ourselves. We cannot mistreat animals, not because they have rights, but because we cannot inflict wanton cruelty without dulling a "shared feeling of their pain" and weakening "a natural predisposition that is very serviceable to morality in one's relations with other men" (443). Kantian morality remains at its deepest level a virtue ethics in which it is the necessity of becoming a particular kind of character that carries the full force of obligation. It is no more self-serving than Aristotle's formulation that the life of virtue involves loving oneself, one's true self, most of all (*Nicomachean Ethics*, 1166a). The difference is that Kant has made explicit the reason this is so: we cannot serve any good other than the good that is disclosed in our movement toward it. We can have no duties toward others unless we first have the duty toward ourselves of binding ourselves toward them. Our obligation is to obligation. There is no going back to something behind duty itself in which we are embedded before we even begin. The possibility of duty toward others lies in the priority of duty by which all obligations toward others are ultimately obligations toward oneself.

This is why Kant insists that we must avoid the amphiboly by which we mistake our "duty *with regard* to other beings for a duty *to* those beings" (442). Duty we have with regard to God is not a duty to God. By recognizing all our duties as divine commands, we do not thereby turn them into divine commands. "Rather, it is a duty of man to himself to apply this Idea [of God], which presents itself unavoidably to reason,

---

must not be regarded as the end and determining ground of friendship – for in that case one would lose the other's respect – but only as the outward manifestation of an inner heartfelt benevolence, which should not be put to the test since this is always dangerous; each is generously concerned with sparing the other his burden and bearing it all by himself, even concealing it altogether from his friend, while yet he can always flatter himself that in case of need he could confidently count on the other's help." *Gesammelte Schriften*, vol. 6, 471.

to the moral law in him, where it is of the greatest moral fruitfulness" (444). Oaths are in this sense absurd, Kant notes, because they have no higher value than the morality of those swearing them (487n). Morality is what grounds religion and therefore cannot include religion as one of its components. This explains why for Kant there is no duty of religion within his ethics, but it does not explain why the reflection on religion comprises the conclusion of *The Metaphysics of Morals*. Perhaps nothing prefigures the wrestling with religion of the next two centuries as Kant's own probing reflections in these pages, for while religion is not included in ethics, it becomes more likely that ethics is included within religion. A convincing argument can be provided as to why faith in an afterlife is irrelevant to the determination of what is required of us, but it is by no means clear that ethics can constitute a realm unrelated to the resolutions that lie beyond its boundaries. Indeed, Kant's whole notion that conscience ought to be regarded as the voice of God within us expresses this realization. We do not need the idea of God to provide an incentive for morality, but we do need the idea of God to convey its reality. Justice does not rest on the expectation of a future life in which rewards and punishments are accorded; rather "it is from the necessity of punishment that the inference of a future life is drawn" (490n). Here we encounter the final form of the paradoxical tension in which Kant's thought moved. While all of these religious extrapolations are irrelevant from the viewpoint of practical reason, it is nevertheless important to recognize them.

We cannot, he insists, form any conception of the way in which the justice and love of God are reconciled. The moral relationship between man and God is one in which one side has only duties and no rights, the other only rights and no duties. It cannot be assimilated to the relations among men. In particular, we cannot comprehend how the punishment owed for the wrong done to an infinite being can be reconciled with the love that is the only possible basis for creation. It seems as if the formal and material aspects of the principle of justice cannot be reconciled, for the requirement that guilt must always be expiated cannot square with the end of serving the happiness of humanity as a whole. Kant does not declare the impossibility of reconciliation. He does not rail against the idea of God as a contradiction in terms. He merely acknowledges his ignorance. "The concept of this is *transcendent*, that is, it lies entirely beyond the concept of any punitive justice for which we can bring forward any instance (i.e. any instance among men) and involves extravagant principles that cannot be brought into accord with those we would use in cases of experience and that are, accordingly, quite empty for our practical reason" (489). What Kant did not do is undertake the step he had thereby made possible in the history of philosophy. He did not yet include his own insight within the account. To have seen that the practice of virtue is bounded by a mystery that is transcendent in its attenuations of justice and love does not constitute sheer ignorance. By demarcating a boundary, we do not simply remain within it. Knowledge of the limits is already a faint but unmistakable glimpse of what is beyond them. Now the existential turn in philosophy would begin to struggle with this realization.

2

Hegel's Inauguration of the Language of Existence

If Kant was the one who brought about the revolution in philosophy that is its modern achievement, Hegel was the one who made the event explicit. This is why we are inclined to see Hegel as the point of reference for the subsequent history of thought. We forget that Kant was the inaugurator of the existential perspective, in large part because he never fully confronted its implications. Hegel by contrast was a more far-reaching thinker, one who was not reluctant to admit his own epochal significance and hint at an even higher status. The megalomania of the nineteenth century was in the air. Yet philosophy was not absorbed by the enthusiasm that surrounded it. Hegel may have been carried away by the prospect of making the turn toward inwardness a permanent achievement, capturing it within the definitiveness of the system, but this did not prevent him from furnishing the means by which the excesses would be resisted and reversed. Hegel thus turned out to be the pivotal thinker, although his significance was other than what he often seemed to indicate. The ironic role of Hegel in the movement of modern philosophy consists in the development of the instruments by which his own missteps have been corrected. This explains the extraordinary prominence he holds for those who came after him. Responses to Hegel are the vehicle by which the unfolding of modern philosophy proceeds because he so thoroughly supplied the instruments of his own critique. We have no choice but to become Hegelian critics of Hegel who accuse the master of not remaining true to himself. Our aim is to out-Hegel Hegel.

This was evidently not his intention, but it is in keeping with the character of philosophy as it emerges in its modern disclosure. Just as there is nothing outside the text, even more so there is nothing outside the philosophical perspective that has become available to us. The modern turn has been to continuously raise the question as to whether the statements of a thinker can be included within their meaning. Is what he does consistent with what he says? Can form and content be reconciled? To the extent that this is precisely the question Hegel applied to Kant, it is only fair that the same inexorability should be applied to Hegel himself. If practical reason has become the means by which we apprehend the whole, practice must become the focus of our attention. Any claim to have absorbed the whole within the practice must be tested against its own practice. This is not merely to repeat the "existentialist" objection that Hegel included everything within his system but Hegel himself. We are familiar with the complaint that life is different from theory. What we need to understand is the degree to which that objection originates within Hegel's practice itself. He is the one who made it clear that philosophy does not deal with objective realities; it is rather that philosophy is constituted by the reality within which it exists. The claim to have finally comprehended the whole within which we are held must strike us, therefore, as a peculiarly perverse return of objectivity. Both in the direction of his thought and in the distortion to which it is subjected, Hegel provokes the question of existence and exhibits the greatest threat to it. In the modes of both openness and closure he remains of decisive significance, as we live within the tensions to which he gave voice.

It is because of his overarching position within the history of thought that we have considerable difficulty in reading him. The tendency toward one-sidedness is very strong as we launch our assault on the part that offends us the most. We may pay lip service to countervailing tendencies within Hegel, but it is difficult to judge the weight to be given them. Our problem is to gain the necessary distance, a task made all the more challenging by the degree to which we are still struggling to enter into the nonobjective mode of reflection that he introduced. His language, too, is a notorious obstacle as he wrestles to make words perform a new function that their derivation from commonsense reference resists. For all of these reasons it is necessary to proceed cautiously, not accepting an interpretation until it has been considered in light of many possible exegeses. If our goal is to uncover Hegel as a whole, rather than any of the partial caricatures that emphasize one feature to the exclusion of the rest, we are best advised to follow the route by which Hegel became Hegel. A genetic account gives us the best chance of catching the integral perspective that illuminates the result. It is a strategy well recommended by his own account of the priority of the process over the end. The meaning of the parts can be judged only in light of the movement that has expanded from the beginning. As mere stopping points along the way, they yield a range of arbitrary possibilities. It is fortunate that we have, therefore, a document that expresses not only Hegel's intention but that of the common project of his contemporaries at their very inception. This is "The Oldest Systematic Programme of German Idealism."

The Program

Whether "The Programme" was actually written by Hegel, as many believe, is not of great importance. The uncertainty of authorship underlines its broadly representative character as a formulation that could have come from any one of several minds at the time.[1] It sets forth the direction of philosophy flowing out of Kant, as the opening suggests. "An *ethics*. Since in the future the whole of metaphysics will collapse into morals – of which Kant, with his two practical postulates, has given only an example and exhausted nothing – all ethics will be nothing more than a complete system of ideas, or, what amounts to the same, of all practical postulates." Now Kant's postulates have become the "ideas," a term not to be confused with our mere representations of objects. Ideas in this sense are the constitutive whole within which we exist. This is why the text goes on to emphasize that most of our so-called ideas, such as the state, the constitution, and eternal peace, are only "subordinate ideas of a higher idea." They do not exist in themselves and must be seen as such. The state in its ordinary sense would thus "cease to exist." In its place would stand the idea of the history of humanity, along with the ideas of a moral world, divinity, and immortality as the encompassing horizon. "Then comes absolute freedom of all spirits, which carry the intellectual world in themselves, and may not seek God or immortality *outside of themselves.*" The sentence must be read as the culminating point of the whole paragraph. It does not make everything internal to human consciousness, as some have suggested. Not only would finding God and immortality within oneself as mere ideas defeat their purpose, which is precisely to

[1] "The Oldest Systematic Programme of German Idealism" is available in Hölderlin, *Sämtliche Werke, Grosse Stuttgarter Ausgabe*, ed. Richard Samuel et al. (Stuttgart: Kohlhammer, 1960), vol. 4, pt. 1, 297–99, and in Frederick Beiser, ed. and trans., *The Early Political Writings of the German Romantics* (Cambridge: Cambridge University Press, 1996), 3–5. The manuscript is in Hegel's handwriting, although the first publisher, Franz Rosenzweig, assumed he had simply copied it from Schelling, whose ideas it seemed to fit more closely. More recently the case has been made for Hegel's authorship; see H. S. Harris, *Hegel's Development Toward the Sunlight: 1770–1801* (Oxford: Oxford University Press, 1972), 249–57. Many affinities between its contents and the ideas of Schlegel, Schelling, Hölderlin, Novalis, and Schleiermacher have been noted.

supply their absence from the self, but this is not what the grounding of metaphysics in ethics really means. The point is that the only source of such ideas lies in our response to them in the practical realm. We do not contain the ideas; they contain us. The injunction against searching for ideas of God and immortality outside of ourselves applies to dogmatic metaphysics. Existential metaphysics consists in living within them.

It is this existential purpose that explains the transition to the idea of beauty in the second half of the document. "I am now convinced," the author declares, "that the highest act of reason is an aesthetic act since it comprises all ideas, and that *truth* and *goodness* are fraternally united only in beauty." Philosophy is replaced by poetry because it is only through poetry that we are moved to action. Without the inspirational force, all ideas are merely dead letters. "The philosophy of the spirit is an aesthetic philosophy." No longer bound to a merely contemplative mode, philosophy is now a living reality shaping the entire world in a new mythology, a "mythology of reason." It is at this point that the vision begins to take wing with the prospect of a new civilizational order joining together the enlightened and the unenlightened. There is, of course, much of the romantic aspiration that beauty will save mankind here, but it is more than a youthful outburst of utopianism. Behind it lies a profound consciousness of epoch, in which philosophy has finally become luminous for the truth and goodness of existence. The transparence of living life is what accounts for the exuberance of the closing proclamation of the realm of freedom and equality that it creates. "A higher spirit sent from heaven must establish this new religion among us. It will be the last and the greatest work of humanity."

The romantic innocence in mistaking the wish for the deed must be seen in light of the philosophical revolution adumbrated in these pages. Confidence that the new epoch with its new religion could be inaugurated arose from a powerful sense of a historical dispensation.[2] Specifically it was the spiritual opening of philosophy as a way of life. The romantic insight had penetrated the opaqueness of symbols to encounter the inner movement that had all along been the secret of their life. The difference was that now the derailment into dogmatism could be avoided, for the existential source had become unmistakably clear. In retrospect we might surmise that this overconfidence was perhaps the

---

[2] For the general context see Frederick Beiser, *Enlightenment, Revolution, and Romanticism: The Genesis of Modern German Political Thought 1790–1800* (Cambridge, MA: Harvard University Press, 1992).

last refuge of dogmatism itself. But at the time the exaggerated expectations were understandable. It was only later when they hardened into a will to remake reality that they became the opposite of their beginning. Even that distortion could not, however, detract from the philosophical revolution itself. The power of the "ideas" had been definitively transformed from an externality remote from human consciousness to the inner dimensions of existence by which we live. The ideas were no longer outside of us, because we were no longer outside of them. Philosophy had become existential in drawing its reflections from the unfolding of its own possibility. It was no wonder that, in the opinion of the early romantics, poetry had surpassed philosophy, which could only reflect on what poetry brought about. In becoming existential, philosophy now pointed beyond itself.[3]

Priority of Life over Reflection

This is clearly the direction announced in Hegel's early theological writings, which set out to find in Christianity what cannot be found in philosophy. He understood philosophy to be merely a process of thinking that must always confront its limit in "the opposition between the thinking mind and the object of thought." Hegel had not yet arrived at his later understanding of philosophy as itself the infinite movement of *Geist* in which religion finds its fulfillment. But the path toward that conclusion had already begun to open within this theological beginning. What looks, therefore, like a rupture from his earlier theological past, the later displacement of revelation by philosophy, turns out to display far more continuity than it appears to do. What changes is not Hegel's attitude toward Christianity but his fundamental conception of philosophy. To understand the far more existential character philosophy acquires for him, we must recognize that it begins in the turn toward life animated by faith and love. So while the early formulation that "philosophy therefore has to stop short of religion" (*Hegels theologische Jugendscrhiften*, 348 / *Early Theological Writings*, 313) may seem at odds with the eventual position he reaches, we will better understand the latter if we bear its existential beginning in mind. Hegel is notorious for the introduction of a new way of philosophizing, but its difficulty will be considerably alleviated if we recall its origin outside of philosophy. Hegel, too, did not regard

[3] This path is well covered in Dieter Sturma, "Politics and the New Mythology: The Turn to Late Romanticism," in Ameriks, ed., *The Cambridge Companion to German Idealism*, 219–38.

philosophy as adequate to the task it had set itself. This is why his earliest writings take up the deeper question of existence. How do we ensure that we are living in relation to the truth that is ultimate and not merely wasting our lives in externalities? Echoes of the eighteenth century concern with transparence, especially as voiced by Rousseau, seem to resonate, but now the search has taken on a seriousness, intensity, and purpose that leave the Age of Reason behind.[4]

The earnestness of the young Hegel, with his friends Schelling and Hölderlin from the Tübingen seminary, coincided with the great social and religious events of the day.[5] Not only was the transition from the vestiges of the medieval past under way in politics, but the inner spiritual ferment of modernity had simultaneously exceeded the boundaries of the Enlightenment. The decrepitude of the past, whether feudal in France or imperial in Germany, had become manifest. What was to form the shape of the future was less apparent. The dramatic starkness of the passage to modernity was less evident in Britain and America as they followed the same path far less consciously – America without possessing any medieval past and Britain by drawing its medieval past into its present. But in Europe the moment lay fully exposed. There was no choice but to embrace the future. Its very openness was in part what inspired the confidence of the first romantic generation that they possessed resources equal to the challenge of their historical destiny. Boundless optimism still radiates from Hegel's retrospective account of the French Revolution in the pages of the *Philosophy of History* as "a glorious mental dawn. All thinking beings shared in the jubilation of this epoch. Emotions of a lofty character stirred men's minds at that time; a spiritual enthusiasm thrilled through the world, as if the reconciliation between the divine and the secular was now first accomplished" (*Sämtliche Werke, Jubiläumausgabe*, vol. 11, 557–58 / *Philosophy of History*, 447). The descent of German philosophy into the pessimism of the later romantics was still several decades in the future, and the interval was marked by the rise and fall of the great project of refounding modern civilization, on which they all converged. Hegel may have typified the epochal ambition, but he was not alone. A widely shared understanding had turned philosophy from its largely speculative role to the activist leadership of modern civilization. Philosophy

[4] On Rousseau see Jean Starobinski, *Jean-Jacques Rousseau: Transparency and Obstruction*, trans. Arthur Goldhammer (Chicago: University of Chicago Press, 1988).

[5] Laurence Dickey, *Religion, Economics, and the Politics of Spirit, 1770–1807* (Cambridge: Cambridge University Press, 1987), locates Hegel's development in this historical context.

now addressed the question of existence at its deepest, that is, religious, level, and it was confident that it could bring about the renewal of the age from this innermost depth.

Hegel's *Theologischse Jugendschriften* are thus not really theological in nature. They are essentially philosophical reflections within the new existential key that permits it to roam beyond the conceptual boundaries that previously contained it. Philosophy has become a living movement to such an extent that Kant's concerns about its inability to provide theoretical knowledge no longer enter into consideration. This is the most remarkable feature of Hegel's unremarkable "Life of Jesus." Christ's announcement of the gospel of the categorical imperative in the text is of such little significance that it was not thought necessary to include it among the English translations. By assimilating it entirely to the Kantian influence, however, we overlook the extent to which it also represents a departure. Absent from Hegel's account is any suggestion that the categorical imperative might not be sufficient, that it might leave questions of the relationship between nature and freedom unresolved, that it says nothing about the ultimate telos of human existence, and so on. What is striking is the confidence that the categorical imperative leads us fully into the divine life of Jesus. This is the good news and the reason Hegel neglects any discussion of the Resurrection. Where Kant felt he still had to deal with such theurgic manifestations, Hegel could follow out the existential logic of the Resurrection that had already occurred within the divine life of conscience. His Jesus never even suggests that men and women believe in him, for he has come to invite them to believe in themselves. They are called to hearken to "the holy law of their reason, to pay attention to the inner judge of their hearts, to conscience, a measure that is also the measure of divinity" (*Theologische Jugenschriften*, 119). It is not that Hegel rejects the theologoumena of the life of Jesus but that they can be neglected in light of existence within them. Kant struggled with the relationship between moral existence and historical religion; Hegel saw more clearly that the former was the only basis for the latter. The question now became whether Christianity could cease to function as a "positive religion."

"The Positivity of the Christian Religion" brings us into the center of the crisis of late eighteenth century Pietism, although it is important to recognize that it is not simply driven by those concerns. The broader framework remains the Kantian turn toward existence in philosophy. It is that discovery of existential openness that gives Hegel the confidence that the positivity of Christianity as exemplified in the conformism of Pietism can be overcome. He may give voice to the alienation of authentic faith, but he in no way despairs of remediation. Indeed, Hegel is brimming with the assurance that he already lives within the light of divinity. Pietism, in contrast, has reached its limits once its social success has established it within the state. The form of Christianity premised on the removal of all externality has now become fully externalized in the enforced discipline of a state church. Where the early Christian community could be formed by the bond of genuine friendship to which each could entrust himself, as the society expands that bond is replaced by the formalities of an external association that mask the absent reality (*Theologische Jugendschriften*, 178–80 / *Early Theological Writings*, 102–3). The rise of new sects to reverse the reification of faith repeated by previous sects is the inescapable pattern of Christian history. Pietism is only the latest, most explicit refusal of all externality of faith, and it too has succumbed to the pressures of routinization. "The fundamental error at the bottom of a church's entire system," Hegel concludes, "is that it ignores the rights pertaining to every faculty of the human mind, in particular to the chief of them, reason. Once the church's system ignores reason, it can be nothing save a system which despises man" (211/143).

The crisis of Pietism makes visible a deeper crisis of Christianity. Judaism was based on the sufficiency of external observance of the divine commands, while Christianity recognized that only the full inner donation of the heart was adequate to the being of God. But as a consequence Christianity came to mandate feelings, "a contradiction in terms" (209/140). The effect of this regime of "legality and mechanical virtue" is well captured in Hegel's poignant description of the vacillation between self-deception and false tranquility in the individual soul. "Often too," he observes, "he falls into despair if he thinks that, despite all his good will and every possible effort, his feelings have still not been intensified to the extent required of him. Since he is in the realm of feeling and can never reach any firm criterion of his perfection (except perhaps via deceptive imaginings), he lapses into a frenzy of anxiety which lacks all strength and decision and which finds a measure of peace only in trusting on the boundless mercy of God. It takes only a slight increase in the intensity of the imagination to turn this condition too into madness and lunacy" (209/141). One can hardly read the passage without sensing that the aching intensity it describes is drawn from experience. Deeper than the complaint of hypocrisy lies the agony of the divided soul (209/141). But here it is treated not as an autobiographical struggle but as redolent of the contradiction that lies buried in the heart of Christianity itself. It is in the nature of the challenge that confronts Christianity in the modern world that it is a crisis that Christianity has drawn on itself. In the hands of a spiritually sensitive young man, Christianity has failed to show him how it can remain true to itself. He is simply caught in the endless contradiction of commanding feelings that cannot be commanded. This is the positivity of the Christian religion.

It may, of course, be that Pietism is particularly vulnerable to this unfolding, while it remains that the history of Christianity in general is the history of a perpetual search for self-renewal. As a historical religion it is essentially a religion of recollection. What makes Hegel sanguine about a fundamental improvement in this condition is that philosophy has at last broken through to the meaning of such *anamnesis*. We now know that the source of the historical symbolizations lies within the existential movement by which we participate in being. This is the breakthrough of Kant's recognition of duty as that which is above everything else. It is in the determination to act only out of obligation that we actualize the true divinity within us. This is what makes it possible for Hegel to reject the suggestion that Christianity is "a positive religion as a whole" (144/173) and to insist that the "convictions of centuries... were not, at least on their subjective side, downright folly" (143/172). The hermeneutical value of this realization becomes evident in the following text, "The Spirit of Christianity and Its Fate," which begins with an extended consideration of the Judaic beginning. Even there, where the externalized relationship to God has been carried furthest, Hegel makes clear, the moving forces remain the inwardness of Jewish existence. It is only because of the contradiction between the spiritual liberation Judaism seeks and the political liberation for which it is mistaken that an opening is provided for the message of Christ. He is the one who proclaims the truth of Judaism in the Sermon on the Mount, not by exhorting fidelity to law, but by exhibiting its source within them. "The Sermon," Hegel observes, "does not teach reverence for the law; on the contrary, it exhibits that which fulfills the law but annuls it as law and so is something higher than obedience to law and makes law superfluous" (266/212). The existential source of obedience to God is disclosed as a "modification of life."

It is through life that what is alien, a power over against us, is reconciled with us. The criminal, Hegel explains, dreads punishment as something from which he must flee, but welcomes it as the fate he has drawn on himself for it is what restores him to the whole of life, from which his actions have separated him. Jesus went even further in recommending that his disciples go beyond the law in granting forgiveness so that reconciliation with the wrongdoer is made complete. This is not merely so that our own unrighteousness might be forgiven, but so that the community of all might be exhibited. "Beware of taking righteousness and love as a dependence on laws and as an obedience to commands, instead of regarding them as issuing from life" (288–9/237). Hegel reads the message of Jesus as salvation from the dead letter of the law to obtain the living reality of spirit, a perfect bond of friendship between those who share the same spirit. "Faith is a knowledge of spirit through spirit, and only like spirits can know and understand one another" (289/239). The problem is that this option for love over legality is still bound to the world it opposes. Hegel sees Jesus as advocating a complete withdrawal from the world in order not to suffer the contagion of its fate. His disciples are required to forsake father and mother, withdrawing from all natural relationships "in order to avoid entry into a league with the profane world and so into the sphere where a fate becomes possible" (286/236). This "beautiful soul" is met with frequently in Hegel's writings, and we must regard its utter self-absorption as one of the principal dangers he discerned in the romantic impulse within Christianity. "A heart thus lifted above the ties of rights, disentangled from everything objective, has nothing to forgive the offender, for it sacrificed its rights as soon as the object over which it had a right was assailed, and thus the offender has done no injury to any right at all." Hegel is here doing no more than pointing out one of the long-standing dangers recognized in eschatological Christianity. In maintaining its purity it runs the risk of ceasing to be real. Withdrawal from the world can be tantamount to the withdrawal from life. If Christianity is to remain true to itself, it must devote itself to its embodiment in a way of life. Up to this point Hegel's reflections remain firmly within the bounds of Christian self-reflection.

More problematic is the final step of his argument, by which he sees the centralization of Christianity around Christ as a fundamental misdirection. He wants to confine the significance of Christ to overcoming the separateness of Judaism through the communion of those who recognize the bond of love between them. Love as "the living interrelation of men in their essential being" (295/246) is what goes beyond the fixity of all concepts. We may still be commanded to love, but "love itself pronounces no imperatives. It is not universal opposed to a particular, no unity of the concept, but a unity of spirit, divinity. To love God is to feel one's self in the 'all' of life, with no restrictions, in the infinite" (296/247). This is the bond that exists among the disciples, who recognize that divinity is what is living between them. For Hegel it is expressed most fully in the "love-feast" of the Last Supper, in which the feeling has become objective in the actions of Jesus (298/249). What prevents it from becoming a full religious event is that the manifestations are to be annulled. "The bread is to be eaten, the wine to be drunk; therefore they cannot be something divine" (300/251). The communion of those who carry the divine within them can be destroyed only by something that suggests the permanence of the divine outside of them. There can be no suggestion of Christ's actions as an external sacrifice for the sin of mankind. "If they are made alike simply as recipients of an advantage, a benefit, accruing from a sacrifice of body and an outpouring of blood, then they would only be united in concept" (299/250). Having entered into the existential mode of philosophizing, Hegel is loathe to permit any hint of an objective perspective to interfere with the full realization of living life. Yet he also does not push the limits to the point of declaring the invalidity of all religious symbolization.

The completion of love is religious; the unity of reflection and love in thought is the intuition of the infinite under the form of the finite. All such symbolization, Hegel perceives, is inadequate. "The infinite cannot be carried in this vessel" (302/253). This is the impossibility Jesus faced when he had to explain who he was. "In the determinate situation in which he appears, the man can appeal only to his origin, to the source from which every shape of restricted life flows to him; he cannot appeal to the whole, which he now is, as to an absolute" (303/255). Referring to himself as the Son, coming from the Father, he must inevitably run the risk of becoming the objectified divinity. Only the opening of John's Gospel provides the possibility for "the recipient to grasp the communication with the depths of his own spirit" (306/256) and thereby provides Hegel with a form of religious discourse more compatible with its content. When the existential mode has been recognized as the most embracing horizon available to us, the partitioning of theoretical analysis has become obsolete. Now the part must be viewed as containing the whole, just as the whole contains the parts. "What is a contradiction in the realm of the dead," Hegel announces in the most striking sentence of the text, "is not one in the realm of life" (308–9/261). Christ is the one who proclaims the good news of the divinity within each one of us, for he shows us that we can recognize him by virtue of the same spark within ourselves. To rescue Christianity from the dead language of the church that settled down to worshiping its founder requires, therefore, a thorough reformation of its traditional symbolizations.

At the core of that reassessment Hegel places the fateful separation of the early Christian community from the world of which it was a part. He sees that it was the impulse to preserve its own beautiful soul, the separated community of love, that rendered its ministry so sterile in regard to the world as such. His critique at this point seems to present the most adamantly anti-Gnostic face, although this does not necessarily inoculate it against its own Gnostic overtones as well.[6] Whatever the judgment may be, the force of Hegel's argument derives much of its impact from a telling identification of the major weakness of the Christian millennia. The impulse to wall itself up within its own life has taken many forms, all equally destructive of the life they are intended to preserve.

[6] I draw attention to this feature because the analysis of Hegel in the conceptualization of Gnosticism has received considerable attention, although few references to it surface in the currently prevalent strands of Hegel scholarship. The fact that this omission stems from the secular presumptions that drive such scholarship should not, however, discourage us from including it within an overall reading of Hegel. As a lost chord in the lively reconsideration of idealism in general and Hegel in particular, it is useful to remind ourselves of the genesis of this Gnostic affiliation, for it originates with Hegel himself. The most notable source is his *Lectures on the History of Philosophy*, where he singles out Jacob Boehme as his great predecessor in dialectical theosophical speculation. A second powerful statement of the relationship is that of Ferdinand Christian Bauer, who, within the Hegelian school, affirms the Gnostic transmission in *Die Christiliche Gnosis* (Tübingen: Osiander, 1835). The first great twentieth century invocation is Hans Urs von Balthasar, *Die Apokalypse der deutschen Seele,* 3 vols. (Salzburg: Pustet, 1937–39). From there it found its way into the work of Eric Voegelin, who formulated it as a general thesis on modernity in *The New Science of Politics* and *Science, Politics, and Gnosticism,* both available in *Modernity Without Restraint, Collected Works,* vol. 5, ed. Manfred Henningsen (Columbia: University of Missouri Press, 2000). The most sophisticated contemporary formulation is that of Cyril O'Regan, *The Heterodox Hegel* (Albany: State University of New York Press, 1994) and *Gnostic Return in Modernity* (Albany: State University of New York Press, 2001). A valuable assembly of the historical evidence is contained in Glenn Alexander Magee, *Hegel and the Hermetic Tradition* (Ithaca, NY: Cornell University Press, 2001). I made my own more modest contributions to the debate in "The Historical Dialectic of Spirit: Jacob Boehme's Influence on Hegel," in Robert Perkins, ed., *History and System: Hegel's Philosophy of History* (Albany: State University of New York Press, 1984), 15–35, and *The Mysticism of Innerworldly Fulfillment: A Study of Jacob Boehme* (Gainesville: University Presses of Florida, 1983). As the remarks in the text indicate, I now find the thesis of Hegel's Gnostic and esoteric background more complicated to assess, for while the textual basis is incontrovertible, the precise weight to be assigned to it is far more difficult to judge. It is possible that Blumenberg is correct in suggesting that much of modernity is to be read as essentially an anti-Gnostic movement, as an attempt to avoid the short-circuiting of existence into a solution beyond it. Blumenberg, *The Legitimacy of the Modern Age,* trans. Robert M. Wallace (Cambridge, MA: MIT Press, 1983), 137–43. The implication is that Hegel, for example, remained more solidly within a traditional Christian orbit while drawing on the heretical critiques to bolster his own case for a rejuvenation of Christianity.

Conflict, Hegel insists, cannot be avoided except at the price of life. This is a theme that would receive enormous elaboration in his later thought. Here it emerges in the context of his own struggle to understand the failure of love in the very community devoted to its realization within history. "This restriction of love to itself, its flight from all determinate modes of living even if its spirit breathed in them, or even if they sprang from its spirit, this removal of itself from all fate, is just its greatest fate" (324/281). It was from that fateful self-separation from history that in Hegel's reading the theological derailments followed, among which was the failure of Christianity to become a religion. Specifically, it had not yet become a living religion. The complaint against the dead letter of historical religion is at the core of the project in which Hegel is engaged. Love, even the divine spirit of love, is not enough. "To become religion, it must manifest itself in an objective form. A feeling, something subjective, it must be fused with the universal, with something represented in idea, and thereby acquire the form of a being to whom prayer is both possible and due" (332/289). This failure of Christianity to satisfy "the supreme need of the human spirit" must be taken seriously. It forms the core of the reinterpretation that engaged Hegel for the remainder of his life.

At its center is the focus of Christianity on the divinity of Jesus. This did give members of the early community an objective means of expressing the spirit that united them, but it also forestalled the self-realization of that spirit. In their prayerful relationship to the risen Lord, the life of the community remained externalized and doctrinalized, while "in the lifelessness of the group's love the spirit of its love remained so athirst, felt itself so empty, that it could not fully recognize in itself, living in itself, its corresponding spirit" (336/294). So long as it remains fixed on the person of Jesus, Christianity is afflicted with positivity. Even the transparence of Christ manifest through miracles and culminating in the Resurrection are not sufficient to dispel the anachronism. Spirit cannot be manifest in the material, because it is the nature of spirit to be that which can be known only through itself. Clothing spirit in a miraculous display is really its concealment. Miracles are a forced conjunction of spirit and body that are essentially opposites. "Their union, in which their opposition ceases, is a life, i.e. spirit configurated (*gestalteter Geist*)" (338/297). For Hegel the resurrection of Jesus and of all who share in his spirit can no longer function as the appropriate identification of his faith. Such a purely physical resurrection has now become an obstacle to the inner resurrection of his spirit within existence. The internalization of eschatological Christianity has reached its limit. Even the recognition that the apostles understood the nonliteralness of the spirit that is present in the miraculous events could not mitigate the demand for transparence.

Miracles had become merely a demonstration of the incapacity of Christianity to deliver on its promise. If man was to be united with God, this could not occur vicariously through a particular individual or physically through a resurrection from the dead. Spiritual union can occur only inwardly. Even the glorified Jesus can express no more than this aspiration without actually fulfilling it. "In all the depths of their beautiful feelings those who felt this longing pined for union with him, though this union, because he is an individual, is eternally impossible" (341/300). By turning its back on life Christianity took a fateful turn, for it sought to hold together in thought what can be united only in life. The turn toward existence undertaken by Hegel convinced him that he had not only uncovered the source of the Christian symbolism, but had found the means of preventing its derailment into externality again. It is one of the insufficiently understood ironies of the history of modern philosophy that the thinker most notoriously associated with the system took his beginning from the realization that life always escapes any effort to contain it. "Life is the union of union and non-union." This is the sense in which the great synthetic effort that followed must be understood, as Hegel himself explains in the "Fragment of a System." "Reflection is thus driven on and on without rest; but this process must be checked once and for all by keeping in mind that, for example, what has been called a union of synthesis and antithesis is not something propounded by the understanding or by reflection, but has a character of its own, namely, that of being a reality beyond all reflection" (348/312). The question is whether we can say anything about that reality without lapsing into the conceptual attempt at containment. In raising it we acknowledge the pivotal place of Hegel in modern philosophy.

The realization that he defines the question that still defines our historical moment should give us pause before concluding that we yet understand him. How is it possible to understand a thinker who is at the limits of our thought? We must, of course, stretch ourselves toward those limits, and a good first step would be to dispense with all of the standard assimilations of Hegel to organic or cosmic analogues.[7] His central

---

[7] It is one of the principal achievements of contemporary Hegel scholarship, especially evident in the approach of such analytic philosophers as Pippin, Wood, Ameriks, Beiser, Pinkard, and others, that organicist and holistic readings have largely disappeared. When Hegel is read as a guide to the problems of the self-realization of freedom, there is no necessity to invoke any further metaphysical realities. An eminent example of this

conception of Geist cannot simply be transferred to some intermediate reality pervading or underlying the whole.[8] Our reading of the *Theologische Jugendschriften* has shown that he employs the term precisely to avoid suggesting that Geist represents any "it" reality. We are contained by Geist, and are not its containers. Like life, Geist is that by which we live, and we can know it in no other way. To call this organic or cosmic still smacks of a tendency to separate ourselves from our existence in order to attain a moment of comforting superiority. This is not Hegel's usage, and his attempt at linguistic fidelity contributes greatly to the unfamiliarity of his language. Perhaps his intentions are clearest in his vision of an integrated social and political community where the danger of false objectifications is minimal. The conclusion of "The Fragment of a System" already held out such a perspective on a community animated by a living spirit, a happy people "whose life is as little as possible separated and disintegrated" (350/317). But it was in his next major writing, *Natural Law*, that Hegel really addressed the social and political dimensions of his existential philosophy. It was here that he took the decisive step beyond the fixity of Kantian morality and right to locate them within the living dynamic of an "ethical whole."

approach is that of Robert Pippin, *Hegel's Idealism: The Satisfactions of Self-Consciousness* (Cambridge: Cambridge University Press, 1989), who insists "that by Absolute Knowledge Hegel is not referring to a knowledge of an absolute Substance-Subject, a Divine Mind, or a Spirit Monad. As he has since the latter half of his Jena years, he is referring to the conditions of human knowledge 'absolutized,' no longer threatened by Kant's thing-in-itself skepticism" (168). For an overview see Frederick Beiser, ed., *The Cambridge Companion to Hegel* (Cambridge: Cambridge University Press, 1993). Whether this analytic approach to Hegel is faithful to the invention of a language of existence is one of the principal questions to be considered.

[8] The "metaphysical" approach epitomized by Charles Taylor's *Hegel* (Cambridge: Cambridge University Press, 1975) sought to do just that. Taylor proposed a conception of cosmic spirit as the only one "which can provide the basis of a union between finite and cosmic spirit which meets the requirements that man be united to the whole and yet not sacrifice his own self-consciousness and autonomous will" (44). The difference between this and the now more favored "nonmetaphysical" approach is perhaps not as great as it appears to be. Both seek to understand Hegel as continuing the Kantian project of grounding autonomy within a whole to which it can never simply be assimilated. As such the project is primarily existential, an exploration of the possibility of existence that can never ultimately comprehend what it seeks without closing off the possibility of existence. In this sense the notorious ambiguity of the Hegelian synthesis may be seen not as a deliberately crafted one but merely as a reflection of the irresolvability within which existence unfolds. In this sense there is no metaphysics other than through our existence within it. Of course, all of this goes with the caveat that Hegel was himself much to blame for the ambiguous implication of closure in his own formulations. On this see Voegelin, "On Hegel: A Study in Sorcery," *Published Essays*, in *Collected Works*, vol. 12, ed. Ellis Sandoz (Baton Rouge: Louisiana State University Press, 1990), 213–55.

"System" of Ethical Life

A system of ethical life is more than a concept of the mutual necessity of universal and particular. *Sittlichkeit* is for Hegel itself a living reality, and his thought becomes an effort to think all of the components within it. Abstractions such as the "rights of man" or goals like "perpetual peace" are dead, and their impact is deadening. None of the parts of a constitution are to be allowed to stand on their own as if they mattered more than the life of the whole. Even war is to be welcomed as what shakes up the society, compelling its members to actively subordinate their individual interests to the common good. Like Burke, Hegel saw clearly the depth of compulsion that lay behind the invocation of abstractions unconnected to any concrete living tradition. But where Burke could only oppose the deformation in the name of historical sense, Hegel understood the existential shift required to make that sense a living reality. It would involve a fundamental revision of the understanding of natural law, one that would take up the incompleteness in its development from classical sources to its renewal in the eighteenth century. "Natural law," he explained pithily, "is to construct how ethical nature attains its true right" (*Natural Law,* 113).[9] To complete this revision in the understanding of natural law, however, Hegel saw that he would have to go farther afield than a conception of nature. As he lays out the project here, it would entail the recognition of the absolute as that within which all the separate spheres subsist. To follow him we must be prepared to take seriously his insistence that the absolute is not itself an existing thing, and therefore more readily accept his unfamiliar depiction. "This ideality of ethics and the form of universality in the laws must, insofar as it subsists as ideality, also be united with the form of particularity. In this way the ideality as such must be given a pure absolute shape, and so must be regarded and worshipped as the nation's God; and this view must in turn have its own vivacity and

---

[9] This is surely no more than a reconceptualization of Kant's formulation of the categorical imperative. "Act as if the maxim of your action were to become by your will *a universal law of nature.*" *Groundwork of the Metaphysics of Morals, Gesammelte Schriften,* vol. 4, 421. The profound rethinking of natural law that occurs in idealism remains one of the least investigated topics, largely because scholars of natural law have little interest in exploring such an interiorization, while scholars of idealism retain little sympathy for the extrincisist vestiges that attach to natural law. What is striking, however, is that for all their critique of a teleological ethics, the idealists still felt compelled to accommodate themselves to the appeal to nature. See also Johann G. Fichte, *Foundations of Natural Right,* ed. Frederick Neuhouser, trans. Michael Bauer (Cambridge: Cambridge University Press, 2000; original, 1796–97).

joyful movement in a cult" (116). When we understand absolute spirit as the life within which we live, we can understand how "by consciously conceding to the negative a power and a realm, at the sacrifice of a part of itself, it maintains its own life purified of the negative" (133). Already, however, the language is veering dangerously close to the suggestion that the absolute, spirit, the infinite are in their own way individual entities.

This is the problem of the elaboration of Hegel's existential insight, in which its very elaborateness is the principal obstacle to its penetration. When we recognize the existential intention of his construction, however, we can place its systematic character in a different light. It is almost as if Hegel sought through comprehensiveness to convey the sense of a living reality. This is the way in which his recurrent reference to a "system" must be taken. Despite the extent to which his own articulateness often defeats the purpose, Hegel really intended the system to be an open one. As a participant within the system of the whole, he could not lay claim to have definitively comprehended it. So while we have the language of a system, we do not possess a system. This explains why, even when his thought is presented in its most systematic fashion in the *Encyclopedia of Philosophical Sciences,* it constantly overflows into lecture "additions" that are frequently larger than the texts they are designed to supplement. The same vitality of philosophy is vividly presented in the great lecture series on history, art, philosophy, and religion that came down to us in that *viva voce* format without benefit of a fixed text. We are confronted with a system that is not a system, because it is a dynamic whole whose movement is not to be stopped but recognized as vital parameters of our existence. "System," it finally turns out, is not Hegel's term for what contains the whole but his way of calling attention to its living reality. The word may connote something dead to us, but to him it was the only way of conveying the interrelationship of all the components of existence. Nowhere is this vitality more apparent than in his generation of various "systems" from the early writings on.

It is noteworthy that all of them have the focus of the title of the very first one, *System der Sittlichkeit,* written for a lecture course in 1802.[10] Other dimensions of the project may have ballooned in the later versions, but its origins remain centered on the question of ethical life. The practical

---

[10] It is always worth keeping in mind that Hegel kept up a lively and deep interest in contemporary political affairs, producing a steady stream of thoughtful essays in parallel with the philosophical writings. In particular we should note his long reflection, "The German Constitution," completed at this time. Virtually his last writing, in 1831, was an extensive essay entitled "The English Reform Bill." *Hegel's Political Writings.*

side of philosophy is appropriately preeminent in its post-Kantian phase. It is important to keep this in mind when ethical life is subsumed within the *Philosophy of Spirit*, in the third part of the *Encyclopedia* following *Logic* and the *Philosophy of Nature*. Thus, while the final shape of the system gives the impression that Hegel bases a moral and political philosophy on a metaphysical foundation, this conventional priority has in fact been rendered obsolete. Metaphysics can no longer provide the first principles of ethical life when philosophy has itself become a mode of ethical life. This is precisely the revolution under way in the history of modern philosophy. It is ethics that now provides the foundation of metaphysics, for we have no access to the order of being other than through our participation in it. Speculation is not a separate avenue toward what is but rather the result of a prior existential openness. This is the insight that Hegel took from Kant and elaborated into what would address Plato's complaint that the most important matters cannot be written down. When philosophy recognizes that the movement of existence can be disclosed only through the movement itself, it ceases to be about something other than what it is. The terms lose their fixity and become moments in the whole of which they are a part.[11]

It is the unfamiliarity of a dynamic language that is the principal obstacle to understanding Hegel when he turns to the execution of the project that the early writings only announce. He no longer talks about what he is going to do, but actually enacts it in the first *System of Ethical Life* (1802–3). Language must play a new role when it no longer refers to a world of objects but to the existential context within which both subjects and objects exist. We might say that language is what constitutes reality. Just as in a contract it is the ideal transfer that makes the real one possible, so we see that ideality is the key moment making reality real. "This much results formally, that ideality as such, and also as reality in general, can be nothing other than a spirit which, *displaying itself as existing*, and wherein the contracting parties are nullified as single individuals, is the universal subsuming them, the absolutely objective essence and the binding middle term of the contract" (*Schriften zur Politik und Rechtsphilosophie,*

---

[11] Robert Pippin has argued that systematic closure "is not a necessary principle of, or a necessary consequence of, Hegel's idealism. This means that there might be some other way to understand the *implications* of Hegel's idealism than that officially attributed to Hegel, and so another way to understand his holism, his account of an 'originary, universal, purposive subjectivity.' But that too is a much longer story." Pippin, *Hegel's Idealism*, 260. That story, I would suggest, can be told only if we enlarge Pippin's speculative reading to its full implication as the existential horizon within which Hegelian reflection unfolds.

439/ *"System of Ethical Life" and "First Philosophy of Spirit,"* 123, emphasis added). From this elemental beginning Hegel constructs a far more extensive conception of the living whole that is the concretely existing people. The intuition of the idea of ethical life is the people. They are no longer conceived of as an abstraction but as a living entity that draws its existence from the idea by which they are constituted. Each individual "reaches supreme subject-objectivity" in this recognition in which particularity and universality are reconciled in being lived. "Between the Idea and reality there is no particularity which would first have to be destroyed by thinking, would not be already in and by itself equal to the universal. On the contrary the particular, the individual, is as a particular consciousness plainly equal to the universal, and this universality which has flatly united the particular with itself is the divinity of the people, and this universal, intuited in the ideal form of particularity, is the God of the people. He is an ideal way of intuiting it" (462–63/144). This does not mean that the collectivity is God or that there is no God beyond the existential tension. Hegel may have left himself open to such notorious misconceptions, but his purpose remains the prioritizing of participation over contemplation.[12]

The extent to which he has departed from the isolated subject is perhaps best recognized in his treatment of the emptiness of freedom against which Kant struggled. "Choice and deliberation," Hegel understood, "is an act proceeding from freedom and the will and so can just as easily be upset again" (484/163). The arbitrariness of individual will, especially when it is aggregated to a whole society, removes any possibility of an enduring public order. Against this capricious majoritarianism, Hegel asserts the authority of the absolute as that alone within which human society can exist. "The absolute government, on the other hand, is divine, is not made, has its sanction in itself, and is simply the universal" (484/163). It is the transition from monarchy and external religion to the form in which a people "takes the divine into itself" (499/177) in enacting its ethical life. In the conclusion attributed by Rosenkranz to this first system, Hegel went on to show how Christ was the point at which this shift from natural religion to a genuinely spiritual form occurred most completely, because Christ is the one in whom the divine force of infinite reconciliation is revealed to be what sustains the ethical life. The truth is

---

[12] For an account of the centrality of recognition as the overarching category of Hegel's thought, see Robert R. Williams, *Hegel's Ethics of Recognition* (Berkeley: University of California Press, 1997).

neither historical nor theological, but existential. This is the revolution Hegel effected in making ethical life the centerpiece of speculation, for "in the organization of a *people* the absolute nature of spirit comes into its rights" (*Jenaer Systementwürfe I, Gesammelte Werke*, vol. 6, 281 / *"System of Ethical Life" and "First Philosophy of Spirit,"* 211). Among the first fruits of this mode of existential analysis are the remarkable insights into the nature of alienated labor that Marx scarcely improved on forty years later. In the *First Philosophy of Spirit* (1803) Hegel could recognize the threat posed by the abstraction of labor in modern industrial society because he located it in relation to the inner dynamic of human existence.[13]

Science Before Science: Phenomenology

By the time he came to write the *Phenomenology of Spirit* (1807), the focus on ethical life appeared to have been dropped in favor of an emphasis on science. He even proclaimed the transformation of philosophy from the love of wisdom to its possession. Closer examination, however, reveals that Hegel had not departed from his earlier existential phase but had enlarged it to include knowledge itself. His new understanding of science was rooted in the recognition of knowledge as itself a mode of existence. Hegel was on his way toward bringing together Kant's theoretical and practical reason, although the status of such an enterprise is characteristically difficult to identify. Heidegger called attention to Hegel's own shifts in title.[14] The most obvious one is that Hegel presents the *Phenomenology* as a "pathway" or "ladder" toward science, which he intended to provide

---

[13] "When he lets nature be worked over by a variety of machines, he does not cancel the necessity from nature; and his living labor is not directed on nature as alive, but this negative vitality evaporates from it, and the laboring that remains to man becomes itself *more machinelike;* man *diminishes* labor only for the whole, not for the single [laborer]; for him it is increased rather; for the more machinelike labor becomes, the less it is worth, and the more one must work in that mode." *First Philosophy of Spirit*, 247. See the discussion of this in Shlomo Avineri, *Hegel's Theory of the Modern State* (Cambridge: Cambridge University Press, 1972), ch. 5.

[14] Heidegger, *Hegel's Phenomenology of Spirit*, trans. Parvis Emad and Kenneth Maly (Bloomington: Indiana University Press, 1994), "Introduction." See also "Hegel's Concept of Experience," in *Off the Beaten Track*, 86–156; and "Hegel and the Greeks," in *Pathmarks*, 323–36, for Heidegger's continuing engagement with Hegel. David Kolb's *The Critique of Pure Modernity: Hegel, Heidegger, and After* (Chicago: University of Chicago Press, 1986) is a fascinating exploration of the relationship because Kolb not only permits Heidegger to speak of Hegel but provides Hegel with the opportunity to speak of Heidegger. A more classically attuned approach is taken by Michael Gillespie, *Hegel, Heidegger, and the Ground of History* (Chicago: University of Chicago Press, 1984).

in its own terms in the *Logic*. We know that the "Phenomenology of Spirit" later appears as one of the elements in the *Philosophy of Spirit,* which is part of the most comprehensive *Encyclopedia of Philosophical Sciences*. The difficulty is clarified by Hegel himself in the title to the first part of the *Phenomenology,* "The Science of the Experience of Consciousness." In the introduction immediately following that heading, he explains that "the way to science is itself already science, and hence, in virtue of its content, is the science of the *experience of consciousness*" (*Phänomenologie des Geistes, Gesammelte Werke,* vol. 9, 61 / *Phenomenology of Spirit,* 56). His own explanation that in the course of the *Phenomenology* we grasp the succession of modes of consciousness in their necessity does not quite resolve the issue, for then the work must be both preparatory to science and science at the same time. The difficulty is inherent in the new understanding of philosophy as a movement in which science becomes possible because we already exist within it even before we begin and there would be no beginning if this were not the case.

Hegel did away with the last vestiges of epistemology that still clung to Kant's breakthrough to the luminosity of existence. We cannot ask about knowledge as if we were capable of stepping outside of it and comparing it with reality. On the contrary, knowledge is possible only because we already exist within the realization that "the Absolute is alone true, or the truth alone is absolute" (54/47). Questions of truth are not questions that can be settled by knowledge in advance of its apprehensions but the living reality within which it itself exists. The key moment within this emergent self-consciousness is the realization of its existential structure. It is at that point that the phenomenology of spirit becomes science. As a view of the whole in which it is, this knowledge must be in the form of a system, understood to be a living system in which all of the moments stand forth in their relationship to consciousness. "In pressing forward to its true existence, consciousness will arrive at a point at which it gets rid of its semblance of being burdened with something alien, with what is only for it, and some sort of 'other,' at a point where appearance becomes identical with essence, so that its exposition will coincide at just this point with the authentic Science of Spirit. And finally, when consciousness itself grasps this as its own essence, it will signify the nature of absolute knowledge itself" (61–62/56–57). The work abbreviates the odyssey of history announced in the preface and presented by Hegel in the several lecture courses. "That the True is actual only as system, or that Substance is essentially Subject, is expressed in the representation of the

Absolute as Spirit – the most sublime Notion and the one which belongs to the modern age and its religion" (22/14).

The meditation on truth begins with sense-certainty, in which we learn that consciousness is what provides the meaning to the "this" of sensation (Chapter 1). From there we move to the perception of things that seem to provide the truth to consciousness until we discover that what makes them objects as such is the intending of them (Chapter 2). In themselves things are merely an assemblage of determinations that coexist indifferently without any essential unity. What brings the determinations together in the moment of recognition is the movement of understanding by which their connection is apprehended. Leaving the sensible we enter the realm of the supersensible that lies behind it and can be grasped by understanding as a "Kingdom of Laws (Chapter 3)." "The supersensible is the sensuous and the perceived posited as it is *in truth;* but the *truth* of the sensuous and the perceived is to be *appearance.* The supersensible is therefore *appearance qua appearance*" (90/89). Understanding attempts to ground the supersensible in the notions of force and law that find expression in the world of appearance, but the order can equally unfold in the opposite direction. Lightning can be explained in terms of the law of electricity, but electricity is then explained in the form of lightning. "Infinity, or this absolute unrest of pure self-movement, in which whatever is determined in one way or another, e.g. as being, is rather the opposite of this determinateness, this no doubt has been from the start the soul of all that has gone before; but it is in the *inner* world that it has first freely and clearly shown itself" (100/101). Consciousness becomes aware that it is itself the decisive moment in explanation. Every consciousness of an object, we now see, is ultimately made possible through self-consciousness.

What had been the determinateness of the object now turns out to be such only for consciousness. Certainty vanished in favor of truth, "The Truth of the Certainty of Self," as Hegel titles the chapter on self-consciousness. His interchange with the terms "certainty" and "truth" indicates the philosophical transformation he is introducing, for it is no longer the outward movement from the self-certainty of the subject but the opening toward the truth of being within which the subject is that constitutes the meditation. "Idealism" is a category so closely tied to the detached observer that it has no meaning as an identifier of his thought. Far from asking whether the observer knows reality, Hegel has launched us on the deeper exploration of what is to count as knowing and what is the ground of its possibility. The certainty of self from which the observer begins does not rest on itself but is rooted in the truth within which the self stands.[15] It is not certainty that makes truth possible, but the reverse. Before all conclusions that can be reached, Hegel insists, there is the movement by which they are apprehended, but the movement itself can be apprehended only by participation in it. It is because existence can be grasped only through existence that the analysis of self-consciousness shifts from the model of contemplation to the practical struggle for recognition. This phase is opened with Hegel's famous meditation on the master–slave dynamic, a gem that is so often excerpted from the context that it is reminiscent of the extraction of diamonds to the neglect of the understanding of geology.

Not concerned with a mere bauble on "conflict resolution," however, his purpose is to unfold the truth of self-consciousness. While the master is sidelined by mere slavish recognition, the slave is the one who carries forward the historical odyssey of spirit. Through his service he discovers that he is the one whose self-consciousness achieves recognition in the freedom of work. His work is for the master, but his thinking is free. The historical appearance of this freedom of self-consciousness, the imperviousness of thought, is Stoicism. It is followed by Skepticism, in which "the wholly unessential and non-independent character of this 'other' becomes explicit for consciousness" (119/123). The result is the "unhappy consciousness" that simultaneously regards itself as the essential and the inessential, unable to relate itself to an essentiality outside of itself, which equally turns out to be inessential. That this is not an epistemological problem is indicated by its existential unfolding into the recognition of the one in whom the essential and the inessential, the particular and the universal, are united. Christ is the religious solution, although not yet the philosophical one. To reach the latter, consciousness would have to recognize that it, too, is the one in whom the universal is realized through the particular. At this stage the best that consciousness

---

[15] Robert Pippin has expressed this with more analytic rigor in explaining how "Hegel is committed to showing that the issue of the deductive legitimacy of any potential Notion (naïve realism, empiricism, atomist metaphysics, post-Newtonian science, Kantian idealism, etc.) involves, first, an account of why, in what sense, such a Notion would have *appeared* or would have been 'experienced' as adequate to Spirit at some time or other (given that there is no other ground for such adequacy) and why, in what sense, it would come to be *experienced* as inadequate." Yet Pippin acknowledges that "it is the generality of this issue of objectivity that, in the interpretation I am presenting, introduces the 'existential' and 'historical' themes other readers find so important in the *PhG*." Pippin, *Hegel's Idealism*, 107.

can do in overcoming its unhappiness is to surrender the particularity
of its acts to the counsel of the mediator, who is the embodiment of
the universal. It may not yet have recognized the truth of Christ as its
own truth, but in finding "that its own action and being, as being that
of this *particular* consciousness, are being and action *in themselves,* there
has arisen for consciousness the idea of *Reason,* of the certainty that, in
its particular individuality, it has being absolutely *in itself,* or is all reality"
(131/138).

The self-certainty of reason must unfold into its truth, which is the
realization of its openness to what is. Mere observation and description
of nature are insufficient, for consciousness is in search of the law of
nature, which it knows because it contains the notion of law within itself.
This is best exemplified in the study of organic nature, in which reason
finds itself, as Kant suggested, in the idea of teleology by which living
things become their concept. This self-realization is, of course, not transparent for the organism but only for us, who can know it because we
are the self-constituting reality of spirit. Organic nature has no history,
while we do. It is therefore to the life of reason itself, the self-ordering
life of spirit constituting history, that we must look for a knowledge of
reality (165/178–79). There we encounter the life of reason that can
be understood only in its own terms, never as reducible to environmen-
tal influences or to its physiological conditions. In a few remarkable
pages Hegel decisively dispatches all the reductionist nonsense of brain–
consciousness discussions by insisting that "man is free" (187/204), for
"*being* as such is the not the truth of spirit at all" (187/205). Man is what
always escapes every category of thinghood, including his own participation in thingly existence. "What merely *is,* without any spiritual activity
is, for consciousness, a Thing, and, far from constituting the essence of
consciousness, is rather its opposite; and consciousness is only *actual* to
itself through the negation and abolition of such a being" (188/205).
Attention must now be turned to this genuine self-activity of spirit, "to
the Notion existing as a universality, or to purpose existing as purpose"
(189/207).

The realization of rational self-consciousness through its own activity is
most completely expressed in the ethical life of a nation. Consciousness
of independent existence is most fully achieved in individuals' willingness
to sacrifice themselves for the good that is greater than themselves. But
while the natural individual may be transformed by the universal medium
of the nation, he does not necessarily recognize himself as such. He
must become explicitly aware of what he is by passing beyond custom

(*Sittlichkeit*) to morality (*Moralität*), acting not only in a way that benefits all but *because* it benefits all. Initially the course is from absorption in selfish pleasure to the insistence on a sentiment of virtue, but reason then recognizes the contradiction in the latter and submits to the universal as law. The "knight of virtue" may aim at "bringing the good into actual existence by the sacrifice of individuality, but the side of reality is itself nothing else but the side of individuality" (212/233). Hegel contrasts this futility of modern virtue with the substantial life of virtue in the ancient city, to which we now return in the recognition that the movement of the individual is the reality of the universal. In this recognition of the individual as the living universal, self-consciousness has grasped itself as the principle of reality as a whole. It is a self-recognition that is so complete that it now runs the danger of circling in a vacuum of self-reference in which individuality serves no goal other than the realization of individuality (215/237).

Again, however, the circle is broken by the movement of action in which consciousness does not have its goal before it yet acts nevertheless. Consciousness discovers that it does not express itself in its action but "exhibits the reality of the individuality as vanishing rather than as achieved" (221/244). The actor always escapes the action. Even the attempt to express himself in the form of universal law valid for all other individuals cannot contain his reality, for as soon as the principle is examined we see that it does not adequately reflect the intention behind it. "Love your neighbor as yourself," Hegel explains, depends for its meaning on a concrete knowledge of how to do good for your neighbor that we do not possess in advance.[16] This has been a fundamental problem within ethics that goes all the way back to Aristotle's insistence that ethics is a practical, not a contemplative, science whose truth is concrete rather than universal. As an issue it comes to a head in Kant's self-legislating morality. Hegel is the one who clarifies the existential source of the difficulty. There can be no moral universals, because morality is ultimately a movement of existence that transcends each of its particular expressions. Only a science that is willing to acknowledge its radical nonattainability in conceptual terms can apprehend it. What is itself the movement of self-examination cannot be fixed within it. Law is in this sense the spiritual

---

[16] Private property can be regarded as incompatible with the universal nature of things, or communism can be regarded as incompatible with the individual nature of need. The validity of principles is not disclosed in advance but only in the movement of ethical consciousness by which they are tested and realized. *Phänomenologie des Geistes, Gesammelte Werke*, vol. 9, 233 / *Phenomenology of Spirit*, 257–58).

reality in which we exist, not what we possess as a formal essence. It is the existing reality of spirit. "The law is equally an eternal law which is grounded not in the will of a particular individual, but is valid in and for itself; it is the absolute *pure will of all* which has the form of immediate being . . . it is not a *commandment,* which only *ought* to be: it *is* and is *valid*" (235/260).

In recognizing the moral world in which we exist, spirit has finally emerged as the truth of all of the preceding modes of consciousness, self-consciousness, and reason. They turn out to be abstractions from it, for while each of them has been constitutive of the reality in which it is, only spirit is aware of the formative role that it plays within the whole. Spirit knows that there is nothing higher than the ethical life of the nation it sustains and by which it is sustained. At this point, however, spirit has only an immediate knowledge of itself as such. To arrive at full self-knowledge it must go through a series of forms, which occupy the largest chapter of Hegel's *Phenomenology* and introduce us to the actual movement of history. Unlike the preceding chapters, this one no longer deals with shapes of consciousness but with actual shapes of the historical world (240/265). The movement originates in the ancient world in which spirit assumes itself to be a formal universality opposed to the natural order. This is followed by the diremption into civilization and faith, a "here" and a "beyond" that can never be brought into reconciliation. Only with the Enlightenment and the emergence of individual freedom is a way found by which the full transparence of spirit might be reached. With Chapter 6 the phenomenology of spirit takes the form of its historical self-realization as displayed through Hegel's formidable command of materials.

The richness of the account is evident in the multiple layers of analysis that he derives from *Antigone.* It is not merely the clash of human and divine laws conventionally attributed to the tragedy, but the inner source of the conflict within the individual–universal tensions of the ethical life. Sittlichkeit is the community that unites individual and universal through the bonds of living custom, but it does not yet recognize itself as such. Instead, it experiences the clash powerfully depicted in *Antigone,* the impossibility of fulfilling both human and divine law. The purest expression of the ethical responsibility of the family toward the individual is the care of a sister toward a brother, especially in regard to the most universal fate of death. It is by claiming the remains and burial that the family ultimately asserts the individual's transcendence of nature. But the state, too, must be able to call on its members to make the ultimate sacrifice in war that affirms the nullity of individual existence. "Just as the family in this way possesses in the community its substance and enduring being, so, conversely, the community possesses in the family the formal element of its actual existence, and in the divine law its power and authentication" (248/276). The community may find its purpose beyond the interests of the individuals, but it can neglect them only at the cost of undermining itself. When such conflict breaks out, the non-transparent ethical community has no way of resolving it and disintegrates into the assertion of individual rights and the masquerade of an imperial unity. "Consciousness of right, therefore, in the very fact of being recognized as having validity, experiences rather the loss of its reality and its complete inessentiality" (262/292).

Unhappy consciousness finds itself again in a twofold world in which consciousness in its purity is opposed to consciousness in its actuality. Only by going through the process of alienation, by completing the work of culture, does consciousness discover itself again. Initially the bifurcation is between an actual world and a world of faith. The self cannot find itself in the actual world, in which wealth and flattery have become the essentials; it searches for its truth in the realm of belief where it is in contact with universal significance. "The notion, however, the actuality of spirit present to itself, remains in the consciousness of the believer the *inner being*, which is everything and which acts, but does not itself come forth" (290/326). Enlightenment is the great force of resistance to the externality of belief, compelling consciousness to become self-conscious of the absolute it carries within itself. The problem is that enlightenment is itself incapable of the same recognition. Pure insight that can penetrate the vacuity of superstition cannot necessarily reach the truth of religion and proves that enlightenment is even more vacuous. "But the absolute being of faith is essentially not the *abstract* essence that would exist beyond the consciousness of the believer; on the contrary, it is the spirit of the community, the unity of the abstract essence and self-consciousness" (298/335). The service enlightenment provides is that of compelling faith to recognize itself as an existential movement. Faith is not a grasping of something "out there" but the living reality by which what is out there is apprehended. Enlightenment charges faith with basing its certainty on historical evidence, with all of the attendant uncertainties of factual transmission over time. By contrast, faith rests on a foundation far more secure than historicity. It carries its source within it, for "it is spirit itself which bears witness to itself, both in the *inwardness* of the *individual* consciousness and through the *universal presence* in everyone of faith in it" (301/338).[17] The next step is for enlightenment to recognize the self-recognition of faith as also its own.

Enlightenment, too, must be brought to realize that its own proclamation, that absolute being is beyond finite consciousness, is already to overstep the limit. It must be made to see that the abstraction of pure thought from all sense reality is also the integration of thought and reality. Kant had embodied the error of the Enlightenment in overlooking the existential import of his own theorizing by which "*thought* is *thinghood*, or *thinghood* is *thought*" (313/352). What made Hegel sanguine about remedying the situation was that Kant had not made the same error in his practical philosophy. There self-legislating reason knew itself to be absolute freedom. "It is self-consciousness which grasps the fact that its certainty of itself is the essence of all the spiritual 'masses,' or spheres, of the real as well as of the supersensible world, or conversely, that essence and actuality are consciousness's knowledge of *itself*" (317/356). As pure universality, however, this freedom eschews any individual expression and can only produce death through "the sheer terror of the negative that contains nothing positive, nothing that fills it with a content" (322/362). Absolute freedom must be left behind as an abstraction that finds its reality within the moral life of spirit. This is the existential moment defined by Kant's wrestling between the imperative of moral purpose and the impossibility of achieving its goal. It is a tension that Kant could resolve only in the postulation of a "Lord of the World" who brings about the harmony between virtue and happiness that morality cannot attain. Hegel zeroes in on the weak point of this postulation, which still lives off its Christian resonance without recognizing the abyss it opens up in acknowledging that God is not really moral (338/381). The ultimate contradiction, one that still preoccupied Nietzsche as the tendency of all moralities to nihilate themselves, consists in morality "being opposed to reality, and to be entirely free and empty of it, and then again, to consist in its being reality" (339/382).

The source of the difficulties, Hegel recognized and sought to explain in often impenetrable language, is that we are attempting to deal with an existential movement as if we were outside of it. When we recognize that the poles of the particular self and the universal principle are not objects

---

[17] This was, of course, the great issue for Kierkegaard, which serves only to suggest how thoroughly he remained within the Hegelian meditation. See *Concluding Unscientific Postscript*, vol. 2, pt. 2, ch. 4, "The Issue in *Fragments*: How Can an Eternal Happiness Be Built on Historical Knowledge?"

but moments in existence, their contradiction is dissolved. This is the reality of conscience in which what cannot be reconciled in theory is reconciled in practice as the concrete realization of the universal through conscience. "Spirit is, in an immediate unity, a *self-actualizing* being, and the action is immediately something *concretely* moral" (342/385). We can no more frame general propositions about the content of morality than Aristotle could when he designated the *spoudaios* as the "norm and measure" of the good (*Nicomachean Ethics*, 113a15–b3). As a concrete unfolding conscience becomes knowledge of what is to be done in the concrete, its knowledge is the "thing itself" (345/389). Yet conscience retains something one-sided in the way in which it thinks of itself as its own, caring only for the self-chosenness of its actions and not whether they are right. In this self-absorbed "beautiful soul," action still springs from selfishness, only now conscience is aware of its inability to escape the tension between particular inclinations and universal duty. But Hegel does not conclude that the romantic conscience is doomed to "waste itself in yearning" (360/406–7). It can encounter the word of reconciliation that emerges from the further unfolding of spirit within existence that is the forgiveness of evil. Again Kant had foreseen the necessity of forgiveness in making the moral life possible, but Hegel carried it further in drawing it into the movement of existence. We now recognize that what not only makes the moral life possible but is its constitutive unfolding is the absolute spirit by which the evil is forgiven. This is not God but "God manifested in the midst of those who know themselves in the form of pure knowledge" (362/409), that is, who have entered into the existential reality of spirit as their constitutive unfolding.

Individual pettiness of the kind so apparent to a valet is not removed, but it has begun to be overcome in the heroism of resolution. A reconciliation occurs when each side sees it is not what it appears to be; the sides are moments of a whole that is greater than they are. In this emergence of self-conscious spirit, the phenomenology reaches its goal, a goal that resolves both the interminable "ought" of Kantian morality and the fruitless longing of romanticism. We cannot despair of the moral struggle, because it is not simply ours to abandon. Not possessing our own existence, we cannot simply walk away from it but must recognize that we are held by a larger reality of spirit. As moments in that greater drama, how much can we know about the whole within which we find ourselves? Conventionally Hegel is read as claiming that there are no limits to our penetration, but our reading so far should give us pause. Here it is important to give full weight to the existential dimension of his thought. Spirit is not discovered as it is in itself, but only as we discern it by living it out. If we ask how, then, we know anything about it, the answer must be: by what it makes possible in our lives. Spirit in that sense does not just appear to us; it becomes real in our existence. When Hegel talks about the self-realization of spirit, it is probably best to maintain such a cautious interpretation and not to rashly assume it means something beyond our relationship to it. Rather than conclude that this phenomenology of spirit is the full reality of God, it is better to see his shift to theological language as recognition of our inability to penetrate beyond what appears to us. Let us postpone the "Hegelian" question of the subsumption of God within self-consciousness to his treatment of it in the last chapter on absolute knowledge.

For now it is worth noting that Hegel's chapter "Religion" explicates the truth of Kantian morality. Not only is God a postulate of the moral life, he is its realization. Morality is the life of God we know by living it. In this sense it is a consciousness of the absolute being that has been present all along without becoming self-conscious as our participation in it. But because we know it only through participation, we cannot dispense with any of the forms of that participation. We are no longer progressing through forms of spirit but must retain them as determinations that are never in some sense superseded. We are approaching a turning point in Hegel's philosophy of history that has never been adequately noted before, in that the philosophy of history is not itself historical. It is rooted in the now of existence in which it in turn locates the historical flow. "The series of different religions which will come to view, just as much sets forth again only the different aspects of a *single* religion, and the ideas which seem to distinguish one actual religion from another occur in each one" (369/417). They differ by the degree to which the consciousness of the divine has become self-consciousness in recognizing its source. But to the extent that this is really a movement of existence, it is never fully penetrated. Determinate forms of religion represent the limits of the self-conscious unfolding of existence. "These, therefore, exhibit spirit in its individuality or *actuality,* and are distinguished from one another in time, though in such a way that the later moment retains within it the preceding one" (366/413).

There is, in other words, something true about every shape of religion, although the direction is toward an inexorable sifting of the divine in light of our self-consciousness of what the divine is. We can know God only because we are already constituted by that knowledge. Initially we look for him outside of ourselves in nature, the realm of being, but still under the aspect of its most spiritualized expression. Hegel regards the conception of God as light as the first stage, the immediate sense-certainty of religion. This is followed by the individualization of the divine in the multiplicity of plant and animal forms. From there we look for the divine in the most abstract human creations, such as the pyramids or obelisks, that only hint at their own self-conscious source when the divine appears in the form of sphinxes. While the pattern Hegel presents may tend toward tidiness, a tendency more accentuated in the later lectures, it does arise from the inner source of the phenomena to which he alludes. This is not simply the history of religion or of the human symbolizations of God. It is the unfolding of the self-conscious source of our consciousness of God. In this sense it remains far superior to the later scientific study of religion, which adopts a largely external perspective. The latter must rely exclusively on empirical accuracy for its account, while Hegel can fill in the empirical gaps from his own exploration of the inner source from which the manifestations have arisen. This is why his analyses retain a validity despite the vast expansion of our empirical knowledge. Nowhere is this more evident than in his expansive "Religion of Art," which comprises his understanding of the Greek world.

A distinct shift has occurred when the source of the knowledge of the divine is recognized to lie within the spiritual workman. Initially he creates only an "abstract work of art" because it is still lifeless, yet it has become transparent for a life beyond it. Unlike the abstraction of the religion of nature, nature has now become symbolic. The life within it is episodically actualized in the cult and acquires permanence in the form of language. Eventually the inner life comes to know "that simplicity of truth as *essential being* which does not have the form of contingent existence through an alien speech, knows it [in the words of Antigone] as the *sure and unwritten law of the gods, a law that is 'everlasting and no one knows whence it came'*" (381/431). The nation is constituted around the oracle but does not yet recognize the oracle as its own. A step toward such self-consciousness occurs when a living man takes over from the statue and enacts the Bacchic and Apollonian moments. The self is beside itself and the spiritual being is outside, however, until the transparence of language unites them. "The perfect element in which inwardness is just as external as externality is inward is once again speech" (388/439). It emerges in the "spiritual work of art," in which the public cult no longer celebrates the particular national spirit but its representation of the universal, in the form of epic. Particular divinities in the epic clash with one another and ultimately must bow before the universal divinity of fate that stands behind them. Epic, the narrative of submission to fate, is succeeded by tragedy, the self-conscious working out of fate as representative for all. Individuality still clashes with the universal substance; action in one direction carries consequences in another, but the necessity in becoming explicit is thereby overcome (395–96/448–49). When the divine ceases to be represented by individual divinities, as a result of this meditation of tragedy, all presentation of individual divinities turns into comedy. It is through comedy, Hegel explains, that dialectical reasoning replaces tragedy.[18]

This is the end of religion in the form of art and the emergence of its truth in religion in the form of the individual self. "The *individual self* is the negative power through which and in which the gods, as also their moments, viz. existent nature and the thoughts of their specific characters, vanish" (399/452). The truth of the religion of art is that the divine is spirit and can be known only through spirit. Behind the work and the action lie the worker and the actor through whose self-consciousness life is imparted. Now Hegel moves on to the form of religion in which that realization has become explicit. It is in revealed religion that God is revealed as spirit, as that which is only by not being what it is. Heretofore we have seen how the self transcends every attempt at self-expression; now we discover that reality is itself the process of going beyond its self-disclosure. Revealed religion turns out to deny its revelation. Spirit is what reveals and fails to reveal; we can know it only by living it. This is the message of Christ, on which Hegel builds the culmination of the phenomenology of spirit. "The self of existent spirit has, as a result, the form of complete immediacy; it is posited neither as something thought or imagined, nor as something produced, as is the case with the immediate self in natural religion, and also in the religion of art; on the contrary, this God is sensuously and directly beheld as a self, as an actual individual man; only so *is* this God self-consciousness" (405/459). Absolute religion is absolute because spirit stands revealed as spirit. No amount of speculation on the divine can capture what Christ communicates through his existence. He lives out the reality of spirit, as that which always goes beyond itself and is itself by going beyond. Christ does not function as

---

[18] This, too, is a theme of abiding relevance for Kierkegaard, who was fascinated by the interrelationship between tragedy and comedy. "The Tragic in Ancient Drama Reflected in the Tragic in Modern Drama," *Either/Or: Part I*.

an idea or a symbol of God but as an immediate existence revealing the existential or spiritual mode of knowing God as the indispensable. Only in Kierkegaard do we find a comparable emphasis on the centrality of Christ within philosophy.

The significance of Christ may be summed up as the realization that spirit can be revealed only through spirit. What "revelation" means for Hegel may be difficult to unravel, but it seems to retain a core sense of the unanticipated. Christ may be recognized when he comes, but he interrupts all preparation. Something of that joyful surprise is still retained in Hegel's most celebratory passages. "Spirit is known as self-consciousness and to this self-consciousness it is immediately revealed, for spirit is this self-consciousness itself. The divine nature is the same as the human, and it is this unity that is beheld" (406/460). The notorious ambiguity of Hegel's formulations become even more evident when he pushes the reflection further in a direction that seems to make spirit a process of divine self-realization. "The absolute being which exists as an actual self-consciousness seems to have come down from its eternal simplicity, but by thus *coming down* it has in fact attained for the first time to its own highest essence" (406/460). Even such statements admit, however, of more than one meaning, for the "highest essence" may refer to God as he is in himself or to our apprehension of him. If we stick to the existential thrust of Hegel's thought, we must give weight to the latter and regard the ambiguity as an effort to remove all externality from the relationship. "The joy of beholding itself in absolute being enters self-consciousness and seizes the whole world; for it is spirit, it is the simple movement of those pure moments, which expresses just this: that only when absolute being is beheld as an *immediate* self-consciousness is it known as spirit" (407/461). The challenge now is to remain within that living reality of spirit and not permit it to deteriorate into the externality of a historical faith.

The self-consciousness that beheld itself in the self-consciousness of Christ must become the self-consciousness of the community of believers. In that way spirit remains actual, not a historical past. If we keep Hegel's focus on the living faith of the community in mind, we will be able to avoid the misimpression that he is presenting a speculation on the being of God. Everything he says must be referred back to the relationship with God, for despite the impression he conveys of embracing a pseudo-Gnostic perspective in which evil is grasped as a divine moment, "*as the wrath of God*" (414/470), his direction remains radically anti-Gnostic. Spirit is a living existential mode, never the congealment of the system.[19] To the extent that the language of system is used, we do not contain but are contained by it. This is why, despite all appearances, Hegel is saying nothing about creation, the advent of evil, or redemption. More and more he is emphasizing that they tell us nothing because such conceptions are arrested moments within the whole in which we find ourselves. "Neither the one nor the other has truth; the truth is just their movement in which simple sameness is an abstraction and hence absolute difference, but this, as difference in itself, is distinguished from itself and is therefore self-sameness" (416/472–73). It is only as moments within the living reality of spirit that the abstractions are true, which "cannot be expressed by the judgment and the lifeless 'is' which forms its copula" (416/473). We are being drawn deeper into the living truth of mystery that is a far cry from the claim to absolute knowledge that awaits us in the final chapter. Yet the suspicion remains that Hegel, too, may have fallen victim to the inescapable tensions of his project. A system of life is an inherent contradiction, for life is always a going beyond system. In the conclusion to his discussion of revealed religion, Hegel still holds out the prospect of finally pulling back the veil of faith. "The spirit of the community is thus in its immediate consciousness divided from its religious consciousness, which declares, it is true, that *in themselves* they are not divided, but this merely implicit unity is not realized, or has not yet become an equally absolute being-for-self" (421/478). We will not be surprised, however, if it turns out that life is more than disclosure.

At every stage along the way, we have seen the object of our attention evaporate within the living dynamic of spirit. How will the claim to absolute knowledge fare differently? By arresting the movement of life itself? It is surely far more likely that absolute knowledge will dissolve in the

[19] The difficulty of finding one's way through these linguistically strained reflections may be illustrated by the personal confession that I was previously convinced of their Gnostic connotation. In particular, Hegel's italicized characterization of evil as the wrath of God struck me as a veritable quotation from Boehme, which, from there, led back to the ancient Gnostic solutions to the problem of evil as a fallen or "other" divinity. What gradually caused me to reconsider was the realization that Hegel did not fit the classic Gnostic paradigm of proposing a solution, a system, that definitively resolved the questions of existence. His interest was too profoundly drawn toward the openness of inquiry to want to effect its final foreclosure. But I do recognize that such a more "orthodox" reading of Hegel is heavily dependent on a major intellectual shift that is prepared to take on board the primarily existential intent of the language he employs. Quentin Lauer, in *Hegel's Concept of God* (Albany: State University of New York Press, 1982), outlines the compatibility with an orthodox theology but without identifying the existential perspective that ultimately explains it. William Desmond, in *Hegel's God: A Counterfeit Double* (Aldershot: Ashgate, 2003), makes virtually the opposite case.

recognition that it, too, has no content that would capture the life of spirit. Perhaps it is significant that the chapter on absolute knowledge is among the shortest in the entire work. It is almost as if the goal when reached is no longer what was sought. Despite the claim Hegel makes to have now reached science, it is not wholly unexpected when we discover that the science is that there is no science. Absolute knowledge is constituted by the awareness of our distance from absolute knowledge. He may seem to have departed from the Socratic model in the ambition announced in the preface to replace the love of wisdom with its possession, but now we realize that he meant to deepen rather than replace the meaning of philosophy. This is not to suggest that there are no aspirations toward system in Hegel or that he was above the temptation to tidy up the unruly patterns of empirical reality. But it is to propose that he never succumbed in his central philosophical quest. He was not the philosopher of history whose achievement definitively removed the possibility of either philosophy or history. No, Hegel's place in the history of philosophy derives from a far more profound contribution. He is the one who really brought about the revolution by which philosophy became the living reality toward which it had always pointed.[20]

Philosophy was then no longer about results, only the movement of existence. It could not present absolute knowledge, only the process of its emergence. This is why when we arrive at the discussion of absolute knowledge it turns out to be, not a resting point, but the rehearsal of the movement through which we have come. "This totality of its determinations establishes the object as an *implicitly* spiritual being, and it does truly become a spiritual being for consciousness when each of its individual

---

[20] An unwillingness to think through Hegel's wrestling with his greatest speculative ambitions while instead focusing on his intermediate explanations of the possibility of knowledge and freedom has marked much of the prevalent scholarship. No doubt the gains in clarifying his contributions on that more modest level have been significant and are likely to be enduring. But one is inclined to feel that a domesticated Hegel is somehow less than the full measure. A "nonmetaphysical" Hegel may be extraordinarily useful while not quite being Hegel. To find our way to a more expansive reading would, of course, require reconceiving metaphysics in such a way that it could be understood as continuous with the dynamic of intellectual and social life that now occupies the foreground. Beyond responsibility for conceptual clarity we must find room for responsibility that carries the full weight of existence. Only then will we be able to at least consider the final chapters, "Religion" and "Absolute Knowing," in the *Phenomenology*. Fairness would seem to require that we at least attempt to make the speculative overreaching of Hegel compatible with the newly appreciated modesty of his ambitions. Simply ignoring or dismissing the issue will not cause it to disappear, for it will continue to haunt the rehabilitation so far accomplished.

determinations is grasped as a determination of the self" (422/479–80). Hegel runs through the stages through which the self-transparence of spirit has passed, culminating in the central conflict between the ideal and the actual bequeathed by Kantian morality and transcended by the forgiveness that makes action possible. "It is only through action that spirit *is* in such a way that it is *really there,* that is, when it raises its existence into thought and thereby into an absolute *antithesis,* and returns out of this antithesis, in and through the antithesis itself" (427/485). The notion is the knowledge of the self's act as all essentiality and existence, "the knowledge of this subject as substance, and of the substance as this knowledge of its act" (427/485). Hegel refers to this variously as "absolute knowing," "comprehensive knowing," and eventually as "science," but what such terms mean specifically is far from clear. If spirit is that which is alive, knowing itself in and through action, then its self-knowledge as science would seem to signal its unreality. Science would signify the nonexistence of spirit, and thus a non-science. Clarity of meaning has all too often been imposed on Hegel's paradoxical conception of absolute knowledge, thereby failing to serve the cause of clarity. Perhaps the best we can say about absolute knowledge is that it represents the limiting condition of a movement that can be known only through itself.

The possibility that absolute knowledge may be such a limiting parameter is strongly supported by Hegel's concluding reflection on its transcendence of time. The passages we have been citing are often quoted as proof of his inclination to bring history to an end, but a closer reading can establish an opposite tendency. Far from ending history, Hegel can be seen to be opening up its possibilities, for in general history comes into view only from the perspective of its end. An eschatological consciousness has always been integral to the full differentiation of history. "Time is the notion itself that *is there* and which presents itself to consciousness as empty intuition; for this reason, spirit necessarily appears in time, and it appears in time just so long as it has not *grasped* its pure notion, i.e. has not annulled time" (429/487). Time is in this sense the possibility of spirit; it cannot be completed without closing the possibility of spirit. Even Hegel's speculation on world spirit consummating itself as self-conscious spirit does not quite establish its attainment. He reminds us that "the content of religion proclaims earlier in time than does science, what *spirit is,* but only science is its true knowledge of itself" (430/488). We recall that his understanding of science, as also of spirit, is that which cannot come to an end in time, thus reassimilating them to the model of religion. Science, like religion, is not what we possess but what possesses us. It is notable that Hegel adopts such more existential language as he approaches the conclusion of the work. "Spirit, therefore, having won the notion, displays its existence and movement in this ether of its life and is *science*" (432/491). Absolute knowing does have the goal of comprehending the appearance of spirit that constitutes history, "the science of knowing in the sphere of appearance," but its real interest remains the life of spirit itself. Comprehended history is not an end in itself but the means by which absolute spirit goes through "the inwardizing and the Calvary . . . without which it would be lifeless and alone" (434/493). Whatever we may make of the slight misquotation from Schiller with which Hegel concludes, it is difficult to deny that the tilt toward life endures.

This is particularly important to keep in mind as we follow the development of the system after the *Phenomenology*. We indicated the difficulty earlier in noting that the *Phenomenology* was presented as a ladder up to the science of the system but then reappeared as an integral part of the system in the *Philosophy of Spirit*. This ambiguity should not surprise us, however, since the *Phenomenology* announced at its end that it had reached "the science of knowing in the sphere of appearance" and was no longer merely about the appearance of spirit. Once science appears, the path of appearance is included within it. This in turn makes sense of a tension that had been present in the language of the *Phenomenology* as Hegel alternated between recounting how the case was "for it," consciousness, and how it was "for us," who had already reached self-consciousness. Only at the end do they coincide, and then appearance is subsumed within the definitive perspective of science. Initially Hegel may not have considered the preservation of the way of appearance so important, since the first exposition of science consists simply of the *Logic*. This is the so-called *Greater Logic* of 1812, which he reissued in 1831 despite the appearance of the "lesser" *Logic* of the *Encyclopedia of Philosophical Sciences* in 1817. In other words, logic continued to dominate Hegel's understanding of what science is even after he determined to expand the boundaries to include the philosophy of nature and of spirit. At the core of the circle, the organic whole, that constitutes science for him is the self-subsisting life of thought that is logic. Hegel saw himself as both continuing the Aristotelian discovery of logic and appropriating its true relationship to being. In penetrating the logic of logic, he inaugurated a new era of philosophy. "Science" is the term that captured for him the sense of at last placing knowledge on the basis of its truth as the self-disclosure of being. "*Logic therefore coincides with Metaphysics, the science of things set and held in thoughts*" (*Encyclopedia of Philosophical Sciences*, pt. I: *Logic*, § 24).

Thinking and Being One as Movement: *Logic*

Thinking and being are one, as the Greeks recognized, although they failed to explain the meaning of this remarkable statement. Hegel had grasped its meaning as the existential turn by which thinking is inseparable from being, for being is not understood through its relationship to thinking but the reverse. The categories of our thought are open to reality because reality is constituted by the same categories, as we discover by living them out. In the voyage of discovery, the goal is to live in truth so that what makes its attainment possible is that we are already there. This is what sets up the two contrasting perspectives, depending on whether or not we recognize what makes our reflection possible. Ultimately the difference between them is purely notional in the sense that truth is there whether we are aware of it or not. The science of logic is thus what makes the phenomenological path toward it possible and also what must then comprehend the movement as an integral part of itself. Yet it is always possible to think of science as existing without any struggle of dialectical confusion behind it. This self-containedness of thought within itself is what Hegel, strictly speaking, means by the term "logic." As the origin and end of the entire historical process, it occupies the centerpiece of his whole conception of philosophy where "content is essentially bound up with form" (*Philosophy of Right*, Preface).

Thought that is dialectical rises above sense into its own element in which it recognizes itself as pervading all. This is for Hegel the pure idea that is the concern of logic. It is the movement of thought by which "it makes these contents imitate the action of the original creative thought" (*Encyclopedia of Philosophical Sciences*, pt. I: *Logic*, § 16). Contrary to the modern view, typified by the assertion that we lack a criterion of truth, Hegel insists that "the objective world is in its own self the same as it is in thought, and that to think is to bring out the truth of our object" (§ 22, lecture addition). This is the meaning of his most famous sentence: "What is reasonable is actual and what is actual is reasonable" (§ 6, quoting his own *Philosophy of Right*). Everything is engaged in the movement to become what it is, to be true to the idea of itself, and thus is apprehended and governed by the world of thought. "God alone is the thorough harmony of notion and reality. All finite things involve an untruth: they have a notion and an existence, but their existence does not meet the requirements of the notion" (§ 24, lecture addition). For this reason they must perish, since they cannot retain their hold on being. We share the same fate but in a way that becomes transparent, thereby moving beyond it. Knowledge of reality is possible for us because we participate in the same process but in such a way that we are not simply subject to it. Kant's critique of pure reason understood the relationship of subject and object, but it did not understand itself. Instead of thinking of the laws of thought as contained within the mind, it must now move toward the recognition of the laws of thought as containing mind, as the life of mind that is at the same time the meaning of life. Logic is indeed metaphysics because the laws of thought are the laws of being. Everything is discrepant from its notion, except God, and follows the inner dialectic of its existence. From the side of individual consciousness, this could be followed as the phenomenology of spirit; from the side of the idea, it is simply the logic of the idea.

The "subjective idealism" of critical philosophy must be replaced with the "absolute idealism" of the idea as, like providence, governing all (§ 45, lecture addition). Hegel assails the tendency to rest with the subjectivity of our understanding, for its identification as such is already its transcendence. "No one knows, or even feels, that anything is a limit or defect, until he is at the same time above and beyond it" (§ 60). We already possess knowledge of the infinite as what makes recognition of the finite possible, but not as an immediate knowledge, as in Jacobi's mystical intuition of God. For knowledge to display its truth there must be a dialectical mediation by which it becomes transparent to itself. The first subdivision of the *Logic* is the "Doctrine of Being," the most indeterminate concept, which struggles toward determinateness until it recognizes, in the second subdivision, the "Doctrine of Essence" as what makes it be what it is. Essence may be what fixes being, but it is not itself something fixed; the ground is itself in need of a ground, for it is struggling to become what it is but is not. This is the meaning of appearance as what is grounded not in itself but in another. In one of the lecture additions, invariably sources of the liveliest presentations of Hegel's thought, he remarks on how welcome it is that things are not simply fixed forever or we might die of hunger. "The apparent or phenomenal," the text then summarizes, "exists in such a way that its subsistence is *ipso facto* thrown into abeyance or suspended and is only one stage in the form itself" (§ 132). Actuality occurs when essence and existence come into coincidence at the point where the thing is in accord with its idea. It is a process we know primarily through our own existence in freedom, which, even in the *Logic*, remains the core meditation. We gain the most profound access to the life of the idea by living it out.

As an "idea" freedom of choice is a contradiction in terms, since the alternatives are always given from somewhere outside of ourselves. But as an Idea, freedom of choice makes eminent sense because it is not simply an abstract choice between options, but the living process by which we make the possibilities our own. Freedom is not the end; it is rather what freedom makes possible. Then we see that the truth of freedom is the necessity of bending itself toward what is necessary. The truth of freedom is disclosed in action, not by thought in advance. If there were such a prior grasp of the necessity of the outcome, the action would, as even Kant recognized, not be free. Instead, freedom is the movement that can never grasp itself fully because it is never fully there, although it can disclose the necessity by which it is constituted. For Hegel necessity, too, is not a bare necessity but rather the movement by which freedom is actualized. It is always very important to preserve the existential meaning of this discussion, particularly when he tends to slip into the language of "mutual necessity," as if one thing implied the other. So while it is true that punishment is implied by our own act of crime, Hegel really means (as Plato did in the *Gorgias*) that punishment emerges as the existential truth of our action. The good man knows he is not free to disobey the law, but this in no way diminishes his freedom: it makes it real. "In short, man is most independent when he knows himself to be determined by the absolute idea throughout" (§ 158, lecture addition). It is always in acting that we demonstrate that we are more than our action and reveal the larger reality within which we exist. At this point we have reached the third subdivision of the *Logic,* the "Doctrine of the Notion."

The notion is the truth of being and essence in the sense of the living movement that constitutes them. "The notion is the principle of freedom, the power of substance self-realized" (§ 160). It cannot be overemphasized that the terms have no meaning outside of the movement they make possible. They are the constitutive dimensions of existence known only from within. The profound revision in the language and conception of philosophy is perhaps best exemplified by Hegel's reformulation of the "ontological argument." In many ways he returns the argument to its original existential setting in St. Anselm's prayerful meditation.[21] It had been well understood by Jacobi and others that the whole enterprise of proving the existence of God was blasphemous, for God cannot be proved in terms of other conditions since he is the unconditioned (§ 50). But Hegel is the one who grasped the significance of the need to

---

[21] See Eric Voegelin, "Quod Deus Dicitur," *Published Essays: 1966–1985*, in *Collected Works*, vol. 12, ed. Ellis Sandoz (Baton Rouge: Louisiana State University Press, 1990), 376–94, for such an approach to Anselm.

recognize God as the ground of himself. It meant that now everything must be viewed in relation to God, not the other way around. God does not proceed from us; we proceed from him (§ 36, lecture addition). The ontological proof is true in the sense that we begin with the idea of God. Its error is to make the being of God immediate to our consciousness, whereas we know only finite being that does not include the necessity of existence. Hegel's revolution is to place the question mark over the character of finite existence. That which does not have its existence within it is untrue (§ 193). We may not yet have the idea of divine self-necessity, but we already live within it as the constitutive horizon of our thought. The other side of "ontological necessity" is that it remains true only of God. "God alone is the thorough harmony of notion and reality" (§ 24, lecture addition). Finite will requires both that its end be realized and that it not be realized. History, although it has an end, cannot reach it within time without ceasing to be history. "Good, the final end of the world, has being, only while it constantly produces itself" (§ 234, lecture addition).[22]

Nature Understanding Itself: *Philosophy of Nature*

As an inarticulate process the idea is realized in nature, and Hegel's *Philosophy of Nature* details the way in which spirit recognizes itself within nature. Nature as evidenced through consumption, reproduction, and death is already a movement beyond itself; it is already constituted by the reality of spirit without knowing it. Despite the poetic quality of this conception, the text does not justify its neglect, because it carries forward the question raised in Kant's *Critique of Judgment:* what does it mean for man to understand nature? Kant had begun to see that the understanding of nature in terms of teleology is essentially a reading in of what cannot,

[22] It is this dynamic character of Hegel's thought that is missed when it is juxtaposed, to its disadvantage, with the more static oppositions of Kant. It is not, for example, that Hegel believed that "concepts produce their own instances," but that concepts are themselves instances of reality as well as apprehensions of reality. One is struck in reading Paul Guyer's objections along these lines by how much the interpretation of philosophers turns on one's own receptivity to their philosophical arguments. "It is simply not true," Guyer concludes, "that one must recognize the existence of something that does not have a certain property in order to conceive of that property as a defect or limit." It is not because we have conceptual apprehensions that a corresponding reality exists, but that we can have such apprehensions only because our concepts are more than internal states of consciousness. All of this is far clearer when we are dealing with the exercise of practical reason. Guyer, "Thought and Being: Hegel's Critique of Kant's Theoretical Philosophy," in Beiser, ed., *The Cambridge Companion to Hegel*, 203–4.

strictly speaking, be found in the organism. Purpose is possible only for a rational being. Even if we understand the variations in terms of randomness, we still attribute rationality to nature as a whole, the survival of the fittest. Reason cannot fail to find itself there. Kant was still troubled about the "subjectivity" of this conception, and we remain mired in similar concerns over reductionism, evolution, mind-body, and a host of other questions because Hegel's resolution of them remains unrecognized. Part of the blame must be placed on the affiliation of his *Philosophy of Nature* with a speculative nature mysticism, but the greatest obstacle continues to be the challenge of absorbing the philosophical revolution he inaugurated. It requires a different way of thinking. Purpose is not something we insert into nature but what the understanding of nature, which cannot understand itself, necessarily is. Nature is spiritualized and understanding arises within nature. We do not impose a meaning on nature but discover nature as a movement toward the reality of spirit. For nature to be, there must be spirit.[23]

Spirit is the disclosure of the possibility of nature. Kant thought in attributing teleology to nature he was going beyond what it strictly speaking contained, but in reality he was showing what nature itself could not. In knowing nature we reveal that nature does not contain itself; it is rather contained within spirit. Nature is not an object but part of the whole that includes spirit and in terms of which it must be understood. Not only do natural entities not contain their existence within themselves, they cannot even be understood except in relation to the self-subsistent reality of spirit. Teleology or reason is not how we comprehend reality but how our reality is comprehended. Through it we recognize the truth of existence. We are the point of the self-transparence of nature. Kant had conceived of knowledge as the imposition of our categories of understanding; Hegel saw that this really meant that nature had adopted our categories as its self-understanding. Contrary to the reductionist conception that everything can be understood through analysis into its most elementary units, we discover that this defeats the possibility of understanding. This is what Kant had seen in relation to teleology, although he failed to grasp what he had seen. In sticking with the notion of his categories as what we apply to phenomena, he overlooked the extent to which the phenomena do not disclose their own categories. Lacking the means of self-interpretation, they point toward what can interpret them. Causality may not be in the

---

[23] One serious effort to reconsider the text is represented by Stephen Houlgate, ed., *Hegel and the Philosophy of Nature* (Albany: State University of New York Press, 1998).

objects themselves but it is in their idea. Only in the case of the teleology of the organism does it become clear to Kant that objects do not reveal ideas but are revealed by them. It is only in relation to spirit that anything can be known. We have no way of stepping outside the life of spirit to understand it in terms of something more fundamental, for even what is fundamental is so from the perspective of spirit. The truth of reality is spirit, and this applies to every single stage up to and including spirit.[24] In the *Philosophy of Nature*, Hegel shows how nature itself points mutely toward this realization, but the moment of transparence arises within the actual life of spirit, the philosophy of spirit, to which we must look for the source of the disclosure.

From Appearance to Science of Appearance: *Philosophy of Spirit*

The essential step consists of recognizing the implication of Kant's "Copernican revolution." "The Kantian philosophy may be most accurately described as having viewed the mind as consciousness, and as containing only the propositions of a *phenomenology* (not of a *philosophy*) of mind" (*Encyclopedia of Philosophical Sciences*, pt. III: *Philosophy of Spirit*, § 415). Now we must turn to a philosophy of mind or spirit in which we move from consciousness to self-consciousness, recognizing that it is not objects that supply the truth but the ideas we bring to them. Appearance is the givenness of objects while all of their determinations are posited by mind, which knows itself to be the source of all reality, at least in idea. Initially this is merely the intuition that mind knows all reality, as when a historian knows intuitively what happened because he knows the whole context so well or the trained scientist who can see what is in the object better than the untrained eye (§ 448, lecture addition). But then this inward intuition is given expression in the concrete imagery of art, the

---

[24] There is no doubt that Hegel called attention to a profoundly nonreductive understanding of nature, one that was continued in fascinating ways by Heidegger in calling attention to the self-limitation inherent in objectification. The problem is that the promise of this philosophy of nature has not been realized, in large part because its practitioners have failed to make the case they set out to establish. We are left, therefore, with evocative statements but a complete absence of attempts to develop a philosophy of nature. Not the least of the difficulties is Hegel's constant recourse to "necessity" without pinning down what kind of necessity is intended. "Nature is to be regarded as a *system of stages,* one arising necessarily from the other and being the proximate truth of the stages from which it results: but it is not generated *naturally* out of the other but only in the inner Idea which is the ground of Nature. *Metamorphosis* pertains only to the Notion as such, since only *its* alteration is development." *Philosophy of Nature,* § 249.

construction of symbols, and eventually the most universal signs of an alphabet.[25] It is in words, the "inward externality," that the constitutive role of intelligence is most evident. Intelligence is in this sense a process of recognition in which thinking and being come together. "It knows that what is *thought, is,* and that what *is,* only *is* in so far as it is a thought" (§ 465). This is the emergence of reason as distinct from understanding, a differentiation derived from Kant but now brought to its culmination. Understanding remains tied to a content that is unrelated to the form of intelligence in which it is apprehended; reason has united the two by recognizing the form of the idea as the source of its content (§ 467, lecture addition). Theoretical and practical reason stand disclosed as continuous, for "when intelligence is aware that it is determinative of the content, which is *its* mode no less than it is a mode, it is will" (§ 468).

The idea is in each instance the truth of the object. It is in the struggle to be what it is that the object maintains itself in being, but it is only intelligence that discloses this process. Nature can only point; its meaning must be supplied by self-consciousness, the point at which the implicit becomes explicit, the *an sich* becomes *für sich.* Absolute idealism does not make consciousness the source of all reality; rather it makes absolute reality the source of consciousness. The idea is the measure, for to the extent that we fall short our reality is defective. This means that everything is viewed in light of the absolute, for only God is fully in accord with himself. But for Hegel this is never an immediate knowledge of God, a mere subjective sense that could easily be set aside as such. In opposition to Schleiermacher and others, he insists that the knowledge of God must be mediated through our own existential movement to live the life of God. Instead of an intuitive knowledge of the absolute we have a constitutive one. We can know God only because we share the same being of spirit, that which contains its own reality within itself, the source of its own being. Like God we are transcendent, never what we are but always more than that. We are not finite but possess finitude within us. As a movement of the infinite we are like God without being God, for our infinitude is never realized. Yet we are constituted by that glimpse of the absolute that is most transparent in our moral existence. Autonomy or self-determination is the mode of existence for all who carry their own

---

[25] Derrida, with his acute sensitivity to grammatology, offers a parallel observation that underscores the affinity with Hegel he would later explore in *Glas.* "Following the same graphic, the alphabet introduces a supplementary degree of representativity which marks the progress of analytic rationality. This time, the element brought to light is a pure signifier (purely arbitrary), in itself nonsignifying." *Of Grammatology,* 300.

being within them. This is what it means to be rational. But where Kant had seen morality as the requirement of autonomy, Hegel penetrated to its ontological truth. To create oneself is to struggle to live in the light of what absolutely is because it contains its existence within itself. As Plato and Aristotle emphasized, without explicating the source of their insight, to live in accordance with the highest is to live the life of the divine. Now that Hegel has uncovered the source in its existential movement, it becomes apparent that this is more than an insight into the structure of morality. It is the structure of reason as such. Not only does practical reason displace theoretical, it forms its core. It is because our existence is constituted by the movement toward being that we are able to apprehend the being of all things.

The priority of the existential means that the moral and the political play a far more central role; they are the philosophy of spirit rather than consequences of it. This is why the second part of the text is "Objective Spirit" and must be read as the actual reality of spirit. Separated out from this context, the analysis of morality and politics is likely to be treated as a series of static oppositions, not the dynamic movement of reality Hegel intends it to be. "If to be aware of the Idea – to be aware, that is, that men are aware of freedom as their essence, aim, and object – is a matter of *speculation,* still this very Idea itself is the actuality of men – not something which they *have,* as men, but which they *are*" (§ 482). Then we can see why he presents it as a reality that can be simultaneously described from an individual or a universal point of view. Rights and duties are thus not opposed, for their distinction is a mere semblance (§ 486).[26] The truth is known only in the existential movement that is the living reality of spirit, which now constitutes an objective or social world. It is not yet absolute spirit, which provides the context in which the social world is constituted. As "objective," however, we are still inclined to slip into the older way of thinking about the social and political as fixed quantities. This is, of course, a long-standing problem in political science that has tended to congeal the historical reality of politics into its episodic stabilizations. Hegel has ironically contributed to this tendency by the very thoroughness of his organic perspective, although this is far from an inevitable consequence of his existential analysis. Indeed, he can equally provide a countervailing pressure by calling attention to the

---

[26] It is because Hegel provides such a profound rethinking of the liberal political vocabulary that he has been seized upon as a resource in its intractable disputes. See Steven Smith, *Hegel's Critique of Liberalism: Rights in Context* (Chicago: University of Chicago Press, 1989).

living character of political unity. Viewed as an existential achievement, the fragility of politics comes to light. This is why his political analysis is often admired more in the details than in its general structure, for the latter seems to move contrary to the former. Hegel depicted the truth of politics as a liberal constitutional monarchy, in which all of the respective forces were held in equilibrium, but this was almost the opposite of what he considered the core of its reality. This is why his liberal political theory discards most of the conventional liberal foundations. His state is not rooted in a contract, nor does it appeal to natural rights, nor does it remove itself from theological meaning. Speculation about a reactionary turn of thought or the pressure of Prussian conservatism is wide of the mark. Hegel is an anomaly in liberal political theory because he profoundly altered the conception of political thought. There can be no theory of politics that would explain its reality in advance, because politics constitutes its own reality. Theory must take its bearings from that living movement, not the other way around, and this places a strict limit on the power of explanation. Only when an age has grown cold can the owl of Minerva spread her wings and philosophy paint its gray on gray. Hegel prefaces the *Philosophy of Right* with that remark to emphasize that theory cannot save politics. The best that theory can do is to live within the same light as constitutes the objective reality of spirit.

There is no penetration beyond the living movement of existence. This is the new old meaning of philosophy. Its value is revealed in its capacity to resolve the interminable alternatives that transfix the consideration of political reality in all other perspectives. Rights versus duties is only the most commonplace rupture, but there is also the question of virtue in the subordination of individual interest to the good of the whole, and behind it all looms the foundational anxiety that the principle of autonomy is unable to resolve. Appeals to nature or to religion, or the many varieties of fundamentalism, are testaments of futility, hearkening for a return of what cannot be and perhaps never was. The best hope is represented by the advocates of a practice, insisting that the failure of theory is not fatal and may even prove salutary for an ordered liberty. Within this long preoccupation with the crisis of liberal democracy, Hegel's achievement stands out even if it is not comprehended. He is the one who has cast philosophical light on the irresolvability. Spirit is that which is ungrounded because it goes beyond every ground and thus cannot be understood in terms of anything else but itself. As soon as spirit is given definition or identification, it is no longer what it is. The arrow of theory has missed its target. This is the insight of the modern philosophical revolution, an insight that, as even Hegel illustrates, is lost as soon as it is grasped. To hold onto it we must remind ourselves of the beginning in the realization that "what is a contradiction in the realm of the dead is not one in the realm of life" (*Hegels theologische Jugendscrhiften*, 308–9 / *Early Theological Writings*, 261). But theory retains its own powers of seduction so that it extends its shroud over the existential self-reflection, returning it to the realm of the dead. One wonders if it was his awareness of this danger that prompted Hegel to expound his philosophy as far as possible through the *viva voce* medium of the lectures. Many of his writings spring out of the lecture context, and it is those living additions that often prove their most compelling projections.

To read the texts rightly we must therefore return them to their living source, the last trace of life itself. Then we can avoid the impression of a glib reconciliation between the interests of the individual and the universal in which they often get couched. Hegel's account of the state is not some liberal apocalypse that is the end of history, although it sometimes wears that air. It is essentially an account of mind or spirit as it lives. This is what he means by "objective spirit." It is the existential movement of spirit that does not possess a self-contained nature but has to live it out, for it is always not what it is. Autonomy was the discovery of Kant, that a rational being is necessarily self-determining, but Hegel was the one who saw that this is not the end but only the beginning. From now on we must recognize that man's nature is historical; the only disclosure of his existence is through its actual unfolding. We cannot step outside of who we are to behold it. The self in self-determination is not a closed entity but the openness toward being by which it is constituted. Not only does the effort to think abstractly objectify what cannot be objectified, but it obstructs the apprehension of the movement of reality as a movement. What determines itself can be known only in the process of self-determination, not through some fixed points outside of it. We may not thereby have reached any definitive clarity, but we are closer to what constitutes existence. It may be difficult to make the language of entities serve this more dynamic function, but this is the only sense in which Hegel's account makes sense. His designation of the state as "the march of God in the world" can be taken as a slogan of absolutism, but its more profound meaning is that it is through the state that our divinity is enacted.

Rather than the antinomy of the ought, we recognize the dialectic of existence that resolves it and marks the transition from morality to ethical life, the objective spirit. "The subjectivity, in this its *identity* with the good, is only the infinite form, which actualizes and develops it" (*Encyclopedia of Philosophical Sciences*, pt. III: *Philosophy of Spirit*, § 512). What it is that compels individuals to find their fulfillment in service to the whole cannot be captured, because spirit is that whose existence cannot be contained in anything but itself. What constitutes life can only be known as life. In this sense there are no individuals, nor are there universal principles; each has reality only as a living movement. "The ethical personality, i.e. the subjectivity which is permeated by the substantial life, is *virtue*" (§ 516). What makes virtue possible is virtue; there is no going behind it to anything else, nor can we know it more deeply than when we actualize it. The family is the most immediate expression of this ethical life, existing in such a way that individuals do not ask what their interest in it is but recognize that they are constituted as centers of interest only in and through it. The family is not what they have; it is who they are. This is why there is really no private property within the family, for they have not yet separated out as individuals. It may appear as if they have subordinated their individual interests to the greater good of the whole, but this is not how it is experienced. Rather the particular persons hold their membership in the family as a liberation of their individuality, which now is sustained by something larger than itself and attains its highest self-actualization in virtue (*Philosophy of Right*, § 162). What makes it possible, Hegel is clear, is not feeling but the substantial ethical life that reaches self-consciousness in the expression of consent. Kierkegaard would go considerably deeper into the question of what makes marriage possible, a decision in time that is to transcend time, but Hegel had identified the core existential structure. Marriage is possible because in some sense individuals are already constituted by wholeness. Given that they are members of civil society, this is not just interdependence but the impossibility of existing in any other way.

Civil society, which is the sphere of ethical life beyond the family, has only the appearance of independent individuals pursuing their own interests. The reality is that they could not exist except as members of a system of needs that gains self-consciousness as the police and corporations. But what makes possible the existence of interdependent individuals is not yet the full inwardness of their existence. That is the significance of the state for Hegel. In many ways the regulatory and welfare functions are already present in civil society, which is why the latter is often confused with the liberal state as the aggregation of individual interests. But the state cannot be conceived of as the product of individual will. Hegel rejects the foundation in contract, insisting that the constitution is not created but grows from the national spirit that has always been. Invocations of an "ancient constitution" or an "eternal contract" express the same sense of the noncontingent character of the political community. Hegel, however, supplies the theoretical insight. The state does not really exist as such, because it is what bears existence within it. Extended over history it is never fully present, for its beginning and end remain shrouded in mystery. All that can clearly be said of it is that the state is what makes itself possible. It is the eternal justice that exists nowhere but through our participation in it. Kant had difficulty with his own conception of freedom as – since it is not subject to the necessity of space-time – exercised in eternity. Hegel saw that the conception was the limit that constituted our existence and could not be known in any other way. It was not that he had reached a solution to the tensions that pervade our political existence, as the nonutopian nature of his political analysis attests,[27] but that he understood why no such solution could even be possible. An answer would abolish life. The theoretical insight into the possibility of freedom that Kant still hearkened after is available only through the practice of freedom. Within existence we glimpse eternity, and the state is its highest realization.

It is this existential context that made possible a nondefinitive penetration of politics. Hegel provided a nonsolution solution to the problems that afflict a liberal polity. He even accepted the conventional formulation in terms of a conflict between liberty and equality. Would the spread of equality mean the death of liberty, as Tocqueville worried? Despite his own misgivings about the rise of an impoverished rabble who would demand the abolition of liberty, Hegel did not share Tocqueville's gloomy forebodings. Equality, he insisted, was an abstraction that would yield before the living reality of liberty as the trajectory of modern states demonstrates. They combine "the supreme concrete inequality of individuals" with "a greater and more stable liberty" (*Encyclopedia of Philosophical Sciences*, pt. III: *Philosophy of Spirit*, § 539). The secret, according to Hegel, lies in the "cannon" that every distinct interest ought to be permitted its full separate expression. Liberty unfolds as a living reality

---

[27] Not only is there the abiding tension within civil society that "consists precisely in an excess of production and in the lack of a proportionate number of consumers who are themselves also producers (*Philosophy of Right*, § 245), but even the state proper seems to be fraught with dangers that remain permanently unresolved. Hegel counsels the need for security "against the misuse of power by ministers and their officials," protections against the misguidance of the Estates and of public opinion, the introduction of bicameralism, and several other cautionary measures along the same lines (§§ 295, 301, 318, 312).

that discovers its own vitality, for "liberty is only deep when it is differentiated in all its fullness and these differences manifested in existence" (§ 541).[28] This is the principle Hegel follows in articulating the constitutional components of monarchy, the executive administration, and the estates. Although he is an acute observer of the constitutional tensions, Hegel firmly rejects any notion of an equilibrium. Each of the components contains the whole as part of a living entity, for they can have no separate existence. No mechanical explanation can account for a life that is not reducible to the parts. Life is that which is self-subsistent, containing its own foundation. Liberty in this sense can be sustained only from itself, not from any of its constituent elements. That may not appear to be a significant advance in insight, but it does decisively remove all of the search for certainty that would render the exercise of liberty more reliable. Liberty, on Hegel's conception, contains itself as objective spirit.

In that self-subsistence, it apprehends itself as divine. Objective spirit is the ethical and political particularization of absolute spirit, "the divine spirit as indwelling in self-consciousness" (§ 552). This is not an accidental or external relationship but one that is constitutive of our moral existence, as Kant demonstrated "when he treats belief in God as proceeding from the practical reason" (§ 552). Contrary to the "monstrous blunder of our times" (§ 552), religion and morality cannot be separated, for it is in religion that morality reaches its truth. Their unity was recognized by Plato, but he lacked the means of making it transparent since the principle of subjectivity had not been adequately differentiated. Religion itself must be seen to rest on individual self-consciousness before its truth as a revelation of the divine life can occur. So long as spirit remains degraded in sensuous forms, not only is the true form of religion absent but the actuality of the state is also obscured. The demand that spirit be revealed as spirit is what marks the transition by Hegel to the third part of the *Philosophy of Spirit*, "Absolute Spirit." His emphasis is on countering the one-sided emphasis of the romantics on the experience of God by insisting that the experience is also a mode of existence. "Religion ... if it has on one hand to be studied as issuing from the subject and having

---

[28] The formulation may be different from the roughly contemporaneous reflections of Tocqueville in *Democracy in America*, 2 vols., trans. Henry Reeve (New York: Vintage, 1956–58), but the issue is the same, namely, how the individual exercises responsible liberty rather than becoming lost within an anonymous whole. Tocqueville's great insight was that the presence of intermediate and voluntary institutions provided the opportunity for genuine political action. "Thus it is by the enjoyment of a dangerous freedom that the Americans learn the art of rendering the dangers of freedom less formidable" (vol. 2, 127).

its home in the subject, must no less be regarded as objectively issuing from the absolute spirit which as spirit is in its community" (§ 554). It is in this section on absolute spirit that Hegel struggles mightily to save the modern principle of subjectivity from its own success and thereby reveals how the entire history of religion can be justified in this new context. We must no longer think, he insists, of absolute spirit as an idea that we contain but as the idea by which our thinking is contained.

Before it is known, that existential movement toward the absolute is first displayed in the form of art. The implication is that once the transparence of the source is established the expression is rendered obsolete, but this is not necessarily supported by Hegel's countervailing profession of the permanent validity of art. The divergence from Schelling in this, as in other points, may be more apparent than real. What is decisive is that beautiful art has "thus performed the same service as philosophy: it has purified the spirit from its thralldom" (§ 562). Spirit can no longer be revealed by its intermediaries but must mediate itself; spirit can be revealed only by spirit. God is self-knowing spirit whom we must know through our own self-consciousness as our knowledge of God. The ambiguity of this formulation probably cannot be unraveled, but it can be salvaged if we take sufficient notice of the conclusion "which proceeds to man's self-knowledge *in* God" (§ 564). What is revealed is the process of revelation as man's self-knowledge in God. Spirit is that which reveals and does not reveal itself because it always lies beyond any of its manifestations. It can be grasped, therefore, only by that which is itself spirit, which shares the same transcendence of its own being, at least to the extent of being able to apprehend itself in the movement. Initially this is grasped in "the divine man who is the idea of spirit," but it has still not gone beyond merely the form of self-consciousness. The assertion of this particular self-consciousness, that of Christ, as absolute leads nowhere. It is a historical conclusion, not a mode of existence, and as such an ironic denial of what it claims to be. "Thinking, so far, is only the formal aspect of the absolute content" (§ 571). It is in philosophy that it lives within its idea.

The last section of the *Philosophy of Spirit* contains some of Hegel's most cryptic formulations, beginning with the declaration that the science of absolute spirit is the unity of art and religion. Philosophy is the culmination of art and religion "in which the diverse elements in the content are cognized as necessary, and this necessary as free" (§ 572). He then launches into a defense of philosophy against the charge of "pantheism," which seemed to provide a means of combining Enlightenment rationalism with the belief in a divine substance. By briefly surveying the so-called pantheistic religions, Hegel demonstrates the utter incoherence of the concept, "for the idolatry of the wretched Hindu, when he adores the ape, or other creature, is still a long way from that wretched fancy of a pantheism, to which everything is God, and God everything" (§ 573). The entire "pantheist" controversy is testament to the failure of Enlightenment rationalism to apprehend the nature of religion. Both art and religion may convey the impression that they refer to objective realities, but their truth is that they know God inwardly. A manifestation of God is not God but functions as a manifestation that does not manifest. The worshiper may not be able to articulate this self-awareness, but it is not any the less present for its unspokenness. Indeed, it is the intuitive awareness of God that makes it possible for finite realities to become the means of his manifestation. He is not in the embodiments but in the movement of spirit by which he is alone apprehended. In contrast to the exoteric symbolizations, Hegel insists that the "esoteric study of God and identity, as of cognitions, and notions, is philosophy itself" (§ 573). Whether this means that philosophy has now abolished art and religion is not immediately apparent. Such an implication can easily be drawn from Hegel's structuring of the conclusion, but his extended meditations in the lecture series devoted to art and religion, as well as the lectures on the philosophy of history and the history of philosophy, point toward the opposite inference. In many ways the thrust of his work is more powerful than his own self-assessments.

Clearly there is more than a strong undercurrent of preference to see history come to its culmination in Hegel's system. Yet everything he did worked against it. History ceases to be a realm of importance once it has arrived at its fulfillment. Hegel did not require Kojève to make him aware of this ironic consequence, and even if he did not reject it forthrightly his example tilts decisively away from it.[29] Once philosophy has become explicitly existential, it arises out of the concrete history of existence. Philosophy now depends on art and religion, as the historical emergence of meaning, as well as its own history, to provide the material of its self-meditation. If philosophy had rendered them obsolete, it would itself be in danger of becoming an abstraction again. Hegel himself generally phrases this as the necessity for spirit to go through all of its historical stages in order, through opposition to them, to arrive at

---

[29] Alexandre Kojève, *Introduction to the Reading of Hegel*, trans. James H. Nichols (New York: Basic, 1969), 159–60. See also Barry Cooper, *The End of History: An Essay on Modern Hegelianism* (Toronto: University of Toronto Press, 1984).

knowledge of itself. But what does this mean? It has an almost mechanical ring to it, yet it can also be given a very different interpretation. The necessity of all of the manifestations of spirit may arise because of its inexhaustibility. To the extent that none of the finite expressions are adequate representations, all of them are indispensable in apprehending the depth of divine richness. The real question is whether spirit, having gone through the process of self-reflection, can reach the point where the manifestations have become superfluous. Is there something irreducible in art and religion that philosophy can apprehend but not replace? Is there a depth beyond manifestation?

This is finally the question that Hegel poses for us and the main source of ambivalence in his thought. His failure to clarify the answer is the principal reason for the failure of his revolutionary transformation of philosophy to take hold.[30] Instead, it had to be reinitiated and generally in opposition to his notorious "system." Schelling was only the first in a long line of successors who thought they had to correct the crucial error that had vitiated his achievement. Yet the very universality of the rejection should give us pause and lead us to consider whether the source of the correction might not have lain all along within Hegel himself. In many respects it was Hegel's own single-minded focus on the revolution he was effecting that obscured for him the need to acknowledge its wider context. His insistence that spirit can be known only through spirit, that it is because we are already constituted by spirit in our self-consciousness that we can apprehend the absolute, concealed from him the mysterious depth from which spirit arises. There would be no spirit unless there was the inexplicable movement toward manifestation. Hegel remained maddeningly inconclusive in dealing with the being of God or the creation of the world, content always to eliminate all objectifying conceptions but never to confront the questions from which they arose. As a consequence he could never acknowledge the permanent validity of myth, which must rather occupy a subterranean position in the presence of art and religion. In truth, however, myth continues to play an indispensable role as the manifestation of spirit, which cannot come to self-knowledge except by going through its symbolization. The self-mediation of spirit through

---

[30] While I am now less inclined to blame Hegel for the ambiguity that afflicts his achievement, I am still inclined to concede that it is the principal obstacle that remains to be overcome in understanding it. In that sense I have modified my position from the one I outlined in "The Ambiguity of the Hegelian End of History," in Timothy Burns, ed., *After History? Francis Fukuyama and His Critics* (Lanham, MD: Rowman and Littlefield, 1994), 171–96.

the process of its historical unfolding is driven not by the urge to reach a conclusion but by the impossibility of spirit being manifest by anything but itself. Any intermediate depiction short of self-transparence would simply be untrue to the nature of spirit.

Hegel's neglect of the context from which spirit arises, the depth of God beyond revelation, can be attributed to his drive to remain strictly faithful to the inner dynamic of spirit. It can be remedied relatively easily because it is implied in the very notion of a process of manifestation. Hegel, as I have suggested, was aware of this dimension but for a range of motives chose to downplay it. Instead, he confined his attention to the discovery of how it was possible for us to know what could never adequately manifest itself. The Hindu worshiper before an ape knew just as well as the philosopher that the embodiment was not what it embodied, which yet functioned as its embodiment. This was possible because the worshiper, too, was not what he appeared to be but was constituted inwardly by the same reality of spirit. His existence may have been in space and time, but his being was constituted by the self-consciousness of spirit. Through the quotation from Aristotle with which the *Philosophy of Spirit* concludes, Hegel reminds us of his descent from the Greek discovery of the unity of thinking and being. His account of thought thinking itself, far from being a departure from Aristotle, is essentially a more profound elaboration of its meaning. *Noesis noesos* consists not of the self-awareness of finite knowing but its meditation on the boundary by which it is constituted. Thought and being are one in the moment in which thinking constitutes being, but that is at the limit where finite thinking apprehends its own possibility within the infinite in which it stands. This is not in any sense the assertion that finite being has grasped the source of its existence but only that its constitution through the infinite has become transparent. Hegel's almost willful ambiguity may have invited the conclusion of self-aggrandizement, but the structure of his reflection negates it. If anything, his implementation of the revolution in philosophy has shown the utter impossibility of definitively grasping the whole that is nowhere available to us except through our existential constitution within it. As what is known only through its self-movement, spirit cannot be known outside of this relationship.

3

Schelling on the Beyond of Existence

The conventional picture of Schelling as the predecessor linking Hegel with Fichte and Kant has only recently begun to dissolve. Schelling's early prominence and the relative paucity of later publications provided some basis for this perception, although it required a neglect of the large body of posthumous writings that continued the existential meditation of philosophy after the death of Hegel. Now that view has become untenable in light of the trajectory that philosophy itself has followed. The position of Schelling as the crucial link between the idealists and the fragmented explorers of existence who followed has begun to be established. Of course, the attendance of Kierkegaard, Engels, Bakunin, Burckhart, and other luminaries at Schelling's Berlin lectures in the 1840s is well known, but its significance has not necessarily been absorbed.[1] This is largely because these brilliant students all subsequently turned their backs on idealism to proclaim the necessity of returning to existence. In the dramatic impact of the gesture, we overlook the extent to which Schelling and, as we have suggested, Hegel pointed the way. If we think of Hegel as having demonstrated that philosophy can be understood only as a

---

[1] Schelling had been invited back to Berlin to weed out "the dragon seeds of Hegelian pantheism," and one presumes that the notoriety of the event had something to do with the assembly of talent it attracted in the audience. The Prussian ministry had placed considerable confidence in the return of an eminence grise to counteract the revolutionary implications of Hegelianism in the hands of a younger generation that had already determined to go beyond the master. It was surely one of those highly visible encounters in which incomprehension was bound to result. See *Schelling: Philosophie der Offenbarung 1841/42*, 408 and passim, for the materials related to Schelling's summons to Berlin. This text is the unauthorized version of the lectures in 1841–42 that was published by Paulus, much to the consternation of Schelling. As such it is an abridgment of the material that is more expansively presented in *Sämmtliche Werke*.

movement of life, that it is only in existence that the tensions are resolved, then Schelling is the one who established the definitive limits to our penetration of the process. Where Hegel was inclined to propound the completeness of the system even in the face of his own evident admission of its incompleteness, Schelling insisted that our very existence precludes the possibility of its systematic comprehension. The reality by which we are constituted of necessity escapes us. Not only did Schelling never complete a system, he never seems to have completed even his proposed literary expositions. In this sense he was not only the first and most forceful critic of Hegel's systematizing proclivities, but also the most powerful witness to the ineradicable limits to philosophy in the mode of existence. While Hegel may have effected the revolution, it was Schelling who grasped its implication.

The impossibility of grounding any knowledge of the whole in the instrumental rationality of modern science becomes inescapable in Kant's *Critique of Pure Reason,* for the categories of our understanding are confined to the sensible intuitions of space and time. Despite the fact that Kant never accepted the "death of metaphysics" that his critique implied and insisted that there would yet emerge a true metaphysics beyond the ruins, his own work largely retained the character of a "prolegomena" toward that aspiration. It was left to the next generation of idealists to show that the disappearance of dogmatic metaphysics did not mean its disappearance as such. Metaphysics now was discovered to be what it had always been, a mode of reflection on the whole by which existence is constituted. Kant's primacy of practical reason had pointed the way, but it had not yet grasped itself as transparent for the reality in which it is. Only with the idealists do Kant's regulative ideas become the constitutive ideas by which existence is possible. They return us to the Greek beginning in which the idea is not only a mental construction of reality but its indispensable source. Thinking and being are the same when thinking is what makes being what it is. Because we are finite beings, our thinking does not, of course, create being, but to the extent that we live in accordance with ideas our thinking is transparent for the constitution of being. Kant had a profound intuition of this existential structure of reflection, but it was Hegel who elaborated it, while revealing one of the profound dangers within it. The constitutive ideas of existence can be absorbed back into the mind; we can suffer from the illusion that we have comprehended the ideas that comprehend us. The achievement of Schelling was to have erected a permanent barrier against this distortion.

With forceful persistence he showed what an existential metaphysics must mean, as the apprehension of an order by which we are held but which for that very reason we can never finally penetrate.[2]

Kant's transcendental inquiry into the possibility of knowledge remained ambiguous as to its own status. Could an inquiry into the possibility of knowledge itself assume the form of knowledge? This was the ambiguity that was most fully exposed in Hegel's system of science, in which the self-mediation of spirit seemed to encounter no limits. Schelling utterly foreclosed this option and, in the process, revealed what the idealist revolution was all about. What had begun as a search for the transcendental ground of the possibility of knowledge was compelled to recognize itself as a search for the ground of the transcendental ground itself, in the realm beyond knowledge. If the categories of the understanding made knowledge possible, the possibility of the categories themselves must lie outside of knowledge.[3] Being is prior to thinking, Schelling constantly asserted, and for this reason cannot be included within it. This means that thinking cannot ultimately illuminate itself but must stand in the light of that which is. Thinking and being can become one only because thinking itself is derived from being and, unlike other beings, knows itself as such. The limit of the self-transparence of thinking is constituted by the awareness of its derivation from being. This is what Schelling announces as his "positive" philosophy, in contrast to the Hegelian emphasis on negation as the most crucial aspect. Hegel ends with unity and emphasizes negation, while Schelling begins with unity and emphasizes the irreducible and impenetrable reality of being. Knowledge cannot go further than acknowledge its own dependence on what *is*, which of necessity must remain beyond its ken.[4]

---

[2] Xavier Tilliette has grasped this significance most powerfully, as indicated by the title of his magisterial intellectual biography, *Schelling. Une philosophie en devenir*, 2 vols. (Paris: Vrin, 1970). See also the useful overview of Schelling on various topics in Jason Wirth, *The Conspiracy of Life: Meditations on Schelling and His Time* (Albany: State University of New York Press, 2003).

[3] This is a point that has been well developed by Andrew Bowie. "Schelling turns the transcendental ideal from a final transcendental possibility into the original ontological possibility of the predicative world of articulated and known nature – a world which, of course, can give rise to Kant's theory but must first be there to do so. Schelling repeatedly stresses in his later work that '*being* is the first, thinking is only the second or what follows.'" Bowie, *Schelling and Modern European Philosophy* (London: Routledge, 1993), 104. See also Wolfram Holgrebe, *Prädikation und Genesis. Metaphysik also Fundamentalheuristik in Ausgang von Schellings 'Die Weltalter'* (Frankfurt: Suhrkamp, 1989), 66–71.

[4] This is, of course, a view of Schelling that is only gradually making its way in the literature. Its beginning can be dated to Walter Schulz, *Die Vollendung des deutschen Idealismus in der*

The echoes that we hear of Heidegger's "ontological difference" and Derrida's "différance" in Schelling's endless deferral of being from knowledge are no accident. They suggest, as Andrew Bowie has indicated, that Schelling is the pivotal thinker who transmits the revolutionary transformation of philosophy in the modern period. He is the one in whom the fragmentation, the inconclusiveness of philosophy is first recognized but, unlike its later manifestations, with Schelling it emerges without the tonality of disappointment. The greatness of Schelling lies in his capacity to present the submission to the mystery of being, not as a frustration of the systematic ambition of speculation, but as an affirmation of the infinite openness of existence. Even his critique of the Hegelian system, for all of its intensity and occasional acerbity, lacks the parricidal invective that marks so much of the treatment accorded it over the following century. Philosophically at any rate, Schelling was the collaborator of Hegel in a relationship that was deeply rooted in their common affinity with Kant's turn toward the existence of reason in its theoretical and practical modes. The significance of Schelling is perhaps best captured by the recognition that, while he never established a school, he nevertheless plays a continuous role in the formation of thinkers who set about their own intellectual voyages of discovery.[5] He is not only the well-known progenitor of existential philosophy through Kierkegaard and others, but the indispensable spur that has made philosophy a living existence for a far wider array of successors. Part of the explanation is surely his extraordinary capacity to anticipate the deeper paradoxes into which contemporary philosophy is led, but an even greater factor must lie in his willingness to see the impenetrable as far more than it appears to be.

Spätphilosophie Schellings (Neske: Pfullingen, 1975), and is particularly associated with the efforts of Andrew Bowie, as in his final chapter of *Schelling and Modern European Philosophy*, "Schelling or Hegel?" But see also Dale E. Snow, *Schelling and the End of Idealism* (Albany: State University of New York Press, 1996), and Joseph P. Lawrence, "Schelling as Post-Hegelian and as Aristotelian," *International Philosophical Quarterly* 26 (1986): 315–30. A particularly important recent contribution that identifies the pivotal role of Schelling is Michelle Kosch, *Freedom and Reason in Kant, Schelling, and Kierkegaard* (Oxford: Clarendon, 2006).

[5] Examples include the dissertations of Tillich and Habermas, as well as his pivotal role in the work of Eric Voegelin. See Jürgen Habermas, *Das Absolute und die Geschichte. Von der Zweispältigkeit in Schellings Denken* (Bonn: Bouvier, 1954); Paul Tillich, *Mysticism and Guilt Consciousness in Schelling's Philosophical Development,* trans. Victor Nuovo (Lewisburg, PA: Bucknell University Press, 1974); and Tillich, *The Construction of the History of Religion in Schelling's Positive Philosophy: Its Presuppositions and Principles,* trans. Victor Nuovo (Lewisburg, PA: Bucknell University Press, 1974). On Voegelin see Jerry Day, *Voegelin, Schelling, and the Philosophy of Historical Existence* (Columbia: University of Missouri Press, 2003).

Schelling was the genuine founder of a metaphysics beyond presence. There is much truth in Bowie's observation that while Derrida concentrated his focus on the loss of presence, Schelling had already shown that even that recognition depends on a prior unity.[6]

The Uncontainability of Thought

It is not enough to point out that "almost every philosopher makes statements which contradict his own explicit account of what can be justified or known."[7] The radical irretrievability of that by which the saying occurs must also be understood. It is nothing less than the impossibility of attending to that which makes the attending possible, for once we have made existence a focus of attention it is no longer that which is doing the focusing. All we can really intend are the traces of what is, namely, that which now is no longer. Only an existential mode that grasps this inescapability on the way can do justice to the situation. This insight is the source of the revolution in philosophy inaugurated by Hegel's insistence on philosophy as a movement of existence. Schelling completes the shift by confronting its most important consequence. The real that perpetually recedes from our grasp can nevertheless be apprehended as receding. Despair over the inaccessibility of truth is misplaced. It is not that we can never make our way toward the true, for on the contrary truth is already so close to us that we exist within it as the possibility of all knowledge. We cannot account for what makes knowledge of the world possible, because we are already constituted by that possibility. A long line of philosophical reflection had formed around the realization that relativism and skepticism cannot ground themselves but must exist within a mode of truth beyond them. Now Schelling made this necessity explicit. If our knowledge of truth is what makes relativism possible, it is precisely because we can exist within this knowledge of truth without objectifying it that we can recognize the relativity of our knowledge. The absolute makes recognition of the relative possible, but it must be an absolute that itself cannot be recognized as such.

---

[6] Bowie, *Schelling and Modern European Philosophy,* 73. Two recent anthologies suggest the range of contemporary thinkers who find an affinity with the metaphysical openness of Schelling: Judith Norman and Alistair Welchman, eds., *The New Schelling* (London: Continuum, 2004), and Jason Wirth, ed., *Schelling Now: Contemporary Readings* (Bloomington: Indiana University Press, 2005).

[7] Hilary Putnam, *Realism and Reason: Philosophical Papers,* vol. 3 (Cambridge: Cambridge University Press, 1983), 226.

The reflection is not that by which the reflection is seen, as Schelling explains. "Just as the eye, in beholding its reflection in the mirror, posits itself [and] has an intuition of itself only to the extent that it posits the *reflecting* [medium], the mirror, as nothing in-itself, and just as it is effectively one act of the eye, whereby it posits itself, beholds itself, and does not posit or behold the reflecting [medium], so the universe (*All*), too, contemplates *itself* by not beholding or positing the particular discretely. Both are One act for it; the nonpositing of the particular is a contemplation and position of itself. And this is the explanation of philosophy's most sublime mystery, namely, how the eternal substance, or God, is not *modified* by the particular or appearance, but how it only *contemplates itself* and how *it is* as the **eternal, infinite substance**" (*Sämmtliche Werk*, I/6, 197–98/"System of Philosophy," *Idealism and the Endgame*, 182). What is recognized is what the reflection as such is not. But this does not mean, as Hegel insisted, that the difference between the self and its reflection is overcome in the moment of recognition. Schelling's whole point is that the recognition is always incomplete. A leap is required to complete it precisely because the reflection is not the self but only its image. While the process of expression may be necessary for the self to come to knowledge of itself, the result never coincides with the aspiration. The self that initiates the movement is never contained in the expression; all that is produced is a reflection of itself. If the self were to be contained in its self-expression, no movement of recognition would be possible. It is because there is a gap that recognition can occur. Resonances of this insight recur in the history of semiology over the next two centuries, particularly in the realization that the impossibility of perfect communication is what makes communication at all possible. Without that deficiency between what communicates and what is communicated, there would be no space for meaning. In this context Schelling's importance looms large not only because he anticipates the critique of the metaphysics of presence, but because he at the same time demonstrates the metaphysical presuppositions of the critique. The absence of presence is not a sheer absence; it is simply a presence that cannot be reduced to presence. We are at the very core of the revolutionary shift toward the perspective of existence.

Perhaps the reason that Schelling's significance in this regard has never been fully recognized lies in his readiness to return to the language of theological reference after his foray into the existential mode of reflection. A similar pattern is evident in the philosophical marginalization of Kierkegaard despite his evident popularity. This misjudgment of Schelling mars the otherwise extremely useful treatment by Andrew

Bowie, who argues for Schelling's own responsibility for the situation.[8] Schelling, he insists, is susceptible to such misunderstanding. It is not simply that his transcendental and theological orientation is out of step with contemporary sensibilities. There is a problem with the consistency of his formulations. If the absolute is that about which ultimately nothing can be said, what is it that accounts for Schelling's evident willingness to develop an extensive philosophy of mythology and revelation in his last writings? How, indeed, can there be a revelation of that which, on his own account, can never really be revealed? Schelling's claim to have reversed the ontological argument is of little comfort, since the fact that he does not begin with a concept of God does not mean that he does not seek to end with it. Rather he leaves himself open to the criticism that the necessity of his absolute is vulnerable to the same criticisms he levels at Hegel. He ought to have remained faithful to his own assertion that positive philosophy is alone open and avoided the inclination to close it in the negative philosophy of necessity. The difficulty is illustrated by Schelling's response to the Hegelian objection. "One could object: an actuality that precedes all possibility cannot be *thought*. One can concede this in a certain sense and say that precisely for this reason it is the *beginning* of all real thought – for the *beginning* of thought is not yet itself thought" (*Sämmtliche Werke*, II/3, 162/ *The Grounding of Positive Philosophy*, 203). In thinking theologically Schelling gives the impression of breaking his own rule and of returning to "Hegelianism."

It may well be that Kierkegaard presents the deepest version of this critique, which arose directly from his attendance at Schelling's late lectures, for the objections, while they seem to be driven by a surface animus against the outmoded character of theological language as such, draw their greatest support from the drive toward existential truth that will not abide any dogmatic substitutes. This is the problematic that is played out in the subsequent history of philosophy, which is really a post-Schellingian development, not only because he marked the end of idealism, but because he bequeathed the incompletely developed meaning of faith that received its most poignant manifestation in the wrestlings of Nietzsche. Whatever the personal obstacles to faith in such later thinkers, there can be no doubt that their most formidable philosophical critique is drawn from the same well as Schelling had unearthed. In thinking through how discourse concerning the transcendent can be conducted, how we might talk about that which can be present only in the mode

---

[8] Bowie, *Schelling and Modern European Philosophy*, 159–68.

of absence, they testify to the enduring power of his positive philosophy that sought to place itself outside of all schemes of conceptual necessity. The luminosity of existence must draw its radiance from that which is beyond all radiance. It is one of the central paradoxes of this long development that the progressive alienation of philosophy from conventional theological perspectives is carried forward by an intensifying awareness of the mystery of transcendent being. Schelling may not have found the means of preserving his discourse from the overtones of Gnostic speculation that still persist within it, but he pointed the way toward the most radical theology of existence as it would emerge in the struggles of his successors. It is noteworthy, for example, that he was a decisive influence in the formation of the nonspeculative philosophy of revelation that we find elaborated in the work of Eric Voegelin.[9]

The shortcomings of Schelling's persevering attempts to refound philosophy are, in other words, capable of being remedied from within the resources of his own account. They contain not a whiff of the systematic ambition that continually jeopardizes Hegel's construction, for Schelling has definitively established the limits of conceptualization. Thought thinking itself, the great transparence of philosophy from its Greek beginning, has reached a turning point in which the limits of transparence have been recognized. Seeing through everything, which had threatened to end by seeing nothing, now acknowledges that its own possibility is derived from something that cannot be seen through. This is not a higher grasp of necessity but rather the acceptance of the inability to grasp the necessity of the last necessity, for no system can ultimately explain the fact of its own existence. This realization evokes one of Schelling's most memorable formulations. "Thus far from man and his endeavors making the world comprehensible, it is man himself that is the most incomprehensible and who inexorably drives me to the belief in the wretchedness of all being. . . . It is precisely man that drives me to the final desperate question: Why is there anything at all? Why is there not nothing" (*Sämmtliche Werke*, II/3, 7; *Grounding of Positive Philosophy*, 94)? The note of existential melancholy is not incidental, for it is an underlying theme of Schelling's reflection in which the boundedness of existence afflicts all aspects, including the speculative and communicative.

---

[9] Voegelin, *The New Order and Last Orientation*, in *Collected Works*, vol. 25, ed. Jürgen Gebhardt and Thomas Hollweck (Columbia: University of Missouri Press, 1999), 193–242. Voegelin agrees with Hans Urs von Balthasar in detecting Gnostic and apocalyptic overtones in Schelling; see Balthasar, *Die Apokalypse der deutschen Seele*, vol. 1, *Der deutsche Idealismus*.

Acceptance of finitude may be the price of thinking as well as existence. Schelling's ability to acknowledge, if not embrace, the fate of existence is surely the first step toward setting thought on the only viable path available to it. The fact that our disputes still revolve within the alternative understandings of language as world disclosure and world coherence testifies to the position he occupies within modernity.[10]

It is a position that is derived from Schelling's refusal to mitigate the tensions that define our existence. Neither the causal nexus of matter nor the self-conscious freedom of thought can be denied. Nor is there a third term to which they can be reduced. The antinomy of freedom and necessity that had so puzzled Kant, the mystery of the connection between the brain and consciousness that still bedevils us, and the whole history of reductionism and dualism reach a moment of enormous clarity in Schelling's realization that they are inescapable dimensions of the same reality.[11] Causality may govern everything under the sun, but it cannot govern the mind by which it is grasped. Only that which determines itself can apprehend the process of causal determination. This does not make mind the only true reality, no more than the force of causality renders everything ultimately material. Neither mind nor matter is ultimate, for both are made possible by that which is other and for which they are modes of disclosure. But that other can never be grasped, Schelling insists, for it is forever outside of the grasping that it makes possible. All easy generalizations have become illicit. This is why the mystery of language cannot finally be penetrated. No amount of analysis of the relationship of the signifier to the signified can get behind the existence of language itself, for it must always presuppose what it seeks to explain. The miracle of the disclosure of reality by language remains. Why do words, even with all their deficiencies, nevertheless say something about what is? No philosophy of language can pierce this veil that must envelope even the efforts to reach behind it. All of these limits have become familiar

---

[10] Habermas's involvement with religious language that exceeds all conceptualizations of it testifies to Schelling's continuing influence in his thought. "Philosophy, even in its postmetaphysical form, will be able neither to replace nor to repress religion as long as religious language is the bearer of a semantic content that is inspiring and even indispensable, for this content eludes (for the time being?) the explanatory force of philosophical language and continues to resist translation into reasoning discourses." Habermas, *Post-Metaphysical Thinking*, trans. William Mark Hohengarten (Cambridge, MA: MIT Press, 1996), 51.

[11] Frederick Beiser has exhaustively recounted the historical development that culminated in Schelling's *Naturphilosophie* as the emergence of absolute idealism, in *German Idealism: The Struggle Against Subjectivism, 1781–1801*.

to us as a result of more than a century of intensive language reflection that centers around the recognition that "no language could say the true about the true, since the truth is founded in that of which it speaks and it has no other means of saying the true about the true."[12] The only explanation, Schelling saw, was the underlying unity between language and reality, between the movement of manifestation and what permits manifestation.

Signification is in this sense possible, because the world is itself a form of signification, a "congealed word," but its disclosure would not be possible without language. As the irruption of meaning without preparation, language is a form of revelation. It is in such terms that Schelling describes the significance of art. Like Kant in the *Critique of Judgment,* he saw art as the test case that illustrated the continuity between consciousness and nature, for in it nature loses its fixity and consciousness simultaneously illuminates the rule of nature. Art is what renders nature transparent to itself in a way that nature can never do alone. Schelling's attention is drawn toward the unforeseeable character of this event, which remains impenetrable even, perhaps most of all, to the artist who undergoes it. He is drawn to that inexpressible point of contact as the "absolute" beyond which we cannot go and from which everything follows. "Now every absolute concurrence of the two antithetical activities [conscious and unconscious, free creation and fateful submission] is utterly unaccountable, being simply a *phenomenon* which although incomprehensible, yet cannot be denied; and art, therefore, is the one everlasting revelation which yields that concurrence, and the marvel which, had it existed but once only, would necessarily have convinced us of the absolute reality of the supreme event" (*Sämmtliche Werke,* I/3, 618/*System of Transcendental Idealism,* 223). Art, like language, cannot explain itself, but it is what makes all explanation possible, for it is disclosure as such. The inertness of what merely is can be brought to transparence because the possibility lies buried within it, but its attainment depends on the presence of that which can render it self-conscious again. Man is the self-consciousness of nature as nature is the hiddenness of self-consciousness. What makes their conjunction possible in thought and language is their connection with the absolute, which, although it cannot be known, can be known in its unknowability. It is this glimpse of oblique self-recognition of the absolute that constitutes the uniqueness of human beings.

---

[12] Jacques Lacan, *Écrits* (Paris: Seuil, 1971), 233, quoted in Bowie, *Schelling and Modern European Philosophy,* 118.

Man is a spark of the absolute, Schelling acknowledges in the only language available to him, that of mythology. We can see that love is more than the explanation of mutual dependence in which Hegel's formulations seem to rest. Love is not love unless there is something supererogatory about it. "God Himself is reconciled to nature by virtue of a spontaneous love, that is, He is not dependent *on nature* and yet He does not want to exist without her. For love does not exist where two beings are in need of each other but where each could exist independently, such as in the case with God who is already *in and of Himself* – *suapte natura* – the being God [*der Seyende*]; here then, each one could be for itself without considering it an act of privation to be for itself, even though it will not want to, and morally cannot, exist for itself without the other. Of such a kind, then, is also God's *true* relation to nature, that is, not a *unilateral* relation. Nature, too, is drawn to God by love and therefore strives with infinite zeal to bear divine fruit" (*Sämmtliche Werke*, I/7, 453/"Stuttgart Seminars," *Idealism and the Endgame*, 221). Love is what explains but itself defies explanation. Schelling's reflections on love here have a long line of successors, from Kierkegaard to Nietzsche to Levinas, in whom it is precisely the instrumental aspect of love that is called to account before the boundlessness of love. Between autonomous beings, love cannot be based on any form of dependency but must arise from the overflow of love itself. Love is love only when it is a free expression of self, and it can be a free expression of self only if it respects the same in the other. Once again the existential marks the boundary of intelligibility. The illumination it provides, however, is both what enables the human relationship of love to serve as a metaphor for the relation between God and the world and, at the same time, underpins the more than metaphorical truth within which the merely human relationship stands. As a microcosm, man is both a part of the whole and the whole in a part.

His is a finite glimpse of the infinite within which he exists. It can be apprehended only on the way, never as a completed process. The recourse to aphorisms by Schelling and the romantics has little in common with the polished nuggets of the earlier moralists. Now the aphorisms are deliberately shaped as fragments because only as such can the whole be evoked that cannot be expressed. "Not we, not you or I, know about God. For reason, insofar as it affirms God, can affirm *nothing* else, and in this act it annihilates itself as a particularity, as something that is outside God (*Sämmtliche Werke*, I/7, 250/"Schelling's Aphorisms of 1805,"

§ 42).'' There are neither subjects nor objects but only the whole that is, which yet cannot be known except through the fragments available to us. Taking up a theme that will prevail throughout his thought, Schelling opposes the self-contained Cartesian subject from which modernity has taken its reference. "The 'I think,' 'I am,' is since Descartes the fundamental error of all knowledge. Thinking is not my thinking, and being is not my being, for everything is only of God, or of the All" (250/§ 44). But reason cannot grasp the all; it can only proceed on Hölderlin's "eccentric path" by which the whole is never comprehended.[13] Reason cannot stand apart from being, because it is never outside of it. We do not possess reason as a faculty or tool but are constituted by it as our being. "Reason is not an affirmation of the One, that itself would be outside the One; it is a knowing of God that itself is in God" (250/§ 47). "Hence the absolute can be eternally expressed only as the absolute and absolutely indivisible identity of the subjective and the objective, an expression which is the same and designates the same as the infinite self-affirmation of God" (253/§ 65). Lacking coherence within themselves, the aphorisms become transparent only when they reach beyond themselves through the evocation of existence within the whole.

Freedom as Metaphysics

All of Schelling's attempts to reflect on the imperviousness of existence to any conceptual formulation came to their first fruition in his *Philosophical Inquiries into the Essence of Human Freedom* (1809), the last work of importance he published during his lifetime. It is no accident that the work has long been regarded as the most powerful statement of his philosophical outlook, for it clearly links Schelling with the whole existential turn in which freedom becomes the pivotal theme. But as always his reflections carry a far deeper resonance beyond the merely anthropological. What made the text so central to Heidegger was that freedom

---

[13] Charles Larmore, "Hölderlin and Novalis," in Ameriks, ed., *The Cambridge Companion to German Idealism*, 149. Richard Velkley has explored this self-limitation of reason in his insightful essay "The Necessity of Error: Schelling's Autocritique and the History of Philosophy," in *Being After Rousseau: Philosophy and Culture in Question* (Chicago: University of Chicago Press, 2002). According to Velkley even Goethe had grasped the existential tension in Kant by which reason demonstrates the impossibility of containing itself. "Goethe, like Schelling, believes that Kant poised himself to discuss the metaphysical realm but held back from doing so. 'Kant resolutely limits himself to a certain circle, and constantly points ironically beyond it,' Goethe writes in one aphorism" (133).

is contemplated in relation to the whole mystery of being.[14] This was also its significance for Schelling. It was in relation to the question of freedom that he addressed the question that had been at the center of his thought, namely, how it is possible for a part to have knowledge of the whole? Given that Schelling sought to avoid Hegel's flirtation with a system of absolute knowledge, the question then became how knowledge of the absolute was possible. It could occur, he saw, only if there was something of the absolute within each of us, if we had not only come from a source beyond ourselves but shared in some way in the very being of the source. Freedom under this perspective receives its most extensive metaphysical meditation in the modern world, for not only is it at the core of our human existence, but it opens upon the mystery of being by which we are constituted. Schelling placed a great deal of importance on the recognition of limits, of the inability of knowledge to penetrate beyond the limits by which it is constituted. In the essay on the essence (*Wesen*) of human freedom, he showed the extent to which the knowledge of limits is itself knowledge. Ever hovering in the background is the Hegelian question of whether knowledge of the absolute is absolute knowledge.

But Schelling always resists that suggestion. In contrast to the self-assurance that spills over into Hegel's claim to absolute knowledge, Schelling is far less certain he has even found the way of presenting his intimations of the whole. The foreword to *Philosophical Inquiries*, which originally appeared at the beginning of a projected collection of his philosophical works, indicates that up to that point his "system" had appeared only in parts whose "essential purport was understood by no one or by very few" (*Sämmtliche Werke*, I/7, 334). "Of Human Freedom" is the concluding piece of the volume, and its location suggested Schelling's confidence that he had at last found the means of conveying the center-piece of his thought. The work itself begins with the definitive rejection of the very idea of a system, which from then on will be one of the distinguishing features of his thought. A system of knowledge he now saw is incompatible with the very idea of freedom, and it is the inability to reach a comprehensive account that guarantees the possibility of freedom. This realization is in accordance with the ancient tradition that

---

[14] Heidegger, *Schelling's Treatise: On the Essence of Human Freedom*. See also Alan White, *Schelling: An Introduction to the System of Freedom* (New Haven, CT: Yale University Press, 1983), who sees the *Essence of Human Freedom* as the highpoint of Schelling's philosophical penetration, which declined in the later "positive philosophy." My own view stresses the continuity of Schelling's project.

"every philosophy which makes claim to unity and completeness is said to end in denying freedom" (336). Most of all, this insight must apply to the self-understanding of freedom itself. The roots of freedom cannot therefore be rendered transparent no matter how far the dialectic extends, for it is in the nature of that which exists that it can never contain its own ground. We begin to discern more clearly in this essay the point of divergence from Hegel. Where the latter had made existence the key to the understanding of freedom, Schelling insisted that understanding can never penetrate the boundary of existence. One of the most crucial turning points within the modern philosophical revolution is becoming clear and the implications stretch all the way to our own time.

It reaches back to the problem of determinism posed by Spinoza, which is in turn followed by the puzzle of freedom and necessity emanating from Kant, and it is part of the larger historical conundrum of man's free will in relation to God's omnipotence. Schelling recognizes that the source of the difficulty lies in the dogmatic character of the reflection. Thinking we can resolve the controversy from the outside, objectively, we fail to see that we already have access to its meaning from within the perspective of life. Dependence is not incompatible with autonomy, since every organic being is dependent on another for its genesis but not for its existence. Living entities contain their existence within themselves as self-subsisting. They may be conditioned, but they are always more than the sum of their conditions; they are capable of the self-movement that overcomes the fixity of the conditions in which they find themselves. None of the prevailing conceptions of the procession of creatures from God adequately captures the communication of life, for it is neither a mechanical production without life nor an emanation from the source that is never separated from it. "God," Schelling insists, "is not a God of the dead but of the living. . . . The procession of things from God is God's self-revelation. But God can only reveal himself in creatures who resemble him, in free, self-activating beings for whose existence there is no reason save God, but who are as God is" (346). Revelation means the emergence of that which is not the source but which nevertheless reflects the source as perfectly as possible. If all things were merely thoughts in the divine mind, they would not be an adequate revelation until they had acquired reality and life. Even thoughts in the human mind take on a life of their own and thus most truly reveal their creator. The separate reality of God's thoughts must be perfect. A "derivative absoluteness," Schelling concludes, "is so little a contradiction that it is the central concept of all philosophy. This sort of divinity characterizes nature. Immanence in God is so little a contradiction of freedom that freedom alone, and insofar as it is free, exists in God, whereas all that lacks freedom, and insofar as it lacks freedom, is necessarily outside of God" (347).

This sentence is a key statement of Schelling's insight, requiring some dissection since it does not immediately render its meaning. To grasp it we must be prepared to adopt the radically existential perspective he is following. Freedom is then not a fixed quantity but a process in which we find ourselves, for it is not ours but the process of divine self-revelation. There is no freedom other than within the movement of freedom. What lacks freedom is outside of this movement of God, and what enjoys freedom does so only to the extent that it participates in the original freedom. The error of Spinoza and all deterministic systems is "by no means due to the fact that he posits all *things in God,* but to the fact that they are *things –* to the abstract conception of the world and its creatures, indeed of eternal substance itself, which is also a thing for him" (349). Even the will is conceived of as a thing caught in the web of necessity, so that there is no way for it to arrive at the constitutive movement by which its freedom is actualized. Only when we recognize that God, too, is a process of freedom that cannot effect any result other than the enlargement of freedom do we perceive the whole within which we exist. "In the final and highest instance there is no other being than will. Will is primordial being, and all predicates apply to it alone – groundlessness, eternity, independence of time, self-affirmation! All philosophy strives only to find this highest affirmation" (350).[15] As the movement of freedom himself, God can give rise only to the movement of freedom. Anything less would be untrue to his divinity.

Yet this is still only the formal possibility of freedom. Real freedom requires Schelling to confront the possibility of the turn away from freedom. What if creatures disvalue the gift bestowed with their existence? This he acknowledges is the "profoundest difficulty" in all systems, whether immanent or transcendent accounts of the whole. "For permitting an entirely dependent being to do evil is, after all, not much better than cooperating with it in causing evil. Or, again, the reality of evil must be denied in some way or other" (353).[16] Either we attribute

---

[15] It was because of this insight that Heidegger proclaimed Schelling's text "the treatise which shatters Hegel's *Logic before* it was even published!" Heidegger, *Schelling's Treatise: On the Essence of Human Freedom,* 97.

[16] Michelle Kosch has made Schelling's confrontation with the challenge of evil the centerpiece of her study of the trajectory from Kant to Kierkegaard. As we have already seen, Kant understood that the possibility of evil constituted a problem for his morality of

responsibility for evil to God or we look for a source of evil outside of God. One alternative renders God inexplicable, the other despairs of any explanation. Schelling is very much aware of the novelty of the position he is developing, for the whole history of European philosophy has foundered on these two possibilities. It was only in his recently presented *Philosophy of Nature* that a way out had been uncovered. There was "first established the distinction in science between being insofar as it exists, and being insofar as it is the mere basis of existence" (357). The distinction between God and the ground of his existence has been universally conceded in philosophy and at the same time rendered nugatory. God has been regarded as containing the ground of his existence, which must therefore be regarded as a mere abstraction. Against this conceptual theology Schelling proposes an existential alternative. "This ground of his existence, which God contains, is not God viewed as absolute, that is insofar as he exists" (358). Even God must exist from that which he is not, for whatever is cannot be that from which it has emerged. The mystery of God is, of course, that he contains his source within himself, but this does not render the distinction any the less real. By virtue of the distinguishability between the two, the differentiation can be made. "God contains himself in an inner basis of his existence, which, to this extent, precedes him as to his existence, but similarly God is prior to the basis as this basis, as such, could not be if God did not exist in actuality" (358).

The same distinction arises when we consider the perspective of things in their independence from God. When we ask how it is possible for things to be independent of God who contains all, we must conclude that they must have their basis in something outside of him no matter how contradictory it may sound. "But since there can be nothing outside God, this contradiction can only be solved by things having their basis in that within God which is not *God himself*, i.e. in that which is the basis of his existence" (359). This is then what becomes the dark unruly force in all things that ultimately defies comprehension. Nature as it emerges presents the view of an orderly and rational realm, but it conceals an inner depth that can break out again in the assertion of its primordial force. "This is the incomprehensible basis of reality in things, the irreducible remainder which cannot be resolved into reason by the greatest exertion

self-determination and, we shall see in Chapter 8, Kierkegaard accepted the possibility of evil as the point at which the ethical transcends itself toward the religious. Schelling's position as the crucial link between them has been insufficiently appreciated until now. Kosch, *Freedom and Reason*.

but always remains in the depths" (360). It is the impenetrable limit of all explanation that seems to be the source of Schelling's experience of the depth, the gravitational darkness from which light emerges but for that very reason cannot itself be light. "Only God – the existent himself – dwells in pure light; for he alone is self-born" (360). Everything else contains a depth that has not been fully pervaded by the light and which remains, therefore, as the self-will in all things that we know most intimately through our inner selves. In language that draws directly on the theosophical speculation of Jacob Boehme, Schelling assimilates the darkness from which the revelation of all things emerges to the darkness of self-will that must be overcome in the moral struggle.[17] "This elevation of the most abysmal center into light, occurs in no creatures visible to us except in man" (363). But it is just for that reason that man is the point at which the process becomes articulate. The struggle of the darkness in all things toward the light of transparence reaches upward, but it becomes the word of awareness only in man. He is the conjunction of what is indissoluble in God "and this constitutes the possibility of good and evil" (364).

This point of self-transparence of the revelatory process is the emergence of spirit, the principle of personality that is a part and yet containing the whole. "It is will beholding itself in complete freedom, no longer the tool of the universal will operating in nature, but above and outside all nature" (364). In the self-transparence of the will the mystery of evil is only heightened, for the turn away from light is all the more unintelligible. Schelling is acutely aware of the illusory tendencies of the age to assign a finite cause. Feebleness, for example, may explain the lack of virtuous actions, "but it cannot be a basis for actions that are positively bad and opposed to virtue" (371). There may be something evil even in animals, but it has not yet come to light; "it is not *spirit* and understanding but blind passion and desire; in short no degeneration, no division of principles is possible here where there is as yet no absolute or personal unity" (372). It is in spirit alone that the fracture of existence between good and evil stands disclosed. Revelation is for Schelling closely tied to the mystery of man's transparence for the order of being. But this must be understood to be the merely human perspective. He rarely suggests, as Hegel does, that he has surpassed that vantage point to become the vehicle for God's return to himself. Revelation is not a necessary movement

---

[17] Robert Brown, *The Later Philosophy of Schelling: The Influence of Böhme on the Works of 1809–15* (Lewisburg, PA: Bucknell University Press, 1977).

from the side of God; it rather serves our self-knowledge emergent in God. There is still no illegitimate move beyond the process in which we find ourselves to turn the whole into an object beheld from outside. We are the ones who are constituted by revelation, not God. The necessary possibility of evil remains, therefore, a necessity from the perspective of God's self-revelation in us. What the principle of evil is in itself we do not know. "For if God, as spirit, is the indivisible unity of the two principles, and this same unity is actual only in man's spirit, then if it were just as indissoluble in him as in God, man could not be distinguished from God at all; he would disappear in God and there would be no revelation and no stirring of love" (373).

It is in relation to the confrontation of good and evil in the heart of man that the deepest mystery is revealed. Nature is a revelation of the emergence of light from darkness, but it is only in history that spirit itself stands forth. Only in the realm of spirit is the principle of evil manifest in itself, not just the dark unruly force, but the turn away from goodness as such. Then alone is the higher ideal of spirit, the ideal of love, called forth in response to the need that has been posed. Prior to that, not only would love not be noticed, but it would not be "revealed" in the sense of apprehended within the spiritual movement. Now, however, it discloses the highest possibility of all, as Schelling recognizes in his Christological turn. It is a fascinating point that intimates the consequences of the philosophical revolution for the orthodox understanding of revelation. When philosophy has itself become a process of revelation, we can anticipate that the ripples will also wash over our reception of "revelation." No longer is revelation a phenomenon that philosophy must confront, as Kant did in terming it "historical religion," but philosophy now locates itself at the very heart of the logic of revelation itself. This is the impact of the meditation on revelation in which we recognize our fall into evil as its most crucial moment. "For as selfhood has made light, or the Word, its own in evil, and for this very reason appears as a higher basis of darkness, so the Word which has been sent into the world in opposition to evil, must take on humanity or selfhood and itself become personal. This occurs only through revelation (in the most definite sense of the word) which must have identically the same stages as the first manifestation in nature – in such a way namely, that here, too, the highest summit of revelation is man, but the exemplary and divine Man, he who in the beginning was with God, and in whom all other things and man himself were created" (377).

Revelation in the strict sense concerns the historical emergence of spirit. In a brief sketch of the pattern of history that would preoccupy

Schelling in his later works, he indicates the growth of transparence as its essential structure. The basis of separated existence that can choose evil does not yet recognize itself as such. As a consequence there is an age of innocence or unconsciousness in which nature may be chaotic but evil itself is unknown. The manifestation of the divine could also not be apprehended in its unity, as that which everywhere transfigured the spirit of self-separation. Instead, the revelation could only assume the form of individual divine beings in a golden age without clear demarcation between good and evil. "The age of the greatest glorification of nature dawned in the visible beauty of the gods and in the glamour of art and significant science, until the principle operating in the deep at last stepped forth as world-conquering, seeking to subordinate all to itself and to establish a firm and enduring world dominion" (379).[18] But this lust of dominion can never create anything real, since the closer the basis of selfhood approaches its actualization, the more tenuous is its hold on existence. Only chaos can ensue from the effort to establish itself without the light of that from which it is derived. The whole process moves toward a moment of great crisis in which the unreality of evil is confronted by the true reality of love. Prior to this the nature of evil had been hidden, but with the approach of goodness it becomes manifest as evil, no longer merely the obstreperous force of destruction. Schelling's vision sees the whole cosmic mystery culminating in the drama of the personal triumph of unlimited love over the abyss of evil. "Indeed, in order to encounter personal and spiritual evil, light appears in personal and human form, and comes as mediator in order to reestablish the relationship between creation and God on the highest level. For only personality can make whole what is personal, and God must become man in order that man may be brought back to God" (380).

Yet the revelation of the mystery of redemption does not reduce evil to a necessary moment in the whole. Schelling insists that "evil ever remains man's own choice" (382) and goes on to reflect on the "formal side of freedom" in which the existential choice is made. Freedom as a movement of existence is not the caricature of a choice between two equally attractive alternatives where, like Buridan's ass, it could starve to death for lack of an impetus either way. Rather freedom follows a deeper "inner necessity which springs from the essence of the active agent

---

[18] This philosophy of mythology would later be expansively elaborated by Schelling, a further indication of the pivotal role of the *Freedom* essay in his work. See Edward Allen Beach, *The Potencies of God(s): Schelling's Philosophy of Mythology* (Albany: State University of New York Press, 1994).

itself" (383). Through the exercise of freedom he follows the necessity of creating himself, although the process cannot be apprehended as a whole. This is because the self-determination does not occur in time but constitutes it. "To be sure, this free act which becomes necessity cannot occur in consciousness, insofar as it is mere self-awareness and only ideal consciousness, since the act precedes it as it precedes being and indeed produces it" (386). Schelling is hewing very closely to Kant's late moral reflections, which are equally puzzling in ordinary language, but they are both seeking to give voice to the common recognition that the choice of good or evil can never adequately be accounted for in finite terms.[19] The source of the decision remains inaccessible even to the person who decides. It is this existential character of the moral life that renders theoretical reflection on it so unsatisfactory and generates the widespread moral confusion of our world. Schelling here shows that the language of a self-contained morality is not sufficient to do justice to the exercise of freedom that is not its own source. "In the strictest sense it is true that, however man be constituted, it is not he himself but either the good or the evil spirit which acts in him, and nevertheless this does no violence to freedom" (389).

Only the language of existence can account for the constitutive dimensions of the moral life in which we are not simply the arbitrary choosers between good and evil but the battleground of being itself. The temptation to follow the glamour of evil is more than a character flaw; it is the possibility of our loss of being. Evil does always promise the enlargement of our hold on being, but it is a masquerade that is possible only by its capacity to trade on that which it is not. Sin, in Schelling's conception, is not real except in appearance, for it cannot rule with the power of the center that has cut itself off from the center in God. In the same way the countermovement of goodness is more than a capacity we may or may not exercise as if it entirely remained at our disposal. We are not just free to take up the side of the good; rather, we find ourselves compelled to follow its movement as a reality. "Religiosity," Schelling emphasizes, is not a subjective feeling we merely contain but a binding of ourselves by virtue of the existential movement in which we find ourselves. "By the very meaning of the word, religiosity allows no choice between alternatives, no *aequilibrium arbitrarii* (the bane of all morality) but only the highest commitment to the right, without any choice" (392). It is best captured

---

[19] For Kant on the eternity of the act, see *Critique of Practical Reason, Gesammelte Schriften,* vol. 5, 97.

in the terms "heroism" and "faith," which no longer have anything to do with holding ideas because they have become the ideas by which we are held. All discussion of morality as if it were something outside of which we could stand has been brushed aside in a recognition of the drama of existence from which the seriousness of morality has always been drawn. Only then do we behold the possibility of the resolution that is possible when morality is moved beyond itself by "the ray of divine love," when "the highest transfiguration of the moral occurs in loveliness and divine beauty" (394).

Having thus reached the luminosity of existence, Schelling is now in a position to address "the chief problem of this whole inquiry." He cannot simply rest with the recognition of the possibility of freedom grounded in the divine self-revelation; he must go on to inquire into the moral status of this movement that is at the same time the possibility of evil. In particular he asks, "What is God's relation as a moral being to evil, the possibility and reality of which depend on his self-revelation?" (394). This is, of course, the most ancient question that differentiates correlatively with the notion of a transcendent God. Once there is a source of the all that is definitively beyond all, the question of responsibility for evil becomes unavoidable. It prompts a whole range of responses that find their most radical expression in the Gnostic division of responsibility between the God of the beyond and the God of the evil creation. Schelling is fully aware of the bifurcation, having, like many of the idealists, immersed himself in the Gnostic and esoteric literature. But his own meditation deviates markedly from the classic Gnostic structure in ways that are far less vulnerable than Hegel's speculations. He is not, as we have seen, interested in the production of a system that could comprehensively contain the truth of being, nor does he believe it is possible. Schelling is oriented far more toward existence in truth than toward apprehending the truth of existence. This difference comes out most significantly in his struggle with "the problem of evil," in which the speculative solution is no longer pursued as an end in itself but solely as an integral moment of the existential response. This is also what makes him different from the orthodox response of resignation before a mystery that cannot be penetrated. The key to his reflections on this "chief problem" is the shift toward existence in which he shows that, although he cannot grasp the speculative necessity of evil, he can stand within the luminosity that radiates its light over the ineradicable possibility of evil. Gnostic duality remains for Schelling at most a human problem; it never touches the divine source within which we exist.

He knew too that the attainment of a solution would at the same time abolish the possibility of freedom. If we could explain our commission of evil, we could no longer be held responsible for our acts; if they are caused, they are no longer free. Evil is the radical capacity of a free being to turn away from being. It is the unsurpassable boundary of our existence that is also the sign of its surpassability. Not only is God free, but freedom is essentially the mode of that which is not simply bound to its existence. We are free because we have a source that is not just our source. Our freedom is one with the freedom of God, and its problems, including the problem of evil, are continuous with the problem of evil in God. The difference, Schelling emphasizes, is that the victory over evil is complete in God, whereas ours always remains incomplete. God's being is fully actual, ours never is. But the only insight we have into the being of God is through our own existential struggle toward being. We can have no other insight into the existence of God from himself except through our own halting efforts to become who we are, our self-determination in freedom, which achieves its highest transparence in the recognition of the divine being in which its possibility is constituted. Not only is Kant's antinomy between freedom and necessity thereby resolved as one that finds its resolution in practice, but the reason its theoretical penetration proved so insuperable is simultaneously disclosed. We cannot see beyond the condition of our existence unless we want to dispense with what makes the seeing possible.

We must be prepared to enter into the struggle between good and evil if we are to understand them and, in particular, how they are resolved in God. Then we recognize that the freedom of God contains the possibility of evil but that his decision has utterly foreclosed the possibility. "Thus since there is in God a tendency working against the will to revelation, love and goodness, or the *communicativum sui,* must predominate in order that there may be a revelation, – and it is this decision which alone completes the concept of revelation as a conscious and morally free act" (397). The closest Schelling comes to ascribing a separate principle that could become a principle of separation within the Godhead is in the initial "longing of the One to give birth to itself" (395). This is not yet the moral freedom of love by which revelation occurs but more "like desire or passion" that urges itself forth without being fully conscious. Only in the second principle does the will of God become personal through the free donation of self, the movement of love that is the divine self-revelation. In God the transfiguration of the principle of self-contraction that makes revelation possible has already occurred, and there is no possibility of anything untransfigured remaining. There is possibility in God, but it has all been realized. What this means is that all necessity has been absorbed into moral necessity. This is one of the most important insights of Schelling's existential metaphysics that resolves the long-standing philosophical problem of how God could be both absolutely rational and free in creating the one possible world. The answer is that the necessity involved is moral through and through. We then see, Schelling explains, "that all follows with absolute necessity from God's nature, that all that lies in its power as possible must also be real, and that anything which is not real must also be morally impossible" (397). Spinoza was not wrong in insisting on the "inviolable necessity in God, but only in taking this in a lifeless and impersonal way" (397). Schelling's final word is that, while God's understanding may be in the form of a system, God himself "is not a system but a life" (399).

To understand God's action we must understand him as existing, that is, as a person. Like all persons he is not what he is, for he always transcends the condition of his existence. The difference with God is that the condition never remains outside of him in whole or in part. "He cannot set aside the condition, for if he did he would have to set aside himself; he can only subdue it through love and subordinate it to him for his glorification" (399). God is the source of his own existence because he contains its condition within himself, which, although it is a dark depth, has been totally united with his glorifying light. We and everything else, by contrast, never attain complete control over our condition of existence, which always remains outside of us and prevents our complete self-actualization. "Thence the veil of sadness which is spread over all nature, the deep unappeasable melancholy of all life" (399). Even in God, Schelling is willing to consider a relative "source of sadness," although it has been wholly transfigured into joy. But because there is nothing left of the untransfigured first principle of existence in God, there is no way that he can be regarded as the source of evil. We cannot even say that evil springs from the dark depth itself, because it is never a mere primordial force but the deliberate resolve to turn away from the transforming power of goodness. "For evil can only arise in the innermost will of one's own heart, and is never achieved without one's own deed" (399). The existence of evil remains incomprehensible because that incomprehensibility remains the source of it. Like the question of why God would create a world knowing the possibility of evil, it "deserves no reply" (402) since it makes no sense to maintain that there should be no love in order that its negative may not emerge.

What we really want to know, however, and what drives this meditation on evil is the question of how it all will end. How will evil be defeated and why has defeat not so far occurred? Schelling's answer is that there is no answer except for the recognition that "God is a life, not a mere being" (403). The answer is not ready-made because it consists of the divine action by which the redemptive transformation of existence has been under way since the beginning of the world. "All history remains incomprehensible without the concept of a humanly suffering God, a concept which is common to all the mysteries and spiritual religions of ancient times" (403–4). History is the self-revelation of God, although not as a matter of necessity but only as a free unfolding of his personality. Good and evil do not exist as separated entities but only within the movement by which the person of God emerges into full existence. This is why we cannot attribute an evil principle to God, for if there were such it could not exist at all, just as goodness has no existence apart from its capacity to subdue the evil principle itself. Only the process of subordination of the dark to the outgoing is real. Before that we can contemplate the source of the duality in the "groundless" or the "indifference" in which they are together, but we cannot think of this as existing. In contemplating the love that is hidden in the depths before existence, Schelling has arrived at the "highest point of the whole inquiry" (406), for it is love that exists from that which it is not but without which nothing could be. Evil as such is a mere counterfeit that cannot exist on its own terms but only through the perversion of love that remains in it. This is why the "absolute identity, the spirit of love, is prior to evil just because the latter can only appear in contrast to it" (409). We cannot, of course, talk of love as preexisting, since love is precisely the movement of self-outpouring by which existence is attained, but it is love that reveals the truth of the movement as a whole. Schelling thus leads us not toward a speculative apprehension but toward the encounter of personality.

We must not, he emphasizes, think of this abstractly, for love can be known only through love. This is the implication of the shift in philosophical reflection by which "we have established the first distinct conception of that personality [of the Supreme Being] in this treatise" (412). All the fixed conceptions of God and man, good and evil, that had prevailed are now rendered obsolete. It is only in reference to the revelation of self-sacrificing goodness that everything makes sense; there is no perspective outside of the divine life that is freely outpoured. "For there is love neither in indifference nor where antitheses are combined which require the combination in order to be; but rather (to repeat a word which has already been spoken) this is the secret of love, that it unites such beings as could each exist in itself, and nonetheless neither is nor could be without the other" (408). No grasp of necessity can adequately account for the light of reason that emerges through creation, since that would be to place reason itself outside of the process. It is only within the struggle to give birth to meaning that reason itself becomes real. There is no higher necessity than freedom. Personality is the highest reality that casts its light over everything else. Reason has its source in the love that freely gives itself as the source of all being and, if it is to remain rational, must hold fast to that constitutive movement. In the concluding pages of this extraordinarily rich essay, Schelling draws together science, art, religion, and philosophy as lines of meaning emanating from the same core. They are properly regarded, in the conception of von Baader, as "procreative," bringing forth in freedom what freedom has implanted within them, for everything is seen rightly only when it is seen in light of what it chooses to be. The law of personality is the principle of revelation that not only lies hidden in all things but is the constitutive principle of their existence. We are close to the formulation Schelling later adopted by which he saw "negative philosophy" as the objectifying preliminary that must be cast aside in order to make room for the "positive philosophy" that cannot be contained in any dialectic because it is the dialectic of life. From this point on, his studies entered a far more open realm that could never be affixed within the pages of a book because they continually burst the bonds of theoretical formulation.

The Ages of the World

Nowhere was this creative overflowing more evident than in the multiple attempts at completing *Die Weltalter*. Revelation is not so much an event within history as the event by which history is constituted. Schelling had broken through to the theogonic understanding of history that would culminate in the great lecture series on mythology and revelation while avoiding any of the Hegelian suggestion that the observer had somehow comprehended the process as a whole. The key was the centrality of freedom. Revelation could be nothing other than a free act, and the response to it must be equally grounded in freedom. Otherwise revelation and freedom would not constitute the highest reality, as Kant sought to suggest but was held back by timidity from proclaiming. Schelling saw through the logic of revelation to the indispensable movement of freedom at its core. God could be God only if he moved himself through his own freedom, and man could not be man if the response called forth anything less. In each case it is the location of the decision in eternity that guarantees its freedom. God is not subject to a process extended over time, and man is not bound to the conditions that time imposes. Neither makes its determination within time. The difference is that God's self-revelation cannot be contained within time, although it intersects with it, while man's self-revelation is never absorbed within the divine, although it is made possible by it. Mystery that is irradiated from the divine side is only glimpsed from the human. God's freedom cannot limit man's because time is incapable of containing what makes its opening possible. Freedom is inexhaustible because the depth from which it springs can never be plumbed, continuous as it is with the depths of God as well as expressive of the divine drama within time. With this shift toward philosophy as existing, Schelling is on the verge of resolving the great pseudo-problems that have bedeviled Western thought since the High Middle Ages. In particular we look back at the nominalist controversies that precipitated the sense of an arbitrary God, whose love could scarcely be trusted to assuage the anxiety of salvation, and see that they were centered around the meaning of divine freedom. The interrelated crises of philosophy and Christianity that such concerns set in motion can now be understood as the failure to take account of freedom as a living reality, within God and man, rather than as a dead incubus threatening existence.[20] Schelling may not have contemplated the full implications of his insights, but he surely understood their crucial significance. He was profoundly aware of the tenuous hold that the philosophical revolution had achieved and struggled mightily to integrate it with a renewed understanding of Christianity. Even more than Kant or Hegel he understood the importance of the relationship, for philosophy had become Christian when it was revelation that provided the space for its possibility. Freedom is not only a mode of revelation but finds its deepest confirmation within the divine freedom.

The ages of the world are theogonic in the sense of an unfolding of the divine life that makes them possible. Schelling's account of them can thus, appropriately, only be a fragment, as Schelling left it in three successive attempts. The text must still be supplemented with the positive philosophy of history toward which it points. In itself *Die Weltalter* is no

---

[20] Blumenberg, *The Legitimacy of the Modern Age;* Louis Dupré, *Passage to Modernity* (New Haven, CT: Yale University Press, 1993); Michael Gillespie, *Nihilism Before Nietzsche* (Chicago: University of Chicago Press, 1995).

more than a compressed statement of our relationship to history that will guide the investigation of mythology and revelation that philosophy must now undertake. The turn toward history is an integral feature of philosophy once philosophy begins to take account of its own historical emergence. That is, once philosophy understands itself again as a mode of existence. Philosophy may be the mode that attempts to penetrate the conditions of its own existence, but it can never overstep them, especially when those conditions have been generated as a free gift of the gift of freedom itself. History is thus the horizon within which philosophical reflection occurs, just as philosophy is the reflection that renders historical remembrance meaningful in the present. For Schelling the terms "history," "philosophy," and "science" become interchangeable once they are understood to be modes of the luminosity of existence by which we stand in the light of that which is. "What is living in the highest science can only be what is primordially living, the being that is preceded by no other and is therefore the oldest of all beings" (*Sämmtliche Werke*, I/8, 199 / *Ages of the World*, Wirth trans., xxxv). Knowledge of the ages of the world is made possible by the presence in us of that which was present from the beginning, and it is the obligation of the historian and the philosopher to reawaken the life that remains deep within them. "What would all history be if an inner sense did not come to assist it? It would be what it is for so many who indeed know most all that has happened, but who know not the least about actual history" (202/xxxvii). Yet this reawakening, this anamnesis, can never be reduced to a mere means of historical investigation, as if the study of history might have an end beyond itself. Schelling emphatically rejects any suggestion that the dialectic of history might be consummated in a science that would render the dialectic obsolete. "The very existence and necessity of the dialectic proves that it is still in no way actual knowledge" (202/xxxvii). Existence in truth is the only and indispensable access to truth. It had long been recognized that knowing is an activity that cannot be possessed in any other way; now Schelling confronts the full consequence that the content of knowledge can only be of that which is itself also in act. Knowledge of life is possible because there is in us that which is the life of knowledge.

The aim of philosophy is to make history living again, and it is surely this conception that lies behind *Die Weltalter* as the "philosophical poem" that announces a new golden age. Where Hegel had sought a reconciliation between thought and actuality that tended to remain in the realm of thought, Schelling held onto the ambition that the transfiguration could be evoked in existence. It is perhaps not too surprising that Hegel should have been successful in constructing a system that yet failed to include reality, while Schelling never managed to complete the magnum opus in which reality was to have provided the ground of thought. The contrast is indicative of the limits of the possibility of making reality real in thought. Schelling's fragmentary system may not have been the failure it appears to be if this is indeed the boundary of the possibility of system. In this sense his *Weltalter* may not have been able to go beyond a visionary intimation of the whole as found in the theosophical speculation he sought to leave behind. Like Hegel and many of the same generation, Schelling had immersed himself in esoteric lore, especially the work of Jacob Boehme. But, also like Hegel, his goal remained different. "Here runs the boundary between theosophy and philosophy, which the lover of knowledge will chastely seek to protect" (204/xxxix). Rather than the immediate knowledge of the whole, he sought the reflective road of science by which the stages of its self-constitution might be recognized. In contrast to the way the farmer knows the totality of the plant, he wanted to be able "to hold the moments apart from one another" within the whole (204/xxxviii). But it may just be that that project cannot be accomplished and that the best we can attain is a fragmentary suggestion of what it cannot contain. It may be that the philosophical poetization of the ages of the world is irretrievably futural. "Perhaps the one is still coming," Schelling concludes in his introduction, "who will sing the greatest heroic poem, grasping in spirit something for which the seers of old were famous: what was, what is, what will be. But this time is not yet come" (206/xl).

In writing this philosophical poem of what cannot be written, Schelling is the real innovator in the modern revolution.[21] His metaphysics of freedom demonstrates the impossibility of containing reality within any account of it, for if it were possible, there would be no further opening

---

[21] The challenge Schelling's project confronts can perhaps be best illustrated by the difficulty that his best commentators have in making sense of his thought. Thus, Edward Allen Beach summarizes the two divergent directions of interpretation represented by Jürgen Habermas and Walter Schulz. The former identifies Schelling's achievement as demonstrating the limits of reason, while the latter seeks to reconcile Schelling with an abiding systematic impulse. Paradox and equivocation seem to be the alternatives, for which Beach, too, has no answer. "In my judgment," he concludes, "the central difficulty lies in the undertaking to conceive (in some manner) of a Reality which supposedly would transcend conceptualization altogether. This project, however, could only succeed if some new mode of 'thinking' were to be developed, a mode which on the one hand would be independent of concepts, and yet on the other hand would constitute the basis for conceptual reasoning. But how should such a thing be possible? For all his efforts, Schelling offers no fully satisfying answer." Beach, *The Potencies of God(s)*, 176.

for reality to occur. More clearly than Hegel, Schelling saw that if history is ended, it is no more; a resolution in theory effects the same in practice. But it is the radical impossibility of closing off possibility that provides the space for what happens. Beyond necessity freedom remains irreducible. Even the necessity of God, the being that cannot not be, does not foreclose the opening, for if it did, there would be nothing that managed to escape the web of necessity. The "pantheism" controversy that had touched Schelling and reached back to Spinoza arose from the long-standing inability of Christian philosophy to think through the relationship between an infinite creator and a finite creation.[22] Now Schelling understood the source of the difficulty in the failure to take account of freedom as a principle of being. Separation of things from God is possible only because they are not necessarily connected to him. His creation of them is free, and from this they in turn derive their freedom. "To speak even more exactly, if it were left to the mere capacity of God's necessity, then there would be no creatures because necessity refers only to God's existence as God's own existence. Therefore, in creation, God overcomes the necessity of its nature through freedom and it is freedom that comes above necessity not necessity that comes above freedom" (210/5). We cannot know the system of reality because we are parts of the system, and what makes independent parts possible is that the system cannot even be comprehended from its divine source. God is the system – "pantheism" is right, Schelling later acknowledges – but only in the sense that he includes that in which he is not God. The freedom of God requires that he not be what he is. Like us, he can know himself only through the revelation of his freedom, which, of necessity, always escapes what it reveals of itself. God, too, is engaged in the enactment of his existence, although it is not distended over time but occurs in eternity.

The challenge for Schelling's thought is not to assimilate God to the model of human existence but to regard it as the converse. Human existence in freedom is made possible because it is derived from the divine model. Freedom is the mode of divine being, although we know about it only through our own existence in freedom. So while *Die Weltalter* is far more focused on the order of being, the principal access is still provided by the essay on human freedom. Schelling reminds us of this experiential source in noting "a law in humanity: there is an incessant

---

[22] On the pantheism controversy see Frederick Beiser, *The Fate of Reason: German Philosophy from Kant to Fichte* (Cambridge, MA: Harvard University Press, 1987).

primordial deed that precedes each and every single action and through which one is actually oneself. . . . In the same way, in the decision, that primordial deed of divine life also eradicates consciousness of itself, so that what was posited as ground in divine life can only be disclosed again in the succession through a higher revelation" (314/85; this passage is similar in the earlier version). The beginning that cannot be penetrated without ceasing to be a beginning is an insight that is derived from our own moral existence, in which it is precisely the capacity to live within the resolution that has been made from eternity that makes moral character possible. Between Kant's location of the decision in eternity and Kierkegaard's evocation of the existential dynamics lies Schelling's thinking in light of the constitutive structure of existence. "Whoever reserves it to themselves again and again to bring a decision to light never makes a beginning. Hence character is the fundamental condition for all morality (*Sittlichkeit*). Lack of character is in itself immorality" (314/85). In order to exist in truth we must live within the movement that has already separated itself from the beginning in order to bring about the realization of the possible. What makes reality possible is the movement of possibility that has not yet reached actuality. "Consequently, the whole unity is also not yet the actual or actualized God" (315/86). But this does not mean, Schelling insists, that there is yet no God, for "God is already the whole God with respect to the possibility (of becoming manifest)" (315/86). It is simply that the separation of God from what is not God opens the space of possibility because God, too, submits to the necessity of existing from a beginning that can no longer be examined.

All existence arises from the negating force that cannot itself give rise to existence except by being overcome. Left to itself the selfish contracting force would leave no room for any other reality, but it can become the bearer of essence by yielding itself. The hold on existence threatens to close off all revelation, and yet there would be no revelation without the force of negation. This is the "fire of contradiction," the deep-seated anxiety Schelling discerns in all reality even down to the inanimate. "Matter, as if posited in a self-lacerating rage, shatters into individual and independent centers that, because they are still held and driven by averse forces, likewise move about their own axes" (322/91). The speculative alchemy of the philosophy of nature is still strongly evident in *Die Weltalter*, only now it has become transparent for the meditation on existence as a whole. Schelling's insight into the continuity between the inner world of spirit and the externality of nature is more than a poetic device, despite the abundant references to the combustibility of matter, for the goal remains the elaboration of a metaphysics of existence. His purpose is defined not by the gold of the alchemists but by "the gold of the gold" (*The Abyss of Freedom: Ages of the World*, 152), the life of the spirit. In this regard he emphasizes the universality of suffering. "It is the path to glory. God leads human nature down no other path than that down which God himself must pass" (1815 *Die Weltalter*, 335 / *Ages of the World*, Wirth trans., 101). All reality, divine and human, must pass through the darkness of being, of nature, in which it is not, in order to break through to the light of transfiguration by which spirit is revealed. Spirit exists from that which it is not and can arrive there only by submitting to the pain of its incarceration. All creation arises from the unconsciousness whose bonds it must burst in a moment of "divine and holy madness" (337/102).

It is this irreducible force of resistance that is overlooked in all the Enlightenment confidence in the capacity of reason to capture reality. The earlier "pantheistic" evocations of divine mystery had collapsed because of their static formulations, and now idealism had sought to emasculate all that is powerful from Christianity itself. In contrast, Schelling insisted on the divine force that resists revelation as what makes all revelation possible. "This is the principle that, instead of confusing God with the creature, as was believed, eternally divides God from the creature. Everything can be communicated to the creature except one thing. The creature cannot have the immortal ground in itself. The creature cannot be of and through itself" (343/107). Far from being a force that is unworthy of God, it is the impenetrable depth that constitutes the divine transcendence. What makes God God, on Schelling's account, is that he exists from that unfathomable darkness that is not yet God but that he nevertheless contains. "For as an active principle, it precedes the principle of the existing God. In existing, this active principle is overcome" (343/107). The "ancient and holy force of Being" cannot be brushed aside in favor of the divine personality of love, for without the struggle of opposition no revelation is possible. Where Hegel had been inclined to permit the dynamics of revelation to abolish the depths beyond revelation, Schelling insisted that the existential presupposition of revelation is that it emerges from a depth that cannot be abolished. All existence is a mode of revelation, and all revelation submits to the requirements of existence. The meditation on the ages of the world is the bridge that leads Schelling toward his final work on mythology and revelation, in which he pursues the central implication of his turn toward existence. A philosophy of existence must eventually become a philosophy of revelation.

Positive Philosophy as Personal

This is the transition that Schelling himself denotes as the movement from negative to positive philosophy. The lectures *On the History of Modern Philosophy* (1833–34), which are partly included in the later lectures, *The Philosophy of Revelation,* are the starting point for this development. By characterizing the achievement of modern philosophy as negative, Schelling opens the door to the positive philosophy contained in the philosophy of mythology and the philosophy of revelation. Both continuity and discontinuity are implied by the relationship, for it is precisely the emergent sense of its own limitation that characterizes the preceding philosophical development as negative and, therefore, as the indispensable point of departure for the entry into its positive fulfillment. In other words, the break is already indicated by the direction of philosophy itself. The existential turn we have been chronicling takes its direction from just such an awareness of the insufficiency of theory and the recognition of its own wider horizon within practical existence. Now Schelling is confronting the previously undiscovered consequences of that recognition. Philosophy is no longer an autonomous discipline but one that must be anchored in the empirical course of history in which mythology and revelation occur. Hegel, too, had acknowledged the relationship between philosophy and history, but it had remained uncertain whether philosophy finally contained history within itself or whether history ultimately escaped its conceptualization. Schelling is unambiguous in his assertion that history, and especially the history of revelation, lies beyond the boundary of ideas. In taking such a step he inevitably risks the perception of irrelevance to the history of philosophy that has been the fate of his late work.[23] Only theologians have demonstrated any enthusiasm for coming to grips with the two great lecture courses he delivered on mythology and revelation.[24] It is this widespread philosophical disdain that makes the understanding of Schelling's philosophical journey into

---

[23] Even those philosophers who have sought to rehabilitate Schelling have sought to separate themselves from his nonviable theological adumbrations. See Andrew Bowie, *Schelling and Modern European Philosophy,* and his "Translator's Introduction" to Schelling, *On the History of Modern Philosophy;* Manfred Frank, *Eine Einführung in Schellings Philosophie* (Frankfurt: Suhrkamp, 1985).

[24] Thomas O'Meara shows how Schelling was a central figure within the Catholic circle that paralleled the Protestant revitalization of theology in nineteenth century Germany, in *Romantic Idealism and Roman Catholicism: Schelling and the Theologians* (Notre Dame, IN: University of Notre Dame Press, 1982). Tillich was, of course, the most prominent twentieth century theologian to call attention to Schelling's significance. But there is also

religion all the more crucial. If it is a legitimate development, it must be understood philosophically.

His own characterization of the project was "philosophical religion," which suggests that he understood it to be a philosophical enterprise distinct from mythology and revelation as such. Yet he abhorred the Hegelian sublation of religion, as well as art, within the history of philosophy. For Schelling the relationship was more properly understood as the reverse, in which philosophy found its culmination in religion, although, for that very reason, a religion conceived of philosophically. In other words, the opening of philosophy toward the history of mythology and the history of revelation is a consequence of the fundamental change in the nature of philosophy taking place in his work. Rational science, the science of reason reflecting on itself, has reached its limits. Even Schelling's development of the identity of reason and reality, the existential connection to the order of being that constitutes its possibility, still fails to get beyond possibility. The whole course of modern philosophy has revolved and, to a considerable extent, still does revolve around the problem that reason constitutes its own source yet cannot provide the ground of its own existence. Pride and revolt at the prospect of submission to an order beyond reason have remained an abiding component of this confusion. The clarity of Schelling's opening toward revelation is therefore all the more remarkable. Its originality is perhaps the best explanation as to why its philosophical significance has been neglected, if not misunderstood, by his best interpreters and the principal reason for underlining its importance. Schelling's insistence that philosophy remains negative until it is completed by the positive truth of revelation is a radical challenge to the self-understanding of reason in the modern world.

His most compelling case is that he arrives at this position by way of the existential unfolding of reason itself. Striving toward that which grounds its own possibility, reason can arrive only at its idea, never its actuality. "It posits the principle only through *elimination,* hence in a negative way. Of course, it deals with the principle as the only reality, but it has it only in *concept,* as mere idea" (*Schellings Werke,* Schröter ed., vol. 5, 744 / *Schelling's Philosophy of Mythology and Revelation,* 193). The critical investigation of possibility arrives only at possibility, never at the existing reality of existence itself. "Everything it knows, it knows as independent of and outside

Hans Urs von Balthasar, although his assessment is more guarded, given his assimilation of Schelling to the Gnostic pattern.

of all existence, and as subsisting in pure thought" (745/193). To go beyond mere possibility to actuality, something more is required than the "what" of reality; a real encounter with the "that" of being is the only adequate affirmation. "It is philosophy which both *seeks* its object and possesses its object and brings it to knowledge. Strictly speaking, positive (philosophy) is implied in the negative (philosophy); it *is* in it, not yet as real but just as seeking itself" (746–47/194). We might say that the necessity for the existential turn has been indicated by the whole history of philosophy, especially from Kant on, but it takes on a new significance when it begins to move existentially in the direction pointed out to itself. The "last crisis of rational science" (747/195) is resolved only when science takes the existential step it had hitherto only contemplated. Negative philosophy ends, Schelling concludes, "with the destruction of the Idea" and the emergence of "a *will* which demands with inner necessity that God should not be a mere idea" (747/195). It is the very drive to know that compels us to move beyond rational science to the personal encounter that is the substantive affirmation of all that reason can know only from the outside. Contrary to the dichotomization of reason and the heart (which in Pascal's formulation has "reasons of which the heart does not know"), Schelling demonstrates that the speculative impulse has its own inexorable movement of the heart.

Faith is not merely the beginning of knowledge; it is its end. There may be a beginning of knowledge in faith, Schelling concedes, but what really sustains its movement is faith in the end by which all knowledge will be fulfilled. In the same way as "the law was the disciplinarian which brought us to Christ, so must the powerful discipline of science precede faith if we are to be justified, i.e. really made perfect through faith, i.e. through the possession of the certainty that eliminates *all* doubt" (vol. 6, 407/212). As a movement outside the realm of reason, albeit one indicated by reason itself, the step cannot be reached without subjective acceptance. To some it comes through as "undeserved grace," to others by virtue of their "life experiences" by which they glimpse the end of their struggle to know. In either case, it is an event that must come to us from the transcendent and be received only by our submission to it. "Revelation calls out to men: only believe, only believe; i.e. dare to regard this as true. In this sense, science itself, as soon as it ascends to the higher domain, requires faith, i.e. the courage and the capacity to be able to regard as true the extraordinary when it presents itself" (409/213). Among "existentialist" thinkers Schelling is unique in connecting the movement of existence with the movement of science. This may have had something to do with the rapid disaffection Kierkegaard evidenced after his attendance at these lectures. One can see how the preoccupation with inner conversion as the means toward the firmer consolidation of science might have appeared suspect to a more youthful disposition, especially one caught up by the full force of the imperative of existence itself. Yet Schelling's service to the paler reality of science should not be any the less valued, especially since its neglect imperils the coherence of any existential understanding of philosophy as well. The objection is, moreover, unfair given Schelling's own inclusion of the moral crisis as concomitant with the intellectual crisis that forms the center of his attention.

He regards the moral law as having a similarly negative impact on the individual, for whom it points out the imperative of duty but leaves him powerless to fulfill it. Kant's assimilation of the moral law to the divine will merely obscures the incapacity of the individual before the requirement of obedience. The point is, Schelling insists, not to ignore the crushing imposition of the law on the individual but to recognize that "this impersonality is the root of the *imperfection which is in the law itself*" (vol. 5, 736 n3/189). Although the law arises from within the person and is never a purely external authority, its universal demands take no account of the needs, interests, or inclinations of the individual. Arising from man's freedom, the law is incapable of bringing about its own realization. "The law is powerless to give man a heart which is equal to the law" (737/189). Instead, it leaves him with a profound sense of his own unworthiness by making him aware of how much even his best efforts fall short of morality. Yet it is precisely in this moment of despair that the purpose of the law is attained in the self that surrenders itself to God. "Without knowing anything about God, it seeks a divine life in this Godless world. And since this search occurs in the renunciation of that selfhood by which the self had cut itself off from God, it succeeds in coming again into touch with the divine" (738/190). It is a state of self-surrender that can take the form of mystical piety, selfless production in art, or direct contact with the intelligible in contemplative science (739/191). But it is a reconciliation that never gets beyond itself to enable the individual to return to the world of action. Existential despair has brought us to the idea of God, even to the contemplative self-abandonment to God. It has not yet entered into a personal relationship with God who reveals himself to us. An existential problem, Schelling insists, can have only an existential solution.

Just as our demand for knowledge cannot rest merely in the idea of its goal, so our moral despair cannot be answered merely by a contemplative response. It is only the positive disclosure of God as a person that puts us in contact with the really real. We can never remain satisfied with the knowledge of God through his effects but must seek to know him as he is in himself. Beyond the idea of God is his reality as a person who can be known only through his self-revelation, which is not just one particular event or does not derive from one particular time in history. "On the contrary," Schelling explains, "just as I am not satisfied, in the case of individuals who are important to me, to know that they exist, but demand continuing proof of their existence, so here: we demand that the divinity draw ever closer to the consciousness of mankind; we require that it be an object of consciousness not merely in its effects but in itself" (753/198). The proof of God consists not of arguments but of a personal relationship that is his self-disclosure throughout the history of the human race. There is finally no way to know him other than as a person, and this entails entry into a personal relationship with him. In the *Philosophy of Revelation*, Schelling found the way to formulate the intimation that had guided his philosophy from the beginning and made him such an adamant foe of all closed systems. It was his intuition that God cannot be captured by the nets of logic, which he had voiced as the centrality of freedom, the ultimate metaphysical beginning, but which he now understood arose from the God who always transcends the nature of his works. In both creation and redemption, the essential meaning can be discerned only through the revelation of the God who is more than what he has done. This was the deepest mystery, one that had fascinated Schelling throughout his life.[25] It lay as the source of his famous question of the why of existence, and there could be no answer until the question reached the astonishing realization of the divine magnanimity. God cannot be contained within reason, because what he does is beyond reason.

This is, of course, not to assert that God acts contrary to reason, but only that we would never arrive at his initiatives by way of reason. Just as when a man goes beyond the requirement of the law to do what is not required of him, the radical discontinuity can only be ascribed to the supererogatory exercise of freedom. "For man not only not to hate, and not to pursue his enemy, but to do him good and even to love him – this is *beyond* reason" (vol. 6, 415/214). An unnecessitated act of love is the pure beginning that Schelling had sought and found only in the self-revelation of God. We may say that the beginning becomes

---

[25] A relatively recent study has called attention to the "personalism" of Schelling's thought, although the focus remains largely on the *Freedom* essay. Temilo van Zantwijk, *Pan-Personalismus: Schellings Hermeneutik der menschlichen Freiheit* (Stuttgart: Frommann-Holzboog, 2000).

transparent for him only in light of the ungrounded and unconditioned revelation that is God's gift of himself. This is the divine foolishness that is more powerful than human wisdom (1 Cor 1: 25), as well as the "absurdity" by which God both affirms and denies himself at the same time. In this insight into the divine gift of self that overflows all the boundaries proposed for it, we are close to the core of Schelling's thought in the tension between form and content. "In man, too, there is this same contradiction: a blind productive power, limitless in its nature, standing – in the self-same subject – over against a sober power which limits and forms it and therefore literally negates it" (417/215).[26] In other words, it is never the determinations of form that reveal the deepest truth of being but rather the point at which they are surpassed by that whose generosity can be disclosed only through itself. The unfolding potencies, which are repeated in the account of mythology, now stand revealed in their experiential source as the negating force is transformed by the free gift of self utterly beyond it.

The linguistic marker of the experience for Schelling is the word "astonishment" (*Erstaunenswerthe*), by which the quest for meaning reaches an end it can never anticipate, for the pure contemplation of himself is the most obvious sense of God's self-sufficiency, while the lowering of himself to involvement with creation can only appear to contradict his divinity. Yet it is in this weakness, his weakness for man, that God is most fully revealed. "In the creation he shows, in particular, the power of his Spirit; in Salvation, the power of his heart. This is what I meant when I said that Revelation – or the deed which is the content of Revelation – is his personal act" (418/216). The meaning of creation is revealed in God's redemptive action by which we know him as he is in himself, in all the unconditioned freedom of his love for us. It evokes a response that remains forever alive, for "the astonishing thing loses none of this capacity to astonish simply because it is now understood" (419/217). Instead, it remains the perpetual answer to the "interminable unrest of the human spirit," which now has reached "the recognition

---

[26] "The secret of true poetry is to be drunk and sober at the same time, not at different moments but at one and the same moment. This is what distinguishes the Apollonian enthusiasm from the merely Dionysiac. To present an infinite content – that is, a content which literally struggles against form and seems to destroy every form – to present such an infinite content in the most perfect, i.e., the most finite form: this is the highest task of art." *Schellings Werke*, Schröter ed., vol. 6, 417 / *Schelling's Philosophy of Mythology and Revelation*, 215. The parallel with Nietzsche's reflections in *The Birth of Tragedy* serve only to underline the role of art within German idealism, a role that was most profoundly conceived by Schelling.

that something has happened than which nothing greater can happen" (419/217). The existential revolution in philosophy has here reached its full realization in the unsurpassable horizon of love. In the presence of that unanticipated and unmerited outpouring, the endless drive for knowledge can advance no farther, for it is literally "struck dumb." Revelation constitutes for Schelling the horizon of philosophy because it is the culmination of the personal horizon of existence beyond which our quest for meaning cannot go. The task for philosophy becomes, therefore, a meditation on revelation, a philosophy of revelation, that must turn its attention to the historically transmitted evidence of the divine intervention in human history. It must take up the question that lies at the center of revelation itself: How do we know that this is from God? How is the revelation of God encountered?

Revelation as Recognition

Schelling understood that the philosophy of revelation must firmly distinguish itself from both philosophical and historical approaches that treat Christianity as a phenomenon within history rather than as the event that constitutes history. Reducible to neither its dogmatic content nor its historical conditions, Christianity arises from a personal relationship that is rather their explanation. God's self-revelation is a personal disclosure and cannot be known in any other way. Instead of asking about the agreement of Christianity with a particular philosophy, as if it were something objective outside of philosophy, we must inquire about the way in which philosophy is contained within Christianity. "Of what kind must that philosophy be which can comprehend and take up Christianity into itself?" Schelling asks, insisting that it is a phenomenon "I want to make intelligible as much as possible out of its own premises. Hence, strictly speaking, I want to let it explain itself" (425/220). In particular, he rejects the attribution of Christ's glorification to the apostles, since the evidence is precisely their failure to recognize his glory. Besides, even if they did contribute to the process, the real question is "How did this country rabbi come to be the subject of such a glorification?" (624/221). Neither his teaching nor his miracles seem sufficient in themselves to authenticate his divinity, and many failed to make such an inference, for it is only when we recognize his divinity that we can see the meaning of what he said and did. Whence, then, comes such a recognition? Schelling's answer is that it derives from a preexisting awareness of Christ before we encounter him. In other words Christ must already be Christ in some sense before he enters history as Jesus of Nazareth. We already are potentially in relationship with him; otherwise there would be no way to move into one.[27]

This is why the *Philosophy of Mythology* is so closely tied to the *Philosophy of Revelation*. Mythology is for Schelling an indispensable *preparatio evangelica*, not just in an accidental sense, but essentially. Without the mythological participation in divinity, we would scarcely be able to recognize and enter into the real participation offered personally through Jesus Christ. The same relationship may also be viewed from the perspective of the historical success of Christianity within a pagan environment, for it indicates the extent to which paganism was already in search of that which it could never find within itself. What was missing, Schelling emphasizes, was the personal disclosure of what could be represented only externally in mythology. Even the Old Testament is merely Christianity in outline, "Christianity in prophecy," not the astonishing personal revelation of the heart of God. "Hence one can say: in a philosophy of revelation the issue is essentially that of comprehending the person of Christ. Christ is not the teacher, as the saying goes, he is not the founder (of Christianity), he is the *content* of Christianity" (427/224). It is important to recognize that Schelling is not here asserting the difference between the lived experience of Christianity and theological reflection about it, as if his purpose were to call his readers back to a practical piety. His goal remains theoretical, a fact that was not lost on Kierkegaard, for he sought to understand how the existential relationship provides the only and indispensable context for reflection. Schelling did not write "upbuilding discourses"; he merely adumbrated their philosophical consequences. In the process, however, he clarified how such existential openness is possible. We are not left to subjectively opt to believe or not to believe who Christ is, for Schelling had gone about as far as it is possible to go in apprehending the horizon that constitutes the possibility of faith.

In this regard, faith is already there even before we begin to believe; otherwise there would be no way of arriving at it. All of Schelling's elaborate discussion about the preexistence of Christ must be seen as an attempt to articulate this insight, for he is not asserting a theological or metaphysical dogma, but continually pushing the boundaries of existential awareness. This is the sense in which the extensive potency speculation

---

[27] This inner Christology seems to track closely to what Kant sought in *Religion Within the Boundaries of Mere Reason, Gesammelte Schriften*, vol. 6, 63–64.

(*Potenzlehre*) is to be taken, despite the pseudo-objective language into which Schelling inevitably slips. He may leave himself open to the misinterpretation of contradicting his own premise of the uncontainability of the beginning in thought, but his intention remains just the opposite. The difficulty is especially acute in relation to the person of Christ because most interpreters assume that they can stand in judgment over the question of who Christ is, not that the question already stands in judgment over them.[28] Recognition of Christ is a re-cognition. He could not be known at all unless we had a prior sense of who he is. When Christ appears on earth, we do not gain any knowledge of who he is, for that is rather presupposed in the acknowledgment he elicits from us. Revelation is thus not a piece of information about the world, but the emergent luminosity of existence present before the beginning. Schelling has gone farther than anyone else in thinking through what the "logic" of revelation must mean, when it is not flesh and blood that reveals who Christ is but the Father who is in heaven. We already know Christ through the Father, so that revelation itself consists in the actual personal encounter by which that pre-knowledge becomes utterly immediate. What God is in substance now is known in his own personal act. Without the prior knowledge of the divine substance, we would not be ready to recognize the person disclosed to us, but the disclosure is for that reason a revelation of personhood that could not be known in any other way.

The distinction is best illustrated in Schelling's account of the sacrifice of Isaac, a story that is all the more significant for its prominence in Kierkegaard's meditations, although, to my knowledge, the connection has not so far been examined. According to Schelling's account, the God who instructs Abraham to sacrifice his firstborn to him is only the God of "relative monotheism," the God whose substantive commands require just such external submission as was performed in all the mythological religions. Abraham, too, is tempted to take this route of outwardly pleasing divinity, although this is not appropriate to the God who appears in human consciousness and stays his hand. "The Angel of Jehovah, however, is not something substantial, but one who simply 'becomes' in consciousness, one who just 'appears.' He is not in consciousness *substantia* but always only *actu,* just the 'angel' of Jehovah, i.e. an appearance, a revelation of Jehovah" (515/258). The revelation of God is always as spirit, and for this he must negate that which he is not, so that the entire

---

[28] It is, after all, Christ who asks, "But who do you say that I am?" (Mt 16: 15).

event presupposes a false conception that is overcome only because its falsity was already implicitly recognizable within it. Revelation is thus a revelation of the higher meaning by which the personal far surpasses all the possibility of meaning that can only be darkly intimated in any other way. The real meaning of the Abraham and Isaac story is not that it prefigures the sacrifice of Christ but that it reveals the God who would sacrifice his own son before he would permit the sacrifice of Isaac. Schelling's *Philosophy of Revelation* is Christocentric because Christ is the authoritative truth of existence beyond which it is impossible to conceive of anything higher.

He is also aware that this recognition of the centrality of Christ's sacrifice puts him at odds with the pervasive modern inclination to contain "religion within the bounds of reason alone." Contrary to the assimilation of God to the standards of rational morality, in which it would have been unreasonable for him to demand the death of his own son on behalf of fallen humanity, Schelling stood firmly on the side of the orthodox conviction of the necessity of Christ's atoning sacrifice for sin. He arrived at this position not by reverting to biblical or traditional authority but by carrying forward the modern discovery of the primacy of personal morality. This is the largely overlooked significance of Schelling's philosophical religion. What the orthodox view had formulated through the medium of an external necessity of sacrifice, he discovered, had its real source in the recognition of the logic of personal disclosure that is the highest mystery of divine reality. Believers have always held onto their traditional formulations because they intuited that they contained the highest affirmation of love. Schelling worked through the meaning of this intimation. The necessity of Christ's saving sacrifice of himself cannot be dispensed with, because it expresses the inexpressible depth of God's love for man. God, Schelling explains, is not free to brush aside the consequences of the fallen human creation, not because he lacks the power, but because he is not morally free to do so. In the first place, justice itself requires that evil be paid, for otherwise there is no restoration of justice, merely the victory of injustice. Second, the imposition of a change would both negate the whole idea of an independent creation and undermine any possibility of evoking a free moral response. Third, the deepest revelation of who God is requires that he disclose himself as the redeemer who takes on himself the whole burden of suffering on our behalf. God, if he is the highest personal reality, must be the one who pours himself out most completely. Schelling unfolds the moral logic of the principle that God is love by radically removing it from all the externality of power theology (561/276).²⁹

He can understand the death of Christ as more than pedagogical because he understands submission to the power of nature in the very act of creation itself. God's relation to man is not merely ideal, as that of a lawgiver, detached from what he has created. Rather Schelling sees God as involved in the world he has separated out from himself and to which he has given the freedom that, at the highest level, includes the capacity even to turn away from God himself. In this sense God has made himself "vulnerable," although not by way of a necessity that entails a diminution of his power, but because of the moral necessity of freedom itself. By freely creating the human reality that in its own freedom can mirror the divine, God has surrendered his omnipotence to the imperative of originating freedom. As a consequence, the revolt in creation, especially man's transgression of the divine order, changes reality not only in man but "in the objective principle of the being and existence posited by God" (594/288). But why was it necessary for Christ to suffer to the point of death? Schelling's answer is that the subjection of Christ had to have been complete; otherwise it would not have completely defeated the divine "unwill," the capacity for self-willed revolt in all existence. Now the principle of free separation from God has been completely united with God by Christ's free self-surrender that held nothing back in the act of submission. "Christ steps over from God to the place of man, covers him over, clothes him, so to speak, so that the Father sees in man no longer man himself but Christ the Son" (597/288). It is God's unwillingness to override this necessity even to save his own son that, on Schelling's reading, discloses the deepest truth. God's justice is impervious, for he will not negate even the principle of freedom that has separated itself from him but wills to conquer it by an even more profound expression of his own freedom. "God is therefore just toward that principle even though it estranged mankind and the world from him. . . . It is, one could say, God's highest law to preserve that *Contrarium*, for it is, in its ground, that in which he rises (when it is finally conquered) to the most powerful affirmation of his deity and sovereignty. He who knows this law has the key to what is enigmatical in the order of the world" (587/286).

---

²⁹ What for Kant was the irreconcilablity of God's justice and mercy is here penetrated within the logic of love. *Metaphysics of Morals, Gesammelte Schriften*, vol. 6, 489.

In all other religions the reconciliation with God takes place in an external manner through the offering of sacrifices. But this does not fundamentally affect the relationship between man and God, and as a consequence, sacrifice leads only to its own repetition. To bring about a definitive change, a final and complete sacrifice is required in which God himself takes on the burden of reconciling all things with himself. This is the radical and unanticipated possibility that bursts forth in the revelation of Christ but cannot be reached by an extension of the preceding order. The mediating potency that is the basis for all separate existence from God must lose its right of independence, which can occur only when the mediating potency surrenders itself entirely and as a whole to God (450/230). "We speak of a love far greater than that love which moved the Creator to create, a miracle of which we can only say: in truth, it is so – something we could never have *expected* or foreseen according to *any* human concepts, indeed, something we would not dare to believe if it had not actually happened" (589/286). The natural order is ruptured by the breakthrough of the divine that now reveals itself, not through another, but solely through itself. Schelling provides an extensive reconsideration of the Christological problems, including the development of his own unique clarifications, but for our purposes it is enough to note the central insight into the meaning of the Incarnation as the full revelation of the one divine person. "There are here from the beginning *not* two personalities, one of which must be negated, . . . but only *one* person, the divine, which reduces its extra-divine being to human being and precisely thereby appears itself as divine" (557/275). Human nature does not disguise the divine but reveals its innermost being. The Logos puts aside only the "form of divinity," while "the process of *becoming* man is none other than this emptying, and the humanity is [not the veil] but the pure expression, the pure product of this emptying, without the material cooperation of another cause" (559/275).

In Schelling's realization that the divine transcendence is not disguised but revealed through its humanity, we see the fruit of the philosophical revolution he carried out. A movement that began with the Kantian celebration of autonomy as the supreme dignity of all rational being, and went through Hegel's insistence that only a living out of the tensional demands of existence is adequate to the idea of autonomy, culminated in Schelling's insight into the exercise of divine autonomy as the deepest revelation of its possibility. It is the freedom of Christ, he constantly emphasizes, that is the key to the entire process, for Christ was under no necessity to pour himself out on behalf of fallen humanity, to empty himself of the form of divinity in order to assume the form of a sinner. Indeed, he was under the necessity of nonnecessity, since only a free act of self-surrender would manifest the love by which the victory could be realized. It would not be love unless it were free, and it would not answer the need if it were less than unconditioned. The discovery of autonomy as the germ of the modern philosophical revolution flowers in Schelling's late meditation on the ground of its possibility in the transcendent autonomy of Christ. It is in our capacity to determine ourselves that we bear the divine image, for the meaning of free rationality is that we must be the source of our own being. We cannot be subject to an authority higher than our own reason. Yet our unconditionality is not itself unconditioned, for it is ours not through our own creation but through a free gift from its source. Our independence is a dependent independence. To the extent that we are subject to forces not of our own making, our souls become the battlefield of a larger metaphysical conflict. This has been the subject of Schelling's meditative explorations in which it is precisely the impossibility of comprehending the dynamic field within which our autonomy is constituted that forms the abiding parameter. Only the light of freedom itself, the impossibility of subservience to any standard other than what is recognized as worthy, provides any possibility of piercing the darkness in which we find ourselves. But Schelling was not closed to the possibility that an answering light might meet our small lamps. He could then contemplate the meaning of autonomy as not only the highest dignity of human being but of being itself, for in the advent of Christ he beheld the supreme metaphysical significance of freedom as the act of love by which all existence is redeemed. This could never be reached by extrapolation from the human condition, but it could be known as its deepest truth once it had happened in history.

Kant could only postulate the redemptive fulfillment by which the kingdom of God might become actual rather than remain invisible to us. It was only on the basis of this hope that we could trust that dedication to duty for its own sake would eventually yield more than the utter abnegation of self it demanded. But he adamantly refused to permit himself any more than hope. He could have no knowledge of its confirmation. Now Schelling takes that additional step by recognizing that autonomy is not exercised within its own setting but is part of the order that makes autonomy possible, and that the ground of that possibility must itself assume the form of autonomy in an even more eminent way. Once we acknowledge that consciousness cannot contain its own ground, for as soon as it attempts it the ground is no longer the ground of the attempting consciousness, we are on the way toward the discovery of consciousness as ungrounded. Only a pure act of freedom can account for a consciousness that is the source of its own being because it is always beyond its source. Fichte had reached this point, but what he had not realized is that the freedom involved is not simply human. Our freedom may be ungrounded in its exercise, but not in its derivation. Human freedom is only a part of the larger constitution of being through its origination in an act of freedom, and Schelling's elaborate *Potenzlehre* is merely one effort to suggest the spiritual structure of reality as a whole in its existence out of that which it is not. The entire preoccupation with Geist that distinguishes German idealism here reaches its apogee in the speculative construction of the process by which God is constituted on the basis of that which he is not. But this must not be understood to be a projection of the human model of self-consciousness onto the divine, for that would presuppose a grasp of what the human model is. It is precisely here that the greatness of Schelling's insight lies, that he insists we do not possess any adequate concept of what human self-consciousness is. To understand the process in which the exercise of self-consciousness takes place, we require the presupposition of an act of divine freedom we can never comprehend. The conception of human consciousness as a self-contained entity is precisely what leads to the antinomies that so puzzled Kant. Schelling, by contrast, has not resolved the mystery of freedom, but he has rendered it luminous for the intra- and extra-divine process by which it is sustained. Ultimately we do not possess freedom; it is freedom that possesses us on whom it is incumbent to respond to the call it has made to us.

In that recognition the inner truth of reality is disclosed as the disclosure of freedom itself. Only the act of freedom, originating in nothing other than itself but always going beyond what is its own, can reveal the innermost spirit of spirit. Where Hegel often yielded to the temptation to comprehend spirit in some other terms, albeit the medium of its own dynamic movement, Schelling had become clear on the irreducibility of spirit itself. Spirit can be known only through spirit. Spirit exists, as Hegel recognized, only in the movement by which it transcends what it is. Schelling, however, was the one who saw the consequence of this, that it can therefore never be apprehended through what it is but only glimpsed in the movement of its self-sacrifice. The going beyond, the giving over of itself by which spirit is, renders it impervious to all except spirit that is connatural with it. If spirit is that which is only by not being what it is, it can be recognized only by that which carries the same movement within itself. Schelling alone of all the idealists understood the implication that spirit can be disclosed only through itself. If freedom is its beginning, the love by which it demonstrates its freedom most completely is its realization. Spirit is by losing itself, and by losing itself most completely it is most completely. The process by which spirit gives birth to the world can only be one in which spirit is by surrendering itself. Creation has its source in a moment of pure freedom. It can be motivated by nothing but love, by which it is moved by nothing beyond itself yet gives itself in the same moment. Creation is thus the supreme act by which the beginning reveals what it is, but it is not yet an act of self-revelation.

So far we have only the negative speculation that is the logic of what must be. Before it assumes the form of such negative philosophy, the same awareness gives rise to its mythological and religious expression. The connaturality of our spirit with spirit itself is elaborated in the rich proliferation of symbols that constitute the development of mythology. In the *Philosophy of Mythology*, Schelling uncovers the esoteric spirit that drives the exoteric substance from within. This is particularly evident in Greek mythology, which provides the clearest instance of increasing spiritualization by which public cults gradually evolve into the mystery religions of initiates who become participants in the suffering transformation of the god. In the successive embodiments of Dionysus, for example, we have the progressive emergence of the consciousness of the divine suffering by which existence is formed and re-formed. Anticipation of the Christian mystery of the incarnation and redemption of Christ is one of the most striking features of Schelling's treatment, yet he is at pains to avoid an assimilation of revelation to the mythological pattern. The representative suffering of the god may be more apparent from the Christian perspective, but it arises from its own experiential source. To the extent that spirit is that which is by sacrificing what it is, the logic of existence reaches even the immortal gods. Not only must they have their own beginning, as recounted through theogony, but their inner reality must follow the same necessity of not being what they are. Self-transcendence is the movement that is profoundly analyzed in Schelling's account of ever unfolding potencies, which he finds confirmed in the figurative language of the myth. It is not yet the personal encounter with spirit that reveals itself in itself. The closest the polytheistic gods come to revelation is in the sharing with initiates of the mystery of the emergence of life from death, of spirit as the movement of sacrificial redemption. Christ marks the distinct advance beyond the universal mystery into the specific mystery of the divine freedom that is God himself.

If freedom is the source of all that is, it can be known only through the personal encounter in which it gives itself personally. This is the centrality of Christ in Schelling's conception, the positive affirmation of what would otherwise have to be reconstructed negatively from the trace. As the reality that can be known only through its effects, the process in which it is not, the positive reality of spirit can be known only through itself.[30] Revelation is in this sense always beyond revelation. What is revealed in Christ is not the universality of God but the particularity from which the free act of love arises. Schelling's achievement in the *Philosophy of Revelation* may have remained unwelcome for philosophers and unabsorbed by theologians, but this does not mitigate its theoretical significance. In ways that have only vaguely been recognized, he carries us forward all the way to the philosophical deconstruction of a revelation that has emerged on the other side of deconstruction. By insisting on the utterly personal character of the revelation of Christ, he enables us to understand the nature of revelation as such. It is never the content, or even the events, that constitute its meaning but that toward which they point. Ultimately the meaning is personal, that opening of self toward another, that can happen only when the disclosure is the gift of self. Revelation cannot take place through parts or proxies; it can be revelation only if the whole of self has entered into it. Schelling's frequent reference to the "still small voice" of 1 Kings 19 identified the awareness of the non-presence of God in the externals of his manifestation. The God who calls us personally cannot be revealed in any way other than through his own person, which, Schelling repeats, cannot be contained in a part. The self-disclosure of God that has been the goal from the first movement of freedom reaches its culmination in the incarnation by which God is revealed through himself. A person cannot be known through a third party, for only the communication of self gives us access to the person. Beyond every revelation is the source that escapes the revelation but that can be encountered as a person.[31] This is why the advent of Christ is pivotal, for it is only through him that the divine gift of self can be apprehended as self. Spirit alone can lay hold of the non-present reality but only when the

---

[30] When we compare this conception of positivity with Hegel's early theological application of the term, we gain some sense of the intricate web by which their thought was connected. See the lecture on Hegel in Schelling, *On the History of Modern Philosophy*.

[31] "An *immediate* relationship to a personal being can, though, *also* be a personal one: I must deal with Him, be in truly empirical relationship with Him; but such an empirical relationship is just as excluded from reason as *everything* personal is excluded from it; *it is supposed* precisely to be that which is impersonal." *On the History of Modern Philosophy*, 170. On the parallel with Kierkegaard see Kosch, *Freedom and Reason*, 120–21.

free gift of self has made the encounter possible by entering as self into it. In the reconceptualization of the transcendence of God as a personal transcendence, we behold one of the most significant consequences of the existential revolution in modern philosophy. Schelling's recognition of the necessity of revelation, and ultimately Christian revelation, is one of the signal turning points in this entire unfolding.

4

Nietzsche

Philosophy as Existence

Schelling's recognition that philosophy could no longer be contained in books marked a turning point in the modern revolution. He continued to draw together vast amounts of material in his lectures on mythology and revelation, but he no longer thought they could be reduced to the stability of the printed word. The living process that Hegel sought, with misgivings, to reproduce in literary form could be apprehended only in the process of life itself. In the *viva voce* format of the lecture, there was at least the possibility of intimating the nonobjective truth that was bound to be misconceived in the fixity of the page. If the whole point of philosophy had become the inwardness that grounded but, for that very reason, lay beyond saying, it would surely be the height of inconsistency to yield to the temptation to express the inexpressible. The position of Schelling in the history of modern philosophy derives in no small measure from his recognition of the full revolutionary significance of this insight. After him philosophy lost its speculative and synthetic ambitions to become fully existential. At the same time, it is because of his own resolute fidelity to the existential imperative that his significance has been so widely overlooked. In the absence of any mature literary formulations, his example remained simply that. His great successors, Nietzsche and Kierkegaard, either neglected or dismissed him, to define themselves in opposition to an earlier phase of idealist philosophy, represented by Schopenhauer and Hegel, when confidence in the capacity for definitive literary statement had not been so disrupted. It is surely an appropriate irony that Schelling's existential insight is precisely what has withdrawn him from the awareness of existentialists.

Tracing the transmission or absence of influences is, of course, not the point of the present investigation. Rather the purpose is to gain an understanding of the context in which the modern philosophical revolution has unfolded. In this sense the absence of any clear connection with a predecessor has given to the work of Kierkegaard and Nietzsche an excessively novel complexion. The impression is easily gained that they were the originators of the modern philosophical revolution, and they certainly did little to dispel it. In many ways they were convinced of their own innovative significance and embodied it in their modes of living as well as in the novelty of their literary forms. But the sense of uniqueness comes with a heavy cost in terms of intelligibility, for it is precisely the impossibility of assimilating them to any prior development that renders Kierkegaard and Nietzsche so notoriously difficult to interpret. Despite the ubiquity of their name recognition, it is arguable that they are the most misunderstood of all modern thinkers. In the absence of any philosophical location of their own, everyone is free to place them in whatever interpretive context they choose. Worse than the misclassification of Nietzsche as a revolutionary or a reactionary, however, is the failure to recognize the new mode of philosophy emergent in his work. If he were seen within the logic of the philosophical turn toward existence that has self-consciously been under way since Kant, the character of his achievement could be more fittingly understood.[1] The disconnection in the history of philosophy that he represents is a burden to both the understanding and the self-understanding of his thought. Even Nietzsche himself placed the emphasis on the discontinuity and thereby virtually invited the vast secondary literature to treat him as if philosophy begins de novo from within his idiosyncratic reflections. A better recipe for the mistreatment of his thought can hardly be imagined.

Indeed, we may say that the single greatest obstacle to the understanding of Nietzsche is the failure to recognize the philosophical revolution of which he is a part. As a consequence, his new way of philosophizing either remains incomprehensible or is mistaken for something it is not. Very often he is viewed as a nihilist despite his protestations to have sought a way of overcoming it. Or his will to power is taken as evidence of his inability to rise above the level of the basest motivations of existence. All of this is before we even confront the race of overmen who are the self-proclaimed masters of the herd of mankind. And we have not even begun to unravel the difficulties of his conception of truth,

---

[1] The situation has begun to be remedied with studies that locate Nietzsche in relation to his predecessors. See R. Kevin Hill, *Nietzsche's Critiques: The Kantian Foundations of His Thought* (Oxford: Clarendon, 2003); Stephen Houlgate, *Hegel, Nietzsche and the Criticism of Metaphysics* (Cambridge: Cambridge University Press, 1986); and Will Dudley, *Hegel, Nietzsche, and Philosophy: Thinking Freedom* (Cambridge: Cambridge University Press, 2002).

which seems to require deception as one of its indispensable features, or the strange ambiguity of Nietzsche's own role as a moralist who takes aim at the very possibility of morals as such.[2] All of these difficulties and more arise from the easy assumption that we know the objects to which his terminology refers. But what if there were no such objects? What if Nietzsche was acutely aware that he no longer lived in a universe of metaphysical hypostases, but that he lived within the luminosity that could be known only through his own existence within it? Then it would become apparent that neither Nietzsche nor we could know what was designated by the "will to power" or by the "overman," but only that they marked the insuperable boundaries of an order constituted by our tensional relationships toward them.[3] Truth was not a correspondence between a subject and an object but the mode of existence that made all talk of correspondence possible. The significance of Nietzsche in the history of modern philosophy, a significance more often intuited than articulated, is that he advanced the philosophical revolution by discarding virtually all of the terminology of morality and metaphysics. His is a radically existential philosophy that scarcely permits itself the language of philosophy by which to render existence transparent.

It is, as in Heidegger's characterization, the quest for metaphysics without metaphysics and is in this sense the further, perhaps the furthest, unfolding of the revolution inaugurated by German idealism.[4]

---

[2] For a sample of the difficulties of placing Nietzsche, see the reflections of Tracy Strong, "Nietzsche's Political Misappropriation," in Bernd Magnus and Kathleen M. Higgins, eds., *The Cambridge Companion to Nietzsche* (Cambridge: Cambridge University Press, 1996), 119–47; and Robert Pippin, "Nietzsche's Alleged Farewell: The Premodern, Modern, and Postmodern Nietzsche," in the same volume, 252–78.

[3] Perhaps there is no better illustration of the problem than the limitations of Walter Kaufmann's reading, especially given his signal role in rehabilitating Nietzsche for an Anglophone audience largely unfamiliar with his thought. Despite the attention Kaufmann lavished on his subject and the clarity of presentation he achieved, it is remarkable that the account remains largely within the perspective of an acute psychologist of philosophical ideas. One might be inclined to conclude that one of Nietzsche's best interpreters learned nothing from Nietzsche but his "ideas" of the will to power, the overman, and eternal return. Kaufmann, *Nietzsche: Philosopher, Psychologist, Antichrist* (Princeton, NJ: Princeton University Press, 1974). By taking Nietzsche too much at his word, Kaufmann failed to penetrate to the meaning of Nietzsche.

[4] It will become evident in this and the following chapter that I do not regard Heidegger's remark that "Nietzsche's philosophy is inverted Platonism" as exhausting the interpretation he offers. The two thinkers are far too intimately linked in the common project for Heidegger's greatest predecessor to be simply dismissed as failing to break free from the metaphysics of presence he opposed and, therefore, ending by becoming defined by the opposition. To do justice to both of them, however, requires the development of a very different understanding of metaphysics. Heidegger, *Nietzsche I*, 188.

Nietzsche's criticisms notwithstanding, it is the continuity with his idealist predecessors that is the key to his thought.[5] Evidently the relationship is the most direct in the case of Schopenhauer, who provided Nietzsche not only the language of the will but also the key by which it was to be interpreted. Perhaps it was inevitable that Nietzsche, the philologist turned philosopher, would gravitate toward the least "professional" member of the idealist circle, but it had the virtues of directing him toward the most existential implications and of anchoring him in the Kantian primacy of practical over theoretical reason. Philosophy, Nietzsche understood from the start, could be thought not from the outside but only by entering into its unfolding. His affinity with the idealists is perhaps nowhere better established than in the critique he launched by way of his break with Schopenhauer. It is the quintessential assertion of dependence on and independence from the master, who now stands accused of not following his own principles seriously enough. The break for Nietzsche is nothing less than a deeper profession of the impassability of the will toward which Schopenhauer points. But the core of their agreement is the recognition of the will as the nonphenomenal reality unencompassable by the boundaries of space and time. This is the key perspective for Nietzsche's long preoccupation with the will to power that is distorted as a pseudo-objective force when it is lifted from its origin within Schopenhauerian idealism. Given the harshness of his later rejection of Schopenhauer, as of Wagner, it is all the more important to recognize that the blaze of his critique derives in considerable measure from the fire that they kindled. This is especially the case in Nietzsche's first book,

---

[5] The location of Nietzsche in relation to idealism has already been performed negatively by the powerful interpretation advanced by Karl Löwith. He sees Nietzsche as the ultimate unraveling of the impossible project of the immanent apocalypse evoked by Hegel in particular. This is not, of course, a wholly negative reading because Nietzsche emerges as a voice of honesty recognizing the bankruptcy of all schemes of historical transformation. See Löwith, *From Hegel to Nietzsche,* trans. David Green (New York: Doubleday, 1967; German original, 1941), for a presentation of Nietzsche as the end point of Hegelianism. While there is much to be said for this view of Nietzsche as the thinker of most rigorous honesty (I subscribed to it myself in *After Ideology: Recovering the Spiritual Foundations of Freedom* [San Francisco: Harper San Francisco, 1990]), there are two problems that necessitate revision. First, it is not clear that Nietzsche had an adequate appreciation of the Hegelianism against which he was reacting. Second, and of more consequence, is the possibility that Nietzsche did not simply fail in the face of the challenge of overcoming nihilism. The latter point is the decisive aspect, for a too ready dismissal of Nietzsche's inconclusiveness overlooks the profoundly existential turn of his philosophy. On the first point see the careful analyses of the relationship to Hegel in Houlgate, *Hegel, Nietzsche and the Criticism of Metaphysics,* and Dudley, *Hegel, Nietzsche, and Philosophy.* On the second point, the present chapter is an attempt to uncover the positive contribution of Nietzsche.

The Birth of Tragedy, which can scarcely be understood without *The World as Will and Idea.*

Tragedy as Lived Contradiction

In *The Birth of Tragedy Out of the Spirit of Music* (1872) the operative assumption is the insight Schopenhauer derived from Kant that the will, as the source of its phenomenal manifestation, can never be made visible as such. Nietzsche later came to reject the distinction between noumenon and phenomenon as the classic escape from reality into an unreal beyond, which he saw as the fatal misstep introduced into Western history by Plato and Christianity. Yet even the rejection testified to the power of the perspective Nietzsche had acquired. His criticism amounted to the objection that Schopenhauer had betrayed his own insight by making of the noumenal world a parallel reality to the phenomenal. Far from insisting on the unattainability of the will, Schopenhauer had instead transformed it into a more tangible realm shorn of the costs of tangibility. In contrast, Nietzsche sought to remain faithful to the original insight that there was no escape from the tension of existence. Hypostatization was to be vehemently rejected even, or especially, when it began from that very rejection. Nietzsche was even willing to risk being regarded as a materialist, obtusely insisting there is nothing more than physical reality, in order to preserve the utterly nonobjective horizon within which existential meaning is possible. It was with Nietzsche that the war on metaphor began in earnest. This is why he is so often regarded as the starting point for the campaign against the metaphysics of presence that has largely defined philosophy throughout the twentieth century.[6] It is a movement that shares with Nietzsche the misidentification of the idealists as the last gasp of the metaphysics of presence, whereas, I have suggested, they are precisely the inaugurators of the revolution in thought that makes it possible to think our way through to a wholly existential perspective. Without understanding this beginning, it is difficult to avoid the misperceptions that have afflicted Nietzsche and his successors. Saying the unsayable is already risky, without adding the dangers of disconnecting it from all previous efforts.

For this reason we may regard Nietzsche's first book as firmly within a Schopenhauerian horizon even while he begins to step outside of it.[7] No

[6] This Continental take on Nietzsche is well represented by the anthology edited by David Allison, *The New Nietzsche* (Cambridge, MA: MIT Press, 1985).

[7] A good overview of Nietzsche's relation to Schopenhauer is contained in Julian Young, *Nietzsche's Philosophy of Art* (Cambridge: Cambridge University Press, 1992).

doubt it was something of this sense of inner continuity that prompted Nietzsche to reissue the volume with a new introduction fourteen years later. The scope of the project that would preoccupy him was already evident in this work. It was nothing less than the philosophical transformation of modern civilization that had its musical counterpart in the operas of Richard Wagner, to whom the volume was dedicated. Both avenues toward the same goal had been opened up by the fundamental reorientation by which the subject lives within a reality he no longer seeks to objectify. In *The Birth of Tragedy* this is the new conception of art that Nietzsche proclaims. We are no longer the creators and consumers by virtue of having produced works of art, for it is much more the case that art is what has produced us. The "whole comedy of art" arises from the misconception that we are the audience and the creators, while the situation is precisely the reverse. "We may very well assume," Nietzsche suggests, "we are already images and artistic projections for the true creator of art, and that our highest dignity lies in our significance as works of art – for only as an *aesthetic phenomenon* is existence and the world eternally *justified* – although, of course, our awareness of our significance in this respect hardly differs from the awareness which painted soldiers have of the battle depicted on the same canvas" (§ 5). This is not how Nietzsche would later advance art as a value higher than truth, but it is arguable that the difference turns on how the insight is formulated. He moved away from the assumption of a "creator," a reality behind reality, to which we might have access through art, as Schopenhauer had suggested. But Nietzsche retained the core understanding of art as a movement beyond the perspective of a subject contemplating an object to arrive at a moment in which the perspective of self-interest is transcended. Even the later identification of the will to power has this focus.

The advantage of beginning with *The Birth of Tragedy* is that we can see the structure of his aspiration before he dismissed its props as illusory. Indeed, this development is already under way in the book, for while Nietzsche continued to use the language of metaphysical "solace" (§ 7) to identify his conception, the force of his analysis inexorably denies the presence of any realm of solace apart from the process of existence. The logic of art itself is that it cannot be satisfied with any deferral of reality outside the immediacy of its expressive means. The poet, Nietzsche emphasizes, is the least likely to be misled by the power of metaphor he wields so successfully. Metaphor functions not as a rhetorical figure but as the veritable reality "he can really see before him as a substitute for a concept" (§ 8). It is this insight that guides Nietzsche to understand Greek tragedy as an irreducible movement that can be misunderstood when it is transposed into its function as catharsis. There is no solace except by undergoing the tragic action. "This insight leads us to understand Greek tragedy as a Dionysian chorus which discharges itself over and over again in an Apolline world of images" (§ 8). It reaches its high point, Nietzsche explains, when it presents us with the impenetrable mysteries of passive and active suffering in the persons of Oedipus and Prometheus respectively. The greatness of Greek tragedies lies in the impossibility of reducing them to a moral content, for they are the supreme expression of the boundaries of the mystery of existence beyond which we cannot go but which we can touch through our participation within them. "The magnificent 'ability' of the great genius, for which even eternal suffering is too small a price to pay, the bitter pride of the *artist:* this is the content and soul of Aeschylus' play, whereas Sophocles, in his *Oedipus,* begins with the prelude to the victory hymn of the *saint*" (§ 9). The decline into dogmatism, by which we attempt to step outside of the mystery by which we are held, is marked by the introduction of the extrinsic perspective of morality into this living whole. Euripides, for Nietzsche, bears initial responsibility, but the real culprit is the rationalist force of Socrates.

Tragedy is finished when the emphasis shifts from undergoing the action to understanding it. Yet the tragic structure of existence has not disappeared when it is no longer recognized as such, for it continues to shine through the logical drive to surpass it. "Anyone who, reading Plato's writings, has felt even a breath of that divine naivete and certainty in the direction of Socrates' life will also have felt that the enormous drive-wheel of logical Socratism is in motion *behind* Socrates, as it were, and that in order to see it one must look through Socrates as if through a shadow" (§ 13). Even the quest for knowledge is urged forward by a primordial will for life that seeks its own satisfaction in preference to all attainment of truth. The "secret of science" stands revealed in the remark of Lessing that "searching for truth meant more to him than truth itself" (§ 15). Nietzsche takes this confession as conclusive proof that science, too, is caught in the tragic wheel of existence in which illusion is the price life requires us to pay for our entrance into it. The discovery of the "sublime metaphysical illusion" at the core of science is tantamount to the realization that it ultimately "must transform itself into art" (§ 15). This is precisely the sequence by which Socrates became "the first man who was capable, not just of living by the instinct of science, but also, and this is much more, of dying by it" (§ 15). He demonstrated, Nietzsche observes, the power of the myth of science, which far surpasses the power of science to justify existence on its own. By supplying the charm of a metaphysical longing for truth, Socrates became the "turning point of history" that saved mankind from the "practical pessimism" that inevitably flows from the recognition of the futility of all existence. "Truth" has saved us from the truth.

But now that Nietzsche had pointed this out, had he not inevitably dissolved the charm of science as an aid to life? Or was his declamation of the truth one more incarnation of the same urge to disguise the horror of existence? What, in short, is the status of Nietzsche's truth claim concerning the "truth?" This is a question with which he struggled throughout his literary career, and it has been at the core of the revolutionary shift in philosophy toward a nonobjective existential understanding of truth. Nietzsche's inability to find the theoretical formulation to capture it may have generated the misimpression that he denied or disdained the truth, but that shortcoming cannot eclipse his valiant struggle to find a mode of living within truth. He knew that no theoretical formulation would be adequate and, in many respects, abandoned the attempt in order to focus his efforts on the truth of existence. In that way he gave the most powerful testament to the momentous change he saw taking place when the Western development of reason had finally turned its sights on itself. Nietzsche was the culmination of a movement of critique that became explicit with Kant (§ 18). This was the impending crisis of modern civilization that he foresaw and for which he struggled to elaborate a response, beginning with the aspiration for the rebirth of tragedy out of the spirit of music. The individual who has seen through the false optimism of science can only turn toward the deeper knowledge of existence within which he has always remained. "When, to his horror, he sees how logic curls up around itself at these limits and finally bites its own tail, then a new form of knowledge breaks through, *tragic knowledge,* which, simply to be endured, needs art for protection and as medicine" (§ 15). The myth to which music and art give expression is not an invention but the unsurpassable truth of the whole in which we find ourselves. No extraneous authentification can be provided other than the affirmation of life itself.[8]

---

[8] This is the focus of two recent studies that, approaching it from very different perspectives, confirm the richness of the legacy of Nietzsche. John Richardson, *Nietzsche's New Darwinism* (Oxford: Oxford University Press, 2004), shows that there is an affirmation of life deeper than the surface dismissal of Darwinism in which Nietzsche frequently engages. Bernard Reginster, *The Affirmation of Life: Nietzsche on Overcoming Nihilism* (Cambridge, MA: Harvard University Press, 2006), demonstrates the value of the affirmation of life as the unifying theme of Nietzsche's life and thought. Such studies provide a way into the enigma of Nietzsche by virtue of remaining close to the animating theme of life, or what I am calling the luminosity of existence. By contrast, the earlier study of Bernd Magnus, *Nietzsche's Existential Imperative* (Bloomington: Indiana University Press, 1978), focuses less on existence than on the idea of the eternal return.

At this point, however, Nietzsche had not reached the implication that life must be lived as art. He still clung, under the influence of Schopenhauer and Wagner, to the redemptive power of music, which can provide immediate access to the mystery of will. Music occupies a privileged position compared with all the other arts because it is not, "as all the others are, a copy of appearances, but a direct copy of the Will itself, so that it represents *the metaphysical in relation to all that is physical in the world*, the thing-in-itself in relation to all appearances" (§ 16). A lengthy quotation from Schopenhauer includes the striking observation that "'we could just as well call the world embodied music as embodied will'" (§ 16). It is for this reason that the spirit of music gives birth to tragedy, as the subtitle of the book indicates, and provides Nietzsche with the expectation that Wagner's music dramas would achieve the same transformative effect in the modern world as tragedy had among the Greeks. Music in continuity with the inexpressible depths of being gives rise to the images and actions in which the drama of existence is transacted. The sacrifice of the individual by which the return to the eternal is accomplished is the Dionysian myth inspired by music and clothed in the Apolline transparency of tragedy. We may think that the music merely supplies an enhancement to the drama unfolding before us, but it is just the opposite, for music is the key to the whole intensity of life that tragedy seeks to disclose. Without their source in a realm beyond images and symbols, a realm that music alone can intimate, the representations would lose the magic they hold over us. "*The tragic myth,*" Nietzsche concludes, "can only be understood as the transformation of Dionysiac wisdom into images by means of Apolline artistry; it leads the world of appearances to its limits where it negates itself and seeks to flee back into the womb of the one, true reality" (§ 22).

Where Schopenhauer would lead reflection behind the veil of existence to attain the quietude of complete self-resignation, Nietzsche seems, even in *The Birth of Tragedy,* to have preferred the intermediate realm enacted through art. Music, he often warns us, can have a suffocating effect if it is not brought into focus by the luminosity of image (§ 21). "Only by myth can all the energies of fantasy and Apolline dream be saved from aimless meandering" (§ 23). The mutuality of the Dionysian and Apolline constitutes the core of the "metaphysics of art" that has become by the end of the book metaphysics as such. When Nietzsche repeats his opening remark that "only as an aesthetic phenomenon do existence and the world appear justified" (§ 24), it is apparent that this has little to do with the pleasure of beautiful forms. It is exclusively an esthetic of the sublime that he intends, for only such can respond to the meaning of existence. As a consequence the metaphysics of art points beyond art toward existence, whose question had all along been the driving force. Even while talking about the rebirth of tragedy out of the spirit of German music, Nietzsche is already hinting at the break from Wagner he would undertake. The elaboration of a new myth, one that would save the modern world from the self-destructive rationalism that threatened to overwhelm it, could not be accomplished through artistic genius alone. A myth that would reawaken modern man would first have to be lived or discovered in life before it could be symbolized, as it was in that brilliant hour of Greek tragedy itself. Without life, tragedy is merely theater. Later Nietzsche would see this more clearly as the logic of the overman, whose emergence is here only in the form of premonitions. "If you could imagine dissonance assuming human form – and what else is man? – this dissonance would need, to be able to live, a magnificent illusion which would spread a veil of beauty over its own nature" (§ 25). We have not yet arrived at the beauty of life lived without illusion.

Cultural Suffocation of Life

That path would take Nietzsche through the break with his philosophical and musical mentors that first became visible in the *Untimely Meditations* (1873–76). At the time, however, it seemed as if Schopenhauer and Wagner were his allies in decrying the *Bildungsphilister*, or cultural philistines, recently ascendant as a result of the Prussian victory over France. The aging David Strauss with the pseudo-religiosity of his *Old Faith and the New: A Confession*, as well as the escapism of historical studies, struck Nietzsche as the symptoms of pervasive cultural suffocation. He looked for revitalization to the mentors that had launched him on the path to courageous existence, and his essays on Schopenhauer and Wagner still overtly held out that promise to his contemporaries. Only later did he see that the realization was already dawning that they, too, had succumbed to the temptation to turn aside from life to seek the comfort of illusion. Thus, the laudatory treatment of Schopenhauer and Wagner could be seen as no longer really about them but as defining the path the only genuinely "untimely one" was to follow. In *Ecce Homo* Nietzsche not only provides a self-commentary on his works but declares that the project was never the production of literary works. The only work worthy of the name and the only truth of requisite authority was to be his own existence. The *Untimely Meditations* was the beginning of a process that had yet to become clear to Nietzsche himself. "The essay *Wagner in Bayreuth* is a vision of my future, while in *Schopenhauer as Educator* my innermost history, my *becoming*, is inscribed. Above all, my promise!" (*Ecce Homo*, III, § 3). Through the testament of his own life, Nietzsche sought the renewal of modern culture that could never be found within the endless proliferation of cultural scholarship.

He railed against the commodification of culture, whether in the mass publication of classics or in the entertainment conglomerates of theaters and festivals – "all these things are merely cash payment by means of which the cultural philistine settles accounts with them so as not to have to follow after them and to go on seeking. For 'All seeking is at an end' is the motto of the philistines" (*Untimely Meditations*, "David Strauss," § 2). The height of this inanity was reached in the figure of Strauss, the philistine become visionary who now professed his own groundless subjective feeling as the new faith. Nietzsche, by contrast, took his stand on the side of that which the present age "continues to count as untimely – I mean: telling the truth" (§ 12). The real meaning of untimeliness became apparent as, not just dissenting from the time, but radically stepping outside of it in order to genuinely exist within time. History had itself become the obstacle to the accomplishment of anything of historical significance, as he argued in "On the Advantage and Disadvantage of History for Life." An absorption in historical studies had obscured the realization that the rendering of historical judgment entailed standing outside of history to strip away the illusions by which life is always concealed. The only question was whether this "superhistorical" would endanger the existential movement by which history was transacted. In this essay Nietzsche again confronted the question of the meaning of existence he had first encountered in *The Birth of Tragedy*, only now with the intimations of the overman and the eternal return that would become clear in his later reflections. There really was no such thing as history, only the eternal simultaneity by which it was possible for us to understand humanity across time, and there was no movement of progress toward a future, only the achievement of greatness that could burst forth at any time. In recognizing that it is "the individuals who form a kind of bridge across the turbulent stream of becoming," Nietzsche formulated a metaphysics of history in which "the goal of humanity cannot lie at the end but only in its highest exemplars" (*Untimely Meditations*, "On the Advantage and Disadvantage of History for Life," § 9). Only an existence that cannot be contained within history can give rise to history.

The first of those whose existence overflowed the bounds of all theorization was Schopenhauer, as evidenced by Nietzsche's treatment of his life rather than his thought. Schopenhauer's role as educator consisted in his way of life. He had already turned away from the comfort and constraint of the academic world that Nietzsche only contemplated departing. Nietzsche had not yet made the fateful decision because he had not yet seen that philosophy required it. Now, however, he began to see that the goal lies not in the production of culture but in the life of the exemplary human being from which it arises. "They are those true *men, those who are no longer animal, the philosophers, artists and saints;* nature, which never makes a leap, has made its one leap in creating them, and a leap of joy moreover, for nature then feels that for the first time it has reached its goal – where it realizes it has to unlearn having goals and that it has played the game of life and becoming with too high stakes" (*Untimely Meditations,* "Schopenhauer as Educator," § 5). Schopenhauer taught Nietzsche the priority of existence, the transcending of natural life by which alone culture is created and by which the crisis of modern civilization might be addressed. At this stage Nietzsche had not yet implicated Christianity in the genesis of the crisis, seeing it as one of the victims of the desultory collapse that now threatened all life. "Christianity is certainly one of the purest revelations of the impulse to culture and especially of the impulse to the ever-renewed production of the saint; but since it has been employed in a hundred ways to propel the mills of state power it has gradually become sick to the marrow, hypocritical and untruthful, and degenerated into a contradiction of its original goal" (§ 6). In lines that could have been penned by Kierkegaard, we see that Nietzsche's intention was nothing less than the renewal through life of Christianity as well. He may have eventually lost faith in the embodiments of the artist, the philosopher, and the saint he had encountered, but he did not lose faith in their possibility as such.

The later invective against Christianity, just like the vitriol poured on Schopenhauer and Wagner, retains the ambivalence of betrayal.[9] Nietzsche's critique that they failed to be true to themselves attests to a deeper affirmation of their truth. The next phase of his development would take him away from the focus on the creation of a culture of tragedy to begin the process of realizing it through life. This was surely the point of the

---

[9] See the castigation of "all of the counterfeiting of transcendence and beyond" that he objects to in Wagner's music. *The Case of Wagner,* Postscript.

shift to the aphoristic style of his next publication, *Human, All Too Human* (1878–80), which seemed designed to capture life in the act without the intermediacy of reflection. Rather than merely talk about a philosophy of existence, Nietzsche now sought to implement it. This aspiration, it would seem, is the key to the rich profusion of insights that tumble from his pen in a work that at once seeks to observe the modern world in its entirety and establish a vantage point beyond it. *Human, All Too Human* far surpasses in scope and ambition the rapier witticisms of the French moralists like La Rouchefoucauld who, for all their brilliance, never surpassed the subjects of their observations. Only Pascal, with his feet firmly planted in Christian existence, provided an adequate exemplar, albeit without the same philosophical self-awareness of the project.[10] The essence, however, even for Nietzsche remained the same. In order for man to reach the truth of himself he would have to step outside of the human. Like Augustine, in the *Confessions,* he could really take the full measure of himself only by placing himself in the presence of God, before whom he could accuse himself and praise God at the same time. We may even regard the title as suggestive of the contemplation of the human from a perspective beyond it. The difference is that Nietzsche no longer understood himself within this theological context, but rather within the modern philosophical shift toward the priority of existence that he sought to complete. The Christian meditative self-examination would now be conducted outside of the Christian framework. That would be at once the achievement and the limitation of Nietzsche and the principal reason that Christianity would begin to occupy a progressively larger share of his attention. It is from this book that the direction began to unfold.

Existence as Metaphysics

The neglect of *Human, All Too Human,* under the influence of Kaufman, is all the more regrettable since it is here that Nietzsche became clear about the character of his project for the first time.[11] He understood that

---

[10] Voegelin, "Nietzsche and Pascal," *History of Political Ideas,* vol. 7: *The New Order and Last Orientation,* in *Collected Works,* vol. 25, ed. Jürgen Gebhardt and Thomas Hollweck (Columbia: University of Missouri Press, 1999), 251–303.

[11] Once again Kaufmann's focus on the ideas of Nietzsche in their mature formulations meant that the texts in which their genesis began were of relatively little interest. Of course, that focus presupposes that Nietzsche had ideas that can be communicated apart from their genesis.

he was no more practicing the craft of the moralist than he was becoming a Christian theologian. His was the philosophically more revolutionary task of establishing a metaphysics beyond metaphysics. He intuited the path on which modern philosophy had been launched, and he had intimations of its source in the classics; he now sought to carry it to the next step by working out what a truly existential vantage point must mean. It would make clear how what cannot be said can nevertheless be glimpsed. If we understand Nietzsche's cogitations as this form of "raid on the inarticulate," we can see why he is not vulnerable to the charge of inconsistency. His critique of morality remains a moral critique despite the self-appellation as an "immoralist," just as his exposure of the untruth of the will to truth is itself an affirmation of truth.[12] This has long been a source of confusion to readers of Nietzsche, who are divided between those who take him for a nihilist and those who take him as the opposite. Either the mendacity he discloses in contemporary morality and science is his deepest intuition, or that very disclosure rests on a faith deeper still. Nietzsche is not always the most helpful in clarifying the tension, but he is certainly aware of it. We might even consider this awareness to constitute his own most profound insight. It is nothing less than the awareness that no moral or intellectual position can provide its own grounds. Existence escapes all efforts to capture it expressively. When he later insists that all moral systems "nihilate" themselves, he points to the power that drives them beyond themselves.[13] The morality of morality is the vital wellspring that cannot be capped. For every moral ultimate, such as obedience to truth or God, we can always ask whether it, too, is good, and this is not merely an instance of the "naturalistic fallacy" whose identification has been so favored by analytic thinkers. It is a demonstration that the saying cannot be contained in the said, because existence is the starting point outside of all starting points. Nietzsche's realization that morality could not be contained in "morality" receives its first exposition in *Human, All*

---

[12] This insight is lucidly developed by Peter Berkowitz in *Nietzsche: The Ethics of an Immoralist* (Cambridge, MA: Harvard University Press, 1995), although he avoids thinking through what the metaphysics of an immoralist must be, namely, ethics.

[13] This is why nihilism is the "uncanniest of all guests." "The end of Christianity – at the hands of its own morality (which cannot be replaced), which turns against the Christian God (the sense of truthfulness, developed highly by Christianity, is nauseated by the falseness and mendaciousness of all Christian interpretations of the world and of history; rebound from 'God is truth' to the fanatical faith 'All is false'; Buddhism of action –)." *Will to Power*, § 1.

Too Human, which must therefore be read as a guide to the inarticulate source of all moral discourse.[14]

The polished fragments, the less by which he takes aim at the more, also mark the shift of his allegiances toward French stylistic brilliance. Dedicating the work to Voltaire and taking the French moralists as his model, Nietzsche takes his leave of German verbosity to follow the example of the only contemporary culture to have taken the Greek admonition of "nothing too much" to heart. Subtitled *A Book for Free Spirits,* the work also signals his attainment of that Apolline freedom that had previously struggled with the Dionysian depths of unconsciousness. Now Nietzsche had found the expressive means of separating the lightness of existence from its inexpressible source. His future preference of Bizet over Wagner, of a gay science over the ponderous weight of speculation, had already become apparent. Nietzsche had discovered the balance of movement and rest by which the dance is sustained. The key is to be found not in discourse but only in action. Life is the means by which life is sustained, and style thereby becomes far more than a matter of style, for it is through the free creation of existence that the transcendence of freedom is finally attained. It is perhaps no accident that Nietzsche's turn toward the priority of existence, of discovering a freedom of style that would be the style of freedom, coincided with the onset of his own suffering existence. The chronic health problems that would afflict him for the rest of his life and within two years necessitate the resignation of his chair had begun. The urgency to find in existence an answer to the question of whether life is worth living now imposed itself on him.

A legitimate question can be raised as to whether the explosion of moralistic analyses in *Human, All Too Human* represents an attainment of equanimity or merely an aspiration toward it. This, too, is a long-standing source of contention in Nietzsche scholarship, but for us the issue is largely beside the point. If we regard the book as an assault on the inexpressible, its source can lie only within life itself. Aspiration is itself

---

[14] "*The effectiveness of the incomplete.* – Just as figures in relief produce so strong an impression on the imagination because they are as it were on the point of stepping out of the wall but have suddenly been brought to a halt, so the relief-like, incomplete presentation of an idea, of a whole philosophy, is sometimes more effective than its exhaustive realization: more is left for the beholder to do, he is impelled to continue working on that which appears before him so strongly etched in light and shadow, to think it through to the end, and to overcome even that constraint which has hitherto prevented it from stepping forth fully formed." *Human, All Too Human,* I, § 178. One suspects too that the remarks on how a man "becomes" rather than being born a genius is also intended to guide our reading of Nietzsche. Ibid., I, § 162.

an existential attainment. Nietzsche could not talk about what could not be formulated unless he knew it in some prearticulate way. This is for readers, too, what constitutes the authority of the moral judgments he brings forth. He can no more explicate the secret of the moral appeal by which he is drawn than they can, for none of us can contain that by which we are contained. This is the problem with which Western moral reflection has wrestled for millennia. We mistakenly thought it had been resolved through the designation of a metaphysical beyond, most recently designated as "the thing-in-itself," by which we could confidently measure truth. But everything we identify as the unconditioned emerges with its own conditions. Nothing that exists can step forward in the full purity of truth and goodness without some element of self-attachment. "Almost all the problems of philosophy," Nietzsche opens his discussion, "once again pose the same form of question as they did two thousand years ago: how can something originate in its opposite, for example rationality in irrationality, the sentient in the dead, logic in unlogic, disinterested contemplation in covetous desire, living for others in egoism, truth in error?" (I, § 1). We might even say it was posed in exactly that way when Jesus asked the young man who wanted to gain eternal life, "Why do you call me good? No one is good but God alone" (Mt 19: 16).

In search of the ineluctable, Nietzsche understood the practice of science, including his own science of philology, as that parsimonious self-discipline by which we confine ourselves to "what the text intends to say but without sensing, indeed presupposing, a *second* meaning" (§ 8). Then perhaps we can get beyond the otherness of a metaphysical world that is "more useless than knowledge of the chemical composition of water must be to the sailor in danger of shipwreck" (§ 9). It may be that our lives are sustained by the illogical, the conviction of our own exceptional status and significance, but the capacity to recognize this has already lifted us beyond self-absorption to become what Nietzsche regards as the exceptional. Mankind as a whole may lack a goal, but each individual is called to become exceptional. "The great majority endure life without complaining overmuch; they *believe* in the value of existence, but they do so precisely because each of them exists for himself alone, refusing to step outside of himself as these exceptions do: everything outside themselves they notice not at all or at most as a dim shadow" (§ 33). It is the attainment of that equanimity of perspective on the human, all too human, that is the goal and the inspiration of the work. Nietzsche's aim had become to "live among men and with oneself as in *nature*, without praising, blaming, contending, gazing contentedly, as though at a spectacle, upon many things for which one formerly felt only fear. One would be free of emphasis, and no longer prodded by the idea that one is only nature or more than nature" (§ 34). The history of the moral sensations, the first of his genealogies, on which Nietzsche launches us in the next chapter is designed not to expose the hypocrisy of our moral life but to enlarge the sympathetic boundaries of our existence. By becoming an immoralist he deepens the role of the moralist.

It is not that Nietzsche rejects the perspective of morality but that he finds it too individualistic. Truth lies in the whole of which we are a part, not in the partiality of the viewpoint available to us. Even when Nietzsche seems to be rejecting freedom in favor of the logic of necessity as determining all things, his goal is to arrive again at the freedom that is possible only when sympathetic understanding has extended to the whole. It is not that we are not free, but we are not free in our individual existence. Schopenhauer's insight is being carried to the higher level of a rule of life that demonstrates conclusively the impossibility of theorizing about it. On Nietzsche's reading, Schopenhauer still tried to hold onto the notion of freedom of the will while simultaneously denying it (§ 39). But the will is always only a part and therefore must submit to the role in which it finds itself. It is only by transcending all partial perspectives that we can find our way through to the "theory of total unaccountability" (§ 105) that is the highest realization of freedom. Of course, we still remain parts, but whether we bear any responsibility for shouldering that mode of existence, as actors in a tragedy, remains unclear, as Nietzsche's focus remains on the liberation from partiality. Later he will return to the acceptance of our fate that even enables us to embrace it, but for now it is the note of release from finitude that dominates. He notes the painful character of the discovery that "good actions are sublimated evil ones," all motivated by the individual's inescapable drive for self-preservation and self-gratification (§ 107). "To perceive all this can be very painful, but then comes a consolation," for it points toward the new human being that emerges from the experience. "It is in such men as are *capable* of that suffering – how few they will be! – that the first attempt will be made to see whether mankind could *transform itself from a moral to a knowing mankind*" (§ 107).

This is the "new gospel" that Nietzsche sees dawning in human history. "Everything is innocence: and knowledge is the path to insight into this innocence" (§ 107). Looking backward at the path we will thereby have traversed, we will see that the aberration of a false morality was simply the means toward "this degree of self-enlightenment and self-redemption."

Gradually, in thousands of years, the new habit of understanding will become "strong enough to bestow on mankind the power of bringing forth the wise, innocent (conscious of innocence) man as regularly as it now brings forth – *not his antithesis but necessary preliminary* – the unwise, unjust, guilt-conscious man" (§ 107). Beyond morality we will have arrived at the purity of its source, that unsurpassable exigency from which even the Sermon on the Mount can be placed under the suspicion of vanity (§ 137). It is a demand of such inexorability that it must sooner or later cast suspicion on itself. Is Nietzsche's own relentless scrutiny of motives not ultimately driven by the same spirit of vanity – of the desire to outdo all other outdoers? The question is legitimate, and it may well even have haunted Nietzsche at some level. But it also has an answer in the fundamental nature of the project he set himself. His purpose was not to occupy a position, to find a formulation that would put the debate over morality to rest, but to find a way of living that would enable the quest to continue. According to his later observation, he sought to find, not a way beyond nihilism, but a way of *living* beyond nihilism.[15] Within that perspective the burden of moral imperatives are lifted, for they are no longer absolute boundaries or foundations that demarcate the limits of our existence. Moral principles are rather stepping stones toward the higher human being. By living beyond morality, "beyond good and evil" as he would phrase it, we arrive at the highest morality, for it is only when we are capable of disregarding our own moral interests that we can act out of the purity of disinterest that makes untrammeled goodness possible. Not since St. Augustine's probing of the ulterior motivations of virtue has such a relentless spotlight been turned on the human heart, nor has it become so clear that the source of the illumination lies beyond our control.

"As soon as a religion comes to dominate," Nietzsche observes of Christianity, "it has as its opponents all those who would have been its first disciples" (§ 118). How else are we to make sense of this remark except to understand it as the ambition of becoming the first disciple of Christianity? Even in its most anti-Christian connotations, Nietzsche's critique draws its strength from the demand of Christianity itself. It may be that the acts of self-denial "are at bottom not moral, insofar as they are not performed strictly for the sake of others; the case, rather, is that the

---

[15] "He that speaks here, conversely, has done nothing so far but reflect . . . as the first perfect nihilist of Europe who, however, has even now lived through the whole of nihilism, to the end, leaving it behind, outside himself." *Will to Power*, Preface, § 3.

other only offers the highly tensed heart an opportunity to relieve itself through this self-denial" (§ 138). But whence does this critique itself arise if it is not from the demand that such acts be done purely for the sake of others? It may well be that Nietzsche never fully reconciles himself to the ultramoral and ultra-Christian implications of his critique. Indeed, he seems to understand historical Christianity as the principal obstacle to the existential transformation he seeks. Yet despite this ambivalence toward the source of his critique, he never fails to recognize the Christian derivation of the demands he imposes. The inexorability of a religion or a morality in its self-critique became one of the abiding features of his thought. We might even characterize it as the defining tension of his work. He came to see more clearly that it had no resolution in thought, and as a consequence, he set out to bring it to a heightened awareness. In that way Nietzsche sought to show that what cannot be reconciled in theory can nevertheless be resolved in life. His goal was never conceptual, but always existential.[16] This necessity follows not just from the existential question from which he began, but from the logic of existence as the only realm in which the contradictions of finitude can be appropriately confronted. The vitality of existence, Nietzsche came to recognize, arises from its capacity to overflow all conceptuality.

Once he had broken through to this realization, he could move easily through the variety of topics that fill out the first edition of *Human, All Too Human*. Art, for example, which is closely tied to religion, displays the same inwardizing tendency. Nietzsche looks wistfully back at the glorious history of art and knows that the faith in divinity that sustained it is no longer present. "It is not without profound sorrow that one admits that in their highest flights the artists of all ages have raised to heavenly transfiguration precisely those conceptions which we now recognize as false" (§ 220). In the absence of the constraints imposed by the subject matter, the inspiration of the *Divina Commedia* and the frescoes of Michelangelo, he wonders if art will any longer be able to attain such heights. The answer, Nietzsche seems to suggest, lies in the capacity of art to absorb the same spiritual vision as its own. No longer looking for

---

[16] The question of the pride of the inquirer can always legitimately be raised. Does Nietzsche come dangerously close to the position of the "judge-penitent" as memorably evoked in Camus's *The Fall*? The hero is the one to confess his own moral failings first in order to preempt the judgment of others and feel a delicious superiority over them. It is the Gnostic impulse to sit in judgment over all reality at its purest. What saves Nietzsche from the Gnostic arrest of the aspiration is that he already knows its seductive power as the perversion against which he struggles most intensely. He knows the temptation of the ascetic ideal perhaps too well, yet it remains to his credit.

confirmation outside himself, the modern artist must step forward with the authority of his own inwardness as the only claim to truth. Nietzsche does not recognize the possibility that artistic self-awareness may disclose something of the whole of reality of which it is a part. It is enough for him to have found his way to preserve the achievements of the great historical development of art in the midst of the crisis of faith that has overwhelmed them. "One could give up art, but would not thereby relinquish the capacity one has learned from it: just as one has given up religion but not the enhancement of feeling and exaltations one has acquired from it" (§ 222). What saves Nietzsche from the charges of emotivism and subjectivism is that such feelings are not an end in themselves. They are inseparable from the mode of existence they sustain. We might thus see him as moving toward an artistic and theological position that eschews all content in favor of a focus on the pure truth of existence. Just as there is no external or cosmic meaning to music, this discovery does not mitigate its interior significance. "In itself, no music is profound or significant, it does not speak of the 'will' or of the 'thing in itself;' the intellect could suppose such a thing only in an age which had conquered for musical symbolism the entire compass of the inner life" (§ 215).

The consequences of this discovery are, Nietzsche goes on to reflect, far more significant in the realm of politics. Democracy is the equivalent of the recognition that the authority of the state rests on nothing more exalted than the aggregated wills of the individuals composing it. In lines that echo Tocqueville and others, he recognizes that, without the aura of reverence religion supplied, obligation collapses and political continuity disappears. "Disregard for and the decline and *death of the state,* the liberation of the private person (I take care not to say: of the individual), is the consequence of the democratic conception of the state; it is in this that its mission lies" (§ 472). Thus, Nietzsche still holds out faith in the emergence of the "individual" beyond mass man. It is this that enables him to sketch a vision of European union as the inevitable direction, once the artificiality of national divisions has been overcome and Germans and Jews both perform their mediating role (§ 475). But the key is the emergence of the individual, whose possibility he has glimpsed in the realization that dignity does not derive from the possession of rights but rather the reverse. "No one talks more passionately about his rights than he who in the depths of his soul doubts whether he has any" (§ 597). The individual, by contrast, has transcended all of the categories and affiliations by which he might be captured. He knows that it is not his thinking that is the cause of his being but that it is his being that is the source of his thinking (I, § 608). However much it might appear that Nietzsche is making reflection subordinate to inclination, his goal remains the imperviousness of a truth that is the source of itself. To the extent that the search for truth cannot be held hostage by any of its intermediate stages, it retains its irrepressible vitality.

This is the theme of the concluding pages, in which Nietzsche provides a glimpse of his own existential movement. If we really want to understand something we must, he advises, give ourselves fully to its loving consideration until we get to the heart of it (§ 621). It is the same with ourselves, whom we really get to know only when we encounter our true selves, the moment when we are at our best. But such episodes of exaltation are also the source of the commitments that entangle us for lifetimes, and what if we are mistaken? "Are we obliged to be faithful to our errors, even when we realize that through this faithfulness we are injuring our higher self?" (§ 629). The conviction that "on some particular point of knowledge one is in possession of the unqualified truth" (§ 630) is the target of Nietzsche's concern. Is the whole movement of existence to be arrested by its ecstatic interruptions? Again it is important to recognize that Nietzsche is not drawn toward fluidity for its own sake, but only as the way toward the existential certainty that is beyond all convictions. If our spirit is free, we will not be captured by the vicissitudes of heat and cold that determine the fate of our convictions. We must, he insists, "kneel down before justice as the only goddess we recognize over us" (§ 637). In this way we will be able to move forward without resting "from opinion to opinion, through one party after another, as noble *traitors* to all things that can in any way be betrayed – and yet we feel no sense of guilt" (§ 637). It is this attainment of a morality beyond morality that removes any sense of guilt and, even if our fate is to become "wanderers on the earth" without a destination, compensates us for the arduousness of the way. One might be inclined to accuse Nietzsche of failing to question such moments of experiential intensity, as he had just insisted, except that his description seems to arise from a level deeper still. It is without content because it is the openness of existence prior to all content. The wanderer, we might say, is constituted by such moments of grace when "if he relaxes quietly beneath the trees in the equanimity of his soul at morning, good and bright things will be thrown down to him from their tops and leafy hiding places, the gifts of all those free spirits who are at home in mountain, wood and solitude and who, like him, are, in their now joyful, now thoughtful way, wanderers and philosophers" (§ 638).

Eternal Liveliness

It was in first writing *Human, All Too Human* that Nietzsche discovered the "philosophy of the morning," as he emphasizes in the preface to the second volume. He had broken with the romantic pessimism of Wagner and was determined "to preserve an equilibrium and composure in the face of life and even a sense of gratitude toward it" (II, Preface, § 5). Living life had made all of its accoutrements superfluous. A genius is one who leads us so thoroughly into the reality that he himself becomes unimportant (II, "Assorted Opinions and Maxims," § 407). The mistake in all of the religious and political preoccupations of his day was that they aimed at making good Germans or Christians without any consideration for the living human reality itself (§ 299). The "pious fraud" by which the effect is taken for the cause was at the core of the crisis of historical religion. "If those glad tidings of your Bible were written in your faces you would not need to insist so obstinately on the authority of that book: your works, your actions ought continually to render the Bible superfluous, through you a new Bible ought to be continually in course of creation" (§ 98). It is this priority of life that Nietzsche finds in the supreme self-renunciation of science, of the demand for truth that has abandoned all certainty. Skepticism is no longer an epistemological barrier to knowledge but rather the inexhaustible wellspring of its existence (§ 20). When we wonder about the value of life lived in this unattainable tension, Nietzsche provides us with a glimpse of the higher reality toward which it leads. In a moving paean to his mentor predecessors, Epicurus and Montaigne, Goethe and Spinoza, Plato and Rousseau, Pascal and Schopenhauer, he describes it as a wandering that draws him through Hades to life again. "May the living forgive me if they sometimes appear to me as shades, so pale and ill-humored, so restless and alas! so lusting for life: whereas those others then seem to me so alive, as though now, *after* death, they could never again grow weary of life. *Eternal liveliness,* however, is what counts: what do 'eternal life,' or life at all, matter to us!" (§ 408). It is perhaps not too great a leap to find here the first announcement of Nietzsche's great theme of the eternal return.

The insight that made it possible is indicated by the title of the last part of the book, "The Wanderer and His Shadow," for the other realm of life beyond life that Nietzsche had glimpsed cannot be apprehended directly. It can only cast a shadow. Language is precisely what misleads us by suggesting we know what it is we are talking about through its presence (II, "Wanderer and His Shadow," § 11). Freedom of the will, Nietzsche is now able to explain, cannot emerge from the realm of shadow without losing its grounding role. We can never obtain access to the pure source of freedom, because visibility requires entry into the realm of causal necessity. Schopenhauer had understood that there is no "thing-in-itself" since freedom is beyond all thingly existence, but Nietzsche was now able to explain why our only access must be through the act of existence itself. Light cannot illuminate light; it can only reach what casts a shadow in it. Free will becomes in this sense an obstacle to the theory of punishment, for if the misdeed was unintentional it cannot be held as culpable, but if the misdeed was intended it followed with a necessity that obviates freedom. If the act is free, it is not intended; if it is intended, it is not free. "The presupposition that for an offence to be punishable its perpetrator must have acted contrary to his intelligence – it is precisely this presupposition that is annulled by the assumption of 'free-will'" (§ 23). The individual is punished because he acted out of willfulness, that is, out of free will, rather than letting rational necessity dictate the course of his action, that is, against his free will. Kant, too, had this problem of motives, and they are still at the core of our contemporary debates about freedom of choice. To act rightly is to act as if one had no choice. What happens then to the vaunted supremacy of free will? It is to recognize that there is no such thing except in the movement by which it is realized. When punishment occurs, therefore, it is never because the individual failed to exercise his freedom but because he failed to deny it. Free will is in this sense the unspecifiable mystery of action that evades every attempt to contain it. As soon as we begin dealing with motives and reasons, we have moved away from the freedom that lies behind them and thereby have lost the capacity to render judgment concerning their source. Nietzsche goes on to develop his "theory of unaccountability," not as a way of absolving individuals of responsibility, but as a way of demonstrating our incapacity to determine guilt. While he is not concerned with clarifying the rule-of-law ramifications, his position would seem to suggest that the legal rendering of judgment must be carried on with the awareness of the impossibility of assigning guilt or innocence. It would seem that it is precisely this intrinsic tension of outer and inward realities that constitutes the self-understanding of the legal process.

The more we know about the factors that led to a crime, the less we are inclined to condemn the defendant's misdeed. Defending counsel seeks to bring "every honest auditor to confess to himself: 'he had to act as he did; if we were to punish, what we would be punishing would be eternal necessity'" (§ 24). In such a way it is possible, Nietzsche realizes, "to lift secular justice off its hinges" (§ 81), as Christ suggested in admonishing men not to be judges of one another. We can never sit in judgment over the primordial freedom that encompasses the whole person. This realization calls into question not only the practice of legal judgment but the much wider amplitude of the judgment of morality itself. Nietzsche's insight is that morality is in conflict with its source. Great art and great virtue are characterized by their capacity to work within limits while simultaneously depicting the finitude of limits. "Dancing with chains" is the favored metaphor. In this light Nietzsche's calling as an immoralist is clearly not to be immoral but to demonstrate the vitality that overflows the bounds of morality itself. If morality is like the rules of artistic expression, especially musical, then the point is to show that, no matter how restrictive the conception, creativity can thrive within them. Indeed, it is the very presence of structure that makes this manifestation of genius possible. For this reason Nietzsche is disdainful of the romantic abandonment of all structure in favor of free-flowing emotion (§§ 149–68). He prefers the law that can be overcome, the abolition by way of its fulfillment, as the only way in which the inexhaustibility of spirit can be recognized. The morality of external conformity may be "on the decline: but the individual virtues, moderation, justice, repose of soul, are not – for when the conscious mind has attained its highest degree of freedom it is involuntarily led to them and comes to recognize how *useful* they are" (§ 212). Man is made for morality, not morality for man.

Like all the great moralists, Nietzsche was able to heap ridicule on the self-limitations that contradict the purpose of any moral impulse.[17] Morality, he sought to show, cannot be contained in any preconceived straitjacket, for it is only the movement of self-transcendence that can be known as such. But for that very reason it can never be fully known. Just as there is never a point at which we can declare our obligations satisfied, there is never a point at which we can declare our self-interest conquered. As an existential movement the moral impulse remains a process emerging from a depth beneath itself and straining toward a transcendence

---

[17] A priceless example is the justification of an army at a time when everyone disavows a desire for conquest. "This is how all states now confront one another: they presuppose an evil disposition in their neighbor and a benevolent disposition in themselves. This presupposition, however, is a piece of *inhumanity* as bad as, if not worse than, a war would be; indeed, fundamentally it already constitutes an invitation to and cause of wars, because, as aforesaid, it imputes immorality to one's neighbor and thereby seems to provoke hostility and hostile acts on his part. The doctrine of the army as a means of self-defense must be renounced just as completely as the thirst for conquest." *All Too Human*, II, "Wanderer," § 284.

beyond itself. It is at its best when it remains within the tension rather than attempts to abolish it. The leap, for example, to communal ownership of the land would be a disaster. "For upon that which he possesses only in passing man bestows no care or self-sacrifice, he merely exploits it like a robber or a dissolute squanderer" (§ 285). Nietzsche's most penetrating insight is that good originates in that which is inferior to it. "Without vanity and egoism – what are the human virtues?" (§ 285).[18] Some element of egoism is indispensable to get the process under way, and it remains the spur to advancement so long as life endures. The chains that Nietzsche at the end of the book wants to remove, the chains of morality, religion, and metaphysics, are precisely the temptations to short-circuit the process rather than continue the struggle to overcome the last vestiges of vanity that fortunately can never be quite erased. Freedom of the spirit is attained not by satisfying externalities or reaching a goal but by living the life of virtue that is its own reward. This is the joy, the banner of peace and good will toward all under which Christianity perished, that Nietzsche sees as the task ahead of him. "The time has, it seems, still *not yet come* when *all* men are to share the experience of those shepherds who saw the heavens brighten above them and heard the words: 'On earth peace, good will toward men'" (§ 350). It is a message not of achievement but of aspiration.

Faith of Living Without Faith

To do good unthinkingly is freedom in action. In the hands of Nietzsche the shift toward existence has become complete. There is no philosophy other than the movement of life itself, as he demonstrates from this point on. *Human, All Too Human* marked the breakthrough to the extraphilosophical perspective of life that is continued in the next two aphoristic works, *Daybreak* (1881) and *The Gay Science* (1882). Nietzsche now forges ahead as an "underground man," fearlessly tunneling away at the foundations of morality because he is sustained by the morality that always surpasses morality. "In us there is accomplished – supposing

---

[18] It seems to me that Tracy Strong ultimately aims at the abolition of this insight in his assimilation of Nietzsche to the politics of permanent revolution. Where Nietzsche recognizes the impossibility of transcending the struggle of existence, the "politics of transfiguration" is precisely the naming of a viewpoint beyond the struggle. Given the perceptiveness of Strong's treatment, one begins to recognize the difficulty of surpassing Nietzsche. Strong, *Friedrich Nietzsche and the Politics of Transfiguration* (Berkeley: University of California Press, 1978), 273–77.

you want a formula – the *self-sublimation of morality*" (*Daybreak*, Preface, § 4). Morality as a whole is exemplified by the institution of marriage, in which we promise what cannot be fulfilled, for it is "contrary to the nature of passion" that it can guarantee lifelong endurance (*Daybreak*, § 27). Instead, we must recognize that every moral commitment, once it has been made, is no longer what it was in the making. Now a substitute takes the place of its reality, thereby exposing its insubstantiality. The unconditional source can never become the focus of attention without in the process becoming conditional. Kant and his successors had sought to express this insight by insisting that the decision takes place not in time but in eternity. For Nietzsche this was still too much like finding another time and place in which it could be located. The problem was that assigning decisive significance to some other reality behind or beyond the present was not only to resort to ideals, but to lose touch with the only reality there is. All morality must therefore undermine itself to the extent that it is ever surpassed by the movement of morality, whose source can never be defined without its being left behind. Christianity too, Nietzsche now understood, must follow the same existential logic. "These serious, excellent, upright, deeply sensitive people who are still Christians from the very heart: they owe it to themselves to try for once the experiment of living for some length of time without Christianity, they owe it to *their faith* in this way for once to sojourn 'in the wilderness' – if only to win for themselves the right to a voice on the question whether Christianity is necessary" (§ 61).

It is not the reasons men adduce that justify their lives; it is their lives that justify their reasons. The authority of Christianity is more clearly evinced in the life it makes possible than in any of its doctrinal summations. The revolution Nietzsche is inaugurating is most clearly evident in the case of Christianity, as he invites us to step beyond the realm of dogma to what can never be adequately expressed but must always remain the source of expression. He explains this further in an aphorism that has often been regarded as a grandiose claim of self-salvation. How can we regard ourselves as lovable in the eyes of God or men if, as Christianity maintains, we are at bottom a detestable assertion of ego? The response that this is an act of mercy provokes Nietzsche to wonder if love of our neighbor is truly an act of mercy. Does it not ultimately reinforce our vanity? "Well, if you are capable of this, go a step further: love yourselves as an act of clemency (*Gnade*) – then you will no longer have any need of your god, and the whole drama of Fall and Redemption will be played out to the end in yourselves" (§ 79). When the phrase "love yourselves as an act of clemency" is read in the context of the whole fragment, it is clear that it is not simply an assertion of the will to self-deification but the removal of the last barriers of ego by which genuine love of the other is prevented. Only the Christian who has no need of Christianity can live it out.[19] Even the passages in which Nietzsche seems to be approaching the revolt against God, "who does not even make sure that his creatures understand his intention," shade off into an almost mystical co-suffering with God. Such a God unable to communicate with his creatures must experience a suffering even worse than the pains of hell. "A believer who reaches this oppressive conclusion ought truly to be forgiven if he feels more pity for this suffering god than he does for his 'neighbors' – for they are no longer his neighbors if that most solitary and most primeval being is also the most suffering being of all and the one most in need of comfort" (§ 91).[20]

Ultimately, however, it is not Christianity that is here the target of Nietzsche's criticism but the presumption it shares with Socrates and Plato that "there exists knowledge as to the essential nature of an action" (§ 116). The motives of our action are at best partially glimpsed and cannot be reduced to the simplicities of morality or immorality. Such castigations serve only to pervert the truth of action through an imaginary mastery that undermines it. The truth of existence can never, in Nietzsche's estimation, be objectified. His recommendation of "deviant acts" that subvert the conventional crystallizations of morality (§ 149) has nothing to do with the advocacy of evil, for his project is precisely to do away with all such categorizations as good and evil. The intervention of thought obstructs the purity, the innocence, of action. In contrast, the muteness of the sea and the rocks preserves their integrity and draws him to follow their example. "I begin to hate speech, to hate even thinking; for do I not hear behind every word the laughter of error, of imagination, of the

---

[19] This is probably the point at which to recall the advice with which Nietzsche concludes the preface: "It is not for nothing that I have been a philologist, perhaps I am a philologist still, that is to say, a teacher of slow reading: – in the end I also write slowly.... this art does not so easily get anything done, it teaches to read *well*, that is to say, to read slowly, deeply, looking cautiously before and aft, with reservations, with doors left open, with delicate eyes and fingers.... My patient friends, this book desires for itself only perfect readers and philologists: *learn* to read me well." *Daybreak*, Preface, § 5.

[20] It is curious that these complex theological reflections get almost no attention within the prevalent analytic reading of Nietzsche, even among scholars who set out to explore Nietzsche's "ontology." See, e.g., John Richardson, *Nietzsche's System* (Oxford: Oxford University Press, 1996), which provides a careful elucidation of Nietzsche's understanding of truth.

spirit of delusion" (§ 423)? Yet this does not become a recommendation for unconsciousness. Rather Nietzsche seems to turn toward a thought that is deeper than thinking, the contemplative life at the core of Plato and Aristotle, what he called "pure seeing." Contemplation and action flow perfectly from the same source beyond them because it is the realm toward which the spirit flies when it is freed from all self-involvement, even that of genius. "The others, who better deserve the name, possess the *pure, purifying eye* which seems not to have grown out their temperament and character but, free from these and usually in mild opposition to them, looks down on the world as on a god and loves this god" (§ 497).

The self-conscious "genius," a type with which the nineteenth century was well supplied, is precisely what must be avoided. August Comte, Nietzsche pointed out, had spent his life in thought and "now it torments him that he cannot be the last thinker" (§ 542). Comte sought to bring the movement of thought to an arrest in his own work, just as Schopenhauer and all the system builders had done. Progress in science, the genuine movement of thought, is carried on only "with a higher and *more magnanimous* basic feeling. 'What do I matter!' – stands over the door of the thinker of the future" (§ 547). Even "truth" must not be allowed to stand in the way of truth, for we cannot allow it to become "boring, powerless and tasteless to us" (§ 507) by turning it into an absolute. Instead, we must be spurred on by the fear that we "might be completely incapable of knowing the truth" to redouble our efforts, lest we find only our own predeterminations where we thought truth would lie (§ 539). In place of the assertion of our own prerogative of willing and creating, we must maintain the inwardness of pregnancy, the pure state of bringing forth in which our responsibility has shrunk to the absolute minimum. "It is in this *state of consecration* that one should live.... This is *ideal selfishness:* continually to watch over and care for and to keep our soul still, so that our fruitfulness shall *come to a happy fulfillment!*" (§ 552). Nietzsche has finally seen his project in all its manifoldness. It is the inexhaustible longing of the spirit that now cannot have a resting place without endangering the longing itself. As "aeronauts of the spirit" it is our destiny to fly ever farther, beyond every finitude, knowing that "it was our fate to be wrecked against infinity" (§ 575).

The Theo-logic of the Death of God

If *Human, All Too Human* (1878–80) marks Nietzsche's break with the romanticism of Schopenhauer and Wagner, and *Daybreak* (1881) the radically existential path he would henceforth follow, it is no surprise that the next book, *The Gay Science* (1882), inaugurates the maturity of his philosophical project. This is why readers generally begin with the latter work and assume they can safely neglect the preceding efforts. It is in *The Gay Science* that Nietzsche follows through on the logic of his critique of morality to proclaim the core implication of the death of God, just as it is here that he first clearly enunciates his characteristic themes of the eternal return, of the will to power, and of the trajectory of overcoming. Only the idea of the *Übermensch* has yet to be formulated, although it is notable that its most vivid carrier, Zarathustra, already emerges by the close of the work. The neglect of the preparatory reflections is thus understandable in light of the newfound clarity that emerges in *The Gay Science*, but it has resulted in a significant loss of clarity in the reading of this and the series of works that now stream forth from Nietzsche's pen. Without knowledge of their genesis, the themes of overcoming and the eternal return are inevitably treated as if they were fixed concepts, the doctrinal contents of Nietzsche's "teaching," and as such they are largely incomprehensible. It is only if we see them not as assignable objects but as the unreachable boundaries of an existential movement that we can really understand their role in Nietzsche's transcendence of the stasis of philosophical language. The early works may furnish abundant evidence of the unsatisfactory state of his achievements in this endeavor, but they remain indispensable if readers are to obtain any sense of the distance he has traveled to reach the fluid conceptions of his maturity. The uncompromising existential imperative of Nietzsche's thought is missed if we assimilate his formulations to the conventional fixity of ideas.

He regarded *The Gay Science* as the most personal of his works because in it he had learned to dance, leaving behind heavy German romanticism to embrace the *gaya scienza* of "singer, knight, and free spirit" (*Ecce Homo*, III, "The Gay Science") of the troubadours. Nietzsche has finally seen that whatever reasons are adduced for our actions, our exhortations to virtue, we can never penetrate to the reason for the reasons. Life escapes us in being lived. There is no vantage point of purity outside the stream of existence by which we might shed every element of egoism. Rather we are borne along by the exigency of passion to become, as in the case of the magnanimous man, a practitioner of a higher form of revenge (§ 49). Whatever stage of moral or spiritual truth we claim to defend, the mind that performs the task has already gone beyond the putative limit it set for itself. This is why a man is "at the peak of his strength when he resists the pressing storm of his feeling and virtually derides it: only then does his mind completely step out of its hiding place – a logical, mocking, playful, and yet terrifying mind" (§ 96). Nietzsche now exemplifies this existential thinking. In *The Gay Science* he can go further in the task of unmasking that he had hitherto carried pretty far because he is simultaneously creating as well. What had previously still caused him the greatest trouble, "to realize that *what things are called* is unspeakably more important than what they are" (§ 58), could at last be addressed. How could he expose the groundlessness of faith that sustained life? The turn to art that he now advocated was far removed from the theatricality of *The Birth of Tragedy,* for he conceived of life itself as an art. "Only as creators can we destroy" (§ 58). Art could provide, he saw, the means of going beyond morality "lest we lose that *freedom over things* that our ideal demands of us" (§ 107).

With the newfound confidence of life as the way, Nietzsche could follow out the ultimate implication of his project: the death of God. The famous episode of the madman who blurts out the news in the marketplace and is greeted with incomprehension, despite the drama of the moment, should not be too closely identified with its author. If we take Nietzsche's own characterization of art as a living process seriously, the artist has always outdistanced his creations. We are perhaps closer to the source when we apprehend the movement rather than the result.[21] The death of God is the dramatic end point of a moral critique of morality on which he had long been engaged. It was the preachers of morality, the quantifiers of what could not be quantified, that practiced the reverse alchemy of "devaluation of what is most valuable." It is only by withdrawing the movement of morality from the public gaze, returning it to the innermost recesses of the soul, that its innocence can be restored. "Isn't it time to say of morality what Master Eckhart said: 'I ask God to rid me of God'" (§ 292). When this thought is carried further, we arrive at the surmise that all religion has not been a mistake to be eliminated but a prelude to the full divinization of man. "Perhaps religion could have been the strange means of making it possible one day for a few

---

[21] Michael Tanner has aptly observed that the direction of Nietzsche's thought is at every phase indicated by what he has to say about music. "It is a plausible case," Tanner concludes, "and rendered more plausible if we think of composers other than Wagner, especially post-Beethovenian symphonists (or perhaps even Beethoven himself) who set themselves to resolve in triumphant conclusions problems which are often undeniably more convincing than the 'happy endings' that must strike ever more hollow notes given the romantic agonies piled on in those ever more imposing first movements." "Introduction," *Daybreak,* xvi.

individuals to enjoy the whole self-sufficiency of a god and all his power of self-redemption" (§ 300). No doubt there are heavy overtones of self-divinization in this formulation, but there is also enough ambivalence, as the reference to Eckhart indicates, for us to judge more cautiously. Is it, for example, plausible to read Nietzsche as driven by megalomania when his entire thrust has been to subject motives to the most searching self-examination? Could it be that he is in the tradition of the mystics whose desire for the living God compels them to push all dogma aside – who even talk about the moment of their own self-causation? These are not easy questions to resolve, if indeed they can be, but the best prospect of dealing with them is surely to follow the central thread of existence that has carried Nietzsche this far. He constantly reminds us of the error of the spectator who "calls his nature *contemplative* and thereby overlooks the fact that he is also the actual poet and author of life" (§ 301).

Self-redemption had become a necessity, not so much because Nietzsche was in revolt against the transcendent God, but because it was only in that way that he could eliminate the manipulative aspect of the relationship. It is always useful to recall his insistence that his critique remains an intra-Christian critique. Christianity, when it is carried far enough, requires the movement toward self-redemption. Only then can our motives be purified, as the source of our actions is no longer tied to the calculation of self-interest but flows freely from unrestricted inner benevolence. Nietzsche has carried Luther's "freedom of the Christian" to the next step by liberating us not only in the sight of God, but even in the sight of ourselves. Giving without thinking of return, even without thinking of giving, seems to be the goal. Perhaps it approaches the advice of Christ, when we intend to do good, not to let the left hand know what the right hand is doing (Mt 6: 3). In some respects Nietzsche hews pretty close to the central theme of the Sermon on the Mount: "Be ye perfect as your heavenly father is perfect" (Mt 5: 48). Redemption as the condition imposed on the event robs it of the sheer unconditional love from which it must flow. But this does not mean that redemption is absent or has been self-generated. It simply means that it is no longer in the future. The pouring forth of unconditional love is possible only because redemption has happened; self-transcendence is the sign of participation in divine transcendence. Nietzsche's closeness to the Christian experience, if not to its dogma, is perhaps best demonstrated by his emphasis on removing every vestige of self-approbation from human action. He does what he has claimed to do in outdistancing Christianity through the rigor of the Christian demands themselves.

This is how he reaches the *fröhliche Wissenschaft* that seems to move in opposition to Christian compassion. There is, he explains, a secret seduction in yielding to the impulse to compassion before the sight of the suffering of others. For the noblest men, the opportunity to sacrifice themselves in a great cause "offers them a detour to suicide, but a detour with a good conscience" (§ 338). The problem is that the demands of conscience cannot be satisfied so easily. Compassion is the trap by which its recipients are made inferior and its dispenser gains an exaggerated self-importance. Far better to live apart from the spectacle of humanity, with its misdirected humanitarianism, if we truly wish to preserve our humanity. "Live in seclusion so that you *are able* to live for yourself!" (§ 338). The only ones whom you can truly help are your friends, those who share the same desire to live the life of freedom beyond all small-minded calculation. Is this not what it means to love another as one loves oneself? "I want to make them braver, more persevering, simpler, more full of gaiety. I want to teach them what is today understood by so few, least of all by those preachers of compassion (*Mitleiden*): to share not pain, but joy (*Mitfreude*)!" (§ 338). Even the relationship with God must approach this situation of pure equality. Nietzsche declares his disdain for the Christian notion of a God who not only sees everything but pities all as well,[22] and we might be inclined to interpret this as indicative of a metaphysical resentment at his own creaturely condition. But we are probably safer in attributing it to the sense that such omnipresence is unworthy of God. A God who really cares about his creatures, who had elevated them to the dignity of rational beings, would surely avoid the stifling communication of his love for us. If the love of God is truly unconditional, it would not even reveal itself. "'If I love you, what does that concern you?' is surely a sufficient critique of all Christianity" (§ 141).[23]

We might say that Nietzsche has carried the Christian message of the divinization of man to its logical conclusion. If we are truly to become God-like, even God cannot help us, for the extension of grace would diminish the divine stature by acceding to the diminution of humanity itself. It has, of course, long been a mystery of Christian theology as to

---

[22] "'Is it true that God is everywhere?' a little girl asked her mother; 'I find that indecent!' – a hint for philosophers! One should have more respect for the *bashfulness* with which nature has hidden behind riddles and iridescent uncertainties." *Gay Science*, Preface to 2nd ed., § 4.

[23] Recent publication of the most private reflections of Mother Teresa, who endured years of the divine silence and concealment, provides an interesting confirmation of Nietzsche's insight. Mother Teresa and Brian Kolodiejchuk, *Mother Teresa: Come Be My Light* (New York: Doubleday, 2007).

how freedom and grace could ultimately be reconciled, and it may be that Nietzsche has done no more than insist that they be reconciled. In the process he has been willing to err on the side of freedom rather than of grace as he paints a portrait of a humanity whose self-sufficiency, albeit a divinely exemplified self-sufficiency, has rendered God obsolete. We may later encounter God when we have reached parity with him, but then it will clearly not be a meeting of God and man, but rather of differently situated gods. Yet even this overt disclosure of the will to become like God cannot quite suppress the source of the aspiration. Nietzsche's critique of Christianity makes its Christian derivation clear. But there may be more than a material dependence here. Could it be that his own account suggests a more personal connection as well? If we take his model of friendship seriously as the only encounter of equals by which true human contact can occur, then perhaps his own experience of liberation has just such a genesis. The suggestion of a revelatory component to Nietzsche, the most infamous atheist, is no doubt a speculative reach that, like all such leaps, can be justified only by the risk itself. What is clear is that he identifies the reserve that must define the mode of every genuine meeting of persons.[24] One wonders, therefore, if it was not that severe self-restraint that was not the essential disclosure of divinity itself within his soul. Such is at any rate the most Christian construction that can be placed on his impressively spiritual invective against Christianity. We are unlikely to get any closer to the experiential source than the most "personal" book, in which he could proclaim that life had not disappointed him. "Rather, I find it truer, more desirable and mysterious every year – ever since the day the great liberator overcame me: the thought that life could be an experiment for the knowledge-seeker – not a duty, not a disaster, not a deception! . . . *'Life as a means to knowledge'* – with this principle in one's heart one can not only live bravely but also *live gaily and laugh gaily!*" (§ 324).

It is arguable that Nietzsche had found a beacon of divinity within himself and that its emergence is closely connected with the affirmation of the eternal return as well as the advent of Zarathustra. The great themes of his thought suddenly come into focus not when they are discovered individually but when their connection with the divine feeling that animates them is perceived. "To finally take all this in one soul and compress it into

---

[24] The friendships that interwove Nietzsche's life no doubt leave their trace in such reflections. One of those friendships, that with Paul Rée, has been carefully explored with a view to its philosophical significance by Robin Small, *Nietzsche and Rée: A Star Friendship* (Oxford: Clarendon, 2005).

one feeling – this would surely have to produce a happiness unknown to humanity so far: a divine happiness which, like the sun in the evening, continually draws on its inexhaustible riches, giving them away and pouring them into the sea, a happiness which, like the evening sun, feels richest when even the poorest fisherman is rowing with a golden oar! This divine feeling would then be called – humanity!" (§ 37). Only then can he receive the message of the eternal return and embrace it with the response: "You are a god, and never have I heard anything more divine" (§ 341). It is from that point of transition to eternity that the return of Zarathustra to humanity, with which the first edition of *The Gay Science* concludes, can begin. The divine feeling is thus not only what makes it possible to accept the return of everything eternally, but even what makes it possible to apprehend it. It is a feeling of eternity that makes possible the affirmation of the whole. No doubt a strong element of uncertainty, of anxiety before the task, still attaches to the account, but for now the sense of liberation predominates more fully even than in *Zarathustra*. How can we assess the event, we might ask, except in terms of a rupture of the ordinary consciousness in which the interminability of the same would be unbearable? Nietzsche may have sought to extend grace to himself, but the trace of his experiences indicates virtually the opposite. Grace cannot be extended to oneself, because it is precisely that which must be received. The sense pervades that one has thus overstepped the bounds of the everyday, to affirm eternity, that one has entered into a realm whose source lies we know not where. It may well be that Nietzsche struggled to find language appropriate to the infinity opening within him. The spatial metaphor of a beyond from which the divine illumination streams could no longer account for the luminosity within which we exist. Grace is neither extended nor received, for it is already present as the condition of the possibility of both. Could it be that Nietzsche's entire critique of Christianity draws not only on the force of Christian morality, but on the theological metaphysics that must account for the intersection of the timeless with time? Could it be that his insight turns on the realization that the rupture is made possible by the containment of time within eternity? Of course, we cannot see how this occurs, but our existence in truth is its disclosure in action.

Zarathustra: Existence as Eternal Return

Philosophy can only be lived, not explained, as the powerful concreteness of Zarathustra makes clear. The limit of aphorism is reached in the vividness of character. Zarathustra is born at the end of *The Gay Science* through words that are repeated as the opening of *Thus Spoke Zarathustra* (1883), almost as if the personification developed by the author had taken over the literary enterprise. Now it is Zarathustra who speaks, not Nietzsche, and it is this intensity of inspiration that accounts for the impact of the work. In every respect this is a work of transformation. From its burning incandescence, Nietzsche will return to the more reflective philosophical implications, but now with an irreversible clarity of purpose. After Zarathustra the authority of existence has displaced all other claimants. It is the end point of the aspiration for a rebirth of tragedy from which Nietzsche had begun, because now life has itself supplied its tragic personification. Zarathustra speaks not only with the voice of authority, but with the authority of a voice. Curiously, however, we yield to its power because it trades on an Old Testament resonance already familiar. Does this suggest the derivative character of Nietzsche's representation? Or does it indicate that even the prophetic voice conveyed its authoritative source indirectly? Such are the intriguing questions toward which Nietzsche points, although he does not provide us with a means of resolving them. He may well have thought that with Zarathustra he had found a more originary source that carried him beyond the biblical horizon, for Zarathustra is affiliated with Zoroaster, the creator of the Persian spiritual movement of light and dark who of necessity must also have transcended them. Surely the key to the Zoroastrian identification is that Zarathustra is beyond good and evil, refusing to be bound by their parameters as the embodiment of a life that can engage in the struggle between them only because it always remains prior to them.[25]

[25] Remarkably little curiosity has been evinced in the vast secondary literature on the precise lineage of the name "Zarathustra." It is almost as if the spell of Nietzsche's literary creation has blocked further investigation of its genealogy. But, of course, there is such a historical descent and Nietzsche sought to reveal it through the name itself. The Persian prophet Zoroaster was selected because he was the one who first erected morality on the basis of a metaphysical distinction between good and evil. No longer merely opposing forces in the cosmos, good and evil were defined by their transcendent character. "I have not been asked, as I should have been asked, what the name of Zarathustra means in my mouth, the mouth of the first immoralist: for what constitutes the tremendous historical uniqueness of that Persian is just the opposite of this. Zarathustra [the original Persian prophet] was the first to consider the fight of good and evil the very wheel in the machinery of things: the transposition of morality into the metaphysical realm, as a force, cause, and end in itself, is *his* work.... Zarathustra created this most calamitous error, morality; consequently, he must also be the first to recognize it. Not only has he more experience in this matter, for a longer time, than any other thinker – after all, the whole of history is the refutation by experiment of the principle of the so-called 'moral world order' – what is more important is that Zarathustra is more truthful than any other thinker. His

The message of his own eternity is the valediction that sustains and structures the speeches of *Zarathustra*. Self-discovery and self-proclamation are one as Zarathustra descends in the opening of the work to dwell among men. No matter the Persian derivation of his name, we are left in no doubt that the pattern of his public ministry is supplied by the Christ against whom he measures his truth. The revolt against God that really gets under way in *The Gay Science* here comes into focus as a critique of Christianity. "Is not pity the cross on which he is nailed who loves man? But my pity is no crucifixion" (*Zarathustra*, Prologue, § 3). Zarathustra is the one who overcomes the lovelessness of pity to proclaim the joyful good news of the overman. The journey of transfiguration on which Zarathustra is engaged is at the same time the work of redemption that affirms the eternity of time. Nietzsche has reached the culminating point of his work, in which the symbols that had emerged in isolation can now be grasped in their mutuality. Where all previous moralities, including the Christian one, had set limits for themselves and thereby brought existence to a halt, Zarathustra announces the annihilation of all values that enables the life of creation to unfold endlessly. The limits that hitherto had been set by Christianity must be exploded if the power of life, the will to power, is to stream forth. In place of love of the neighbor he extols the love of the friend, "the creating friend who always has a completed world to give away" (*Zarathustra*, I, "On Love of the Neighbor"). Zarathustra muses that the Hebrew who died on the cross might have recanted in favor of this teaching of giving without even contemplating the cost (I, "On Free Death"). "Verily, such a gift-giving love must approach all values as a robber; but whole and holy I call this selfishness" (I, "On the Bestowing Virtue"). Ever outstripping its own attainments, "a gift-giving virtue is the highest virtue." The disciples of Jesus became, like all disciples, believers in him rather than in themselves and thereby proved how small their faith was (I, "On the Bestowing Virtue"). By the end of the first book, as Zarathustra departs from the town of the Motley Cow to which he had been attached, the divinity within has surpassed all other

doctrine, and his alone, posits truthfulness as the highest virtue; this means the opposite of the cowardice of the 'idealist' who flees from reality; Zarathustra has more intestinal fortitude than all other thinkers taken together. To speak the truth and to *shoot well with arrows*, that is Persian virtue. – Am I understood? – The self-overcoming of morality, out of truthfulness; the self-overcoming of the moralist, into his opposite – into me – that is what the name of Zarathustra means in my mouth." *Ecce Homo*, "Why I Am a Destiny," § 3. For a fine summary see Paul Corey, "Speaking Immorality through the Mouth of a Moralist: The Irony of Nietzsche's *Zarathustra*," paper delivered at the American Political Science Association annual meeting, 2006.

external divinities. *"Dead are all gods: now we want the overman to live –* on that great noon, let this be our last will" (I, "On the Bestowing Virtue").

As Zarathustra withdraws again to his cave, the emergence of the over-man requires the death of God. "But let me reveal my heart to you entirely, my friends: *if* there were gods, how could I endure not to be a god! *Hence* there are no gods" (II, "On the Blessed Isles"). Creation, "the great redemption from suffering," necessitates the absence of cre-ator gods. As yet, however, it is no more than the cry of revolt. Necessity from the side of the human will cannot determine reality, for it is only if it is a divine necessity that the twilight of the gods actually happens. It is not enough for Zarathustra to deny God; God must nihilate him-self. Has God become a divine impossibility? That is the question toward which Nietzsche draws near and explains why the centrality of Christian-ity grows, for it is in Christ that the innermost personhood of divine love is revealed. The crisis of metaphysics is specifically a crisis of Christian theology, of the failure to see that "if a little charity is not forgotten, it turns into a gnawing worm" (II, "On the Pitying"). It is only when God is pictured in this way that the problem becomes clear, for his all-seeing pity not only overshadows man but eats away at the very essence of God himself. "Thus spoke the devil to me once: 'God too has his hell: that is his love of man.' And most recently I heard him say this: 'God is dead; God died of his pity for man'" (II, "On the Pitying"). Divinity has drained away when the demand of love has outstripped his static relationship to man. Now we sense, with Nietzsche, that love does not permit the luxury of self-awareness but goes on to sacrifice even itself in the name of love. Beyond pity, love does not seek a relationship to the other, but rather the full self-overcoming of the other. "'Myself I sacrifice to my love, *and my neighbor as myself*'" – thus runs the speech of all creators. But all creators are hard" (II, "On the Pitying").

The love that is ever bringing forth surpasses the love that loves from its own benevolence. We see in Nietzsche the impact of the great seismic shift from a conceptual metaphysics to a metaphysics of existence that can never be contained in any of its expressions. He is the point at which the philosophical revolution reaches its theological apex. The conventionally pictured God of Christianity is rendered obsolete when love has ceased to be a fixed quantity. But, we are inclined to ask, is this not the truth, perhaps the truth of the truth, of Christianity? Grounds for suggesting this are to be found in Nietzsche's own recourse to Christian formulas, like "love of the neighbor as oneself," in order to specify his critique of Christian theology. Did Nietzsche understand himself to be engaged in an intra-Christian critique? Or was he tied to the self-image of its destroyer? We might recall that prophets have always come to bring a sword, not peace, and that the path of creation lies through the destruction of our own self-enclosure. Moreover, the destruction is never the end but the prelude to the movement of creation that is the eternity of life itself. But the most crucial evidence of Nietzsche's Christian genealogy, to borrow his own term, is his insistence that the critique emerges as a self-critique. If we take him at his word, this means that what emerges is at once a negation and a transcendence of Christianity that is possible only from within what it contains. It may be that we have been too much captured by the received conception of Nietzsche as the great antitheologian to stop long enough to consider whether this is possible without also being a great theologian. Even Nietzsche gives little hint of such self-awareness, but it is just possible that he would also not have been too surprised by it.

A far stronger case for Nietzsche's transformed Christianity can be made in the discovery of the eternal return, the culmination of the trial of Zarathustra that unfolds in Book II. I am inclined to interpret the famous "Night Song" with its complaint about ever giving without receiving as a stage through which he must pass rather than as an expression of Nietzsche's deeper ambivalence.[26] The episode occurs in the context of several other explorations of the tension of existence as overcoming, as the inexhaustible will to power, that is nevertheless tempted to halt before the will to truth that creates "a world before which you can kneel" (II, "On Self-Overcoming"). Zarathustra is even tempted to succumb to the vision of the Soothsayer that "all is empty, all is the same, all has been" (II, "The Soothsayer"), a formulation that reminds us how far Nietzsche really is from nihilism. The unstillable will to life within him saves Zarathustra from this despair, at least to the extent that he can be a bridge to the future. He can grasp what redemption must be, but he has not yet apprehended it. "To redeem those who lived in the past and to recreate all 'it was' into a 'thus I willed it' – that alone should I call redemption" (II, "On Redemption"). Like Augustine before his conversion, he can see what he must do but is incapable of doing it because the spirit of revenge, "the will's will against time and its 'it was'" (II, "On Redemption"), has not yet been removed. That is the effect of the great epiphany of Book III, the acceptance of the eternal return, with which Nietzsche brought the first edition to a close.

---

[26] For a different take see Voegelin, "Science, Politics, and Gnosticism," *Modernity Without Restraint*, in *Collected Works*, vol. 5, ed. Manfred Henningsen, 265–68.

The buildup to it is no accident. Eternal return is the very summit of Nietzsche's thought, which has tested the limits of his readers as well. The notion espoused by Kaufmann, for example, that this represents Nietzsche's belief in the scientific necessity of everything recurring, is surely among the flattest interpretations. It fails to do justice to the full meaning of the overcoming by which the eternal return is reached, or regards it as a merely external challenge. As the teacher of the eternal return, Zarathustra is hardly the propounder of a wacky pseudo-science.[27] Rather he is the one who has grasped that the movement of overcoming is itself an eternal return. To the extent that the will to overcome requires the departure from all that was, it cannot take place unless it is already a movement outside of time. The moment is eternal. It may be renewed endlessly and thus generate time, but the condition for its possibility is that it transcends time. Kant, we recall, was the first to draw our attention to the impossibility of locating the will within space-time causality so that the mystery of the relationship remained indecipherable. Nietzsche has now carried the speculation further by shifting attention from the space-time context to the inner dynamics of the will willing to go beyond itself. The eternal return is thus not a postulate about the external conditions in which we find ourselves but the inward reality disclosing its nondisclosure. In this sense the eternal return is a leap of specification toward what makes possible yet can never itself be a possibility. This does not preclude Nietzsche's explanation of the moment as the point from which eternities stretch in either direction and therefore generate the

---

[27] See Kaufmann, *Nietzsche: Philosopher, Psychologist, Antichrist*, 326–28. To be fair to Kaufman, however, it must be recognized that Nietzsche provided more than a little justification for the purely scientific interpretation. There are passages in the notebooks in which he recounted his excitement at having discovered the mathematical necessity of eternal return in the physical universe. But he carefully avoided including any of this speculative physics within the published works, sensing that it would directly conflict with the rejection of propositional metaphysics. Rüdiger Safranski has provided a more sensitive account in *Nietzsche: A Philosophical Biography*, trans. Shelley Frisch (New York: Norton, 2002), ch. 10, "Eternal Recurrence and the *Gay Science*." Bernard Reginster gives an incisive analysis of the range of interpretations that have been proposed for Nietzsche's concept of eternal return. See his *Affirmation of Life*, ch. 5. He takes the affirmation of life as the key to unlocking Nietzsche's thought. "And so, the ethics of power, which defines good in terms of activity and precludes a permanent, once-and-for-all satisfaction, represents a paradigmatic way to live up to the distinctive requirement of the doctrine of the eternal recurrence" (15). One can only smile at the innocence with which Reginster and much of the literature takes the Christian understanding of eternity to be "a life free from change and becoming" (227) without further comment. St. Thomas defines eternal life as "the simultaneously whole and perfect possession of interminable life" in his nuanced discussion in *Summa Theologiae*, I, Q. 10, a.1.

return and departure of everything endlessly. In many ways Nietzsche, too, struggled to keep the inward meaning of the eternal return in focus, for it was no piece of information but the lodestar of his thought.[28] By means of the eternal return he was finally able to understand the will to power and the overman in whom it was most fully realized. All willing aims at the eternal return because it seeks to will eternally. "Wants deep, wants deep eternity" (III, "The Other Dancing Song").[29]

The will that seeks to rest in the finitude of the moment is the perversion of willing because it wills its own annihilation. Now Zarathustra has found the affirming redemption he had in the previous part only glimpsed. "To redeem what is past in man," he now proclaims with conviction, "and to re-create all 'it was' until the will says, 'Thus I willed it! Thus I shall will it' – this I called redemption and this alone I taught them to call redemption" (III, "On Old and New Tablets"). Redemption is not itself a past but the eternal present of all willing that for that reason can never be contained in a moment. If "man is a bridge and no end," the movement of life can be sustained only by that which can never be included in it, because it is the inexhaustible source of the movement. The eternal is thus beyond purpose. Now Zarathustra can affirm the critique of all teleology at a far deeper level for it is the nonteleological, the eternal return, that saves the will to life from self-suspension. "'By Chance' – that is the most ancient nobility of the world, and this I restored to all things: I delivered them from their bondage under Purpose" (III, "Before Sunrise"). The way of the creator, which is hard and cruel, is made possible only by the refusal to acknowledge any way as *the* way (III, "On the Spirit of Gravity"). He has been freed from the conceit of the knowledge of good and evil. "I disturbed this sleepiness when I taught: what is good and evil *no one knows yet*, unless it be he who creates" (III, "On Old and New Tablets"). Indeed, it is precisely what is called evil, the selfishness of the will to power, that is the means of realizing the good that is itself beyond good and evil. The emergence of good from evil, which Nietzsche had earlier discerned, can now be recognized as more than it appears to be, for good and evil are the unspecifiable moments

---

[28] Heidegger gives full weight to this recognition. See Chapter 5.

[29] Laurence Lampert has perhaps best articulated the central significance of the eternal return in his *Nietzsche's Teaching: An Interpretation of "Thus Spoke Zarathustra"* (New Haven, CT: Yale University Press, 1986): "The blessing of eternal return permits mortal man to be at home on the earth under the open sky, and it permits the return of gods who consecrate the world of mortals. Eternal return is the teaching that lets being be" (176).

of an unreachable eternal return. The long Western preoccupation with purpose is over when purpose has become eternal.

We live in the eternity of purpose that makes all purpose possible. Nothing stands higher than this glimpse of what cannot be glimpsed, as Nietzsche recognizes in assigning it the status of divinity. Now we understand the death of God more profoundly as a requirement from the side of divinity itself. God's pity for man may have been the cross on which he died, but it was also the means of the divine resurrection. A bounded divinity is no divinity at all. There is no twilight of the gods, Zarathustra insists; instead "they *laughed* themselves to death." This happened when one of them in a moment of forgetfulness proclaimed himself the only God there was. "And then all the gods laughed and rocked on their chairs and cried, 'Is not just this godlike that there are gods but no God?'" (III, "On Apostates"). It has become laughable that the one God would assert an exclusive prerogative of divinity but would not rather see his nature poured forth over all creation. Conserving one's substance is the very opposite of what constitutes divinity. We are close here to the heart of Nietzsche's thought as he sought not only to purify Christian morality, but the very foundation of its theology. No God would proclaim the jealous word that "there are no other gods but me." Instead, God would freely dispense his divinity to all who were willing to take it upon themselves through continuing the divine overcoming of self. The proliferation of gods is ultimately not just a necessity from the side of human self-transcendence; it is the very outpouring of life that is the mark of divinity itself. None of this is, of course, any longer a matter of theology, as if we could stand outside the movement of divine outpouring and comprehend it, but our own participation within it. Virtually the last word of Part III is Zarathustra's admission that life has become "dearer to me than all my wisdom ever was" (III, "The Other Dancing Song").

The fourth part of *Zarathustra* (privately printed and circulated in 1885) is, despite the vividness of the different characters encountered, something of a coda to the radiance of the eternal return. This is the part in which Zarathustra encounters his disciples, those who have in various ways been seeking him, although the arrested stages of their development often prevent them from realizing this. In many ways this is still about Zarathustra, since the personae represent different stages of incompleteness on the way to the overman. The two kings are in search of the higher man, who alone can give kingship its truth. The leech is the "conscientious in spirit" who has not driven his conscientiousness far enough. The magician turns out merely to be an actor, portraying an ascetic of the spirit without the asceticism of honesty. The retired pope connects the death of God with the piety of Zarathustra that would not let such a God live. The ugliest man murdered God but ended by despising himself and could not find the strength to overcome man. The voluntary beggar has given away all his riches but has still not learned "the ultimate and most cunning master-art of graciousness" (IV, "The Voluntary Beggar"). Finally there is the shadow who has followed Zarathustra's breaching of all limits, "nothing is true, all is permitted" (IV, "The Shadow"), but still cannot lay hold of the reality of life itself. None of them can find the higher man, because they have not realized, as Zarathustra has, that he is already within his own cave. The folly of Zarathustra's mission had been to think the higher man could be proclaimed. "And as I spoke to all, I spoke to none" (IV, "On the Higher Man"), a remark that provides the subtitle of the work. It is only when he returns to find them returning to piety that he realizes they have found their own way, for it is a "festival of the ass" they have invented as the first mark of their own self-overcoming. Now they can begin to share with Zarathustra the meaning of the eternal return. Joy, the movement of life, does not seek results but the movement that is itself eternally. "*For all joy wants – eternity*" (IV, "The Drunken Song").

Beyond Categories of Thought

With *Zarathustra* Nietzsche had at last found his voice; the remaining works would constitute variations on the interrelated themes he announced there. This was especially the case with the next book, *Beyond Good and Evil* (1886), which, he wrote to Jacob Burckhardt, "says the same things as my *Zarathustra*, but differently" (quoted by Kaufmann, Preface, x). Now he sought to explain what Zarathustra could present by living it, and to the extent that his message is the defectiveness of all categories for life, Nietzsche too encounters the limits of language. These are not just the "prejudices of philosophers," as the opening set of aphorisms suggests, but the impossibility of comprehending the existential setting of thought. It is Nietzsche's efforts to think beyond the limits of thought that renders these last works so impenetrable. The elevation of the subject over his thoughts, as identified by Descartes, has ceased, for "a thought comes when 'it' wishes and not when 'I' wish, so that it is a falsification of the facts of the case to say that the subject 'I' is the condition of the predicate 'think'" (§ 17). We do not have thoughts; it is rather thoughts that have us. Nietzsche's own philosophical symbols must be read in this way as efforts to identify what lies beyond the boundary of consciousness because it provides the fecundity of what emerges in consciousness. The "will to power" is thus neither a will nor a power but the source of both. Nietzsche introduces it here as a warning against "superfluous teleological principles" (§ 13) that reify the very movement beyond itself that constitutes all teleology.[30] Higher than truth for every philosopher, therefore, stands the will to power by which life is gained in transcending it. "Truth" is only a stage, while life is that by which it is held and therefore the truth beyond "truth."[31] A scholar is, in Nietzsche's view, someone indifferent to truth; a philosopher lives toward the beyond of truth (§ 6).

We are entering a new era when the philosophical revolution overturns the priority of reality over appearance that has virtually defined the tradition.[32] "It is no more than a moral prejudice that truth is worth more than mere appearance; it is even the worst proved assumption there is in the world" (§ 34). With Kant we might wonder how such a principle might be proved except in terms of itself. But Nietzsche has gone further in locating the issue within existence, as life that perpetually generates perspectives that cannot be comprehended without stepping outside of life. "Let at least this much be admitted: there would be no life at all if not on the basis of perspective estimates and appearances; and if, with the virtuous enthusiasm and clumsiness of some philosophers, one wanted to abolish the 'apparent world' altogether – well, supposing *you* could do that, at least nothing would be left of your 'truth' either. Indeed, what forces us to suppose that there is an essential opposition of 'true' and 'false?'" (§ 34). The life of truth is yet beyond any truth comprehended, but it is this unattainable truth that enables Nietzsche to recognize the finitude of all truth. I am inclined to conclude that the closely connected paragraph that begins, "Whatever is profound loves masks" (§ 40), is to be taken in this sense and that this is an important guide to Nietzsche's language. The terminology of the "will to power," "the overman," and so on is

---

[30] Nietzsche himself references Spinoza here, but he could just as easily have pointed to the analysis of Kant's *Critique of Judgment*. For an account of his reading of the latter see Hill, *Nietzsche's Critiques*, ch. 3, "Early Nietzsche and the *Critique of Judgment*."

[31] "Perhaps nobody has ever been truthful enough about what 'truthfulness' is." *Beyond Good and Evil*, § 177.

[32] "Shouldn't we be standing on the threshold of a period that would be designated, negatively at first, as *extra-moral*? Today, when we immoralists, at least, suspect that the decisive value is conferred by what is specifically *unintentional* about an action, and that all its intentionality, everything about it that can be seen, known, or raised to 'conscious awareness,' only belongs to its surface and skin – which, like every skin, reveals something but *conceals* something more?" Ibid., § 32.

not so much intended to deceive as to draw us into the hiddenness of life. Over it all is the warning that what is disclosed is already dead. Life can never really yield to the pessimism of reconciliation "with whatever was and is, but wants to have *what was and is* repeated into all eternity" (§ 56).

Where Christianity still lived in relation to a false eternity beyond the now, modern society had collapsed everything into the immediacy of "the dwarf animal of equal rights and claims" (§ 203). Nietzsche's consciousness of his historic task is accentuated by this realization as he portrays the "genuine philosophers" who look toward the future and turn their "hammer" on the past. "Their 'knowing' is *creating*, their creating is a legislation, their will to truth is – *will to power*" (§ 211). They resolutely reject the dream of the modern world, which is the abolition of suffering, because they recognize its deadly implications. "In man *creature* and *creator* are united" (§ 225); an excess of pity for the creature indicates an absence of pity for the creator. Such is the choice confronting the modern world. Either it must sink below even the Christian level in its quest for reassurance or it must advance beyond the substitutes through which it has sought the same security. Germans have retarded the evolution beyond themselves by turning aside to "fatherlands," while the Jews alone have displayed the necessary endurance, although they cannot give birth to the future. Without a social carrier, Nietzsche nevertheless feels compelled "to touch on what is *serious* for me, the 'European problem' as I understand it, the cultivation of a new caste that will rule Europe" (§ 251). Nietzsche's unlucky endorsement by the Nazis still prevents us from recognizing the extent to which he rejected the position of a German thinker in favor of expressing a unifying vision for Europe (§ 256). But it may also be that we are not yet ready for his vision of "what is noble" as accepting "with a good conscience the sacrifice of untold human beings." The difficulty is indicated by the extent to which the preceding statement is often interpreted as endorsing such mass destruction, whereas it is for him really only a test of the limit of our love of life. Will European or modern man have the faith to sustain a life that lives beyond itself? "Their fundamental faith simply has to be that society must *not* exist for society's sake but only as the foundation and scaffolding on which a choice type of being is able to raise itself to its higher task and to a higher state of *being*" (§ 258). Nietzsche concludes with doubts about the capacity of his works to intimate what is great and can only in the "Aftersong" invoke the appearance of "the guest of guests," Zarathustra.

For Nietzsche life, the life of Zarathustra, has become the means of knowledge rather than the other way around. He goes on in the fifth book of *The Gay Science* (1887), "We Fearless Ones," to explore what this suspension of knowledge really means. If all forms of knowledge, theological and moral, must be rejected as an obstacle to life, what are we to make of the faith that still grounds this movement? "We godless anti-metaphysicians" are compelled to recognize that "it is still a *metaphysical faith* upon which our faith in science rests" (§ 344) and wonder, if we are truthful, as to what the value of truth is. This is the "relentless, fundamental, deepest suspicion concerning ourselves that is steadily gaining more and worse control over us Europeans and that could easily confront generations with the terrible Either/Or: 'Either abolish your venerations or – *yourselves!*' The latter would be nihilism; but would not the former also be nihilism? That is *our* question mark" (§ 346).[33] The way to confront the crisis, he now realizes, is to follow out the priority of life up to the realization that knowledge always fails to account for its source. A solitary person, Nietzsche explains, would never even develop the need for consciousness but would find himself sufficiently absorbed in the business of living. What emerges into consciousness must therefore be only the smallest and most superficial generalization of the uniquely personal richness of life beneath it. "This is what I consider to be true phenomenalism and perspectivism: that due to the nature of *animal consciousness,* the world of which we can become conscious is merely a surface- and sign-world, a world turned into generalities and thereby debased to its lowest common denominator" (§ 354). Nietzsche rejects the long-standing philosophical distinction between appearance and reality. "We simply have no organ for *knowing,* for 'truth'" (§ 354). With this profession Nietzsche has, as Heidegger notes, overturned the millennial Western conception of metaphysics.[34] Moreover, he recognizes this as the truth of the modern world, in which we have all become actors and not builders (§ 356), despite the great efforts of the German philosophical tradition to forestall it. They were, in Nietzsche's judgment, only "delayers" (§ 357).[35] This was finally the error of romanticism, that it sought a new fixity where none can be found and betrayed its own source in a pessimism of weakness rather than of strength. Now Nietzsche insists on asking the question of every new

---

[33] It is noteworthy that Nietzsche acknowledges here the coinage of the term "nihilism" by Turgenev in *Fathers and Sons* (1862). See Gillespie, *Nihilism Before Nietzsche.*

[34] Heidegger, *Nietzsche, Gesamtausgabe,* 6.1, 589–94/*Nietzsche III,* 154–58.

[35] "But the oddest thing is: those who exerted themselves the most to preserve and conserve Christianity have become its best destroyers – the Germans." *Gay Science,* § 358. One wonders, of course, if this makes Nietzsche, who points it out, the preserver of Christianity?

creation whether it "was caused by a desire for fixing, for immortalizing, for *being*, or rather by a desire for destruction, for change, for novelty, for future, for becoming" (§ 370). We can no longer ground this preference for becoming over being, because "the human intellect cannot avoid seeing itself under its perspectival forms" (§ 374), but that does not prevent us from living within this unknown infinity of interpretations. Even when we have become "good Europeans" who have left behind the insularity of the Germans, we are far from being driven by our unbelief. "No, you know better than that, my friends. The hidden Yes in you is stronger than all the Nos and Maybes that afflict you and your age like a disease; and you must sail the seas, you emigrants, you too are compelled to this by – a *faith*" (§ 377).

No Being Behind Doing

The consciousness of proclaiming a new faith marks all of Nietzsche's works after *Zarathustra*, and it is important to read them in connection with this common project. They tumble forth in close proximity, as Nietzsche indicates on the title page of *On the Genealogy of Morals* (1887): "A Sequel to My Last Book, *Beyond Good and Evil*, Which It Is Meant to Supplement and Clarify." By focusing on the positive purpose, we can avoid becoming distracted by the powerfully negative critiques that they also contain. This is particularly the case with the *Genealogy*, whose analysis of *ressentiment* as the root of conventional morality has often caused us to forget the extent to which genealogical analysis was only preliminary to what could not be analyzed. There is no genealogy of actions that spring from strength; it is only the reaction that seeks to avoid action that gives rise to a gap between thought and deed. Nietzsche, we might say, sought to eradicate ulterior motives whose intervention perverts the meaning of action. It was for this reason that he took aim at the notion that morality could be separated from its realization, as if there were a pre-moral moment in which a free choice was exercised in favor of good or evil. "But there is no such substratum; there is no 'being' behind doing, effecting, becoming; 'the doer' is merely a fiction added to the deed – the deed is everything" (I, § 13). The existential truth of action is gained, as Zarathustra showed, in life rather than through the devious interpositions of thought. "We are unknown to ourselves" is the opening statement of the *Genealogy*, and the remainder of the book is intended to forestall every attempt to look for self- knowledge other than by living it out. When morality has become existential, existence is its only guide.

That is why the fate of the few who carry existence farthest must interest us vastly more than the many who have merely sought to avoid it.[36]

By being turned into an "animal with the right to make promises" (II, § 1), such vigorous and forceful individuals who lived completely in the present found their existence deferred. Bad conscience had split them in two. They could no longer be who they were, as the very power that had previously been directed outward was now internalized against themselves. Ultimately the debt incurred by their missteps could not be discharged, and the idea of an irredeemable debt mounted to the point of devaluing all existence. It was at this stage that the "horrifying expedient" that constituted the genius of Christianity burst forth. "God himself sacrifices himself for the guilt of mankind... the creditor sacrifices himself for his debtor, out of *love* (can one credit that?), out of love for his debtor!" (II, § 21). Nietzsche's insight into the existential truth of Christianity has reached a new height, one almost indistinguishable from Christianity except for his reservation that it only "afforded temporary relief for tormented humanity." He did not want to be bought off by any palliative remedy. His own faith in redemption would not permit it. We might even say that the growing specificity of Nietzsche's rejection of Christianity in these late works is directly connected with the increasingly redemptive turn of his project. Nietzsche sought the redemption Christianity could not provide, and its first tantalizing glimpse had been vouchsafed to him in the figure of Zarathustra, who from that point on grounded his faith in its coming. He knew that "the *redeeming* man of great love and contempt" must come some day, so that "he may bring home the *redemption* of this reality: its redemption from the curse that the hitherto reigning ideal has laid upon it" (II, § 24). But would the Antichrist not suffer the same fate of unreality as the Christ from whom he had been derived? Could the existential tension beyond good and evil be sustained if Zarathustra were no longer anticipated? Is Nietzsche's own faith merely a variant of the "ascetic ideal"?

The lengthy treatment of the ascetic ideal in the third essay seems to provide a basis for grappling with these questions. Nietzsche was very conscious, as he had indicated in *The Gay Science,* that he was still driven by a faith not too dissimilar from the one he rejected. "They are far from being free spirits: *for they still have faith in truth*" (III, § 24). Or was

---

[36] "But grant me from time to time – if there are divine goddesses in the realm beyond good and evil – grant me the sight, but *one* glance of something perfect, wholly achieved, happy, mighty, triumphant, something still capable of arousing fear! Of a man who justifies *man,* of a complementary and redeeming lucky hit on the part of man for the sake of which one may still *believe in man!*" *Genealogy,* I, § 12.

he like the scientists whose self-subordination to truth had merely furnished the latest refuge for the ascetic ideal? Was he the only one who saw the problem? "From the moment faith in the God of the ascetic ideal is denied, *a new problem arises:* that of the value of truth" (§ 24). Unless we can see that truth itself has become the great danger, we will end, Nietzsche foresaw, by worshiping "the *question mark* itself as God" (III, § 25). Atheism is not the antithesis of the ascetic ideal but this ideal in its purest form – "it is the awe-inspiring *catastrophe* of two thousand years of training in truthfulness that finally forbids itself the *lie involved in belief in God*" (III, § 27). In contemplating this awesome spectacle of Christianity's self-overcoming, Nietzsche is brought to the limits of "my problem, our problem." Its formulation appears to be its own sufficient answer: "what meaning would *our* whole being possess if it were not this, that in us the will to truth becomes conscious of itself as a *problem?*" (§ 27) But this is no longer an intellectual problem, one more hiding place for the ascetic ideal as a further variant of the will to truth. Now Nietzsche can leave the question in its inconclusiveness because it marks the beginning of a final acceptance of existence as the only viable horizon for human consciousness. The momentousness of this last step is indicated by the announcement of a new literary project, *The Will to Power: Attempt at a Revaluation of All Values* (1883–88), on which he intends to embark. No doubt it would be an expression of the truth of life as forever exceeding the life of truth. It was not that Nietzsche ceased to believe in truth, indeed to pursue it, but that he now recognized that he could not contain it. Rather it was life that provided the unsurpassable boundary of truth and thereby the only possibility of glimpsing it. Truth can never be made our ideal, for it always arises from a context of life that lies outside of it. It is only by living life in the full amplitude of joy and suffering, not by willing "against life" (III, § 28), that we have any access to the glance of truth along the way.[37]

Christ Who Has Become Wholly Inward

The writings that follow, for all of their streaming intensity, do not break new ground. Nietzsche has reached the life-affirming philosophy that can no longer be contained in the "concept-mummies" (*Twilight of the*

---

[37] This insight into the uncontainability of truth is one toward which many interpreters of Nietzsche grapple without fully recognizing what they have reached. A large part of the reason for this failure is the profound unfamiliarity with the kind of philosophizing it entails. See, e.g, the lengthy "case study" of Nietzsche's conception of truth in Simon May, *Nietzsche's Ethics and His War on "Morality"* (Oxford: Clarendon, 1999), pt. 2.

Idols, "'Reason' in Philosophy," § 1) hitherto produced by philosophy. He now sees that his own initial question about the value of life, whether it is worth living, is an "unapproachable problem" since it presupposes we can take up a position outside of life. "When we speak of values, we speak with the inspiration, with the way of looking at things, which is part of life: life itself forces us to posit values" ("Morality as Anti-Nature," § 5). He can now allow himself to contemplate the distance he has traveled, in *The Twilight of the Idols* (1888), which he originally titled *A Psychologist's Idleness*. We note, too, that it is the idols who have fallen, not the gods, to whom we are still close in the task of redeeming the world ("The Four Great Errors," § 8). From that perspective Nietzsche can issue a series of acute observations on the familiar topics of art, marriage, society, Germany, the Greeks, and so on. He has reached a capacity for penetration that renders these among his most arresting formulations. Within a page he can dispatch the defining paradox of liberal institutions, which "cease to be liberal as soon as they are attained" ("Skirmishes of an Untimely Man," § 38). He can pinpoint the fatal flaw of his erstwhile mentor with newfound accuracy. Schopenhauer perpetrated "the greatest psychological counterfeit in all history" by interpreting the most life affirming in art and heroism as the deepest expression of the will to negate life (§ 21). Nietzsche could now look back and see that his own trajectory had not been the Schopenhauerian one of searching for release from life but that of finding its deepest affirmation, which he first encountered in the Dionysian festivals. "Here the most profound instinct toward the future of life, the eternity of life, is experienced religiously – and the way to life, procreation, as the *holy* way" ("What I Owe to the Ancients," § 4). The psychology of the tragic poet was not about reaching a point above life but finding the point within it that enabled him to say yes to all. It was in this transcendence of all values that Nietzsche could say that "*The Birth of Tragedy* was my first revaluation of all values" (§ 5).

   At this point Nietzsche dropped the previously announced title *Will to Power* and made what had been its subtitle the title of the new work, *The Revaluation of All Values*. It is difficult to assign any definitive significance to this revision, but it does suggest that he wanted to emphasize the completion of the Zarathustra epiphany. His final book, *The Anti-Christ* (1888), was to have been the first essay in this project, which was intended not so much to advance Nietzsche's own thought as to complete the transvaluation of all previous values. The importance of *The Anti-Christ* lies in the deeper understanding of Christianity it contains and thus of Nietzsche's relationship to it. In retrospect the work is essentially a clarification but one that would be difficult to attain without it. Several earlier passages could be cited to demonstrate the distinction he develops between Christ and Christianity, but few would have the trenchancy of his observation here that "in truth, there was only *one* Christian, and he died on the cross" (I, § 39). The distinction is an important one because it helps to explain both his invective against Christianity and the sympathies that would attune his project to the figure of Christ. While the affinity with Christ should not be given too much weight, the ambivalence was sufficiently important to be built into the title. *Der Antichrist* can be translated just as appropriately as *The Anti-Christian,* while the subtitle developed from *An Attempt at a Critique of Christianity* to *A Curse on Christianity.* Nietzsche comes in many passages remarkably close to Kierkegaard's insistence that a Christian today must anathemize Christendom.[38] Indeed, what seems to arouse his "blackest melancholy" is the mendacity of modern Christians whose self-congratulation masks their utter failure to grasp what following Christ must mean (I, § 38). It was the church that since the beginning turned the redemptive good news of how Christ lived into the redemption that became available to all who merely believed. "Evidently the small community did *not* understand the main point, the exemplary character of this kind of death, the superiority over any feeling of *ressentiment*" (I, § 40).[39] Only "we spirits who have *become free*" (I, § 36) have the capacity to understand what nineteen centuries of Christianity have missed, that there is no immortality worthy of the name but the immortality exemplified by the way one lives.

When Christianity has become wholly existential, it must jettison all dogmatic formulations as false. In pushing the implication of existential truth to this extreme, Nietzsche has brought to light one of the most enduring tensions of Christianity. Whether fidelity to the imperative of existence in truth would not also require dogmatic expression as the means of ensuring its transmission is a question he does not consider. But the fact that we can raise it suggests that there are even for great

---

[38] "If one were to look for signs that an ironical divinity has its fingers in the great play of the world, one would find no small support in the *tremendous question mark* called Christianity. Mankind lies on its knees before the opposite of that which was the origin, the meaning, the *right* of the evangel; in the concept of 'church' it has pronounced holy precisely what the 'bringer of the glad tidings' felt to be *beneath* himself – one would look in vain for a greater example of *world-historical irony.*" *Antichrist,* § 36; see also §§ 37–41.

[39] Max Scheler's recognition of the significance of Nietzsche's naming of *ressentiment* is still worth reading. See the excerpt from his book in Robert Solomon, ed., *Nietzsche: A Collection of Critical Essays* (Notre Dame, IN: University of Notre Dame Press, 1980), 243–57.

thinkers dimensions that simply cannot arise within their thought world. Perhaps those of us who are less affected by the animus that drove Nietzsche or, in a parallel fashion, Kierkegaard may be able to make the necessary adjustments that would save the nineteen centuries of history so brusquely dismissed. For the teacher of the eternal return it is, for example, a little unbelievable that the same insights have not previously occurred. Indeed, the whole history of philosophy and Christianity might be reconstructed as the history of this tension between the formulated truths and the truth of "living life." Awareness of the tension is unlikely to have escaped human notice in that long historical struggle, just as its explication now is unlikely to abolish it. Doctrinal definitions and disputes have always sought their authorization in the way of life they claimed to defend but could never contain. Correlatively, it was always by transcending the merely verbal expressions that the living reality of faith was ever realized. The radically existential thrust of Nietzsche's thought, forswearing any conceptual content, runs the perennial danger of dogmatic recapture that is virtually unavoidable when a literary enterprise constantly denies itself. In the absence of any terminology to identify what one is positively about, the only guide to interpretation consists of the targets of one's critique. Even for Nietzsche it became difficult to explain himself. Nowhere was this more problematic than in his tortuous relationship with Christianity, which, he insisted, merely followed the path along which Christianity overcame itself. But what was the character of such a self-overcoming if not a self-deepening? To the extent that the critique arises from within Christianity, it cannot lead outside of it.[40]

Nietzsche was clearly aware of the extent to which he was driven by the same faith he critiqued both in metaphysics and in Christianity. His meditation carried him a considerable distance but, in the case of Christianity, rarely back to the admission of his own Christian derivation. Without carrying it to a conclusion, he left the tension plainly visible for all to see, even though few have had the temerity to confront its shocking implication. Could the most notorious critic of Christianity have been its deepest witness? The suggestion is audacious enough to have at some point brushed Nietzsche himself, although he gives little evidence of it even in the voluminous notebooks he left behind. The notebooks really provide source material for the published works, which they confirm in various ways but do not advance beyond. What he does do, however, is make the

---

[40] For an account of Nietzsche that parallels this suggestion see Giles Fraser, *Redeeming Nietzsche: On the Piety of Unbelief* (London: Routledge, 2002).

issue visible in the text, not only by severing his critique of Christianity from his admiration for Christ, but also by rooting his rejection of God in God himself. "That we find no God – either in history or in nature or behind nature – is not what differentiates *us,* but that we experience what has been revered as God, not as 'godlike' but as miserable, as absurd, as harmful, not merely as an error but as a *crime against life.* We deny God as God" (I, § 47). At one level this can be read as the failure to find God, but because it is a rejection, it is more than that. "If one were to *prove* this God of the Christians to us, we should be even less able to believe in him" (§ 47). Proof of a Pauline external God has become incredible in light of the truth of God he knows within himself. Nietzsche may not have a deep inner sense of God but he has enough to know that a reified God is a fraud. The revolt he announces is not against the inner idea of God but against its external deformation, for the whole force of Nietzsche's critique is derived from the heightened awareness of what God must be. We begin to understand more clearly why Nietzsche was compelled to turn to Christianity in his last work. Even when he could not fully recognize it, the inexorable thrust of his quest for a life without ressentiment led him to affirm unconditional love as the only one worthy of the name. The existential truth of Christianity can require even the abandonment of God. Could it be that Nietzsche reminds us, no doubt in his idiosyncratic way, of the cry of Jesus forsaken: "My God, my God, why have you forsaken me?" (Mt 27: 46; Ps 22: 1)? Given the profound self-consciousness of the philosophical shift he had inaugurated, it is perhaps not so surprising that it should entail an equally radical rethinking of revelation.[41]

That focus on the status of his own insight is what accounts for the strikingly lucid formulations that pepper the last *Notebooks* (1885–88). In part they are composed of material he had discarded, but they also contain fragments from which a whole new phase of his reflection might have sprung. Gone is the uncertainty about his metaphysical faith in truth, to be replaced by the realization that all faith is a movement beyond itself. The paradoxical structure of existence can now be accepted because it is no longer a theoretical problem; it is rather the boundary glimpsed from within the movement by which existence is sustained. "The view that *truth* is *found* and that ignorance and error are at an end is one of the most potent seductions there is. Suppose it is believed, then the

---

[41] It is this tragic character of Nietzsche's relation to Christianity that I earlier tried to bring out, especially by way of its clarification with the parallel trajectory of Dostoevsky. See *After Ideology.*

will to examination, investigation, caution, experiment is paralyzed: it can even count as criminal, namely as *doubt* concerning the truth" (*Will to Power*, § 452). The pursuit of truth requires the nonattainability of truth. It is because Nietzsche himself is no longer concerned about the tendency of the highest values to "nihilate" themselves, no longer sees it as doubt concerning their truth, that he can embrace it as the indispensable means by which we can exist. He is very close to the insight of Schelling that the world is made possible through the withdrawal of God, which also implies that revelation means the withdrawal from revelation. But Nietzsche has arrived at this metaphysical insight through a far more thoroughly existential meditation. His has been the struggle to overcome ressentiment, to go beyond metaphysical revolt to the life-affirming being of becoming. Now he could find the language to express this because he was confident that it could no longer be confused with a theoretical statement.

It is with all the awareness of the revolutionary significance in the history of Western philosophy that he can now pronounce, "To impose upon becoming the character of being – that is the supreme will to power" (§ 617). The entire theoretical stance with its orientation toward a world of constancy has been displaced in the realization that it is inconstancy that has furnished all possibility. "That *everything recurs* is the closest *approximation of a world of becoming to a world of being.* – high point of the meditation" (§ 617).[42] But Nietzsche is no longer concerned that the approximation will be taken for identity. The eternal return is not the surreptitious return of being; it is its definitive elimination from existence. Even though he still uses the language of metaphysics to bring about the eradication of metaphysics, insisting that the advent of being would have brought about the termination of becoming (§ 1062), the denotation has become entirely existential. Truth and its problem of faith in another realm can be dismissed when there is no truth beyond the existence it makes possible. In one of his most memorable dicta, reminiscent

---

[42] Stephen Houlgate has contrasted the analytic reading of Hegel as escaping metaphysics with Nietzsche's apparent embrace of an antimetaphysics of life that remains entangled in the categories of metaphysics. No doubt this accurately reflects the limits of the analytic retrieval of idealism. Nietzsche and, significantly, Heidegger lie beyond the pale. The difficulty with this reading is that it fails to recognize the extent to which the analytic meditation is already implicated in a metaphysical relationship and the degree to which the reflections of Nietzsche and his successors took their beginning from that realization. Even the analytic overcoming of metaphysics is a move within metaphysics. See Houlgate, *Hegel, Nietzsche and the Criticism of Metaphysics.*

of the long odyssey from *The Birth of Tragedy* as well as the long modern preoccupation with the privileged position of art, Nietzsche can now provide a summation. "We possess *art* lest we *perish of the truth*" (§ 822). Far from the desiccated effeteness of "art for art's sake," art has achieved its redemptive promise when it has become a way of life (§ 853). Beauty is not only our connection and our consolation in existence, but the means by which we respond to the pull of existence. That is its deepest meaning. It is not the products, the works that soon become obstacles to their own reception, but the life that is made possible. Art for Nietzsche is, like truth, morality, and faith, a revelation of what cannot be revealed. With this realization the existential revolution in modern philosophy has reached a clarity that cannot easily be lost. That achievement is the fruit of Nietzsche's single-minded meditation and the reason the arc of his influence extends all the way to the present.

5

Heidegger's Achievement Despite the Betrayal of Philosophical Existence

If we regard Nietzsche as the furthest reach of the philosophical revolution wrought by German idealism, Heidegger represents the moment of its greatest danger. The undiminished fascination with the "problem" of Heidegger does not simply derive from a curiosity about his personal failures, no matter how absorbing such a preoccupation may be. It is a controversy that has irrupted at regular intervals since 1933.[1] New information about his complicated relationship with Nazism has, far from resolving the debates, only whetted appetites for more. No doubt there are morbid dimensions to the interest itself, but there is more in it than ordinary prurience. Even when we may not have admitted it to ourselves, we sense that the fate of philosophy itself is bound up with the verdict on its most impressive practitioner in the twentieth century. For all of Heidegger's lamentable character flaws, even his detractors cannot deny the elemental force of his philosophical genius. "The gale that blows through Heidegger's thinking – like that which still, after thousands of years, blows to us from Plato's work – is not of our century." So wrote Hannah Arendt, who intuited in him something of the "primordial" that was at once fascinating and appalling.[2] This is why the debate over

---

[1] Heidegger's notorious involvement with Nazism erupted into controversy in three distinct phases. The first was immediately following the war in 1946, when he was deprived of his professorship and subjected to denazification. The second was after the publication of *An Introduction to Metaphysics* in 1953 when the young Jürgen Habermas was provoked to ask about the tendency of his philosophy to exonerate Nazism. The third, and by far the largest explosion, occurred after the publication of Heidegger's rectoral address in 1983, prompting the historical investigations of Ott and Farias that established the extent of Heidegger's Nazism.

[2] Quoted in Rüdiger Safranski, *Martin Heidegger: Between Good and Evil,* trans. Ewald Osers (Cambridge, MA: Harvard University Press, 1998), 417. The full text of the celebratory talk Arendt gave on Heidegger's eightieth birthday is in Hannah Arendt and Martin

Heidegger cannot easily be put to rest, for we sense that it implicates far more than the failure of a particular man. Does it not cast a pall over the entire project of the modern existential revolution in philosophy, if not on the entire history of philosophy itself? No doubt this is a very Heideggerian question to pose, but then that too only attests to the difficulty of separating ourselves from the flawed genius of philosophy's contemporary evocation. In this sense Arendt is perhaps only the most obvious instance of the problem that, even when we succeed in carving out independent lines of reflection, we still must take account of the Heideggerian primordiality.

Confronting the issue in this way carries us well beyond the prevailing debates over whether Heidegger's philosophy necessitated his support of National Socialism. There are, of course, few defenders today of the prevarications Heidegger himself was the first to circulate, that his dalliance with Nazism was a temporary lapse in political judgment. One of the benefits of the extensive reexamination of the record in recent decades has been to develop a fairly clear picture of Heidegger's relationship. Thus, it is well known that the years of his most active party engagement were 1933 and 1934, after which he became largely disillusioned with it as the carrier of a genuine spiritual renovation within German society. But his willingness to admit this disaffection did nothing to diminish the faith in the revolutionary project from which it sprang. Heidegger may have ceased to be a National Socialist in politics, but he remained one in idea. This distinction is indispensable if we are to comprehend the far greater failure of his silence in the long succeeding years. For no matter how much weight we might give to his expressed disavowals, including those impressively made while he was under surveillance by the National Socialists, the inability to come to grips with the scale of the catastrophe to which he had once lent his support is the crucial factor. The brief flirtation with National Socialism, which has received the bulk of attention, is outweighed by a lifelong apocalyptic preoccupation. This is illustrated by the way in which a remark that, coming from any other thinker, could be construed quite innocently is, from Heidegger, fraught with ominous overtones. One thinks particularly of his 1949 observation that "agriculture is now motorized food industry, essentially the same as the manufacture of corpses and gas chambers."[3] Only a thoroughly

Heidegger, *Letters: 1925–75*, ed. Ursula Ludz, trans. Andrew Shields (New York: Harcourt, 2004), 148–62.

[3] Bremen lecture, 1949; quoted in Safranski, *Martin Heidegger*, 414. Typical of the prominence of the passage is its culminating position in Richard Wolin's indictment, *The Politics*

apocalyptic imagination could fail to distinguish between the holocaust and agricultural mechanization, and only a thoroughly monomaniacal intellect could lack the sensitivity to notice the moral difference. The staggering failure of repentance, not his readiness to cooperate with a totalitarian regime, is the indictment that overshadows Heidegger's philosophical greatness and causes us to wonder about the connection. Could it be that it was because he could not be mistaken about philosophy that he could not acknowledge his mistakenness about politics? Is the existential unfolding of philosophy implicated in Heidegger's own existential failure?

These are hard questions to raise because, unlike the atmosphere of moral superiority in which the journalistic discussions of the case have been conducted, they compel us to include self-examination within the investigation. If the obtuseness of Heidegger is more than a personal failure and, perhaps, implicates the direction of philosophical thought itself, there is far more at stake than individual mendacity. We must assess the extent to which it was the intellectual trajectory of our era that distorted the capacity to recognize such misdoing. Moral failure always remains personal, but it is philosophy that sharpens or blurs our perception of it. An inchoate anxiety about the complicity of philosophy in Heidegger's guilt is ultimately the most significant factor behind the periodic reexaminations. It has made the case of Heidegger the ironic contrast to the trial of Socrates, in which it was also the fate of philosophy that was at stake. The difference is that now we are not as sure that philosophy will be able to acquit itself, although the philosopher may have escaped execution. That lack of confidence derives directly from the greatest representative of philosophy in our time, whose failure causes us to ask whether there is a greater achievement of philosophy than that reached by him. The self-examination of philosophy in light of the Heidegger tragedy remains a philosophical enterprise.[4] It would

---

of Being: The Political Thought of Martin Heidegger (New York: Columbia University Press, 1990), 168.

[4] The difficulty of gaining a perspective on the "case" of Heidegger is best illustrated by the challenge it represented to his students. One of the ablest, Karl Löwith, sought to encapsulate the phenomenon within an intellectual history of European nihilism that eventually debouched into Heidegger's "decisionism." See the essays of Löwith edited by Richard Wolin in *Martin Heidegger and European Nihilism* (New York: Columbia University Press, 1995). The problem with this approach is that it assumes that Heidegger's thought can be encompassed within the categories of intellectual history, while the only genuine critique is to be reached by following his thought to the self-critique that points beyond it. That latter path is the one followed by Levinas and Derrida, as we will see in the next two chapters.

perhaps not be a wholly surprising outcome of this tortured episode if philosophy's leading genius should become the catalyst for a deepening of philosophy beyond him. Having confronted the anxieties to which his defection gave rise, we may ultimately be better able to surmount the betrayal that caused it. In this sense the real greatness of Heidegger may lie in the release of philosophy into an openness more open than he could conceive.

The Loneliness of the Primordiality of Truth

Before we can make any such assessment, however, we must follow the path by which he became the breaker of paths. The man who referred to himself as the perpetual beginner, ever on the way and never arriving, had his beginning at an inauspicious moment in the history of philosophy. The turn of the century was in many respects a low point. Nietzsche's departure from the groves of academic philosophy had marked the exhaustion of the impulse from which German idealism had sprung. Now philosophy had reverted to the routine of scholarship, always its most tempting retreat, against which Heidegger would continually strain. So despite his lifelong immersion in university life, Heidegger conveyed the unmistakable impression that philosophy could really be done only outside of it, and he sought to address a community beyond the institutional neighborhood. The thinkers to whom he was drawn in the early years were invariably those who ruptured the placidity of the intellectual realm in calling attention to the vitality outside of it. Already one can sense in his responses to Dilthey, Bergson, and Scheler, the intensity of spirit that overflows the capacity of linguistic expression to contain it. Heidegger was from the first in search of philosophy as a way of existence. No doubt it was this intensity that made such a powerful impression in the classroom despite the evidence that many of the students did not understand him. From the very beginning he was an elemental force in search of the nourishment from which it could be fed. Philosophy was not for him a livelihood; it was his very life. The contrast with such humanist learning as that exemplified by Ernst Cassirer could not have been greater, for he could not be deflected from the trail of the numinous.

It was that quest of the living reality that led Heidegger to place his confidence in "the treasure of truth" of the church and then to turn against it as "the system of Catholicism."[5] His *Habilitationschrift* on Duns Scotus (or pseudo- Scotus) is guided by the same interest in the unfathomable,

[5] Safranski, *Martin Heidegger*, 67.

for the nominalist demonstrates the inability of universals to capture the mystery of the particular. But it was through Husserl's phenomenology that Heidegger found the royal road of access to the *haecittas*, the 'this-now-here' of things. Phenomenology was based on the awareness by which consciousness, in being aware of objects, is also aware of itself and its relationship to them. By turning toward the process of perception, it is possible, therefore, to gain an awareness of the primordial relationship between subject and object that makes perception possible. Phenomenological reduction is, as Hegel suggested, the truth of perception. From this exciting discovery in the immediate dynamics of perception, it did not take Heidegger long to apply it within the larger dynamics of existence as a whole. It was in this way that he, along with many others, carried the potential of phenomenology beyond the boundaries of scientific rigor Husserl had visualized for it. No doubt Heidegger's immediate historical situation in military service during the closing years of World War I had something to do with this existential enlargement. All around he witnessed the collapse of the cultural invincibility so dominant in Germany before the war and now realized its inner fragility. What is remarkable about his response to defeat and disintegration is the tone of resounding confidence he struck. When the hollowness of the old social and political order had been exposed, the time was ripe for the birth of an authentic order of truth as the only impregnability. It was in the midst of the devastating German collapse that Heidegger was seized by the sense of a historical mission his philosophical genius must serve. All of the elements were present in germ long before the advent of either National Socialism or his own philosophical maturation.[6]

The direction of his thought is disclosed by the style that combines the intensity of analytic dryness with an eschatological penumbra. By practicing the hard craft of intellectual self-purification, he hoped to pierce the veil of mystery that is sensed but not comprehended. Religious symbols and metaphysical structures had become opaque, but they had not diminished Heidegger's thirst for a glimpse of what they formerly contained. The only difference is that now he would not be deflected by mere representations. Only being itself would satisfy his longing as he set out on his long personal odyssey to reach it through the transparence of existence. It was no doubt a sense of the same combination of rigor and depth that drew him toward a more profound reading of Aristotle. He explains his intention in the introduction to his *Phenomenological*

---

[6] See the sentiments of letters quoted in ibid., 87–88, 102.

Interpretations of Aristotle (1922). "Any philosophy that understands itself in what it is must know, as the factual How of the interpretation of life – especially when it still has a 'surmise' of God – that the snatching back of life performed by it represents, religiously speaking, a raising of a hand against God. But only thus does it present itself honestly to God, that is, according to the possibilities available to it as such; in atheistic terms, keeping itself free from a tempting anxiety that merely pays lip service to religiosity."[7] The existential turn in modern philosophy has reached a fascinating moment when it is burdened with the task of responding alone to the tension of existence. Where previously art and religion could also carry the responsive unfolding of existence, now philosophy is the only reliable mode. To the extent that art and religion are subsequently drawn into the quest, it is rarely in their own right but only to the extent that they can illuminate the philosophical awakening. Heidegger's association with the label of existentialism may carry its own confusions, but it does serve to alert us to the intensity of the existential dimension in his thought, for it is not just that philosophy furnishes a guide to existence, but that existence has become philosophical.

Along with Jaspers, Heidegger discovered the indispensability of existence as the "snatching back of life" from the realm of inertness it leaves behind. The problem of being and time was already on his horizon.[8] Heidegger would shortly begin the great work of snatching what cannot be captured and thereby transform the nature of philosophical language. His place in the history of philosophy is still rooted in this one book, *Sein und Zeit* (1927), and there is considerable basis for this perception since it was there that he demonstrated the power of existence over thought. From that point on thought would have to move within the movement of existence. The journey would take Heidegger too far from this beginning, but it would still be a path that originated from this first irruption. Perhaps nowhere were the revolutionary implications more manifest than in the dramatic exchange with Cassirer in Davos, April 1929. Clothed in the prophetic mantle of existence, Heidegger could hurl an anathema at the idealist cultural vision of the most distinguished liberal democrat. In his quest to understand the symbolic forms created by freedom, Cassirer had allowed freedom to be collapsed into

---

[7] Quoted in ibid., 110.
[8] Safranski points out Heidegger's awareness of his parallel with Karl Barth. "'Snatching life back' from a false Beyond – this is now the most important task for Heidegger and Barth. Martin Heidegger tears life loose from God; Karl Barth tears God loose from life." Ibid., 112.

its own products. "To what extent is it the task of philosophy," Heidegger counters, "to allow liberation from anxiety? Or is it not its task radically to deliver man to anxiety?"[9] This philosophical high noon was a moment of supreme self-disclosure. The greatness of Heidegger could not save him from the overreaching by which his thought betrayed itself. Railing against cultural incarceration seemed to become a refusal to accept the same fate as the price that is paid by all that exists. The denouement, in which political action becomes a means of transcending politics, had already been set. In this sense Heidegger was no different from the many Germans whose disdain of politics prompted their own disastrous political misjudgment, but he did provide an insight into the philosophical source from which such a paradoxical attitude might spring. Disdain for politics arises from disdain for the everydayness as the path by which existence can daily be renewed.[10] The tragedy is that the wrong arises from the right, which nevertheless remains right; the path should rather have been moderation rather than abandonment.

To understand Heidegger's infatuation with National Socialism one must go beyond the superficial assignment of blame to his "decision-ism," especially as this is usually located in the discussion of authenticity in *Being and Time*.[11] It is not that Heidegger believed in nothing and therefore could believe in anything. No, he found himself on the thresh-old of Nazism as a result of the steps he had taken to stand within truth rather than outside of it. It was the whole Western tradition derived from Plato that had turned truth into an externality in which the question of our relationship to it could become problematic. The freedom toward which Heidegger sought to draw nigh was not a radical emptiness, but a deeper discovery of the truth already lived, although knowable only as such. It was an opening into an expanse without fixed signposts but not an opening without direction. So why did the direction point toward *der Führer?* "Let not axioms or 'ideas' be the rule of your Being. The Führer himself and alone is the present and future German reality and its law."[12]

---

[9] Quoted in ibid., 187.

[10] See the description of Heidegger's political views by Hermann Mörchen in 1931. Ibid., 226–27.

[11] Charles Guignon explains why *Being and Time* "is not merely cataloging facts about existentiell cases of Dasein;" see his "History and Commitment in the Early Heidegger," in Hubert Dreyfus and Harrison Hall, eds., *Heidegger: A Critical Reader* (Oxford: Blackwell, 1992), 135.

[12] "Appeal to German Students," November 2, 1933; quoted in Safranski, *Martin Heidegger,* 232–33. On the Heidegger's relationship to Nazism see Victor Farias, *Heidegger and Nazism,* trans. Paul Burel and Gabriel R. Ricci (Philadelphia: Temple University Press,

Even Jaspers, who had sought to warn Heidegger of the political intoxication, was still fascinated by the phenomenon because he sensed that its roots were philosophical rather than political.[13] This was why Heidegger would later admit that he had only dreamed politically, never that his philosophical quest had become a mode of dreaming.[14] If need be he was prepared to concede not to his own mistake but to an "error of Being" it had been his burden to bear. The results, of course, varied between the ludicrous and the pathetic as Heidegger called on the unemployed workers to become "capable of *Dasein*" by subordinating themselves to the national effort.[15] In the end, however, it was not so much that Heidegger left the party as that the party left him. No political movement could preserve the purity of spirit he required, because no party could become philosophical. Compromises with reality would become inevitable. National Socialism had, after all, been only a political revolution, while the inner metaphysical revolution would now have to be carried forward by Heidegger alone until it could again become the formative basis for a national community.[16] From that point on Heidegger would feel free to include remarks critical of National Socialism in his writings, while he retained the consciousness of his own revolutionary significance. The difference is that now he no longer laid claim to any special capacity to pronounce on the political and progressively withdrew from that sphere.

The remarkable thing is that this major philosophical thinker abrogated any political philosophy. It is not just a failure of Heidegger's character, as Arendt and Jaspers both recognized, that caused his inability to undertake the movement of repentance that would have been required to restore a true measure of political reality. The requirement was articulated most profoundly by Jaspers in his reflection on German guilt. "Anyone who, as a mature person, in 1933 had the inner conviction that

1989), and Hugo Ott, *Martin Heidegger: A Political Life,* trans. Allan Blunden (New York: Basic, 1994).

[13] See Safranski, *Martin Heidegger,* 252.

[14] "In a later letter (April 8, 1950) he would concede to Jaspers that he had dreamed 'politically' and had therefore been mistaken. But that he was politically mistaken because he had dreamed 'philosophically' – that he would never admit, because as a philosopher who wished to discover the essence of historical time he was bound to defend – even before himself – his philosophical interpretative competence for what was happening in political history." Ibid., 234.

[15] Ibid., 260.

[16] See his broadcast lecture, "Creative Landscape: Why Do We Stay in the Province?" March 1934, quoted in ibid., 278.

was rooted not only in political error but in a life experience enhanced by National Socialism, cannot now become pure except through a remelting that would have to go deeper than any other."[17] The problem now was that Heidegger no longer felt any need to sift the political, for the ethical life the political sought to guard had itself been overtaken by the primordial meditation on being. When the rest of postwar Europe was struggling with the meaning of the crisis through which it had passed, desperate to erect a barrier against a repetition of its totalitarian nightmare, Heidegger had already overleapt the palliatives to open toward the only luminosity available to us. It is a remarkable testament both to the consciousness of his philosophical mission and to the moral blindness that remained inseparable from it. As he insisted in the "Letter on Humanism," written at the point of his own material and psychological nadir, it was not that he rejected the demands of the ethical but that he could not give them priority in light of the mystery of being in which they are embedded. What he failed to see was that an ethical demand that had become secondary was no longer an inescapable obligation. It was almost as if the existential revolution had betrayed itself in forgetting that it is precisely through fidelity to the demand of existence that the opening toward being takes place. Had Heidegger returned to a metaphysics of presence that would relieve him of the burden of responsibility toward what can never be present because its presence remains our responsibility?

The enigma of Heidegger continued to baffle his closest and most sympathetic readers. Arendt had shown the possibility of a genuine political philosophy in his thought even while he had misplaced himself in the "temporary alliance between the mob and the elite."[18] But it was Jaspers, with whom Heidegger enjoyed a friendship that was closest to one between equals, who really identified the source of the problem. Even in 1950 Heidegger had written to him in doleful tones about the "homelessness" of their time in which an "advent" was to be greeted "whose furthest hints we may perhaps still experience in a soft murmur and that we must capture in order to save it for a future." Jaspers would, of course, have nothing of a murmured apocalypse. "Does not a philosophy

---

[17] Jaspers, *Die Schuldfrage;* quoted in Safranski, *Martin Heidegger,* 339. See also 314 for the assessments of Jaspers and Arendt.

[18] Hannah Arendt, *The Origins of Totalitarianism,* new ed. (New York: Harcourt Brace Jovanovich, 1973), 326. For an interesting investigation of the complementarity of their thought see Dana Villa, *Arendt and Heidegger: The Fate of the Political* (Princeton, NJ: Princeton University Press, 1995).

that surmises and poetizes in such phrases in your letter, a philosophy that aroused the vision of the monstrous, once more prepare the
ground for the victory of totalitarianism by severing itself from reality?"
Heidegger's advent is nothing but "pure dreaming, in a string of so many
dreams that . . . have deluded us through this half-century."[19] One would
be inclined to conclude that Heidegger had learned nothing from his
own responsibility for the monstrous, an impression confirmed by the
mendacity of the *Der Spiegel* interview in 1966.[20] But an abundance of
caution should guide our judgments in the area of a man's soul, especially
when there are alternative explanations. Heidegger's disdain of public
confessions of repentance may have arisen from the offensiveness of the
implication that he was capable of murder.[21] Besides, the significance of
Heidegger does not turn on his personal merits or defects but on the
extent to which they are or are not embedded in his thought.

Again Jaspers continued to meditate on the central issue, coming to a
piercing summation of the differences in a philosophical note in 1965.
"H: Thought itself is Being – the talking around it and pointing to it
without ever getting there. J: Thought has existential relevance – which,
in the inner action of the meditating person it demonstrates (provision-
ally, expresses) and in the practical life brings to realization – without
this being possible to happen in the philosophical work." Heidegger, too,
had contemplated this difference, since it was also what divided him from
existentialism as a whole. In his view Jaspers no longer took philosophy
seriously once he subordinated it to the task of moral enlightenment,
turning it into a "moralizing psychology of human existence."[22] Heidegger, it would seem, misunderstood Jaspers, but we cannot preclude the
possibility that the reverse was also the case. The point, however, is not

---

[19] Quoted in Safranski, *Martin Heidegger,* 386. Writing to Arendt in 1949, Jaspers could be
more reflective. After noting that Heidegger "is entirely in his Being speculation, he
writes '*Seyn.*' Two and a half decades ago he backed 'existence' and basically distorted
matters. Now he backs more essentially . . . I hope he doesn't distort it again. But I doubt
it. Can one, as an impure soul . . . can one see greatest purity in insincerity?" But then
he rebalances the estimation: "The strange thing is that he knows about something that
hardly anyone notices today, and that his surmise is so impressive." Quoted in ibid., 374.

[20] Safranski, drawing on Karl Schmitt, notes that the interview, appropriately titled "Only a
God Can Save Us," had elevated "fellow-traveling as a form of resistance." Ibid., 420.

[21] Safranski is at his best in this summative reflection. "If, therefore, one understands
Heidegger's critique of the modern age also as philosophizing about Auschwitz, then
it becomes clear that the problem of his silence is not that he was silent on Auschwitz.
In philosophical terms he was silent about something else: about himself, about the
philosopher's seducibility by power." Ibid., 421.

[22] Quoted in ibid., 387–88.

to settle the issue but to find the question by which to bring Heidegger's vast enterprise into focus. This terse juxtaposition seems to do that. Heidegger's dismissal of Jaspers's philosophy is of most value for what it tells us about Heidegger's own philosophy. It could not be in service to human existence, since it responded to the higher call of being as its shepherd or guardian. We might say that Heidegger sought to reach through thought what Jaspers thought could be reached only through existence. But were they different, especially when thought is itself our mode of existence? There can be no doubt that Heidegger's thought strains the limits of thinking and, in that sense, carries the existential revolution to its limits, perhaps even to the breaking point. What, then, is that limit? Was Jaspers right that thought could not overstep them, or was Heidegger correct in insisting that it already had in acknowledging them? Such are the questions that must now occupy us as we struggle with Heidegger's writings while also keeping an eye on the enigma of his personality. Could it be that his existential downfall is somehow rooted in the blind spot of thinking beyond the self? If it is, what does this say about the value of the turn toward existence as the only viable path of philosophy in the modern world?

We must, in other words, approach the Heidegger problem as our problem, since he is the one who has walked farthest along the philosophical path on which we find ourselves. He is the point at which the modern philosophical revolution becomes irreversible. This is not only because of his association with the "existentialist" movement but, most importantly, because of his drive beyond it. Heidegger grasped the significance of the existential shift in modern philosophy, but he also recognized the danger of its dissolution into subjectivism. Such a fate would negate the whole prospect of philosophy finding a way of surmounting the isolation of the subject from a world of objects it can manipulate but never really know. Instead, Heidegger sought to extend the project of German idealism with a corresponding ambition for the role of philosophy in the world. This is why, despite his "existentialist" phase, he never really subscribed to its absolutization of individual subjectivity. The notorious *Kehre* in his thought after *Being and Time* was not so much a departure from the direction he had pursued as a deeper self-recognition of its meaning. An initial overemphasis on Dasein could easily be revised toward the meditation on being because this had all along been its implicit purpose. The same single-minded quest would later drive Heidegger to stretch the carrying power of language to its limits in order to more adequately intimate the unattainable horizon of all thought. The effect can be dizzying, but it remains comprehensible once we bear in mind its derivation from the modern turn toward existence. Once we recognize that philosophy in the modern era has been driven by the realization that its source must forever remain outside of its expressions, the surface impenetrability of the language becomes less baffling. What distinguishes Heidegger's achievement in this regard is that he definitively locates the subject, existence or Dasein, within the realm of truth.[23] Human existence not only carries within it the capacity for truth, but is already a mode of openness toward it. With Heidegger the shift toward existence was completed, and he had the capacity to demonstrate its explication as the implication of the Western philosophical tradition. Nowhere is his significance better attested to than by the fact that his critics, many of whom offer indispensable correctives, must now do so within the mode of philosophizing he established.

The Primacy of Being: Fundamental Ontology

Being and Time marked a turning point in 1927 that has defined the arc of philosophy in our time. Not even its author could fully escape its shadow, such was the power and originality of the work, for despite his relentless intellectual efforts over the next fifty years, he never succeeded in bringing the fruits together with such compressed intensity. We would have to look back to Hegel's *Phenomenology of Spirit* to find a work of comparable impact. The parallel extends even further than the supernova brilliance at the beginning of their respective careers, for they are works of such astonishing richness that they provided their authors with a seemingly endless vein to mine. Much has been made of the famous turn from Dasein to *Sein* in the years after *Being and Time,* but Heidegger himself never seems to have emphasized any discontinuity. On the contrary, whenever he returns to the analysis of *Being and Time,* it is always to emphasize the continuity with the reflection on being within it, which he now claimed to understand better. For most great thinkers there are no "breaks," only an ever deepening grasp of the intuition that seized them even before they were able to name it. In the case of Heidegger we might say that it is this single-mindedness that constitutes his greatness and at the same time opened the way of his failure. Even though much of the work may have digressed into an inquiry into human existence, its

---

[23] An excellent guide to this beginning point in Heidegger is Daniel Dahlstrom, *Heidegger's Concept of Truth* (Cambridge: Cambridge University Press, 2001).

real purpose remained the quest for being identified in its title. When Heidegger later concluded that he could not complete the second part of the book, this was not because it was impossible but because it would have entailed too radical a revision of its beginning (preface to seventh ed.). The quest for being would draw him deeper, but it was possible, as he himself would suggest, only because it had already been there before the beginning.

In *Being and Time,* Heidegger was aware of inaugurating a new era in philosophy that went considerably beyond the steps taken toward it by his immediate predecessors. An extensive revision in the self-understanding of human nature had already been under way in the personalism of Scheler, Bergson, and others. The materialism and reductionism of the human sciences had been exploded by the critique of psychologism offered by Husserl. But it was Heidegger who realized that the category of philosophical anthropology was no longer adequate for the break-through incipiently leavening modern civilization. A whole new way of thinking was needed, and it could be reached only if contemporary reflection abandoned its piecemeal emphasis on particular problems and undertook a more comprehensive inquiry into the whole within which it found itself. Philosophy must return to its primordial role of an inquiry into being. It was this realization, and the willingness to expend all of his concentration on it, that turned Heidegger into the preeminent philosophical voice of our time. His has been from first to last the path of being. This is why he did not want the analyses of *Being and Time* to be confused with philosophical anthropology, however rich their contributions to that discipline might be. The term he preferred was "fundamental ontology." In other words the illuminating discussions of anxiety or death were not to be taken at face value or for their intrinsic interest, but primarily as contributions to a far more fundamental inquiry into being as such. Heidegger sought from the start to restore philosophy to its Greek beginning as an inquiry in its own right, never to be subordinated to anything else.

Later he would drop even the term "ontology," since the science of the being of entities is itself derived from the understanding of being as such. But that would represent a deepening rather than a departure from the ontology of Dasein with which he began. Initially he conceived of "the ontological analysis of Dasein as laying bare the horizon for an interpretation of the meaning of being in general" (§ 5); eventually he would conclude that it is being that provides the horizon for an understanding of Dasein. In either case it is being at which he aims.

Heidegger's gaze is only secondarily on the human world as he fixes his attention on the source of illumination he discovers within and beyond it. He has leapt out of the mundane realm of problems to find the horizon within which they become worthy of contemplation. Something of the excitement of that enlargement is still evident in the remarks about the method of phenomenology he is now able to grasp in its more primordial significance. The dedication of *Being and Time* to Husserl reflects Heidegger's acknowledgment that it was Husserl who made the work possible through his rigorous clarification of phenomenological analysis. It would no longer be possible for anyone to be perplexed by the Kantian dichotomy between noumenon and phenomenon. Husserl had definitively disposed of the problem by showing that the phenomenon is always an appearance of something, which it shows and conceals at the same time. "Appearing is an *announcing*-itself through something that shows itself" (§ 7A). Heidegger, however, was the one who grasped the ontological significance of the achievement, for he saw that it was now possible to contemplate being in a far more fundamental way than the juxtaposition of appearance and reality had permitted. There is no being behind appearance because appearance is itself a mode of being. "Phenomenology is our way of access to what is to be the theme of ontology, and it is our way of giving it demonstrative precision. *Only as phenomenology, is ontology possible*" (§ 7C).

The displacement of epistemology with metaphysics, a transition under way since Kant, has now been completed. There is no longer any possibility of grounding metaphysics in epistemology, since any account of knowledge must itself presuppose an account of the being that knows. Phenomenological reflection is no longer a contribution to epistemology, an ambiguity that persisted in Husserl, but is already a metaphysical exploration. Heidegger still held onto the notion that he might be able to give an account of the being that knows, of Dasein, and thereby arrive again at being, but he later concluded that this was not possible. The capacity of Dasein to provide an avenue on being arises only because being is what opens up Dasein. Luminosity does not flow from existence but flows into it from the being it can never contain. This is the turn Heidegger makes from the truth of being to the being of truth in the period after *Being and Time*, as he follows out the guiding inspiration of the work more profoundly. The result would entail not a rejection but a revision of what he had written there. If we characterize *Being and Time* as a study of the self-unfolding of human existence, the later work would disclose why it must assume this form. There can be no nature of man, not only because it is his responsibility to become what he is – existence precedes essence – but because he can never contain the being by which he is in being. Heidegger would later see this more clearly, but it was already intuited in his first great work. From the start he was on the trail of being, not of man, because he was convinced that it is being that opens up the deepest access to man rather than the other way around. "The two sources which are relevant for the traditional anthropology – the Greek definition and the clue which theology has provided – indicate that over and above the attempt to determine the essence of 'man' as an entity, the question of his being has remained forgotten, and that this Being is rather conceived as something obvious or 'self-evident' in the sense of the *Being-present-at-hand* of other created Things" (§ 10).

When we adopt the questionableness of being as the starting point, as the opening quotation from the *Sophist* suggests, the entire structure of taken-for-granted knowledge disintegrates. It is with Heidegger that the revolutionary implications of the modern philosophical revolution become apparent. Part One of *Being and Time*, "Preparatory Fundamental Analysis of Dasein," outlines a radical revision of our self-understanding and our relationship to the world in which we find ourselves. This is followed by Part Two, "Dasein and Temporality," in which the implications of the historicality of human existence are elaborated. Despite the surface similarity of this division to the traditional progression from psychology to ethics, it is clear that the character of the inquiry has changed profoundly. Gone are all fixed points of reference, to be replaced by what Heidegger referred to as the "liquefying" of traditional conceptions. Hegel and the idealists had introduced the novelty of a moving philosophical language, in which the terms take their meaning from the particular phase they have reached, but now Heidegger carried it farther by depriving language of any reference apart from the movement of existence it makes possible. The contortions imposed on a language of entities when it is made to subtend the fluidity of existence are a notorious source of complaint against Heidegger, but it must be remembered that they are not pursued simply for their disorienting effects. Dissolution of the crystallizing tendency of language is an inescapable consequence of the prioritization of existence. The achievement of Heidegger was to demonstrate not only that this is the culmination of the modern revolution in philosophy, but that its logic has been embedded in Western philosophy from its inception.

It is not the case, he emphasizes, that there is first man and then he has a relationship to the world. "Taking up relationships toward the world is possible only *because* Dasein, as being-in-the-world, is as it is" (§ 12). We never simply encounter entities within the world as they are in themselves but always within an already constituted world of significance. The brilliance of the phenomenological analyses on which Heidegger embarks is often so mesmerizing that one can readily understand why many readers, and even the author himself, could tend to overlook the primacy of the connection with being; for he makes it clear that our capacity to perceive anything, from equipment to signs, is possible only because we already inhabit a world disposed to such perceptions. The availability of things as ready-to-hand is possible only because of the presence of a world of the ready-to-hand that is not itself ready-to-hand. Right from the beginning Heidegger shows that the category of the useful is dependent on what is not simply useful because it simply is, as the prior that cannot be encapsulated within what it yields. "*The 'wherein' of an act of understanding which assigns or refers itself, is that for which one lets entities be encountered in the kind of being that belongs to involvements; and this 'wherein' is the phenomenon of the world*" (§ 18). In contrast to the Cartesian notion of being as substance, as constant presence, Heidegger is at pains to show that being is precisely what is not present or at least not in the mode of things. The possibility of encountering things is that we are not simply things ourselves. Even the most embracing container of space is not to be found in externality but in relation to our capacity to "de-sever" space. Like the mystery of time that will occupy Heidegger more extensively, space is possible only for beings who do not simply live in space because they constitute it.[24] "*Space is not in the subject, nor is the world in space. Space is rather 'in' the world in so far as space has been disclosed by the being-in-the-world which is constitutive for Dasein*" (§ 24).

In this way Heidegger begins to unlock the potential contained in the revolutionary shift from a philosophy of essence to one of existence. Without the obstacle of hypostatized entities, we can more readily glimpse, without contemplating, the movement by which we are. The original thrust of the German idealists has once again been resumed. But there is also something different about the phase represented by Heidegger. It is not only that he displayed little interest in or inclination toward the political world, but that he never thought that his meditation should eventually generate a philosophy of right. Despite the heroic effort he undertook

---

[24] "Churches and graves, for instance, are laid out according to the rising and the setting of the sun – the regions of life and death, which are determinative for Dasein itself with regard to its ownmost possibilities of Being in the world." *Being and Time*, § 22.

to rescue the subject from its isolation in a world of objects, the result never seems to return us to the primordiality of a social whole. Even when the challenge of historical destiny is later taken up, the strangely unreal quality of the discussion arises to a large extent from the individualistic nature of the perspective. All is weighed in light of the impact on the self, which seems to exist within a characteristically lonely crowd. It is almost as if Heidegger, having decided that "*the substance of man is existence*" (§ 43c), cannot risk the suggestion that there may be a preexisting substantiality within the social realm. Meaning that emerges from the unfolding of Dasein cannot also be found before Dasein provides the clearing for it. Perhaps Heidegger never fully escaped the subjectivity of the existentialists.

What makes the situation complicated is that, to the extent that our inquiry is philosophical, we are not simply concerned with rendering a judgment about a particular thinker. We must also consider whether his defects are fatal or permit a remedy through the further extension of his thought. Could it be that the concern with authenticity that seizes hold of him as soon as he considers "being-with," the world of the "they," could be enlarged to include the recognition that Dasein cannot meet the demand alone? It may well be that Heidegger's emphasis on what is "ownmost," the primordial behind which we cannot go, tilts his inquiry toward the individualist perspective. After all, we have no access to the movement of existence except through our individual existence. Dasein is irreducibly personal. It is no wonder, then, that the public is the realm of the inauthentic, while the solitary is the only refuge of the authentic. But it is not just the case that Dasein discovers itself through the "clearing away of concealments and obscurities" (§ 27). Heidegger's own effort comes to us through the medium of social communication; by publication it becomes a part of the public realm. To the extent that it is not simply coopted but remains a witness to authenticity, it is a power with public status, thereby showing that the public is not simply the realm of the inauthentic. Moreover, we might assume that Heidegger's own journey of authenticity is not simply self-inspired but instead the fruit of the resonances that come toward him. Clearly he intended to give voice to a call that would rejuvenate a national destiny, but he seems never to have included such a practice within his account. If he did, he would not have regarded national destiny in such an external fashion, as if it were something whose irruption could occur all at once without precedence or consequence.

With Heidegger we have reached the point at which the modern philosophical revolution has progressed so far that it is in danger of undermining itself. It has so firmly established that there is nothing outside the movement of existence that it is inclined to identify its own emergent luminosity with existence itself. This is not just a matter of political inexperience confusing authentic man with inauthentic society, but a far more deep-seated blindness Heidegger was never able to overcome. Confessing a political mistake causes no more than ordinary embarrassment, but to admit to philosophical disorientation would entail a far more extensive adjustment. It would require a fundamental rethinking of the modern philosophical revolution. The shift toward existence may have opened up unrivaled access to the constitution of our being, but it provided no illumination of the empirical connections within which we live. A single-minded focus on being comes at the price of overlooking the knowledge of beings. The political blindness of a man like Heidegger can indeed hardly be explained by ordinary ignorance. To understand it we must be prepared to acknowledge a philosophical scotosis that hindered the normal course of acquaintance with the world. The eschatological style, which he never completely abandoned, arose directly from the eschatological character of his existential analysis. Heidegger's genius was in compelling us to see that our existence is a movement from what is never fully present, because what makes present defies the possibility of presence, but his mistake was to extrapolate that structure to the movement of history as a whole. Having found the eschatological setting for existence, he could only conclude that this is all there is. No doubt other motives of self-aggrandizement were also at work, but they are of little interest compared with the fatality embedded in the philosophical revolution he was engaged in advancing. It is because of the latter that Heidegger has become the great teacher of the past century forcing those who would revise him to find their way through him.

The question he compels us to ask is whether the distortions he sponsored are the result of carrying his project too far or not far enough. At first glance it may appear that it was his single-mindedness that constituted his fatal flaw, and we can readily understand how such an obsessive focus can block out competing views of the reality within which we find ourselves. But if the revolution he sought to promote was genuine, if, that is, he was a philosopher, we are more likely to find its corrective in a greater fidelity to its unfolding. It may be paradoxical to demand of those who would emulate a thinker who spoke constantly of opening and clearing to go further in the same task, but it is a divergence that really only masks a deeper agreement. The pattern is well illustrated by the thinkers who come after him. As his most formidable critics they are his most faithful disciples; we might even say they are such out of the necessity under which he has placed them.[25] This is why it is so important to acquire well the insights he made available. It is through the full appropriation of his philosophy that we obtain the most reliable means of correcting the distortions to which he himself succumbed. In many ways the value of *Being and Time* is still that it provides us with the most unguarded reflections of Heidegger's philosophical odyssey, and thereby alerts us to the points at which it requires a deepening that even the later works do not always provide. For all of its powerful originality, we do well to remind ourselves of the extent to which it falls short of its own aspiration. The liquefying of concepts, the new way of philosophizing through existence it forces upon us, causes us to overlook what the text itself seems often to have forgotten – that is, that the movement of existence is not all of existence, that the eschatological "not yet" does not mean not yet at all. Heidegger himself turned from existence to the path of being, and as we follow him, we will continue to ask the question of whether he went far enough.

Being Is Prior to Knowing

The pattern of Heidegger's self-correction is well illustrated as he launches into his exploration of the way that Dasein can get lost in the "they." Being-in-the world is at the same time a being-with others from whom one does not at first distinguish oneself. What is striking about the analysis is not the warning about the dictatorship of the "they," the point at which "everyone is an other, and no one is himself" (§ 27), but the extent to which Heidegger insists that the loss of self can never be total. Only that which can never be lost can in any sense be "lost," for it loses that which it never really possessed. The "they" can be a force over against the individual only because the individual can never finally

---

[25] This will become evident in the following chapters on Levinas and Derrida, but it is also noticeable among commentators who have been struck by Heidegger's "way" of thinking. See David Wood, *Thinking After Heidegger* (Cambridge: Polity, 2002); Reiner Schürmann, *Heidegger on Being and Acting: From Principles to Anarchy*, trans. Christine-Marie Gros (Bloomington. Indiana University Press, 1987); Miguel de Beistegui, *Thinking with Heidegger: Displacements* (Bloomington: Indiana University Press, 2003); and Gail Stenstad, *Transformations: Thinking After Heidegger* (Madison: University of Wisconsin Press, 2006).

be overcome by it. For this reason the question of how the self can be connected with others is never problematic, since it is already so related before the question even arises. The strength of the existential analysis is that it allows us to surmount problems that have always appeared to be either insuperable or redolent of an infinite regress. "'Empathy' does not first constitute being-with; only on the basis of being-with does 'empathy' become possible: it gets its motivation from the unsociability of the dominant modes of being-with" (§ 26). In other words, what looks like the beginning of a long reflection on the authenticity of the self, which necessarily must pull against the inauthenticity of the "they," is anchored in a "with-world" (*Mitwelt*) that is prior to the concern of Dasein about itself. Dasein may come to awareness of its authentic self through the effort of "clearing away," but it is a clearing that can never finally over-leap the wholeness from which it begins. Clearing is made possible only by what cannot be cleared. At this point, however, the analysis can only point toward such ultimate implications, as it sets out on the long path of "authenticity" for which *Being and Time* became famous.

For now Heidegger is concerned with the clearing as such, the "being-in as such," in which the capacity for understanding is at stake. Dasein has the possibility of understanding because it can be in the world without being in it. This is also what distinguishes understanding from its inau-thentic double of "idle talk," the mere subscription to what everyone thinks that masks the absence of understanding for oneself. Understand-ing is precisely what calls for us to be in the world without losing ourselves within it. The reason why the question of authenticity arises for Heideg-ger here is that his analysis is an account not of understanding as such but of the being that it is. An existential epistemology directs our attention toward what knowledge is rather than what it does, and thus brings us that much closer to a knowledge of knowledge. Initially it is the possibility of an attunement to a state of affairs, a projection of possibility as such, but always in such a way as to avoid absorption within it. "In every case interpretation is grounded in *something we see in advance* – in a *fore-sight*" (§ 32). Heidegger emphasizes the primordiality of care (*Fürsorge*) as what structures our understanding of things, so that they are never encoun-tered in their nakedness but always in relation to the disclosure we bring to them. The Kantian categories of the understanding have reached their culmination in Heidegger's location of their existential source.[26]

---

[26] The analytic reading of Heidegger, not surprisingly, sees him in light of the Kantian tran-scendental perspective. See Mark Okrent, *Heidegger's Pragmatism: Understanding, Being,*

We might say that it is because Dasein carries the question of its being within itself that it is capable of projecting that question on all others and therefore of understanding them as such, in relation to their being. The primordiality of care that Heidegger announces at the beginning of this chapter is not just some generic care, but the care about being that is at the core of Dasein. This is the very movement of its existence and what it can bring in advance to all things as disclosure. "An entity for which, as being-in-the-world, its being is itself an issue, has, ontologically, a circular structure" (§ 32).[27]

Dasein can disclose being because it carries the question of being within it as its deepest care. For that which unfolds its own existence, thinking and being are the same. Summarizing the most famous observations of Parmenides and Aristotle, Heidegger makes clear the existential basis for all science. "Being is that which shows itself in the pure perception which belongs to beholding, and only by such seeing does being get discovered. Primordial and genuine truth lies in pure beholding" (§ 36).

---

and the Critique of Metaphysics (Ithaca, NY: Cornell University Press, 1988), and William D. Blattner, *Heidegger's Temporal Idealism* (Cambridge: Cambridge University Press, 1999). It is perhaps inevitable that Heidegger would sooner or later be assimilated to the antimetaphysical example of Wittgenstein or Quine, but one can hardly avoid the impression that he does not sit quite so comfortably in that estimable company. For all of the analytic rigor with which his "arguments" can be presented, there is the small matter of Heidegger's own realization that the arguments did not simply function in a wholly separate realm. Thought is itself an event within being. This is why it can never be fully penetrated, even by itself. For the thinker on the path of the primordial, the transcendental can hardly suffice. But just as one can do an analytic reading of Heidegger, so it is possible to do a Heideggerian reading of analysis. So what looks like a conception of philosophy that "is concerned to discover necessary features and concomitants of systems that are capable of generating semantic content" (Okrent, *Heidegger's Pragmatism*, 296) is itself an existential openness to being without metaphysics. Heidegger reveals more clearly than the analysts how it is possible to be both antimetaphysical and more deeply metaphysical at the same time. A key reason is that he remains concerned with existence, not simply with meaning or, more correctly, with meaning that overlooks its own existential horizon. For a powerful exposition of the issues see Cristina Lafont, *Heidegger, Language, and World-Disclosure*, trans. Graham Harman (Cambridge: Cambridge University Press, 2000). When Heidegger makes truth dependent on meaning, Lafont argues, he has abandoned the transcendental standpoint and thereby rendered his own statements about truth and meaning questionable. The only way of avoiding either relativism or dogmatism is to assimilate the theory of meaning to a "fallibilist" viewpoint. The obvious objection is that this, too, is a version of transcendentalism. But neither Heidegger nor Lafont gives much consideration to such an objection, because the "fallibilist" moniker is merely a way of pointing toward the unencompassibility within which all theorizing takes place. No theory of meaning can include its own existential horizon, nor, Heidegger understood, can it really say anything about itself.

[27] "Mathematics is not more rigorous than historiology, but only narrower, because the existential foundations relevant for it lie within a narrower range." *Being and Time*, § 32.

Such pure beholding is far from the everyday reception that occurs without thinking, without the struggle toward truth that recognizes what it sees as the being toward which its own existence bends. Science and understanding are possible only because Dasein is always already on the way toward it; this is what it means to know. Just as in discourse it is not the saying but the hearing that grounds the possibility, Heidegger emphasizes, in introducing an auditory metaphor to convey the existential movement that generates understanding. "Listening to . . . is Dasein's existential way of being-open as being-with for others. Indeed, hearing constitutes the most primary and authentic way in which Dasein is open for its ownmost potentiality-for-being – as in hearing the voice of the friends whom every Dasein carries with it" (§ 34). The advantage of this metaphor over seeing is that it is less instantaneous and therefore better conveys the sense of a movement within time. Heidegger even employs the more antiquated variants of "hearkening" (*Horchen*) to get across the primordiality of the event as an understanding that is already there before we understand. Discourse, composed of speaking and silence, is grounded in hearing. "Only he who already understands can listen (*zuhören*)" (§ 34).

For Heidegger understanding is itself a calling from which, as a consequence, it is possible to have a falling away. Any talk of a fall in human nature cannot explain the possibility that it must presuppose. Temptation and the struggle against fallenness are primordial because they are the tension that constitutes existence. The truth of being is accessible to Dasein because it is itself the struggle for the truth of being. The long modern preoccupation with epistemology is now concluded in Heidegger's recognition that it has been largely an exercise in futility. How can knowledge of the world be grounded in the being of a subject that has not itself been grounded (§ 43a)? Heidegger carries the inquiry beyond the mutuality of the subject–object relationship in which phenomenology had left it, to show that it is only by rising to a meditation on being that the question of truth can be addressed. Far from providing a resolution, the epistemological question is itself an expression of the anxiety that arises from Dasein's precarious hold on being.[28] Anxiety in

---

[28] "To *have faith* in the reality of the 'external world,' whether rightly or wrongly; to "*prove*" this reality for it, whether adequately or inadequately; to *presuppose* it, whether explicitly or not – attempts such as these which have not mastered their own basis with full transparency, presuppose a subject which is proximally *worldless* or unsure of its world, and which must at bottom, first assure itself of a world. Thus from the very beginning, being-in-a-world is disposed to 'take things' in some way, to suppose, to be certain, to have faith – a way of behaving which itself is always a founded mode of being-in-the-world." Ibid., § 43a.

this ontological sense now becomes the motif for the analysis of Dasein, the "thrown projection" that carries the possibility of projecting understanding because it perpetually struggles against the closure of its own thrownness. Viewed in this light the modern epistemological digression seems more like an attempt to escape the call of existence that is Dasein. By contrast, Heidegger insists on fidelity to the movement of existence by which Dasein in remaining true to itself becomes the point at which truth can be uncovered. Being is prior to knowing because knowing is itself a mode of being.

The superiority of existential ontology to the previous epistemological muddle is well demonstrated in the concluding section of Division One. "Asserting is a way of Being towards the Thing itself that is" (§ 44a). When we seek to confirm our assertions through perception, we do not depart from this primacy of being by, for example, seeking to understand it in some terms other than being. "Representations do not get compared, either among themselves or in *relation* to the real thing" (§ 44a). Knowing cannot be understood in terms of a congruence between the psychical and the physical, not only because that is not what we mean by knowing but also because the psychical and the physical must themselves be known in terms of their being. We always arrive back at the irreducibility of being as that at which we must arrive. "What is to be demonstrated is solely the being-uncovered of the entity itself – *that entity* in the 'how' of its uncoveredness. This uncoveredness is confirmed when that which is put forward in the assertion (namely the entity itself) shows itself *as that very same thing.* The confirmation is accomplished on the basis of the entity's showing itself" (§ 44a). This, of course, does not give us what the epistemological pursuit always seemed to promise, even if it never delivered, namely, a foolproof method of verification. But Heidegger has alerted us to the chimerical character of such a quest that bespeaks nothing so much as the anxiety in the face of being it seeks to suppress. Neither a method nor a technique of confirmation is available because we cannot step outside the vantage point of truth that constitutes the being of knowledge. All we can do is accept the uncertainty of the quest for knowledge that makes it possible, while recognizing that the quest in uncertainty is not incidental but constitutive of our existence. "To presuppose 'truth' means to understand it as something for the sake of which Dasein *is*" (§ 44c). The end of Division One in the understanding of truth as uncoveredness, *al-etheia,* cannot avoid the inquiry into the being that does the uncovering which is conducted in Division Two.

Ecstatic Temporality: Dasein Chooses Its Own Hero

Now the reason for the difficulty in understanding the possibility of knowledge becomes apparent. As that which does the uncovering, Dasein can never get at the uncovering as such, but always understands it in terms of what is uncovered. But this is to misunderstand the nature of uncovering, which is the same as the misunderstanding of Dasein itself. This is what Heidegger refers to as the "falling" of Dasein, which, since it can never actually fall, now finds itself as the struggle to maintain the truth of its existence. The possibility of truth arises from that being whose existence is constituted by the truth of its existence. Knowledge means, therefore, not the awareness of the "ready-to-hand," but the inaccessible movement by which the ready-to-hand becomes "ready-to-hand." It is the uncovering by which uncoveredness is effected, which is possible only for a being whose own existence is the process of self-uncovering. It is possible for us to know things in their existence because we are ourselves the very process of existence. Consciousness of reality is thus not only a way of being-in-the-world; it is through our being-in-the-world that we become conscious of reality. "Entities with Dasein's kind of being cannot be conceived in terms of reality and substantiality; we have expressed this by the thesis that *the substance of man is existence*" (§ 43c). With this remark Heidegger has reached the promised land held out by German idealism. The unity of theoretical and practical reason occurs not as a theoretical synthesis but as the pre-existential unity whose unfolding constitutes existence.[29] Neither in contemplating nor in acting can we step outside of the existential preconditions, but we must recognize that it is who we are that is implicated in each case. What varies is the degree.

Once Dasein is understood as Dasein, as existence, there can be no way of getting at what it is as an essence or an entity. Existence is that which is never present or is present only as it exists. The only access we have to Dasein as a whole is through the moments in which existence as a whole is glimpsed from within its movement. No vantage point is superior to that in which Dasein puts its own existence as a whole into question. The analysis, Heidegger makes clear, has not yet reached that primordial perspective by thinking of care as the pervasive structure, but

---

[29] With a forward trajectory rather than one that looks back to German idealism, William McNeill explores this point well in *The Time of Life: Heidegger and Ēthos* (Albany: State University of New York Press, 2006); see especially ch. 2, "Care for the Self: Originary Ethics in Heidegger and Foucault."

must now extend to "the being of Dasein in its possibilities of *authenticity* and *totality*" (§ 45). The event, or rather nonevent, that brings the being of Dasein as a whole into focus is death. Death is, of course, the end of all existence, not just of Dasein, but it does play a particular role in Dasein, for it is only there that death reaches into consciousness. In a certain sense, Heidegger points out, only man can die, for only man can be aware of death as the end of his existence. As the existence that has an end, Dasein is constituted by the question of its meaning as a whole. "Thus the whole existing Dasein allows itself to be brought into our existential fore-having" (§ 45). This in turn raises the further question of whether Dasein can indeed exist authentically within this question of its authenticity. He finds confirmation for this possibility in the existence of conscience, or more correctly in the realization that Dasein "*wants to have a conscience.*" The primordial being of Dasein is thus a mode of care that becomes visible within temporality. "Within the horizon of time the projection of a meaning of being in general can be accomplished" (§ 45).

With the account of being-toward-death, Heidegger has reached the horizon of temporality that constitutes existence. Death is not itself an event within time but the end of temporality for us. The *memento mori*, a Christian tradition to which Heidegger deliberately alludes, is the ultimate perspective on existence. Any discussion of the conventional topic of a life after death must find its reference in this full existential meaning of death as precisely what frees us from lostness in particularities (§ 53). That enlargement of horizon opened by death is initially manifest in the anxiety that is a fear not of death, or of anything particular, but of the loss of "that potentiality-for-being which is one's ownmost" (§ 50). Death brings to light the problem of authenticity as the encompassing question of our existence, specifically as the voice of conscience. It is what draws us back from the inauthenticity of the "they" to hearken to the only call that can reach us authentically. "The call is from afar unto afar. It reaches him who wants to be brought back" (§ 55). The analysis of conscience that follows is among the most powerful of the book, an indication of its centrality within his thought. "*Conscience discourses solely and constantly in the mode of keeping silent*" (§ 56). In conscience Dasein calls itself, yet the call also comes from beyond the self as Dasein in its "uncanniness." It is subjective and objective at the same time. "The fact that the call is not something which is explicitly performed *by me*, but that rather 'it' does the calling, does not justify seeking the caller in some entity with a character other than that of Dasein" (§ 57). The thoroughly existential character of this analysis is extended to the primordiality of guilt, not as a fixed state, but as the movement against which conscience continually pulls. Authenticity is ever the drawing away from inauthenticity. Guilt is the recognition that Dasein never has control over its own basis of being but is constituted by the struggle to achieve it. "Dasein is not itself the basis of its being, inasmuch as this basis first arises from its own projection; rather, as being-its-self, it is the *being* of its basis" (§ 58).

It is because Dasein never achieves what it is but is always on the way to it, through the exercise of its freedom, that "*Dasein as such is guilty*" (§ 58). This primordiality of guilt that Heidegger develops must be understood in a fully existential sense as a condition that can never be known because we already live within it. He particularly rejects the notion that it is a moral guilt, which would imply that we have already committed some culpable action, whereas Heidegger means that guilt defines the very possibility of action. Authenticity or inauthenticity, the freedom to be or to fail to be true to ourselves, is possible only for a being that already finds itself within such a tension before it even begins. "The primordial 'being-guilty' cannot be defined by morality, since morality already presupposes it for itself" (§ 58). But what, we might ask, of the morality of morality? Is this not what Heidegger himself is sketching in his account of authenticity as more primordial? His use of moral language to account for the existential movement suggests that the latter is irreducibly moral. It is surely no accident that the more notorious aspects of *Being and Time* begin to raise their head from this point on in the text when authenticity is discussed as if it were a pre-moral decision. Where previously the call of conscience had been deftly analyzed in ways that echoed our moral experience, now we seem to be severing those connections in favor of a primordial freedom that must be exercised outside the bounds of any guidance. One can understand Heidegger's reluctance to admit any "read-to-hand" moral norms, but what about the normative structure disclosed in the exercise of freedom itself? It is almost as if the excitement of the discovery of existential primordiality has caused Heidegger to forget that the discovery is itself an existentiell, not a leap outside of existence. Has Heidegger, in other words, betrayed his own deepest intuition? And if he has, what does this imply about the vulnerability of the existential shift of modern philosophy that he virtually completes?

The distorted greatness of Heidegger's thought becomes increasingly evident as he leads Dasein down the path to its disclosure (*Erschlossenheit*) in resolution (*Entschlossenheit*) (§ 60). Since conscience cannot precede its call to action, resolution becomes the pivotal moment. "As resolute, Dasein is already *taking action*" (§ 60). In the account that follows we begin to see one of the great dangers of the existential revolution whose unsurpassability by us suggests its unsurpassability as such. This is how a thinker of the stature of Heidegger could find himself asserting that action, both in theory and in practice, has nothing to do with morality. Simply because good and evil are not disclosed before we begin does not mean that they are not disclosed as we begin. "Dasein's authentic existence can no longer be *outstripped* (*überhölt*) by anything" (§ 62). By following "the *unwavering discipline* of the existential way of putting the question" (§ 65), Heidegger arrives at maximum clarification when the resolution is held fast in the moment of vision. "It means the resolute rapture with which Dasein is carried away to whatever possibilities and circumstances are encountered in the situation as possible objects of concern, but a rapture which is held in resoluteness. The moment of vision is a phenomenon which *in principle* can *not* be clarified in terms of the '*now*'" (§ 68a). One is inclined to see in this understanding of "ecstatic temporality" the fatal step of *Being and Time* that, despite itself, seems to jump outside of time and existence. The suspicion is confirmed by the transition from the individual to the collective ecstasies in the penultimate chapter, "Temporality and Historicality." Dasein does not live simply in tensions with the inauthentic "they," but must at some point throw in its lot with the destiny of its own generation in historical existence. It is when it is broadened out to a political movement that the shocking character of ecstatic resolution becomes apparent.

Indifferent to the past or the future, the collective Dasein seems concerned only with the purity of its own moment of decision as the guarantee of its authenticity. While there is much to admire in Heidegger's insistence that every generation bears responsibility for itself, there is also something appalling in the rejection of responsibility it bears toward any others. Existence as the possibility of history has eclipsed existence in history. What counts is simply that each generation take up the call to which destiny has beckoned it, without considering the worthiness of the destiny to which it has been called. By separating itself from history, Dasein has submitted itself more completely to it. This is why Heidegger must reject any "connectedness" in history, for having emphasized the priority of existence, he cannot contemplate the possibility of a connection within history that is existential. In the most infamous remark of the book, he notes "the possibility that Dasein may choose its own hero" (§ 74), almost as the ultimate gesture of disassociation. Temporality and the historicality through which it is collectively realized exist for the sake of Dasein, Heidegger emphasizes in the final chapter, in which he shows that he has merely made Aristotle's definition of time existential. The problem is that, once human existence has absorbed the entire focus of attention, the tendency to forget that it is not the whole of existence becomes almost irresistible. One suspects that Heidegger too sensed, if he did not always perceive, the danger and that this accounts for the famous "turn" away from the existentialism of *Being and Time*. At root the problem with existentialism is that it is not existential enough, for the focus on the moment of ecstatic self-resolution all too easily suggests that we are once again contemplating a complete entity. In contrast to the view that history cannot contain man, there is the view that man cannot contain history. We live in history, not because we are a part of it, but because it is a part of us.

Any fair rendering would have to concede that Dasein can never really understand itself, not even in the flash of resolution in which it projects its own thrownness. The best it can do is realize the moral truth of action, which, because it can never realize the whole of moral truth, must always remain the concrete truth of action. Dasein, Heidegger gradually came to realize in the years after *Being and Time*, cannot provide the opening toward being, because Dasein can open only within being. In other words the path he began to walk pointed away from the self-creation of Dasein of the nihilistic apocalypse toward which Heidegger felt drawn, but it is not clear that he ever managed to cut the link with its deepest roots in his own development. Fascination with destruction, we recall, entered his soul in the waning years of the First World War. The impact of such formative events lingers long after their philosophical context has shifted considerably. In Heidegger's case not even the confrontation with the full consequences of Nazism proved sufficient to dislodge it. The turn on which he now embarked never progressed to the point that it would require an overturning of his first convictions. It results in the curious case of the philosopher who is better than the man, although this does not mean that they are really divided. From our perspective the interest is, of course, far more in the philosophy than in the man. The limiting danger of the existential revolution in modern philosophy having been revealed, the significance of Heidegger now centers on the extent to which he pointed out the road of its self-correction. Without going through repentance, his philosophical drive was sufficient in itself to mark the way of remediation.

The Turn from Dasein to Being

The self-disclosure of Dasein now occurs not through its self-resolution but through the opening toward being in which it finds itself. Talk of authentic self-creation was in danger of becoming mere talk, forgetting that there is no authenticity except in living it out. Heidegger realized that the greatest danger of existentialism was that it could all too readily revert to the psychologism it had sought to avoid. He now saw that his meditation in *Being and Time* had left itself open to that misinterpretation, and he set out to rigorously discard every vestige of the psychological in his thinking. This is what gives his thought the quality of the primordial. He sought not to talk about thinking but to get behind it through the mode of living within it. Despite this clarity about the direction to be followed, however, it is difficult to conclude that Heidegger actually followed out his own indication. Even while recognizing that Dasein exists within the luminosity of being, and not the other way around, he still clung to the priority of that recognition itself. Preferring again to talk about the danger of talking, he nevertheless fell into the same pattern of deferral. More than once the endlessly incipient character of his thought has been noted. Heidegger's predilection for the metaphor of paths and pathways carried its own mode of entrapment, for it suggested that the beginning could substitute for the undertaking. Admittedly this is a difficult issue to unravel in his work because much of his insistence on being ever a beginner can be read as an even greater insistence on the impossibility of ever getting back before there is a before. Yet the very relentlessness of that insistence all too readily yields to the relentlessness of the insistence. Talk about being does not advance us beyond talk about authenticity if it is not more than talk. But worst of all is the great danger that such a primordial deepening can suggest a transcendence of existence. Then we are left not only without the illumination of being but without the awareness of our lack. For Heidegger the turn away from the self-enclosure of existence in *Being and Time* to the opening of existence toward being aggravates, rather than alleviates, the danger with which he struggles. Is the quest itself greater than that of which it is in quest? Is the search more primordial than the primordial?

The course that Heidegger follows is not so much a revision of the earlier work as a clarification of it. This is what has made his infamous

Kehre, or "turn," so difficult for commentators to pin down.[30] It clearly represents a break with the phenomenological analyses of *Being and Time* but always in the direction of going more deeply into their metaphysical significance. Heidegger's turn is a turning within as he tracks the metaphysics of *The Fundamental Concepts of Metaphysics* (1929–30). The previous confidence that metaphysics would be disclosed once we had reached an understanding of man has now evaporated. "These detours (*Umwege*) are really false trails (*Holzwege*), paths which suddenly stop, which lead up a blind alley" (§ 3). Now he sees that the fundamental concepts must include the question and avoid the illusion of the critical stance that fails to put the "I" into question. If philosophy is not to be the remnant left when all of the Aristotelian sciences have found their place, the origin of the coinage "meta-physics," then it must locate itself in relation to the awakening or fundamental attunement out of which it arises. One such mood is boredom, the disclosure of our nonabsorption in the manifold of interests. The philosophy of culture that categorizes the "symbolic forms" of meaning exemplifies the boredom with that which is now outside of us (§ 18c).

"Things can leave us empty only along with that being held in limbo that proceeds from time" (§ 23d). The awakening that is the moment of vision, of rupture, that announces philosophy as existence is very much at risk. Heidegger wonders about its possibility "when an event like the Great War can to all extents and purposes pass us by without leaving a trace" (§ 39). The priority of philosophy over life is suggested by his ominous wish "for someone capable of instilling terror into our Dasein again." But for now Heidegger contents himself with the far less horrifying role of suggesting the metaphysical setting of modern science. By comparing animal and human existence, he shows that the indispensable framework of a world is precisely what is lacking in the former as the condition of knowing. In an extraordinarily rich analysis, Heidegger shows that the teleological perspective that we apply to animals cannot be the perspective of the animals themselves, for they do not "adapt" to their environment but are rather captured by it. Kant's insight into the regulative role of teleology is here recognized in its metaphysical primordiality. We have access to the being of things only because we exist within the transparence of being. It is possible for us to be bored only

---

[30] A good survey of the diversity of avenues into this phase of Heidegger's odyssey is to be found in the contributions in James Risser, ed., *Heidegger Toward the Turn: Essays on the Work of the 1930s* (Albany: State University of New York Press, 1999).

because we cannot be captivated by things. Instead we live within the expectation of awakening by which our openness to being is disclosed in an ecstatic moment of resolution that Heidegger identifies as the illumination of vision. Genuine action, as opposed to the reactivity of animal existence, occurs when the resolution is made with the whole of our being as an attunement to being. This is why "resolute disclosedness is not some present at hand condition that I possess, but on the contrary is something which possesses me" (§ 70a). The rarity of such moments of *ecstasis* does not in the slightest diminish their significance, for they are the point at which the primordiality of our openness to being bursts forth. Their preciousness is what explains Heidegger's readiness to see in their irruption the whole purpose of existence. Within the modern philosophical revolution, he is the point at which the luminosity of existence is identified with its transformation.

Heidegger's temporary susceptibility to Nazism was possible only because of the fatality of his projection of the philosophical revolution onto the historical reality. Philosophy now emergent as a mode of existence was inseparable from its civilizational impact. Nowhere was this consciousness of historical apocalypse more evident than in the volume of private meditations written in 1936–38 but withheld, on Heidegger's instructions, until the publication of the lecture courses would have sufficiently formed a climate for its comprehension. It was published on Heidegger's centenary under the titles he had designated. Exoterically it was to be known as his *Contributions to Philosophy,* a work that would mark his position in the pantheon. Esoterically, the title *Vom Ereignis,* would best denote the achievement of a new mode of philosophizing out of the movement of being or, be-ing, as an event, appropriation, or "enowning."[31] In other words the work was written with the longer historical view in mind, not as a reflection intended for immediate exposure within his own time. It is a fascinating moment in Heidegger's biography, just after distancing himself from the Nazi Party when history had left him alone to carry its burden. No doubt history had found in him a suitable partner who did not shrink from its interiorization. He could support the task because, while history may have left him, he had never left history. It is

---

[31] It is probably fair to say that the recency of the publication of *Beiträge* has meant that it remains a largely unabsorbed component of the literature on Heidegger. A beginning has, however, been made with Charles E. Scott et al., eds., *Companion to Heidegger's "Contributions of Philosophy"* (Bloomington: Indiana University Press, 2001). A useful monograph is Richard Polt, *The Emergency of Being: On Heidegger's "Contributions to Philosophy"* (Ithaca, NY: Cornell University Press, 2006), whose analysis parallels some of my own.

no accident that these were also the years when Heidegger was absorbed with Nietzsche, the last philosopher to step outside of the academic circle to address the crisis of modern civilization. He resumes the Nietzschean struggle with the death of God, understood no longer as an event of history but as *the* event of history. Within "reservedness Da-*sein* attunes itself to the *stillness* of the passing of the last god" (§ 5). Now the opening that Nietzsche accomplished really does lead beyond nihilism to existence within the openness. Poetry becomes the language of philosophy because it alone has the capacity to return words to their moving source. "More readily than others, the poet veils the truth in image and thus bestows it to our view for keeping" (§ 5). Heidegger was perhaps correct in judging that the time was not yet ripe for the literary-philosophical tour de force that *Beiträge* represents. Who but Heidegger, Hannah Arendt noted, would in 1935 have conceived of the convulsion of National Socialism as merely a chapter within the larger convulsion unleashed by "the encounter between global technology and modern man" (*Introduction to Metaphysics*, § 57)?[32] The fate of humanity turns on the philosophical struggle.

Nowhere does it dawn that philosophy might reach its denouement while history continues unregenerate. Heidegger remains too close to the philosophical character of the problems of history to recognize that there is more to history than its philosophical problems. The enthusiasm is perhaps understandable in light of his attainment in this most creative of decades of the philosophical mastery that had eluded him in *Being and Time*. The titles of all eight chapters that make up *Beiträge*, "Echo," "Playing Forth," "Leap," "Be-ing," and so on, suggest the priority of activity on which philosophy has long set its sights. Philosophy would no longer philosophize about existence but would philosophize out of it. Where previously Dasein could still be regarded as a kind of being, now Dasein can be understood only in relation to be-ing. The last vestige of the anthropological or psychological has been eliminated with the realization that "only the great occurrence, innermost enowning, can save us from being lost in the bustle of mere events and machinations" (§ 23). So far philosophy has risen only to the "guiding question" of the beingness of beings, but even to ask it presupposes a more primordial "grounding question" that exists within be-ing. "A being is. Be-ing (the antique *Seyn*) holds sway" (§ 34). By thinking through the stance that made *Being and Time* possible, Heidegger is on the way to turning the language of beings

---

[32] Arendt, "Eightieth Birthday Speech" in *Letters*, 160.

into the language of be-ing. "All saying has to let the ability to hear arise within it" (§ 36).

Preoccupation with Destiny as the Obstacle to Destiny

More primordial than the moral perspective is the openness that makes the moral perspective possible. By beginning with the question that requires a decision, we already locate ourselves outside of it. *Being and Time* with its emphasis on resolution had left itself open to that "existentialist" misperception; Heidegger now seeks to remain more faithful to the movement of existence itself. But this is not in any sense a withdrawal from action. It is rather a deeper ingress into the very movement by which authenticity is reached, not as a goal of its own, but as it exists in its openness to being. The great danger of autonomous morality has always been the tendency to regard it as a self-contained realm. Now Heidegger is anchoring it more profoundly in the metaphysics that Kant intuited and all of his successors have sought to unfold. "*The truth of be-ing is the be-ing of truth*" (*Contributions to Philosophy*, § 44). Philosophy no longer discourses about existence; it has become transparent as the mode of existence, which is what the historical really is. The astonishing aspect, however, is how rapidly Heidegger moves from that discovery of historical existence to the assumption of a historical impact. Philosophy is for him what constitutes the existence of a people open to its historical existence. One wonders how this can be when the people lack philosophical awareness. Yet Heidegger evinces no hesitation. The danger of lostness in beings and goals has mounted to an extreme from which the apocalypse must burst forth so that "'culture' and 'worldview' become the means for the strategy of struggle for a will that no longer wants a goal" (§ 45). In the absence of a party of the revolution, Heidegger still held onto his faith in its people, even though the shift to "the people" returned him to the language of abstraction. His blindness to the inconsistency can be explained only by the intensity of his conviction concerning what was at stake.

Truth itself is what is being decided (§ 47). Working on this text, which he had already decided to withhold from publication, Heidegger was free to admit to himself the full historical significance of the philosophical revolution he was implementing. For his contemporaries all that was left was the "echo of the essential sway of be-ing in the abandonment of being" (§ 50). Within a regime of machination in which "only the representable *is*" (§ 51), he alone could see that its possibility derives from what is non-representable. By contrast, the masses of humanity lost in their schemes of "gigantism" intended to conceal their state of lostness are no longer even "deemed worthy of finding the shortest way of annihilation" (§ 54). The wasteland Heidegger paints is even more unrelieved than the nihilism diagnosed by Nietzsche because it does not even include the latter's lingering admiration of science. That most vaunted achievement of the modern world is seen by Heidegger as yielding nothing but calculability that bears no relation to knowledge. "What is 'scientifically' knowable is in each case *given in advance* by a 'truth' which is never graspable by science, a truth about the recognized region of beings" (§ 76.3). The situation is no different for the historian whose discipline gains more information about everything except the perspective from which it is viewed, "the present of history in which the historian lives but which he cannot know historically" (§ 76). With Heidegger the critique of objectivist patterns of knowledge unfolding since Kant has reached its limit, and nothing of the achievements of the modern world are left standing. In the sweep of his denunciation it is perhaps not surprising that Heidegger's imagination flowed toward the apocalyptic question of "whether modernity is grasped as an end and an other beginning is inquired into, or whether one sticks obstinately to the perpetuation of a decline that has lasted since Plato, which one can still ultimately manage only by persuading oneself that one's having no inkling is an overcoming of tradition" (§ 69).

Heidegger, it seems, is alone in recognizing that "the *great turning around* is necessary, which is beyond all 'revaluation of all values,' that turning around in which beings are not grounded in terms of human being, but rather human being is grounded in terms of be-ing" (§ 91). He complains that *Being and Time* in its essential meaning has not been understood to the extent that "in their essential sway space and time remain hidden" (§ 98). Readers have focused on the existential encounter with death, but they have failed "to ponder what was thought *ahead* regarding being-toward-death" (§ 161). Heidegger's drive to inwardize the language of philosophy left behind, perhaps, not only his readers but even his own ability to express it. In *Beiträge* he redoubled his efforts at transparency in order to rescue them from the inconclusive condition in which they had been left in *Being and Time*.[33] The grounding question that he

---

[33] "*Being and Time* is therefore not an 'ideal' or a 'program' but rather the self-preparing beginning of the essential swaying of be-ing itself – not what *we* think up but – granted that we are ripe for it – what compels *us* into a thinking that neither offers a doctrine nor brings about a 'moral' action nor secures 'existence'; instead 'only' grounds truth as the free-play of time-space, in which a being can again become 'a being,' i.e. come to preserve be-ing." *Contributions to Philosophy*, § 125.

sought was not to be mistaken for a question about the ground of things but was rather the ground of questioning as such. Before there is any thinking about being, there is the be-ing within which thinking occurs. The shift toward existence has now become complete in the insistence that philosophy has no external reference; all of its fixed concepts have been dissolved within the movement of existence from which they were derived. Heidegger's "contribution" is to have completed the revolution and confronted its full significance. The complaint that the result is sheer dissolution is beside the point, for the previous fixity of concepts has been shown to be false. The real question is whether the more thoroughly existential opening does indeed open us toward be-ing. If there is no longer a morality over against us, is there a morality within which we exist? To the extent that the latter is the case, we must entrust ourselves to its movement, rather than merely talk about it. The tragedy of Heidegger, which found such painful public expression, is here revealed in its most philosophical form. By becoming captivated with the radicalness of his philosophical breakthrough, he failed to remain true to his own imperative.[34] An apocalyptic imagination, his best readers would later discern, attests to a failure to live within the apocalypse.

It is the insistence on a revolutionary outburst that is his most astonishing quality, for this seems to move exactly counter to his own discovery. If the revolution still has to be awaited as a historical event, it cannot have happened within his own philosophical reflection. Moreover, a social and political upheaval is precisely what cannot constitute the inner path of the primordial in thinking. But worst of all is the implication that the shift toward the movement of grounding has not already taken place or that its taking place could be blocked by the failure of some external reality. An e-vent that still awaits an event is perhaps never likely to arise. Equally, it is impossible that the events in which its joining has been missed could be characterized as an absolute nonevent. The gulf that Heidegger paints between be-ing and being seems perpetually in danger of becoming another being. In contrast, we might suggest that the upshot of his thought is the impossibility of a revolutionary breakthrough; the revolution is precisely what cannot happen, since it is the opening to all happening as such. It is perhaps not so surprising that the

---

[34] Richard Rorty has sought to articulate this insight but without grasping the inner logic of the pattern in Heidegger's own trajectory. A deeper appreciation of the fatality is evinced by Mark Okrent. See Rorty, "Heidegger, Contingency, and Pragmatism" and Okrent, "The Truth of Being and the History of Philosophy," both in Dreyfus and Hall, eds., *Heidegger: A Critical Reader*, 209–30, 143–58.

underlying tension within the modern philosophical revolution should reach its apogee here. To the extent that he is the one who has carried forward the turn toward existence, there remains the last obstacle of interpreting the turn itself. Is the existential revolution an event within history or the event that constitutes history? Heidegger is a unique figure in contributing both positively and negatively to the question, and it is not wholly clear which contribution is the more important. What matters is that after him there is no longer any possibility of misplacing the meaning of the existential opening. As the e-vent that makes all events possible, it can never be included within them. The crisis of modernity, of the uprooted masses lost in the machinations of a mad gigantism, cannot overwhelm the primordiality of the primordial, nor can it bring about a definitive elimination of technological forgetfulness.

A philosophical reading of Heidegger must, in other words, be acutely sensitive to the nonphilosophical obiter dicta scattered throughout his writings. Only by rigorously separating them will we be able to grasp his real contribution in making the language of beings transparent for the truth of be-ing to such an extent that it can be used even against his own distortions of it. Dismissive of moralities, as of worldviews (as he had characterized the work of Jaspers), Heidegger fails to see that they never exist as such, but only because they derive from the morality of morality. The disposition of be-ing is always already there even when it is covered by the language of being. Nowhere is the issue more clearly encountered than in his extensive discussion of "the stillness of the watch for the passing of the last god" (§ 133). No doubt much of the reflection here is under the shadow of Nietzsche's *Götzendämmerung* as the defining sense of our abandonment in the midst of beings. In this vein the penultimate chapter is entitled "The Last God." But its meditation moves continually toward the realization that there is no "last god," because lastness is the be-ing of gods. It may indeed be that the Christian God with his stolidly spatiotemporal presence can be imaginatively removed, but then that only leaves his absence as the lingering suspicion that that had all along been the mode of divine presence.[35] Heidegger seems to acknowledge

---

[35] For a sympathetic reading along these lines, including a thoughtful critique of Jean-Luc Marion's ambivalent appropriation of Heidegger, see Laurence Paul Hemming, *Heidegger's Atheism: The Refusal of a Theological Voice* (Notre Dame, IN: University of Notre Dame Press, 2002). Also useful, especially for underlining the significance of the reading of Schelling, is Frank Schalow, *Heidegger and the Quest for the Sacred: From Thought to the Sanctuary of Faith* (Dordrecht: Kluwer, 2001). The mystical affinities have been well explored by John Caputo, *The Mystical Element in Heidegger's Thought* (Athens: Ohio University Press, 1978), and Sonya Sikka, *Forms of Transcendence: Heidegger and Medieval Mystical Theology*

this in his observations about the closeness of god and enowning. "In this remoteness and its undecidability is manifest the sheltering-concealing of that which we, following the enopening, called god" (§ 242). But then the other cry of Zarathustra's heroic resolve is heard, demanding steadfastness in our aloneness. No redemption is possible, only the self-recognition that opens up "immeasurable possibilities for our history" (§ 256). The "Ones to Come," the title of a chapter that fully exemplifies the danger of falling in love with one's own rhetoric, refers to those greeted by Heidegger as "mace bearers of the truth of be-ing" (§ 248). The extraordinary tension between the surface and the depth of his reflections is eventually resolved in favor of the former as he fantasizes about the historical emergence of a people prepared to make its own history.

Rhetorical self-aggrandizement, Heidegger's great fatality, is so much on display in this work hubristically retained for a future that can comprehend it that it tends to mar the indisputable achievements he had reached.[36] This is the work in which the unmastered intimations of *Being and Time* have finally been mastered. A new literary freedom now characterizes his reflections as he roams authoritatively through the range of philosophical problems. The assimilation of "being and thinking" first evoked by the Greeks and resumed in earnest by the idealists can be rendered by the formulation "being and time," which is at last understood. "In the first, 'thinking' means the guiding-thread along which a being is questioned unto its beingness: the representing assertion. In the other, 'time' means the first indication of the essential sway of truth in the sense of the clearing of the free-play – a clearing which is open as removals-unto – in which be-ing is sheltered and, sheltering, first expressly gifts itself in its truth" (§ 259). To the extent that truth is not what we possess but what possesses us, the externality that attaches to its dimensions must be eliminated. The opening that is time is profoundly distorted when it is pressed into service as the discipline of history. By claiming to "have" history, we cease to be historical. Our very historical existence is endangered when it is understood in terms of what Heidegger, in an oblique critique of Nazism, refers to as its nonhistorical preconditions. "Blood and race

---

(Albany: State University of New York Press, 1997). The pseudo-Dionysian theme of naming God with its reverberations in Heidegger, Marion, and Derrida is ably presented by Thomas Carlson, *Indiscretion: Finitude and the Naming of God* (Chicago: University of Chicago Press, 1999).

[36] For a study that tracks the rhetorical excesses of Heidegger and at the same time demonstrates the excessiveness of just such a focus, see Gregory Fried, *Heidegger's Polemos: From Being to Politics* (New Haven, CT: Yale University Press, 2000).

become the carriers of history. *Pre*history now gives history its character of validity" (§ 273). The Greeks, by contrast, were so historical that the horizon of history remained undifferentiated for them. The existential revolution in philosophy has here been carried to the point that all of the obstacles to existential openness have virtually been eliminated. So why does Heidegger insist on dwelling on historical "destiny" and on the irruption of the "people" who will achieve it? The answer can only be that he fails to take his own discovery seriously enough. Why not get on with historical existence without discoursing endlessly about it?

"*Be-ing as enowning is history*" (§ 273). But that recognition is not necessarily history. It may be history, so long as it retains its existential thrust and does not deviate into merely discoursing about it. With Heidegger we might say that the existential revolution confronts its final temptation. By holding onto its contemplative priority, it suggests the possibility of turning the existential shift away from the demand of existence. Can the fruits be retained without undergoing the struggle? Even to raise the question is to point toward a character flaw, which is not of either relevance or interest. What is significant is that the misappropriation is philosophically flawed. Heidegger's fascination with historical transformation, including the projection of his own "Dead Sea Scrolls" into the future, betrays the very notion of history at which he has arrived, for history is not something present but that whose nonpresence is immediately manifest through our action. "History" may indeed be produced, but it is so by not being what makes historical existence possible. The central insight of the existential revolution, that it is impossible to contemplate what does the contemplating, that language is forever removed from its source, is in danger of being lost in Heidegger's reversion to rhetorical reification. Historical destiny is impossible because history is precisely our evanescence from destiny. Even the discovery of our openness toward be-ing does not escape the fate of that movement itself. It is not a statement that can comprehend the condition of its own emergence. Our destiny is that we have no destiny, because we exist historically. Historical destiny is, in this sense, a contradiction in terms. Dasein can enown be-ing because there is no point at which it can be captured by being.

The Truth of Being Is the Be-ing of Truth

Heidegger's tendency to be enthralled by the primordiality of the truth about truth does not in any way detract from the discovery itself. Its self-betrayal does not mitigate the existential revolution. He had given the

existential shift of modern philosophy an incontrovertible direction
and attempted to express it in a series of writings on the new conception of truth. Their brevity and originality combined to obscure their
reception among his contemporaries, who had already fixed him as an
"existentialist" from his *Being and Time* phase. One is inclined to agree
with his own judgment that it would be only after the publication of the
lecture courses on the history of philosophy that his culminating position
would become clear. Now that that has happened, we can more clearly
decipher the often enigmatic formulations he provided and recognize
that their significance is quite separate from the historical adumbrations
he often attached to them. This is particularly the case with the *Introduction to Metaphysics,* which he delivered at the University of Freiburg in
the summer of 1935 shortly after distancing himself from the party. The
text is replete with contemporaneous references, but it endures as an
introduction to the metaphysics that must now be beyond metaphysics.
Of particular note is that the longest section, comprising almost half the
book, is devoted to a meditation on the meaning of *to gar auto noein
estin te kai einai,* often translated as "thinking and being are the same"
(Chapter 4.C, "Being and Thinking"). Heidegger, however, opens it up
as the defining statement of Western metaphysics now to be recovered
in a more originary fashion than its conventional distortions. The separation of being and appearance in Plato began the privileging of being
as presence, *ousia,* over being as coming-to-presence, *parousia.* But there
would be no presence of being without the coming to presence of be-ing,
which is in turn accessible only to that which is in the mode of be-ing, as
thinking. The meaning of the famous statement for Heidegger is then
that thinking and being belong together because thinking is the coming
to presence of being. It is only in light of be-ing that thought is possible.
Dasein is not, as could have been mistakenly adopted from *Being and
Time,* the way to being; rather being is the way to Dasein. The great mis-
turn of Western philosophy has at last been reversed by a refusal of the
domination of thinking over being and a retrieval of the dependence of
thinking on being.[37]

Now the question becomes whether this fundamental achievement will
overcome the nihilism of "values" arising from the elevation of idea and

[37] "The essence of being human opens up to us only when understood through this need
compelled by being itself. The being-there of historical man means: to be posited as
the breach into which the preponderant power of being bursts in its appearing, in
order that this beach itself should shatter against being." *Gesamtausgabe,* vol. 40, 171–
72 / *Introduction to Metaphysics,* 163.

ought over being. The excitement of Heidegger is that he holds out such promise but at the same time demonstrates the difficulty of delivering on it. In particular, there is the tendency to overlook the impossibility of thinking leaping ahead of itself to illuminate its opening to be-ing. Thinking is now firmly contained within the movement of be-ing and, unlike before, can claim no light of its own. The luminosity of existence radiates only through its own movement within be-ing. Temptations toward an impatient leaping-ahead remain as strong as ever, especially when combined with inclinations toward sweeping dismissals of the opacities previously in place. In the case of Heidegger there is the exacerbation of the intensity of the breakthrough he has achieved. Truth may no longer be found in propositions, but will there be the perseverance to bear witness to its emergence in life? The fact that Heidegger more often than not trails off into rhetorical vagueness does not in any way diminish the import of his work in generating the question. In many ways it is his recovery of the existential movement of truth as its most originary meaning that is the decisive contribution. Truth is possible only because we already exist within it, for we cannot go back beyond the truth of truth. The be-ing of truth is the truth of being, although we must constantly remind ourselves that the "is" there does not constitute a proposition. It merely depicts the outermost limits of our thinking that cannot be reached by thought because thought is itself subsequent to being. "Truth," Heidegger observes in a later note to his 1930 lecture "On the Essence of Truth," "signifies sheltering that lightens as the basic characteristic of being. The question of the essence of truth finds its answer in the proposition *the essence of truth is the truth of essence*" (*Gesamtuasgabe*, vol. 9 / *Pathmarks*, "Essence of Truth," § 9).

The modern philosophical revolution has reached its denouement when Heidegger no longer speaks about truth but out of it, recognizing that we can never grasp the truth of truth. That by which the grasping occurs always remains ungraspable. We merely stand within its unconcealment, *aletheia*. As a return to primordiality, the luminosity of existence, it is of revolutionary significance, for not only does it mark an epoch within history but it constitutes the historicality of history. Heidegger struggles, not always successfully, to keep these two meanings of history apart, that is, as the opening that brings historical existence to light that yet can never be grasped within history. Often the temptation to identify the originary meaning of history with the events within history became irresistible, especially during the years leading up to and during the Second World War. Apocalypse has always proved a notoriously difficult notion to control. The opening of history all too easily slides into an opening within history, even when we recognize that immanentization of the eschaton marks the end of history. Apocalypse requires its nonoccurrence if we are to be faithful to it. Knowing, however, does not remove the temptation, as Heidegger demonstrates within his profound philosophical meditations that yet are peppered with asides about contemporary events. Philosophy, which is transacted within the opening that constitutes history, is put to work to editorialize on current affairs. The reversal in which the eternal is applied to the temporal does not vitiate the philosophical illuminations, but it does demonstrate the difficulty in maintaining their separation. In this respect the value of Heidegger's negative contribution is almost as much as that of his positive contribution. The man with his concrete allegiances, sympathies, and prejudices can never be fully removed even when we take our stand within the unattainable truth of truth.

One can imagine that the declaration of American entry into the war in Europe must have been experienced as insupportable. Little in the way of apocalyptic proclivities would have been required to acquire the sense that Germany was now besieged on all sides. Lecturing in 1942 on Hölderlin's hymn "The Ister," Heidegger perceived it to be nothing less than the resolution of "the Anglo Saxon world" to annihilate Europe, the homeland that constituted "the commencement of the Western World." But as in all projections of the apocalypse, the extremity of darkness cannot extinguish the light destined to triumph. "Whatever has the character of commencement is indestructible. America's entry into this planetary war is not its entry into history; rather, it is already the ultimate American act of American ahistoricality and self-devastation (*Hölderlin's Hymn "The Ister,"* § 10, Review)." It would be easy to dismiss the greatness of a thinker who yields so readily to such mythic self-deception, but it remains more useful to understand him, especially as a guide to the difficulty of living within the apocalypse rather than preempting it. Heidegger may have taken leave of the National Socialist idea of the priority of the political, and indeed was under surveillance in his lectures, but he still had not fully taken on board his own insight that the polis cannot be understood in terms of the political. The polis is rather the site of the political and thus beyond it, a possibility that arises only because humans, "in ascending within the site of their essence, are at the same time without site" (§ 15). How, then, was it possible to caricature the political reality of other peoples as simply "measurelessness?" "The latter is the principle of what we call Americanism; Bolshevism is only a derivative kind of Americanism" (§ 13). The foreshortening of the obiter dicta is in stark contrast to the lovingly elaborated meditation on the figure of Antigone, who exemplifies the grounding of the political beyond itself. Antigone unlocks the political so profoundly as the site of "a becoming homely in being unhomely" (§ 20) that it can never be locked up again.[38]

Holiness Beyond God: Nietzsche's Failure

It may be that what caused Heidegger to overlook his own insight into the nonreducibility of the political to the political was the sense of the dramatic character of his breakthrough. No previous intimations had intimated so primordially; they could never be recognized in their commonality with him. This is, of course, the source of all apocalyptic assertions. The unprecedented has irrupted. What preserves the tension of apocalypse is the sense of its permanence in what comes before and after. In Heidegger's case a central element of rupture is his penetration beyond the fixities of traditional religiosity to its source in the holy. No doubt a conventional view is that he tends toward an atheistic perspective, especially as evidenced by his readiness to discount the God of Christianity. But it is just such nonchalant dismissal that indicates a realization that this was never the truth of divinity, perhaps not even of Christianity.[39] Such an impression is confirmed by the intensity of his conviction of having reached beyond the gods to that from which they derive their divinity. Compared with the Western reification of divinity in the mode of beings, Heidegger mounts higher to the be-ing of the gods. Hölderlin through his hymns is the prophet of this new religiosity opening toward

---

[38] Despite his frequent dismissals of the political as the realm of the external and his preference for *ēthos*, as the inner realm of our dwelling, there is a continuous striving to enlarge the latter into the former. Nowhere is this more evident than in Heidegger's engagement with the more limited public realm of education. See the intriguing investigation by Iain D. Thomson, *Heidegger on Ontotheology: Technology and the Politics of Education* (Cambridge: Cambridge University Press, 2005). In general on this see Fred Dallmayr, *The Other Heidegger* (Ithaca, NY: Cornell University Press, 1993); Michael Lewis, *Heidegger and the Place of Ethics* (London: Continuum, 2005); and McNeill, *The Time of Life*.

[39] See his response to the question of identifying being and God at the Zurich Seminar, 1951: "Being and God are not identical, and I would never attempt to think the essence of God through being. Some of you perhaps know that I came out of theology, and that I harbor an old love for it and that I have a certain understanding of it. If I were yet to write a theology – to which I sometimes feel inclined – then the word 'being' would not be allowed to occur in it." Quoted in Hemming, *Heidegger's Atheism*, 291. One should also give some weight to the report that, despite his unchurched status, he continued in his old age to attend Mass at St. Martin's Church whenever he was in Messkirch, "seating himself in the choir stalls where he had sat as a boy bell ringer." Safranski, *Martin Heidegger*, 47.

the holiness of the gods. "What is to be said in this hymnal poetry is the holy, which, *beyond* the gods, determines the gods themselves and simultaneously, as the 'poetic' that is to be poetized, brings the dwelling of historical human beings into its essence" (*Hölderlin's Hymn "The Ister,"* § 23)." The demigod status of the poet is matched by the philosopher, who can grasp the movement by which he is grasped. This is particularly the impact of his reading of Nietzsche, the most notorious pronouncer of the death of God, but for that very reason the one who leads Heidegger most deeply into the God beyond God. Heidegger's abiding temptation to abolish revelation thus arises from the sense of having reached the revelation of revelation. Its characteristic error is the failure to see that that is not itself revelation, but only the opening toward it.

It has long been recognized that the lectures on Nietzsche are key to the understanding of Heidegger because they are the key to his self-understanding. This is surely why he lavished such attention on Nietzsche, lecturing more continuously on him than any other thinker (1936–40). It was in Nietzsche that the philosophical apocalypse had become apparent. For Heidegger he marked the end point of Western metaphysics, a judgment that sits uneasily with the realization that the end was present from the beginning and that its arrival signals the recognition of its beginning. In his treatment of individual philosophers, Heidegger was open to nuance, but in dealing with the culminating figure he was drawn toward absolute utterance. This is not to suggest that the volumes on Nietzsche are an oversimplification, for on the contrary, they remain among the most insightful analyses of Nietzsche ever written and are among the richest reflections Heidegger ever penned. It is to recognize that their role in Heidegger's self-understanding is utterly distinctive. When the entire history of philosophy, not to mention the history of revelation, has narrowed to its essential clarification in one figure, there is a great temptation to overlook the historical unfolding it illuminates. In the eagerness to make history, we are inclined to abolish history. What is forgotten is that history cannot be made if there remains no history. Revelation wherever it occurs cannot abolish its own context without simultaneously destroying itself. Perhaps especially in his extensive treatment of Nietzsche, we discern a tendency to bring the conversation to a close and a failure to recognize that the conversation cannot be concluded precisely because its expression cannot contain its reality. The tragedy of Heidegger on a philosophical level, quite apart from its political ramifications, is that the closer he approaches the primordial the more he is in danger of betraying the connection.

Nietzsche, it appears, brought the temptation into the open because he, too, had taken it upon himself to address the crisis of modern and ultimately Western civilization. In carrying forward what Nietzsche had failed to achieve, Heidegger frequently suggests the attainment of a solution, even though his solution is that there is no solution other than living it out. This is the whole point of the rejection of technical mastery, the culmination of the philosophical revolution that prioritizes luminosity over intentionality. Yet even when such foreclosing proclivities are *most* present, there is no denying the philosophical significance of the Nietzsche–Heidegger penetration. Where we are inclined to regard the death of God as a pronouncement about history, they were able to see it as the opening of the divine that constitutes history. "What to common sense looks like 'atheism,' and has to look like it, is at bottom the very opposite" (*Gesamtausgabe,* vol. 6.1, *Nietzsche,* 423 / *Nietzsche II,* Krell trans., 207–8). The God who had to die is more present in his disappearance than ever before. This is the impact of the "telling silence" that is the mark of thinking. In this sense Nietzsche's de-deification of nature in the direction of chaos is not godless but the uncovering of "the path on which alone gods will be encountered" (6.1, 315/II, 94). It is a task that Heidegger likens to negative theology, the withholding of all humanly relative perspectives that obstruct the encounter.[40] The theological significance of Nietzsche, on Heidegger's view, is that here the question of God has been raised in all its primordial force. In an aside that would hardly surprise a believer, he wonders "whether the god possesses more divinity in the question concerning him or in the situation where we are sure of him and are able, as it were, to brush him aside or fetch him forward, as our needs dictate" (6.1, 288/II, 68). A far more expansive formulation, shorn of gratuitousness, is that "a question is always bathed in a light that emanates from the question itself" (6.1, 405/II, 187).

As always Heidegger is most profound in the actual reflection but flirts with derailment in thinking about it. The tension is most evident in a treatment of Nietzsche that must view him as the end of metaphysics that is simultaneously its resurrection (6.2, 178–79/IV, 148), yet cannot credit him with the same degree of self-awareness. How, we might ask, was it possible for Nietzsche to occupy this position without knowing it

---

[40] "What Nietzsche is practicing here with regard to the world totality is a kind of 'negative theology,' which tries to grasp the Absolute as purely as possible by holding at a distance all 'relative' determinations, that is, all those that relate to human beings. Except that Nietzsche's determination of the world as a whole is a negative theology without the Christian God." *Nietzsche,* 6.1, 315 / *Nietzsche II,* Krell trans., 95.

in some sense? How was it possible for Heidegger to find it within his writings if it was not already there? It may indeed be that "the inner form of his thought was denied the thinker" (6.1, 436/III, 12), but was it not also possible that he understood his purpose as a living out of what could not formulated? Could it be that Heidegger's fatality consists of the opposite tendency to make language do what it cannot? The power of Heidegger's analysis of Nietzsche can often deflect us from considering this possibility, although it remains the core of the charge that Heidegger betrayed his own insight. When philosophical acumen has reached such a level, we are inclined to overlook the neglect of the existential focus of the original. Philosophy has surpassed life. Whatever may be the limitations of Nietzsche's self-understanding, there can be no doubt that he was driven by the question of how he should live. In contrast, one is struck by the paucity of space devoted in Heidegger's voluminous reflections to the moral struggle that so engaged Nietzsche. The single-minded focus on the question of being not only seems to suggest that its penetration resolves the existential questions but, more dangerously, tends to subsume them under the former. The opening toward be-ing that Heidegger so magnificently accomplishes, in many ways justifying his claim to have restored metaphysics to its source, does not obviate the imperative of living it out. The resurrection of metaphysics is not yet our resurrection.

The strange distortion of Heidegger's genius having been noted, it nevertheless remains that it was through his engagement with Nietzsche that he reached a towering moment of clarity. The affinity with Nietzsche was deep. Heidegger recognized in him a struggle similar to his own to overcome the early perceptions of his thought.[41] But the real importance was that Nietzsche provided the perfect foil, in his exploration of the limits of metaphysics, for Heidegger to demonstrate his own insight into the metaphysics of metaphysics. Nietzsche had brought the logic of Western metaphysics to its ultimate conclusion in recognizing the will to power as its source; all that remained was to realize the meaning of this insight itself as no longer bound by the same fatality. Knowing is a "re-presenting," a fixating of nature in such a way as secures technological

---

[41] "If there is something like catastrophe in the creative work of great thinkers, then it consists not in being stymied and in failing to go farther, but precisely in advancing farther – that is to say, in their letting themselves be determined by the initial impact of their thought, an impact that always deflects them. Such going 'farther' is always fatal, for it prevents one from abiding by the source of one's own commencement." *Nietzsche,* 6.1, 301 / *Nietzsche II,* Krell trans., 81.

success (6.1, 477–78/III, 50–51). If all truth is a mere "holding to be true," what does that truth hold onto (6.1, 547–48/III, 116)? This objection is not for Heidegger the standard relativizing of the relativizers that Nietzsche himself recognized, but a far deeper question about truth as a mode of existence that Nietzsche could only live without finding its linguistic expression. He had never been able to overcome the problem that metaphysics always "transforms being into a being" (6.2, 312/IV, 208), the subject setting a ground or cause or divinity outside itself and thus rendering the relationship nihilistic. "Thinking," Heidegger emphasizes, "is not an independent activity over against being . . . thinking belongs to being itself" (6.2, 321–22/IV, 216–17). As an event within being thinking has access to being only as what cannot be contained within thinking but rather as that within which thinking itself stands in relation to being. In a particularly luminous formulation Heidegger announces, "*Being is the promise of itself*" (6.2, 333/IV, 226). Nietzsche, by contrast, remained mired in the subject–object relation that necessarily took being as a "value" and thereby rendered its value as nought. The best he could achieve was a negative theology that merely negated the theology of intentionality but failed to go beyond it. He could reverse Plato, but he could not disconnect himself from Plato. The diagnosis of nihilism failed to reach its mark because he had not understood the opening it had thereby created. "Nietzsche's concept of nihilism is nihilistic" (6.2, 44/IV, 22).

Instead of seeing through the death of God, the negating of theology, to the "uncanniness" (*Unheimlichkeit*) of what cannot be rendered objectively because it is still more embracing, he was held by the "deepening dark" of absence and homelessness (6.2, 358/IV, 248). Nietzsche had not been able to see the withdrawal as an advent. The hold of millennial patterns of philosophizing prevented him from recognizing the radical character of the demand that the end of metaphysics now imposes on philosophy. "The essence of the destitution of this era in the history of being consists in the need of needlessness. Because it is more essential, and older, the destiny of being is less familiar than the lack of God" (6.2, 359/IV, 248). Nietzsche's critique of the tradition whose crisis he witnessed had not gone deep enough. He had been able to understand the innovation of knowledge as power, announced by Descartes, but he still understood it only psychologically (6.2, 164/IV, 132). He was entangled in his castigation of "truth as error" because he did not think truth in relation to being. A resolution would have required him to follow the path of Heidegger in uncovering the crucial misstep by which truth is dissevered from being and becomes merely an idea. This is the real impact of Plato. It is in the hands of Plato that being as idea, as that which lets beings be and therefore cannot be in the same sense, slips into the mode of a being. "Being is shown in the character of making-possible and conditioning. Here the decisive step for all metaphysics is taken, through which the *a priori* character of being at the same time receives the distinction of being a condition" (6.2, 201/IV, 169). Everything follows from this fatal oversight, including the conception of being as the utmost being whose pure presence is ultimately never quite enough to forestall the doubt about its presence that Nietzsche suffers as the death of God. To really go beyond nihilism, more is required than a reversion to its Platonic or Christian origins. It must entail, Heidegger insists, the willingness to dwell with "this uncanniest of all guests" (6.2, 43/IV, 21).

Truth as Appearance: Nietzsche's Achievement

Nietzsche could only point metaphysics in the direction it must go. Hegel is regarded as the last metaphysician because his project was to show how becoming becomes being; Nietzsche marks the end of metaphysics as a project when being becomes becoming. Without fully grasping what he accomplished, Nietzsche provided the formula for the resurrection of metaphysics. "To stamp becoming with the character of being – that is the supreme will to power" (quoted in 6.1, 592/III, 156). Heidegger dwelt on this pronouncement from the *Late Notebooks* as the key to Nietzsche's metaphysical perspicuity. What blocks Nietzsche from reaching the same level of self-realization is that being remains for him identical with beingness. He has not yet grasped that, to the extent that our thinking occurs within being, being can be reached only through the revelatory event by which the whole within which we are is glimpsed. Being remains for Nietzsche indistinguishable from beings, an undifferentiated jumble opaque to all but the most utilitarian significance. Yet he was on the way to the more primordial reading of being in his apprehension of the priority of becoming. "Being ultimately steps into the arena with its opponent, becoming, inasmuch as the latter claims being's place" (6.2, 11/III, 172). The withdrawal of being has not yet been recognized as its self-disclosure, so that its luminosity can fall only indirectly on the movement it leads forth. Nietzsche's "transvaluation of values" is, on Heidegger's reading, mute testament to the opening toward being by which we move beyond good and evil to stand within the primordial. Existence draws us where eye has not seen.

The interpretation becomes, therefore, fraught with ambiguity, for the same terms must bear the possibility of pointing in opposite directions. Of all of Nietzsche's readers, Heidegger is most willing to dwell within the tension. This is why he is able to regard the will to power as the final expression of the drive for technological dominion and as the first step in freeing ourselves from the blindness of unmastered mastery.[42] Or he can understand the overman as both the completion of the last man and as the liberation beyond the human. But it is on the eternal return that he lavishes the most attention, for it functions as both the culminating symbol of Nietzsche's thought and the point of its most fascinatingly inconclusive self-recognition. Eternal return, too, carries the opposing directionalities, for it can be read as the endless recurrence of the same or as the moment of transcendence by which it is illuminated. "If being as a whole is eternal return of the same, then for mankind, which must conceive of itself as a will to power within this whole, there remains only the decision as to whether it would sooner will a nihilistically experienced nothingness than no longer will at all, thereby in the latter case surrendering its essential possibility" (6.2, 281/III, 234). It is at this point, when being as a whole in its consummate opacity has finally overshadowed the truth of being, that the deepest question, the question of the truth of this insight into the correlation of will to power and eternal return, begins its inexorable emergence. Heidegger leaves the question hanging at the end of a chapter, but he titles the immediately following one "Justice."

He cannot, of course, find justice as a guiding theme in Nietzsche, but it does enable Heidegger to grasp the essence of his metaphysics as a "letting-appear" that is identical with "justice." This also converges with Heidegger's own interests, for it cannot be said that he sought out the priority of justice. His instinct was always to hold back from the realm of morality as the realm of values whose very positing is "the cause of nihilism" (6.2, 251/III, 206). Heidegger's thought is drawn back to the priority of thinking that can recognize the limitation of morality. Justice is of interest primarily to the extent that it is indispensable to the emergence of truth (see III, ch. 21, "Truth as Justice"), the main focus of his engagement with Nietzsche. It was Nietzsche's wrestling with the problem of truth that fascinated Heidegger because he had glimpsed

---

[42] "The conditions of such dominion, namely, all values, are posited and realized through a total 'mechanizations' of things and the breeding of human beings." *Nietzsche*, 6.2, 277 / *Nietzsche III*, Krell trans., 230.

the central philosophical problem of our scientific civilization. When we ask what a science is, we are no longer asking a question that can be addressed from within that science. "The fact that every science as such, being the specific science it is, gains no access to its fundamental concepts and to what those concepts grasp, goes hand in hand with the fact that no science can assert something about itself with the help of its own scientific resources" (6.1, 332/II, 112). Nietzsche had understood this problem as the imposition of perspectives from life that chafed against the accompanying realization of them as only perspectives. How they could be held together became apparent only through Nietzsche's discovery of the eternal return. Contrary to the opposing interpretation of the eternal return as the acknowledgment of universal sameness (6.1, 392/II, 175), Heidegger takes it as a proclamation of the redemptive release from nihilism (6.1, 365/II, 146–47). They are, of course, two sides of the same coin but one that is weighted toward eternity rather than the return. Eternity is an escape from the return precisely because its apprehension contains and for that reason cannot be contained by time. This is why Heidegger insists that Nietzsche's eternal return, whatever scientific figments may occasionally have been attached to it, really concerns "the inner structure of a thought's truth" (6.1, 386/II, 168). As a thought about being as a whole, it cannot be included within being as a whole but must take its stand within being. "Accordingly those who are thinking are more than, and something other than, mere *particular cases of what is thought.* . . . Out of this moment alone the eternity of what is thought in the thought looms large" (6.1, 386–87/II, 169). When being is thought as time, time is grasped as being.[43] Nietzsche had discovered being as becoming (6.1, 592/III, 156).

This is why art loomed so large for him. Like Schelling he recognized it as the preeminent instance of the becoming of being. Heidegger seized upon this elevation of art as "worth more than truth" (6.1, 143/I, 141), for it provides access to the primal question of the essence of truth. Nietzsche may not have been able to formulate it in that way, but he certainly intuited the perspicuousness of art. Not only the will to power and the eternal return but the entire complex of problems surrounding semblance and truth that had never been fully penetrated came together

[43] "Here it is essential to observe that feeling is not something that runs its course in our 'inner lives.' It is rather that basic mode of our Dasein by force of which and in accordance with which we are always already lifted beyond ourselves into being as a whole, which in this or that way matters to us or does not matter to us." *Nietzsche,* 6.1, 100/ *Nietzsche I,* Krell trans., 99.

in the rapture of art. The artist does not really create or impose form on things but rather becomes the point at which the radiance of the work bursts forth. He does not invent beauty but is led forth by it along the path of life enhancement that is the exemplar of the will to power. "Rapture (*Rausch*) as a state of feeling explodes the very subjectivity of the subject. By having a feeling for beauty the subject has already come out of himself; he is no longer subjective, no longer a subject. On the other hand, beauty is not something at hand like an object of sheer representation. As an attuning it thoroughly determines the state of man" (6.1, 124/I, 123). Nietzsche may never have been able to escape the juxtaposition of art and truth, but for Heidegger it opened the way to recognizing their correlation. Even today the best way of understanding his conception of truth is in the model of the artist who leads forth what is true. Heidegger might even be forgiven for yielding to the temptation of momentousness in his most fundamental idea, for it shows how the modern philosophical revolution implies a fundamental shift in the understanding of science itself. Nietzsche glimpsed the notion that science is a form of art, but only Heidegger saw the issue through to its core. When we take art as the model of truth, what makes science science is that it too follows the path of be-ing. Just as art is not interested in the difference between appearance and reality, so neither is science. Semblance is not the way that truth hides itself but rather the way by which truth is. Both the artist and the scientist are drawn by the same eros of form "as what allows that which we encounter to radiate in appearance" (6.1, 119/I, 119).

Thinking and Being Are the Same

That thinking and being are the same is the pivotal insight of Heidegger's immense philosophical effort. It was endlessly elaborated in successive accounts of the nature of truth by which he worked his way back to the original Greek understanding of aletheia. He had finally broken with the dominance of intentionality by glimpsing the more primordial openness of luminosity behind it. What had been missed through all the self-confidence of the sciences was that no science can even begin to give an account of itself from within its own horizon. We will no more know what history is by returning to the study of history than the mathematician can explain his discipline in the language of mathematics. "The essence of their sphere – history, art, poetry, language, nature, man, God – remains inaccessible to the sciences" (*Was Heisst Denken? Gesamtausgabe,* vol. 8, 35/ *What Is Called Thinking?* 33). No intellectual discipline can speak of the essence out of which it speaks. "Physics as physics can make no assertions about physics" (*Gesamtausgabe* vol. 9, 59 / "Science and Reflection," in *The Question Concerning Technology*, 176). By subordinating everything to its method, science cannot really know whether its method does not prevent nature from revealing itself rather than permit its disclosure (9, 57/174). In that entry into *skepsis*, the "seeing-ahead" (*Zusehen*) ("Hegel's Concept of Experience," *Holzwege, Gesamtausgabe,* vol. 5, 152 / *Off the Beaten Path*, 114) apprehends that from which it is as that which can never be apprehended but which for that reason guards all coming to presence of truth. This is the deepest principle of philosophy first enunciated by Parmenides in his incomparable statement that "thinking and being are the same." It has provided the most enduring avenue for Heidegger's meditation as he sought to draw us away from absorption with what is present to call our attention to the presencing from which it is. What we call laws of thought, the principles of identity and sufficient reason, are not simply the regulative principles of our thinking but the primordial self-disclosure of being. We do not impose them but are ourselves imposed upon by them as the very possibility of our thinking at all. Thinking and being are the same in the sense that it is only by standing in the light of being that we can perceive what is. This is an insight discovered not by a method available to us in advance but by submitting to the movement of being by which it is disclosed. Truth is irreducibly poetic, for it is not we who possess it but it that possesses us. Our task is only to give thought expression as art, in which alone the sameness of thinking and being is unfolded.

Heidegger's prioritizing of art over science in the path of truth is a remarkable culmination of the intimation that originated with Kant's third critique.[44] Kant's sense that esthetic judgments did not fit within his conception of phenomenal knowledge, since they attested to our subjective capacity to judge objectively, had set the reversal in motion. Hegel had grasped the idea of art as a mode of absolute knowledge, although he had ambivalently suggested its supersession by philosophy while at the same time retaining the meditation on art within philosophy. Schelling had gone further in recognizing that art puts us in touch with the primordial creative movement of reality as a whole, a possibility that is available to us only because of our connection with the process of the

---

[44] Richard Velkley has elegantly traced this meditation to Rousseau who, of course, always stands behind Kant. See the concluding essay, "Heidegger's Step Behind the Greeks," *Being After Rousseau*, 138–50.

divine self-emergence. Working with the same problematic, if not always in continuity with his predecessors, Nietzsche had given voice to the primordial significance of art in his declaration that "art is worth more than truth." In its baldness the assertion might be taken as a preference for art over truth, but it is to be more properly read as a recognition of art as the only viable mode of truth. Not only does Heidegger bring out this inner meaning, but he brings out its full significance in relation to the world of science to which Nietzsche, at first, gave his uncritical admiration and later ended with misgivings concerning its relationship to truth that he could never fully clarify. Through this engagement Heidegger was able to reach the transparence that had eluded Nietzsche. The primordiality whence art derived its significance was understood in reference neither to an ontological beginning nor to a psychological state but as the disclosure of the movement of disclosure by which all knowing occurs.[45] Philosophy's expulsion of art from the polis, never an event to be taken at face value, was now resolved in the self-recognition of philosophy as art.

When philosophy is confronted by the realization that truth is not something that it apprehends but rather that by which it is apprehended in advance, the relationship to truth is indistinguishable from that of the artist to beauty. He is drawn by beauty to create, but he does not create beauty. Art reveals, therefore, the primordial mystery of luminosity by which we are related to beings. In his 1936 essay, "The Origin of the Work of Art," Heidegger employed Van Gogh's famous painting of his rumpled old shoes to illustrate this idea. The shoes have been separated out from their usefulness to reveal the superabundance of their being from whence their utility can be derived. But before they are useful, they simply are. It is this insight into being made that distinguishes a work of art in which usefulness as such has been discarded. In this sense Van Gogh's famous painting is an artistic reflection on art. "In the work of art the truth of the being has set itself to work . . . the opening up of beings in their being, the happening of truth" (*Holzwege*, 21–24 / *Off the Beaten Path*, 16–18). In a later "Addendum" to this essay Heidegger indicates his dissatisfaction with the conception he had reached here, in that it still was too closely tied to the subjective apprehension of the movement. What he really sought to grasp was that the movement of the disclosure, making all disclosure of truth possible, could not itself be grasped. He explains

---

[45] In general, see Julian Young, *Heidegger's Philosophy of Art* (Cambridge: Cambridge University Press, 2000).

that "setting-into-work of truth" means "truth's setting itself into work." "Art is then conceived as disclosive appropriation (*Ereignis*) (74/55). Schelling's most fundamental insight had reached its final implication. Art, Heidegger had seen, could provide the full exemplification of the interrelation of truth and being, yet it could also be drawn back into an objectifying tendency that concealed its origin. What was needed was a movement in which being and thought would unfold their relationship more inextricably. This Heidegger found in the realm of language, to which he now devoted the last great creative phase of his career.

Language as the Home of Being

This was not in any sense a deflection of the focus on art but a deepening of it, as Heidegger sought to open philosophy to its own ungraspable openness. His formulations are often inscrutably oracular, but this is an inevitable consequence of a project that not only comments on language, but comments by means of the very linguistic self-transcendence that discloses the origin of language. Philosophy both acknowledges the primacy of poetry and absorbs it.[46] The result is that it no longer sounds like philosophy. Rather than the extensive discourse on being that marked the works of the middle period, especially *Beiträge* and the *Nietzsche* lectures, now being no longer plays such a central role. Instead, Heidegger has found a way of opening toward being without necessarily naming it. This has the distinct advantage of precluding the misidentification of being as an object over against us, to be considered in the mode of propositional metaphysics. But it did lead to formulations of baffling impenetrability for the unsuspecting reader. A classic example is the 1950 essay "The Thing," in which Heidegger linguistically unveils the mystery behind some familiar entities of our world. A jug is not the everyday utensil we take for granted; it is the "holding vessel" for the nothing. The potter does not make the jug, he shapes the void (*Gesamtausgabe*, vol. 9, 171 / *Poetry, Language, Thought*, 169). Even further, we can contemplate the role of the jug in pouring out its contents and realize that the jug can be a jug only because of the gift of outpouring. "The gift gathers what belongs to giving" (175/173). The jug is thus not present as a thing but more primordially as the presencing that grants it the possibility of being present.

---

[46] A good guide to this phase because of its literary sensitivity is Gerald L. Burns, *Heidegger's Estrangements: Language, Truth, and Poetry in the Later Writings* (New Haven, CT: Yale University Press, 1989).

"The jug is a thing insofar as it things" (179/177). The same holds for the world itself, which cannot be conceived of as a thing or in relation to its cause or ground. Instead, it must be held out into the nothing that we apprehend as death but that is the opening in which everything becomes transparent for what it is. "The thing things world" (182/181).[47]

This is just one example of the amazingly original retrieval of language by which Heidegger sought to save modern man from the homelessness of the linguistic dwelling he had built for himself. Thinking he is the master of language, man has become deaf to the stillness within which he speaks. Everyday language is a forgotten mode of poetry rather than the other way around. The challenge is to recognize that, when we speak, it is not first of all we who speak but language that speaks in us. "Man speaks when, and only when, he responds to language (*der Sprache entspricht*) by listening to its appeal (*Zuspruch*)" (194/216). This is what it means to learn to discover language as language, rather than as a phenomenon for investigation by a detached observer who overlooks the fact that his investigation relies on language as its medium. Poetry, therefore, looms large as the only mode of self-reflection that might glimpse the container by which it is contained, the great existential task of philosophy since Kant took the first step of reason's self-contemplation. "Language is the house of being" (*Gesamtausgabe*, vol. 12, 156 / *On the Way to Language*, 63) is one of Heidegger's repeated observations that reminds us of the continuity with the underlying philosophical meditation. The accent now, however, falls heavily on the problem of dwelling as the answer to homelessness and still with the tone of apocalyptic foreboding that the "battle for the dominion of the earth has entered a decisive phase" (201/105). Poetry, rather than any more specific historical carrier, holds forth the greatest promise because only poetry can really address the inability to listen that has afflicted our world. We have become blind to what opens the possibility of dwelling and therefore have become homeless in our dwelling. But Heidegger reminds us, in an admirably poetic turn, that blindness is itself only a possibility for a being endowed with sight. "When the poetic appropriately comes to light, then man dwells humanly on this earth" (*Gesamtausgabe*, vol. 9, 208 / *Poetry, Language, Thought*, 229).

---

[47] Burns is probably correct in referencing Joyce's *Finnegan's Wake* as the only comparable project of linguistic self-commentary. "One could not write a grammar for such a language: that is, one could not say in what the logic of such a language could consist. One would have to say that 'in the Nichtian glossary which purveys aprioric roots for aposteriorious tongues this is nat language at any sinse of the world.' It is otherwise than language." Ibid., 163.

The answer to the wasteland generated by the technological domination of thought is to listen to the opening that the catastrophe itself invites. Such is "The Turn," the title of a lecture Heidegger gave during the bleak years when the only forum available to him was the Club at Bremen (1949). He envisions the turning of the oblivion of being into the truth of being, a path that he had been on since his 1930 essay "On the Essence of Truth" (*Pathmarks*). Now he can proclaim this insight as the truth of technological civilization. "The saving power is not secondary to the danger. The selfsame danger is, when it is *as* the danger, the saving power" (*Gesamtausgabe,* vol. 79, 72 / *Question Concerning Technology,* 42). In that penetrating formulation Heidegger had reached the core of the problem of technology as the problem that arises because technology is not technological. It is only because we cannot be controlled by technology that the question of our control by technology arises. This is the conception of "enframing" (*Gestell*) he develops within these lectures, of which the most expanded one is "The Question Concerning Technology."[48] Widely recognized as a classic treatment of the impossibility of reaching a technological means of controlling technology, the full extent of its contribution has still not been absorbed by the widespread preoccupation with the crisis of the unmastered mastery technology has generated. We can readily see that the enframing that reduces all to a "standing reserve" (*Bestand*) of usefulness eventually comes to include man himself within its scheme. But how many are prepared to ask the mind-opening question of what the instrumental as such is? We take for granted that we do not need to raise it because we are, after all, so familiar with using things for our ends. Heidegger's greatness as a thinker is that he is not deflected by surface obviousness from asking the deepest questions. Through the question itself he has already opened up the realm beyond technology by which it must be understood. "Such a realm is art" (36/ 35), the precinct (*templum*) of the holy (*Gesamtausgabe,* vol. 5, 310 / *Poetry, Language, Thought,* 132).

The Fatality of Apocalypse

The accompanying apocalyptic vision arises through the projection of Heidegger's meditation onto the historical process. "Only where the

---

[48] Richard Rojcewicz has devoted a perceptive volume to this essay, *The Gods and Technology: A Reading of Heidegger* (Albany: State University of New York Press, 2006). Michael Zimmerman, *Heidegger's Confrontation with Modernity: Technology, Politics, Art* (Bloomington: Indiana University Press, 1990), has shown how the engagement with technology can be viewed as the nexus of Heidegger's political and philosophical interventions.

consummation of the modern age attains the heedlessness (*Rücksichtslösigkeit*) that is its peculiar greatness is future history being prepared" (*Gesamtausgabe*, vol. 5, 112 / *Question Concerning Technology*, 153). He held onto this view from 1938, affirming it with even more resoluteness after his return to teaching in 1951. At that point he could boldly ask what the Second World War had decided. Apart from the division of Germany, it had for Heidegger only confirmed his judgment of modern democracy, expressed in the words of Nietzsche, "as the *form of the decline of the state*" (*Gesamtausgabe*, vol. 8, 72 / *What Is Called Thinking?* 67). No institution could endure in the absence of the will that attested to man's fidelity to a higher calling than his own willfulness. Even Nietzsche's admiration for Russia, "the *only* power today that has endurance in its bones," is quoted before being withdrawn as "not identical with today's political and economic system of the Soviet republics." The sentiments are no doubt astonishing, perhaps evidence of Heidegger's own consistent record of political misjudgment, but what makes them of interest is their derivation from the deepest recesses of his thought. It was not just that his philosophical breakthrough, the attainment of the goal of the philosophical revolution, had dissolved the crisis of nihilism modernity had spawned. What rendered it apocalyptic was that the difference between the philosophical and the civilizational had disappeared. The apocalypse had begun in his own work. This was what made it possible to shift confidently from the meditation on being to historical pronouncements without any of the uncertainties and hesitations by which empirical judgments are usually informed. Gradually, however, the tension of apocalyptic certainty began to erode, worn away by the ebbing of impending doom and the return of undeniable social well-being. By 1962 it was "uncertain whether world civilization will soon be abruptly destroyed or whether it will be stabilized for a long time, in a stabilization, however, which will not rest in something enduring, but rather establish itself in a sequence of changes, each of which present the latest fashion" (*Gesamtausgabe*, vol. 14, 75 / *Time and Being*, 60).

Prediction may have become impossible, but the structure of apocalypse remains. The fascinating impact of Heidegger's thought arises in no small measure from his conviction that philosophy is itself apocalyptic, "destining the fate of man." Philosophical meditation rather than decisive action has become the arena of history. This peculiar reversal of thought and life is in marked contrast to Nietzsche's insistence on overcoming the spirit of revenge as the way to life rather than merely thought. For Heidegger "the question of revenge is after all not the question of being" (*Gesamtausgabe*, vol. 8, 92, *What Is Called Thinking?* 87). At best deliverance from revenge is a transition to the truth of being. But are they not in the end identical? Can there be an opening toward being that is not also a living out of its illumination? Can there be an illumination that does not arise from living within it? Kant had seen the limits of theoretical reason and thereby pointed philosophy on the path of practical reason as its deepest disclosure. The idealists overcame Kant's hesitation that the latter constituted the disclosure of being, with Hegel virtually subordinating practical reason to its theoretical significance. What had not yet been determined was whether practical reason could be contained within its theoretical significance. Schelling, Kierkegaard, and Nietzsche insisted that practical reason, existence, necessarily overflowed all its conceptualizations. Now Heidegger asks whether theoretical reason as a mode of practical reason does not therefore extend to the whole of it. Is thought tantamount to action? It is tempting to conclude that it is, given the closeness that arises when both thought and action are recognized as existential, or ultimately modes of practice. When thought has become a living process, it is easy to forget that there is living beyond thought. But fidelity to the character of what is living requires it. Any foreclosing of the horizon of living is a betrayal of the fundamental mandate of being. There is no opening of being except through its actual opening in life. Contemplation always cleaves to an unsurrendered residue, while life refuses to be contained even by the self-understanding it has generated out of itself. What overflows can be only in the mode of overflowing, never in the mere thought of it. Apocalypse, even in the form of the unconcealment of being, does not preclude the being of apocalypse as unconcealment.

The sense that nothing more is required once one has thought the opening of being comes across most strongly in Heidegger's disavowal of ethics. There is no imperative to live the opening, as if it entails an opening beyond what thought has glimpsed.[49] What is overlooked is that thought cannot provide a resting place without arresting the very movement from which it, too, draws its dynamic. It may indeed be that "morality as a mere doctrine and imperative is helpless unless man first comes to have a different fundamental relation to being" (93/89), but

---

[49] The emphasis for Heidegger always falls on thinking rather than living, as, for example, in the conclusion to the *Principle of Reason*, 211: "Or are we obliged to find paths upon which thinking is capable of responding to what is worthy of thought instead of, enchanted by calculative thinking, mindlessly passing over what is worthy of thought? That is the question. It is the world-question of thinking. Answering that question decides what will become of the earth and of human existence on this earth."

it is also the case that the relation to being is equally bereft without the lived unfolding that is the ethical source of ethics. Heidegger, it seems, mistakes the radicalness of his thought for the thought of radicalness. For him there can be no ethics beyond the thinking of being, "the abode of man" that is the most basic meaning of the term ("Letter on Humanism," *Gesamtuasgabe,* vol. 9, 354/ *Pathmarks,* 271). It may indeed be the case that we can derive no "directives" for our practical lives from such knowledge because "such thinking is neither theoretical nor practical. It comes to pass before this distinction. Such thinking is, insofar as it is, recollection of being and nothing else" (358/272).[50] But what of the being of such recollection that is not recollection because it is lived before it? The prioritizing of what is prior privileges the contemplatively prior without justifying the exclusion of the simply prior. Apart from the suspect inferences that may be drawn from this determination, there is the larger problem that thought without the full amplitude of existence implies its containment within itself. The shift toward existence, even when it concedes that existence cannot be contained within thought, must remain watchful lest it suggest that it may nevertheless comprehend the thought of the shift itself.

The case of Heidegger remains a fascinating one in which the most antiapocalyptic resolution nevertheless could not separate itself from its own apocalyptic profession. His thought could not attain its goal because it held too fast to the goal of thought. Despite Heidegger's best efforts to present a thought that dissolved the proclivity of thought to freeze itself, he nevertheless succumbed to the same fatality. He had not taken on board the imperative of existence from whose unsurpassability the openness of thought arises. Railing against a metaphysics of presence can still yield a metaphysics of presence if the nonpresent presencing is merely thought. What guarantees the openness of thought is not merely that the openness cannot be contained in thought, but that the openness is more than thought itself. The truth of being is the being of truth, not merely its thought. In this sense, the shift of philosophy toward existence is not simply an event over and done with but an enduring in life that is larger than philosophy. It is an imperative that must go all the way down, not resting at its conceptualization. The tragedy of Heidegger is not

[50] The an-archy of Schürmann's reflection on this, *Heidegger on Being and Acting,* is not the sheer destructiveness of the anarchists but the disclosure of principle through action rather than before it. This is surely the direction of the deconstructionists and their path out of Heidegger, but it is not clear that Schürmann gives the most perspicuous formulation of that project. Levinas and Derrida add considerably more.

just that his philosophical brilliance became associated with an extraordinary series of social and political misjudgments but that he failed to distinguish between the two. He saw clearly that philosophy originated beyond philosophy but mistook that insight for its realization. When the event of discovery eclipses what is discovered, the outcome betrays the achievement itself. A single-minded dedication to the opening of being was not enough to save him from withholding from being. This is the shrinking back from the full demand of the existential we have previously identified as one of the reasons for Heidegger's unwillingness to credit Nietzsche with the full authority of life. By being less concerned with the problem of truth, Nietzsche had also borne a deeper witness to truth. The unwillingness to recognize this emanated from the enduring blind spot in Heidegger's thought. By remaining a philosopher, he became less of a man. This was the flaw of his character so painfully noted by admirers who sensed its tragic import. His greatness as a man was his unsparing devotion to philosophy. In the minds of his most sympathetic readers this was sufficient to outweigh the moral failures, especially given the unavailability of any human beings without sin. Yet there was always something more than personal failure at stake. In the hands of its most profound twentieth century practitioner, the fate of philosophy was implicated. Heidegger shows that philosophy itself is the greatest victim of the absolute assertion of its cause. He is the flawed genius who makes that plain in relation to both his predecessors and his successors.

6

Existence Without Refuge as the Response
of Levinas

The tragedy of philosophy, although inseparable from the tragedy of Heidegger, was nevertheless different. In its finality toward openness, philosophy exceeded the limitations of even its most brilliant practitioners. This was the post-Heideggerian path in which philosophy employed his undeniable accomplishments to remove the restrictions that accomplishments as such impose. Philosophy can no more regard itself as the end point than it can encompass that by which it is. The existential shift under way since the time of Kant, having been diverted from its further realization, could now resume its unfolding. Even a contemplative apocalypse could not stand in the way of the apocalypse of contemplation. The value of a great thinker is not confined to his positive contributions but extends to the errors that are not just mistakes. Philosophical errors are glimpses of the fatality of philosophy itself. Any account of the full measure of Heidegger must take both dimensions into consideration. His best readers are thus challenged not only to reach up to the revolutionary opening of philosophy he wrought, but also to extend it through the exercise of a self-critique at which he proved insufficient. Such a profound critique and extension is the work of Emmanuel Levinas, whose existential thrust opened up a new phase in the unfolding of the modern philosophical revolution. His was the voice of an authority distinctly different from that of the mentor from whom he progressively withdrew.[1]

---

[1] Levinas attended Heidegger's lecture courses in the period after the publication of *Being and Time* and was present at the "triumph" of the confrontation with Cassirer at Davos in 1929. Later he would regret his approval of Heidegger and question his own inability to discern the beginnings of the Nazi connection even then. "I held it against myself during the Nazi years to have preferred Heidegger at Davos." See Samuel Moyn, *Origins of the Other: Emmanuel Levinas Between Revelation and Ethics* (Ithaca, NY: Cornell University Press, 2005), 95. This is an indispensable guide to the intellectual environment in which Levinas developed, although, as with much of the historical literature on the period,

With Levinas the luminosity of existence was now recognized as prior to existence itself.

His most famous formulation of the divergence from Heidegger is the insistence that ethics is prior to ontology.[2] In this encapsulation Levinas makes use of a conventional philosophical language to convey an understanding of philosophy that is far from conventional. He is very much aware of the questionableness of the identifications of "ethics" and "ontology," as if they could be treated as self-contained entities apart from the movement by which they emerge. Almost the only genuinely Heideggerian element of the formulation is the language of priority. But it is in that element that Levinas seeks the extension. He intends to show that the prioritizing movement by which philosophy lives in the unconcealment of being contains the crucial implication of unreachability as such. It is not that ethics precedes ontology, but that ethics itself is never reached because it is always "before." The prioritizing movement, if it is taken seriously, means that even the philosophical appropriation can never be appropriated.[3] Instead, there is already a bond of responsibility in place even before we begin to contemplate it. Our only access is through the movement of responsibility that recognizes its incapacity to fulfill a demand whose primordiality renders it inexhaustible. We have no resting point, no moment of sufficiency in which contemplation is possible. It is only through responsive action that the only luminosity that is available becomes available. The prioritizing exigency forces an inexorable deepening of the existential turn in the history of modern philosophy. Not only is existence a condition for the unfolding of the philosophical meditation, but now it must be acknowledged that there is no philosophizing other than at the limits of existence. When philosophy

it operates with the assumption that Heidegger's philosophy is indistinguishable from relativism. For the biography of Levinas see Salamon Malka, *Emmanuel Levinas: His Life and Legacy*, trans. Michael Kiegel and Sonja M. Embree (Pittsburgh: Duquesne University Press, 2006), especially 45–52, on the same Davos encounter.

[2] "Ethics as First Philosophy," *The Levinas Reader*, 75–87. This principle is well explored by various contributions in Simon Critchley and Robert Bernasconi, eds., *The Cambridge Companion to Levinas* (Cambridge: Cambridge University Press, 2002), especially those of Critchley (1–32) and Putnam (33–62).

[3] One can discern the presentiment of this direction in Levinas's early essay "Reflections on the Philosophy of Hitlerism" (1934), in which he tries to pinpoint the philosophical distortion at its core: "*Universality must give way to the idea of expansion,* for the expansion of a force presents a structure that is completely different from the propagation of an idea." The essay is reprinted with a brief introduction by Levinas in Asher Horowitz and Gad Horowitz, eds., *Difficult Justice: Commentaries on Levinas and Politics* (Toronto: University of Toronto Press, 2006).

has understood its task to be an opening toward being within which we are, this can be done in no way other than through an openness transcending all safeguards in advance. The existential turn of philosophy has placed all of the burden on existence.

Existence Antecedent to World

It is fascinating to follow the way that Levinas works this existential intensification of *Being and Time* in his first book, *De l'existence à l'existant* (1947; *Existence and Existents*). He saw that the central emphasis of Heidegger on existence as ecstatic, as thrown, already privileges the subjective point of view. Anxiety before nothingness, the fall from being, can readily arise when everything depends on the unassisted efforts of Dasein to maintain itself. Confronting its uttermost possibility of death then becomes the most authentic horizon for its existence. Levinas, by contrast, does not begin with nothingness, from which Heidegger never fully separates his reflection, but rather sees the superabundance of being as the beginning within which a nothingness can arise. He begins where Heidegger strains to reach in his movement from Dasein to the unconcealment of being. For Levinas being is already in unconcealment. This is why his philosophical meditation is radically nonsubjective. It is anchored in what is before subjectivity arises and orients itself toward that which subjectivity can never include within itself. Schelling's insight into the noncomprehensibility of the condition of comprehensibility is resumed in the full rigor of its consequences. This is also why Levinas's meditation is definitively noncontemplative. It is rooted in the realization that the contemplative stance already holds at a distance what cannot be known through holding at a distance. What is prior to contemplation, to subjectivity, is available only through the movement of existence itself. It is never accessible through a partial engagement but draws on our existence as a whole. Levinas is thus the point at which the so-called "existential" movement is shown not to be existential enough. Existence is not something we have at our disposal and become anxious about losing. Nothingness is a possibility only because there is a fullness from which it can withdraw. "It is because the *there is* has such a complete hold on us that we cannot take nothingness and death lightly, and we tremble before them. The fear of nothingness is but the measure of our involvement in being" (*De l'existence à l'existant*, 21 / *Existence and Existents*, 5).

Levinas fully confronts the implication of the priority of existence even over Heidegger's thematization of world as its setting. "Existence is not synonymous with the relationship with a world, it is antecedent to the world" (26/8). This enables him to see the real meaning of Plato's famous characterization of the good as beyond being, thereby avoiding the confusion generated by the misidentification of the good as a being that must therefore fall under being. That is an insight Levinas only announces in *Existence and Existents,* for its elaboration would form the major thrust of his reflections. For now he was concerned mainly with becoming clear about the main line of his "ontological" difference with Heidegger. To do this he conducted a phenomenological analysis of experiences selected to highlight the difference. For Levinas the illuminative glimpses are provided by fatigue and indolence. In indolence we experience the impossibility of getting out of existence, a contract we cannot shake off, no matter how much we may be inclined to do so. We would rather not exist, or not exist in this way, and yet we must. In fatigue the onerousness of effort comes to the fore, and we become acutely conscious of "this lag that occurs between a being and itself" (42/19). Effort makes us painfully aware of the instants through which we must pass, as opposed to the effortlessness of melody that cancels duration. "Effort is an effort of the present that lags behind the present" (45/20). Levinas emphasizes that this is a "peculiar form of forsakenness" quite unlike the metaphysical loneliness so well known to modern man. "It is not the solitude of a being forsaken by the world with which it is no longer in step, but of a being that is as it were no longer in step with itself, is out of joint with itself, in a dislocation of the *I* from itself, a being that is not joining up with itself in the instant, in which it is nonetheless committed for good" (50/24).[4] Even when it is not active, an existent is engaged in the act of existence. Its involvement is that of what Levinas calls a "hypostasis."

He explains that the whole essay is concerned with this "upsurge of an existent into existence" in which the relationship with being is disclosed as already there before it is reflected upon. Reflection is itself possible only because of the unreflective movement that precedes it. Caught up in the sincerity of desire, we cannot say what the world is unless we withdraw from that immediacy. It is only by not being in the world that we can reduce it all, as Heidegger does, to the status of tools. "For a soldier," Levinas notes in lines that he probably penned as a prisoner of war,

---

[4] "Concern is not, as Heidegger thinks, the very act of being on the brink of nothingness; it is rather imposed by the solidity of a being that begins and is already encumbered with the excess of itself." *De l'existence à l'existant,* 36 / *Existence and Existents,* 15.

"his bread, jacket and bed are not 'material;' they do not exist 'for ... ,' but are ends" (65/34). The multiple activities of daily life, eating and drinking, moving and resting, do not have an ulterior purpose beyond themselves. "All that is not for the sake of living; it is living. Life is a sincerity" (67/36). Within that authenticity of living, contemplation is a special case of appropriation by which we possess things at a distance. "This power of an agent to remain free from any bond with what remains present to it, of not being compromised by what happens to it, by its objects or even its history, is just what knowing qua light and intention is" (78–9/43). Suspension, or the *epoché*, is not just phenomenology's disclosure of existence; it is the very existence of knowledge as such. "Our existence in the world, with its desires and everyday agitation, is then not an immense fraud, a fall into inauthenticity, an evasion of our deepest destiny. It is but the amplification of that resistance against anonymous and fateful being by which existence becomes consciousness, that is, a relationship an existent maintains with existence, through the light, which both fills up, and maintains, the interval" (80/44). A hypostasis has been realized, but to understand it more fully Levinas seeks to glimpse what cannot be glimpsed because it lies beyond the boundary of the movement by which the hypostasis emerges. It is "the central concept of this study, that of anonymous existence" (80/44).

An initial illumination of this anonymous existence is provided by art, in which objects are withdrawn from our appropriation of them to stand in their own light. Perception gives way to sensation, *aesthesis*. Much of modern art, Levinas insists, is concerned to call our attention to the nonassimilation of its elements to our schemes of representation. Prior to the luminosity of forms, art seems to say, lies the formlessness of the *there is* (92/51). The *il y a* is a key conception for Levinas, for it designates "existence without existents," the very limit of thought whose noncomprehensibility by thought has occupied the history of philosophy since Kant. As the universally indeterminate absence that is nevertheless universally present, it is accessible to us only through the boundary apprehensions of primordial chaos. But it is not the threat constituted by the danger of falling away from existence that is dispositive, but the threat of never escaping the anonymity to reach into the luminosity of existence. It is the nothingness of being rather than the fall from being that marks the horror. "We are opposing, then, the horror of the night, 'the silence and horror of the shades,' to Heideggerian anxiety, the fear of being to the fear of nothingness" (102/58). Where Heidegger still conceived of nothingness as the distinctive contribution of Dasein and as, therefore, a thought of nothingness that could maintain itself outside of being, Levinas struggled to reach the point at which Heidegger too ultimately aimed in finding thought itself to be embedded within being. Levinas was simply more consistent in recognizing the enveloping darkness such a conception must intimate. "A presence of absence, the *there is* is beyond contradiction; it embraces and dominates its contradictory. In this sense being has no outlets" (105/60). Consciousness, he emphasizes, is "not the locus of this nothingness-interval."

What is unique about consciousness is not that it can hold itself apart from being but rather that it has the capacity to slip away from being through sleep. It may be paradoxical "to define consciousness by unconsciousness" (115/64), but it is the proximity of the two that constitutes the "scintillating" quality of consciousness. The possibility of sleep is "a participation in life by non-participation" that becomes acutely evident when we are afflicted by insomnia. Again the localization from which consciousness arises and to which it may return is very different from Heidegger's Dasein. "The latter already implies the world. The *here* we are starting with, the *here* of position, precedes every act of understanding, every horizon and all time. It is the very fact that consciousness is an origin, that it starts from itself, that it is an *existent*" (121–22/68). Now we can understand Levinas's selection of the term "hypostasis," for it is "the transmutation, within the pure event of being, of an event into a substantive – a hypostasis" (125/71). Even Heidegger with his focus on the event had not taken so bold a step into the recognition of the substantiveness of the event itself. For him substance remained under the shadow of the rise of subjectivity in modern philosophy without making the Levinasian leap into the substance of subjectivity. Yet it was just such boldness that allowed Levinas to pierce the mystery of time that can be neither contained nor infinitized. Evanescence, he could now see, was precisely the way that what could not be possessed could be possessed. In the instant, time is lost and taken up again. "Time does not flow like a river. But the present brings about the exceptional situation where we can give an instant a name, and conceive of it as a substantive" (125/71). Existence is no longer synonymous with duration but rather with the interruption of duration by which the eternity of substance is effected. "A beginning does not start out of the instant that precedes the beginning; its point of departure is contained in its point of arrival, like a rebound movement" (131/75). Every instant is the instant of creation.

But like creation the instant, once it has occurred, is bound to itself. The freedom of existence is inseparable from the existent. Levinas questions the prevailing sense of existence as ex-istence, an ecstatic movement outside of the self that is doomed to futility. For him existence is more properly seen as the readiness to assume the self-limitation that makes existence possible. "The freedom of the present finds a limit in the responsibility for which it is the condition. This is the most profound paradox in the concept of freedom: its synthetic bond with its own negation. A free being alone is responsible, that is, already not free" (135/78–79). The question, then, is how this fixity of the existent can once again be dissolved so that the opening of existence can be sustained. This is the point at which Levinas breaks with the phenomenological method that can never radically rupture the definitiveness of the ego. What is needed must come from beyond the self as the revelation of what is inescapably prior to it. This is Levinas's greatest insight into the philosophical significance of the other. The other is not an *alter ego*, but the event that shatters the existent. We do not go beyond in the way that always implies we have never really gone beyond, because we are abruptly lifted outside of ourselves. Left to ourselves we have only hope, the hope of liberation from the enchainment of the instant and not just the mere compensation with which it is often confused. Ordinarily time is the economy of compensation, "the forgetting of the unforgiven instant and the pain for which nothing can compensate" (154/92). Machines perform the same function of compensating time by alleviating it rather than transforming it. Hope, Levinas emphasizes, aims at a time that is more fundamental. "The true object of hope is the Messiah, or salvation" (156/93).

This is the rupture by which the substantiality of the subject beyond subjectivity is established. We are more than ourselves through the relationship with the other. Outside of the calculus of reparations is the opening toward the infinite. "To hope then is to hope for the reparation of the irreparable; it is to hope for the present" (156/93). The reparation that is impossible in time is precisely what constitutes time. "Is not the future above all a resurrection of the present?" (157/94). Time is not the mere duration of frozen instants but the unanticipated liberation by which in every instant a new beginning is made. "What is called the 'next instant' is an annulment of the unimpeachable commitment to existence made in the instant; it is the resurrection of the 'I'" (157/94). Kant's location of action in eternity, having been conceived in terms of dialectic and ecstatic, is now taken for what it is. The "I" is thus not an event within time but the point at which the event of eternity constituting time becomes transparent. "*The 'personality' of a being is its very need for time* as for a miraculous fecundity in the instant itself, by which it recommences as other" (157–59/94–5). That alterity cannot, however, come from the self but must come to it from the other. Dissolution of the instant through otherness, the rupture of time by which time is constituted, comes to us through sociality. Levinas has not yet given sociality the precision of the face of the other, but he does understand it to be the situation of the "face-to-face" that is quite different from the collectivity of merely being alongside one another. The other already lays the claim of need on me. "Intersubjective space is initially asymmetrical" (163/98). The other is present as absence, as that which is other. It is, Levinas emphasizes, the failure of communication in eros that marks its distinctive quality, the impossibility of returning to the self. "Asymmetrical intersubjectivity is the locus of transcendence in which the subject, while preserving its structure's subject, has the possibility of not inevitably returning to itself, the possibility of being fecund and (to anticipate what we shall examine later) having a son" (165/100).[5]

Alterity Precedes Unity

Time and the other are what make self-transcendence possible. This is what provides Levinas with the title of the four lectures he delivered at Jean Wahl's Philosophical College in 1946–47. *Time and the Other* extends the break with phenomenology, so powerfully undertaken by *Existence and Existents*, by admitting that "we find ourselves at a level of investigation that can no longer be qualified as experience" (*Le temps et l'autre*, 34/ *Time and the Other*, 54). The ego, Levinas emphasizes, "is not initially an existent but a mode of existing, that properly speaking it does not exist" (33/53). In the solitude of contemplation, the "I" may dominate the external world but it remains enchained within its own hypostasis. To really be itself, the "I" must no longer be itself, because it is in the time of its transcendence toward the other. Death is not, as with Heidegger, the ultimate lucidity of existence, but rather the limit of lucidity that points toward a luminosity beyond the light of consciousness.[6] The relationship with otherness opened up by death points us toward a future that cannot

---

[5] The extent to which virtually all of the themes of Levinas's mature works are announced is a remarkable feature of this 1947 work. It is one of the reasons Edith Wyschgorod's *Emmanuel Levinas: The Problem of Ethical Metaphysics,* 2nd ed. (New York: Fordham University Press, 2000; original, 1974), which appeared before the publication of *Otherwise Than Being,* remains a valuable guide. John Llewelyn uses the remarkable unity of Levinas's intellectual development as the key to his genealogical account, *Emmanuel Levinas: The Genealogy of Ethics* (London: Routledge, 1995).

[6] "Death in Heidegger is an event of freedom, whereas for me the subject seems to reach the limit of the possible in suffering. It finds itself enchained, overwhelmed, and in some

be grasped, precisely because it must be lived. Time, the future, which cannot come from the subject, can arise only from "the face-to-face with the Other" (68–69/79). It is at this point that Levinas develops two dimensions of the relationship that had only been alluded to previously, the feminine and fecundity, which constitute two dimensions of otherness. By the "feminine" he does not means a specific gender identity, but the hiddenness of love by which the other perpetually withdraws into mystery. "The caress is a mode of the subject's being, where the subject who is in contact with another goes beyond this contact" (82/89). But the real mystery is how the subject can become other to itself. Paternity is the answer, resuming Schelling's meditation on God's creation of human freedom, of which Levinas seems unaware but which he relates to the same problematic. "It is thus not according to the category of cause, but according to the category of father that freedom comes about and time is accomplished" (86/91). This prioritizing of plurality represents a departure from the dominance of the Eleatic emphasis on being as one, for it makes unity a derivation from an irreducible duality. "Time constitutes not the fallen form of being, but its very event" (88/92).

Ought Before Is: Morality as First Philosophy

With that formulation of time as the event of being Levinas set himself definitively outside of the Heideggerian orbit that still sought to assimilate time to being rather than the reverse. The sharpness of the disagreement was even progressively heightened as a means for Levinas to clarify the understanding of his own project. Some element of caricaturization is thus inevitable, making it all the more necessary to keep the continuity in mind if we are to gain an accurate picture of the relationship. This is especially the case as we approach Levinas's most Heideggerian work, *Totalité et Infini* (1961; *Totality and Infinity*), which fairly bristles with the apocalyptic tone so familiar from our reading of Heidegger. One thinks in particular of the wholesale condemnation of the totalizing tendencies pervading the modern world. Yet the work sets itself against the last vestige of the metaphysics of presence represented by Heidegger's speculations. The puzzle is resolved only when we recognize that the correction of Heidegger is inextricably connected with Heidegger in a mode of self-correction. Notable in the apocalyptic tone is the transformation

---

way passive. Death is in this sense the limit of idealism." *Le temps et l'autre*, 57–8 / *Time and Other*, 70–71.

of apocalypse through eschatology. A move that has been well known in church history is now given philosophical demonstration as Levinas points out the full interior significance of apocalypse as the revelation occurring in every now. This is how he can simultaneously agree and disagree with Heidegger so profoundly. Without even adverting to Heidegger's dalliance with Nazism, Levinas definitively removes its source within the retention of theoretical primacy in the modern philosophical revolution.

The totalizing drive that has dominated the modern world is now to be disrupted by prophetic eschatology. It is an astonishing transformation of the opening denoted by Heidegger that he yet could not avoid deferring to a future event. Levinas's achievement was to insist that the opening had already occurred and that its occurrence constitutes openness as such. It is in *Totality and Infinity* that the moral significance of the prioritizing of existence over existents, of the opening toward otherness over the stabilization of the "I," becomes evident. Indeed, the impact of the book as implementing a revolution in moral philosophy is what accounts for its prominence among Levinas's writings. Contemporary moral theory may not yet have caught up to its implications, but this is largely because they lie outside the limits within which moral reflection still operates.[7] One measure, however, of the breakthrough Levinas achieved in this book is that he reached the goal set by Hegel in his critique of Kantian autonomy. The "ought," Hegel pointed out, lay too much on the side of subjectivity without any stronger connection to the "is" than the wish. This lack of seriousness was what robbed Kantian morality of its seriousness, which Hegel sought to reconnect through the dialectical movement from ought to is. But Hegel never managed to impart as much conviction to this solution as Levinas achieved here through his insistence that the ought is what already is before we even raise the question. The project of justifying morality, which has so preoccupied modern reflection, was incapable of resolution so long as morality remained a part of philosophy – that is, so long as the primacy of the theoretical still held sway. Only Levinas had the forthrightness to grasp the reversal by which the ungraspable could be reached. "Morality is not a branch of philosophy, but first philosophy" (*Totalité et Infini*, 281 / *Totality and Infinity*, 304).

It is a transfiguration in thought rather than in history that Levinas pronounces in the preface when he foresees that "the eschatology of

---

[7] For an impressive attempt to place Levinas's ethics within a wider countermovement against the limits of moral reflection, see Richard A. Cohen, *Ethics, Exegesis and Philosophy: Interpretation after Levinas* (Cambridge: Cambridge University Press, 2001).

messianic peace will have come to superpose itself upon the ontology of war" (x/22). But this is no mere change in thought, a utopian dream, for it is a change in the reality of thought itself. History may not yet be transfigured, but its truth has when its measure is no longer immanently derived but originates in an openness definitively beyond it. "Eschatology institutes a relation with being *beyond the totality* or beyond history, and not with being beyond the past and the present" (xi/22). Apocalypse is the infinity that overflows every present and does not have to be awaited because it is already there before any awaiting is possible. Levinas thereby removes the last vestige of intentionality, of the sense of adequacy between thought and being, to recognize the utter non-adequacy of thought to contain that by which it is contained. "All knowing qua intentionality already presupposes the idea of infinity, which is preeminently *non-adequation*" (xv/27). One might be inclined to respond that even a grasp of non-adequation is ultimately a form of adequation, but Levinas is aware of that suggestion. He insists on the radical otherness of the source that precludes the possibility of immanence. "Infinity does not first exist, and *then* reveal itself. Its infinition is produced as revelation, as a positing of its idea in *me*" (xv/26). The impossibility of consciousness grasping itself, a recognition at the core of the idealist revolution, has now reached its full implication in the revelation that alone can illuminate it. But it is never simply a disclosure as such. To the extent that it is the *existence* of knowledge that is involved, nothing less than the full openness of existence can make its disclosure possible. We can know only by opening ourselves fully, not by holding back in contemplation from a distance. In this sense "ethics is an 'optics'" (xvii/29).

Yet the claim of Levinas reaches further than the centrality of ethics to our perspective on the world. It is nothing less than the constitution of the world from the ethical relationship. This is the focus of the first part, "The Same and the Other," in which it is the breakthrough of the other that underpins meaning. Levinas has definitively broken with the lonely subject, who must build bridges from the sameness of the self that never quite reach the other side. It is because Levinas starts with otherness, specifically with the preeminent otherness of the other, that the absurd no longer exists.[8] Transcendence has hitherto been the goal of philosophy, but it has remained a transcendence within the grasp of the self. Levinas, by contrast, begins with the other, the superabundance of meaning that

---

[8] On the genesis of the other as the pivot of Levinas's thought see Moyn, *Origins of the Other*, especially ch. 5: "Levinas's Discovery of the Other in the Making of French Existentialism."

is already there before the movement toward exteriority even begins. Only the relationship with a person, an other, can properly constitute a transcendence by means of a distance that is surpassed and retained at the same time. The waiting on presence and disclosure, the return of the gods anticipated by Heidegger, has already happened in the revelation of the person that always lies beyond revelation. Intentionality as the model of knowing can never include the intentionality of intentionality. This much had become clear, but the hold of the model has not been fully broken until, as Levinas insists, we abandon the aspiration for an intentional grasp. All forms of objective knowledge entail the possession that is just what precludes transcendence. "The 'intentionality' of transcendence is unique in its kind; *the difference between objectivity and transcendence will serve as a general guideline for all the analyses of this work*" (20/49).

Metaphysical Atheism as the Possibility of Revelation

Transcendence with all of its implications for discourse is made possible by separation or what Levinas calls "metaphysical atheism." This has nothing to do with a nontheological metaphysics but is rather a way of evoking the radical separateness whose overcoming makes communication possible. We may be dependent beings, but it is our independence that makes it possible to overlook the former. Atheism is a possibility for a being no longer tied to its source, although it is precisely this possibility that makes the opening toward otherness also possible. "Metaphysical atheism" captures this rich relationship, in distinction from plain atheism. "The idea of infinity, the metaphysical relation, is the dawn of a humanity without myths. But faith purged of myths, the monotheist faith, itself implies metaphysical atheism" (50/77). Revelation, in other words, requires atheism because it is the revelation of what cannot be contained in the embodiments of its revelation.[9] The unnoticed parallel with Schelling is striking and derives from the same dynamic of communication between persons. Levinas has, however, carried the insight farthest into a philosophy of language. "Truth arises where a being separated from the other is not engulfed in him, but speaks to him" (33/62). Discourse, whether it occurs between man and man or between man and God, involves the overcoming of separation that yet fully preserves it. Otherness is indispensable to communication. This is why for Levinas a

---

[9] "The idea of Infinity *is revealed*, in the strong sense of the term. There is no natural religion." *Totalité et infini*, 33 / *Totality and Infinity*, 62.

philosophy of revelation implies a philosophy of discourse. "*The absolute experience is not disclosure but revelation:* a coinciding of the expressed with him who expresses, which is the privileged manifestation of the Other, the manifestation of a face over and beyond form" (37/65–66), yet always with the proviso that a meeting of persons can take place only through the full donation of self by which justice is underpinned. "The Other is not the incarnation of God, but precisely by his face, in which he is disincarnate, is the manifestation of the height in which God is revealed" (51/79).

Truth arises from the justice that calls itself into question, or is already a suspicion of its own freedom in action. Knowledge thus does not originate within the subject but arises from a source that is already beyond him. It is the consciousness of failure in knowing and of immorality in action that is primary in such a way that the subject is under suspicion before there is even a subject. Levinas carries Nietzsche's hermeneutic of suspicion to its irreducibly social implication. But this primordiality of the other also means that the subject is not abandoned to nihilism. Instead, he finds himself already within a world of meaning even before he begins to reflect. "It is because phenomena have been taught to me by him who presents himself – by reviving the acts of this thematization which are the signs – by speaking – that henceforth I am not the plaything of a mystification, but consider objects. The presence of the Other dispels the anarchic sorcery of the facts: the world becomes an object" (72/99). Signification may still generate a gulf between sign and signified, but it is not unbridgeable; the signifier, whose absence testifies to his presence, is the token of reassurance. The space of discourse, which is also the space of thought and freedom, is opened up by the relation to the infinite that overflows all relation. This, Levinas suggests, is what was glimpsed in Plato's formulation that the good is beyond being. Creation *ex nihilo* conveys the same insight that the source is moved not by need, by a deficit, but by desire, an abundance that overflows itself into a free creation. The countermovement of return is correspondingly reflective of that freedom by refusing the temptation toward totality in the name of the infinity present in each person. It is in the opening toward the other that the infinity of freedom is disclosed.

At Home with the Other

Having established the fundamental relation of the same and the other as the context for discourse, Levinas goes on in the next part, "Interiority and Economy," to detail the consequences for our immediate experience. The "I," or interiority, is already a movement beyond being in the enjoyment that answers need. In its autochtony "enjoyment accomplishes the atheist separation" (88/115). Without any of the distance entailed by Heidegger's conception of instrumentalization, need and enjoyment are the spontaneous opening beyond the self. Instinctively we are at home in the world, which becomes alien only in light of the reflective distance that the satisfaction of need makes possible. The insecurity of our condition becomes manifest as the death of the ministering gods, the opening to true transcendence which, for Levinas, is always beyond need in the freedom of its own desire. For now, however, the insecurity of existence that cannot be possessed is masked by mythic presence and relieved by human labor. Man is not simply thrown into the world but abides in it "from a private domain, from being at home with himself, to which at each moment he can retire" (125/152). The uncertainty of the satisfaction of our need is suspended as in a "still life (*nature morte*)" (131/158). Insecurity is not abolished. Labor has merely postponed the moment of nonsatisfaction and death, but in doing so, it has generated the time within which consciousness arises. "Consciousness does not fall into a body – is not incarnated; it is a disincarnation – or, more exactly, a postponing of the corporeity of the body" (140/165–66). The task of consciousness is not, however, to confront its own incapacity but to radically transcend it in the openness toward the other. Then the real meaning of the only temporary satisfaction of need becomes apparent as the offering to the other that goes beyond need.

Levinas had taken a first step beyond Heidegger in the analysis of need as arising from being at home in the world. The disengagement that can see the world as standing reserve for our use is possible only because it is first there in the immediacy of enjoyment. Now Levinas is able to clarify how that self-consciousness can arise within a world that, despite its ultimate bleakness, remains a home to us. "This withdrawal implies a new event; I must have been in relation with something I do not live from. This event is the relation with the Other who welcomes me in the Home, the discreet presence of the Feminine" (145/170). The feminine, presumably as mother, is the first disclosure of disclosure beyond need. To enter into the luminosity it offers, the "I" must abandon its engagement with possession. In order "to see things in themselves, that is, represent them to myself, refuse both enjoyment and possession, I must know how *to give* what I possess" (145/171). It is the other, the astonishment of the infinite in the finite, that both constitutes consciousness and saves it from its isolation. "The Other – the absolutely other – paralyzes possession, which he contests by his epiphany in the face" (145/171). Representation, the freedom of thought by which we can hold everything at a distance, has its source not in the self but in the opening toward the other that places the self and all that it holds in question. Morality underpins intentionality, not the other way around. It is dispossession that makes thought and language possible, because a common world arises only where the world I thought I possessed has been put in question by the primacy of the other. "Being, the thing in itself, is not, with respect to the phenomenon, the hidden. Its presence presents itself in its word" (156/181). Signification is possible when the relationship of sign to signified becomes transparent through the signifier, whose presence can never be made present. "The signifier, he who gives a sign, is not signified" (157/182). This is the surplus of speech, the living language over its mute written expression, that is still never contained in the speaking. Only beings that can place their center of gravity outside of themselves can speak to one another. "The ground of expression is goodness" (158/183).

It is striking to suggest to a world riven by moral anxiety that it is already constituted by the moral truth of order before such self-concern can arise.[10] The formulation may be novel, but it evokes a sense of recognition once it is voiced. One had always suspected that the crisis of nihilism targeted by Nietzsche would never have drawn forth so prolonged and so profound a meditation unless there prevailed a far deeper intimation of truth than could be reached by the forces swirling at the surface. The problem was that we were at a loss as to how to identify such subterranean constants. Once identified, every candidate seemed to be consumed in the maelstrom of values. "By the assessment of something as a value," Heidegger remarked, "what is valued is admitted only as an object for human estimation" ("Letter on Humanism," *Pathmarks*, 179). In many ways the whole existential revolution in modern philosophy has been driven by this intuition of a living truth validating its own authority through itself. Now Levinas has shown us how we are to conceive of such moral truth impervious to the withering effect of subjectivism. Our failure to live up to the moral exigencies, which so oppressed Nietzsche, leaves their obligatory force untouched. Levinas can identify the irrefragable

---

[10] Bettina Bergo, *Levinas Between Ethics and Politics: For the Beauty That Adorns the Earth* (Dordrecht: Kluwer, 1999), presents a vigorous defense of Levinas's account of ethics as prior to all foundations. This is a particularly useful treatment because it is developed in opposition to the criticism that Levinas reduces ethics to mere social relationships or the "political."

power of morality because he no longer treats it as an identifiable component of our common world. Morality, as he shows in the third part, "Exteriority and the Face," is what constitutes the very possibility of such a world. It is such a powerful reconceptualization that it reminds us of the deepest line within the classic tradition, in which the common is not an ideal but what emerges from persons no longer enclosed in their private realms. With Levinas morality is finally at the point of surmounting its millennial derailment in the form of ideals. The only way of grounding a moral order, he reminds us, is to recognize that it alone is what cannot be grounded. It alone is indispensable.[11]

Morality as Grounding World

Exteriority, by which the subject is inexorably drawn outside of himself, evinces a power far more invincible than the aspiration for morality. What Levinas seeks to elicit is the imperviousness of moral truth. The face is never contained in its manifestation. Rather it "speaks to me and thereby invites me to a relation incommensurate with a power exercised" (172/198). In the face, we encounter an infinity stronger than murder that can therefore be the source of the prohibition against murder. As a consequence of this indefeasibility, moral injunctions are what underpin the universality of reason, convincing even "the people who do not wish to listen" (175/201). But what does that mean? It surely does not render it impossible to lie or to commit murder, nor can breaches of the moral law leave the law as such untouched. What Levinas has in mind is something more primordial, as that which is presupposed by the very attempt at its denial. The moral order not only coincides with reason, but is reason as such. Infinity plays the same role for Levinas as it does in Descartes's Third Meditation, whose ontological argument has been misread when the infinite is viewed as an idea within thought. The point Levinas reiterates is that the infinite is what makes thought possible and therefore overflows it. Thought in this sense is the publicly available modality of reason, never a private language between intimates or a mystical connection of pure inwardness. It is essential to Levinas's prioritizing of ethics that it underpins the world of public rationality. The opening toward the face of the other is never a wholly private "I–Thou" affinity, for it is always

---

[11] It was, of course, the great insight of the totalitarian catharsis that, as the title of Solzhenitsyn's Nobel Prize speech indicates, "One Word of Truth Outweighs the Whole World." See Walsh, *After Ideology.*

transacted within the priority of the universally human. "The third party looks at me in the face of the Other – language is justice. It is not that there first would be the face, and then the being it manifests or expresses would concern himself with justice; the epiphany of the face as face opens humanity" (188/213).

The humanity that is constituted by such multiple disclosures of infinity is inescapably pluralistic. It seems doubtful that Levinas is familiar with the extensive discussion of pluralism among liberal political theorists, but they would certainly benefit enormously from more familiarity with his.[12] In the hands of Levinas, pluralism is not a brute irreducibility of politics but rather the indispensable mode in which infinity is possible. To the extent that the infinite is what cannot be contained in the finite, a plurality of self-transcending centers is the only means of its disclosure. The independence and yet exposure of the other, of being, is what opens the possibility of time. As called forth by the command of the other, my freedom is placed in the service of postponing his death. "It is not finite freedom that makes the notion of time intelligible; it is time that gives a meaning to the notion of finite freedom" (199/224). Space and time are for Levinas inescapably social, for they are constituted by a multiplicity of centers and an extension of service. It is interesting, too, that he connects this pluralism with freedom but reverses the relationship mooted by the liberal theorists. For Levinas it is not freedom that generates pluralism but rather pluralism that calls forth the dimension of freedom. "It is therefore not freedom that accounts for the transcendence of the Other, but the transcendence of the Other that accounts for freedom – a transcendence of the Other with regard to me which, being infinite, does not have the same significance as my transcendence with regard to him" (200/225). The last clause indicates the nonreciprocity to which a more profound view of pluralism must lead. Pluralism is not an indifferent relationship between objects, but a personal opening on infinity that must consequently fall most heavily on me. Whatever may be perpetrated by the other, I am never relieved of my responsibility of responding to the face whose command lifts me utterly beyond myself. Having been seized by the impossibility of annihilating the other, his death has become impossible for me (208–9/232).

---

[12] A thoughtful reading of Levinas in light of the pluralist imperative is provided by Ruki Viksker, *The Inhuman Condition: Looking for Difference after Levinas and Heidegger* (Dordrecht: Kluwer, 2004), although the impulse toward critique has perhaps obstructed the final measure of sympathy needed. When pluralism is taken as an irreducible, it is difficult to concede the priority of the infinite from which plurality as such flows.

The formulation suggests an unattainable moral rigor, but this would be to misread Levinas's innovation. He does not mean that it has become physically impossible for me to kill the other, only that such killing would not kill the presence of the other within my conscience. In this sense he is very close to the ordinary meaning of conscience as precisely that which we cannot suppress despite our efforts to do so. What this means is not that politics is only occasionally pierced by the light of morality but that it ultimately can never escape the luminosity of existence. "War and commerce presuppose the face and the transcendence of the being appearing in the face" (197/222). Levinas devotes only a few cryptic comments to the relationship of commerce, possibly as a result of a lack of sympathy, but one could see his analysis being extended into the recognition that a market is constituted by moral boundaries it cannot contain. It is violence, as the most fundamental problem of politics, that absorbs most of his attention. "Violence bears upon a being both graspable and escaping every hold" (198/223). It is in the very meaning of violence, Levinas insists, that it aims at annihilating that which cannot be annihilated. Where discourse had been possible in the donation of the self to the other, who can never be included within the framework of power, the determination to do so nevertheless breaks out. Violence as such "does not aim simply at disposing of the other as one disposes of a thing, but, already at the limit of murder, it proceeds from unlimited negation. It can aim at only a presence itself infinite despite its insertion in the field of my powers. Violence can aim only at a face" (200/225). Even the Marxist analysis of the alienation of the producer from his product must be removed from its economic reference to be understood primordially as an assault on the infinity of the worker (202–3/227).

The crucial insight that Levinas labors to convey in this meditation on violence aimed at a face is that it is never successful. When morality is no longer an option available within being but our very mode of being, the futility of its betrayal is evident. Indeed, it is the very impossibility of violence that is its deepest disclosure. Levinas here opens a line of reflection that again leads back to the classic understanding of evil as nonreality, that which is incapable of being, only now with the accent of unreality identified as the limit of existence. "Violence does not stop Discourse.... It is produced only in a world where I can die *as a result of someone* and *for someone*" (216–17/239). We cannot escape the infinite call of the other, as we are inexorably drawn from fear of death to the fear of committing murder. But this transformation is not one that occurs in a lightning flash; it is rather the growth of a responsibility that strengthens as we enter more fully into it. In thus purging itself of its enjoyment of separation, the "I" does justice to the singularity of the other that entails doing more than justice. Infinite responsibility entails an infinite response. "The sole possibility in being of going beyond the straight line of the law, that is, of finding a place lying beyond the universal, is to be I" (223/245). Levinas comes remarkably close to Kierkegaard's insight that the individual transcends the ethical into the religious, a parallel insight that flows directly from the same prioritizing of existence.[13] It is in that singularity of the infinite that the opening of existence becomes possible in the full sense as the procreative opening of other existents. "The fecundity of subjectivity, by which the I survives itself, is a condition required for the truth of subjectivity, the clandestine dimension of the judgment of God" (225/247). Not even Kierkegaard with his extensive meditation on marriage had carried the inquiry to the point where paternity is recognized as the primary opening and redeeming of time.

Paternity as the Truth of Love

His notion of paternity constitutes Levinas's most radical challenge to the metaphysics of intentionality within the culminating part of the work. "Beyond the Face" makes it clear that the analysis does not rest with the disclosure of the other but that it necessarily entails a relationship with the nondisclosive other. Far from constituting an epiphany, the face of the other is what marks the impossibility of epiphany. We are so used to thinking of freedom in terms of its putative possessor, the subject, that it is something of a shock to encounter Levinas's assertion that freedom derives its justification from the other. The drama of the self is played out beyond the self. "The freedom of the I is neither the arbitrariness of an isolated being nor the conformity of an isolated being with a rational and universal law incumbent upon all. My arbitrary freedom reads its shame in the eyes that look at me" (230/252). It is because we do not determine our own destiny that the fate of freedom is transacted in a

---

[13] The precise contours of Levinas's relationship to Kierkegaard are a major unexplored topic in the literature. What is clear is that the suggestion was not particularly welcome. "To judge from his postwar essays on the subject, Levinas rejected the founder of existentialism with no little irritation." Moyn, *Origins of the Other,* 186. A large part of the explanation may be that Levinas did not want his own analytical rigor to be tainted by the implication of a subjectivist leap associated with Kierkegaard. In other words, it is likely that the prevailing superficial assessment of the "existentialist" is to blame. This is an impression that the more philosophical reading of Kierkegaard in Chapter 8 is intended to dispel.

realm beyond the subject. "Hence we must indicate a plane both presupposing and transcending the epiphany of the Other in the face, a plane where the I bears itself beyond death and recovers also from its return to itself. This plane is that of love and fecundity, where subjectivity is posited in function of these movements" (231/253). The anchoring of philosophy in what it can never comprehend or contain has now reached its positive affirmation. Responsibility is not what limits freedom but what constitutes its reality as freedom. Modern philosophy, which began with the centering of attention on the self, has now recognized that its very project is constituted by what lies beyond it. This is the other half of the Cartesian beginning, as Levinas reminds by his constant reference to the Third Meditation.

The infinite he shows was there from the very beginning. Even when the subject seemed most absorbed with itself, in the movement of love it was held fast by otherness. Love may seem to head toward immanence, but it is defined by transcendence. It is "a movement by which a being seeks that to which it was bound before even taking the initiative" (232/254). Eros is "*the equivocal* par excellence" (233/255) because, while seeming to be a choice of destiny, it is really a predestination. In an analysis that is more reminiscent of Plato's *Symposium* than Levinas acknowledges, he shows that eros is precisely what cannot be defined, because it is perpetually what is not yet. "Nothing is further from *Eros* than possession" (243/265). Instead of jumping from there to the contemplation of eros as spiritual, however, Levinas directs us toward the implications for the physical. The body is not a thing or, rather, it is a thing that demonstrates its incapacity for thingly existence. A caress aims not at what can be reached but at what is beyond reach. The pornographic caress is precisely an attempt to possess what cannot be possessed. and as such, its primary untruth is toward the eros it ostensibly makes available. We might speculate, going further than Levinas, that pornography functions by triggering an eros it cannot contain. He simply leaves it with the observation that erotic nudity is "an inverted signification, a signification that signifies falsely" (241/263). The profanation of love is a possibility because of its equivocal character as a nondefinitive movement beyond the self to the other. Love seeks the other but returns to the self as the locus of its satisfaction. What lifts love definitively into that plane of the other is when it generates an other, a child.

The ambiguity of eros is resolved when it bears fruit in an other that is distinctly other. Through voluptuousity the subject is "initiated into a mystery" beyond the self, but it has not yet utterly severed the connection with self. Love is love only when it loves an other as an other, not just as an other self. The child is that unmerited event by which an other is "more exactly, me, but not myself" (249/271). Transcendence has reached its goal when it has engendered, beyond its own finality, the finality of the transcendence of an other. I can love myself in the child but never as myself; it is always as other that the child is loved. The category of causality, Levinas notes, no longer applies. "The father does not simply cause the son. *To be* one's son means to be I in one's son, to be substantially in him, yet without being maintained there in identity" (255–56/278–79). Levinas might well have quoted the New Testament formulation of loving the other as oneself to delineate this difference between loving the other as an expression of oneself, and thus still contained within the self, and the love of the other as an *other* self. Paternity provides him with the clearest evocation of this insight because it aims at the freedom of the son. The relation to the father is sacrificed for the sake of the independence of the son. Only a free other is an adequate embodiment of the father, for the child is an embodiment that goes beyond embodiment as a new embodiment of its own. This rich vein of reflection is only sketched in the concluding pages of the book, but sufficiently to indicate that for Levinas paternity provides the model of human relationship. "The I as I remains turned ethically to the face of the other: fraternity is the very relation with the face in which at the same time my election and equality, that is, the mastery exercised over me by the other, are accomplished" (256/279). Fraternity is not an idea added to that of man but its very "ipseity" (257/280).[14]

The fraternity that becomes transparent in paternity is, for Levinas, not an event that occurs in time but the event that constitutes time. Kant's problem of how free beings can exist within an order of causality is now resolved by the reversal of priority that was implicit in the shift of philosophical attention from what it contains to that by which it is contained. Once again the unnoticed connection with Plato of the *Symposium* is striking in Levinas's observation that philosophy, too, is a movement that aims at the engendering of an other. "Philosophy itself constitutes a moment

---

[14] We can glimpse some measure of the original contribution of Levinas to ethics in this analysis of paternity by simply comparing it with the prevailing rights language surrounding parenthood today. It is always worth recalling Heidegger's reluctance to address ethics apart from being, for Levinas showed how powerfully ethics is rooted in the very meaning of being. One has only to glance at the moral thicket that has overtaken human fertility interventions to recognize the need for just such a radical rethinking of conventional approaches.

of this temporal accomplishment, a discourse always addressed to an other" (247/269). Both philosophy and generation, Plato insists, aim at the same goal of immortality, which Levinas identifies as infinite time. "Fecundity continues history without producing old age" (246/268). The difference is that Levinas pictures this touching of the infinite not as the highest point of being but rather as an event beyond the being it opens up. The transcendence that transcends itself, "the goodness of goodness" (247/269), is the innermost meaning of time. In uncovering this insight Levinas is not so much departing from the tradition of metaphysics, with its logic of oneness and being, as revealing unsuspected depths within it. Being that is one carries within it the unfolding toward oneness of the other. It was simply that Levinas discovered in paternity a powerful metaphor for the intuition of an opening that would not inevitably return to the source contemplating it. I am my child in a way that breaks up the "Eleatic unity." "In this transcendence the I is not swept away, since the son is not me; and yet I *am* my son. The fecundity of the I is its very transcendence" (254/277). The work of time is not in the attainment of immortality; it is rather immortality that enacts the work of time.

It is because we are not bound to being that we can take our distance with regard to being. Time is that mode in which the beginning does not determine but holds open the possibility of a new beginning. This is not just fecundity but more generally the new beginning that is made possible through forgiveness. "Forgetting nullifies the relations with the past, whereas pardon conserves the past pardoned in the purified present" (259/283). Resurrection, Levinas repeats in a formulation he first employed in *Existence and Existents,* is the principal event of time. Heidegger could never quite separate his thinking about time from the apocalyptic event that closes it, a fatality that constituted the central temptation of the modern world. The only way the opening of existence can avoid its self-betrayal as immanent is to recognize that it is constituted by an infinity that transcends all instantiation. "It is not the finitude of being that constitutes the essence of time, as Heidegger thinks, but its infinity" (260/284). Time is a discontinuous continuity of death and resurrection. It is this nonimmanent apocalypse that makes possible both the openness of history and its equidistance at every point from its goal. "Truth requires both an infinite time and a time it will be able to seal, a completed time." It is, Levinas concludes, "messianic time," which at once completes time and guarantees its completeness. In keeping with the unfathomable mystery of openness, the question of whether this triumph of eternity is "a new structure of time or an extreme vigilance of messianic consciousness" (261/285) is beyond the scope of the work. To settle it would be to enter into the realm of theology, in which the idea of God substitutes for his presence. By contrast Levinas insists on "the surplus of truth over being" (267/291), which, in displacing the primacy of intentionality, has been one of the principal theses of his study (270–71/294). Knowledge, whether theological, philosophical, or political, reverts to the impersonal that can be grasped rather than remain faithful to the transcendence of the personal that can only be respected.

Substitution Is Signification

The challenge is to work out the implications for knowledge once its origination in existence has been acknowledged. This is the task that Levinas addresses in his next great book, *Autrement qu'être ou au-delà de l'essence* (1974; *Otherwise Than Being or Beyond Essence*), which, as the title indicates, elaborates the metaphysics of otherness. Where *Totality and Infinity* had focused on ethical alterity, *Otherwise Than Being* turns to the implications for the entire language of philosophy. A far-reaching revision is entailed, which, despite Levinas's tendency to regard it as a break, is more properly seen as the culmination of the prioritizing of existence within modern philosophy. The ambivalence is not specific to Levinas. It is implicit within the historical tension of modernity that has simultaneously exalted the instrumental mastery of the subject and strained against that mastery in the name of the transcendence that contains it. An emphasis on one side to the exclusion of the other often suggests a forgetfulness that is not the case. Levinas, too, is sometimes guilty of this imbalance, as when he rails against the dehumanizing impact of ideology but fails to consider his own sympathy toward Marx as a variant. A less one-sided selection would recognize that Marx not only opened up the utopia of otherness, but also generated the ideology of most universal destructiveness. What saves Levinas's analysis from this objection is that it is essentially pre-political and that it leads to a far richer set of political implications than the few attenuations he suggests in passing. The point, however, is not to find fault with his political sympathies, which are at any rate relatively undeveloped, but to draw attention to their source within the innermost tension of the modern world. Even a thinker who no longer sought solutions could not avoid occasionally framing his project in such terms. Resistance against totalities absorbs something of the totalizing pattern. It is simply that Levinas went farther

than most in elaborating what a metaphysics of existence must avoid by
way of reification. He invites us to carry the process forward by recognizing that it is a process emergent from the very historical existence it
critiques.

A first step is provided by the preconceptual philosophical language of
Otherwise Than Being in light of the unsurpassable movement of transcendence toward the other. "Transcendence is passing over to being's *other*,
otherwise than being" (*Autrement qu'être*, 3 / *Otherwise Than Being*, 3). Levinas intends his language to be taken carefully as delineating an opening
prior to the enduring or presence that is *esse*, being or essence (he does
not use "essence" in the sense of form, or *eidos*). In the first chapter,
"Essence and Disinterest," he moves away from the interest that draws us
toward being in order to glimpse the disinterest of the prior openness
irreducible to being. It is, Levinas explains, the audacity of skepticism
that denies saying and says so (9/7). Before freedom there is the debt
to goodness contracted in the face of the other. This responsibility in
which I am chosen is not a relationship with a thou, as in Buber's characterization, but with an *illeity* (from *il*, he) that defines a concern with
an other unlimited by his concern with me. It is a past before every possible present, utterly impervious to eventualities. "In its *being* subjectivity
undoes *essence* by substituting itself for another" (16/13). Substitution in
this primordial sense is one of the most crucial developments of Levinas
throughout the book. It is a term that carries the weight of transcendence, "the glory of transcendence," while emphasizing a leaping ahead
to the place of the other that makes signification possible. "Substitution
is signification."[15] It is not that we necessarily offer an expiation for the
other, but that "sacrifice without reserve" (18/15) is the orientation of a
subject outside of time and therefore capable of the time of signification.
Only a subject outside of being is capable of the transcendence of being
signification requires. The intention toward an other discovers that it
originates from the other in a way that is reminiscent, Levinas reminds
us, of the Platonic good beyond being. "To reduce the good to being, to
its calculation and its history, is to nullify goodness" (22/18).

The exposition of this insight leads to a far deeper revision of the
language of subjectivity that no longer needs an elaboration in the form
of fecundity. It is not that the relationship to the other, in the face and

---

[15] It is no accident that this formulation and the focus on language carry echoes of Derrida,
whose semiological philosophy was already prominent at this time. Levinas had learned
much from the most famous critique to which his work had been subjected in Derrida's
"Violence and Metaphysics: An Essay on the Thought of Emmanuel Levinas."

paternity, has ceased to be pivotal for Levinas; it is simply that it has been more fully interiorized in the other-directionality of the subject. The second chapter, "Intentionality and Sensing," thus shows that the presupposition of the preexisting subject fails to account even for intentionality itself. Over and beyond the disclosure of being is the being of disclosure, which is not present but must always be past. This "diachrony" is the root of the distinction Levinas makes between subjectivity and consciousness. The latter is always correlative to "a present represented," while the former "signifies an allegiance of the same to the other, imposed before any exhibition of the other" (32/25). In many ways the logic of Heidegger's quest of the primordial reaches its limit in Levinas's assertion of the priority of a past that can never be present because it is what renders every present possible. The question of how that can be conceived of is answered by the relation to the other, who is never what is disclosed. Truth becomes, then, not the discovery of what is present outside the subject but the process of recovering what can never really be recovered or, for that reason, never really lost. Where in *Existence and Existents* Levinas had understood how the movement of existence structures subjectivity, now he is able to understand subjectivity as a movement of existence. "Being's essence is the temporalization of time, the diastasis of the identical and its recapture or reminiscence, the unity of apperception" (37/29). He is, moreover, conscious of the radical challenge this represents to the prevailing ontology that refuses any possibility outside of being. How can possibility be if it does not occur within being? It is the principal question of a work that evokes "otherwise than being."

It is also the principal question at the heart of the modern philosophical revolution that has struggled to articulate what cannot be articulated because it is what makes articulation possible. "If saying is not only the correlative of a said, if its signifyingness is not absorbed in the signification said, can we not find beyond or on the hither side of the saying that tells being the signifyingness of diachrony?" (49/38). Levinas answers in the affirmative but insists that the "signifyingness of diachrony" is not within being as present but rather as that which is prior because it opens the space and time of presence. It is the time of being rather than the being of time. The "otherwise than being" is the temporality of being. If time were within being, there would be no separation by which being could be apprehended. In this sense time is not so much an event within being as the event of being's self-disclosure. "The work of being, essence, time, the lapse of time, is exposition, truth, philosophy" (38/30). Temporality is the movement by which being diverges from itself in order to return to itself, but always in such a way that the return never attains closure. Where Husserl makes sensing the originary consciousness of time his focus, Levinas insists that sensing is irreducibly temporal. We do not sense time; rather we sense because of time. Even with Heidegger there was still the prospect of intentionality grasping time, but for Levinas intentionality is inseparable from time, which, therefore, cannot be grasped as such. This then enables him to address the question of whether time lies within being by showing that the presupposition of the question is that being, an event, can be apprehended without time. But it is precisely because being is temporal that there opens up the distance by which it can be known. "The temporal modification is not an event, nor an action, nor the effect of a cause. It is the verb to be" (43/34). Only that which is temporal can be sensed and intended so that temporality is irreducible.

Language springs from this past that cannot be included in a present. That is, it is inescapably temporal. Just as sensibility is the process by which "the qualities of perceived things turn into time and into consciousness" (44/35), so language is the movement by which they turn into the said. Before it is a noun, language is a verb. "It is only in the said, in the epos of saying, that the diachrony of time is synchronized into a time that is recallable, and becomes a theme" (48/37). But again it is not the arresting of time in the said that constitutes the essence of language, but the very impossibility of such simultaneity. Language attests to the unattainability of re-presentation. "Here language does not double up the being of entities, but exposes the silent resonance of the essence" (51/40). While Heidegger still held out the suggestion that language opened a path to being, Levinas insists that it is the impossibility of reaching being that constitutes its essence. Even in art, the preeminent case of a said that can stand apart from the saying, there is an inexorable pull back into the verbal movement before it. This is what Levinas sees as the meaning of the restless proliferation of forms in modern art, a relentless drive for innovation. Only by keeping open its own possibility of renewal is art true to itself. "The said, contesting the abdication of the saying that everywhere occurs in this said, thus maintains the diachrony in which, holding its breath, the spirit hears the echo of the *otherwise*" (57/44). This, Levinas emphasizes, is not to reach an authentic reality beyond appearance, but to reach without reaching the question, the "utopia" or non-place, from which the quest must spring. "It will be possible to show that there is question of the said and being only because saying or responsibility require justice" (58/45).

Condition of Possibility as Beyond Possibility

In the Levinasian analysis, consciousness is "other-wise," to give the title of the work its different meaning. It is in relation to the other that conscious-ness obtains the glimpse of itself that it cannot know directly because, in line with the modern meditation since Kant, that is the condition for the possibility of knowing. Levinas has finally made it clear that the condition of possibility cannot be a possibility, but must rather be beyond possibility. Even sensibility, he shows us in this first chapter, can only be glimpsed in the opening toward the other that lies before all opening. This "supreme passivity of exposure to another" can be expressed only through "a quasi-hagiographical style" that must not be confused with sermonizing but rather related to the consciousness beyond self-consciousness (61/47). Before all saying, there is the exposure to the other by which one is severed from one's own inwardness, a transcending of one's being that is dis-interested. "This being torn up from oneself in the core of one's unity, this absolute non-coinciding, this diachrony of the instant, signi-fies in the form of one-penetrated-by-the-other" (64/49). Everything that comes under the heading of identity, self, corporality, essence is precisely what we are not, for such terms denote what we are ready to give up in openness to the other. "This *despite oneself* marks this life in its very living. Life is life despite life – in its patience and its ageing" (65/51). Time is this passing of existence, senescence, that is not "I" because I have already been chosen by the other as what constitutes my uniqueness. It is not the being toward death that identifies me but the transcendence of death that has already occurred in my submission to the other. But this in turn means, although Levinas does not quite phrase it thus, that life is a dying to oneself in responsibility toward the other. The "I" consists in not holding onto itself, for only in not being an "I" do I become an I. Without quoting the formulation of Christ that he who loses his life will gain it, Levinas shows how this proclamation is more than an exhortation. It is the unsurpassable boundary of our existence. Exhortation still has a role, but the appeal could not be heard unless it had already been heard.[16]

Having thus shown that intentionality presupposes more than inten-tionality, Levinas now carries the "an-archic" implications further in the

---

[16] This is a perspective that seems completely lost in Leora Batnitzky, *Leo Strauss and Emmanuel Levinas: Philosophy and the Politics of Revelation* (Cambridge: Cambridge University Press, 2006), whose obvious sympathy with Strauss renders Levinas conceptually opaque.

third chapter, "Sensibility and Proximity." The interiorization of openness to the other, the distinctive ontology of *Otherwise Than Being*, is rooted in the proximity that has no beginning. Sensibility is now not just an openness or a passivity from which the "I" cannot sever itself; it is a bond or fraternity that undergirds the vulnerability of the subject as the possibility of communication. To follow Levinas here we must remind ourselves of the meaning of communication. It is never the mere exchange of information, but always entails the full donation of self to the other. Over and above what we talk about, we give ourselves to one another.[17] We cannot analyze the capacity to communicate from the elements involved, a semiology of parts, but must rather begin with the whole, whose transferability precedes all discrete exchanges. Communication is precisely the awareness that what we talk about is not who we are, that speaking is no more than a symbol of the incommunicable openness of the self to the other. This is what Levinas means by "proximity." It is in contrast to the universality of the medium of language by which communication actually occurs. Proximity is in this sense what explains the mystery of language by which the particular can become the vehicle for the universal and yet make possible the meeting of two concrete individuals. Human beings can communicate, can touch one another, not just because they have access to the sensible, but because that access is always more than sensibility. It is a sensibility that is shot through with proximity to the other. Heart can speak to heart because their speaking is always more than speaking. Sensation is not an obstacle to transcendence but its origin.

It is in subjective sensation, the point of maximum self-enjoyment, that the process of "coring out" (*dénucléation*) really begins. Signification arises from the altruism of sensibility that is continuous with its egoism. One first has to "enjoy one's bread, not in order to have the merit of giving it, but in order to give it with one's heart, to give oneself in giving it" (91/72). Vulnerability is the sense of the other that precedes any action toward him. Levinas, in contrast to his earlier application of the metaphor of paternity, now employs maternity as a means of conveying the intimacy of a relationship in which we become responsible for bringing forth an

---

[17] Heidegger's awareness of the reputation for obscurity his own linguistic innovations had attracted was revealed in an incident recounted by Safranski: "Carl Friedrich von Weizsäcker once told him the Jewish anecdote about a man who perpetually sits in a tavern. When asked why he does so, he answers: 'Well, it's my wife.' 'What about your wife?' 'Oh, she talks and talks and talks . . . ' 'What does she talk about?' 'That she doesn't say.' When Heidegger heard the story he said, 'Yes, that's how it is.'" *Martin Heidegger,* 311.

other. Closer even than the face is the bond of maternity that substitutes itself for the other. "Maternity, which is bearing par excellence, bears even responsibility for the persecuting by the other" (95/75). The language of free consent, like the language of being, not only cannot capture this connection that is prior to freedom, but is even a refusal of the anarchic responsibility. "In this plot I am bound to others before being tied to my body" (96/76). In a formula of supreme succinctness Levinas declares, "Signification is witness or martyrdom" (98/77–78). The Cartesian dichotomy of mind and body is no longer an issue once the body is recognized as a primordial vulnerability toward the other. "Hospitality, the one-for-the-other in the ego, delivers it more passively than any passivity from links in a causal chain" (99/79). Behind and before all thematization and reciprocity there is the exposure to being affected by the other that is the sensibility of the body, signifyingness as such. Levinas no longer talks about the face of the other, because the primordial bond is not manifest in the face that is no more than a trace. "It escapes representation; it is the collapse of phenomenality" (112/88). Proximity does not create a common present but rather disturbs it. "One can call that apocalyptically the break-up of time" (113/89). The meditation on sensibility has brought Levinas to the boundary of theology, which, with its reduction of mystery to the dominating model of intentionality, he leaves aside. Speculation and faith may complete, but they cannot advance beyond, the prior openness of proximity from which our deepest sense of the infinite is drawn. "This debit which increases is infinity as an infinition of the infinite, as glory" (119/93).

Good Before Being

Having thus reached the infinite, Levinas is at the point from which metaphysics takes its source, but now without the reification of being that has marked the Western tradition since its inception. "Substitution," the topic of the fourth chapter that was the germ of the whole work (note 1 to Chapter 4), definitively removes the primacy of the subject, for the starting point lies in the radical otherness that cannot be absorbed within its contemplation. The self substitutes itself for the other before it is a self. Existence that is otherwise than being opens being that lies definitively beyond being. It is a "recurrence" to a responsibility that arises before the self, as if the self is orphaned before it is even born (133/105). The self is unable to contain itself in the mode of consciousness but already finds itself in infinite passivity before it finds itself. "It is a recurrence to oneself out of an irrecusable exigency of the other, a duty overflowing my being, a duty becoming a debt and an extreme passivity prior to the tranquility, still quite relative, in the inertia and materiality of things at rest. . . . This recurrence is incarnation" (139/109). Responsibility for the other to the point of substitution, expiation of the persecution, is our own expulsion from being. Creation launches us into a relation of responsibility without our grasping or assenting to it. Absolute passivity of creation is what Western philosophy has missed in its assumption that it can contain the idea of creation rather than the other way around. The easy confidence of reason is upended by this acknowledgment of its own assignation of a responsibility it can never satisfy, for we are compelled to discover, like Kierkegaard, that "the more just I am, the more guilty I am" (143/112).[18] It is in the language of creation rather than ontology that this priority of obligation is best expressed. Levinas, while he does not clarify matters theologically, does recognize the value of the *ex nihilo*, for "in creation, what is called to being answers to a call that could not have reached it since, brought out of nothingness, it obeyed before hearing the order" (145/113).

The good that is before being is what chooses me before I choose it. Original goodness precedes original sin. It is because we are already invested by the hidden good that we have community with the other before with ourselves. "This responsibility commits me, and does so before any truth and any certainty, making the question of trust and norms an *idle* question, for in its uprightness a consciousness is not only naivety and opinion" (154/120). Such idle questions are of course raised, indeed preoccupy political philosophy, because the articulation of a public mode of discourse has required the thematization of the prethematic relation to the other. Levinas recognizes this necessity as one that arises because the other is not just an other but is a third party in respect to another. The common world of such indirectly related others can be constituted only through the objectifying language that overlooks their distinct otherness. Political philosophy must, then, assume the task not of justifying the primacy of this publicly authoritative set of norms but of recalling their derivative character.[19] The "death of God" only

---

[18] See Kierkegaard, "The Upbuilding That Lies in the Thought That in Relation to God We Are Always in the Wrong," *Either/Or*, Part II.

[19] "This antecedence of responsibility to freedom would signify the Goodness of the Good: the necessity that the Good choose me first before I can be in a position to choose, that is, welcome its choice. That is my pre-originary *susceptiveness*. It is a passivity prior to all receptivity, it is transcendent. It is an antecedence prior to all representable

suggests the subjectivity of values; it does not touch upon the primordial inescapability of God. "The impossibility of escaping God lies in the depths of myself as a self, as an absolute passivity" (165/128). The egoism of consciousness is not what is primary, as becomes evident in our very mortality by which sacrifice attests to a meaning beyond the self. We "can have responsibilities and attachments through which death takes on a meaning. That is because, from the start, the other affects us despite ourselves" (166/129). This is a line of reflection that confirms the path of the present study, which took its beginning from Kant. He was the first to clearly insist that ontology cannot measure the human, for the categorical imperative is prior to God and immortality.

In thus invoking the revolution introduced by Kant, Levinas discards the ambiguity of the subject that still attaches to it.[20] The existential shift of modern philosophy does not install the autonomy of the imperious subject but rather definitively transcends it. The subject, Levinas insists, is not free, or more accurately, he is free only because he is not free. Law is not derived from freedom, for freedom is derived from law. It is a reversal of accent that in the way of revolution returns the modern to the ancient starting point, only now with a more deeply held awareness of its genesis. Both ancient and modern had struggled to conceive of the relationship between the subject and the infinite. Now Levinas was able to show that the infinite is neither a presence nor an absence but the priority by which the subject is constituted. In "Subjectivity and Infinity," the concluding chapter of the work, he shows that it is precisely the subject's inability to contain that by which it is contained that opens up its access to the infinite, that makes it an infinity of openness. The hold of phenomenality, subjectivity in the ordinary sense, must be broken if we are to see the pre-phenomenal openness of subjectivity in its primordial sense. It is "non-indifference to the other" (177/138) that holds open a

antecedence: immemorial. The Good is before being." *Autrement qu'être ou au-delà de l'essence*, 157 / *Otherwise Than Being*, 122.

[20] The significance of Kant for Levinas should never be underestimated. In many ways Levinas's disaffection from Kierkegaard can be accounted for by his desire to link his reflection with the compelling force of Kant's transcendental rigor. It is surely only a matter of time before contemporary analytic scholars grasp the connection and exploit Levinas's provocative linguistic inversions for their semantic import. In the meantime a good beginning has been made by Catherine Chalier, *What Ought I to Do? Morality in Kant and Levinas*, trans. Jane Marie Todd (Ithaca, NY: Cornell University Press, 2002), who draws attention to their common inspiration in an utterly disinterested morality. For the wider relationship of Levinas to the Age of Reason, see Melvyn New, ed., with Robert Bernasconi and Richard A. Cohen, *In Proximity: Emmanuel Levinas and the Eighteenth Century* (Lubbock: Texas Tech University Press, 2001).

presubjective passivity by which the subject is constituted. Ethical responsibility for the other is what makes the subject, rather than the other way around. "Signification as proximity is thus the latent birth of the subject" (178/139). In this capacity to be chosen, a capacity before any capacity, the disclosure of the infinite occurs in and through the subject. "The subject is born in the beginninglessness of an anarchy and in the endlessness of obligation, gloriously augmenting as though infinity came to pass in it. In the absolute assignation of the subject the Infinite is enigmatically heard: before and beyond" (178/140).

The panegyric to the glory of the infinite is so powerful that one is inclined to forget that it is not an attainment but an inspiration. Like Kant, Levinas has to struggle to prevent this exaltation of human dignity from becoming a theme if it is to constitute the horizon of existence. We do not achieve the infinite but rather bear witness to it. For us it is an infinity of guilt in which, in the words of Dostoevsky, "each of us is guilty before everyone and for everyone, and I more than the others" (186/146).[21] The formulation is strange within a world in which guilt or innocence denotes a fixed quantity, but in relation to the ethical there are no stopping points. Enough is never reached when it is the infinity of movement that discloses the infinite. "Before they call I will answer," Levinas remarks of this quotation from Isaiah (65: 24): it is a formula that must "be understood literally. In approaching the other I am always late for the meeting" (192/150). It is only because of this existential priority of ethics that a readiness to communicate without reserve can make communication possible. "Before putting itself at the service of life as an exchange of information through a linguistic system, saying is witness; it is saying without the said, a sign given to the other" (192/150). The problem is, however, that language does arrest the passing of the infinite by which it becomes possible. Thematization becomes sophism, which philosophy must resist with the force of prophecy.[22] The problem, against which the whole modern philosophical revolution struggles, is that philosophy has forgotten its prophetic origin and become entangled in its own linguistic thicket. Its work of disentanglement must begin with the enigma of revelation it shares with theology.

[21] Dostoevsky, *Brothers Karamazov*, trans. Constance Garnett (New York: Modern Library, 1950), 384.

[22] It is doubtful that Levinas was aware of Bodin's theory of prophecy and its relation to the periodic revitalization of spiritual truth. On Bodin see the relevant chapter in Voegelin, *History of Political Ideas*, vol. 5: *Religion and the Rise of Modernity*, in *Collected Works*, vol. 23, ed. James Wiser (Columbia: University of Missouri Press, 1998), especially 188–90.

Levinas has already delivered a few glancing blows at this problem, but now he addresses it head on. In line with the idealists, he recognizes that the infinite cannot be reached by way of a demonstration from the finite, which would be to suggest its dependence or continuity with the finite. But what of the God who speaks in me and yet cannot be counted on by me? The situation in which the God that is revealed in me is not in me is, Levinas asserts, "the very pivot of revelation" (196/154). The transcendent is precisely that which transcends and thus can be known only through revelation, albeit a revelation that does not reveal. Even in revelation the transcendent remains transcendent; that is its revelation. It is possible for me to glimpse the infinite only because I am constituted by it, by the same movement in which I transcend without reserve. "The enigma of the Infinite, whose saying in me, a responsibility where no one assists me, becomes a contestation of the Infinite" (196/154). This is very close to the Schellingian understanding of revelation as an encounter of persons that for that reason always transcends the means of signification. "The statement of the beyond being, of the name of God, does not allow itself to be walled up in the conditions of its enunciation" (199/156). This then leads to the inversion of the prevailing understanding of the reception of revelation as one in which "the revelation is made by him who receives it." Or perhaps we should say that revelation occurs when the subject holds itself open to the command that comes to it before its own existence. Religion and politics, in which the command has become thematic, present the continuous challenge of reverting to the revelation by which they are constituted.[23] It is in this sense that the almost aphoristic style of *Otherwise Than Being* is to be understood. "A book is interrupted discourse catching up with its own breaks" (217/171).

Philosophy as Faith

After this book Levinas's writing assumed a punctuated form through a series of essays that, even when assembled into the later books, bear the mark of their interruptions. It is striking that, unlike the largely meditative approach of the books, the later essays are more focused on

---

[23] The difficulty of striking the balance is perhaps underlined by Levinas's own defense of political elitism with its implicitly totalizing connotations. "One can call it utopian, yet it is the exact situation of men, at least in our time, when intellectuals feel themselves to be hostages for destitute masses unconscious of their wretchedness." *Autrement qu'être ou au-delà de l'essence*, 211 / *Otherwise Than Being*, 166.

the relationship to his predecessors. Moving from a style that seemed to eschew any extensive reference to the history of philosophy, we now catch a glimpse of what Levinas did in his lectures on the history of philosophy. Of particular interest is the volume *Dieu, la mort et le temps* (*God, Death, and Time*), which contains his last two lecture courses at the Sorbonne (1975–76). The value of what he did in this more philosophically referenced phase of his career is not just confined to the clarifications provided by the necessity of engaging with the thought of others, for the engagement also provoked further developments of his own thought, which now entered a third phase, following those marked by the two great books. A new freedom and lucidity are evident in his thought, as the often enigmatic formulations of the books are pressed to yield a transparence that had previously escaped them. That is why this last phase of Levinas's career was more than a series of lectures and occasional essays, for they are all rigorously underpinned by the same thrust toward a revolution in the language of philosophy. We might say that with Levinas the shift of modern philosophy toward the primacy of existence has reached a full awareness of its consequence. Now philosophy takes its direction from an otherness it can never possibly contain. It is in these late writings that Levinas's own awareness of his achievement is becoming clear as he sees that it means the definitive removal of the ambiguity of intentionality that had remained within the history of philosophy from its Greek beginnings up to Husserl and Heidegger. The openness that made thought possible always seemed to be threatened by the enclosing reach of thought. Levinas's intuition of a horizon of thought prior to thinking, as he had first announced it in *Existence and Existents,* could now be more confidently developed as the innermost intuition of philosophy itself. It is in conversation with its deepest practitioners that the conversation of philosophy is advanced.

This is why the critique of Heidegger developed most sharply in these late writings is best understood to be an extension of Heidegger's own path. Levinas takes him to task, in a pattern not too different from Heidegger's own reading of the history of philosophy, for not fully recognizing the implication of his own thought. The topic of the lecture "Death and Time" must inevitably take account of the seminal analyses of *Being and Time,* but it cannot end there. Levinas finds Heidegger to be insufficiently existential in his inability to shake free of the model of intentionality that holds even death within itself in the manner of being. By contrast death, Levinas insists, is to be seen as the radical nonpossibility that makes all possibility possible. Death is not just to be endured but rather what provides endurance. "It is through death that there is time and there is Dasein" (*Dieu, la mort et le temps*, 64 / *God, Death, and Time*, 53). Levinas finds in the earlier reflection of Kant a simplicity that could address the problem of death, not as a passivity, but as what calls forth courage. Meaning is thus not always an event of being but rather the nonevent that remains outside of all existence. The transcendental ideal was merely an awkward indication that "reason has ideas that go beyond being" (71/60). It was only within practical reason that the radically existential character of Kant's philosophy could become clear as "the possibility of thinking a beyond of time by way of hope" (75/63). Moral obligation is carried forward by its own superiority to everything there is, including God, but for that reason it can more adequately reveal the transcendence of God. "We must behave as if the soul were immortal and as if God existed" (77/65). But this hope is not just a defect of knowledge, as Kant felt; it is more than knowledge because it is more than being. "Hope must thus be analyzed as this very temporality itself" (77/65). Western philosophy has sought to grasp the meaning of the negative, as Hegel suggested, but it has failed to reach its existential truth as the ungraspable. Curiously it is in the philosophy of social hope espoused by the Marxist Ernst Bloch, with its avoidance of any ultimate penetration of death, that the existential role of death comes to the fore. Death does not defeat life but makes it possible as the limit to be overcome.

Levinas, we might say, takes the collectivist orientation of utopian humanism and individualizes it. It is in relation to the other that the character of death as beyond being is disclosed. "What we call, by a somewhat corrupted (*frelaté*) term, love, is *par excellence* the fact that the death of the other affects me more than my own. . . . We encounter death in the face of the other" (122/105). Time with its culmination in death is therefore not a deficiency, a falling away, but the overabundance that cannot be contained, the way of being of the infinite. What time sets in motion is a search for what cannot be apprehended within time. Time is in this sense "an awaiting without something being awaited. A patient awaiting. The patience and endurance of the beyond-measure, to-God [*à-Dieu*]; time as to-God" (132/115).[24] The Kantian postulate of God has reached an astonishing confirmation in the preeminence of existence, as Levinas leads the modern philosophical revolution to the threshold of faith, only now a faith that has found itself philosophically shorn of all dogmatic

---

[24] The term *à-Dieu* is Levinas's play on "farewell" and "to God," which in both instances suggests taking leave of being, although with different but related tonalities.

admixtures.[25] As infinite patience, time is a question, a prayer, that precedes all questioning because it is "a putting in question of the one who questions" (127/110). Death is not the end but "a pure being seized" by my responsibility for another. "The relationship with the Infinite is the responsibility of a mortal being for a mortal being" (134/117). It is in taking up this responsibility that the disclosure of the infinite occurs by which, as in Abraham interceding for Sodom (Gn 19: 23–33), I become aware that "I am, myself, ashes and dust."

The priority of knowledge of the infinite to knowledge of myself is taken up in the parallel lecture course, "God and Onto-theo-logy," in which Levinas tackles Heidegger's dismissal of theology directly. He recognizes Heidegger's great achievement in recovering the verbal meaning of being, *Sein*, the act of being, as opposed to *Seiendes*, beings. The "ontological difference" between being and beings calls attention to the existential glimpse of what makes existence possible. Levinas correctly sees Heidegger as the culmination of the shift of modern philosophy toward the priority of existence that encompasses theoretical reflection, but he wonders about his readiness to jettison theology as merely the misidentification of being with beings. Is God, then, just another being conveniently assigned to the beginning of the world process? Or is he more properly understood to be beyond being?[26] In other words, Levinas asks, "did onto-theo-logy's mistake consist in taking being for God, or rather in taking God for being?" (141/124). His objection is that for Heidegger being remains somehow thinkable, whereas God lies utterly beyond thought, approachable only through the responsibility for the other that he imposes on us. The strength of Levinas's critique of Heidegger derives from the latter's retention of the language of appearing or uncovering by which being, even when it lies beyond appearance, is still drawn inexorably within it. Kant's identification of God as what cannot be thought, as lying beyond the categories of thinking, seems preferable,

---

[25] While tending to underline the differences between Kant and Levinas, a tendency made inevitable by the simple juxtaposition without intermediaries, Catherine Chalier is nevertheless brought to concede their convergence on the question of God. Levinas, in her view, avoids both agnosticism and fideism in seeking "another path. Claiming that that religion and that God 'do not exhaust the message of Scripture,' he paves the way for a more demanding and more living notion of God. And although that God does not found ethics for Levinas any more than for Kant, the thought of God comes to mind thanks to ethics." Chalier, *What Ought I to Do?* 160.

[26] For a parallel reflection out of Heidegger, one that provides a path toward Christian theology, see Jean-Luc Marion, *God Without Being*, trans. Thomas A. Carlson (Chicago: University Press, 1991; original, 1982).

but even "Kant keeps the idea that the ultimate meaning of a notion is in its being" (178/155). It has proved difficult to break with the idolatry of knowledge that always seeks itself to worship, the problem of "bewitchment" first expounded by Don Quixote (193/168). The hold of being as presence must be more thoroughly broken, without the attenuations that still attach to it in Heidegger's treatment, if we are to glimpse the radical transcendence within which we exist. Already we live beyond death in the limitless responsibility we bear toward the other. We should, Levinas suggests, take more seriously Kant's "Copernican revolution" by which the categorical imperative surpasses God and immortality. "Meaning is not determined through the to-be or the not-to-be. It is being, on the contrary, that is determined on the basis of meaning" (212/184).

The infinite is that which cannot appear, for it is that which lays open the self by which all appearing and signification can occur. Levinas is thinking through the meaning of transcendence, which since Plato has been afflicted by the ambiguity of appearance. "Here, bearing witness is the exception to the rule of being: in it the Infinite is revealed without appearing, without *showing* itself as Infinite" (225/197). The subject who is inspired by the infinite does not pronounce its name, yet in the "here I am" attests to it. In many ways Levinas is showing how God cannot be a being but must rather approach the hiddenness of Heidegger's being. The advance beyond Heidegger may simply be to do away with the metaphor of concealment with its inevitable incorporation into unconcealment. God is not a "thou" in dialogue with me, for he is the voice of command, the third person, or *Illeity*, that I alone hear in responding to the "thou" of the neighbor. "As Illeity, God is in-finite, outside of the structure wherein the gaze might take charge of his shock and include him in a *logos*" (232/203). This is in contrast to art and theology that attempt to fix the transcendent God, who always overflows the word in a glory that "undoes its dwelling" (233/204). We cannot question God because he puts us in question before all experience, the insomnia or wakefulness of consciousness. As his favorite formulation, Levinas returns to Descartes's Third Meditation, with its Augustinian resonances: "*my perception of the infinite, that is God, is in some way prior to my perception of the finite that is myself*" (246/217). This is not just the failure of thought, but a relationship with the infinite effected by the failure.

We do not derive our idea of God even from our existential attunement toward him, for that still inverts the relationship. God is the exigency of our existence as that which can never be attained. How, then, Levinas asks, is it possible for God to remain near and yet never be assimilated, the object of desire ever unreachable? The answer is contained in the word "holy," by which "the desirable commands me to what is undesirable" in yielding everything to the other (252/223). It is "the enucleation of the transcendental subject" that resolves the Kantian antinomy between duty and happiness. From a past before I was, I discover myself as under an obligation toward the other that can never be satisfied. "As such the 'me' is a wakefulness or an opening of a self absolutely exposed and sobered from the ecstasy of intentionality" (252/223). Kant had glimpsed but could not clarify the centrality of God within the moral life. Now Levinas could explain that it is God who ultimately kicks away the last consolation of himself and institutes "the reversal by which the desirable escapes desire. The Goodness of the Good inclines the movement to which it appeals to set it aside from the Good as desirable and to orient it toward the Other – and only thus toward the Good" (253/223). As transcendent, God cannot be contained within my desire; I can reach God only by going beyond my desire. God is goodness itself. "He does not fill me with good but compels me to goodness, better than the good to be received." This is a remarkable extension of the aspiration of Kant's *Religion Within the Bounds of Mere Reason*, which should perhaps now be titled "Religion Beyond the Limits of Mere Reason." Levinas shows that the trajectory of Kantian autonomy is not toward independence from God but toward a dependence that mandates our independence. When the gospel of love is finally taken seriously, we see that it leads not toward being but beyond it in a loss of self that is "otherwise and *better* than being" (253/224). God is not a goal but what enables and compels me to love without a goal. "In this way God is different from every neighbor. And transcendent to the point of absence, to the point of his possible confusion with the agitation of the *there is*" (253/224). Looking back we can see that it was this inner purification of faith that has driven much of what appeared to be atheism, justifying the appellation of its most infamous proponent, Zarathustra, as the "most pious of the godless."

In the case of Levinas the irony seems to pass unnoted. His admiration for the other famous atheist, Marx, may have prevented him from appreciating the extent to which his own work proclaims the end of Marxism. False idealism is displaced by the demand for the true idealism that had all along been its only source. Not only does Levinas fail to identify Marx himself with ideology, preferring to take him at face value as the great exposer of ideology (see "Ideology and Idealism," in *Of God Who Comes to Mind*), but he seems to neglect completely the antitheistic revolt that made Marx the culmination of messianic activism. One explanation for the latter pattern is that Levinas was so convinced he had understood the inner significance of eschatology that its historical misapplications could be completely overlooked. This may well be the case, but it remains strange in the context of French intellectual life in the seventies, on which the publication of Solzhenitsyn's *Gulag Archipelago* had worked such a devastating effect. The book provoked a sea change in the perception of communism as no longer a movement accidentally perverted by Stalin but one that was from its inception implicated in totalitarianism.[27] Such blind spots are, of course, largely of interest as a warning for our own susceptibilities, for in contrast to the case of Heidegger, they played no role in the unfolding of Levinas's thought. While Heidegger's thought retained an apocalyptic structure as its great tension, Levinas undertook the most profound reorientation of apocalypse since Augustine.[28] It is for this reason that his relationship to Marx is an ironic one of restoring to transcendence what Marx aspired to make wholly immanent. "Permanent revolution" had now become the eschatological boundary of existence, not a historical condition.

Time as *à-Dieu*

It is the same with Levinas's separation from Heidegger, for he has seen the impossibility of achieving the apocalypse when it is what we live within. This is the clarification of the understanding of God that is the centerpiece of his later writings. *De Dieu qui vient à l'idée* (1986; *Of God Who Comes to Mind*) is not only the title of one of the most important such collections, but the central conception of God as coming to mind rather than merely being contained within it. The wakefulness prior to intentionality arises from the patience or passing without presence. "But does not dis-inter-estedness, as this leavetaking and this *adieu*, signify an unto God [*á-Dieu*]?" (*De Dieu qui vient à l'idée*, 87 / *Of God Who Comes to Mind*, 50).[29] It is time as an awaiting for the ungraspable that does not

---

[27] One wonders, too, about the response of Levinas to the earlier devastating indictment of Marxism in Camus's *L'homme revolté* (1951) and the ensuing very public break with Sartre. As the reaction of Levinas is summarized by Moyn, *Origins of the Other,* 224–25, the culpability of the ideological rationale for totalitarianism is not addressed. On Camus see Walsh, *After Ideology,* 62–65.

[28] It is for this reason that his analysis of politics could be simultaneously realistic and prophetic without any danger of confusing the two within the delusions of wishful thinking. See the good account of Howard Caygill, *Levinas and the Political* (London: Routledge, 2002).

[29] The centrality of this theme in Levinas is best indicated by its adoption in the title of Derrida's final memorial, itself an invaluable entrée into Levinas's thought, *Adieu to Emmanuel Levinas.*

nevertheless seek to grasp but that sees itself as grasped. The "in" of infinite is not, Levinas emphasizes, sheer negation; it is the inspiration of the finite that is its duration. God is not what moves me to love of the neighbor or what prevents me from loving, but the watchfulness that makes love possible. In contrast to Heidegger's "waiting for God," Levinas evinces the God whose disclosure has already seized me with "fear for the neighbor" (89/51). Malebranche is singled out, in the essay "God and Philosophy," as the one who saw most clearly that "God is his own idea" and not ours. "We are out of the order in which one passes from the idea to the being. The idea of God is God in me, but it is already God breaking up the consciousness that aims at ideas, already differing from content" (105/63). What this means is that God cannot be known, cannot be the object of desire, but must always remain beyond desire. That is what Levinas, like Kant, calls the holy. A parallel with Luther's critique of motivation might also be adduced, since it invokes God as freeing us from motivation in order to make it possible for us to love. Levinas is merely elaborating the structure of such earlier adumbrations of holiness as what commands me to love the neighbor, the very epitome of the undesirable. The imperative that makes me a hostage before all desire is the "enucleation" effected by the God beyond being (113/68). "The Infinite concerns me and encircles me, speaking to me through my own mouth. . . . The religious discourse prior to all religious discourse is not dialogue. It is the 'here I am,' said to the neighbor to whom I am given over, and in which I announce peace, that is, my responsibility for the other" (122/74–75).

Luminosity is not a light but rather the afterglow of an illumination that is always past when it reaches us. The modern philosophical shift from intentionality to its existential container has been preoccupied largely with delineating the distinction, especially as defining the unattainable boundary of intentionality. Husserl and Heidegger demarcate this phase of its articulation. Levinas accomplishes a distinct advance within this unfolding by recognizing its most fundamental implication as the evacuation of presence. Not only is luminosity not a light we shine but, as the light within which we exist, it always reaches us as past. We cannot be present to that by which we are, for it necessarily precedes us. This is more than an "ontological difference," a distinction that Heidegger abandoned because of its implication that all is nevertheless reducible to ontology. The difference, Levinas would suggest, is prior to difference. As the one who announces all difference, God cannot be included within difference, for he is irrevocably before what is constituted from him. Responsibility for the other may be the point of epiphany, but it is not itself an epiphany, for it rather points toward that which is before all epiphany, before all other. The significance of Levinas's idea of God, which he generally formulates as the "beyond being," should perhaps be more accurately characterized as the "before being."[30] If Kant is the beginning of the modern philosophical revolution, Levinas may well be its conclusion. With him the priority of God to being, the inspiration from which the whole critique of dogmatic theology and metaphysics has drawn its strength, has reached a definitiveness not likely to be reversed.

Heidegger's guiding intuition that the problem of God lay not in theology but in ontology was right; it was simply that he did not quite grasp what a radical revision of ontology this would require. This is why he still talked of the unconcealment of being as if the unconcealment could be unconcealed. Tied too much to the dominance of space, he could not really embrace the submission to time as the exigency under which our existence must labor. Only with Levinas does the time of existence emerge in its full existential necessity. Existence is then the time of that which must work out its existence in relation not to a future it might dream of eclipsing but to a past it is ever incapable of catching up with. The fullness that draws it forward is nevertheless past; otherwise it would exercise no appeal. "Vulnerability is the power to say '*adieu*' to this world. One says '*adieu*' to it in growing old. Time endures in the form of this *adieu* and this *à-Dieu*" (134/83). The philosophical revolution requires a revolution in philosophy whose articulation remained the ultimate goal of Levinas's work. This is evident in "The Meaning of Being," the third and final part of *Of God Who Comes to Mind*, which began with "The Rupture of Immanence," followed by "The Idea of God." When the primacy of intentionality is displaced by the luminosity of existence, the discourse of philosophy must be "otherwise than being" because it is led by what is before, infinitely before, being. The responsive unfolding

---

[30] It is a conception that is challenging even for Levinas's sympathetic readers. See, e.g., Jeffrey Bloechl, who concludes his *Liturgy of the Neighbor: Emmanuel Levinas and the Religion of Responsibility* (Pittsburgh: Duquesne University Press, 2000) with the characterization of "the crisis facing religion after metaphysics – not the death of God, but God's return as little more than a cipher" (285). But one can surely point to a very similar structure in the Augustinian "experience," which is strictly speaking the complaint of a failure to experience. "I have learned to love you late, Beauty at once so ancient and so new! I have learned to love you late!" *Confessions*, X, 27. Derrida characteristically calls attention to the most provocative formulation of this theology in one of Levinas's Talmudic writings, the conception of "the Torah before Sinai." *Adieu to Emmanuel Levinas*, 65; see also the concluding quote, 123.

of existence prioritizes what is before existence as an abundance it can never contain. What is perhaps most striking about Levinas's reflection is that it has completely shed the subjective isolation that Heidegger could never quite discard. Fullness, not poverty, is what draws existence from beyond being.

The entire Western spiritual tradition, philosophical and revelatory, has struggled with the linguistic means of expressing the rupture of transcendence. How can the "beyond," a term coined by Plato, avoid the fate of immanence? The priority of prayer over theology, of the life of the church over the history of dogma, always derived from the intuition that the divine could be reached only through existence. Now Levinas had provided the theoretical expression of this insight in the form of a theory that immediately discards itself. Before thinking, there is dialogue. "In effect, for Buber, the Thou *par excellence* is invoked in the invisible Eternal Thou – nonobjectifiable, unthematizable – of God. For Gabriel Marcel, to name God in the third person would be to miss Him" (221/144). Where thought always begins with the *cogito* in order to assimilate all being to itself, the very meaning of presence, it is only in dialogue, the responsibility for the other, that the beyond being is glimpsed in a way not reducible to presence. In a challenge to all speculative theology, Levinas surmises that all thought is "essentially atheism" (241/160). As a reprise of St. Anselm he does not want his "greater than can be thought" to be taken as yet another way into the proof of God's existence – a suggestion that appalled the scholastics as much as the idealists for its impropriety. Levinas is merely describing the circumstance in which "the meaning itself of the word 'God' comes to mind. And it does so more imperiously than a presence could do" (252–53/168).[31] When it is not my death that defines the parameter of existence but the even more irrefragable responsibility before the death of the other, ontology must take its reference from the question of my right to being. I participate in the infinite not by possessing it but through infinite responsibility. "The question *par excellence,* or the first question, is not 'why is there being rather than nothing?' but 'have I the right to be?'" (257/171).

The displacement of theoretical reason by practical reason, initiated by Kant, has become definitive when the latter has become the source of the former. It is not just that thinking about being cannot be separated from

---

[31] Levinas at this point notes the parallel with Augustine. "In Book 10 of his *Confessions,* Saint Augustine opposes to the *veritas lucens* [truth that shines] the *veritas redarguens,* or the truth that accuses or puts in question." *De Dieu qui vient à l'idée,* 256 / *Of God Who Comes to Mind,* 170.

being, a revision of ontology that still holds out the ambiguous prospect of remaining within ontology. Now Levinas has shown that there can be no ontology other than what cannot be included within it, because it is already there before there is a there. The "heart has reasons of which reason does not know," not just because of the depth of intuition, but because reason draws its openness from its predisposition toward the other. "It is as though I were destined to the other before being destined to myself" (249/165). The right of reason, its freedom, equality, autonomy, can never again be taken as dispositive, for it takes its validity only from the call of infinite responsibility. A sense of profound unease had always been associated with the imperious assertion of the authority of reason. Its closed universe, especially in the construction of ideological systems, had seemed the height of irrationality. As an instrument, reason skirts dangerously close to its own self-destruction. It has been just such an ominous prospect that has stirred the modern philosophical revolution, whose goal has all along been the restoration of reason to its rightful subordination to the good. As the highest point of our spirit, reason is itself only when our spirit strains to be what it is at its utmost. The face that elicits responsibility for the other is the beginning without beginning because it is what calls us into being.

Levinas may not always have found the most perspicuous formulation for the existential eschatology he glimpsed, but he marked out the meaning of the philosophical revolution through the prioritization of ethics. "In the disposition by the I of its sovereignty as an I, and in its modality as detestable, signifies the ethical, but probably also the very spirituality of the soul" (265/177). With echoes of Plato's *Gorgias* in "the possibility of dreading injustice more than death, of preferring the injustice undergone to the injustice committed," we can discern the return to the origin of philosophy within a way of life. The major difference is that now we can see more clearly why ethics must insist on this priority. Ethics cannot be grounded in reason, no more than reason can be given an ethical veneer. All such reversals overlook the grounding of reason in ethics and the unavailability of ethics to any donation of self less than the whole. "This is a turning around that starts from the face of the other where, at the very heart of the phenomenon in its light, there signifies a *surplus* of meaning that one could designate as glory" (264/176). In the final brief essay of the volume, Levinas connects this supererogatory meaning with art in ways that suggest the insight of his modern predecessors into the advantage of its immediacy over philosophy. In relation to the predispositional self-sacrificing capacity, he wonders "whether poetry is not defined precisely by this perfect uprightness and by this urgency" (267/179). By serving something higher than itself, art may open the road of ontology that is prepared to ask about the value of its own truth. The question that so ceaselessly troubled Nietzsche, of the value of truth, can now be asked with more awareness of the infinite love from which it arises. "Is it certain that the truth justifies, finally, the search for truth, or that the search for the truth is justified by itself, as though the truth coincided with the Idea of the Good" (269/180)?

7

Derrida's Dissemination of Existence as *Différance*

Levinas completed the prioritization of practical reason that began with Kant, but it was Derrida who unfolded the profusion of theoretical consequences. It was Derrida who saw the full significance of the philosophical revolution that Levinas had made irreversible. In this sense Derrida represents the culmination of the movement we have been following, especially with respect to the correction of its tragic self-betrayal in Heidegger. Derrida was thus more like Hegel in inaugurating a new mode of philosophy, or rather in giving shape to the new mode of philosophy that has emerged in our time. Of course, he was utterly opposed to the systematizing proclivities of Hegel, whom he excoriated in his famous *Glas*, but he occupied a similar position in uniting a bewildering array of developments hitherto apprehended only in isolation. Derrida held together in life what Hegel had also seen as an existential unity despite his inclination toward conceptualization. It is the definitive rejection of the temptation toward theoretical coherence that marks the achievement of Jacques Derrida and at the same time marks the incoherence of his deconstruction philosophy.[1] He resumed the project of German idealism, which

[1] The notoriety of Derrida, by which he became the favorite whipping boy for erstwhile defenders of the "canon," generated enough heat to warm the dwellings of all involved. Fulminations against the nihilism of deconstruction were as satisfying to the expostulators as the controversy was beneficial to the expanding fame of their target. A particular high point was the "Cambridge affair" in 1992, when the prospect of an honorary degree for Derrida provoked an orchestrated campaign of opposition. A forgettable ceremonial event was transformed into a *cause celèbre*. Not since Kierkegaard's exploitation of the "*Corsair* affair" has philosophy enjoyed such publicity of the cave. Since those heady days, of course, cooler heads have prevailed and the vaunted incoherence of deconstruction has come to be seen as a far more coherent unfolding of the very tradition it seeks to address. For a good example of this more measured judgment informed by a substantial reading of Derrida, see Michael Naas, *Taking on the Tradition: Jacques Derrida and the Legacies of Deconstruction* (Stanford, CA: Stanford University Press, 2003). A useful

had set itself the task of integrating the Kantian bifurcation of theoretical and practical reason. What had now become clear was that the integration could never be accomplished theoretically. Schelling, that most neglected voice in the whole conversation, was after all right. Theory cannot comprehend that by which it is comprehended; the priority of practice includes the practice of theory itself.[2] Derrida labored to show how the coherence of reason depends on the differing and deferring of its boundary. It cannot and must not reach its goal. The revolutionary self-understanding of reason here projected is at times so far-reaching that some of its consequences seem not to have been foreseen even by Derrida himself.

It is not just that the measure of his work could not be fully taken so long as it remained in process, a situation that has been altered only slightly by his recent death. Of far greater significance is the extent of the odyssey through which Derrida wandered from his early semiological reflections to the messianic musings of his last works. Given that his reputation was fixed by the early phase, it was perhaps not surprising that he should complain in his most autobiographical "Circumfession" that his fate was "to be read less and less well over almost twenty years, like my religion, about which nobody understands anything" (154). One is inclined to suggest that it is precisely his religion that has raised the greatest obstacle to his readers. Those who admired in Derrida the relentless power of deconstruction, the merciless hollowing out of the meaning of texts, were surely ill prepared for the metamorphosis into a Kierkegaardian heightening of existence.[3] Equally, those who abhorred the destructive effect of difference without restraint were hardly prepared, if they cared

overview of the range of contexts in which Derrida's thought has been taken up is provided by Michael Thomas, *The Reception of Derrida: Translation and Transformation* (London: Palgrave, 2006).

[2] It must be conceded that two of Schelling's best contemporary readers, Manfred Frank and Andrew Bowie, take pains to distinguish Schelling from Derrida. They each take issue with what they see as Derrida's elimination of the subject as the ground of the possibility of self-reflection. What they fail to consider is that Derrida's différance represents a further application of Schelling's insight of the impossibility of the subject returning absolutely to itself in the movement of self-reflection. A full reading of Derrida would have dispelled this misunderstanding. Manfred Frank, *What Is Neostructuralism?* trans. Sabine Wilke and Richard Gray (Minneapolis: University of Minnesota Press, 1989; original, 1983) and "Is Self-consciousness a Case of *Presence à Soi?*" in David Wood, ed., *Derrida: A Critical Reader* (Oxford: Blackwell, 1992), 218–34; Andrew Bowie, *Schelling and Modern European Philosophy*, 67–75.

[3] A notable exception is John Caputo, *The Prayers and Tears of Jacques Derrida: Religion without Religion* (Bloomington: University of Indiana Press, 1997).

to follow his work, to acknowledge the prioritizing of faith that it came to represent. What matters, however, is that his work does remain in continuity, if it does not aspire toward a unity. There were no sharp breaks, no need to disclaim its earlier versions in light of the later developments. Continuity was there from the start, but as with any existential movement, it could not be known in advance. Only the path itself would disclose it. This is why it is even more essential to follow the full trajectory, not to assume that its direction was fixed from the beginning. Then we can discover, perhaps along with Derrida himself, that there never was a purely semiological phase of his work but that it had all along simply been a way of doing philosophy. Despite the affinity with literary theory, deconstruction has never simply been a concern with texts, for its preoccupation has been the engagement with metaphysics that can no longer be made present in texts. It is this philosophical aspiration that has become apparent only as Derrida's work has unfolded. His stature as a philosophical mind of astonishing depth and penetration has only lately begun to be distinguished from his early literary brilliance.

Meaning as the Noncoincidence of Signifier and Signified

The problem of seeing the full scope of Derrida's contribution to metaphysics arises in large part from the difficulty of taking him at his word. His call for a new metaphysics in *De la grammatologie* (1967; *Of Grammatology*) seems so pervasively tied to the end of metaphysics as we know it. Most readers of the work that marked his first public impact would draw from it the powerful critique of the metaphysics of presence he limns as its ultimate implication. By displacing the priority of speech in favor of writing, the *grammē*, as the origin of language, he announced the end of phonocentrism and the logocentrism that follows from it. The proclamation burst the almost instinctual privileging of the living word of speech that had long dominated literary theory. Writing was always regarded as the dead letter, a necessary concession, but never more than a poor substitute for the living voice at its origin. With this bold assertion Derrida swept away more than two millennia of prejudice against writing from Plato to Saussure. It was an audacious move but one that Derrida was confident he could sustain, for it was never really a theory of signification at all, but a profound insight into the existential movement through which all philosophy and, therefore, all meaning must pass. Right at the beginning he had had an insight that would occupy the center of his thought. The rest would be the unfolding of its rich and unforeseeable implications. By confronting the prevailing prejudice against writing, Derrida had been able to make a momentous discovery about signification. Meaning depends not on the coincidence of sign and signified but precisely on their noncoincidence. It is only by the movement toward a signification that cannot be reached that the opening of language, of communication, becomes possible. Writing is where that nonpresent intentionality is most evident.

Heidegger was the clearest point at which writing assumed the form of erasure in his famous silence of being, which, in *The Question of Being*, he wrote as "~~Being~~." Derrida was particularly struck by what this crossing out without actual erasure suggested. For him it was an insight into the whole possibility of language deriving from the absence of the signified. Hegel was the beginning of this, but it was in Husserl that the connection with writing was made. Derrida's study of Husserl's *Origin of Geometry* was surely the source for his prioritizing of writing, since it was there that he found the realization that writing was not only an auxiliary for science, but the condition of the possibility of ideal objects, of objectivity.[4] It was in Saussure that the issue had been clarified even while it had failed to be understood. The famous semiologist had recognized written notation as what "exiles us" from presence (*De la grammatologie*, 60 / *Grammatology*, 40), but he had been unable to see that it is precisely such difference that makes all intentionality possible. Writing is what is originary because in it we behold "a becoming sign of symbol" (69/47). Derrida finds Pierce to have advanced beyond Husserl in recognizing that "*manifestation* itself does not reveal a presence, it makes a sign" (72/49). Everything begins with the trace and there is no original of the trace. Contrary to Husserl's attachment to a transcendental experience in which pure presence is reached, Derrida calls attention to "the unheard difference between the appearing and the appearance" (95/65). The Cartesian meditation that set modern philosophy off in search of epistemological certainty, the assurance of presence, had now reached its end with the full acknowledgment of the unattainability of the existential horizon within which it seeks to take place. "*The trace is the différance* which opens appearance and signification" (95/65).

Signification is possible, Derrida seems to be saying, not because of an original to which we might make recourse, but because even the

[4] For a perceptive account of what Derrida learned by going through and beyond Husserl, see Paola Marrati, *Genesis and Trace: Derrida Reading Husserl and Heidegger* (Stanford, CA: Stanford University Press, 2005). Derrida's fifteen-year engagement with Husserl is likewise extensively explored in Joshua Kates, *Essential History: Jacques Derrida and the Development of Deconstruction* (Evanston, IL: Northwestern University Press, 2005).

original is in the position of a signified to us. We do not ground signification; it is what grounds us. The Heideggerian opening or uncovering of being has become what opens us, not what is opened before us. As with Levinas's prioritizing of the other, Derrida locates us in relation to signification rather than the other way around. The displacement of the subject as the starting point is virtually complete. That the signified "is *always already in the position of the signifier*" is a proposition that signals the replacement of a metaphysics of speech with one derived from the model of writing (108/73). As a hermeneutical orientation this shift has vast consequences, for the disappearance of a substantive measure of the text, the role that the authoritative immediacy of speech exercised, now leads to "the axial proposition of this essay, there is nothing outside the text" (233/163; see also 227/158). But what does Derrida mean by this pronouncement? Is it an invitation to descend to a bottomless morass of subjectivism? The frequency with which this sentence is mindlessly repeated often seems to suggest such an outcome. But it hardly squares with the serious reading of philosophical texts on which Derrida embarked. To find the meaning of his most infamous pronouncement, we are better advised to follow the way in which he sought to apply it, rather than just fill it with our own speculative suspicions. Then we will have a better chance of catching the real implications of the philosophical revolution that Derrida above all drew out for literary theory. It is no accident that he found his first reception within such circles rather than the philosophical academy, for the unsurpassability of writing suggests a very different way of reading texts in their originary abundance. The end of linear writing, which takes its point of reference in an origin, now suggests that there is no going beyond, only a going through texts. It is an exciting development in literary theory when we begin to approach works with the assumption that they contain more than they can say. The best readers have always understood that books write their authors, rather than the other way around, but Derrida provided the philosophical formulation of this intuition.

When he insists that there is nothing outside the text, he is reminding us that the poem exists only in the writing of it. There is no poem in advance or outside, just as there is no going back to a beginning before there is a beginning.[5] Writing is the process by which the text is.

---

[5] Michael Oakeshott's notion of the "poetic" bears a remarkable resemblance to Derrida's insistence that there is nothing outside the text. According to Oakeshott, "A poetic utterance (a work of art) is not the 'expression' of an experience, it *is* the experience and the only one there is. A poet does not do *three* things: first experience or observe or recollect an emotion, then contemplate it, and finally seek a means of expressing the

Signification is itself our mode of existing, or rather our existence is a signification. Derrida is giving semiotic expression to the existential character of knowing, which can never know itself from the outside but always from within the movement of existence. The correlate of the principle that there is nothing outside the text is that outside the text there is nothing. Existence is textual. We can unfold it only through the further textual weaving that is writing. We write our existence, or existence is writing. Either way we never get beyond the struggle for signification as if an end point might be reached wherein signification is no longer needed. That, of course, would be the end of history attributed to Hegel, which is tantamount to the closure of history. This is surely why Derrida calls grammatology a "positive science." By breaking with the book, the end of linear writing that seemed to move toward a conclusion, its own abolition, he extols the virtue of a writing that, while it still may be enclosed in books, points beyond its own inevitable finitude to remind us of the participatory character of all books. The textuality that Derrida invokes illumines the endlessness that will not let any formulation conclude the conversation. Nothing is outside the text of existence, which precisely because it cannot be hermeneutically consolidated opens up the space and time of existence. Reading and writing become interrelated modes of existence by which we no longer rest in the comfort of an absolute beginning or end but seek to catch "what wrote itself between the lines in the volumes" (130/86).[6] When the text has become the only opening available to us, it is the pursuit of what the text itself pursues that constitutes both the possibility and the impossibility of reading.

The innovation of allowing texts to read us is exemplified by Derrida in the second part of the book, which is devoted to Rousseau's essay on the origin of language. At first glance Rousseau appears to be "the most energetic eighteenth-century *reaction* organizing the defense of phonologism and of logocentric metaphysics" (147/99). Like his ethnographic successor, Lévi-Strauss, Rousseau believes firmly in the possibility of stripping away the grammatological accretions to arrive at the original truth of the voice. The origin of language lies in the immediacy of passion before

---

results of his contemplation: he does *one* thing only, he imagines poetically." *"Rationalism in Politics" and Other Essays*, expanded ed. (Indianapolis, IN: Liberty Fund, 1991), 525.

[6] "That is why, beginning to write without the line, one begins also to reread past writing according to a different organization of space. If today the problem of reading occupies the forefront of science, it is because of this suspense between two ages of writing. Because we are beginning to write, to write differently, we must reread differently." *De la grammatologie*, 130 / *Of Grammatology*, 86–87.

the layering of articulation has had a chance to intervene. By returning again to that elemental beginning, it will be possible to reestablish the emergence of language purged of the distorting effects its accidental unfolding has caused. The dream of a science of language, the attainment of pure transparency, is set in motion as the irresistible project of European thought. It is an aspiration that Derrida skillfully deconstructs from within, calling attention not just to the self-contradiction in which Rousseau's own literary undertaking is caught, but to the indispensable opening of possibility it also sustains. Derrida refers to this space of possibility as "*différance*."[7] Rousseau in the *Confessions* can disclose himself only by not actually disclosing himself; instead, he must allow his writing to stand in place of his self. "Without the possibility of différance, the desire of presence as such would not find its breathing space. That means by the same token that this desire carries in itself the destiny of its non-satisfaction. Différance produces what it forbids, makes possible the very thing that it makes impossible" (206/143). The contradiction of Rousseau the writer who condemns the artificiality of writing is more than ironic. It is the supreme instantiation of what cannot be instanced because in every saying it remains unsaid.

"Différance," that inimitable coinage of Derrida, is his great contribution to the modern philosophical revolution. It is really his term for existence. Differing and deferring constitute the movement of existence, which cannot reach its goal of transparence without ceasing; nor, correlatively, can it know itself as a transparence without ceasing to exist. So long as we exist, we differ and defer from an origin, which is the blind spot of the movement of existence itself. Neither Rousseau nor Derrida is concerned solely with language, for their real interest is a concern with existence. This also explains their affinity for revolutionary politics, which is ultimately a heightening of the movement of existence rather than a purely political predilection. The difference between them is that Rousseau exhibits a naive expectation that the gap between aspiration and fulfillment might be closed, while Derrida knows the ominous consequences of such a resolution in closing the very movement by which it is sustained. For Rousseau the goal of politics is to retrieve the immediacy of gesture, while Derrida's politics are largely gestural. The convergence between them is closest in relation to the *Social Contract*, the work that brings out most clearly Rousseau's awareness of his own différance from nature. It is precisely by not being natural that the political community

---

[7] See the essay "Différance" in *Margins of Philosophy* for a full account.

can sustain its continuity with nature most fully. The political is the opening of différance, just as it is the opening of existence. Retreat of the signifier frees attention for the signified, reaching its limit in the alphabet as pure signifier. Letters signify nothing but open the possibility of signification. "The movement of supplementary representation approaches the origin as it distances itself from it. Total alienation is the total reappropriation of self-presence. . . . Within the political order . . . 'we gain the exact equivalent of what we lose, as well as an added power to conserve what we already have'" (*Social Contract,* Bk. I) (*De la grammatologie,* 417 / *Of Grammatology,* 295). The alphabet, which effaces itself better than any more immediate signifier, is like the sovereignty of the political that is all the more real for not simply being an immediate presence of sovereignty.

Existence as Always Exceeding Structure

The full philosophical import of the openness wrought by différance becomes apparent in the companion book to *Of Grammatology,* published in the same year, *L'écriture et la différence* (1967; *Writing and Difference*),[8] which he suggested could be inserted as the middle section of *Of Grammatology*.[9] This is the work in which Derrida takes leave of his mentors by showing how their insufficient attention to language jeopardized the philosophical revolution in which they had been engaged. For all of his intellectual originality we may consider Derrida, in the context of the modern philosophical revolution, to be the moment of its consolidation. He may appear to be the innovator, but *Writing and Difference* makes clear the extent of his dependence on his immediate predecessors. It is a relationship that Derrida would continue to explore up to the midpoint of his career, culminating in his most famous study of Hegel, *Glas.* Philosophy, too, partakes of the textuality of existence, for it is only by discharging our debt to the past by way of its critique that we can engage in the act of philosophizing.[10] There is no philosophy outside of the opening in which it is pursued, as Plato sought to make clear in distinguishing it from merely writing. The significance of Derrida's insights is that he now shows the limitation of this prejudice, which erects speech into a realm of

---

[8] There is also a third volume from the same year, *Speech and Phenomena* (*La voix et le phénomène*), which looks back to the work on Husserl.

[9] Derrida suggests several relationships between the volumes in *Positions,* trans. Alana Bass, 4–5.

[10] Michael Naas is one of the few commentators to have taken up this Derridean insight in his treatment of Derrida, *Taking on the Tradition.*

pure presence it never was. The modern philosophical revolution thus restores Plato to Plato in the sense of more adequately regaining the vitality of his aspiration. As an engagement with texts, philosophy must recognize that it has always been the impossibility of closing the gap with speech that has been the possibility of its life. We exist through writing and difference.

It is only God, Derrida suggests through a powerful inner motif of *Writing and Difference,* that can be fully present to himself. His theology is remarkably traditional in its orientation, although it is radically unfamiliar in its formulation. The reason lies in its thoroughly existential character. God is not some one or other that can be known as a presence, for he is the movement within which we exist, the presence we can never attain without the closure of what opens the possibility of existence. "Meaning is neither before nor after the act. Is not that which is called God, that which imprints every human course and recourse with its secondarity, the passageway of deferred reciprocity between reading and writing?" (*L'écriture et la différence,* 22–23 / *Writing and Difference,* 11).[11] The whole history of Western metaphysics is implicated in the misidentification of form with the force that inspires it, driven by the mistaken aspiration of closing the gap of secondarity to regain the original. It is the aim of man becoming God that, Derrida can now make clear, marks the impossibility of existence. At the level of structure this is the error of defining it in terms of its goal, which, if it were attained, would signal the end of its existence as such a structure. Derrida does not adumbrate the line of reflection from Kant on the understanding of living things, but there is more than an echo within his theme of poststructuralism. For what exists, what lives, structures can never be anything more than secondary; otherwise their existence is over. This is preeminently the case with meaning, the main concern of Derrida, who arrived at this realization by way of his reading and extension of Husserl. In the latter's removal of the logical and psychological structures of knowledge, he saw the direction he must go.

Structures can be grasped only because we are not grasped by structures. "The Idea of truth, that is the Idea of philosophy or science, is

---

[11] Derrida quotes St. John Chrysostom: "It were indeed meet for us not at all to require the aid of the written Word, but to exhibit a life so pure, that the grace of the spirit should be instead of books to our souls, and that as these are inscribed with ink, even so should our hearts be with the Spirit. But since we have utterly put away from us this grace, come let us at any rate embrace the second best course." That second best course, Derrida observes, is "the circularity and traditionality of Logos. The strange labor of conversion and adventure in which grace can only be that which is missing." *L'écriture et la différence,* 22 / *Writing and Difference,* 11.

an infinite Idea, an Idea in the Kantian sense. Every totality, every finite structure is inadequate to it" (237/160). This "irreality or ideality of meaning" (249/166) is the great discovery of phenomenology, but the account of its reality would carry Derrida beyond the limits of Husserl. Two of his teachers in particular lifted him into the existential openness that continued to elude Husserl. Foucault's project of a history of madness that refused to privilege reason was an instructive example, because it showed how reason and unreason could be held together without assuming a higher unity of reason between them. Only such an approach could give an account of the existence of reason, as an emergence that is not rigged by its preordained victory over unreason. Instead, reason is the struggle against the silence of madness in which success is not known in advance. Madness is in that sense the threat within which reason lives, the other from which it can never fully secure itself. "From its very first breath, speech, confined to this temporal rhythm of crisis and reawakening, is able to open the space for discourse only by emprisoning madness" (94/60–61). But that it is not able to deliver us permanently from the struggle is the great insight of Foucault's often misunderstood work. His existential sociology badly needs the philosophical context provided by Derrida if it is not to be seen as a concession to relativism or even madness itself. The requisite philosophical acuity is derived from Derrida's ability to simultaneously break with the Cartesian dream of the invincibility of the *cogito* by going deeper within the Cartesian reliance on divine reassurance. "For, finally, it is God alone who, by permitting me to extirpate myself from a Cogito that at its proper moment can always remain a silent madness, also insures my representations and my cognitive determinations, that is, my discourse against madness" (90/58).

A similar relationship of advancing philosophical articulation is evinced in the most notable essay of *Writing and Difference,* the one dealing with the thought of Emmanuel Levinas, "Violence and Metaphysics." Derrida recognized the significance of Levinas's break with the incompletely existential openness of Heidegger. It is only the encounter with the unforeseeable other that opens time beyond any possibility of its recapture within the economy of the subject. The event that remained ambiguous for Heidegger now definitively exceeds all totalities as a presence before presence, a trace. "Levinas calls it *religion.* It opens ethics. The ethical relation is a religious relation (*Difficile liberté*). Not *a* religion, but *the* religion, the religiosity of the religious" (142/96). In contrast, to subordinate the relation with someone to the relation with being is the violence of metaphysics that fails to acknowledge the priority of ethics.

Responsibility to the other precedes being as existence. Even responsibility to God cannot take priority, for it is only through the face of the other that God is revealed. Derrida wonders if Levinas would agree with the formulation of Jabès: "All faces are His; this is why HE has no face" (160/109). Evidently Derrida suspects that Levinas would not quite agree with this formulation, because he could hardly subscribe to the position that the revelation of God is his nonrevelation. The difference is not, however, as substantial as it appears to be, for we have already noted it in the chapter on Schelling, who thought more deeply about the revelation of God than most. Revelation of persons, supremely in the case of God, is their nonrevelation. To be a person means never to be contained in the means of one's self-disclosure. What has been lacking in Levinas, as well as Schelling, has been the linguistic means of indicating this. "By making the origin of language, meaning, and difference the relation to the infinitely other, Levinas is resigned to betraying his own intentions in his philosophical discourse. The latter is understood, and instructs, only by first permitting the same and being to circulate within it" (224/151). It is a warning no less serious for the collaborative spirit in which it is offered, and it goes a long way toward explaining the linguistic contortions into which Derrida is prepared to go in order to avoid the fate of a "Hegelian" recapture of the language of différance.[12]

This insistence is driven by more than a desire for linguistic hygiene, for it reflects a deep awareness of the requirement of metaphysics today. All of the great critiques of metaphysics, of Nietzsche, Freud, Heidegger, suffered from the fatal defect of implicating themselves in what they sought to disclaim. There is "not a single destructive proposition which has not already had to slip into the form, the logic, and the implicit postulations of precisely what it seeks to contest" (412/281). Even Derrida's own critique of the signification of presence must employ the very concept of a sign. Like every structural proposition it can operate only "by not taking into account, in the very moment of this description, its past conditions" (426/291). What distinguishes Derrida is not a solution to this insoluble situation but a full awareness and acceptance of its imperatives.[13]

---

[12] It must be emphasized that Derrida's famous essay is directed toward the Levinas of *Totality and Infinity*, before Levinas himself thought more deliberately about the language of the philosophical revolution in which he was engaged. It is arguable that the impact of Derrida's critique is to be found in the closer linguistic path followed by *Otherwise Than Being* and the later works.

[13] It is not clear, as Simon Critchley suggests, that there would be a Levinasian counterargument that the acknowledgment of différance is already to betray the priority of the other, for Derrida is merely drawing attention to the only linguistic means of acknowledging

Différance, he acknowledges, is the condition of existence. "Consciousness of speech, that is to say, consciousness in general is not knowing who speaks at the moment when, and in the place where, I proffer my speech" (263/176).[14] Up to now the shift of philosophy toward existence had sought to make use of the language of objects, thereby arresting and denying the very movement of existence that is history. With Derrida the contradictoriness becomes inescapable. *Bricolage,* "borrowing from the ruins" (418/285), is not just an incidental event; it is the very mark of what makes our existence possible. Even the term "negative theology" is not quite adequate because it still implies too much of a presence that could be known or signified. When experience is no longer ultimate, Derrida prefers to emphasize a "negative atheology" (431–32/297) as its condition.

The Vital Inability of Philosophy to Master Its Margins

There are no readily available terms to identify the philosophy of différance. Even the familiar markers that have long been attached to contemporary philosophy have become unsatisfactory. It is in this sense that Derrida confirms the thrust of the present study by emphasizing the misreading of recent philosophy that has dominated the scene. The misinterpretation of Heidegger by Sartre and the French existentialists is a pivotal case in which the longing of man to become God, "a useless passion," is taken as emblematic of a whole unfolding. Derrida in a collection of essays addressed to the self-understanding of philosophy, *Marges de la philosophie* (1972; *Margins of Philosophy*), exposes the inaccuracy. At best, we have seen, the project of human self-divinization was a misimpression that could indeed be drawn from Hegel and his successors. Derrida, too, recognizes this in his reading of them. But it made no sense to regard the transfigurational project as their defining philosophical concern. What made such overtones of interest was that they occurred within a bona fide philosophical meditation, one that sought to render the tension of existence more luminous and not simply abolish it. It was a serious misreading, going directly contrary to Heidegger's own

that priority. Critchley, *The Ethics of Deconstruction: Derrida and Levinas,* 2nd ed. (West Lafayette, IN: Purdue University Press, 1999), 176.

[14] This is an insight that has been well noted within the whole idealist tradition, especially by Schelling. For a later formulation of it see Eric Voegelin, "On the Theory of Consciousness," *Anamnesis,* in *Collected Works,* vol. 6, trans. G. Niemeyer and M. J. Hanak, ed. David Walsh (Columbia: University of Missouri Press, 2002).

protestations in the "Letter on Humanism," Derrida emphasizes in "The Ends of Man," to take anthropology and humanism "as the milieu of his thought" (140/118). Theism or atheism made no essential difference to the fundamental question of the metaphysical unity of man and God. The latter was the prior question of conditions of possibility that had driven the philosophical quest from Kant on and had redirected attention toward the existential opening prior to any contemplative discourse. It is instructive and confirmative to see Derrida sketch this deeper and more inward reading of modern philosophy that we have been following as, if not always its truth, at least the truth of its best aspiration.

The struggle of philosophy with itself is really the subject of *Margins of Philosophy,* an engagement that is extended in the two following works, *Dissemination* and *Glas,* which deal with Plato and Hegel, respectively. Philosophy is unique, Derrida suggests, in implying that it can deal with its own margins, with the boundaries that constitute it.[15] He questions what philosophy has always insisted on, its capacity of "thinking its other" (*Marges de la philosophie,* i / *Margins of Philosophy,* x), of dealing with and mastering its own limits. As we might expect, his counterassertion is that philosophy cannot escape the différance it aspires to overcome, for it submits itself to the very finitude it intends to surpass. The unsurpassability of margins is emphasized through a device he later favors extensively, the writing of his text with marginal surrounds or parallels (here in "Tympan," later in *Glas* and "Circonfession"). Despite this appearance of taking issue with philosophy's self-assurance, Derrida is himself engaged in continuity with its effort to deal, albeit more respectfully but for that reason all the more adequately, with its limits. The relationship with his predecessors is ambivalent. His discussions may be couched in terms of their marginalia, but they address the heart of the matter. A prime example, including the title, is the most famous essay of the collection, "*Ousia* and *Grammē:* Note on a Note from *Being and Time.*" The topic is the longest footnote in *Being and Time,* in which Heidegger emphasizes the inability of Hegel to go beyond the Aristotelian conception of

---

[15] The remarkable convergence of Derrida with analytic philosophy is most in evidence here. While Rorty and others have noted the similarity, it is most fully explored by Samuel C. Wheeler, *Deconstruction as Analytic Philosophy* (Stanford, CA: Stanford University Press, 2000). The major point of commonality, Wheeler argues, is that there is no "magic language," an ultimate point of reference to which appeal can be made in resolving disputes. There is only interpretation, language, and différance. The big difference, it seems to me, is that Derrida preserves a wry appreciation of the status of even such transcendental propositions. He understands that language is more than talk because it is the very opening of existence.

time because he has already absorbed it in according it the meaning of the "now." For Derrida this apparently technical discussion opens up the major issue of the metaphysics of presence, whose dominance has clouded the history of Western philosophy. He recognizes the superiority of Heidegger's analysis of time as precisely that which cannot be present, not be now, since it is that from which things can become present. The objection, as I read him, is that Heidegger still thinks he has thereby arrived at an understanding of time as a mode of presence, rather than as that which can never be understood or defined because it is inscribed in all such undertakings. For Derrida, and this is his crucial insight, difference cannot appear as such (77/66). "In order to exceed metaphysics it is necessary that a trace be inscribed within the text of metaphysics, a trace that continues to signal not in the direction of another presence, or another form of presence, but in the direction of an entirely other text" (76/65). Presence is then no more than "the trace of the trace, the trace of the erasure of trace" (76–77/66).

Derrida is endlessly creative in finding new ways of saying what cannot be said.[16] Another extended essay in the volume approaches the issue from the perspective of metaphor, "White Mythology: Metaphor in the Text of Philosophy." An "exergue" (outside the text) explains that white mythology is the draining away of the sensory in every metaphysical metaphor. It is in our interest, Derrida argues, that in the general economy of existence, as opposed to the restricted economy of the actual economy, metaphor promises more than it delivers. In the text of philosophy, metaphor is endless loss. Philosophy cannot dominate the concept of metaphor, from either outside or inside, "by using a concept of metaphor which remains a philosophical product" (272/228). Only a blind spot remains for philosophy, but it is from that endless proliferation of metaphor that it lives. Yet even that realization is not enough to stanch the drive to surpass metaphor by returning to its proper source. "Metaphor, then," Derrida concludes, "always carries its death within itself. And this death, surely, is also the death *of* philosophy" (323/271). This double genitive, transitive and intransitive, is precisely the tension of philosophical existence, which can be neither abolished nor resolved. Derrida is not about to suggest a further resolution that would be tantamount to its abolition. For him the accent falls, as it did for Kierkegaard, entirely on the side of existence that brings together what can never be united in thought, a dislocation that opens the very possibility of

---

[16] See Derrida, "How to Avoid Speaking: Denials," *Languages of the Unsayable: The Play of Negativity in Literature and Literary Theory*, 3–70.

existence. Recalling Schelling's reflections on the "I" that glimpses itself in the mirror, Derrida sees it as the opening of time that distances itself from its origin. "Valéry has recognized that the specular agency, far from constituting the I in its properness, immediately expropriates it in order not to halt its march" (339/285). Like the signature that makes it possible for the signer to be present when he is not, it is also what implies his nonpresence. Within the structure of iteration, intention can be present without being completely present to itself. This is the opening of existence.

Plato's *Pharmakon*

Having thus established his relationship to his immediate predecessors, Derrida goes on to address the two great historical challenges to his philosophy of writing. The first is Plato's insistence on the priority of speech and the impossibility of reducing philosophy to its text. Again the disagreement is not an opposition. Both Plato and Derrida have the same goal of opening the space for philosophy, which means that Derrida must become a more faithful exponent of Plato than Plato himself. This ambivalence is captured in the dual meanings of the title of the major essay in *Dissemination,* "Plato's Pharmacy." The *pharmakon* that denotes writing in the *Phaedrus* is both a remedy and a poison, and it is the inextricability of this opposition that is its essence. On Plato's analysis, the letters that are intended as a remedy to the problem of forgetting are also what encourage forgetting, since they make remembering less necessary. For Derrida the key insight is that remembering is already a kind of forgetting in the way in which writing depends on forgetting, an opening up of the distance from an origin that recedes endlessly. Writing, he suggests, opens up a possibility that cannot be contained within it in the way in which Plato's text cannot be closed within itself. The *Phaedrus* or any of the dialogues do not encompass an origin but point rather toward a range of problems beyond themselves. If writing "as a *pharmakon* cannot simply be assigned a site within what it situates, cannot be subsumed under concepts whose contours it draws, leaves only its ghost to a logic that can only seek to govern it insofar as logic arises from it – one would then have to *bend* into strange contortions what could no longer even simply be called logic or discourse" (*La dissemination,* 118 / *Dissemination,* 103). Plato's dream of a memory without a sign has become impossible, and it is for this reason that we can locate ourselves "on the eve of Platonism," which can also "be thought of as the morning after Hegelianism" (122–23/107–8).

Before taking leave of Plato, however, we must note the extent to which we never take leave of him. This is because the critique of Plato can never simply remain what it is, for it always turns out to have been an exploration of Plato's self-critique.[17] In Plato's lifelong avoidance of taking writings literally, Derrida finds the awareness of erasure by which the opening of difference becomes possible. He notes in particular "the stunning hand Plato has dealt himself" as he "plays at taking play seriously" (181/157), especially in the famous passage from the *Laws* on man as a plaything of the gods. It should not surprise us, therefore, that Derrida goes on to select from the *Timaeus* (48e–51b) one of the most important concepts of his later elaborations of difference. This is the formless *khora* at the origin of all. It is the perfect term for the trace that disseminates without remainder of itself. "It is a matrix, womb, or receptacle that is never and nowhere offered up in the form of presence, or in the presence of form, since both of these already presuppose an inscription within the mother" (184/160). The originary inscription that cannot be inscribed is the furthest reach of Plato beyond Platonism. It is Plato's answer to the problematic of truth that was set in motion by Parmenides and reaches over the entire history of metaphysics: how to speak about that which comes before all speaking and therefore cannot be spoken about. It has been addressed largely as a problem of language. Derrida, despite his extensive linguistic investment, has reached a clarification by recognizing that it is primarily a problem of existence. Difference is the existence of language before language. It is that heightened attention to existence that he brings to the Platonic formulation. "The disappearance of truth as presence, the withdrawal of the present origin of presence, is the condition of all (manifestation of) truth. Nonpresence is presence. Difference, the disappearance of any originary presence, is *at once* the condition of possibility *and* the condition of impossibility of truth" (194/168).

Hegel's System Read as a Book of Life

An even more extensive return that is not a return to the same is evinced in Derrida's reading of Hegel, the other great other of his thought. The Hegel of the system capable of containing the whole of history would

---

[17] Catherine Zuckert has acknowledged the importance for Derrida of thinking through the relationship to Plato. However, her reading of Derrida remains too much in the shadow of Leo Strauss to really engage the novelty of Derrida's Plato. Zuckert, *Postmodern Platos: Nietzsche, Heidegger, Gadamer, Strauss, Derrida* (Chicago: University of Chicago Press, 1996).

seem to be the principal challenge to a philosophy of difference without reconciliation. But as we have seen, this is not the only way to read Hegel. His own beginning was much closer to the movement of existence escaping its capture in thought, and much of the significance of the system remained its tensional openness to what could not be included within it. This is the path of Derrida's journey through Hegel that emerged in the formidable *Glas* (1974). It is a powerful testament to the raw force of unrecoverable existence, différance, that now overflows the textual analysis of Hegel in the form of a parallel analysis of the avant-garde playwright Jean Genet, with numerous interpositions along the way.[18] As a work it exhibits a bewildering strangeness in presenting Hegel in the left-hand column and Genet in the right, but the unfamiliarity soon disappears as the technique of juxtaposition is accepted. It is, after all, little different from the polyphonic novels of Dostoevsky in which the authorial voice has largely been ceded to the character of the moment.[19] If we take seriously Derrida's insistence on the end of the book, the incapacity of any book to include its source within itself, the ceaseless overflow of existence whence writing derives, the result must surely be a book that concedes its nonencompassing status. In a sense *Glas*, whose title intimates a bell, SA (*savoir absolu*), and several other possibilities, is the point at which Derrida rises to the challenge presented by Hegel. It is both a correction and an extension of Hegel that attempts to deal with the realization that life cannot be included within the system and does so by not including it. *Glas* is Derrida's attempt to do justice to his own observation that "the Hegelian system commands that it be read as a book of life" (*Glas*, 96 [all references to left column unless indicated] / *Glas*, trans. Leavey and Rand, 83).[20]

---

[18] Christina Holloway has pointed out that Derrida uses Genet in a similar way to Sartre, whose *Saint Genet, comédien et martyr* (1951) viewed him as the pure existential type, in contrast to the systematizing exterior of Hegel. Holloway, *Derrida: Deconstruction from Phenomenology to Ethics* (Oxford: Polity, 1998), 84–95. A companion volume to the translation of *Glas*, *Glassary* (Lincoln: University of Nebraska Press, 1986), contains comprehensive notes on the text by John Leavey, an extensive literary essay by Gregory Ulmer, as well as a brief contribution from Derrida on the problems of translating his most stylistically ambitious work.

[19] Mikhail Bakhtin, *Problems of Dostoevsky's Poetics,* trans. R. W. Rotsel (Ann Arbor. MI: Ardis, 1973), 20, 90.

[20] The significance of Derrida's existential reading of Hegel has often been overlooked because it does not fit easily within the conventional picture of Hegel as the author of a conceptual system against which all advocates of openness must voice their opposition. An exception to this pattern is Simon Critchley, who observes that here Derrida "works within – rather than with – the text" to read it from within its own dynamic. "Within

The analysis begins with Hegel's account of the transition within life from its mute beginning to speech. This allows Derrida to dwell continuously on the role of the family, the relationship of persons among whom life is actually lived, exploring eventually Hegel's own family life to the extent that it is available to us. The tension between text and existence is Derrida's abiding fascination, and it is his principal contribution to Hegel studies to have shown that it absorbed Hegel as well. Animal copulation generates neither memory nor monuments nor speech. It is only in the family that the movement of language begins, although it is the very movement beyond the family. As a consequence, Derrida notes, "the family speaks and does not speak" (14/8), occupying an intermediate status between the natural and the universal. Yet it is through the family that Sittlichkeit, the idea of freedom, becomes conscious when the father, in raising and educating the son, loses him from the family. Love as the innermost life, by which in losing myself in an other I also gain myself in the other, makes of the family the prime instance of reconciliation (*Aufhebung*). It is the model of the divine outpouring by which God becomes an other in the Son but in the process gains himself even more fully within the Spirit of love. Derrida makes much of the contrast that Hegel underlines between this inwardness of love that is at the heart of Christianity and the harsh externality that characterizes the Jewish relationship to God and, by extension, the relationship of the family. It is a contrast that underpins Hegel's harsh judgment of the contemporary marginalization of Jews in European society as a fitting reflection of their existential obstinacy in alienation. Incapable of rising above their "servile earthboundness" (65/54), the Jews could never live within the freedom of the spirit that endowed modern nations with rights, property, and a civil constitution.

What is remarkable about this reading, despite Derrida's understandable sensitivity to the cavalier historical dismissal of his own race, now a mere foil for the Christian triumph of freedom, is that he seems to agree with its philosophical substance. He understands that Hegel is not engaged in the elaboration of a merely mechanical scheme of reintegration. It is a genuinely living reconciliation of love by which the finite overflows with what it cannot contain. While the Jewish tabernacle

and through this commentary, this experience of language, Derrida leads the reader to focus upon certain privileged moments in Hegel's text that cannot be fully mastered by the dialectical method and that perhaps constitute the unthought towards which Hegel's thought tends." Critchley, "A Commentary upon Derrida's Reading of Hegel in *Glas*," in Stuart Barnett, ed., *Hegel After Derrida* (London: Routledge, 1998), 225.

remains empty, incapable of containing its representation, "a signifier without a signified" (59/49), the Christian discovery is that the finite can become the vehicle for the infinite when it is loved as the infinite. "One is no longer limited to loving a finite being: one loves a finite being as infinite" (44/35). Moreover, this is the nature of love, as it is of the family and morality, whose disclosure is tied to the advent of Christianity. "One can love the other only as an other, but in love there is no longer alterity, *Vereinigung*" (76/64). This, Derrida suggests, is the meaning of Hegel's statement in the "Positivity of the Christian Religion" that to love is to feel oneself in the whole of life "with no limits, in the infinite." Love is itself an infinite movement. "Love, the sensible hearth of the family, is infinite, or it does not exist" (76/64). In thus pushing Hegel to the boldest formulation, Derrida lifts the debate out of the sterility of contrasting theologies to draw us into the existential movement that is more profoundly inward. The force of love is evinced in its transformation of the law. Love is what abolishes the law by going beyond fulfilling it. Kant had understood this too, but it was Hegel who explored its real significance. It meant, on Derrida's reading, nothing less than the overabundance that "throws off balance the principle of equivalence, commerce, the economy of exchange that regulates *justice*" (70/59). Love is what renders impossible the return to a stable condition of the system because it never returns to itself but continues to infinity without remainder. Could it be an Aufhebung that forgets or loses itself? "*Pleroma* will have been the name of this de-bordering fulfillment of synthesis" (70/58).

It is almost as if Derrida is learning more from Hegel than the latter has to teach. This possibility is suggested particularly by Hegel's insistence that Christianity is the truth of love as an infinite movement, whereas for Derrida the relationship seems to be reversed and infinite love is what confirms the truth of Christianity. He follows Hegel's account of how Christianity fails to deliver on the promise of spirit it had instituted and falls victim to a new externality of dependence on the person of Jesus. Christianity has "succeeded in lifting the Jewish limitation," but it "repeats, a little higher up, the Jewish cutting" (106/92). The march of spirit must be resumed outside of Christianity before its truth can be fully unfolded. The moment of self-recognition that is reached when natural existence is jeopardized in war or capital punishment is indicative of the path that must be followed if the intermediaries of spirit are to be pervaded by self-transparence. Spirit is always what dies to itself in nature in order to emerge from it. This notion of "the suicide of nature" (134/117) is what draws the focus of Derrida's attention. "That it is subject to the law of what it is the law of, that is what gives to the structure of the Hegelian system a very twisted form so difficult to grasp" (139/121). Derrida has put his finger on the central temptation or tension of Hegel's thought. The conflict stems from an inability or an unwillingness to decide whether to remain faithful to a wholly internal movement of life or to seize the opportunity to leap outside of it to an assessment of the value of its result. In his analysis of desire as that which remains by not remaining, Hegel approaches the Derridean notion of différance, but he loses it by reaching out for it. In thinking of the child as the death and the life of the parents, Hegel makes of the ambiguity itself the focus that eclipses everything else. "The ever so slight difference of stress, conceptually imperceptible, the inner fragility of each attribute produces the oscillation between the presence of being as death and the death of being as presence" (151/133). Derrida takes the oscillating itself as emblematic of the speculative temptation to cheat death. "The Aufhebung is the dying away, the amortization, of death. That is the concept of economy in general in speculative dialectics" (152/133).

It is to rescue Hegel's dialectic from this economy, to restore it to its inwardness, that Derrida now turns in the second half of *Glas*. Again it is the role of the family that proves to be the point of access. Derrida notes that the family is treated before morality and formal right in the *Phenomenology* but after it in the *Philosophy of Right* (154/135) by way of alerting us to the problematic status of the relationship. As in the master–slave dialectic, the question is how the movement from singularity to the universal is to be assessed. Is it a pure loss of self without return? Or is there a return without the self? The irresolvability is brought out best in relation to the family. "The family does not yet know the universality-producing labor in the city, only the work of mourning" (162/143). But unlike the individual who either loses himself in the struggle for recognition or gains recognition from a slave whose otherness he can no longer recognize, the family endures within its own realm. The question of gain and loss is less susceptible to the economy of speculative dialectics. This seems to be the reason for Derrida's focus on the relationship between the family and the work of spirit. It is in relation to the family that the failure of Aufhebung is most apparent. What cannot be resumed on the higher level of unfolding persists with an obstinacy that attests to its own primordiality. We are approaching the major insight into existence as nonrecoverable precisely because it is what constitutes the possibility of existence. Like Kierkegaard, Derrida learned from Hegel the absolute unrecoverability of the moment. "There is on this edge [*fil*], on this blade, the instant before the fall or the cut [*coupe*], no philosophical statement possible that does not lose what it tries to retain and that does not lose it precisely by retaining it" (158/139).

Antigone is the epitome of this condition in her refusal to bow before the law of the universal in the state. Derrida tracks Hegel's fascination with the Aeschylean masterpiece, which parallels the continuing irresolvability of tensions within Hegel's own family life. He had to balance the demands of obtaining a post that would make it possible for him to marry and support a family with those of caring for his sister, who had undergone a mental breakdown. The thinker does not escape the vicissitudes of existence as if the world of thought could contain them without remainder, for it is precisely the nontransferability of existence that is its opening into thought that yet can never exhaust its source. There is no closure back on the beginning. Derrida exemplifies this insight in his own treatment, which is simply interrupted by the personal letters of Hegel, juxtaposed without mediation or reduction to the text of Derrida. There are no seamless jointures, only the irreducibles of existence. This is the significance of Antigone, who represents the unassimilability of the existential, the family, in relation to the larger whole it makes possible. She cannot yield the family prerogative of burying the dead brother to the universal law of the living brother. The individual cannot finally be sacrificed to the state, for even as a corpse there is something left over. It is this brother–sister relationship at the boundary of the natural and the universal orders that, Derrida suggests, so fascinated Hegel. At the intersection of the realms, the relationship could not be definitively assigned. "Isn't there always an element excluded from the system that assures the system's space of possibility?" (183/162).[21] Hegel seems to approach this possibility but then opts to draw it all back into the system by way of the Aufhebung. In so doing he enters into his own tragedy, the undoing of the very Aufhebung in which he had placed such faith.

Rather than simply remaining at its unassimilated limit, the family, in Hegel's account, "dissolves itself and goes out of itself" (188/166). Incorporating existence is to lose existence. "Relieving a limit is guarding it,

---

[21] "Like Hegel, we have been fascinated by Antigone, by this unbelievable relationship, this powerful liaison without desire, this immense impossible desire that could not live, as capable only of overturning, paralyzing, or exceeding any system and history, of interrupting the life of the concept, of cutting off its breath, or better, what comes down to the same thing, of supporting it from outside or underneath a crypt." *Glas,* 187 / *Glas,* trans. Leavey and Rand, 166.

keeping it, but here guarding (a limit) is losing it. To guard what loses itself is to lack. The logic of the *Aufhebung* (re)turns itself at each instant into its absolute other. Absolute appropriation is absolute expropriation. Onto-logic can always be reread or rewritten as the logic of loss or of spending without reserve" (188/167). We gain life only by living it; the price is life itself. The reconciliation that is no reconciliation does not avoid the tragic law of action that reoccurs at every moment of concrete action. Ethical action, as Sittlichkeit, always includes unconscious crime. As the action of a singular individual, it cannot do justice to the universal toward which it is directed, nor can the universal encompass the singularity of the individual through whom it is realized. The dialectic of the finite–infinite is the core of Hegel's insight. His only failure is in thinking it can be resolved without destroying the possibility of action. Derrida's account is difficult to separate from Hegel at this point, evidenced by his employment of lengthy quotations without comment (210–11/187–88), because the convergence is almost complete. All that separates them is the Aufhebung. Without it there is the dialectic whose irresolvability is the condition that opens existence. At times it is not even clear if Derrida is accusing Hegel of this speculative sleight-of-hand that subsumes and abolishes at the same time. The pattern is one I have already noted in my treatment of Hegel in Chapter 2, in which the presence of unresolved tensions, especially in the *Philosophy of Right*, sufficiently attests to Hegel's awareness of the issue. His reference to the ironic role of women in relation to the state, whose suppression of private interest ultimately serves its reemergence, is adduced by Derrida. But it is in relation to romantic love that the priority of existence is evidenced most strongly. Hegel identifies the deception of romantic love, which would appear to constitute a leap into a fulfillment that can be acquired only over a lifetime, as the very paragon of an Aufhebung. Derrida picks out this critique because it reveals so clearly how "the lure of the false infinite, hides a deadly coldness under the ardent discourse of passion" (217/194). In taking from it the consequence "that there is no infinite love without marriage," Derrida has drawn Hegel as close as possible to the existential implication pronounced by Kierkegaard.

There is no goal of fulfillment, only the movement of existence that opens time. Submission to the necessity of self-limitation, repression, does not even let itself be thought. "The question is already strict-uring, is already girded being" (215/191). There is nothing outside existence, just as there is nothing outside the text. No explanation is given in advance or in the end; we know only that the upsurge of the natural requires the suppression of the natural. To say that shame, the prohibition against appearing nude, is the truth of marriage is not to understand the latter in terms other than itself. It is to acknowledge the priority of existence over its concept. "More precisely: shame, which is *still natural*, spiritually accomplishes itself in the conjugal bond" (220/196).[22] Both Kierkegaard and Marx, Derrida notes, recognized this failure of Hegel to deliver on the culmination he promised would ultimately save him. It was the turn toward existence that he so decisively began that was the main "contribution" of Hegel. A limit had been reached, Derrida insists, when the question of existence could no longer be raised because existence had become the horizon of the question. Life occurs within its movement and nowhere else. Having thus placed Hegel in the context of his revolutionary significance, the context of Derrida's own différance, it is now possible in the concluding pages of the left column of *Glas* to take up Hegel's own theological conclusion.

The viewpoint of finite subjectivity, as philosophically defined by Kant, cannot think the infinite of God. Thinking God can occur only through God himself – that is, through God's self-revelation, a movement that cannot be contained in specific events because it is what contains them. "God is the very act of self-manifesting, of being *there*" (238/213), Derrida notes, before launching into a lengthy digression on Freud and Hegel's relation to Kant. When he returns, it is to take up again the relation between absolute religion and absolute knowledge. "Absolute religion is not yet what it is already: *Sa*. Absolute religion (the essence of Christianity, religion of essence) is already what it is not yet: the *Sa* that itself is already no more what it is yet, absolute religion" (244/218). The disclosure of a person is always the disclosure of nonfinite disclosure, and this is preeminently the case with the self-disclosure of God. In other words the claim that absolute knowledge, *savoir absolu*, constitutes an advance beyond revelation cannot be sustained. The claim can be retained only if it is turned into its opposite as the assertion of the impossibility of absolute knowledge. Derrida does not quite give the issue this formulation, but he does point toward it in underlining the opposition between revelation and knowledge. He notes that "the absolute of revealed religion would have a *critical* effect on *Sa*. It would be necessary to keep to the (opposite) bank, that of religion and the family, in order to resist the

---

[22] Derrida notes how Hegel's treatment of the incest prohibition foregrounds the contradiction within the system. "An index: the incest prohibition breaks with nature, and *that is why* it conforms more to nature." Ibid., 223/199.

lure of *Sa*" (248/221). In the end the only absolute knowledge is that there is no absolute knowledge, for the attempt to attain it closes off the only possibility of knowledge within the movement of existence. But this is the opening of existence as time. Absolute knowledge "imposes on itself a gap [*écart*] in signing itself. The *Da* of *Sa* is nothing other than the movement of signification" (256/229). The right-hand column drawing from Jean Genet had all along consisted of a rich elaboration of this movement of signification that remains a movement because it is ever incapable of coinciding with its goal. To the extent that there is any absolute knowledge, it consists in this glimpse of impossibility that is not itself an absolute glimpse. "Consciousness represents to itself the unity, but it is not there" (247/220).

Apocalypse Restored to Eschatology: Engagement with Heidegger

There is no doubt that Derrida has reached in *Glas,* his most ambitious volume, a clarity (we are inclined to say a nonclarity) that marks his work as the furthest reach of the modern philosophical turn toward existence. It sounds the knell (*glas*) of philosophy as a conceptual system, accomplishing its own obsolescence and the opening of philosophy as a movement ever on the way toward its own initiation. What he had grasped earlier as the problem of différance, that no text could ever enclose itself within itself, is now understood to be the problem of existence that depends on never coinciding with the goal it sets itself. Hegel, as the most notorious case of this tension, had proved the exemplary means of clarification. Now Derrida could move on the self-understanding of the modern world that had taken its direction for so long from the variants of Hegelianism. The apocalyptic outlook that had hung over that world could now be removed or, more properly, removed by the restoration of its eschatological status. The turn toward religion that became increasingly pronounced in Derrida's writings from this point on was not an incidental biographical aside. It was intimately connected with the removal of the burden of apocalypse. Very much like St. Augustine, whom he increasingly invokes, he understood that the foreclosing effects of an imminent apocalypse can be removed only by the opening toward the full internalization of existence in apocalypse.[23] In this sense Derrida

---

[23] So far the discussion of the Augustinian parallels have been limited to the impact of the *Confessions* on Derrida's own *Circumfession*. A remarkable conference at which Derrida participated took place in 2001 on the relationship, but neither he nor any of the other participants seem to have explored the broader character of the parallel. The resulting

is neither postmodern nor postapocalyptic, for he has entered into the existential mode of apocalypse that cannot be contained within historical events or texts. The engagement is announced in his 1981 lecture, "On a Newly Arisen Apocalyptic Tone in Philosophy," a title intended to demarcate the beginning of the impending apocalypticism identified by Kant in his late essay, "On a Newly Arisen Superior Tone in Philosophy" (1796).

Kant had discerned the rise of the aspiration to "philosophize under the influence of a higher *feeling*" (*Gesammelte Schriften,* vol. 8, 395 / *Raising the Tone of Philosophy,* 58) as precisely what would turn philosophy into a matter of tone rather than reason. As a leap into the end of history, the short-circuiting of philosophy parallels Derrida's preoccupation with the closure of existence. Hindsight, however, provides him with a far richer perspective on the fatality of the apocalyptic imagination. Kant could apply the power of his polemic only against a rising threat; Derrida could enter so deeply into its seductive hold that he emerged on the other side. What he carried out in *Glas* is here formulated as a project, one that he will elaborate over successive studies of such great apocalypticists as Nietzsche, Heidegger, and Marx. For now Derrida attacks it in the more muted enlightenment sounding of a tone. The significance of a tone, he explains, is that it is the mode in which apocalypse can insert its claim, for it is a revelation that is imminent but precisely for that reason cannot yet exist. Kant could only warn that its advent would spell "the death of all philosophy" (398/62). Derrida understands it to be the différance secreted within the heart of all revelation, the double bind that at once forbids the revelation of the name of God but fulfills it only by the revelation itself. Tone is then the way that what exceeds the discourse can indicate itself. It is the revealing over and above the revelation itself. "Truth is the end of the instance of the last judgment. The structure of truth here would be apocalyptic. And that is why there would not be any truth of the apocalypse that is not the truth of truth" (*D'un ton apocalyptique,* 69 / *Raising the Tone,* 151). The primordiality of apocalypse launches Derrida on an analysis of the Apocalypse of John in which he sees the multiple layers of the sending of the message as inseparable from the meaning of revelation. Tone is not dispensable, for "it always refers to the name and to the tone of the other that is there but as having been

volume is, however, an invaluable testament to the enduring character of the Augustine connection. John Caputo and Michael Scanlon, eds., *Augustine and Post-Modernism: "Confessions" and "Circumfession"* (Bloomington: Indiana University Press, 2005).

there and before yet coming, no longer being or not yet there in the present of the *récit*" (77/156). Even Derrida's account of the apocalypse cannot avoid apocalyptic language.[24] He cannot extricate himself from the imperative "Come" under which the injunction to write arises, for writing does not permit us to leap outside of existence, although it may continuously insinuate this possibility. A new formulation is needed to characterize the situation of philosophy today, and Derrida announces it at the end of the essay as "an apocalypse without apocalypse, an apocalypse without vision, without truth, without revelation" (95/167). The elaboration of this existential "Come," "the apocalypse of apocalypse," would occupy Derrida for the next quarter century.

It is what had eluded Nietzsche in his effort to understand how the truth of truth always overflows the border of truth. The insight could be glimpsed but it could not be formulated, and as a consequence he could only circle endlessly around the truth of nontruth. "Nietzsche," Derrida concludes, "might well be a little lost in the web of his text, lost much as a spider who finds he is unequal to the web he has spun" (*Spurs*, bilingual ed., 100).[25] But it is Heidegger who represents the greatest challenge to the evocation of an apocalypse without apocalypse since, as we have seen in Chapter 5, he grasps the insight but cannot retain it. Instead, the idea of apocalypse follows the course of its self-betrayal. The extrication of the question from its Heideggerian phase promised the most in its unfolding, which is why Derrida's study *De l'esprit: Heidegger et la question* (1987; *Of Spirit: Heidegger and the Question*) looms large in his own philosophical odyssey. It emerged at the height of the last wave of revelations concerning Heidegger's Nazi connections with their inevitable implication of his philosophy. Derrida's way into the controversy is necessarily oblique, as is to be expected from a thinker who sees texts as contained in life rather than the other way around. A more conventional characterization is that he begins with the philosophical texts and works back toward their setting in life, but that would not quite capture the hermeneutic of différance, of the trace and distance, that continuously imprecates all writing. It is

---

[24] "That I have multiplied the distinctions between closure and end, that I was aware of speaking of discourses *on* the end rather than announcing the end, that I intended to analyze a genre rather than practice it, and even when I would practice it, to do so with that ironic genre clause I tried to show never belonged to the genre itself; nevertheless, for the reasons I gave a few minutes ago, all language on apocalypse is also apocalyptic and cannot be excluded from its object." *D'un ton*, 84 / *Raising the Tone*, 160–61.

[25] The text dates from the Cerisy-la-Salle colloquium in 1972.

an approach that is borne out by the results, which go much farther than most analyses of Heidegger in correlating the philosopher and the functionary. No judgment of Heidegger's philosophical culpability can be rendered from outside his philosophy. It must rather be viewed as a movement that had for him its origin in the philosophical work that now must be brought to confront the question of whether it remained faithful to itself. The fact that the path coincided with the one on which Derrida himself was moving, indeed that he traversed the path opened by Heidegger, is what generated the sympathetic reconsideration.[26]

Derrida is very much aware that his title, *De l'esprit*, is a very French one that would not have been approved by Heidegger. No doubt he chose it to underline that difference. Heidegger, despite the highly charged spirit of his work, deliberately avoided all the terminology of an objectivist metaphysics that would suggest soul, spirit, psyche, and so on. He rigorously set aside all accounts of a subject to further the opening toward being within which the subject stood. But, Derrida seems to suggest, it was precisely the eschewal of all spiritual language that left him open to its political misapplication. Most notoriously in the "Rectorship Address," he spiritualizes Nazism by way of the "metaphysics of the subject" that he had simultaneously rejected. "Metaphysics always returns, I mean in the sense of a *revenant* [ghost], and *Geist* is the most fatal figure of this *revenance* [returning, haunting]. Of the double which can never be separated from the single" (*De l'esprit*, 66 / *Of Spirit*, 40). Heidegger's problem is that he wishes to avoid this doubling of spirit so that it both informs the philosophical meditation and the historical reality from which it springs. This is what explains the numerous political obiter dicta that pepper his texts as we have seen. They are more than just his personal musings, for they take the form of oracular pronouncements that evoke the future. Even in the *Introduction to Metaphysics*, Derrida notes, the political retreat it represented did not constitute a retreat from the political. He refuses to accept that the doubling is inscribed in spirit. "It is *of spirit*" (67/41), as Derrida suggests by the title of his work. The gap cannot be closed between the movement of spirit and the trace it leaves within historical reality, unless the apocalypse has been reached, in which the full

---

[26] The significance of the engagement with Heidegger in *De l'esprit* is indicated by the appearance of an anthology dedicated to the volume. It includes not only Derrida's sympathetic readers, but other more impartial voices and one highly critical, Gillian Rose. David Wood ed., *Of Derrida, Heidegger, and Spirit* (Evanston, IL: Northwestern University Press, 1993).

self-transparency of spirit is realized. For now spirit is inscribed by the doubling in which it is never what it is. Existence is différance, apocalypse without apocalypse.

It is possible that it is impatience with limits, this tensional existence, that tips Heidegger into the annihilation of spirit within history, the apocalypse realized. Derrida suggests as much in a lengthy discussion of the parallels with Husserl and Valéry, who, with Heidegger, had developed their sense of an impending crisis of European civilization. In the spectacle of spirit turning against itself in the instrumentalized material civilization it was bringing forth, they beheld a crisis, an apocalypse of spirit, that could not long endure. The unsupportability of the crisis of spirit weighed heavily "in this imaginary symposium, in this invisible university where, for more than twenty years, the greatest European minds [*esprit*] met" (100n/124n). In the case of Heidegger the weight of apocalypse without apocalypse so burdened him that it caused him not only to lend his philosophical prestige to the *Führer* locomotive, but even to engage in the retroactive desecration of his own texts. Derrida takes note of the notorious erasure of the dedication of *Being and Time* on the occasion of its second edition, an action that seemed to suggest the rewriting of its philosophical debt to Husserl as a rewriting of its history. But there is Heidegger's even more interesting misquotation of himself in the *Introduction to Metaphysics*, a mutilation that Derrida may be alone in noticing. In the "Rectorship Address" the word *Geist* is in quotation marks, but in the later passage they are removed without comment (106–7/66–67). It is an episode that intrigues Derrida with his ear for the noncoincidence of texts and their origin, although he does not explain it any further. One suspects that he takes note of it because it exemplifies the difficulty Heidegger has in making "spirit" in its civilizational sense coincide with the movement of spirit to which his own philosophy responds. It is a difficulty nowhere more acutely marked than by his own retreat from public support of the Nazi Party in the interim between the two texts. As with his characterization of German as the only language in which spirit can be said, one senses the deep contradiction with the spirit that always differs from the said. Heidegger, Derrida concludes, is capable of calling forth "the most serious or the most amused reflections" at the same time. "It's always horribly dangerous and wildly funny, certainly grave and comical" (109/68).

He has hit upon the key problem of Heidegger, the gravely comic self-betrayal we noted in Chapter 5. The relentless quest for the origin of spirit implies its attainability, and the failure to admit its unattainability undermines the validity of the quest as such. It is the refusal to decide between spirit as a noun and a verb, as the flame or what inflames (133/84). Vacillating between these alternatives, Heidegger is ever claiming to have surpassed any specific stabilization of spirit as penultimate to the one toward which he is moving. It is simultaneously a philosophy of the way and of the destination, or, as he would say, of the "destining," without ever being able to bring them into relationship with one another. The ever-approaching and never-arriving character of his thought is not the problem, for it is what constitutes our existence so long as we exist. It is what Derrida has pinpointed in his différance. What is problematic is Heidegger's refusal to accept it as such. It is the source of his dissatisfaction with every unfolding of spirit that is driven by the expectation that there must be some unfolding that does not fall short of its promise. This is why language is ceaselessly tortured to make it say what cannot be said because the saying is always already outside of the said. It is, of course, the power of poetry that brings us to the brink of the sayable, thereby suggesting the possibility of a linguistic apocalypse. But again it only leaves us on the brink (145–46/93–94).[27] In the end it is Heidegger's refusal to live within the apocalyptic expectation that is the source of his desire to accomplish it. This is the centerpiece of Derrida's analysis that emerges when he poses the question of faith to Heidegger.

Despite the elaborate philosophical and linguistic apparatus, Heidegger has not taken one step beyond the self-understanding of faith as living in the "not yet." "It is with reference to an extremely conventional and doxical outline of Christianity that Heidegger can claim to de-Christianize Trakl's *Gedicht*" (178/108). The objection is heightened by Derrida's posing of it in the form of a dialogic questioning of Heidegger by "certain Christian theologians." They might ask if it is not the case that "the archi-originary spirit, which you claim is foreign to Christianity, is indeed what is most essential in Christianity" (179/110). It is what the theologians, too, have been seeking and makes them closer to him than he thinks. But Heidegger would say in reply that he is not opposing anything of the Christian mysteries of fall and salvation but

---

[27] Referring to Paul de Man's playful variation of Heidegger's "*Die Sprache versrpricht sich,*" Derrida notes that "language or speech promises, promises *itself* but also goes back on its word, becomes undone or unhinged, derails or becomes delirious, deteriorates, becomes corrupt just as immediately and just as essentially. It cannot not promise as soon as it speaks, it is promise, but it cannot fail to break its promise – and this comes of the structure of the promise, as of the event it nonetheless institutes." *De l'esprit,* 146 / *Of Spirit,* 93–94.

"simply trying, modestly, discreetly, to think that *on the basis of which* all this is possible. That (on the basis of which . . .), because it has always been veiled, *is not yet what makes it possible*" (182/111). Derrida is as good a lawyer for the defense as for the prosecution because he knows what Heidegger's response must be almost as well as Heidegger himself. The latter would hardly have been floored by the objection with which he was familiar from various Christian theologians, having numbered himself among them at one point. He would not accept that he was saying the same as the theologians but that "the thinking access to the *possibility* of metaphysics or pneumato-spiritualist religions opens into something quite other than what the possibility makes possible" (183–84/113). It is here that Derrida lowers the boom. The theologians, he surmises, would not take exception to Heidegger's formulation; they would agree with it more emphatically and thereby dispose of it. Yes, they would insist, it is "just what we're saying . . . we are appealing to this entirely other in the memory of a promise or the promise of a memory. That's the truth of what we have always said, heard, tried to make heard. The misunderstanding is that you hear us better than you think or pretend to think" (184/113). It is a powerful objection, so staggering that Derrida had to voice it by not voicing it himself. One wonders if it does not mark a seismic shift in his own development into the notably religious phase of his thought when he has recognized its religious character. Apocalypse without apocalypse occurs nowhere other than in the life of faith. "The spirit which keeps watch in returning [*en revenant*] will always do the rest. Through flame or ash, but as the entirely other, inevitably" (184/113).

Retrieving Marx as Purely Spectral

It may well be that it was this attainment of the apocalypse of apocalypse as faith that enabled Derrida to finally distance himself from the failed or, as he would call it, the "spectral" apocalypse of Marx. The result was one of his most lucid volumes, *Spectres de Marx* (1993; *Specters of Marx*), in which he came to terms with the political sources of his thought to an extent that previously had not been possible. Of course, the volume arose directly from the collapse of communism as a political movement in 1989, and was part of the generalized grieving the Left was compelled to undergo in the succeeding years. But as usual, Derrida provided something far more interesting than the cloying nostalgia of those days. He thought through what Marx and Marxism must always have been. To fail as an apocalypse does not mean that one could or should have succeeded. It means that one has never been anything other than the apocalyptic framing of the present, a spectral return that could not do other than return spectrally. Instead of yielding to the endemic mood of disappointment, Derrida finds in Marx what he had always found, namely, its apocalyptic appeal, only now more properly understood to be an apocalypse that could never be realized or could be realized only at the cost of its significance. Notably absent from his reflection is any reckoning of responsibility for the murderous destructiveness that seventy years of Marxism had perpetrated; nothing of the impact of the revelations of Solzhenitsyn's *Gulag* in the seventies linking communism with totalitarianism surfaces in Derrida. Perhaps this is because, as he explains, he had long abandoned de facto Marxism, although never "out of conservative or reactionary motivations, or even moderate right-wing or republican positions" (*Spectres de Marx,* 36 / *Specters of Marx,* 14). The question "whither Marxism?" has for Derrida's generation the same age as the questioners. The collapse of the Soviet Union did not precipitate their reflection on the end of history, for they had been brought up on "the canon of the modern apocalypse." But the event did bring into focus the connection with totalitarian terror that many of them had known for a long time. We recall Derrida's arrest in Prague in 1981 for his support of the dissidents of the Jan Hus Foundation. Never a mere fellow traveler, Derrida had long been engaged with the central question that the collapse of communism posed. How is it possible to live toward a fulfillment that historically can never arrive? It is, of course, the central question not only of the modern world, but of the philosophy of history opened by Augustine's *saeculum senescens.* "Such was no doubt the element in which what is called deconstruction developed – and one can understand nothing of this period of deconstruction, notably in France, unless one takes this historical entanglement into account" (38/15).[28]

Only now does it become clear that deconstruction has not just been about texts; its primary thrust has been to deal with existence in the end of history. The situation is not novel. It is certainly that of Augustine and Christian civilization, and Kierkegaard made the question of existence in relation to the culminating event of history the centerpiece of his meditation. What Derrida introduces through the semiological avenue is a greater awareness of the way in which the end can be present without

---

[28] Derrida refers to Maurice Blanchot's "The End of Philosophy," an essay from 1959 that took account of the books of former Communists from the fifties who had concluded that the ideology had reached its end. *Spectres de Marx,* 39 / *Specters of Marx,* 16.

being present. Existential fidelity is not just an exhortation; it is the only mode by which we can live in relation to what we are not. This is precisely what he finds living in Marx, or should we say, it is that in which Marx is still living. Derrida in his title evokes Marx's famous opening of the *Manifesto,* which in turn evokes the specter that was haunting Europe. This theme is subtly interwoven with the opening ghost scene of *Hamlet,* in which it is the ghost of the dead father who stirs the living son to life. "The time is out of joint" becomes for Derrida the motto of existence, because it is disjointure that sets in motion a train of action we are enjoined to undertake without knowing the beginning or the end. "The question of justice, the one that always carries beyond the law, is no longer separated, in its necessity or its aporias, from that of the gift" (53/26). We are given the gift of providing a justice we do not already have. The other requires it of us, and we cannot escape the risk of committing injustice along the way. Derrida's point, however, is not to call attention to the tragic predicament of human action. It is to understand it to be the ineluctable movement of existence. The original injustice, the primordial disjointure the imaginative projection of an apocalypse seeks to remedy, cannot be abolished, because it is no longer present. This is the meaning of apocalypse, revelation, Derrida seeks to retrieve from its immanentization in the present. For all of his disclaimers against finding the true Marx, he still aims at something similar in focusing on the truth of Marx. All haunting is from the past, not the future. It is present only in its nonpresence, as a ghost, but for that very reason can even less be ignored. We are implicated in its cry for justice. It is this messianic call of the other that is "an *ineffaceable* mark – a mark one neither can nor should efface – of Marx's legacy, and doubtless of *inheriting,* of the experience of inheriting in general" (56/28).

It is a curious turning of the tables that no longer accuses Marx of falsely proclaiming himself a secular messiah, but applauds him as a witness to the messianic as such. Religion may be the truth of Marx, but only because Marx is already the truth of religion.[29] The strangeness arises only because we routinely read Marx as if he is talking about historical reality outside of himself. Everything shifts when we see him as unfolding

---

[29] Caputo serves as a particularly good guide to this phase of Derrida's thought. "Unlike reductionist critique, or transformational criticism, deconstruction first identifies the way in which Marx himself unwittingly borrows the irreducible resources of religion and depends upon them and then makes it plain that such borrowing is self-consciously true of deconstruction itself – whose kinship with negative theology was spotted 'early on.'" Caputo, *Prayers and Tears,* 148.

his own existence. Then what he analyzes with such claim to scientific rigor turns out to have no more substantiality than the ghost of Hamlet's father. But like the latter, it is no less real for all of that. Indeed, the ghost is the reality of reality, what sets it in motion but cannot be contemplated outside of that. Derrida has found the most succinct statement of this unattainable horizon of existence. "In the incoercible difference the here-now unfurls" (60/31). Even the infamous "permanent revolution" can now be retrieved within this more existential reading as the imminence that never arrives (62/33). It is Blanchot who guides Derrida to this most essential character of Marx, which he names "a voice of unceasing contestation" (66/35), a thinking that always overturns the limits of any thinking whether economic, scientific, or religious. Marx is thus the voice of différance, of the inveterately heterogeneous, of the revelation that cannot occur because it has always already occurred. "The opening must preserve this heterogeneity as the only chance of an affirmed or rather reaffirmed future. It is the future itself, it comes from there. The future is its memory.... Is there not a messianic extremity, an *eskhaton* whose ultimate event can exceed, *at each moment,* the final term of a *phusis,* such as work, the production, and the *telos* of any history?" (68/37). This, it would seem, is not just Marx without Marxism, it is Marx without Marx.

It is by restoring Marx to his eschatological status that Derrida is able to deal with the pseudo-apocalypse of the end of history, especially in the liberal democratic guise of Fukuyama. The task is relatively simple, since Fukuyama himself reveals the confusion in the claim. On the one hand the triumph of liberal democracy is taken as the announcement of the end of political history, while on the other it is acknowledged that the existing liberal democracies fall short in various ways of being what they are. Apocalypse requires endless modulations, for nothing is more hazardous to speculate about than the future. The muddle arises from the failure to understand the role of an eschatological expectation, which, by definition, can and must never be realized without the abolition of time. It is not that Derrida is opposed to liberal democracy but that he wants to distinguish between its idea and the historical movement it provokes. There is no possibility of closing the gap between ideal and reality because it is precisely that tensional aspiration that constitutes history. "That is why we always propose to speak of a democracy *to come,* not of a *future* democracy in the future present, not even of a regulating idea, in the Kantian sense, or of a utopia – at least to the extent that their inaccessibility would still retain the temporal form of a *future present,* of a future modality of the *living present*" (110/64–65).[30] This is an important clarification of a central problem that has arisen ever since Kant suggested the role of regulative ideas, although the origins go all the way back to the notorious ambiguity of the Platonic Ideas. Derrida has virtually concluded the debate by removing them entirely from the realm of attainables, real or ideal, and recognizing their status as eschatological indices of our existence. The debate over the end of history, liberal, Marxist, or Platonic, is endless because it fails to recognize that the oscillation between idea and event is irresolvable so long as it does not do justice to our existence within the irresolvability. We already live within the end of history, and so there can be no end of history.

Having thus disposed of the epigone, Derrida can now go back to the source of this round of endist speculation in Alexandre Kojève. He was the Marxist who thought through the logic of the end of history in relation to Hegel, its most assignable proponent. Kojève had most famously pronounced its implication as the end of philosophy, of all thought and striving, of everything that seemed to constitute the relish of existence. All that would be left would be animality or, at best, the reversion to a formalist snobbery indifferent to its contents. But Derrida does not take this apocalypse of unconsciousness as the limit it has often seemed to represent. Kojève may have evoked the nightmare of instrumentalization, a regime of power utterly without purpose, but he has not for that reason evoked the limit of his own evocation. This is Derrida's insight. It enables him to turn around the Kojèvian projection to view it not as an apocalypse of limits but as the limit of apocalypse. Kojève provides us not with an apocalypse but with its existential role. It is a pure apocalypse

---

[30] What Derrida means by "democracy to come" is best explored in the way in which he goes about applying it to specific cases, such as the problem of immigration or national reconciliation. See *On Cosmopolitanism and Forgiveness* and *Politics of Friendship* (*Politiques de l'amitié*). The measure of Derrida's contribution to political theory still remains to be taken. A large challenge to any such effort is the profound intellectual shift his thought entails within the conventional political vocabulary. Such concepts as sovereignty, founding, and democracy must be seen as no longer representing fixed entities but rather as the unattainable horizons within which politics is conducted. A good start has been made, however, by Richard Beardsworth, *Derrida and the Political* (London: Routledge, 1996), and Alex Thomson, *Deconstruction and Democracy* (London: Continuum, 2005). Beardsworth attempts to place Derrida in a wider context of Kant, Hegel, and Heidegger, while Thomson sticks more closely to Derrida and especially *The Politics of Friendship*. Symptomatic of the problems faced in explaining Derrida's political theory is the difficulty of translating his thought into non-Derridean terminology. Thomson, for example, ends up talking about the pattern of "depoliticization and repoliticization," which hardly diminishes the obscurity of the original.

without content, an apocalypse without apocalypse. We live within an end, but it is always not yet. The fact that we are occupied with Kojève's vision is the clearest indication that we have not yet succumbed to it. "Apparently 'formalist,' this indifference to the content has perhaps the value of giving one to think the necessarily pure and purely necessary form of the future as such, in its being-necessarily-promised, prescribed, assigned, enjoined, in the necessarily formal necessity of its possibility – in short, in its law. It is this law that dislodges any present out of its contemporaneity with itself. Whether the promise promises this or that, whether it be fulfilled or not, or whether it be unfulfillable, there is necessarily some promise and therefore some historicity as future-to-come. It is what we are nicknaming the messianic without messianism" (124/73). When history is over, we are left with the purity of promising as such. It is in this that Derrida finds the "spirit" of Marx (127/75).

It is a position that is reminiscent of Dostoevsky's insistence, even after he had broken with revolutionary socialism, that he remained a Christian socialist.[31] When socialism is recognized as a political misplacement of religion, it can always return as the religious placement of the political. The nonrealizable apocalypse is the brotherhood of all men. This perhaps explains Derrida's unwillingness to consider any serious revision of his view of capitalism's subtending of liberal democracy. One senses a certain tone of relief that he can at least return to blasting the ills of liberal capitalism. At least in listing the "ten plagues" that afflict it, he is on familiar territory. Inveighing against the evils of unemployment or national xenophobia does not require any sustained consideration of the concrete complexities that frame them. The notion that politics might be a realm of inherent limits does not disturb the declamations. This preservation of a radical tone even when the expectations have been tempered to the point of pure expectation is surely one of the strangest aspects of deconstruction. It permits the most famous practitioner of the art to overlook the extent to which his philosophical achievements tilt inexorably toward a conservative politics of limits. Old habits die hard, and moderation remains one of the least attractive positions to defend. What matters, however, is that the acknowledgment of the apocalypse beyond politics returns politics to the realm of more modest inquiries along the lines of better or worse. There is surely no reason to expect any greater political insight from a philosopher whose interest, for all of its civic-mindedness, remains philosophical.

[31] On this dimension see Walsh, *After Ideology*, 209–10.

Even Marx, Derrida reminds us, is a guide not so much to economics as to the philosophical background economics cannot provide for itself. It is the same with Derrida himself. A politics of gesture may border on the self-serving, but its selectivity is far less significant when we recall that the thrust is primarily philosophical rather than political. Like Dostoevsky, he aims at a spiritual rather than a political revolution. This is how Marx could shift from being a pseudo-religious figure to being a religious figure to whom we owe a debt of mourning. Marx's own "ontologization" of his messianic promise cannot remove the witness it contains to a messianic imperative as such. "Even where it is not acknowledged, even where it remains unconscious or disavowed, this debt remains at work, in particular in political philosophy which structures implicitly all philosophy or all thought on the subject of philosophy" (150–51/92). Derrida may not be a reliable guide to politics, and he is certainly far from the spirit of practical compromise its imperfection requires, but he does unwaveringly point us toward what in politics is more important than politics. In the hands of one who is willing to suffer, the politics of gesture is transformed into the politics of witness.[32] The closest model is the "power of the powerless" exemplified by the dissidents who stared down the totalitarian regimes or the tireless witnesses to human rights and dignity that do not provide political solutions but something far deeper that politics cannot do without. Beyond law and justice, there is the love that every human being deserves. Politics may not be able to provide this, and we have the inept cruelty of bureaucratic welfare regimes to confirm it, but it cannot do without it. It is this depth beyond the political for which Derrida aches that is the core of his political thought. The "attempted radicalization of Marxism called deconstruction" (151/92) is nothing less than the apocalypse that each human being outweighs the whole of history.

The truth of politics is the noble, we should now say eschatological, "lie" that all men are brothers. Deconstruction is the political form of this realization. The historical disappearance of Marxism affects nothing in this regard, for it was never more than a ghost and "a ghost never dies" (163/99). No matter how tightly work is bound into the economy as a commodity, the worker always escapes it. Deconstruction is thus no more than a philosophical formulation of what is well known intuitively, for

---

[32] Levinas identifies one of the most powerful instances in which the gesture overwhelmed the reality in which it occurred in Sadat's 1977 visit to Israel. See Levinas, "Politics After," in *Beyond the Verse*, 194.

in every system of valuation the one who does the valuing cannot be included within it. Capitalist economies have their own acknowledgment of this in the politics of liberal democracy, which rigidly excludes the commodification of human beings. The language of human rights is the eschatological boundary of a capitalist economy.[33] Derrida does not, of course, formulate it in such terms, largely, one suspects, because a lifetime of Left leaning has left him ill prepared to find in liberal politics anything more than the abstractions Marx roundly dismissed. In not recognizing any specters but his own, Derrida gives evidence of the trauma he so rightly diagnoses as the source of the totalitarian convulsion. The concept of trauma, which he picked up from Freud, is a useful way of conceiving of the totalitarianisms of the Right and Left that arose in response to the shock of the modern rupture with all natural humanity. Unmitigated capitalism was simply the epitome of the wider crisis of modernity in which man had become the slave of the technology he had created. It is a trauma that reverberates still in Heidegger and even today within the Muslim world, and always with totalitarian echoes. When the trauma is so profound, the call for a total solution is almost inevitable. Deconstruction is thus a distinctly post-totalitarian philosophy that, in true psychoanalytic fashion, deals with the trauma by recognizing the spectrality of its sources. The crisis is past once we recognize that our involvement with it is possible only because we already exist outside of it.

An alternative formulation is that the crisis is never past because we always exist within its tensional parameters. We can neither succumb nor escape in any definitive sense. It was Marx's terror of the former, the prospect that humanity could be reduced to its exchange-value, that provoked his dream of the latter, the projection of a world utterly free of exchange-values. But existence cannot be abolished by either the threat or the remedy. The commodification of things, Derrida points out, can never be exorcised of the spectral haunting that would restore them simply to the status of things. Marx himself acknowledges as much in conceding that the use-value always has inscribed within it the exchange-value it holds in the eyes of others (256/161). This is the ineliminable haunting Derrida details. "To haunt does not mean to be present, and

---

[33] In this regard the Chinese situation presents an intriguing test case, since it is a deliberate experiment in capitalist economics without the rights-based individualism associated with such a practice. Will the inevitable freedom of the market expand into personal and political freedom, or will the lack of such robust defenses of liberty undermine the viability of the market? The tensions within this development cannot remain uncertain forever.

it is necessary to introduce haunting into the very construction of a concept. Of every concept, beginning with the concepts of being and time. That is what we would be calling here a hauntology. Ontology opposes it only in a movement of exorcism. Ontology is a conjuration" (255/161). As with textuality, we never get back to a time before inscription, no more than we reach an end of it. Existence is pervasively haunted, just as economics is. This is the debt to Marx that Derrida carries forward, albeit in a form that would hardly have been intelligible within Marx's invocation of scientific authority. That is, that even within an apparently closed universe of exchange, the appearance is "exceeded by a promise of gift beyond exchange" (254/160) because a system of exchange neither furnishes nor restores its own free possibility. This insight into the non-automaticity of markets is not novel, but Derrida formulates it with an astonishing philosophical breadth that links the eschatological promise to the wider crisis of modernity in its religious and technological dimensions. In the end, however, a comprehensive formulation eludes him, and Derrida contents himself, by way of a conclusion, with a formulation of the problem. "What costs humanity very dearly is doubtless to believe that one can have done in history with a general essence of Man, on the pretext that it represents only a *Hauptgespenst,* arch-ghost, but also, what comes down to the same thing – *at bottom* – to still believe, no doubt, in this capital ghost. To believe in it as do the credulous or the dogmatic. Between the two beliefs, as always, the way remains narrow" (278/175). The work of finding this eschatological way of modernity occupied the final religious phase of Derrida's thought.

Existence as Eschatology: Time as Gift

Having shed the politics of eschatology, Derrida could now begin to work out the eschatology of politics. Needless to say, this endeavor did not deal with theological dogmas but remained within the existential preoccupation with what exceeds intentionality. The connection with différance is again by way of enlargement rather than a break, so that it is impossible to demarcate distinct phases within Derrida's thought. We must rather expect to find the beginnings of this eschatological discussion in the earlier writings, for example, in his work on the gift. The first unpublished seminar took place in 1977–78, but it was only in 1991 that it became a public lecture and, no doubt spurred by his contemporaneous reflections on Marx, was published as *Donner le temps. I. La fausse monnaie* (1991; *Given Time: I. Counterfeit Money*). Gift as a theme was not new for

Derrida, but as with other advances in insight, a new level of lucidity had been reached in this volume that enabled him to link gift with the abiding themes of being and time. The title suggests as much. His real interest is in time as given, as gifted, in a way that suggests the unassimilibility of its eschatological framing. Derrida comes closer to a satisfactory formulation of the meaning of time than does the longest footnote of *Being and Time*, because he is now willing to follow through the logic of the existential shift pursued only incompletely by Heidegger. Time as existence is made possible by what exceeds it, so that time cannot be understood from within itself. It is only as the rupture of an impossible gift that time is. Heidegger may have had the language of the gift, but he never fully opened to it as gift. As always the distinctly Derridean contribution is the recognition that the "discursive gesture is from the outset an example of that about which it claims to be speaking" (*Donner le temps*, 85 / *Given Time*, 62).[34]

It is in this sense that his own beginning is informed by Mauss's famous study, *The Gift*, and also Baudelaire's short story "Counterfeit Money." Each is taken as a gift from which meditation on the gift can begin. Beginning always arrives as a rupture, a pure gift irreducible to what was there before. The attempt by Mauss to erect the whole understanding of economy on the basis of the gift is, in Derrida's view, to misunderstand the meaning of the gift. What distinguishes the gift is precisely the impossibility of its assimilation to an economy. "There is gift, if there is any, only in what interrupts the system as well as the symbol, in a partition without return and without division [*repartition*], without being-with-self of the gift-counter-gift" (25–26/13). Once a gift is perceived as such, it sets up the circulation, the economy, of a return that annuls its character as gift. "*At the limit, the gift as gift* ought *not appear as gift: either to the donee or to the donor*. It cannot be gift as gift except by not being present as gift" (26–27/14). Derrida does not quote Christ's eschatological advice from the Sermon on the Mount, "Let not your right hand know what your left hand . . . ," but it seems to be the closest parallel. If the gift is an eschatological instant, it does "not belong to the economy of time" (30/17). Similarly the forgetting that is so constitutive of the gift "is no

---

[34] "One cannot be content to speak of the gift and to describe the gift without giving and without saying *one must* give, without giving by saying one must give, without giving to think that one must give but a thinking that would not consist merely in thinking but in doing what is called giving, a thinking that would call upon one to give in the proper sense, that is, to do more than call upon one to give in the proper sense, that is, but to give beyond the call, beyond the mere word." *Donner le temps*, 85 / *Given Time*, 62.

longer a category of the *psyche*" (38/23). The gift is thus the impossible, beyond being. Only in that way can it give being and time, and the possibility of thinking them on the basis of the nonpresent. "In this sense one can think, desire, and say only the impossible, according to the measureless measure of the impossible" (45/29). Mauss, on Derrida's analysis, approaches this in his conception of the gift as providing time, since it cannot be immediately reciprocated, but then veers away from it by reabsorbing the gift as an event within time. He understands the gift to be more primordial than economy and seems to appreciate its eschatological "madness" in the ceremony of potlatch by which gifts are destroyed to preclude the possibility of their return. But Mauss still holds back from submitting his own discourse to the same madness.

Derrida, by contrast, recognizes that even the social scientist cannot evade the imperative that constitutes the object of his study. "One cannot be content to speak of the gift and to describe the gift without giving and without saying *one must* give, without giving by saying one must give, without giving to think that one must give but a thinking that would not consist merely in thinking but in doing what is called giving, a thinking that would call upon one to give in the proper sense, that is, to do more than call upon one to give in the proper sense of the word, but to give beyond the call, beyond the mere word" (85/62). It is because Mauss has not understood the eschatological character of the language of the gift that he ends by seeming to betray it in an endorsement of moderation that robs the gift of its prodigality. A measured gift reabsorbs it within economic calculation. "Indecent mediocrity," Derrida seems to say, is the way that the gift can be comprehended by a social science that has put itself outside of the gift. Only a reflection that submits itself to the unmerited grace of the gift can begin to understand what it can never fully understand because it lives within it. There is no resting point outside of the gift from which its value could be assessed. Derrida does not formulate it in terms of the eschatology of the person, but that is precisely what is indicated. We cannot value a gift because there is no gift but the gift of oneself, and conversely, we cannot only give a gift because we give ourselves. It is because of the eschatology of the person, that by which every existing attribute is exceeded, that an anthropology of the person misses the indispensable. There is no security in logic against the logic of the gift. We cannot inure ourselves against the risk of counterfeit money so long as we live within the unexpectedness of the gift, that is, so long as we exist.

The structuralism of Lévi-Strauss was the last attempt to close the system in the form of a guarantee, if not within the intentions of the actors, then within the whole in which they participate. But structures can no more indemnify themselves than can individuals. A signature, once it has been dispatched, cannot preclude its forgery.[35] "The problem remains intact, the problem of knowing whether one *gives* tokens and whether one gives when one gives tokens or signs or simulacra" (118/90). Structures, as conceived of by structuralism, are simply arrested moments within a circulation that cannot be arrested without abolishing the movement within which the analysis itself exists. What Derrida sketches, therefore, are eschatological glimpses of what cannot be contemplated directly.[36] This why he finds Baudelaire's story "Counterfeit Money" to be the treatment that more nearly does justice to the supererogatoriness of the gift. It is the story of two friends who, on emerging from a tobacconist, give different coins to a beggar. The one who gave the most generously reveals that his coin was a counterfeit and that his feigned generosity was not an exercise in malicious amusement but reflected his genuine conviction that generosity could be practiced cheaply. It was, in the words of the narrator-friend, this intention of obtaining "paradise economically" that was so "unforgivable." This little gem of a story evokes a deft, scintillating analysis of its inexhaustible facets. At the core of Derrida's account is the unsurpassability of the category of the gift itself that enables him to connect it with the narrative of both the story and its treatment. The story is not a report of an event; rather the story is itself the event, namely, the impact that the friend's action has on his friend, who finds it unforgivable. "What happens happens to the narration, to the elements of the narration itself, beginning with the fiction of its supposed subject" (155/121). It is, Derrida suggests, only because of the condition of narration that the events take place.

  This is an astonishing formulation of what he has been trying to say for a considerable period of time. To make our knowing the cause of events known is surely an inversion of the reigning convention in philosophy and common sense, but this is only, he argues, because the possibility of narration has already been built into the event. Narration, Derrida seems to be saying, is the event, from which events can indeed be events.

---

[35] "The accredited signatory delivered it up to a dissemination without return." *Donner le temps*, 130 / *Given Time*, 100.

[36] It strikes me that this is precisely the point of convergence with Marion, who provides a parallel analysis of the given and gift while failing to take account of the extent of agreement with Derrida. Jean-Luc Marion, *Being Given: Toward a Phenomenology of Givenness*, trans. Jeffrey L. Kosky (Stanford, CA: Stanford University Press, 2002). Also relevant to this discussion is the first volume in a trilogy on the gift by John Milbank, *Being Reconciled: Ontology and Pardon* (London: Routledge, 2003).

There is nothing outside the narration, for that is what we exist within; the leap outside of narration is the leap outside of existence. But the narration cannot include the event that gives rise to it; otherwise the narration would contain itself, a redundancy that afflicts all presumptions of closure. "There must be event – and therefore appeal to narrative and event of narrative – for there to be gift, and there must be gift or *phenomenon of gift* for there to be narrative and history" (156/122). As gift the event is unanticipated, provoking but not determining the narration. The aleatory that is "phenomenologically impossible," because always from beyond our horizon, is not, however, the product of pure chance. It must somehow be intended for it to be received as a gift. "This," Derrida remarks, "is the paradox in which we have been engaged from the beginning" (157/123). Gift must be intentional and yet exceed intentionality, for "everything stemming from the intentional meaning also threatens the gift with self-keeping, with being kept in its expenditure." Again Derrida does not formulate it quite in this way, but is not this impossible convergence of the intentional and the unintentional the eschatological boundary? The gift cannot be penetrated, because to do so would signal its end. "In giving the reasons for giving, in saying the reason of the gift, it signs the end of the gift" (187–88/148). In the case of the story this unfathomability is indicated by the impossibility, shared even by the author, of knowing whether the coin was indeed counterfeit, since it might as easily conceal the authenticity of the gift within it. Such is the eschatological, rather than the psychological, secret of literature.

It is a line of reflection that is carried to an even higher level of intensity in the sequel to *Given Time,* Derrida's *Donner la mort* (1992; *The Gift of Death*). The eschatological and even Christian direction becomes explicit as Derrida engages with the work of Patočka and Kierkegaard. Patočka's *Heretical Essays on the Philosophy of History* (1975) move within the Nietzschean meditation on the self-transcendence of Christianity, hence the "heretical" character, in response to the crisis of Europe. The technological abdication of responsibility, culminating in the totalitarian convulsion, heightens the imperative of responsibility within which we live. Patočka points toward the religious as the exercise of singular responsibility irreducible to either the dogmas or ontologies that have historically concealed it. Christianity contains at least the possibility of recognizing the singular exercise of responsibility because in it the soul is, quoting Patočka, not related to an object "but to a person who fixes it in his gaze while at the same time remaining beyond the reach of the gaze of that soul" (*Donner la mort,* 44 / *Gift of Death,* 25). Responsibility is called forth through the personal encounter that is outside of any thematization of it. In that sense, Derrida notes, responsibility is related to heresy as *hairesis,* choice, outside of any dogmatic formulation, within the inaccessible secret of its command through a gaze that cannot be seen. It is as the gift that cannot announce itself that "Christianity has not yet come to Christianity" (49/28). Derrida extends Patočka's analysis into a reflection on the secret of the gift that is the gift of death, the event that brings home the irreplaceable exercise of singular responsibility.

The secret of the person is the absolute singularity that cannot be named in the language of generalities or roles. It is accessible only in the singularity that is apprehended in the possibility of my death, as the event that marks the limit of my uniqueness. This uniqueness is also what enables me to give myself even to the point of dying for the other. "In this sense only a mortal can be responsible" (64/41). The eschatology of the person by which it always eludes its disclosure, the secret to which Derrida points, is the possibility of death. Only an existence that can contain itself can give itself, but it can do so only by virtue of the possibility of not being itself. Death is the ultimate means by which the gift of self is possible, as we recognize in Christ's admonition that there is no greater love. The gift of death is thus both the gift of giving and the limit of giving. The secret of giving is that it always involves the giving of self, precisely what cannot be given. Death is the event that marks both the highest bestowal of the gift and the highest nonbestowal of the gift. One can die for the other, only because one cannot die for the other. Death is thus the eschatological horizon of giving as the giving of self. The paradox can be carried farther than Derrida takes it through the recognition that it is only because we cannot die that we can give ourselves in death. The possibility of death would then become its impossibility. In that sense, only immortals can die. Dying for another, Derrida observes, "is not given in the first instance as an annihilation. It institutes responsibility as a *putting-oneself-to-death* or *offering-one's-death,* that is, *one's life,* in the ethical dimension of sacrifice" (73/48). The meditation at this point veers toward the recognition of its Christian provenance or at least toward the evocation of a revelation apart from its specification. We might as well conclude "that this concept of responsibility is Christian through and through and is produced by the event of Christianity" (75/50).

No doubt Derrida is following the lead of Patočka in this observation, but he seems to extend it through his own endorsement. *The Gift of Death* is not just Derrida's entry into an explicitly religious mode of reflection; it is also a surprisingly Christian take for a thinker who had not previously located himself within this orbit. His treatment evidences not only a closer attention to Christian texts, but an advancing sympathy in their interpretation. When he asks how responsibility is possible, Derrida finds himself edging up to the idea of the Incarnation, the becoming finite of the infinite. "Only infinite love can renounce itself and, in order to *become finite,* become incarnated in order to love the other, to love the other as a finite other" (77/51). The good cannot remain transcendent but must put on mortality in order to reveal itself as the infinite love that dies for the other. A Christian logic is at work here that does not depend on Christian revelation but might at some point recognize itself there. We are dealing here with the inward revelation that is prior to all revelation. The unfolding occurs through the awareness of our deficiency manifest as a guilt that is there before we even begin. "Guilt is inherent in responsibility because responsibility is always unequal to itself: one is never responsible enough" (77/51). Trembling afflicts us as the condition under which we assume our responsibility as we become aware of our inequality to what we are called to do. To explore this existential priority, Derrida turns to Kierkegaard's *Fear and Trembling* in an analysis that leads him toward the heart of Christian faith. Abraham, the "knight of faith," turns aside from the public language of ethics to answer the call that can come only in the secret of his uniqueness. He cannot account for what is unaccountably his. "Absolute duty demands that one behave in an irresponsible manner (by means of treachery or betrayal), while still recognizing, confirming, and reaffirming the very thing one sacrifices, namely, the order of human ethics and responsibility. In a word, ethics must be sacrificed in the name of duty. It is a duty not to respect, out of duty, ethical duty" (96/66–67). The logic of Kant's rejection of any motivation for duty now becomes clear as an existential imperative that always exceeds itself. Secrecy and différance guard the possibility of existence.

Action cannot remain at the level of universals. It must become singular, unique, irreplaceable, as what exists. But this means, Derrida explains, the sacrifice of the ethical that Kierkegaard has identified as the religious core of the individual. "I cannot respond to the call, the request, the obligation, or even the love of another without sacrificing the other other, the other others" (98/68). We must all find our Mount Moriah on which we offer the inexplicable gift of death as the price of fidelity. Faith as the relation to a person is the eschatological boundary of action. The sacrifice faith calls forth is not in this sense part of the action within time, for it has already occurred. This is the meaning of the moment in which God stays the hand of Abraham before he can kill Isaac "*when there is no more time*" (103/72). It is the instant within which time is contained and that we grasp, not by knowledge, but by faith. The absolution that it brings cannot be given reasons, for it is prior to all giving of reasons within the imperative of response to the other. As "witness of the absolute faith," Abraham must bear witness by not witnessing. "He must keep his secret" (104/73). His faith can be known only if it is entered into, never reduced to the certainty that enables us to stand outside of it. The absolution Abraham lays hold of within the secrecy of faith cannot be known in any other way. Even the promise of disclosure within Christian evangelism, Derrida seems to suggest, is only a deepening of its mystery. "We share with Abraham what cannot be shared, a secret we know nothing about, neither him nor us" (112/80).

This is also the response to the "political" problem of sacrificing some others in fulfilling our responsibility to other others. Derrida is a more political thinker than Kierkegaard, and he cannot be satisfied with the latter's suggestion of the transitional status of ethics. Now it is not clear that this is exactly Kierkegaard's position, since the ethical is ultimately viewed from the religious point of view, but it is a conventional reading that Derrida uses while simultaneously enlarging. The clarification is really the work of Levinas, who brings together the face of God and the face of the other within an ethics that is religious. Can there be an ethics outside of the religious? "If every human is wholly other, if everyone else, or every other one, is every bit other, then one can no longer distinguish between a claimed generality of ethics that would need to be sacrificed in sacrifice, and the faith that turns towards God alone as wholly other, turning away from human duty" (117/84). Levinas had already made this point in relation to Kierkegaard, Derrida reminds us, by pointing out that the culmination of the Abraham and Isaac story is its ending. By staying his hand from the sacrifice, God indicates that the highest fulfillment of the religious imperative is the return to the ethical prohibition against murder (110/78). Far from a disjunction, the ethical and the religious are correlative. They are equally rooted in the inexplicable singularity of responsibility before the other who commands me before I have received the command. It is because we cannot distinguish between the ethical and the religious imperatives, for both move toward the impenetrable uniqueness of responsibility, that we cannot also carve out a separate realm of the political. Derrida rejects Carl Schmitt's distinction between the public and private by which we might treat different categories of enemies differently. Responsibility before the other does not allow of distinctions, because it is prior to all distinctions.

The eschatological horizon of action cannot be abolished simply because it cannot be realized, for it endures as the secret of a politics that can never comprehend it. The "genius of Christianity," Derrida concludes in a revision of Nietzsche, is that it never sought to abolish this eschatological tension but instead preserved it within the secret life of faith (157/115). The secret is the life of faith.[37]

The Imperative of Exceeding Every Imperative

The life of faith is the secret of the person, a mystery so deep according to Augustine as to be hidden from him in whom it is. Derrida is not satisfied with simply noting this situation but wants to bring it vividly to attention. It is the luminosity of existence that exceeds every embodiment. Only a Kierkegaardian term like "passion" can suggest it, and "Passions: An Oblique Offering" is the title of the first essay in a collection that revolves around the mystery of the person, *Sauf le nom* (1993; *On the Name*). Derrida brings Kant's meditation to act only out of duty to its limiting implication in this essay in discharging his obligation of responding to a collection of "critical readings" of his work. "The internal contradiction in the concept of politeness, as in all normative concepts of which it would be an example, is that it involves both rules and invention without rule. Its rule is that one knows the rule but is never bound by it. It is impolite to be merely polite, to be polite out of politeness" (*On the Name*, 9). Just as the secret of the person is his noncontainment in the name, so morality cannot be reduced to a task whose fulfillment can be assigned, since it must overflow its own mere requirement. Kant's problem of not acting out of a sense of moral obligation, as a feeling, is here clarified as the existential impossibility of including that from which one exists within existence (15–16). Derrida points out in the essay that he can neither respond nor fail to respond to his "critical readers," for either way diminishes them, so he settles for the "oblique offering" that simply notes the problem itself. "This non-response is more original and more secret than the modalities of power and duty because it is fundamentally heterogeneous to them" (29). He preserves the secret, the passion, from

---

[37] "To speak of the secret between God and Abraham is to also say that, in order that there be this gift as sacrifice, all communication between them has to be suspended, whether that be communication as an exchange of words, signs, or promises, or communication as exchange of goods, of things, of riches or property." *Donner la mort*, 132 / *Gift of Death*, 96.

which conversation springs as the inaccessible singularity concealed even in the name.

It is the movement of confession that Derrida now draws from the example of Augustine, whose question of why he needs to confess to God what God already knows marks the secret of all interpersonal communication. Derrida writes his own confession, *Circumfession*, when he is on a prolonged visit to his dying mother.[38] He carries with him selections from Angelus Silesius's *Cherubinic Wanderer*, on which he meditates in "Sauf le nom" (*Sauf le nom*, 113 / *On the Name*, 85). The essay was originally a postscript to a volume on Derrida's relationship to negative theology, and that designation is retained as the subtitle. Postscript is the countersignature that effaces the name, thereby saving it, in the manner of negative theology that functions by interrupting what it sets out to say. "It is a matter of holding the promise of saying the truth at any price, of testifying, of rendering oneself to the truth of the name, to the thing itself such as it must be named by the name, *that is, beyond the name*" (80/68). Yet this, Derrida emphasizes, is not a mystical absorption or perhaps, as he better explains, what a mystical absorption must be. It is the unsurpassable boundary of communication that cannot include itself, the personal that escapes all attempts at identification, the point at which the failure of language is glimpsed as the possibility of language. "'God' 'is' the name of this bottomless collapse, of this endless desertification of language" (56/55–56). He uses the term *khōra* to denote this space or place by which language can strain beyond itself in prayer. "It asks God to give himself rather than gifts" (57/56). This apophatic character of language, by which it continually exceeds what it contains, is what creates the possibility of translation. Meaning can be universalized because it is never strictly what it says it is. "What makes philosophy go outside itself calls for a community that overflows its tongue and broaches a process of universalization" (84/70). Derrida comes very close to Levinas's identification of the face of the other as the face of God, for both are safe from their name. Communication is only in the giving of persons that cannot be given, a giving that is given exemplarily in the *kenōsis* of God. "The other is God or no matter whom, more precisely, no matter

---

[38] The "Circumfession" was published as a lower-half text interacting with the pages of Geoffrey Bennington's *Derridabase*, an overview of his life and thought. Derrida had once again ingeniously avoided entrapment in the conventions of biography or autobiography to suggest that life is always more than can be said.

what singularity, apart from whom every other is totally other" (92/74). This is the meaning of "radical atheism" (103/80).

What is needed to speak of what exceeds existence is a language beyond the language of being.[39] In thus confronting the problem of existence as a problem of language, Derrida returns to his semiological beginnings, only now with deeper awareness of their metaphysical character, in the third essay in *On the Name, "Khōra."* The term is taken from Plato's meditation in the *Timaeus* on the space or place within which philosophy and the work of creation takes place. "Khōra" is the name for what cannot be named, what every name fails to name. Derrida shows that Plato was aware of the problem and developed a language that submitted to the fate of self-effacement it talks about. It is an insight into the mythic status of the language of myth that was lost when Aristotle conceptualized its content, as in identifying khōra with matter. An intermediate language was precisely what was necessary, Plato recognized, to indicate the process of intermediation. Khōra is a third genus between the sensible and intelligible, defying the logic of noncontradiction because it is what contains such a logic of boundaries. The name is made possible by virtue of the unnamable. "*Khōra* reaches us, and as the name. And when a name comes, it immediately says more than the name: the other of the name and quite simply the other, whose irruption the name announces" (*On the Name,* 89). Derrida recognizes in Plato the ambition of speaking about that which cannot be spoken since it is what yields the space of speaking. Its political significance is precisely the one that Plato saw in linking the *Timaeus* to the discussion of the best regime in the *Republic.* The question of realization could not be separated from the realization of the question. There is no separate event of actualization as if the container could be assimilated to what it contains. Every actualization occurs through a giving place, a giving place that itself is never given place. This is khōra, not *the* khōra as a thing, but simply khōra (97). Socrates resembles khōra in giving place by effacing himself before the reception of the gift of the discourse that he brings. This is the meaning of the tale of Critias concerning the prehistory of the Athenians that must come to them from the Egyptians, "a tale about the possibility of the tale" (115).

[39] This is the way in which Derrida responds to the question, posed by Richard Kearney, as to why he says, "I rightly pass for an atheist," rather than "I am an atheist." "It's the same question. If I knew, I would say that I'm an atheist or I'm not, but I don't know. I don't know for the reasons that I've been trying to explore for years and years. It depends on what the name of God names." Roundtable in John Caputo and Michael Scanlon, eds., *Augustine and Post-Modernism: "Confessions" and "Circumfession,* 38.

Each tale becomes the means of receiving a further tale in the unfolding of a secret without a secret. "Though it is not a true *logos,* no more is the word on *khōra* a probable myth, either, a story that is reported and in which another story will take place in its turn" (117). Instead, khōra is the movement initiated by Socrates away from a simulacrum that never arrives at more than a simulacrum yet explains how it is possible for the *politeia* to have an origin older than itself.[40] As with writing, what the city inscribes is never the movement of inscription itself. "So it is Athens or its people who, as the apparent addressees or receptacles of the tale, would thus be, according to the priest himself, its utterers, producers, or inspirers, its informers" (122).

Derrida's meditation of existence has carried him "beyond the limits of truth" in a way that is reminiscent of the wrestling with antinomies that began with Kant and became an overturning of language in Nietzsche and his successors. But Derrida has moved away from the static implication of an antinomy and now announces the "aporia" within which existence is enacted. It is a shift that he embraced in the 1992 lecture that was published as *Apories* (1996; *Aporias: Dying – Awaiting [One Another at] the "Limits of Truth"*). The lecture is one extended meditation on death that deals extensively with the existentially constitutive analysis of being toward death in *Being and Time.* Heidegger, Derrida observes, has more clearly penetrated the existential meaning of death than any cultural survey, no matter how comprehensive,[41] yet he ultimately seeks to hold the mystery at bay within his triumphal resolution of authenticity. By mastering the antinomies, he has abolished them. This is the betrayal of existence noted in Chapter 5. Derrida seeks to avoid this derailment by thinking of existence as itself aporetic. "There, in sum, in this place of aporia, *there is no longer any problem*" (*Aporias,* 12). Where antinomies had suggested a problem that was out there waiting for us to solve, now there is the acknowledgment that we already exist within the problem or aporia from which we cannot separate ourselves. We are asked to endure the antagonism of tensions within duty as the very possibility of duty, as

---

[40] Eric Voegelin's analysis of the same texts moves remarkably along the same lines of appreciating that myth cannot be reduced to its concept, that the only adequate account of myth is itself mythic. It was an insight that he traced to its Platonic origin. Voegelin, *Order and History,* vol. 3: *Plato and Aristotle,* in *Collected Works,* vol. 16, ed. Dante Germino (Columbia: University of Missouri Press, 2000), ch. 5, "*Timaeus* and *Critias.*"

[41] Derrida uses Philip Ariès, *Essais sur l'histoire de la mort en Occident du Moyen-Age à nos jours,* to show that even within a cultural historian of death, there lies the awareness that he has really not understood the subject from within. As a consequence Ariès is caught in the aporia of not being able to delimit the subject of his study. *Aporias,* 42–52.

our duty. "The most general and therefore most indeterminate form of this double and single duty is that a responsible decision must obey an 'it is necessary' that owes nothing, it must obey a *duty that owes nothing, that must owe nothing in order to be a duty,* a duty that has no debt to pay back, a duty without debt and therefore without duty" (16). It is not just that we have a duty to cross the limits of truth, of reality as it presents itself, but that duty is that very transcendence of borders. Forgiveness, Derrida insists, cannot be limited if it is to be forgiveness. It must be infinite. That is the aporia within which it exists. The duty of hospitality is always to go beyond the duty of hospitality. But the aporia within which duty exists cannot even be known as such. It remains like death the impossible border of existence (78–79) at which we await the arrival of one another without really knowing the secret by which we are held. It is because the aporia marks the limits of circumspection that we can do no more than repeat what has already been repeated in the religions of the Bible. Like Marranos we remain faithful to what we have forgotten (80).

Hospitality: The Impossible That Has Become Possible *as* Impossible

The last phase of Derrida's remarkable personal and intellectual odyssey is marked by the recognition that we cannot get beyond texts of religion. Where previously he had followed the Heideggerian impulse toward religion without religion, now he is more inclined to acknowledge that we cannot do without religion, for we at best merely repeat its components. Even the worldwide resurgence of fundamentalism can be taken in stride from within the aporias of existence that refuse resolution. It is a phase that comes into focus with the publication of *Acts of Religion* (2002), which, as with so many of Derrida's books, brings together previous addresses and writings but now with a new awareness of where they were headed. Probably the most theoretically significant is the first essay, "Faith and Knowledge: The Two Sources of 'Religion' at the Limits of Reason Alone," whose italicized first half was a talk at a conference in Capri, 1994, to which Derrida added a postscript for publication in 1996. The subtitle alludes to Bergson and Kant, whose universalist thrust seems to draw out Derrida's reflections but not in such a way that would lead him to break with the particular expressions. He remains deeply suspicious of the philosophical sublation of religion, as in Hegel, but even in Heidegger's impulse toward a more originary "revealability." Derrida wonders about religion within the limits of reason alone, "a religion which, without again becoming 'natural religion,' would today be effectively universal." Would "the idea itself remain, in its origin and in its end, Christian?" (53)?[42] The address does not answer such questions, possibly because it was enough to point in the direction the discussion might follow. Derrida merely announces that the "two fountains" are the messianic and khōra, as that which has yet to arrive and its pure possibility. Neither has any content, but for that reason they do not replace the historically emergent texts of religion. Rather they are Derrida's way of insisting on the unsurpassability of religious particularity.

The "Post-Scriptum" is where the more extended consideration takes place. The question of universalization then takes the form of the temptation to set up reason as independent of faith. Derrida rejects the suggestion with a disavowal of their separation as strong as any Catholic affirmation of integrity. The difference is that he can more than affirm because he has glimpsed the unattainable existential necessity from which it arises. We might, he suggests, "try to 'understand' how the imperturbable and interminable development of critical and technoscientific reason, far from opposing religion, bears, supports and supposes it" (65–66). The common source of religion and reason is the unscathed (*l'indemne*) around which faith and knowledge revolve. There can be no knowledge without what exceeds knowledge, "the absolute witness," God, access to whom is granted only through "fiduciary trustworthiness." The two sources of both religion and reason are faith and the unscathed. Heidegger had sought a more originary experience of the unscathed, the holy, without allowing room for faith. Levinas seemed the reverse in holding firmly to faith while remaining silent about the sacred toward which it is drawn. Derrida proposes to hold them together within a unity that cannot be found as a unity but only lived within a concreteness that bears the particularity of religion. It is the experience of witnessing that brings about the convergence of the unscathed and the fiduciary. "Even the slightest testimony concerning the most plausible, ordinary or everyday thing cannot do otherwise: it must still appeal to faith as would a miracle. It offers itself like the miracle itself in a space that leaves no room for disenchantment" (98). Even critique cannot go outside of the text that is existence. Faith and knowledge remain the two sources that cannot be separated from one another (76–77).

---

[42] Derrida's provocative conclusion from Kant, that "Christianity is the death of God," should not be taken as his last word on it, just as it was not Kant's last word either. *Acts of Religion*, 51.

Now the treatment of the Tower of Babel that Derrida offered in 1980 makes sense, for it is the story not just of the confusion of languages but of the city of God, whose name must be translated and cannot be translated. This is the law of translation, law as such, whose source is God in the unattainable beyond. "Translation becomes law, duty and debt, but the debt one can no longer discharge" (111). God is the messianic promise that sustains and precludes the possibility of translation. Where Derrida had begun with the assertion that there is nothing outside the text, he now seems to conclude that there is nothing but God, who is nothing, outside the text. The sacred text is no longer a carrier of meaning but of existence. "It is the absolute text because in its event it communicates nothing, it says nothing that would make sense beyond the event itself" (133). This is why the unraveling of the relationship between such Jewish thinkers as Hermann Cohen and Franz Rosenzweig with their German philosophical background cannot finally be plumbed. It is simply part of the worldwide convergence of the human family united around the dual emergence of technological science and the authoritative language of rights. We cannot fully understand the relationship between them precisely because we live within it. All the attempts at explanation, Derrida seems to suggest, end up explaining it away, as if they might claim to have reached a perspective of objectification. But we cannot simultaneously claim to live within what we have held at a distance. This is the entire problem of the existential perspective, a perspective we cannot abandon without abandoning existence. It is the secret of deconstruction that is the secret of life. There is no truth of truth, for there is no perspective outside of truth. This is the "seism" of deconstruction that happens to "the logocentric-Judeo-Protestant truth," "without one being able to decide if it comes from inside or from outside" (159).

This is why deconstruction does not focus on ethics or justice, yet speaks continually from within them. It understands the mystical foundation of the authority of law, observed by Pascal and Montaigne, in which it is precisely the reduction to a principle that destroys it.[43] The difference between deconstruction and critique is clarified in the other extensive essay of *Acts of Religion*, "Force of Law: The 'Mystical Foundation

---

[43] "Pascal cites Montaigne without naming him when he writes, in *pensée* 293, 'one affirms the essence of justice to be the authority of the legislator; another, the interest of the sovereign; another, present custom, and this is the most sure. Nothing according to reason alone, is just in itself; all changes with time. Custom creates the whole of equity, for the simple reason that it is accepted. It is the *mystical foundation* of its *authority*. Whoever carries it back to first principles destroys it.'" Ibid., 239. The *pensée* is number 94 in the Sellier edition.

of Authority,'" an expansion of the address first delivered at the Cardozo Law School in 1989. Law is "essentially deconstructible" while justice is not, because while we live within law we do not wholly live within it (*Force de loi*, 34 / *Acts of Religion*, 242). There is still the possibility of hold-ing law at a distance; justice is closer to us than we are ourselves. It is in this sense that Derrida declares, "*Deconstruction is justice*" (35/243).[44] As such it cannot speak of that out of which it speaks, no more than the law can. Derrida's great contribution to the philosophy of law is the recognition that the root of law is not just mystical or hidden, but an aporia, a hiddenness that constitutes its existence. There cannot even "be a full experience of aporia, that is, of something that does not allow passage. *Aporia* is a nonpath" (37–38/244). The eschatological language Derrida had previously employed to account for the borders that cannot be crossed, or rather that we cannot cross even when we undertake to cross them, now acquires a new precision. "Justice is an experience of the impossible: a will, a desire, a demand for justice the structure of which would not be an experience of aporia, would have no chance to be what it is – namely, a just *call* for justice" (38/244). Justice is incalculable, an attempt at reconciling singularity with the universal norm that can never be brought into coincidence. This is why it is impossible to say "I am just," for we are ever on the way toward what we have not arrived at. Justice is always the demand for infinite justice. It is the moment of responsibility of the singular toward the universal that must remain an "unsatisfied appeal" (46/249) as the very possibility of justice.[45] Any finitization has

---

[44] In such a ringing declaration we see why deconstruction is not pragmatism and certainly not the purely ironic pragmatism identified with Richard Rorty. Whether deconstruction can be related to the more metaphysically open pragmatism of William James is another matter. The contrast with Rorty is, however, very instructive, for it brings out the extent to which deconstruction clarifies the existential imperative that is only peripherally asso-ciated with pragmatism. Rorty draws from the ironical stance an admonition toward solidarity, while Derrida understands that irony takes its stand within an existential com-mitment it can never transcend. Rorty still assumes that theoretical and practical reason can be separated, while Derrida is more profoundly attuned to their philosophical inte-gration inaugurated by Kant. The exchanges between Derrida and Rorty on this topic seem never to get beyond polite preliminaries. See Chantal Mouffe, ed., *Deconstruction and Pragmatism* (London: Routledge, 1996). For a reading of Rorty's liberal irony as an existential imperative, see Walsh, *The Growth of the Liberal Soul*, 53–56. Kierkegaard is, of course, the great neglected authority on irony.

[45] We begin to understand the Gnostic revolt most powerfully pronounced by Ivan Karam-zov's insistence, "I would rather be left with the unavenged suffering. I would rather remain with my unavenged suffering and unsatisfied indignation, *even if I were wrong.*" Dostoyevsky, *Brothers Karamzov*, 291. The revolt consists precisely in the refusal to live within the "unsatisfied appeal" of justice, for the determination to master justice abol-ishes the possibility of existence.

already lost contact with its source, yet there is no contact except through the effort at finitization. Derrida elaborates by distinguishing three aporias within this overarching one. The first is the "epokē of the rule." Justice requires following a rule but never as if it were merely a matter of following a rule. In that sense justice requires the suspension of the rule of justice. The second aporia is the "haunting of the undecidable." Forced to make a decision as to whom justice will be applied, it can never eradicate the ghost of the excluded others whose claim was equally just. The unique singular has not been subsumed under the concept but remains to haunt it. The third aporia is "the urgency that obstructs the horizon of knowledge." The demand of justice exists before reflection on it is possible; all horizons in which it might become visible have been obstructed by its urgency. Justice cannot be known because it can only be lived.

Having thus linked deconstruction and justice more thoroughly than in any of his previous writings, Derrida was prompted to add a prolegomena and a postscript, which, as he would know better than anyone, are an author's attempt to capture what the text has so far failed to reach. Provoked by Walter Benjamin's *Kritik der Gewalt,* these additions extend the aporia of justice into the aporia of the law itself. Derrida finds Benjamin's juxtaposition, of the divine violence that annihilates the law with the mythic violence that installs it, to be a formulation that moves in the direction of deconstruction. Not surprisingly it falls short only in its claim to critique, a far too determinate prospect that suggests a higher viewpoint beyond the justice within which we must exist. Derrida seems to say that Benjamin's critique of violence, of the violence by which all law is established, has yet to discover its own non-source. Critique cannot itself be subject to critique or, therefore, repeat the violence it excoriates. Only as deconstruction does critique work. This insight also gives Derrida a more balanced approach to the main target of Benjamin's critique in the flagrant inconsistency of parliamentary democracy, a prejudice he shared with many of his early twentieth century contemporaries. The target seemed to offer itself in its simultaneous imposition of a public law with a flagrant disregard for the lawlessness of private life. Deconstruction, by contrast, assumes a transcendent starting point that never suggests the possibility of its social-political realization. It permits Derrida to more adequately appreciate the virtues of a form of government that acknowledges its self-limitation. The violence of law is still preferable to lawless violence. It is not clear that this is exactly Derrida's position, but it is close to it in his "unreserved taste, if not an unconditional preference, for what, in politics, is called republican democracy as a universalizable model" (*Acts of Religion*, 47). Indeed, we might say that Derrida provides one of the most powerful conceptions of "republican democracy" that rigorously eschews any representation of the absolute. Law is transcendent because its founding is never present (*Force de loi*, 90 / *Acts of Religion*, 270). Nowhere is this more visible than in the defense of life that may be justified through the taking of a life. This is not merely reducible to the confrontation of one violence with another, for it is the opening toward the mystical source of law, the beyond of law that cannot be included within it. "What is sacred in his life is not his life but the justice of his life. . . . It is life beyond life, life against life, but always in life and for life" (126/289).

Existence is ever constituted by what it can never touch. Like the silkworm secreting what it can never see, we live within "the absolute delay of the verdict" (*Acts of Religion*, 350). Like the *tallith*, the childhood prayer shawl that Derrida contemplates on his way to Buenos Aires, there is no unveiling of its meaning. "You will never know anything about it, and no doubt neither will I" (350). Yet it is precisely our being held hostage in existence that opens the possibility of hospitality, the great theme of Derrida's last writings, especially as represented here by the aptly titled, "A Note on 'Hospitality'" (1997). "To be hospitable is to let oneself be overtaken" (361). As an opening of self without limit, hospitality is a madness, a going beyond rules because it is the source of rules. "Deconstruction," Derrida finally announces, "is hospitality to the other" (364). Like the earlier themes of forgiveness and the gift, a hospitality that falls short of a complete self-giving is not hospitality. It must be eschatological if it is to remain what it is. Hospitality is thus one of those links by which we are drawn through death to life beyond life. "When hospitality takes place, the impossible becomes possible but *as* impossible" (387). The eschaton is not in the future, for it is already now, but as the now that exceeds all possibility of presence in a moment of time. We live within its possible impossibility in which dying to life is life. When the whole of existence is pledged, nothing finite can encompass it. The fault that must be forgiven must be unforgivable if it is to be worthy of forgiveness (386). It is for this reason, Derrida insists, that God, "the God of mercy, is the name of he who alone can forgive . . . the only one to whom I can abandon myself, to the forgiveness of whom I can abandon myself" (389). In the hope that hopes for the reparation of the irreparable, Derrida gives voice to the eschatological presence that has always been the nonrevelation of revelation. Faith has always been inseparable from existence. Now deconstruction has made it clear that existence is inseparable from faith. It is in this sense that we should read the questioning meditation of time posed toward the end of the essay, in which the incompleteness of Heidegger's exploration seems to have been answered. "Does not the essence of time consist in responding to that exigency for salvation? Does not the analysis of economic time, exterior to the subject, cover over the essential structure of time by which the present is not only indemnified, but resurrected? Is not the future above all a resurrection of the present?" (393).[46] In pointing toward the Christian eschatology of existence, we might regard Derrida as pointing forward, as he might say, to the texts of Kierkegaard.

[46] The remarkably Christian character of these reflections carries enormous implications, not only for understanding the trajectory of Derrida's thought and for what it reveals about the modern philosophical development from which it arises, but even for apprehending the meaning of Christianity itself. Some sense of the ramifications can be gleaned from Theodore W. Jennings, *Reading Derrida / Thinking Paul: On Justice* (Stanford, CA: University of Stanford Press, 2006); see especially "Derrida as 'Christian Philosopher,'" 170–76.

8

Kierkegaard's Prioritization of Existence over Philosophy

The placement of Kierkegaard at the end of a study of the modern philosophical revolution must seem anachronistic. Surely the chronological pattern virtually imposes itself on a movement guided by the inner logic of its conversation. How could Kierkegaard be the exceptional voice whose contribution has not adequately been taken into account? The question challenges the depiction of the central line of modern philosophy as an unbroken discussion from the time of Kant's initiation of the existential shift. Within a context in which the respective positions were subjected to intensive scrutiny, was it possible that a major figure could be overlooked? The possibility of such an oversight reminds us of the parochial aspects of even the most ambitious philosophical projects. We realize that the revolution we have been examining has, after all, been a largely German and only lately French affair. We have said nothing about the emergence of pragmatism in America, nor have we mentioned the rise of the philosophical novel in Russia. The neglect of a solitary thinker who, while connected with the German mainline, published all of his reflections in a language spoken by only a tiny minority in Europe should not strike us as surprising. In other words we must be prepared for surprises. Indeed, even the connection between the "existential" and the "idealist" phases has been something of a more recent discovery. Within the sharp delineation of differences, the lines of continuity often become faint. The idiosyncrasy of Schelling's decision not to publish his late works deprived us of one of the most salient points of connection. So it is perhaps not so astonishing that the chronology of modern philosophy, which seemed to have stepped over what it never really knew, should now find that it can never really pass by what it has yet to pass near.

For a figure like Kierkegaard who does not appear within his own time, the problem is exacerbated by the vagaries of the moment of his discovery.[1] Plucked from his historical setting, his interpretation is fixed by the setting of his reemergence. His identification by Heidegger in the pages of *Being and Time* ensured a permanent linkage with the decisionism that marked the reception of "existentialism."[2] Kierkegaard would be inextricably tied to the analysis of existence as anxiety from which release could be achieved only through a leap of faith into the absurd. Even today it is difficult to shake this perception of him as an advocate of the irrational ground of decision, a position that dooms the will to an ultimately arbitrary resolution.[3] As the quintessential "existentialist," Kierkegaard was in no position to disavow a label that had not even been invented when he lived. He could not, like Heidegger, eventually outgrow it to be taken seriously as a thinker with more range than had at first been perceived. The path was difficult enough for Heidegger, but he could at least fight his own battles to be taken seriously as a philosopher of being, not simply existence. Some element of that first impression still attached to Heidegger, but it was unshakable for one whose thought had been arrested in the moment of its discovery. The constancy of the dead, as Kierkegaard himself would have noted, necessitates that the possibility of change toward them must rest with the living. Are we then capable of the kind of development that would make possible a reconsideration of Kierkegaard? At this point we cannot even take up the question without overcoming the greatest obstacle that lies in the way, for Kierkegaard has been even more indelibly marked as a "religious thinker."

---

[1] For a fascinating accounting of the slow emergence of Kierkegaard before his "discovery" in the period after the First World War, see Habib C. Malik, *Receiving Søren Kierkegaard: The Early Impact and Transmission of His Thought* (Washington, DC: Catholic University of America Press, 1997). Roger Poole provides a useful overview of the more familiar aspects of the Kierkegaard reception. "The Unknown Kierkegaard: Twentieth Century Receptions," in Alastair Hannay and Gordon D. Marino, eds., *The Cambridge Companion to Kierkegaard* (Cambridge: Cambridge University Press, 1998), 48–75.

[2] It was, of course, Jaspers who, eight years before *Sein und Zeit*, featured the thought of Kierkegaard in his *Psychologie der Weltanshcauungen* (1919).

[3] Kierkegaard functions as such a straw man in Alasdair MacIntyre's *After Virtue* (Notre Dame, IN: University of Notre Dame Press, 1984), 39–42. An interesting experiment in reconciling MacIntyre's "virtue ethics" with an "existential virtue ethics" was conducted in the anthology edited by John Davenport and Anthony Rudd, *Kierkegaard After MacIntyre* (Chicago: Open Court, 2001). The result, despite MacIntyre's unwillingness to budge, demonstrates an impressive range of convergences. For a more fully developed account of virtue ethics along Kierkegaardian lines, see Rick Anthony Furtak, *Wisdom in Love: Kierkegaard and the Ancient Quest for Emotional Integrity* (Notre Dame, IN: University of Notre Dame Press, 2005).

This convenient label also originated with Heidegger, for whom it removed the burden of exploring him more fully, especially in the decades after *Being and Time* when translations had become more plentiful. A thinker who had already foreclosed himself to thinking by affirming religion could not ultimately be taken seriously as a thinker. He could not be a philosopher of being if he had already identified it with the being of God. This requirement, especially as enunciated by Heidegger, has considerable merit, and it would constitute a weighty presumption against Kierkegaard if it were the case. But it is not. Indeed, we might say that it was his central preoccupation to avoid the kind of hasty recourse to the divine that would have brought the process of questioning to a comfortable and comforting conclusion. He was so painfully aware of the difficulty, if not impossibility, of being a religious thinker that he employed a range of stratagems to distance himself from it. He might have aspired to be a religious thinker, but even in his most explicitly devotional writings, the *Upbuilding Discourses*, which Heidegger admired for their philosophical acumen, Kierkegaard made clear that he was himself the audience more than their author. Yet if even a Heidegger could not quite perceive the issue, namely, that no one can legitimately claim to be a religious thinker, it is perhaps understandable that Kierkegaard has been so warmly embraced by theological circles as just such. His usefulness within theological and devotional reflection has simply overwhelmed any resistance to the notion that Kierkegaard is essentially a religious thinker. Ironically, and perhaps just as he feared, it has been by his sympathizers that Kierkegaard has been most profoundly misunderstood. They have missed his most abiding insight that it is only by remaining outside religion that one performs the greatest service toward it. Kierkegaard's prescience concerning the danger his work confronted is perhaps the strongest confirmation that we have not advanced beyond him but have rather yet to catch up to where he is.[4]

Of course, it is also evident that Kierkegaard's formulations do not quite fit so neatly into the current state of the conversation. The preceding three figures, Heidegger, Levinas, and Derrida, took note of him,

---

[4] Fortunately this is a situation that is beginning to change in the latest spate of theological approaches to Kierkegaard, in which the need to take account of the philosophical revolution he effected is at least acknowledged. See Anthony Rudd, *Kierkegaard and the Limits of the Ethical* (Oxford: Clarendon, 1993); David J. Gouwens, *Kierkegaard as Religious Thinker* (Cambridge: Cambridge University Press, 1996); Murray A. Rae, *Kierkegaard's Vision of the Incarnation* (Oxford: Clarendon, 1997); and David R. Law, *Kierkegaard as Negative Theologian* (Oxford: Clarendon, 1993).

often quite extensively, but never with the expectation that he might have attained a perspective they had yet to reach. He was illustrative rather than instructive. In particular, the far more technically articulate mode of their philosophizing seems to have left Kierkegaard's leaps of philosophical imagination far behind. They may point back to him, but does he extend them further? Is the philosophical revolution deepened in Kierkegaard or merely retarded in a literary exposition? One small indicator of the former is the growing tendency of readers, especially Derrida, to turn to Kierkegaard as the beacon toward which their own reflections were drawn. Increasingly, Kierkegaard is viewed not just as the past but as the future toward which philosophy tends. If we think of the modern philosophical revolution as the displacement of theoretical reason by practical reason, as the reversal of the priority of the subject in intentionality to include the luminosity of existence that precedes it, then Kierkegaard was the one who most fully lived within that ineluctable shift. He had arrived or, as he would say, existed within the arrival toward which the others were still striving. He was less handicapped by the problem of language as a result of his capacity for imaginative leaps that brought him where language would not go. In this way he became a genius of language. He knew how saying could avoid saying. As a consequence he remained an enigmatic thinker the full scope of whose thought has yet to be appreciated. He could be admired by many along the way but understood by far fewer. Only now do we possess the existential understanding of language that enables us to recognize Kierkegaard for the philosophical genius he was. The question of how he can reenter the philosophical mainstream today is therefore in large part answered by the reflective bridge that philosophy has since built over to him. His contemporary status is what we now attempt to address.[5]

Socrates' Irony Is Existence

Kierkegaard's capacity to overleap and rejoin the subsequent development of philosophy arises from the earnestness with which he lived out

---

[5] The uniqueness of Kierkegaard is that he has been an author to whom readers turn in order to discover what they need to know, never merely for the sake of mastering a body of knowledge. His relationship to readers has always been personal. This is the secret of his appeal. But there are points at which that existential impact is expressed in a wider public recognition. Several volumes have argued just such a convergence with the postmodern moment. See Martin J. Matuštík and Merold Westphal, eds., *Kierkegaard in Post/Modernity* (Bloomington: Indiana University Press, 1995); James Giles, ed., *Kierkegaard and Freedom* (New York: Palgrave, 2000); as well as Davenport and Rudd, eds., *Kierkegaard After MacIntyre*.

its revolution. He could intuit what remained to be articulated because he had entered with his own existence into it. Heidegger may have devoted himself to the life of philosophy, but only Kierkegaard gave himself to the philosophical life. Where others had grasped the philosophical priority of existence, that ethics precedes ontology, he had understood that even such an interest in the philosophical implications jeopardizes the purity of heart that existence requires. Philosophical illumination recedes in significance, as it must, when the mandate of existence is conceded. The reason Kierkegaard occupies such an extraordinary position in the modern philosophical revolution is that he complied most completely with its logic. Not even philosophy could come before the imperative of existence. This was surely the meaning of the prioritization of practical over theoretical reason, but old habits die hard. It has always been difficult to shake the sense that ultimately it was all simply to see what theoretical enlargement would take place. From Hegel's speculative turn away from existence, to Heidegger's apocalyptic leap out of it, to Derrida's linguistic distance from it, the task of shaking off the dominance of theory has not been easy. Perhaps the difficulty arises from the starting point of these thinkers within theory, a condition that did not so strongly define Kierkegaard. Almost from the beginning he seemed, like Nietzsche, more driven by the question of how he should live. It was this existential earnestness that compelled both of them to pursue the answer outside of all institutional supports. But unlike Nietzsche, Kierkegaard was not so encumbered by the burden of finding the answer within himself alone. The self-limitation of Nietzsche is answered by Kierkegaard's greater self-opening. As with the whole philosophical shift toward existence we have been tracing, Kierkegaard arrived at its end by virtue of his existential dedication to it. The answer to the question of how one should live was actually to be lived, not just talked about . He exemplified Hegel's dictum that "what is a contradiction in the realm of thought is not necessarily one in the realm of life."[6]

This is not to suggest that Kierkegaard found all of the linguistic means of making the prioritization of existence transparent. In many ways his

---

[6] This is not to say that Kierkegaard resolved the contradictions in life, for he may more accurately be described simply as having lived them. Yet even that is sufficient to ensure that his life remains a topic of considerable interest. He has been well served by recent biographies, of which the most comprehensive is Joakim Garff, *Søren Kierkegaard: A Biography,* trans. Bruce H. Kirmmse (Princeton, NJ: Princeton University Press, 2005). But Alastair Hannay, *Kierkegaard: A Biography* (Cambridge: Cambridge University Press, 2001), remains a useful source. A masterful account of the historical setting is provided by Bruce Kirmmse, *Kierkegaard in Golden Age Denmark* (Bloomington: Indiana University Press, 1990).

existential intuitions could not be adequately understood until the development of the more expansive language of existence we have seen. His
relative obscurity is due only partly to his publication in Danish; to a far
greater extent, it derives from his incompatibility with the philosophical
medium at the time. It was a situation of which he was acutely aware. His
response was the inventive proliferation of literary devices to indicate
the impossibility of objectifying the process from which the struggle for
articulation arises. While he eschewed becoming a theorist of semiological limits, Kierkegaard became an incomparable practitioner of the art
of overcoming and not overcoming them. Indeed, he understood the
fate to which his writings were exposed with uncanny accuracy. It is in
this sense that his frequent animadversions against the public success
of his works are to be understood, for he knew that the more popular
they became the more they would be misunderstood. His premonitions
have been largely confirmed. But now that the revolution in thinking,
to which his wholehearted enactment contributed, has more fully and
inescapably unfolded, we are perhaps for the first time in a position to
recognize the depth of his insight. Without determining whether he or
the history of philosophy has been asleep, we can safely say that a mutual
reawakening has occurred. When the "single individual" (*hiin Enkelte*)
(Preface, *Eighteen Upbuilding Discourses*, 5) has reclaimed his place as the
only indispensable entry into the philosophy of existence, we encounter
again the thinker who, as the solitary individual, devoted all of his writings to such a one. In this way Kierkegaard more genuinely grounded
solidarity than at any time since the founding of the Academy.

In many ways Socrates, the philosopher who lived rather than wrote,
provided the model for Kierkegaard. This was surely the inspiration that
led him to write his dissertation, *The Concept of Irony, with Constant Reference
to Socrates*. Kierkegaard had sensed the importance of irony as a concept
through which the modern world might be understood, a choice that
has been confirmed by the extent to which irony has been taken over
by the self-understanding of that world. The vacuity of an age that had
vastly extended its instrumental power while simultaneously severing its
connection with any substantive purpose would increasingly epitomize
the ironic. But while Kierkegaard understood that fatality, and made its
romantic variation the focus of his study, he understood that the mere
observation of the ironic suffers from what it diagnoses.[7] Irony is not

---

[7] The broader pattern of irony in the modern world, by which the rejection of God
becomes the impetus for his return, has been noted in Walsh, *After Ideology*, 13–15.

primarily a standpoint of critique; otherwise it merely repeats the self-distancing it excoriates. At its most fundamental level, irony is a mode of existence that does not in any sense absolve us of the obligations of existence. Many of our contemporary ironists are prepared to concede as much, but their inaction displays the extent to which they have not taken it to heart. Kierkegaard, in contrast, had seen the temptation all the way through and thereby emerged from it. As an existential stance, irony carries us beyond irony. This is why for him the "constant reference" was always back to Socrates, the man who not only critiqued but who went beyond by living out the struggle he addressed. Philosophy, Kierkegaard noted in the final thesis (xv) at the beginning of his study, begins with doubt, but human life begins with irony. Even Schelling, whose lectures on the philosophy of revelation Kierkegaard attended shortly after completing the dissertation, failed to deliver on his promise of a return to "actuality."[8] It was the announcement of a program, not its implementation in existence. Socrates alone loomed large as the figure who had remained faithful to the imperative of living philosophy rather than discoursing about it.[9] This is why for Kierkegaard he opened the meaning of irony at its deepest level.

As the living embodiment of irony, Socrates could support the duality by which it points in opposite directions simultaneously and which even Plato, on Kierkegaard's reading, was inclined to reduce to the manageability of a single dimension. Irony in its full Socratic mode is both a healthiness that rescues the soul from relativity and a sickness that overwhelms its capacity for resolution (77–78). This ambivalence in the figure of Socrates, which is well known from the variously spiritual, rational, and comic portraits left by Plato, Xenophon, and Aristophanes, arises from the variety of perspectives that yet fail to see Socrates as an existence that defies comprehension. The answer, Kierkegaard insists, is that "Socrates's existence is irony" (127). Only if irony is understood to be the movement of his existence can we make sense of the most basic tension by which Socrates continually points toward the idea and yet never reaches it (154). The charges against him of impiety, disloyalty to

[8] Kierkegaard's reaction to Schelling is well summarized by Howard V. and Edna H. Hong in their "Historical Introduction" to *The Concept of Irony*. This volume of the work also has Kierkegaard's "Notes of Schelling's Berlin Lectures."

[9] The centrality of Socrates for Kierkegaard is only now beginning to be given sufficient weight, another indication of the influence of the "religious" label that has dominated the Kierkegaard reception. A recent instance of the shift is Jacob Howland, *Kierkegaard and Socrates: A Study in Philosophy and Faith* (Cambridge: Cambridge University Press, 2006), who takes Kierkegaard as an important guide to the meaning of Socrates.

the state, and injuring the youth are all from one perspective justified, for he does seduce by stirring up a desire for knowledge he cannot subsequently satisfy (188). But the pinnacle of his irony is that he also saves men from the corrosive consequences of his dialectic by carrying it so far that they glimpse the true, the beautiful, and the good as utterly beyond all other cares within this life (197). Socrates is the Hegelian power of the negative, not conceptually, but as the demand for ideality, the idea in life. He is "a magnificent pause" (198). Socratic irony could not be further from the "sickly egotism of later irony" (213) that afflicts the modern world. This is the subject of the second part of Kierkegaard's study, which is now equipped to analyze it in light of the healthy irony of Socrates.

The crucial characteristic of modern irony is that it holds back from the opening toward existence that irony invites. Having disclosed the relativity of all things, the force of "infinite absolute negativity," its practitioners settle down to a play of masks and roles that deflects the critique away from themselves. The ironic subject resembles the religious in denouncing vanity, but it does not include itself within such denunciations. As a consequence it does not see that the world-historical task lies within itself. Kierkegaard understood that romanticism springs directly out of the boredom that the ironic perspective creates; the individual is set free from all anchors and drifts aimlessly between the alternatives of the "monastery" and the "venusberg." Latter-day ironists have not so much gone beyond good and evil as simply failed to include their own failure within the critique. If they had, they would eventually recognize that the only reconciliation between universal morality and particular circumstances is the one that they effect in life, a reconciliation that can be effected only if they live in relation to it as the all-encompassing imperative of their existence. Kierkegaard had seen his essential thought at the very beginning of his journey. "Only the religious is the true reconciliation, infinitizes actuality" (297). The poets who fail to get beyond poetry are the ones who end up making the "Kierkegaardian" leap of faith, whether into Catholicism (Friedrich Schlegel) or into the deification of poetic existence (Tieck) or into a mysticism of negativity (Solger). A great poet like Shakespeare never loses control of irony; he masters it through irony. The real value of irony lies in its existential force, for it compels us to submit to the same critique by which we dissect the world. The romantics mistook irony for the goal of their longing, as if they had reached the perfection within which their lives should have been led, for it is in existence that truth is realized. "Actuality acquires validity through action" (329).

Self-Oblivion of the Esthetic

The problem for Kierkegaard was that actuality could then not be written about. How was he to communicate a truth that could not be communicated but which at best could be intimated indirectly? He was not the only one to recognize the problem, for it is inseparable from the recognition of the existential appeal as the pivot of the human person. As I have shown in *After Ideology*, Dostoevsky was to develop the polyphonic novel as the means by which the author's point of view could be withdrawn to allow the characters to speak for themselves. Only the truth that emerged indirectly from the test of "living life" could express an authoritative utterance. Kierkegaard, almost two decades earlier, had worked out a similar means of distancing himself from his creations. In many ways he carried the approach further than Dostoevsky because he was not just interested in the proclamation of truth; his goal was its realization in existence, especially in the only existence over which he had any control, his own. Indifference to the popular success of his works was not simply a ruse. The books were written only secondarily for other people; their primary target remained Kierkegaard himself, as he reminds us on numerous occasions (*Concluding Unscientific Postscript*, 623). This is the most profound meaning of his principal literary device of pseudonymous authorship.[10] The various signatories not only allow Kierkegaard to say things contrary to the "religious point of view" from which everything is written, but permit him to grapple more openly with the tensions that are never left behind within that point of view. Religion is not a perspective that Kierkegaard possesses; it is rather one that possesses him. This is why even in his second literary device, of simultaneously publishing religious works under his own name, the authorship still ultimately escapes the author. "From the very beginning, I have stressed and repeated unchanged that I was 'without authority.' I regard myself as a *reader* of the books, not as the *author*" (*Eighteen Upbuilding Discourses*, xv). In thus disclaiming authorship even of the works to which his name

---

[10] Mark C. Taylor, *Kierkegaard's Pseudonymous Authorship: A Study of Time and the Self* (Princeton, NJ: Princeton University Press, 1975), is a useful beginning on the topic but now needs to be supplemented in light of subsequent semiological developments.

is assigned, Kierkegaard is the first writer to explicate the problem of différance. Textuality is as unsurpassable as existence.[11]

The romantic irony was the conviction that the text, the literary production, could reach a truth superior to existence, but instead it devalued what it claimed to exalt. This is the meaning of *Either/Or* (1843), the great literary production with which Kierkegaard burst on the cultural scene. Written in close continuity with *The Concept of Irony,* this was the first of the indirect writings that were part of an ambitious project intended not so much to expose the inadequacy of the esthetic but to intimate the insufficiency of its development. The unhealthy irony that failed to subject itself to the same examination must be replaced by the more thoroughgoing healthy irony. That would lead back to the religious point of view from which everything had been written, but for now that was concealed behind the name of the pseudonymous editor, Victor Eremita, whose victory is as inaccessible as a hermit. Indeed, the author of the first collection of papers that constitute Part I is unknown, or is known simply as "A;" the second collection comprises the papers of "B," although he is identified as Judge William. The anonymity of the first group of purely esthetic writings indicates that they arise from the primordial force of sensuality prior to personality itself. It is only with the emergence of the ethical concern in the second set that distinct individuality steps forth with a name. In the case of the most famous of the literary effects, the "Diary of a Seducer," which culminates Part I, even "A" cannot be assigned as author but must stand outside the papers as a mere editor. Horror before the abyss of evil renders particular authorship inconceivable. It is a sophisticated layering of textual différance that extends to the organization of the disparate texts. Their inner coherence is belied by the haphazard circumstance of their discovery in a writing desk purchased by Victor Eremita. Randomness at the esthetic level arises from the impenetrability of the religious horizon within which the reflections unfold.

Indeed, reflection at the esthetic level is barely possible, for it must rise to a universal standpoint even to articulate itself. The papers of "A" are thus not sheerly esthetic but are reflections that have at least in part begun

---

[11] In other words the question of pseudonymity must be seen in connection with the substance of Kierkegaard's thought, not as a merely external strategy of communication. See ibid. I do think that Derrida's notion of différance as unfolded in his own Kierkegaardian development casts considerable light on the issue. The topic of Kierkegaard's pseudonymity was not, so far as I know, dealt with by Derrida. One such effort in this direction is Roger Poole, *Kierkegaard: The Indirect Communication* (Charlottesville: University of Virginia Press, 1993), which is, however, too readily inclined to conclude Kierkegaard's inconclusiveness.

the process of separation by which the individual exists. This is indicated by the title of the first group of fragments, aphorisms under the heading "Diapsalmata," a term coined from the *Selah* that indicates a pause in the psalms at which reflection might take place. These meditations *ad se ipsum*, for himself, unfold the absurdity of an existence untouched by the opening toward which it points. "On the whole, I lack the patience to live" (25). The author can sense the meaninglessness of a world in which earning a living is the only purpose for living, or in which people think they can cheat even God by "trimming coins a little" (28), yet he is unable to take the first step beyond it. Driven by a longing for longing, he is like one already dead, indifferent to everything that happens. Real decision escapes him as he vacillates endlessly between decisions. In a reference to the title of the whole collection that indicates it is more than a choice between the perspectives of the two writers, "A" and "B," the author notes that "true eternity does not lie behind either/or but before it" (39). Lost as he is without possibility where even the sun does not reach, the only thing left to touch him are the sounds of music that can draw him out of himself. Reflection on Mozart's *Don Giovanni* is the beginning of the next document, "The Immediate Erotic Stages, or The Musical Erotic."

The analysis of the opera is a tour de force in which the author, perhaps Kierkegaard too, admits to being "indescribably happy in having understood Mozart even remotely" (135). Music is the only medium in which the sensuous differentiated by Christianity can be presented as the sensuous. This insight was Mozart's genius in fashioning the figure of Giovanni, who is primarily a musical force rather than a force of deception. He is neither crafty nor immoral but simply the one in whom the power of desire, of the sensuous, has come to full expression. It is through the immediate erotic of the music that he is able to seduce the other characters, who are all reflections of the passion that animates him. Outside of all ethical categories, Giovanni is the elemental force of life that only music can depict in its immediacy. "Thus he does indeed deceive, but still not in such a way that he plans his deception in advance; it is the power of the sensuous itself that deceives the seduced, and it is rather a kind of nemesis" (99). It can be understood only at a distance from outside the world of sensuous abandonment in which Giovanni lives. This is the position of the Commendatore, the ghost who in death is impervious to the appeal. But it is also the perspective from which the analysis itself has taken place. The mood of the work can be recognized only when one is not subject to it. Irony is thus present as that toward which the action points but cannot comprehend, for like the ghost that cannot be killed, "irony is and remains the disciplinarian of the immediate life" (120). The "demonic zest for life" that Giovanni evinces arises from an underlying anxiety that cannot arise in consciousness as he "fleetingly speeds on over the abyss" (129). In Giovanni's eventual dissolution in sound, Mozart has found the means of conveying the power of the immediate erotic that cannot permit itself the breathing space of self-awareness.

By contrast, the dawn of reflection arises only through the perspective of death that allows us to contemplate life. This seems to be the meaning of the "Fellowship of the Dead" (*Sumparanekromenoi*), to which the next three compositions are addressed. As with the indeterminacy of authorship, there is no way for us to know whether the author has membership in this association or not. The text remains equally uncertain as to whether the writer suffers from the incapacities he diagnoses. He seems not to, in the fragment "The Tragic in Ancient Drama Reflected in the Tragic in Modern Drama." Our age, he announces, is moving toward the comic in which the vacuous self-assertion of the subject dominates all. The result is the despair that falls far short of the tragic by which the healing of suffering might be evoked. In placing all responsibility on the subject, we have deprived him of inwardness, and thereby of the connection with a fate that is shared by others who might suffer in sympathy with him. "It is conceited enough to disdain the tears of tragedy, but it is also conceited enough to want to do without mercy" (146). The insight into tragedy here is considerably deeper than that of Schopenhauer and even Nietzsche, both of whom place the emphasis on individual catharsis. Our author alludes to Hegel in placing the emphasis on the sympathetic bond it creates with the one who sufferers, rather than merely the experience of pain (147). Perhaps the difference can be explained by the fact that his interest lies less in the ethical than the esthetic, within which he searches for an appropriate expression of human existence.[12] When the esthetic thus tries to capture the depth of sorrow surrounding existence, it is inevitably stretched toward the nonesthetic categories of fate, of guilt, and of original sin. In going beyond individual guilt, "hereditary guilt, like hereditary sin, is a substantial category, and it is precisely this substantiality that makes the sorrow more profound" (150). When the

---

[12] "Intrinsically, the tragic is infinitely gentle; esthetically it is to human life what divine grace and compassion are; it is even more benign, and therefore I say that it is a motherly love that lulls the troubled one. The ethical is rigorous and hard." *Either/Or: Part I*, 145.

esthetic is enlarged to its full dimensions, it goes beyond the individualism of the ethical to arrive again at the concreteness of the religious. The tragic is the first evocation of the insight that the person is known most deeply when he is not known at all, for beyond the self are the great unknown forces that reach into it.

Inwardness is the realization that we do not contain ourselves but are rather contained. All that is visible are "silhouettes" or the unhappiness of the "unhappiest one" who can neither abandon nor succeed in the effort of recollection. Illumination is sought through a chance encounter with the beloved at a comedy of "First Love," but nothing is left beyond the laughter of irony at the futility of such expectations. Finally the reflections of "A" arrive at the root of his unhappiness in boredom, for which the "Rotation of Crops" provides an answer. "Boredom rests upon the nothing that interlaces existence (*Tilveraelsen*); its dizziness is infinite" (291). To overcome it one must live as much as possible in the moment, without hope or seriousness, or anything that might prompt the fatal awakening of recollection. Now the esthetic project, remembrance in poetry, becomes the means of avoiding the esthetic life with its vacuity. The ultimate irony of the esthetic life is that it continuously removes itself from the esthetic life. This is the great idea behind "The Seducer's Diary," which is as far from the world of sensuality as one can get. The seducer here is virtually the opposite of Giovanni, for he practices a form of seduction that seeks to dominate the soul rather than the body, thus evidencing an abyss of evil of which Mozart's figure is largely innocent.

Seducer Seduced Most Completely

Seduction for the diarist is the means by which he seeks to cheat existence by triumphing over it while never engaging in it. Giovanni is submerged in the erotic to the point of self-oblivion, a far lesser mode of escape than that of the diarist, whose goal is to transcend without suffering the burden of living. The seducer is at the antipode of the tragic, for he represents the extreme of the refusal to respond to the pull of responsibility by which he might exist. Thinking he can contain himself absolutely, he loses himself most completely as a human being. It is one of Kierkegaard's great literary achievements to have presented a portrait of such vacuity. An ironic result has been presented in a perfectly ironic mode. This is why we cannot know the author of the diary, for the papers were taken surreptitiously by "A," their editor, although he received from Cordelia, the victim, the letters the seducer sent to her. It is only through Cordelia that we know his name, Johannes, signed at the close of the letters. Their insertion by the editor at the appropriate points in the diary is indispensable to understanding the externals of a process that the inwardness of the diary could never adequately explain. At least with the letters, we have the surface intelligibility of their effect. The editor remains, however, the one who pieces it all together, and in this sense he preserves, despite all the careful stratification, the same ambivalence of his status throughout Part I. "A" could not serve as editor unless he was in on the secret, as indeed Cordelia and we as readers ultimately become as well. Perhaps even Kierkegaard "can scarcely control the anxiety that grips me every time I think of the affair" (310), for the interest in the diary of a seducer betrays our own susceptibility. "He has spread the deepest secrecy over everything," "A" observes, "and yet there is an even deeper secrecy, that I myself am in on the secret and that I came to know it in an unlawful way" (310). Can it, we might ask, ever be known lawfully?

It is only because we might become accomplices in seduction that we can glimpse what it is about. The seducer is simply the one who has carried farthest the possibility of cheating existence by means of its transfiguration into poetry. "In the first case, he continually needed actuality as the occasion, as an element; in the second case, actuality was drowned in the poetic" (305). Not quite good enough to be a poet, he was nevertheless capable of turning his life into a scheme of poetic interest, thereby becoming the kind of vaporous man "whom I had once known without knowing him" (306). This is how he became the kind of seducer for whom pursuit is of greater interest than the prey. He reveled in bringing a young girl to the point of complete surrender, when he could break it off and exit without detection. The experience of being in love far surpassed actual loving with its inevitable transition to deeds in which the poetry is lost. Even the physical consummation presented but a momentary enjoyment soon gone, while he sought the more enduring. "No, if one can bring it to a point where a girl has but one task for her freedom, to give herself, so that she feels her whole happiness in this, so that she practically begs for this devotedness and yet is free – only then is there enjoyment, but this always takes a discerning touch" (342). It is at this point that the seducer works to introduce "a respectable young man" around whom the love interest of Cordelia must circulate. So while Edward, the young man, occupies the center of her attention, Johannes works tirelessly in the background to make himself the indispensable presence in both their lives. Through the engagement of Cordelia to

Edward, he works constantly to effect his own substitution for the latter, but only when Cordelia recognizes Johannes as the true object of her affection. "My art is to use amphibolies so that the listeners understand one thing from what is said and then suddenly perceive that the words can be interpreted another way" (370). He is no ordinary deceiver, as he insists, for his intention is not to steal but to have Cordelia give the gift of her freedom to him. "I am intoxicated with the thought that she is in my power" (377).

Dissatisfied with merely capturing her heart in the way of an ordinary lover who knows that he has captured by not capturing, by allowing her to be herself, Johannes wants to translate her into the realm of "infinite possibility" far beyond the actual. The high point is reached, not when he poetically infinitizes her, but when she takes a hand in her own imaginative transcendence of reality. The turning point in this scheme is reached when he shifts direction in their burgeoning relationship by breaking off contact. He sends no more letters. Then he becomes the object of *her* overheated imaginings. "The point now is to guide her in such a way that in her bold flight she entirely loses sight of marriage and the continent of actuality, so that her soul, as much in pride as in her anxiety about losing me, will destroy an imperfect human form in order to hurry on to something that is superior to the ordinarily human" (427–28). His self-congratulation is almost uncontainable as he exults, "Let God keep his heaven if I may keep her" (429). It is the culmination of womanhood, according to Johannes, for she is awakened to the erotic by a man but then is the one who compels him in that irony of love by which "the victor submits" (431). The coyness and cruelty that are thereby awakened in a woman is far more unbounded than the mere incidental cruelty of Bluebeard, who disposes of his wives after he has once enjoyed them, or of Don Juan, who simply abandons them in the pursuit of the next conquest. Johannes convinces himself that the wanton cruelty of women arises from their greater attunement to unlimited possibilities, as he has prompted them in Cordelia. Free from reality now, she has entered the moment that is eternal in its infinite possibility. She is like the bride adorned outside of all time. Now she coincides with Johannes's trajectory by insisting that they break off their "engagement," lest it sully the perfection of the love that unites them. The goal of evoking a love free of all externalities has been achieved. "What does erotic love love? Infinity. – What does erotic love fear? Boundaries" (442). A love that lives by the moment dies by the moment, for once it has reached its consummation it dies out exhausted with itself. Everything interesting

about Cordelia has evaporated, "and I never want to see her again" (445).
The whole romantic affinity with the mutuality of love and death comes
into focus in the project of the seducer, for it is precisely the aspiration to
detach the eternal from time without enduring the vicissitudes of living
it out. But what is successful as poetry cannot be successful as life. An art
that surpasses existence is tantamount to the conceptual reconciliation of
the system that supersedes reality. The infinite that flames in the moment
leaves only ashes behind. That is the irony that can be perceived in the
seducer, though he has not yet been able to perceive it in himself. For
that a very different kind of man is needed, one who is not terrified by the
ashes in which all love falls short but knows that the différance between
aspiration and attainment is precisely the space and time within which
existence itself is unfolded. Instead of capturing eternity within time, he
is prepared to work to transfer time into eternity. Such an individual is
"B," the author of Part II, whose identity can be known because he takes
up his place as a visible member of human society.

Ethical as the Possibility of the Esthetic

Judge William is a public official, a far more substantial presence than the
elusive "A," who finally recedes behind the veil of editorship of the diary.
It is indeed only through "B" that we gain a real sense of the person of
"A" as a result of the relationship of friendship on which the writings are
based. The writings of "B" assume the form of letters (although they do
not begin that way) to "A" that appeal for a change of heart. Friendship
is invoked as the inspiration by which "A" might be drawn from his
proclivity toward holding the world at a distance. Conventionally Judge
William's interventions are taken as the beginning of the ethical phase
of the meditation, the alternative to the esthetic appeal of the romantic
perspective extolled in Part I. But this is to overlook the significance of
irony in Kierkegaard or his insistence that everything has been written
from a religious point of view. The irony here is that the judge is a
defender, as the title of his first "letter" indicates, of "The Esthetic Validity
of Marriage." Not only does he begin at the level at which his friend
locates himself, but he is able to show that the esthetic carries a finality
toward ethical action within it, just as the embrace of the ethical entails
the realization that it is subsumed within the religious. The difficulty
for "A" and for readers is the tendency to read the judge's reflections
as mere moral exhortation and to overlook the extent to which they
arc first addressed to himself and only later readdressed as a letter to

his friend. But simply because William is a respectable citizen does not mean that respectability is the source of his appeal. What makes him respectable, a person of weight, is not an attainment but rather the prior decision to embark on the task of existing. His panegyric to the ordinary becomes extraordinary only by virtue of his awareness of the existential opening it requires. In the commonsense reflections of Judge William, we find a most complete exemplification of Aristotle's observation that the truth of ethics lies in action. Existence is no longer a topic but a concrete movement that does not shrink even from the concreteness of the religious within which it unfolds.

As the guardian of the concrete William is the one who most fully affirms romantic love, in contrast to his friend, who seeks to live wholly in the moment of its awakening. It is only if romantic love opens toward the ethical commitment of marriage that it can preserve its truth, which is precisely its readiness to stand within the eternal. "Although this love is based essentially on the sensuous, it nevertheless is noble by virtue of the consciousness of the eternal that it assimilates, for it is this that distinguishes all love [*Kjaerlighed*] from lust [*Vellyst*]: that it bears a stamp of eternity" (21). It is the movement toward the eternal that rescues it from the merely sensuous. Marriage thus finds its essential meaning only within Christianity. "In the religious, love again finds the infinity that it sought in vain in reflective love" (30). By contrast, reflection, preoccupation with preserving itself, is the romanticization in which love withdraws from its own infinite movement. It may begin in the sensuous, but it is scarcely aware of itself as sensuous until reflection focuses the self-attention of love. Left to itself, love spontaneously leads the lovers toward "an obligation they impose upon themselves face to face with a higher power" (56). This, William insists, is no mere expression of a transitory mood but the very reality in which their mood has validity. It is not something they possess but the différance by which all that they are is bestowed on them as a gift. "The way it happens is that in taking their first love to God the lovers thank God for it" (57). Conquest or superiority has no place in a relationship in which each receives the other as a gift. It is by thus taking their love from God that they are freed of the burden of finding its source within themselves with all its impossible struggle to possess what cannot be possessed. By humbly receiving the other from God, they open the space of love before them. What in the erotic embrace is only an illusory eternity is here translated into "the eternity of eternity" (58).

First love is "abstract," in the sense that it is all possibility but not yet a concrete unfolding. "In order to make this real, marriage enters in" (60), but then it is no longer an object of contemplation but the mode within which we exist. Marriage is a secret inner life without any other reality than the lives of the husband and wife, for whom it is the secret that even they cannot penetrate without holding it apart from themselves. The problem with all romantic portrayals is that they suggest that the preliminaries are the essence and stop short of the reality of the life of love that is incapable of portrayal. What is presented cannot be lived, and what is lived cannot be presented. The secret as Derrida formulates it is that there is no secret, nothing that could be formulated as such. Our author declares that marriage has no "why" (63). Even why one should love only one and not others or all others remains an impenetrable boundary, yet a boundary that sustains the possibility of love toward any. "If I do have any understanding of the whole subject, the defect in earthly love [*Kjaerlighed*] is the same as its merit – that is preference [*Forkjaerlighed*]" (62). Spiritual love moves toward the universal, embracing all human beings, while earthly love moves toward the particular, embracing one to the exclusion of all others. Why this is so has no answer, for there is no way of justifying the preference that lies at the heart of love. All that can be said is that it at the same time affirms the universal reality of love as the uncontainable infinitude of each person, by which every other is indeed to be preferred to all others. Kierkegaard addresses this paradox more deeply than Levinas or Derrida because he contemplates it in its most accessible manifestation in marriage, which is "absolute in itself and also within itself points beyond itself" (62).

The religious attenuations intimate the mystery that cannot be portrayed but only lived, as they open the very possibility of such living. As particular beings we cannot possess the universal but can only know it through the submission by which the universal takes possession of our particularity. "Like every human life, every marriage is simultaneously this particular and nevertheless the whole, simultaneously individual and symbol" (90). This is why Kierkegaard can only suggest the reality of marriage through the concrete reference of a character who is married. It is also why the church in its ceremony reminds us, he explains, of the marriage of our first parents and does not hesitate to include the acknowledgment of sin as present from the beginning. To say that children are conceived in sin may not seem to make sense in finite terms, but it makes a great deal of sense within the infinite movement of marriage itself. Not only does the child become more precious by the suffering through which it is born, but "that a child is born in sin is the most profound expression of its highest worth, that it is precisely a transfiguration of human life that everything related to it is assigned to the category of sin" (92). The interest here is not in providing a justification of sin but in seeing how its acknowledgment is what leads human existence to its highest level. We might say that the existential significance of sin stands higher than its theological significance. The *felix culpa* is its consequence not just in the advent of Christ but in the eradication of pride it effects in existence. "Sin has come in, but when the individuals have humbled themselves under this, they stand higher than they stood before" (93).

The esthetic in marriage, as in the unremarkability of the ceremony, is the inner life it makes possible between two human beings. By contrast, the friend "A" is frozen before the prospect of infinite possibility. William compares him to the *Flying Dutchman,* the legendary ship that can sweep across the ocean without ever landing anywhere. It is the false infinity of his own reflection, rather than the infinite that is the gift of his self-giving. "Alone in one's boat, alone with one's sorrow, alone with one's despair – which one is cowardly enough to prefer to keep rather than to submit to the pain of healing" (84). He must rather carry the principle of doubt that restrains him from commitment to the point that it begins to assault itself; then he has the possibility of becoming a completely different person. That is not yet beauty, but it can become so when the doubting of doubt turns into the unfolding of a concrete way of life. "Beauty," in contrast to the externality of its romantic conception, "consists in this, that immediacy is acquired in and with the doubt" (95). Marriage as its actual living out, rather than its imaginary fixation, is what is truly poetic. "What the first love lacks, then, is the second esthetic ideal, the historical. It does not have the law of motion in itself" (98). The esthetic validity of marriage is therefore not a competing poetic account but the more faithful living out of that first poetic impulse. We are back at Plato's preference for reality over its poetic imitation, only now the reality is more clearly identified as temporal existence rather than its eternal form. But we have also understood the former as the source of the Platonic preference for the latter. The incompleteness of the Platonic revolution, with all its dispersed confusion in the history of philosophy, has been completed in the existential revolution. Now, William explains, "I turn everything around and say: The esthetic is not in the immediate but in the acquired; but marriage is precisely that immediacy which contains mediacy, that infinity which contains finitude, that eternity which contains temporality" (94).

The esthete is the one who is so preoccupied with losing the mystery of love that he fails to enter into it. Clinging to the first natural intimations, he resists the transfiguration that love works within him. Because he was not prepared to enter with his whole self into the shared consciousness of marriage, he could not discover the infinite power of love. The erotic beginning, a species of self-love, is not properly love itself but only what must be surrendered if love is to emerge from it. It is a giving of self that can occur in no way other than as a complete self-giving. Marriage is thus not an event in time but the rupture of eternity by which time is constituted. To the extent that the mutual giving of selves is not contained in any of its manifestations, it is a strictly eschatological event, although Kierkegaard does not use that term. His letter writer prefers to emphasize the eternity by which marriage has already surpassed all its temporal vicissitudes. It is from this that he derives his "conviction that nothing is able to crush the esthetic in a human being" (123), because it is constituted by a faith that has already attained the truth that remains to be confirmed within time. With this announcement of the theme of faith, the transition of the esthetic to the religious becomes explicit. The esthetic is transfigured by faith that makes it real, for "the person who has the courage to transform the outer trial into an inner trial has already virtually surmounted it, since by faith a transubstantiation takes place even in the moment of suffering" (124). The difficulty in following William's reflections here is to get hold of this eschatological conception of faith, which has nothing to do with faith in a future. It is already realized in the eschatological opening of self by which the infinite is realized. For the married man, fidelity is continually acquired within time because it has already been received in eternity. Eternity does not approach him afterward; it is already his existence in time. "Like a true victor, the married man has not killed time but has rescued and preserved it in eternity" (138). Compared with this true inner history, what happens in historical time pales in significance, just as esthetic poetry is a mimesis of what can be portrayed only by living it out. We have reached the culmination of Kant's intuition that he had found room for faith, as well as Hegel's insight that love transcends duty. By responding to the call of duty, faith lays hold of the eschatological moment, the complete self-donation by which all is received in return, in which duty is completely fulfilled.

Freedom Is Eternity of Choice

The reason for his friend's inability to make such a decision lies, of course, deeper than a faulty understanding of marriage. It arises from the very core of his personality in the crisis that is addressed in "The Balance Between the Esthetic and the Ethical in the Development of Personality." Even the tone of Judge William's appeal has shifted as the issue of the refusal of human responsibility by "A" is broached more directly. Can he even be a friend to William or anyone else? He has reached the crossroad at which his understanding of "either/or" as endless vacillation (159) must be juxtaposed with the "either/or" of Cato that constitutes ethical resolution. The problem is not that "A" has chosen wrongly but that he has failed to choose at all. By refusing to choose absolutely, with his whole self, he merely chooses for the moment, which drifts into yet another moment. Esthetic existence is the refusal of freedom, contrary to the self-proclamation of its freedom. The analysis here brings us much closer to a clarification of that much misunderstood concept of freedom than any of the attempts by successors in the history of philosophy.[13] Kierkegaard utterly eliminates the notion of arbitrariness that has afflicted the notion of freedom by locating it squarely at the core of human existence. It cannot be exercised arbitrarily, because it cannot be exercised with anything less than the whole of our being. The significance of the ethical is not that it is a choice but that it is the meaning of choice. We do not therefore choose between good and evil – this is not our "either/or" – but more fundamentally we choose to choose. Then the choice is disclosed. "As soon as a person can be brought to stand at the crossroads in such a way that there is no way out for him except to choose, he will choose the right thing" (168). This is what is missed, not only by "A," but by the age that discourses about the end of history as a means of avoiding action within history.

It is an epoch that has yielded to the enervation of depression, that "hysteria of the spirit" that fails to gather itself together out of its dispersion (188–89).[14] But the letter writer has little sympathy for its victims.

---

[13] The best study, informed by careful analysis and scholarly investigation of the connections, is Michelle Kosch, *Freedom and Reason in Kant, Schelling, and Kierkegaard*. See also her essay, "Freedom and Immanence," in Giles, ed., *Kierkegaard and Freedom*, 121–41, as well as the other contributions to this fine anthology. Also of interest in this context is Timothy P. Jackson, "Arminian Edification: Kierkegaard on Grace and Free Will," in Hannay and Marino, eds., *The Cambridge Companion to Kierkegaard*, 235–56.

[14] Sensitivity to this peculiar mood of enervation when the abundance of possibilities robs all possibility from human existence was widespread in the nineteenth century. One thinks not only of Nietzsche and Dostoevsky, but of Matthew Arnold and Tocqueville. It is perhaps instructive to recall how the issue surfaced for the latter in the context of the rise of mass democracy with its elimination of all authority of rank. "The reproach I address to the principle of equality is not that it leads men away in the pursuit of forbidden enjoyments, but that it absorbs them wholly in quest of those which are allowed. By these

He holds to "the ancient doctrine of the Church" (185) that regards depression as a sin. Culpability is manifest in the despair that lies at its root. The disappointment that arises when each of its passing infatuations proves false gives way to the realization of the despair from which such futility arises. It is not, in other words, a despair over anything specific but a disclosure of the deeper condition that drives the joyless quest of joy. "Consequently, it is manifest that every esthetic view of life is despair, and that everyone who lives esthetically is in despair, whether he knows it or not" (192). You are ludicrous, William explains, with your momentary enthusiasms (199) that rob you of the solidity on which a friend could rely (204). The answer to such despair is to despair even more thoroughly, not over the particular but over the insufficiency of any particularity. "Generally speaking, a person cannot despair at all without willing it, but in order truly to despair, a person must truly will it; but when he truly wills it, he is truly beyond despair" (213). The problem of the esthetic is that it does not wish to break with the despair in which it wallows, while despair itself points toward the impossibility in which it is grounded. "When a person has truly chosen despair, he has truly chosen what despair chooses: himself in his eternal validity" (213).[15] The choice of the absolute is at the same time the choice by the absolute. William is able to steer clear of the metaphorical confusions of Hegel's self-identification with the absolute by sticking closely to "my category" of choosing. "I choose the absolute that chooses me" (213) is the formulation that perfectly captures the mutual emergence of the self and the absolute.[16] In refusing to choose this or that as the absolute, I stand in relation to that which is absolutely beyond me, which can therefore be known only through the movement of self-transcendence it makes

means a kind of virtuous materialism may ultimately be established in the world, which would not corrupt, but enervate, the soul and noiselessly unbend the springs of action." Tocqueville, *Democracy in America*, vol. 2, 141.

[15] Many, William points out, conquer doubt by losing themselves in ideology, yet they retain despair in their hearts, perhaps even more so. "In this respect, I think that our age will advance, provided I may have any opinion at all about our age, inasmuch as I know it only from reading the papers and a book or two or from talking with you. The time is not far off when we shall experience – quite likely at a high price – that the true point of departure for finding the absolute is not doubt but despair." *Either/Or: Part II*, 211–13.

[16] "When I choose absolutely, I choose despair, and in despair I choose the absolute, for I myself am the absolute; I posit the absolute, and I myself am the absolute. But in other words with exactly the same meaning I may say: I choose the absolute that chooses me; I posit the absolute that posits me – for if I do not keep in mind that this second expression is just as absolute, then my category of choosing is untrue, because it is precisely the identity of both." Ibid., 213.

possible. There is no self prior to the choice of the absolute, just as there is no absolute outside of the obligation it imposes. This means that our movement toward it must always begin with the awareness of our deficiency. Our choice is marked by repentance.

By acknowledging his self-dispersal in multiplicity, a man "repents himself back into himself, back into the family, back into the race, until he finds himself in God. Only on this condition can he choose himself. And this is the only condition he wants, for only in this way can he choose himself absolutely" (216). He does not know himself before he chooses, and therefore his choice is the response of love toward God who loved him first and knew him before he knew himself. Repentance is the luminosity of existence. While demurring against any theological encroachment, it is this discovery, William claims, that is the distinctive achievement of Christianity, for while many have felt the burden of guilt under which humanity labors, only Christianity has recognized that repentance is already the movement by which it is lifted. When repentance has become the absolute choice of the self, the self is received into the absolute. "The greater the freedom, the greater the guilt, and this is the secret of salvation" (218). Repentance and forgiveness emerge at the same time. In a reprise of the idealist glimpse of the absolute thinking itself in me, our author understands good and evil to be the correlative differentiations that emerge only with my choice.[17] But he shies away from their language of the absolute, just as he does from the mystic who has similarly chosen the absolute but not in an absolute way. There is too much of the particular in the mystic's enjoyment of the status of divine favorite that withdraws him from responsibility within the world. The mystic does not choose himself ethically, through repentance, but metaphysically in an almost esthetic mode. It is for this reason that he does not live the full meaning of temporality as the horizon of his finite enactment of the infinite. By leaping into the eternal he, like the philosopher, abandons the realization of eternity within time. We cannot, in the view of the married man and public official, turn away from our obligations in this world. "The particular beauty of temporality is that the infinite spirit and the finite spirit in it are separated, and it is the particular greatness of the finite spirit that temporality is assigned to it" (250).

[17] "That is to say, my thinking is an element in the absolute, and therein lies the necessity of my thinking, therein lies the necessity with which I think it. It is otherwise with the good. The good is because I will it, and otherwise it is not at all. This is the expression of freedom, and the same is also the case with evil – it is only inasmuch as I will it." Ibid., 224.

It is in this way that the ethical transfigures the esthetic by assuming the concrete as its task. The relationship thus has to do not with an external obligation to duty but with what is in accordance with one's innermost being. It is the religious, the Christian, that discloses the concreteness of the ethical in which the universal becomes the responsibility of the individual who has given himself entirely to it. "What is required of me is the universal; what I am able to do is the particular" (263). The paradox of irreconcilable imperatives that still troubled Levinas and Derrida had already been resolved in William's recognition that its acceptance is the irremovable condition of ethical action. Beauty, the transfiguration of the esthetic, consists in the realization that nothing a person accomplishes matters more than the person himself, his only true accomplishment. "'It is every human being's duty to have a calling'" (291), not for what the calling achieves but for what it effects within him.[18] The universal emerges in its true beauty in the individual who lives it out with his whole being. Marriage is not about the incidentals of the particular individuals involved, their feelings, compatibilities, and so on, but about the process by which they transcend them in the movement of mutual love. It is a relationship that brings into view the extent to which friendship in general is rooted not in indeterminate sympathies but in the permanence of absolute self-giving. Judge William notes that Aristotle, too, made friendship the starting point for an ethical life. Only someone who has chosen absolutely can give and receive the same from another. It is because his "friend" has never been able to give himself as a whole that William doubts the possibility, despite all that has been said, that they can truly be friends. Bemoaning his inability to find the universal in any particular relationship, "A" has overlooked its presence within the eschatological openness of every human being. Thinking he is always in the right, "A" has never been able to build himself up with the meditation that forms the "Ultimatum" of the book, which is a sermon, not penned but transmitted by "B": "In Relation to God We Are Always in the Wrong."

[18] "Think of an author. It never enters his head to consider whether he is going to have a reader or whether he is going to accomplish something with his book; he only wants to grasp the truth – that alone is the object of his pursuit." Ibid., 297. The appearance of Kantian echoes (all duties as duties to oneself) in Kierkegaard's formulations should not surprise anyone who has been following the argument of the present work. But it does certainly challenge the conventional reading of Kierkegaard. For the details of Kierkegaard's Kantian dimensions, see Ronald M. Green, *Kierkegaard and Kant: The Hidden Debt* (Albany: State University of New York Press, 1992), and Kosch, *Freedom and Reason*.

Différance as Upbuilding Discourse

The last word of Part II is, like the last text of Part I, not by the putative author but comes to him from another source, a pastor out in the remoteness of Jylland. It is introduced as a thought for "upbuilding" that connects *Either/Or* and the other pseudonymous writings with the parallel series that Kierkegaard published under his own name as *Upbuilding Discourses*.[19] The latter were intended to show that his own point of view had from the start been religious, while the pseudonymous authors had merely presented the esthetic way toward it. But this did not mean that Kierkegaard was himself a religious author, for he never claimed to speak with religious authority. He was rather himself as much in need of upbuilding as Judge William or "A," which explains why that form of discourse could find its way into an esthetic work. It is because Kierkegaard always regarded himself "as a *reader* of the books, not as the *author*" (*Eighteen Upbuilding Discourses*, xv), that they are called "upbuilding [*opbyggelig*] discourses" rather than "discourses for upbuilding." He could not claim to have reached what he dispenses to others. Indeed, he eventually reverts to pseudonymous authorship for the works of his second period, as in *The Sickness unto Death*, when the pseudonyms must present what is above him, just as they earlier produced what was below him. In each case the abiding insight is that the religious cannot be communicated directly. To the extent that the religious is what defines us, we are never in the position to define it. We can only depict the way toward it in the manner of a poet whose theme is the movement in which he himself is involved. This is why Kierkegaard in his late reflection on the problem of authorship, *The Point of View*, eventually identifies his subject as "becoming a Christian." He is neither a religious nor an irreligious author but one on the way toward the horizon of faith. One might observe, as Derrida would, that it is the différance that opens the whole space of writing for him. Neither the signed nor the unsigned works capture Kierkegaard as a fixed quantity, for he has thought through the meaning of a writing existence.

All of the writings are in the manner of an upbuilding in which the author is as much the reader because there is no truth outside of its

---

[19] The *Upbuilding Discourses* have received scant attention within the Kierkegaard literature, but one sign of a change in that pattern is the fine study by George Pattison, *Kierkegaard's Upbuilding Discourses: Philosophy, Literature and Theology* (London: Routledge, 2002).

existential appropriation. As the pastor in Jylland, the pseudonymous author of the discourse that could easily have been signed, concludes his sermon, "Only the truth that builds up is truth for you" (354). The echo of William James's "truth is what works" is not accidental, nor is the reminiscence of Heidegger's "truth as the concealment of unconcealment" surprising, and even Nietzsche's observation that "truth is the least well established of our prejudices" resonates here. Kierkegaard had understood that the opening toward truth could not be included as a truth. Instead, he designated it as an "infinite relationship," a relationship that by definition could never be encompassed. This is why for him there are no theological doctrines, such as original sin or divine redemption, as if we could contain the knowledge by which we are contained. When we acknowledge that "in relation to God we are always in the wrong," we are not providing a report on a state of affairs; we are adumbrating the unsurpassable movement by which our existence is constituted. There is no truth to be contemplated here as if we could briefly step outside of our existence to view it. We are rather continuously held by what we glimpse, for if we were to behold it apart from us, we would have lost that by which we are sustained. This is the great anxiety, to which the pastor refers, in the possibility that we could be in the right and God in the wrong. Existence would have closed in on us. He rejoices that it is not so, not because the Gnostic thesis has been disproved, but because it is existentially impossible. "Every time the cares of doubt want to make him sad, he lifts himself above the finite into the infinite, because this thought, that he is always in the wrong, is the wings upon which he soars" (352).

What Kierkegaard seeks to express in the *Upbuilding Discourses* cannot, in other words, be said directly either. It is simply a different kind of indirection than the pseudonymous works in which the source of the problem is less explicitly acknowledged. The superiority of the discourses arises from this greater lucidity that is yet not self-transparence. Where *Either/Or* revolves around the inability of erotic love to preserve itself unless it transcends itself, the parallel *Two Upbuilding Discourses* (1843; contained in *Eighteen Upbuilding Discourses*) centers on the gift of eternity that renders possibility within time. The first discourse is a meditation on the "expectancy of faith" by which faith has already reached what it seeks to attain. It is through the eternal that one conquers the future, "an expectancy of the future that expects victory – this has indeed conquered the present" (19). Unlike the quest for certainty in the esthetic, faith cannot be disappointed by any finite outcome. It is already the assurance it seeks. This is also why the second discourse reflects on the thought that "every good and perfect gift is from above" (Jas 1: 17) for it is not the relief of particular trials that is best but the assurance of their complete overcoming through faith. Such a faith can be received only when we have abandoned all claim to our own finite perspectives, including our right to complain against God's indifference to our sufferings, in order to receive the gift of infinite overcoming as the only "good and perfect gift." Even the love of God is then not our love, for we become aware that we are inadequate to the task and can love him only through the gift of his love within us. "In repentance, you receive everything from God, even the thanksgiving that you bring him, so that even this is what the child's gift is to the eyes of the parents, a jest, a receiving of something that one has oneself given" (46).

Freedom Exceeds the Universal

The same reality of faith by which the infinite takes hold of us, rather than the other way around, is explored from the outside, poetically, in the following esthetic works, *Fear and Trembling* and *Repetition*. The former is the one work that even Kierkegaard recognized would "make my name imperishable," while the latter bears remarkable resemblance to the circumstances of his own life. That biographical affinity with Kierkegaard's decision to break off his engagement with Regine Olsen perhaps explains the poetic power of the works but does not in any sense determine their meaning. Indeed, his struggle through these texts was precisely to reach the poetic distance they achieved. The irreducible singularity of his relationship with Regine was left behind as he sought to explore the universalities of existence. It was an exploration that remained under pseudonymous authorship as befitted poets who could not quite grasp the religious meaning toward which their works pointed.[20] Johannes de Silentio would have to remain silent about the movement of faith he admired in the reflection on Abraham in *Fear and Trembling*, while Constantin Constantius would attain a surface constancy that fell far short of the living eternity evoked by the religious category of *Repetition*. But

---

[20] See the quote from Haman affixed as the motto of *Fear and Trembling*: "What Tarquinius Superbus said in the garden by means of the poppies, the son understood but the messenger did not."

it is perhaps the very deficiency of the authorial perspectives that lends strength to their creations, for they present more extensively than the *Upbuilding Discourses* the distance that still must be traveled if their aspirations are to arrive at their destination. We begin to understand more clearly the relationship between the two genres of writing if we recognize that the goal so unambiguously proclaimed in the *Discourses* can be reached only through the arduous ascent pseudonymously undertaken toward it.

Abraham is perhaps one of the authors, for he provides the text of his witness to the faith that sustains existence. Johannes de Silentio reads him as the "knight of faith" whom he had admired from childhood but had not yet been able to emulate. To be able to sacrifice Isaac and yet believe that the sacrifice will not be demanded of him can only be designated as the "absurd." "He had faith by virtue of the absurd, for human calculation was out of the question, and it certainly was absurd that God, who required it of him, should in the next moment rescind the requirement" (35–36). The farthest that Johannes de Silentio can follow is the movement of infinite resignation by which he surrendered all to God but not the countermovement by which he also received it all back.[21] That must appear to be "absurd," a "leap into eternity," to one still bound by human calculation. The reason of faith remains closed to him. This is why he presents his reflection in the form of a "dialectical lyric" on the "problemata" of the Abrahamic paradox, "which no thought can grasp, because faith begins precisely where thought stops" (53). One of the regrettable consequences of the popularity of *Fear and Trembling* is that the struggle of the pseudonymous author is very often attributed to its ultimate author. The place and purpose of the text in Kierkegaard's overall literary project are often forgotten. As a result, the accent that de Silentio places on the absurdity and even irrationality of faith is too readily taken as Kierkegaard's own estimation. Not only does such an assumption fly in the face of Kierkegaard's guiding conviction of the reason-sustaining force of faith, but it even fails to read de Silentio's own progress through the problemata by which faith becomes eminently more reasonable. He may not succeed in becoming a knight of faith himself, but he does go a considerable distance toward uncovering the movement of reason itself in that direction.

---

[21] This is surely why the text has generated such a range of possible interpretations. They are well summarized by John Lippitt, *Kierkegaard and "Fear and Trembling"* (London: Routledge, 2003).

This enlargement of reason toward the boundary of faith begins with the first problem, "Is there a teleological suspension of the ethical?" Does the ethical universal that since Kant has been its own telos nevertheless move toward a telos beyond itself? The question has been embedded in the existential shift from its beginning, for if the individual undertakes the realization of the universal, does this not mean that he at some point stands higher than the universal? Levinas had realized this in the prioritization of the face, and Derrida had discerned the différance by which every singularity escapes its identification. A human being is not just a part of the whole; he is also a part that contains the whole. This is what Kierkegaard calls the "paradox of faith that the single individual is higher than the universal" (55), that he is never simply absorbed without remainder into his service of the universal but remains in the unabsorbed uniqueness by which he is one with the absolute. Even with Hegel this insight into the relation of the individual and absolute had been percolating without erupting into clarity. Now with the meditation on the case of Abraham, faith emerges as the unique, irreplaceable responsibility of the individual before God. Mediation, by which the universal steps in to explain the response of the individual, is no longer possible when the individual is called in his uniqueness to surrender the all that only he can yield up. This is the question that defines our author's second problem, "Is there an absolute duty toward God?" Is the duty toward God not just a duty, but the summit of the ethical as such? Many readers of the text have taken it as a juxtaposition of the demands of faith against the demands of duty, but it is more properly read as an exploration of Abraham's readiness to go beyond merely doing his duty to obey the voice of God that in inwardness is the source of all duty. Do we have a duty to go beyond merely performing our duty? The problem with duty is that it is already a separable part of ourselves, an obligation we may be able to meet with plenty to spare. But how do we perform a duty into which we place the whole of ourselves? We must find a way of showing that we are doing our duty not simply out of the necessity of duty, but out of a supererogatory abundance by which we give ourselves without reserve. This is the meaning of Abraham, the "knight of faith," for he "concentrates in one single point the whole of the ethical that he violates, in order that he may give himself the assurance that he actually loves Isaac with his whole soul" (78). He is not simply enduring a trial but grasps by faith the victory of the ethical through his inward relation to the absolute. "The paradox of faith, then, is this: that the single individual is higher than the universal, that the single individual . . . determines his relation to the universal by his relation to the absolute, not his relation to the absolute by his relation to the universal" (70).[22]

The difficulty, then, is that the relationship cannot be disclosed. "Was it ethically defensible for Abraham to conceal his undertaking from Sarah, from Eliezer, and from Isaac?" is the third and most extensive problem of the text. It is by his relation to the absolute that the individual is an inwardness, containing the possibility of the total gift of self that for that very reason cannot be mediated by its manifestations. The self can be given, but it cannot be contained in the means by which it is conveyed. Truth or falsity exceeds verification within the form of universals, for they are rooted in the possibilities of absolute closure or absolute openness, the demonic or the religious. Just as the movement of disclosure cannot be arrested in any of its mediations without betraying itself, so its culmination in the inexpressibility of faith is merely confirmation of the absolute gift of self that exists nowhere but in the giving itself. The esthetic merely throws a cloak of love over the inner struggle of love to become a love that goes beyond duty. To the very end the outcome is uncertain, as it is with the self-revelation of Dostoevsky's most profound characters. So long as some unsurrendered element of the self is left, the possibility of reversal remains. The analysis focuses on the moment of decision, not because it remains an arbitrary leap, but because there is no outcome other than the existence constituted by its enactment. In the story of Agnes and the Merman, he discovers that he cannot possess her as booty, for she has already given herself to him in all innocence. The question then is whether he will be able to overcome the repentance that afflicts him to reach the positive affirmation by which he can offer himself in return. Can he receive her forgiveness with his repentance, or does the repentance mount to a demonic closure? It is the question of whether he is capable of the movement of faith by which in losing all he simultaneously gains all. "In other words, when the single individual by his guilt has come outside the universal, he can return only by virtue of having come as the single individual into an absolute relation to the absolute" (98). Outwardly nothing has changed, while inwardly everything

---

[22] C. Stephen Evans, *Kierkegaard's Ethics of Love: Divine Commands and Moral Obligations* (Oxford: Oxford University Press, 2004), reaches this same position by way of an analytic account of the logic of divine command morality. The approach yields less interesting results in the case of *Fear and Trembling* than it does in relation to *Works of Love*. Part of the reason for this is that the issue of Abraham's obedience to a divine command to sacrifice Isaac is not well integrated with the larger discussion of commanding love that occupies the center of Evans's attention.

is different, as befits an event in which the infinite is transacted in the finite. Abraham's silence is justified as inexorable.

Ours is an age that cannot understand the movement of faith, de Silentio explains, because it has not reached beyond the ethical. The alternatives of the demonic or the divine remain closed to it because it does not understand the necessity of surmounting the challenge of sin. "An ethics that ignores sin is a completely futile discipline, but if it affirms sin, then it has *eo ipso* exceeded itself" (99). This consideration has not arisen in the case of Abraham, because in an esthetic work he is being conceived in immediate categories, but the need to account for his incomprehensibility must be addressed in a footnote that concludes, "As soon as sin emerges, ethics founders precisely on repentance, for repentance is the highest ethical expression, but precisely as such it is the deepest ethical self-contradiction" (98). Incapable of reaching the boundary of faith, our age also cannot understand the misshapen demonic natures, like Shakespeare's Gloucester, who are capable of bearing anything except sympathetic love. In many ways they are closer to the movement of faith because they are stirred by a singular passion for depravity that already lifts them outside the universal. They are already in the grip of the absolute, by which "they are either lost in the demonic paradox or saved in the divine paradox" (106). But their singularity can never be communicated. They remain within the ironic silence of Socrates and Abraham, incapable of explaining to a society incapable of understanding. This is the loneliness of the knight of faith who cannot share his gift with others, for each must arrive at it on his own. The inaccessibility of language arises because each unique person must undertake his or her unique movement of faith. No substitution is possible. The epilogue permits itself just one reflection on the value of the silence of faith in comparing it to the Dutch merchants who sink their ships at sea because the price of their commodity on land has fallen too low. Is this submergence of meaning the point of Kierkegaard's vast literary enterprise?

Repetition as the Eternal Possibility of Time

The one thing that does emerge from these depths is Kierkegaard's fascination with the transition from the demonic mastery of the esthetic to the divine unmastery of faith. In the companion work, *Repetition*, Constantin Constantius, a pseudonym that suggests an incapacity for repetition, the subject is a young poet who has fallen in love. Constantius recounts, through his own report and the letters addressed to him by the young man, the psychological experiment by which he attempted to turn the episode into a demonic triumph over the demand of love. The young man has already poetized the experience and has determined to break off the relationship for its imperfection, so that he is susceptible to the promptings of his older companion to manipulate the situation from the perspective of his superiority. It is the most autobiographical of Kierkegaard's works because of the resemblance to his relationship with Regine Olsen. But it is more properly viewed as underlining the dissimilarity, since the young poet falls short of the true religious viewpoint toward which he aspires. Nevertheless, the young man does resist the poetic exploitation of the relationship suggested by Constantius, the false repetition of mere sameness in the theater, although he cannot find his way toward the full repetition in life made possible by faith. Repetition is the same movement as faith by which what is lost is at the same time fully restored; in the surrendering of the beloved, she is loved even more deeply. Instead, the young man arrives at the boundary of faith, an esthetic affirmation of religion, when he turns away from the false counsel of Constantius to contemplate the other great knight of faith, Job. From this "God's-hand poultice" (204), however, he cannot make the full repetition of faith but rather enters accidentally into the equivalent liberation when the news of the beloved's engagement to another is announced. The thunderstorm that would have broken his self-obsession has hit him, so that he now can live, although life has removed the immediate obligation from him. "My poet now finds a legitimation precisely in being absolved by life the moment he in a sense wants to destroy himself. His soul now gains a religious resonance" (228). Repetition has been glimpsed poetically precisely because it has not been embraced existentially.

In *Repetition,* Kierkegaard has carried forward the critique of the poetic project, with which he had himself a more than passing familiarity, to the point where the incapacity to understand itself is its defining characteristic. "It is characteristic of the young man," Constantius concludes, "precisely as a poet, that he can never really grasp what he has done, simply because he both wants to see it and does not want to see it in the external and visible, or wants to see it in the external and visible, and therefore both wants to see it and does not want to see it. A religious individual, however, is composed within himself and rejects all childish pranks of actuality" (230).

The difficulty is that such perfect composure cannot be represented, for it leaves no room for reflection on itself. Kierkegaard is the first thinker to fully confront the limitation of a metaphysics of presence that is incapable of capturing what cannot be present. The luminosity of existence cannot include the source of its luminosity, because it cannot stand outside itself. This insight implicit in the modern philosophical revolution has only slowly disclosed its inexorability, although Kierkegaard seems to have grasped its scope from the very start. It is this extraordinary farsightedness that accounts for both his anomalous position and the convoluted character of his writings. The parallel series of pseudonymous and acknowledged texts was more than a communication strategy in an age of nominal Christianity. It had much to do with the structure or, rather, nonstructure of his realization. We must take him seriously when he insists that the writings were his own reading as well. What he tried to formulate directly in the *Upbuilding Discourses* he could also grasp as the direction insufficiently unfolded in the esthetic writings. Both genres are a form of "upbuilding" that the author/reader requires in his existence that lies outside of them. With approximations from the before and after, he is more capable of reaching the now that never becomes a now that can be named. Kierkegaard returned again and again to the poetic at which he excelled because it directed toward, without entering, the path he had to follow; the summative discourses formed a beacon of reassurance, a vision of the goal he had yet to reach.

The relationship is particularly close between *Repetition* and the *Three Upbuilding Discourses* (1844; in *Eighteen Upbuilding Discourses*) that appeared simultaneously with it. They deal with the complete victory of love. "Love will hide a multitude of sins" is the theme, not for reflection, but for enlargement. Love has already reached the goal toward which it aspires, thus answering the problem of the distance that the esthetic existence places between itself and its fulfillment. Love hides a multitude of sins because it has already covered the space within which they might become visible. Love has already reached what desire seeks. This is why desire is never what it is. It is a "fraud" that lets a person "keep only a superficial, passing intimation of authentic being [*Tilvaer*]" (76). Love, by contrast, forgets itself in love, as in the case of Mary Magdalene, whose weeping at the feet of Jesus causes him to say that her sins are forgiven because she has loved much. She has already reached the end that is the theme of the third discourse, "strengthening in the inner being." Victory is attained even though we are still on the way toward it. Love is the attainment of faith that surpasses all tangible attainments. "Then he will rejoice in quite another way than the fortunate person does, because he who has the whole world and is as one who does not have it has the whole world – otherwise he is possessed by the world" (90). He is free of the anxiety that even the most extensive possession of wealth and power cannot escape. Unlike the "shudder" that arises with the realization "to have power and not know *for what* purpose one has it" (91), there is only the peace that has already reached all that it seeks. What makes human love possible is that it has already received the gift of love that is the gift of God himself. Our earthly fathers are only a faint sign of this but sufficient to move Kierkegaard to dedicate the whole series of *Upbuilding Discourses* to his own late father.

God as Différance: Expectancy Cannot Be Disappointed

These reflections are followed by *Four Upbuilding Discourses* (1843), *Two Upbuilding Discourses* (1844), and *Three Upbuilding Discourses* (1844) in close succession, tumbling from the pen of Kierkegaard as if they formed the meditative center of his own and, by extension, our existence. As such they are unfathomable. This is what constitutes their difficulty, marking them as far more than "edifying" pieties. We can never fully understand that to which they point, because they ultimately point toward us. Job intimates the limitation of knowledge, for we can learn nothing from what he said, only what he did. Knowledge always seems to promise something good, the delectable fruit forbidden us, but it always comes with the doubt that coils around the human heart (*Eighteen Upbuilding Discourses*, 127). To escape its grip we must turn doubt on itself, disdaining the false promise of knowledge from which it derives its strength. "Every good and perfect gift comes from above" is what builds us up beyond the stranglehold of knowledge. "False doubt doubts everything except itself; with the help of faith, the doubt that saves doubts only itself" (137). With that succinct formulation, Kierkegaard has pinpointed the revolutionary movement by which modern philosophy has superseded itself. Admittedly it has launched us into a linguistically bewildering condition in which all the structures of our intentionality have become reversed, but it is an opening or a clearing in which we can breathe at last beyond the imprisonment of our own necessity for domination. This is why, Kierkegaard insists, we cannot know "the secret hiding place of the good" (135) since it comes to us from above. Our gift, insofar as we have any thing to give, is the gift of love by which we give nothing but ourselves, as the gift we have received. To the extent that we give only particular effects, we do not give ourselves; to the extent that we give ourselves, we give what we do not have. We can give to others only because we have received the gift of giving. Both "giver and receiver are inseparable in the gift" (157) by which the self is forgotten in the love that surpasses them. This is the infinite movement of patience, "to gain one's soul in patience," by which we can gain what we possess. The formulation is identical to that later elaborated by Derrida, in emphasizing that différance of the soul from itself that constitutes its life. "It was the infinity in the life of the world in its difference from itself" (165). Existence in faith is existence within that difference by which the soul gains itself in patience, for there would be no existence if the esthetic leap to a conclusion had been possible. Contradiction with the world is the self-contradiction of the soul. "If it were not in contradiction, it would be lost in the life of the world; if it were not self-contradiction, movement would be impossible" (166). The "above" that cannot be possessed guarantees both its completion and its incompletion.

This meditation is deepened in the next publication, *Two Upbuilding Discourses,* which deal with patience and expectancy as the tension of existence. It is a tension that cannot wish for its release, for then it would lose the very thing toward which it aspires. "Even if the wish were fulfilled, it would be to a person's loss; he would lose the best, the holiest, to be what God has intended him to be, neither more nor less" (*Eighteen Upbuilding Discourses,* 190). Our whole life is "one nightwatch of expectancy" (206). Not needing to be paid like a day laborer, we are prepared to work our whole life long without receiving anything by which our expectancy might be diminished. Next to God it is the memory of one who is dead that so forms the soul in expectancy that is more than its fulfillment, for "the person who loves one who is dead serves his entire life for his love" (210). The constancy of the dead, reminiscent of the *Sumparanekromenoi* (Fellowship of the Dead), is what constitutes the constancy of life. Those who have chosen expectancy cannot be disappointed, for they have already received the eternal that never changes. "The error of the one doubting [*Tvivlende*] and of the one despairing [*Fortvivlende*] does not lie in cognition, since cognition cannot decide with certainty anything about the next moment, but the error lies in the will, which suddenly no longer wills but on the contrary wants to make the indeterminate into a passionate decision. Even at the last moment there is a possibility, or rather there is no last moment before it is past" (215). Impatience is lost in the "maybe [*maaskee*]," while patience has already received the assurance of the "it must happen [*det maa skee*]" (217). Patience that has already laid hold of everything without laying hold of anything is the singular relation of the individual with God, for "there is truly only one eternal object of wonder – that is God – and only one possible hindrance to wonder – and that is a person when he himself wants to be something" (226).

God who is known before a person knows himself is the deepening meditation of *Three Upbuilding Discourses*. Before Nietzsche employed Diogenes' story of the madman with a lantern in the marketplace, Kierkegaard refers to it here with the same application to the modern occlusion of God (245). How are we to find what we have lost? Nietzsche uses the occasion to announce the death of God that is the apotheosis of man, while Kierkegaard sees that the latter is already the reversal of the former. We have not lost that for which we search. All we need is that recognition itself. Beyond the universality of the question is the singularity of the questioner, who cannot be contained within the speculation he unfolds. It is the memory of that transcendence that opens the possibility of questioning, of the search that is fulfilled in the glimpse of what cannot be glimpsed. Nietzsche is still far from seeing clearly that the question of God already contains the relationship to God that cannot be contained. Since Jacobi and the idealists, modern philosophy has been wrestling with this great implication, but Kierkegaard has overtaken even the post-Heideggerians in grasping its full extent. The question remains within the difference by which recollection is always a recollection of an earlier recollection. We never get outside the text of the divine revelation, because we can never contain that by which we are contained. Our only apprehension is through existence. The despair of "nihilism" is shaken off when we have begun to live outside ourselves in the thought that "God's word abides forever" (248). But this is no return of metaphysics or theology; it is the transcendence of dogma by which existence is possible. It is the upbuilding thought that cannot have a source or it would not be what upbuilds.[23] "Spiritually, the fulfillment is always in the wish, the calming of the concern in the concern, just as God is even in the sorrowful longing that is the lack of him" (250). There would be no cry of the madman if there was not already the revelation of God. Even the thought of death "liberates a person, saving him from being a bond servant who wants to belong only to the earth, from being a cheat who does not want to belong to God" (282).

---

[23] "Above all, generality is not for upbuilding, because one is never built up [*opbygges*] in general, any more than a house is erected [*opføres*] in general." *Eighteen Upbuilding Discourses*, 276.

Philosophy as a Fragment: The Knowledge of Faith

The series of intensifying discourses that here reach a culmination now make possible a more far-reaching statement of the philosophical revolution they have inaugurated. It begins with *Philosophical Fragments, or a Fragment of Philosophy,* edited by S. Kierkegaard but authored by Johannes Climacus, a monk of Mt. Sinai (570–649) who wrote the *Ladder of Paradise.* The pseudonym is intended to suggest the relation to a ladder of ascent made available by one who has yet to reach its summit, just as the title suggests that philosophy is available only as a fragment that points outside itself. The work also includes *Johannes Climacus, or De omnibus disputandum est: A Narrative* as the account of the ascent from the modern philosophical immersion in systematic doubt. Thus, the overturning of modern philosophy is conceived of as a separate part of the larger project of *Philosophical Fragments,* which is aimed at the revolution that goes beyond Socratic philosophy by affirming it more completely. *Johannes Climacus,* which is presumably the self-reflection of Climacus, was written first but placed second in the *Philosophical Fragments.* Perhaps this means that the ladder by which the ascent might be undertaken, as it has been attempted in modern philosophical doubt, is not actually a viable way. That at any rate is the outcome of the reflection of Johannes Climacus, especially when he undertakes in the second part to think on his own. Doubt, he then recognizes, cannot be resolved either by knowledge or by reality, since it arises from the interest of consciousness in the relation between the two. As such it is a mode of existence by which the relation between ideality and reality is probed in our becoming conscious. There is no getting behind doubt to something more fundamental by which it could be resolved. Where the modern skeptics imply that doubt can be put to rest through the advance of knowledge, the ancient skeptics saw more clearly that it is only the removal of interest that quiets its restless drive. "From this it is apparent the doubt is the beginning of the highest form of existence [*Tilvaerelse*], because it can have everything else as its presupposition" (170). In doubt we recognize our incapacity to go beyond the existential condition in which we find ourselves.[24]

---

[24] The philosophical pattern of Kierkegaard's thought comes most in evidence in these works, and its affinity with the dialectical movements of idealism in general is clearly recognizable. But because so much of *Philosophical Fragments* and *Concluding Unscientific Postscript* takes aim, even in the titles, at the whole notion of a system of philosophy and at Hegel in particular, the relationship of Kierkegaard to idealism has been difficult to unravel. Recent scholarship has, however, considerably clarified the situation. Like the

To reach a point where doubt could be removed would be to reach a point where existence had been arrested. This temptation to step outside of existence in order to enjoy it has already been encountered in the esthetic refusal to actually live our existence; the philosophical equivalent is the construction of the system by which doubt would be erased through the comprehension of itself. In both cases the underlying presupposition is that existence can be held at bay while we remain within existence. The Kantian equivalent would be the assertion that practical reason can be comprehended by theoretical reason without recognizing that the latter is already a mode of the former. What practical reason can understand about itself is severely limited, Kant recognized, unless it abdicates the very responsibility by which it is constituted. When philosophy is defined by the luminosity of existence, philosophy itself can provide no more than a fragment. This was certainly the Socratic beginning in ignorance, but it could not hold firm and wandered into such claims to knowledge as that virtue could be taught. Fidelity to Socrates would demand more than fidelity. It would be nothing less than the new beginning that is the new beginning with which no human being can dispense. When there is no stepping beyond the existence in which we find ourselves, the question must remain firmly contained within its horizon. "Can a historical point of departure," the title page of *Philosophical Fragments* asks, "be given for an eternal consciousness; how can such a point of departure be of more than historical interest; can an eternal happiness be built on historical knowledge?" When existence cannot be surpassed, we must search within it for its surpassing truth. What does not await our knowledge in order to be must always and everywhere have been.

The task for philosophy is therefore the awakening to what it already knows but can never, for that reason, reduce to knowledge. Kierkegaard here joins up the Hegelian recognition of truth as movement with the Derridean insistence on the irreducibility of différance. But he goes beyond them in existential thoroughness. The movement in which philosophy is engaged is not a general condition but the concrete existence of the philosopher himself. To the extent that truth is not possessed but

relationship with Schelling that Kosch has helped to illuminate, Jon Stewart, *Kierkegaard's Relation to Hegel Reconsidered* (Cambridge: Cambridge University Press, 2003), has finally put paid to the oversimplification of Kierkegaard as the archcritic of Hegel. Much of the invective against Hegel, Stewart explains, was directed against Danish Hegelians, while Kierkegaard himself moved through three phases of admiration for Hegel, critical distance, and then silence in regard to him. The relationship to Hegel may thus be more accurately described in the same terms as that with Socrates: fidelity by going beyond the mentor.

pursued, the awakening must begin with the recognition of the philosopher's own untruth. He not only is afflicted by untruth, but exists within it. This means that he lacks the very condition by which he might recognize his untruth, a limitation that no teacher can overcome, for it requires a transformation that can be worked only by the Creator. "The teacher, then, is the god himself, who, acting as the occasion, prompts the learner to be reminded that he is untruth and is that through his own fault" (15). He must be brought to recognize his state of sin. Yet the work of God is inexpressibly delicate, for he does not want to devastate the learner with the truth but instead to raise him up to the equality in which love itself can be liberated. Unity can be brought about by an ascent toward God, but since that would be unbearable to sinful self-consciousness, it must be effected through the descent by which God dwells in hiddenness among human beings. Climacus compares the situation to that of the king who falls in love with a lowly maiden and must therefore take on the suffering of the contradiction: "not to disclose itself is the death of love; to disclose itself is the death of the beloved" (30). We are saved by the impossibility of piercing the différance that is contained only within the divine suffering.

That realization is the limit of our self-reflection, designated by Climacus in the central fragment entitled "The Absolute Paradox (a Metaphysical Caprice)." We recall that Climacus is only the author of *The Ladder of Paradise,* not the one who has reached its summit. Paradox is the ladder he offers us, for it is paradox that is the way toward the goal and not the goal itself. "This, then, is the ultimate paradox of thought: to want to discover something that thought itself cannot think" (37). Erotic love is constituted by the same unsurpassable tension. "A person lives undisturbed in himself, and then awakens the paradox of self-love as love for another, for one missing" (39). Existence in thought and love emerges from what it is not, the unknown we may call, Climacus suggests, "*the god*" (39). Demonstration of the existence of God is futile, since all efforts at demonstration flow from the conviction of divine being in the same way that demonstration always presupposes existence. This is not a logical presupposition but an existential one as the unknowable from which the movement of knowing flows. "The whole process of demonstration continually becomes something entirely different, becomes an expanded concluding development of what I conclude from having presupposed that the object of investigation exists" (40). Reasoning never ends with existence but originates from it. "I do not demonstrate that a stone exists but that something which exists is a stone." Spinoza, Climacus explains in a coda to German idealism, had failed to grasp the meaning of his inclusion of existence within the essence of God as such an existential condition for our thinking about God. Demonstration is futile when it turns to what overflows demonstration itself. "The paradoxical passion of the understanding is, then, continually colliding with this unknown, which certainly does exist but is also unknown and to that extent does not exist" (44). Existence and nonexistence are equally inapplicable to God, who is the impetus of the reflection that seeks him.

Yet understanding constantly strains to leap over the difference between itself and the God it knows is beyond it and, in that struggle, cannot shake the impression that it has merely created that of which it is conscious. Climacus prefigures Derrida's focus on différance and under-stands it in the same unbridgeable sense.[25] He asks only how we become conscious of it if we cannot break out of the self-containment of under-standing. Apart from the question itself as a mode of transcendence, there is the source of awareness of the need for the question that lies deeper still. If understanding is to truly come to know the difference, "it must come to know this from the god," even though that precludes truly understanding it (46). To the extent that the difference is something that originates within us, it arises from that which separates us from God, our own responsibility for sin. Now the full terror of the divine approach becomes clear as the heightening of awareness of separation that is correlative with what is required for reconciliation. "Thus the para-dox becomes even more terrible, or the same paradox has the duplexity by which it manifests itself as the absolute – negatively, by bringing into prominence the absolute difference of sin and, positively, by wanting to annul this absolute difference in the absolute equality" (47). It is in this way that God provides not only the knowledge of himself but also the condition in which we can grasp it. This is the resolution of faith by which the endless circling in difference, simultaneously produced and rejected by the understanding, comes to rest. When the paradox gives itself, it also gives the passion of faith by which it may be entered (59).

The situation is no different whether it occurs to the contemporary or to one who comes later, for there is no getting outside the movement

---

[25] If the human being is "to know something about the unknown (the god), he must first come to know that it is different from him, absolutely different from him. The under-standing cannot come to know this by itself (since, as we have seen, it is a contradiction); if it is going to come to know this, it must come to know this from the god, and if it does come to know this, it cannot understand this and consequently cannot come to know this, for how could it understand the absolutely different?" *Philosophical Fragments*, 46.

of faith. Anticipating Heidegger's insistence on the "ontological difference," Climacus explains that "the only thing that cannot come into existence is the necessary, because the necessary *is*" (74). When it enters existence, the necessary can no longer be grasped in its necessity but only through faith in the actualization of possibility. The contemporary does not have a noticeable advantage, because he is not an eyewitness to the necessary but must simply hold by faith its emergence in existence. There is no leap outside the text to a presence that dispenses with reading it. The historical revelation is the means by which we are occupied with the eternal as that which is not historical. Faith is what mediates the ontological difference, but never in such a way that it is reduced to a knowledge of difference. It is the mode by which what is not manifest is held without being assimilated to what is not. Belief is a resolution that has excluded doubt. "It believes the coming into existence and has annulled in itself the incertitude that corresponds to the nothingness of that which is not" (83). The relationship to something historical is precisely a relationship to what is not historical. Through this understanding of faith, Climacus has clarified what still remains obscure in Heidegger, namely, how consciousness of the ontological difference arises when it is not a consciousness of something. "As is well known, Christianity is the only historical phenomenon that despite the historical – indeed, precisely by means of the historical – has wanted to be the single individual's point of departure for his eternal consciousness, has wanted to interest him otherwise than merely historically, has wanted to base his happiness on his relation to something historical" (109). Faith, on this analysis, takes its stand on the recognition that it has nothing on which to take its stand other than the movement of faith itself. When philosophy has thus entered into the movement by which it is constituted, it can justifiably claim to have gone beyond the uncertainty of its Socratic beginning. Philosophy cannot grasp that by which it is itself grasped, except through the movement of faith that grasps the historical as not being what it is. In the "Moral" with which the book ends, philosophy has become faith.[26]

---

[26] "This project indisputably goes beyond the Socratic, as is apparent at every point. Whether it is therefore more true than the Socratic is an altogether different question, one that cannot be decided in the same breath, inasmuch as a new organ has been assumed here: faith; and a new presupposition: the consciousness of sin; and a new teacher: the god in time. Without these, I really would not have dared to present myself for inspection before that ironist who has been admired for millennia, whom I approach with as much ardent enthusiasm as anyone. But to go beyond Socrates when one nevertheless says essentially the same as he, only not nearly so well – that, at least, is not Socratic." Ibid., 111.

Freedom Enacted Through Repentance, Not Anxiety

It is almost as if to demonstrate the power of this revolution in philosophy that Kierkegaard turns in the following work to its psychological application. *The Concept of Anxiety* is subtitled *A Simple Psychologically Orienting Deliberation on the Dogmatic Issue of Hereditary Sin,* a sure indication that the application is neither simple nor psychological. We have followed Kierkegaard far enough by now to know that such a deliberation will not be about the psychology of anxiety but rather about the irreducibility of anxiety to its psychological dimensions. This is why the subtitle warns us of the "dogmatic issue of original sin." Psychology does not designate a self-contained realm, because it is in turn contained within the contours of dogma. The ambivalent status of *The Concept of Anxiety,* floating between the psychological and the dogmatic, seems to have affected its authorship as well. Initially Kierkegaard intended to append his own name to the work, but then shifted to the pseudonymous author Vigilius Haufniensis, "the watchman of Copenhagen." Such an author could presumably limit himself to watching over or anticipating the dogmatic issue he was not required to address directly. One begins to suspect that the device of pseudonymous authorship that had initially appealed to Kierkegaard as a literary device of indirection was becoming a necessary consequence of his own philosophical position. Could it be that pseudonymity is the only available mode of authorship? Or does it mean that pseudonymity collapses entirely when the author is forced to concede his inability to dispense with it? Perhaps it is in *The Concept of Anxiety* that Kierkegaard begins to realize that he can never say more than "the watchman of Copenhagen."[27]

The categories of watchfulness cannot be surpassed, for we cannot understand sin in relation to psychology. It is always the other way around, or rather it is that the psychological is contained within the dogmatics of sin. Anxiety does not exist apart from sin, as the title of the first chapter indicates, "Anxiety as the Presupposition of Original Sin." It does not "explain" the origin of sin so much as coincide with it. "This is the profound secret of innocence, that it is at the same time anxiety" (41). By projecting its actuality outside itself, spirit first senses its nothingness,

---

[27] Writing in his journal, Kierkegaard commented on *The Concept of Anxiety:* "After all, I always have a poetic relationship to my works, and therefore I am pseudonymous. At the same time as the book develops some theme, the corresponding individuality is delineated. For example, Vigilious Huafniensis delineates several, but I have also made a sketch of him in the book." Quoted in notes to *Concept of Anxiety,* 222.

which is its anxiety. "In the moment actuality is posited, possibility walks by its side as a nothing that entices every thoughtless man" (50). Man becomes aware of his synthetic nature, including the differentiation of the sexes, as what is to be but has not yet been overcome. Sin that breaks out from this anxiety has no source other than itself and therefore is original with each human being.[28] Once sin has thus erupted, of course, subsequent generations are more conscious of it, as Vigilius suggests in the second chapter, "Anxiety as Explaining Sin Progressively." This is where the awareness of the loss of spirit, of immortality, arises.[29] It is especially manifest in the modesty by which spirit senses the loss of itself in the sexual, the contradiction by which the immortal is contained within the genus that is propagated. The erotic is the false overcoming of this contradiction, an illusory immortality, that deepens the condition of sin. Now anxiety reaches its apogee. "At the maximum we find here the dreadful fact that *anxiety about sin produces sin*" (73). Looking back to the esthetic works, especially *Either/Or,* we can understand more fully their implication that love heads toward the transcendence in which "the spirit is so victorious that the sexual is forgotten, and recollected only in forgetfulness" (80).

But before that consciousness of sin and repentance can be reached, it must pass through what the title of the third chapter refers to as "Anxiety as the Consequence of That Sin Which Is the Absence of the Consciousness of Sin." Anxiety is at this point inchoate, fearing nonbeing rather than the radical nothingness that sin is, but is for that reason on the way toward a genuine sense of spirit. "It is quite remarkable," Vigilius observes, "that Christian orthodoxy has always taught that paganism lay in sin, while the consciousness of sin was first posited by Christianity" (93). Fate is the relation to spirit as something external, a becoming guilty through fate rather than through freedom. The genius thus engaged remains in sin because he has not yet reached repentance, the turning point in which anxiety is confronted and surmounted. Mere guilt is not sufficient, for it must also be acknowledged as such within that movement whereby "as soon as guilt is posited, anxiety is gone, and repentance is there" (103). This is the great theme of guilt and repentance

[28] If a man seeks to explain sin scientifically, "if he magnanimously wants to forget himself in the zeal to explain all of humanity, he will become as comical as that privy councilor who was so conscientious about leaving his calling card with every Tom, Dick, and Harry that in so doing he at last forgot his own name." Ibid., 51.

[29] It is worth recalling that the book is dedicated to Martin Møller, who wrote on the immortality of the soul.

around which Kierkegaard's writings have revolved since *Fear and Trembling*. When Vigilius had announced in the introduction that an ethics without sin and repentance is "shipwrecked" (17), he seemed to suggest that Greek ethics lacks a means of addressing its inevitable failure. Now, however, it becomes clear that his objection identifies a deeper inability of Greek philosophy to perceive the movement of freedom by which spirit becomes responsible for itself. Guilt is the indispensable first step in that movement because it is only through repentance that freedom becomes free. Rather than be captured by fate, freedom is captured by guilt, whereby it reaches the freedom of repentance. The anxiety that impinged on the Greeks lacked awareness of what it was, namely, guilt, and therefore also an awareness of temporality as the loss of eternal by which guilt is acquired and also lost. Anxiety as "the relation of freedom to guilt" remains a fixation until it becomes explicitly, as the title of the fourth chapter indicates, an "Anxiety of Sin."

Then anxiety moves beyond itself through repentance. If freedom were to remain in the good, it would know nothing of evil, like God, but because freedom is never what it is, the possibility of evil arises within it. Yet this does not mean that freedom chooses between good and evil as if it were apart from them. Rather, freedom is the differentiation of good and evil that anxiety discloses. "To speak of good and evil as the objects of freedom finitizes both freedom and the concepts of good and evil. Freedom is infinite and arises out of nothing" (112). The movement of freedom, however, depends on moving beyond repentance, by which it can become held fast. The psychological condition must be broken by the urgency that arises from what is beyond it. This is faith, which, without annihilating anxiety, "extricates itself from anxiety's moment of death" (117). We are beyond the realm of psychology here because the movement of freedom cannot be explained in terms of anything other than itself. Anxiety now is twofold, for it is anxiety in the face of evil but it is also anxiety at its incapacity for the good. "The bondage of sin is an unfree relation to the evil, but the demonic is an unfree relation to the good" (119). One is an excess of freedom, the other a deficit of freedom. Each is a possibility of freedom, which, if it is to remain free, must overcome the anxiety in the face of evil and of good that arises within it. There is no "answer," for any such formulation would merely delay the realization "that truth is for the particular individual only as he himself produces it in action" (138). Anxiety in the face of evil once it has arisen becomes a paralysis in regard to the good that is the demonic fixation by which an "inclosing reserve" is chosen over action. This is the romantic and systematizing proclivity to hold existence at bay. The quest for proof, whether emotional or intellectual, must be replaced by the inwardness in which immortality is seized rather than merely contemplated. The difficulty is that "men are not willing to think eternity earnestly but are anxious about it, and anxiety can contrive a hundred evasions. And this is precisely the demonic" (154). That demonic hold of anxiety, Vigilius concludes in his final chapter, must be broken by the saving power of faith through which the individual lays hold of the infinite. Psychology loses its grip when it encounters the unlimited openness of dogma. Like the hypochondriac who experiences real injury as a relief, "he who in relation to guilt is educated in anxiety will rest only in Atonement" (162).

Immobilized in Ethical Without Religious

Kierkegaard had finally hit the target toward which all his writings had tended. He could now see clearly what it was that held the human heart back from the responsibility that beckoned it. It was nothing less than the ethical itself, that articulation of the universal that in its very explication of duty set up a distance between itself and the individual charged with its fulfillment. At last the meaning of the religious, the unsurpassable category of the singular that he had struggled with in *Fear and Trembling* and *Repetition,* could break out of its inscrutability. Far from being in conflict with the ethical, the religious is what removes the hesitation that is the principal obstacle to its actualization. Something of this interrelationship has been present ever since the first Christian encounter with Greek philosophy, and it has endured as a mysterious undertow even within the arc of modern philosophy we have surveyed. Even when the imperative of duty stands higher than faith, the linkage cannot quite be severed. A pervasive intuition of their mutuality was too strong even within the rigors of purified reason. But not even the extraordinary linguistic sensitivity of a Derrida could delineate the indispensability of faith as Kierkegaard did in this last phase. His single-minded focus on existence was able to provide an opening into the mystery that had always been clothed in the ontotheological language of grace. The struggle against the opacity of metaphor that had always constituted the vitality of the theological tradition reaches a culmination in his elaboration of a wholly existential faith. The sheer novelty of his achievement is not only what has delayed its reception, but also what exacted such a heavy cost in Kierkegaard's own struggle toward it. It was only as he approached the end of his projected authorship that he reached an understanding of what he wanted to say.

The two great "concluding" works, *Stages on Life's Way* and *Concluding Unscientific Postscript,* mark the achievement.

Stages, whose very title identifies the continuity that is more than literary, is presented as the "narrative" that had been missing from *Either/Or.* Structurally they are similar. Each is a loose collection of writings discovered by chance and published extraneously. In the case of *Stages,* the final editor bears an even less identifiable relationship to the work than the editor Victor Eremita; now the work is simply stitched together by Hilarius Bookbinder for the amusement of his children and only later is he prevailed upon to publish them. As usual this is only the first layer of pseudonymity. We also meet Judge William and several of the other authors, but by far the longest contributions come either from or through Frater Taciturnus. As his name indicates, the later author can present but not talk about what it is that he presents. The religious perspective dominates the work without providing access to its inner unfolding. Where the analyses of *Either/Or* remained close to the esthetic material on which they operated, now it is clear that the esthetic must find its full unfolding in the religious. Even though the authors are incapable of such a movement through the stages themselves, they recognize that this is the logic of the characters involved. The transparence of the poetic for the religious has reached the point where a wholly new conception of the poetic is itself under way. This is what accounts for the greater fluidity of expression. It raises anew the question of whether there is any religious expression of the religious, an issue that has lain at the core of Kierkegaard's elaborate experiment in pseudonymity. What is clear is that it is the religious that at last provides the "narrative" of the esthetic and the ethical.

The banquet of the opening text, "In Vino Veritas," modeled on Plato's *Symposium,* seems to set the mood of a celebratory farewell. We are treated, through the recollection of one of those present, to the speeches on erotic love given after dinner by Victor Ermita, Johannes the seducer, Constantin Constantius, an unnamed young man, and a fashion designer. The young man initiates the series of speeches by declaiming against the possibility of understanding love as the reason that he will not love. Thinking about life, he must let everything pass. Constantin tries to set his mind at ease with the observation that the soaring of erotic love inspired by a woman is all jest, nothing to be understood. Victor Ermita builds on this theme to show that it is precisely the impossibility of understanding erotic love that inspires the ideality of man by which he reaches beyond immediacy for the infinite. The fashion designer contributes his unique perspective on the utter madness of the feminine that is seduced by femininity, fashion, itself. Finally, Johannes the seducer recommends his own gallant means of surpassing erotic love by turning it into a sport, the cleverness of those who "eat only the bait." In terms already familiar from the diary, he counsels them "to enjoy the deception without being deceived" (79) as the means by which they might attain the eternity promised by love but never delivered unless one loses one's life to it. On their way from the banquet, the guests wander past the house of Judge William, whom they see conversing with his wife. It is a glimpse of the reality of marriage that remains impenetrable to the observers, one of whom, Victor Ermita, stealthily removes certain papers of the judge but is intercepted by the unnamed narrator, who now becomes the conduit for the next writing, "Some Reflections on Marriage, in Answer to Objections by a Married Man."

The voice of Judge William has the same unassuming solidity as his earlier reflections in *Either/Or,* but now he speaks with a fluidity derived from greater existential transparence. His reflections are prefaced by a motto that underlines their juxtaposition to the counsels of the seducer: "The deceived is wiser than one not deceived."[30] It is those who avoid the deception of marriage in the name of pursuing the highest that miss the object of their search because they have overlooked the only means available to human beings. If he had stayed with Penelope Ulysses might have learned as much as he obtained from all the marvels he encountered on his wanderings. "Marriage" William regards "as the highest *telos* of individual life," for anyone who avoids it "crosses out the whole of earthly life in one single stroke and retains only eternity and spiritual interests" (101). Existence without marriage is arrested. What is principally of interest in the subsequent reflections is the explanation of how existence is constituted through an act that takes place within it. This is the deception that is so much the target of romantic anxiety, the loss of erotic love when it is no longer permitted its freedom. The concern is answered by a stirring defense both of marriage as such and of the understanding of existence as contingently grounded in the noncontingent. How is it possible for us to be bound by a resolution that is made in a moment that itself has no constancy? Judge William's understanding now is that marriage is not immediate. It is not like falling in love that now awaits something else to follow from it in the same way that seduction is followed by betrayal. Marriage is different. It does not await some eventuality to determine what it is, "for resolution is present from the very

[30] The remark is derived from Gorgias by way of Plutarch. See *Stages on Life's Way,* 693, n.2.

beginning" (103). The resolution of marriage is not an event in time but the event that constitutes time by removing the suspense that still attaches to the falling in love. Not dependent on any outcome, it sails over the probabilities that might shipwreck it. The ethical, Judge William reveals, is contained within the religious. "The genuinely idealizing resolution then has this characteristic: it is signed in heaven, and then it is countersigned in temporality" (112). One who refrains from marriage out of fear of the challenge of temporality is "a poor wretch who goes through time with his eternal resolution and never gets it countersigned." He is the "rueful knight of reflection," deceived by his own fear of deception, proclaiming like Thales that "out of love of children he will not have any children: the saddest of sayings" (123). By valuing existence so highly, they disvalue it entirely. A young girl is only a phantasm, all possibility; an older woman has found the actuality of motherhood. Initial beauty is insignificant; it is the beauty ever more deeply disclosed by love that counts.[31] But all of this arises if falling in love unfolds not into the false infinite of reflection but into the true infinite of faith. "The resolution is a religious view of life constructed upon ethical presuppositions, a view of life that is supposed to pave the way, so to speak, for falling in love and to secure it against any external and internal danger" (162).

The problem is that once the religious is reached, it might also point beyond marriage. When one is related only by the singularity of the God relationship, there is nothing left of the ethical universal to guide one. Could it be that I am the exception? This is the question that preoccupied Kierkegaard in his relationship to Regine Olsen, although it cannot obviously concern a happily married man like Judge William. He acknowledges it only by way of the contrast with the unexceptionality of marriage. In the case of marriage the religious secures the universal; in the case of the exceptional individual the religious calling goes beyond the universal. Judge William recognizes that such a summit of faith exists, although he is not familiar with it. He does know, however, that such a false infinite often becomes an excuse for avoiding the resolution of marriage, and he warns against the short-circuiting of love. Medieval recourse to a monastery was, in his view, such a foreclosure of existence as if it could "trick spirit out of the divine" (182). Neither in marriage nor in the exceptional life outside of it is there a substitute for the immediacy of

---

[31] "Is an author less rich in ideas because ordinary observation finds nothing, while the reader who has made him his sole study nevertheless discovers an ever-greater wealth?" Ibid., 141.

existence. The resolution that sustains it is contained nowhere but within the resolution itself. Faith is the horizon of faith. For Judge William the life of the exception is the most terrifying of all, precisely because it is sustained by a faith and an existence unknown to him. "Indeed, I shall add this as the worst of terrors, that the very person who wants to be an exception never finds out in this life whether he is" (183). But, we might ask, is this not also true of marriage? It is simply that the judge knows from within the faith that sustains the married life and thus has reached the assurance that is nowhere available but through living it. In neither case has it been possible to "tear open the sealed dispatch that is only to be opened out there and that contains the orders from God" (181).

But what if the orders are that he should not get married, especially if he has already made the ethical determination that he will? This is the situation of the unnamed young man, whose diary and other effects are dragged up from Soborg Lake by Frater Taciturnus, who also provides a "Letter to the Reader" to accompany it. In title, "Guilty / Not Guilty," and in its anonymous derivation, the diary alludes to the "Seducer's Diary" of *Either/Or*. But its closest antecedent is *Repetition*, as Taciturnus confirms in pointing out his own similarity with its author, Constantius. In *Repetition* the young man regains the religious esthetically and by accident; here the breakthrough to the religious is inexorable. The reason is that the young man in "Guilty / Not Guilty" already exists within the ethical and is thus incapable either of the poetic infinity of the seducer or of the esthetic infinity of *Repetition*. He already exists within the universal and has only to acknowledge the contradiction between his own finitude and the infinite commitment he assumes, between his temporality and his eternity, which is resolved only in the movement of faith by which the singular is already located within the divine. The young man here does not remain on the threshold of decision, an "either/or," but has only to live it out completely within the religious alteration of "guilty / not guilty." His problem is perhaps closest of all to that of the ultimate author, Kierkegaard himself, in that he undertook to get married without examining whether he was capable of it. He thought it would be possible to conceal his depression from his bride but then came to realize that such an "inclosing reserve" by which he failed to give himself completely in marriage would subject her to a cruel fraud (394). His impediment is related to the false infinite of the esthete, in that it has its seat in "the power of the imagination and possibility is its nourishment" (391). But it is recognized as a sickness that life rather than poetry must overcome. This is how he arrives at the religious as what provides the possibility of life. It is the realization that "eternity takes away possibility" (391) because it has already completed what remains to be traversed in time. Meanwhile, however, he must struggle with the vicissitudes within time, which now include the burden of guilt he has incurred in relation to his intended. How, then, does faith sustain him? By making it possible for him to live out the condition in which he finds himself. Out of love for his betrothed, he cannot marry her and is borne up by the assurance of love itself. "In faithfulness to her, my resolution is with all my power to remain faithful to the ideas and to my spiritual existence so that I may be convinced by experience that it is spirit that gives life" (396). Refusing to be a seducer and incapable of becoming a married man, he reaches up to the highest meaning of faith.

Yet in the view of Taciturnus he has not quite reached it. Perhaps there is no way for us to tell from the diary, since the resolution occurs in life rather than on paper. Or it may be that the "Letter to the Reader" by Taciturnus must remain silent about the innermost mystery of the soul. That possibility is strongly supported by the author's repeated insistence that he has not himself reached the religious stage and can therefore only comment on it from the outside. Taciturnus's position might be more correctly characterized as pre-religious, for he knows what the religious must be and how it must appear from the outside. In this sense his letter details the external emergence of what is inwardly emergent in the preceding diary. As its ultimate author he is naturally in the best position to identify the literary genre and explain how an "imaginary psychological construction" is required to go beyond the poetic. Poetry was all about the unhappiness of love in the face of obstacles outside, for they enabled it to celebrate love without actually loving. But what about the obstacles to love that arise from within it? These are the ones that can be explored only through the vehicle of the "imaginary psychological construction" that permits us to approach its existential movement. To understand love we have to see that it is not an immediacy but rather a movement that at its apex must reach up to the religious. Viewed externally it bears simultaneously the marks of the tragic and the comic. "This then is the task I have assigned myself: an unhappy love affair in which love is dialectical in itself and in the crisis of infinite reflection acquires a religious aspect" (415–16).

Yet love does not reach the God relationship by which it would be secured. It remains only at the transitional level of the ethical by which it is simultaneously tragic and comic in its failure to be what it is. In the young man of *Stages* we are far from the false infinity of the seducer, but we have not reached the true infinite within which married life is realized.

Anxiety before the good is what holds him back from the life of the good. In this sense the young man falls into the category of the "demonic." By remaining with the ethical, he falls short of the ethical. His is the case that shows most clearly that the ethical calls for the religious because there is no stopping point for love before the complete giving of self. Both the esthetic and the religious head toward that infinite movement, the one falsely the other truly, but the ethical is the point of arrest by which the movement is recognized but not actualized. This is why it is both tragic and comic. What is admirable in the young man's movement of repentance does not reach the peace toward which it is already heading. By remaining in suspension, love has become the demonic. "It is not the dialectical that makes a person demonic – far from it, but it is remaining in the dialectical" (437). Without following the movement all the way toward the religious, he becomes incapable of carrying out the ethical, for if it is carried out only under an external compulsion, it has lost the inwardness that is the reality of love. The idea that we fulfill the law only by going beyond it is, of course, the message of Christ that has been resumed in the modern philosophical revolution we have been following. Here it is presented with particular vividness through its opposite. In the young man, whose situation is perhaps Kierkegaard's most autobiographical, we are able to contemplate by way of his "inclosing reserve" more of the movement toward faith than is otherwise possible. Demonic self-containment heightens the hiddenness it refuses.

The young man does the right thing in breaking off a relationship that cannot become a real union of minds, but engineers the break from the woman's side rather than bearing all of its responsibility himself. In that sense his love did not go all the way. He reaches its goal but not through its means. Both tragic and comic, he is the subject of an imaginary psychological construction because he has not reached the religious healing that is wholly inward. Taciturnus confesses that such a resolution lies beyond his own capacity too, yet he is close enough to recognize that it entails the real unity, not just the combination, of the tragic and the comic. "To be joyful out on 70,000 fathoms of water, many, many miles from all human help – yes, that is something great! To swim in the shallows in the company of waders is not the religious" (470). Self-torment, he notes in language almost identical to Nietzsche's, is merely a halfway house "due to one's being unable to work one's way through to joy" (470). This is what it means to be immobilized in the ethical. It is less an incapacity than an inability to take seriously what it already takes too seriously. "There are," Taciturnus explains, "three existence-spheres, the esthetic, the ethical, the religious.... The ethical is only a transition sphere, and therefore its highest expression is repentance as a negative action" (476). In repentance the ethical already moves beyond itself, for it recognizes its own beginning in sinfulness for which it can never sufficiently make amends. A man who goes through life on the assumption "that he is not a criminal but not faultless, either, is of course comic" (479). He regards himself as a finite product rather than the infinite movement that contains it. Repentance is the most dialectical moment of that movement, for it is the point at which the realization of the inadequacy of any of its moments becomes transparent. There is no stopping point except within that realization itself. Repentance for sin is not simply a matter of returning to a previous condition but of living within a movement that goes ever deeper without ever reaching an end. The realization that repentance is the way of that unending enlargement is its joyful secret (483). It is a movement that is so dialectical that merely exemplifying it, like the seducer who has "become not the deceiver but the deception (492)," can have the effect of regaining the infinite significance of the individual. The happy obscurity of writing in Danish within modest Copenhagen underlines such an author's disdain of any extraneous valuation (487).

Truth Is Subjectivity: Immortality Demonstrated by Being Lived

The reflections on authorship set the scene for the culminating work in this series, the *Concluding Unscientific Postscript to Philosophical Fragments* by Johannes Climacus, although now it is edited by S. Kierkegaard. The veil of pseudonymous authorship is about to slip away as we approach the religious or, more accurately, recognize that the religious can never be spoken about for it can only be lived. This is why *Concluding Unscientific Postscript* can indeed live up to its name despite appearances to the contrary. It can look back on the path that has been traversed and, in the manner of an unscientific postscript, evoke its concluding significance. Thus, we are not immersed in the existential struggle of characters but are now free to formulate the lessons learned by them. Having traversed the great variety of concreteness preceding the *Postscript*, we are less likely to confuse its conclusions for its substance. The author is now free to discourse about his results with less danger of misinterpretation. Such a risk remains, however, as evidenced by the prominence that the work occupies among readers of Kierkegaard, but it was probably a risk judged worth taking if he was at any point going to be able to express his intentions in the entire literary project directly. The mastery of the task that he had now achieved gave him a new facility and freedom of expression that distinguishes the *Postscript* as the work in which Kierkegaard was best able to locate his self-understanding within the modern philosophical movement. A newfound distance concerning his project made it possible to explain it even to himself. The need to interpose pseudonymity had virtually ceased and now made possible "A First and Last Explanation," in which the device is revealed as the indispensable means of its communication.

The work resumes the issue of *Philosophical Fragments,* the question of whether a historical point of departure can be given for eternal consciousness, but now viewed more "systematically" in terms of an understanding of why the existential horizon is the only one in which the question can be handled. It is a systematic or comprehensive account of why the perspective of the system must be abandoned. While mounting a formidable critique of the systems of German idealism, it can also be read as carrying them forward to their innermost inspiration of life as the ultimate sustaining unity. Kierkegaard's deep reading of his philosophical forebears is often disguised by the extent to which he uses them as a foil for his own original meditations, yet it is undeniable that the *Postscript* is replete with awareness of his own tangential approach to their project. This explains the need to address them throughout, in order to emphasize his rejection of anything that approaches a concluding conceptualization. Having thus established his distinctiveness, he is free to organize his thoughts in a remarkably systematic division within the two parts. If the question is that of "my relation to Christianity," it can be addressed from an objective and a subjective point of view. The former leads to a consideration of the historical necessity by which the Christian truth emerges; the latter yields an overview of the necessity of individual appropriation as the only possible access to its truth. System has finally reached its meaning as the horizon within which we live that cannot, therefore, be presented systematically. But for that reason Climacus is now free to approach it "systematically."

Part 1, "The Objective Issue of the Truth of Christianity," is divided into the historical and speculative approaches. By the historical Climacus understands the new biblical criticism, of which he is very much aware and admires. His only concern is to point out that its promise of relevance to faith is highly questionable. The "duplexity" of historical scholarship arises because if scripture is inspired, a critical examination can only call it into question, while if it is not inspired, critical examination would only betray itself in suggesting that it was (26).[32] He warns against the danger of living one's life within the parentheses that confuse knowledge with faith. Far better to concede that the books were not by the authors imputed or were not inspired, from which nothing follows for the existence of either such authors or Christ himself. "To that extent, the believer is still equally free to accept it, equally free, please note, because if he accepted it by virtue of a demonstration, he would be on the verge of abandoning faith" (30). Any attempt to render the objective truth of Christianity fails, not because it cannot be done, but because it misunderstands what the apprehension of Christian truth must be. In a formulation that reinforces the affinity with German idealism, Climacus insists on the impossibility of propositional truth. "If truth is spirit, then truth is inward deepening and is not an immediate and utterly uninhibited relation of an immediate *Geist* to a sum total of propositions, even though this relation is confusingly given the name of the most decisive expression of subjectivity: faith" (37). Heidegger might well have referenced this source for his own conception of truth as the concealment that enables all grasping of truth. It is the insight that was deflected within the project of a speculative grasp of the truth of Christianity, as Climacus explains in the second chapter. The idea that the dialectical living within truth can be fulfilled or resolved is only the speculator's illusion that he can "be exclusively eternal within time" (56).

The issue of truth lies within subjectivity, or as it is later formulated in the extensive second part of the work, "truth is subjectivity." A preliminary first section acknowledges the contribution of Lessing, from whom various theses on the appropriation of truth are derived. Lessing understood that the problem of communicating the truth arose from the impossibility of its appropriation in any way other than through an existential "leap" (93). Correcting "Magister Kierkegaard's" dissertation along the way (90), Climacus clarifies this crucial formulation of the issue with the help of Lessing's reflection on Aristotle's assertion of the impossibility of "passing from one genus to the other (*Posterior Analytics*)." The historically contingent events cannot become the means of reaching the necessity of eternal truth. The "incommensurability between an historical truth and an eternal decision" can be overcome only through a "leap" (*Sprung*) (98). Climacus is careful to elaborate on this most crucial insight in order to explain why Lessing comes closest to its realization, in contrast

---

[32] "Luther's rejection of the letter of James is alone enough to bring him to despair." *Concluding Unscientific Postscript*, 26.

to the overly subjective treatment it receives by Jacobi, Mendelssohn, and even the author of *Fear and Trembling*. Neither emotional nor arbitrary, the leap is rather an appropriation of truth by which subjectivity is transcended. But it was the greatness of Lessing to recognize that it could never be attained without abolishing the condition of its appropriation.[33] If he were given a choice by God between truth and striving for it, he confesses that he would choose striving because "*pure truth is indeed only for you alone*" (106). Lessing had been inoculated against the disease of the system because he understood that it abolishes existence. This is why, Climacus explains, the system of Hegel has no ethics (119). An age infatuated with the system that completes existence is comic in its "world-historical absentmindedness" that forgets what it means to be human (120). "The systematic idea is subject-object, is the unity of thinking and being; existence, on the other hand, is precisely the separation" (123). Existence is différance but it is best discovered through laughter.

With all of these preliminaries out of the way, Climacus is free to go on in the most substantial second section of Part II, "How Subjectivity Must Be Constituted in Order That the Issue Can Be Manifest to It." First there is "becoming subjective," in which the real meaning of freedom is recognized. It has nothing to do with undertaking actions of world-historical significance but rather of seeing their significance within the eternal. Socrates did not "talk about what the times demanded," yet in minding his own business he had a world-historical effect (147). Besides, "trying to restrain the age directly is as futile as for a passenger on a train to try to stop it by clutching the seat ahead of him. . . . No, the only thing to do is to get off the train and restrain oneself " (165). It is in the inwardness of freedom that the meaning of good and evil is disclosed; in the perspective of history it is irrelevant. Indeed, it is only for subjectivity that the distinction arises as the choice by which its existence is determined. In the same way, immortality is not reducible to a tangible quantity, for it is the inner dimension of a being whose existence is transacted within the perspective of eternity. To the extent that the "postulates" of God,

---

[33] This is a very different understanding of the "leap" than the conventional attribution to Kierkegaard of a "leap of faith." The latter is surely one of those instances of the entrapping power of a metaphor that, no matter how frequently corrected, proves extraordinarily difficult to dislodge. Thus, it surely comes as news to most who are familiar with the name of Kierkegaard that, as M. Jamie Ferreira points out, "Kierkegaard never uses any Danish equivalent of the English phrase 'leap of faith.'" "Faith and the Kierkegaardian Leap," in Hannay and Marino, eds., *The Cambridge Companion to Kierkegaard*, 207. For her far less volitional account see Ferreira, *Transforming Vision: Imagination and Will in Kierkegaardian Faith* (Oxford: Clarendon, 1991).

immortality, and freedom are proved, Climacus notes, the faith by which they sustain existence correspondingly declines (177). It is only in subjectivity that we have access to that by which we are constituted. In this light our author can find a more satisfactory formulation for the finite–infinite commitment that had presented such an obstacle to the understanding of marriage. It is a difficulty that arises only because we have not yet understood "the contradiction, which it clearly is, that an immortal spirit has become an existing being" (180).

Having established the priority of subjectivity, Climacus explains in the following chapter how the appropriation of truth takes place. Madness consists in an inwardness that affixes itself to the finite, like Quixote, or an inwardness that forgets itself entirely in taking the external for its own reality, as in the preoccupation with history. Either way it is tragic and comic precisely because it fails to see itself as such. What cures the madness is therefore the realization that our only hold on truth is the movement toward it. "Only momentarily can a particular individual, existing, be in a unity of the infinite and the finite that transcends existing. This instant is the moment of passion" (197). Socrates did not demonstrate immortality in order to live but lived it as his way of demonstrating it. By drawing on his example, Climacus reaches the most famous formulation of the conception of truth that has been at the core of the modern philosophical revolution. "*An objective uncertainty, held fast through appropriation with the most passionate inwardness, is the truth,* the highest truth there is for an *existing* person" (203). What must be kept in mind if this famous sentence is not to be misunderstood, as it frequently is when excerpted out of context, is that the "objective uncertainty" betokens not the absence of truth but only our absence from it. Ignorance, as Socrates understood, is the condition from which philosophy begins. The only thing that Climacus and the modern philosophical revolution add is the recognition of the necessity of ignorance. Ignorance is not just a factual condition that might some day be remedied, but the irremovable horizon of our existence. What is paradoxical or absurd is not the notion of eternal truth but the idea that the existing person has access to it. That is the boundary that can never be surpassed. The paradox cannot be resolved, as attested to by the absence of any Danish word for "*aufheben*" (222), because it is indispensable to existence. Having seen this for himself, Climacus can now acknowledge its significance for an age that has set itself precisely the opposite task of going beyond faith through knowledge. He can even permit himself an appendix at the end of this chapter that recounts the series of books that have appeared in Denmark, beginning with *Either/Or*, and have converged on the same goal of prompting a return to existence from the escapes of the esthetic and the ethical that have predominated.

When existence is constituted around the glimpse of the eternal that of necessity can never be more, the center of emphasis must be the actuality of existence. The following chapter, "Actual Subjectivity, Ethical Subjectivity; the Subjective Thinker," can be appropriately brief. It can consist largely of a warning about the calamity facing mankind if it fails to turn aside from the Gnostic dream of escaping existence. The danger is nothing less than the loss of humanity, the "horror of existence because it is godforsaken" and the reversion to herdlike mentalities that Nietzsche would warn about three decades later (356). The reminder, which can be no more than a reminder, of the necessity of existence is a prelude to the final chapter, "How Can an Eternal Happiness Be Built on Historical Knowledge?" which returns to the original question of the truth of Christianity as the highest illumination of the paradox of existence. This is the general question of existence that is heightened by the Christian paradox of the entry of eternal divinity into time. Climacus, however, does not go beyond acknowledgment of the tension, for as a humorist, he can bring us only to the boundary of the religious that he is himself seeking (451). He can see what the Christian is without fully entering into it, a condition that shares the paradoxical character of Christianity itself. "The individual's eternal happiness is decided in time through a relation to something historical that furthermore is historical in such a way that its composition includes that which according to its nature cannot become historical and consequently must become that by virtue of the absurd" (385). The "absurd" is not the irrational but a synonym for the paradoxical, that which cannot be comprehended, for it is what provides the possibility of comprehension. Christianity is charged with demonstrating this truth that cannot be demonstrated because it can only be lived. No way of communicating the message of Christianity is available other than the witness that is borne in life. This is the meaning of the leap that undertakes what initially is lunacy, yet through its enactment discloses its validity. Eternal happiness can be laid hold of only by existing within it. Ethics, too, is held by this paradox of taking a stand on what cannot be demonstrated, but it is only in Christianity that the inescapably existential character of the paradox becomes clear. Faith is the realization that "the existence of the absolute ethical good can be demonstrated only by the individual who, himself existing [*existerende*], expresses that it exists [*er til*]" (424). But it must be a Christianity that has abandoned its own illusion of a shortcut to God by entering a monastery, which ventures very little, or the modern temptation to elide itself with knowledge or emotion, an extremity that ventures nothing at all.

The difficulty of the venture is the measure of its truth, for it is only if faith entails a struggle that it draws the entirety of the self into the relationship in which it is related to God. A humorist, like Climacus, can grasp it externally as a contradiction between aspiration and achievement, but it is only the religious man who enters into the trial by which he lays hold of the eternal. Even *Fear and Trembling* is regarded as attempting to depict too completely the knight of faith, precisely what cannot be depicted because it is really the "knight of hidden inwardness" (499). The contradiction cannot be mastered; it can only be lived. Irony, by which the distance between appearance and reality is concealed, is to be favored over humor, by which the distance between the two is explicit. "Immediacy has the comic outside itself; irony has it *within* itself" (521). Irony is the link between the ethical and the religious, indicative of the realization that the demands of the ethical can never be adequately fulfilled. This is the moment of repentance by which the religious man lives within the impossibility of exonerating his infinite guilt. He has passed through the stage by which he seeks to overcome his guilt in a particular instance by the discovery that even such an effort indicates that he is "essentially guilty" (528). "The totality of guilt comes into existence for the individual by joining his guilt, be it just one, be it utterly trivial, together with the relation to an eternal happiness. That was why we began by saying that the consciousness of guilt is the decisive expression for the relation to eternal happiness" (529). In leading us thus to the boundary of faith, which, by definition, cannot be presented further, Climacus has lived up to his name and his nature.[34] The editor, S. Kierkegaard, can step forward in an appendix to acknowledge as much. This is followed by "A First and Last Explanation," in which the pseudonymous authorship in its entirety is admitted by Kierkegaard in a leave taking that is at the same time not a leave taking. While acknowledging that he is the ultimate author, Kierkegaard recommends that the pseudonymous authors continue to be cited as such, for he is only a "*souffleur*" (prompter) or a "secretary." Consistent with these texts' guiding insight that they are written not primarily for the public but for their author, the single individual, Kierkegaard's literary device reveals a far-reaching transformation of our understanding of writing that finds full explication

---

[34] "Faith is the objective uncertainty with the repulsion of the absurd, held fast in the passion of inwardness, which is the relation of inwardness intensified to its highest." *Concluding Unscientific Postscript*, 611.

in Derrida. When the book writes the author, there is nothing outside the text. We should not be surprised, therefore, that the announcement of neither the actual authorship nor its conclusion should actually be what it claims. *Concluding Unscientific Postscript* marked only the end of Kierkegaard's first authorship.

Saying What Cannot Be Said: The Age

Postscript did, however, constitute the end of a distinct phase in Kierkegaard's development. Never again would he feel the need to enlist such a range of pseudonymous collaborators, or invent characters as a poetic means of working out what could be worked out only in life. Now Kierkegaard was in full possession of what he wanted to say, or at least as fully as any writer can expect to be. There were still surprises and he continued to write "upbuilding discourses" of various types, only now the distinction between them and the more exploratory genres began to disappear. All of his writings converged on the "upbuilding" of which the author was as much in need as the reader. He had worked through to the conclusion of the existential revolution of modern philosophy in grasping that its truth could only be lived. Nothing more could be said, for the saying would necessarily become a nondoing. Philosophy, therefore, now became a way of not-saying as the opening of existence. This is the meaning of Christianity, which has from its beginning been a way of life rather than a doctrine and always finds its rejuvenation by deepening its actuality rather than by comprehending it. The insight, barely glimpsed by Kant, that theoretical reason constitutes a principal obstacle to practical reason, has now become unmistakable. What the status of the insight is, theoretical or practical, cannot finally be determined for it partakes of both, a sure indication that the distinction cannot ultimately be maintained. There is no getting outside the practical imperative of existence, even to theorize. Once that unsurpassability is acknowledged, we gravitate toward that horizon that can never be reached because we always remain within it. Christianity is the transcendence that eternally enlarges existence. In this sense Nietzsche was right that there was only one Christian and he died on the cross.

When the accent has fallen so heavily on existence, it is natural that the second phase of Kierkegaard's career would take a dramatic turn. He would exist in a far more public mode than his previous pursuit of anonymity had suggested. But even in his public notoriety he was careful to remain hidden. How do you bear witness to inwardness in public? Kierkegaard's answer was that you take care to be misunderstood, at least by the public. This is surely the meaning of his strange provocation of the "*Corsair* affair," by which he goaded a local literary rag into attacking him. Something similar occurred in his more hesitant but still fateful confrontation with Bishop Mynster and the ecclesiastical establishment. It was almost as if Kierkegaard, instead of inventing characters, had himself slipped into the roles as a means of ironic communication. By being what one is not, one calls attention to what cannot be called to attention directly. Kierkegaard bore the social incomprehension and isolation that resulted with great, if not unbroken, equanimity. No doubt he had the consolation of living as purely as possibly within the mandate of eternity when all mundane approval had been withdrawn from him. It was a remarkably self-sacrificing witness and the deepest service possible for an age that so badly needed it. Having come to understand that one can do nothing for another human being, least of all for a whole age, Kierkegaard was free to do everything he could for all of us. It was a clarity that definitively broke with the schemes of emancipation that dominated the modern imagination, through the realization that the world can be saved only one solitary individual at a time. Indeed, there is hardly a "world" or an "age" at all when we see that each individual exists within an eternal scale of measurement that utterly outweighs any finite calculation. It was to the pellucid formulation of that insight that Kierkegaard's last works are dedicated.

The preeminence of Kierkegaard in the modern philosophical revolution rests on his refusal to merely talk about the limits of language and his insistence on actually overcoming them. In the late works he says what cannot be said. This is their novelty and strangeness. He has solved the problem by knowing that we can communicate what otherwise cannot be said by living it. Existence, the thread that the Greeks were so concerned about losing, has now been regained as the indispensable support of philosophy. To the extent that the achievement has been realized, our exposition can be comparatively brief. It is announced right after *Postscript* with a literary review of the novel by Thomasine Gyllambourg, *Two Ages* (1845). The two ages revealed through the characters of the novel were the revolutionary and the postrevolutionary, with their corresponding traits of passionateness and passionlessness. It provided Kierkegaard with an opportunity to locate himself within a historical context pervaded by revolutionary nostalgia. He could point out that the revolutionary impulse, for all its apparent vitality, was essentially a negation of existence rather than the affirmation it claimed to be. Perhaps it was the age of formlessness and leveling that followed that drew closer to the awakening to the eternal that was required, at least by evincing its own bankruptcy. But what could be done when the revolutionary promise had collapsed? It would have to be recalled to the existential truth it had mistaken for a historical event. The equality of all human beings before God has nothing to do with an age, but only with their irreducibility to the features of an age. Theirs is an equality in responsibility that exists nowhere other than in its exercise. The individual of such insight has no message for the age: that is his message. Such individuals "will be *unrecognizable,* like plainclothes police carrying their badge secretly and giving support only negatively" (107).

An interesting failed attempt at prophetic witness was the case of the deposed pastor, Adler, who, precisely because he claimed to have been given a revelation, showed that he had had no revelation. It was an episode that again provoked Kierkegaard to write, both for the clarification it yielded and because of the affinity with his own project. Adler had even managed to sound eerily close to some of the pseudonymous authors. *The Book on Adler* pushed the understanding of revelation to its limits by way of "The Difference Between an Apostle and a Genius," which was published separately. The apostle "has no other proof than his own statement," while the genius carries the proof of his authority within himself. By claiming to possess an inspiration, Adler identifies himself with the latter rather than the former. Adler had been unsuccessful in defending himself before the bishop by claming that he had received no new doctrine, only the instruction to publish the fact of his reception of a revelation. But this, Kierkegaard notes, is the crucial distinction, for it concerns whether the source of authority is within or without. If it is within, the individual remains a Hegelian because he has retained mastery over it. Only if the revelation is wholly from outside, from Christ, is it one within which the individual lives with no possibility of detaching himself from it. Even the claim to have received a revelation is already a separation from it because it has become one more barrier to carrying it out. "Most men live in relation to their own self as if they were constantly out, never at home," so that even religious enthusiasm finds expression in resolutions to be taken up in the future and never in the present (*Book on Adler,* 103–4).[35] Everything is done to avoid acting. In a postscript Kierkegaard diagnoses the recent revolutions of 1848 as a similar failure

[35] "It is always well to know that you are immortal, in order to be on the safe side when at some time you die; but that, most likely, will not be for some years. Thus they do not at the same moment think the thought of death together with the consciousness of immortality; they do not bear in mind that every moment one does not have the consciousness of immortality within oneself one is actually not immortal." *Book on Adler,* 105.

to act by making action something external to the self (315–20). A man who had received a revelation would act upon it rather than talk about it, for he would realize that the revelation is that there is no revelation apart from his living it out. The individual is outside the universal in his God relationship.

Love Cannot Fail

Life exceeds reflection on it. If philosophy is to intimate its own incapacity, it must locate itself within the same existential movement. Something of that transparency is reached in the first of these culminating works in Kierkegaard's development, *Works of Love: Some Christian Deliberations in the Form of Discourses*. The deviation from the form of "discourses" seems intended to emphasize that the author himself is engaged in the deliberations, for they are not "works on love" but "of love" itself. At last he had found the means of bringing together erotic love (*Elskov*), friendship (*Kjerlighed*), and Christian love. It is the command "You *shall* love" that allows love to be itself, for then it is anchored in nothing beyond its own eternity (38).[36] Equally, only when it is love of the neighbor "*is the selfishness in the preferential love rooted out and the equality of the eternal preserved*" (44). Both erotic love and friendship are defined by their object, while love for the neighbor is defined by the love (*Kjerlighed*) that is God himself (66). The sentiments are so simply expressed that one could be inclined to read them as mere exhortations to Christian love, but this would be to miss Kierkegaard's essential insight that love of the neighbor is the realization of all other love. It is the unsurpassable horizon of love. "*Love for the neighbor has, namely, the perfections of eternity*" (65). The performance of duty for duty's sake that had so occupied Kant has now been reached in the love that fulfills the law because it is free, loving only out of love. But this means that the God relationship takes priority over all others in a person's life, where priority is not just formal but existential in the same way as Levinas sought to suggest it. The luminosity of Kierkegaard's formulations arises from the even more single-minded focus he devoted to this central idea.

The most intimate relationship of each human being, he emphasized, is with God because he is the one before whom the possibility of

---

[36] "The command is one that frees our love from the accidents of our inclinations and misfortunes of our lives. Such a commanded love can be ours in a deeper sense than is possible for an emotion that is rooted in what is momentary." Evans, *Kierkegaard's Ethics of Love*, 197.

confidentiality can be unfolded. Between human beings confidentiality "ultimately becomes only confidentiality about confidentiality. Only God *is confidentiality*" (152). The openness of one human being to another arises from their prior openness to God, who is openness itself. This is the eschatological, the element of the inexpressible that remains within their openness to one another. This is why their confidentiality cannot be broken or lost. It abides whatever the consequence. Love does not depend on finding a particular response or on finding a particular person. It goes out unconditionally toward the person who is present (174). "When it is a duty in loving to love the people we see, *there is no limit to love; if the duty is to be fulfilled, love must be limitless, it is unchanged, no matter how the object becomes changed*" (167). Love is an infinite debt: "*the one who loves by giving, infinitely, runs into infinite debt*" (177). Once love begins to take a measure of itself by means of something finite, it is out of its element; it is like an arrow swiftly moving so long as it does not stop to think about itself. Again this is not an avocation, but the very reality from which love lives. "Before infinity's requirement even your greatest effort is but child's play, by means of which you will not be able to become self-important, since you learn to understand how infinitely much more is required of you" (185). Love is free to love when it has become an infinite duty to God by which all that is giddy and selfish has been removed from it. It is in relation to God who is love that duty becomes the complete forgetfulness of self. "The deficiency in even the most noble human enthusiasm is that, as merely human, in the ultimate sense *it is not powerful itself, because it has no higher power over itself.* Only the God-relationship is earnestness; the earnestness is that the task is pressed to its highest because there is one who controls with the power of eternity; the earnestness is that the enthusiasm has a power over itself and a control upon itself" (190).

The duty to love by which love is freed to love forms the first series of deliberations. In the second series Kierkegaard deliberates on the transformation of love that is thereby effected, not as a result, but as the mode of its existence. Love builds up through love itself, thereby joining with the divine initiative that alone "loves forth love" (217). Unlike the seducer, the one who loves cannot be deceived, because he seeks nothing in return. He cannot be tricked out of the gift he tenders unconditionally (242). Love cannot be disappointed, because it already lives within the eternity of its hope. The secret of love is that it never seeks its own, for it has already abandoned itself to the love by which it lives beyond itself. Love knows that "the only true object of a human being's love is *love,* which is God, which therefore in a more profound sense is not any object, since he is Love itself" (264–65).[37] The one who loves, loves anonymously and, in words that recall Derrida's analysis of the gift, "he gives in such a way that it looks as if the gift were the recipient's property" (278). Love covers a multitude of sins with forgiveness rather than become privy to them. It cannot fail because love abides. The individual may fall away from love, but love itself cannot fall away because it is eternal. By holding to love, death is overcome because eternity has already been reached. "After all, how would the love that abides waste away? Can immortality waste away? But what is it that gives the human being immortality, what else but the love that abides" (311)?

The mercifulness of love is most in evidence when it can give nothing and do nothing. Then the victory is for love itself. This is above all our relationship toward the one who is dead. It is in relation to the "works of love" that Kierkegaard's enigmatic references to the company of the dead become clear, including the awareness of the meaning of his own name.[38] Love is glimpsed most profoundly in relation to the dead, for whom nothing more can be done and from whom nothing more can be received. "*The work of love in recollecting one who is dead is a work of the most unselfish love*" (349). Someone dead, who is unchanging and does everything to make himself forgotten, can be held onto purely only by love. It is in such a work of love that love is praised because it makes us aware that we are nothing apart from the love by which we are sustained in love. When love receives nothing, when it loves the unlovable, it can rejoice most completely in love. This is for Kierkegaard the meaning of Christianity, which "turns our attention completely away from the external, turns it inward, and makes every one of your relationships to other people into a God-relationship" (376). We might say that Christianity is the awareness that we do not exist from ourselves but rather from the infinity by which we are held inwardly. God, as the infinite we can never surpass, is the one within whom we exist. He does not require anything from us, yet he requires everything of us while, at the same time, making us see that nothing is from us (379). Beyond the gift is the giving we have already received as a gift. There is no stepping outside of existence. We

---

[37] "To be able to seek love and oneself to become the object of love, yet without seeking one's own, is reserved for God alone. But no human being *is love.*" *Works of Love*, 264.

[38] "The number of confessors does not create a kind of company any more than 'the number of the dead creates a kind of company' in the quiet garden. *Purity of Heart Is to Will One Thing, Upbuilding Discourses in Various Spirits*, 150–51. See Joakim Garff, *Søren Kierkegaard*, 3, on the derivation of *kirkegaard*, "churchyard" or cemetery, as the family name.

have only the choice of opening to the infinite disclosed in each moment or turning away from it. Depending on which we choose, we become capable of either believing in the forgiveness we have begun to make our own or disbelieving it because our whole lives have made it incredible (380). To the loving, God's rigorousness appears to be leniency, but to the unloving, his leniency is rigorousness. "God's relationship to a human being is at every moment to infinitize what is in the human being at every moment" (384). Love is in that sense the infinite from which we exist infinitely.

Despair as the Opening Toward God

Kierkegaard's capacity to evoke existence continued to grow through these luminous late works. The author, who had thought his task complete, was no doubt as surprised as anyone at the deepening responsibility placed on him by the ever more transparent reach of his language. A body of work that could have culminated with *Works of Love* is followed by a return to pseudonymity under the pressure of existential lucidity. *The Sickness unto Death: A Christian Psychological Exposition for Upbuilding and Awakening* is authored by Anti-Climacus, a pseudonym that designates the writer's higher standing than Climacus's. Anti-Climacus has reached the religious level that was the object of Kierkegaard's own upbuilding, while Climacus remained firmly outside of it. To the extent that the Christian designated the horizon of existence, it would be inappropriate for Kierkegaard to suggest that he had actually reached that toward which he too strained as long as he lived. Above all he wanted to avoid any hint that he had a plan to resolve the ills of the age. Any such implication would place Kierkegaard himself outside as master of the plan, rather than as the deepest witness to his own need of the plan. He shuddered to think, in line with Fénelon, of how "dreadful for a man if God had expected more of him" (xviii). Kierkegaard, too, needed a "religious poet" in order to exist beyond himself in the infinite. Where earlier he could diagnose anxiety as the arrest of existence that fails to unfold itself, especially in *The Concept of Anxiety*, he now lays bare the deepest source of that refusal as a turn away from God in *The Sickness unto Death*. As with most of the writings after the planned first authorship, there is no parallel series of upbuilding discourses. They are all in that mode and take their point of departure from a scriptural meditation, an instruction given in advance. In this case it is the remark of Jesus before he raises Lazarus: "This sickness is not unto death" (Jn 11: 14).

What then is the "sickness unto death" that even rising from the dead could not cure? Sickness unto death is despair, that turning away from existence that cannot ultimately be accomplished. Either the attempt is made to escape existence, including even suicide (which still aims at a certain existence), or the impulse is to overcome despair by means of the very same self that is in despair. This is why the person in despair is never despairing over something, but rather over himself, "or to put it even more accurately, what is intolerable to him is that he cannot get rid of himself" (19). It is that deathlessness that is eternity's claim on him, as evidenced by his incommensurability with anything less than the infinity of God. All who have not become Christian are thus in despair; they differ only in the extent of their self-awareness. Even happiness, that moment of rest in the beautiful, is despair because it is an arrest of the spirit that knows it cannot be arrested. "It requires extraordinary reflection, or more correctly, it requires great faith to be able to endure reflection upon nothing – that is, infinite reflection. Consequently, even that which is utterly beautiful and lovable, womanly youthfulness, is still despair, is happiness" (26). The only waste of life is one that fails to find itself in despair before what is and thereby fails to behold its infinite relation to God. Returning to the problem of self-reflection that had formed the core of German idealism, especially Schelling's attention to its unattainability, Anti-Climacus now grasps its existential source in the "mirror of possibility" (27). But it must not be the mere contemplation of possibility that impedes action. Only that possibility that has become necessity carries existence forward. Salvation from despair arises through the realization that "for God everything is possible" (39).

The great misconception of this text is that it provides an "anthropology," for here we can separate the "anthropological" from the "ontological" or "theological" even less than in *The Concept of Anxiety*. Such distinctions no longer work when philosophy has become thoroughly existential and now moves within the realization that there is nothing outside the text of its own unfolding. Kierkegaard saw this more clearly than anyone. His celebrated observation about the creator of the system living in a shed outside cannot itself yield a further system.[39] Anti-Climacus leads us all the way down to the source of failure. Despair over being a self is seized

[39] "A thinker erects a huge building, a system, a system embracing the whole of existence, world history, etc., and if his personal life is considered, to our amazement the appalling and ludicrous discovery is made that he himself does not personally live in this huge, domed palace but in a shed alongside it, or in a doghouse, or at best in the janitor's quarters." *Sickness unto Death*, 43.

by a defiance that aims at mastering its condition. "This is a simulated earnestness. Like Prometheus stealing fire from the gods, this is stealing from God the thought – which is earnestness – that God pays attention to me; instead, the self in despair is satisfied with paying attention to itself, which is supposed to bestow infinite interest and significance upon his enterprises, but it is precisely this that makes them imaginary constructions" (69). Despairing of being a self, it nevertheless remains a self in need of the eternal. Its mastery is its despair. In words that eerily prefigure Zarathustra, although, for that very reason, probably not Nietzsche, who stood outside his most famous character, Anti-Climacus notes the ultimate infuriating prospect that "eternity could get the notion to deprive him of his misery" (72). It is in the demonic, the deliberate closure against the good, that the opening toward God is most clearly evoked. Nothing less than God can break the hardness of heart that has gripped the self. The second part of *The Sickness unto Death* turns to the realization that "despair is sin."

Despair is like sin, not mere weakness, but rather its deliberate endorsement. Sin is in this sense always against the spirit. It is overcome only by faith in which "the self in being itself and in willing to be itself rests transparently in God" (82). Christianity lifts the self outside of all self-limitation by virtue of its "offense," the absurd and incredible realization that God cares about the self. It is for this reason that Christianity cannot be defended, for that would disparage what has reality only as a movement of faith (87). The problem is not ignorance, as Socrates suggests, but the turning away from the good that is sin. It is overcome only by faith in its overcoming. Even modern philosophy, with its *cogito ergo sum*, is already a movement from knowing to being and, in this sense, always points beyond itself toward what it cannot comprehend. Such an offense against reason is most completely expressed in Christianity. It does not even posit that we can know what sin is before we have begun to turn away from it through faith, for in itself sin "is ignorance of what sin is" (96). The general principle is formulated by Anti-Climacus with a penetration that is hardly surpassed by Heidegger. "The secret of all comprehending is that this comprehending is itself higher than any position it posits; the concept establishes a position, but the comprehension of this is its very negation" (97). It is in this sense that the Christian teaching about sin is not a dogma to be comprehended but "a paradox that must be believed" (98) if it is to be acted upon. Hereditary sin is not an item of information to be accepted or rejected. It arises from the realization that the individual is always more than the species through his existential movement beyond any species determinations. In this sense he bears the full weight, and more, of sin transmitted by the species. He is both more sinful and more capable of perfection (120). What had been glimpsed more obscurely in *Fear and Trembling* as the superiority of the individual to the universal can now be grasped more clearly through the religious movement. The relation to God by which the individual is always more than he is, the overcoming of despair, is the point of his greatest existential transparence. This, Anti-Climacus concludes, is "the definition of faith" (131).

To Be the Truth Is the Only True Explanation of What Truth Is

Having thus reached the core of Christianity, Kierkegaard now felt himself ready to address the problem of Christendom directly. *Practice in Christianity* was his critique of that establishment Christianity that had completely occluded the truth of Christianity. But it was a critique that took the form of a defense of Christianity and, as we might expect, under the form of his own upbuilding by way of the pseudonymous Anti-Climacus again. The question of why Christ does not reveal himself more directly, the complaint that the Grand Inquisitor would later voice of Christ's apparent indifference to the misery of men (60), is now understood to be not merely incidental to the revelation of Christ, but its very essence. He reveals himself by not revealing himself. This is why we learn nothing from history about him, for "Christ himself *willed* to be the abased and lowly one" who is seen only by faith (33). His compassion for human beings was not limited to what they might be able to endure; it went deeper still. "Blessed is he who is not offended by me" is the secret of his communication with men and women. Offense is what opens the possibility of faith. "He is love, and yet at every moment he exists he must crucify, so to speak, all human compassion and solicitude – for he can become only the object of faith" (137). With this insight that concealment of self is the way to draw the other out of himself, we are launched into a sermon by Magister Kierkegaard that Anti-Climacus included in the volume. It follows the implication that the suffering of the follower of Christ must also be deepened. Our suffering, too, is the way by which Jesus lifts us up toward himself, freeing us from the reward of the relative to receive the eternal inwardly. Christ seems to turn away from marriage, the world, ordinary life because he is ever moving us toward the joy that is deeper. "Thus Christ is the truth in the sense that to *be* the truth is the only true explanation of what truth is" (205). Thinking and being, whose unity was glimpsed by the pre-Socratics, are really united only through existence.[40]

In the same way, the great theological conundrum of grace and freedom also resolves itself within the existential movement. In *For Self-Examination*, Kierkegaard under his own name as a doer rather than an achiever of the word gives witness to the inward deepening of which he himself is as much in need as the "present age," for whom it is intended. Grace and works must be held together as Luther, on a more accurate reading, intended. "Christianity's requirement is this: your life should express works as strenuously as possible; then one thing more is required – that you humble yourself and confess: But my being saved is nevertheless grace" (17). Like the gambler, who is saved if he gives up gambling just for an hour but lost if he postpones the first step, there must be no gap between knowing and doing. There is no "I" left over when in doing my all I deny that the initiative is in any sense my own.[41] Everything must be surrendered, as Abraham was prepared to sacrifice the one he loved most, in the movement of the spirit that transcends life. Relying on nothing, we lay hold of God. This is the only meaning of hope worthy of the name. "It is against hope, because according to that purely natural hope there was no more hope; consequently this hope is against hope" (82). In the same way, it is only when love in loving the unlovable goes beyond itself that love can truly be called love. Faith is the point at which we glimpse what cannot be more than glimpsed because our existence is contained within it. Even when writing directly about faith, as Kierkegaard is doing here, it can be only under the premise that he strains toward becoming, but is not yet, a man of faith.

Judge for Yourself!, the title of the companion work, captures the limit of our perception. Christianity does not trade on probabilities of success. It knows it will not be victorious and in this is its victory, the victory of

---

[40] "The being of truth is not the direct redoubling of being in relation to thinking, which gives only thought-being, safeguards thinking only against being a brain-figment that is not, guarantees validity to thinking, that what is thought is – that is, has validity. No, the being of truth is the redoubling of truth within yourself, within me, within him, that your life, my life, his life expresses the truth approximately in the striving for it, that your life, my life, his life is approximately the being of the truth in the striving for it, just as the truth was in Christ a *life*, for he was the truth." *Practice in Christianity*, 205.

[41] Luther "forgot what he himself was too honest to know, what an honest soul he himself was." *For Self-Examination*, 24.

God. "Become sober," Kierkegaard counsels, so that "one's understanding is action" (119).[42] Pull away from the establishment Christianity that moderates the unconditional demand and supports it with scholarly justifications. Recognize that only the imitation of Christ can support the imitation of Christ. While the Middle Ages mistook Christian existence for entry into a monastery and Luther's rejection of works became a work itself, now it must become apparent that the truth of Christianity lies nowhere but in the hiddenness by which it is lived. "One single act done in true self-denial and renunciation of the world is infinitely more awakening" than the ambiguous witness of "one million clergymen" (124). Faith, to the extent that it is based on something other than faith, is not really faith. As an even more acute psychologist than Nietzsche, Kierkegaard could unerringly detect the gap that opened between the thought and the deed. Only the deed that sprang directly from its source could bear witness to the truth by which it was constituted. My task, he explained, is not just to bear with the adversity that assails me, but "to find joy and blessedness in this" so that offense does not intervene between faith and existence (204). Thinking about the transformation that is thus worked, the soul can look back, in Kierkegaard's own prayer, and say that "what I suffered or that which pained me was really that in this adversity I saw a proof that everything had gone wrong for me. But now when you, kind Governance, explain it to me and explain yourself to me, I now wish only to remain out there in an understanding with you" (207).

[42] "An expert judge [Pascal] in this matter has said that one rarely sees anyone who writes humbly about humility, doubtingly about doubt, etc." *Judge for Yourself!* 119.

Epilogue

Modernity as Responsibility

A study that has sought to be a meditation on the priority of existence over all reflection cannot have a conclusion. We cannot abandon the central insight of the enterprise merely because we have reached an end of the account. Falling back into conventional patterns would suggest we have reached an answer when all along we have emphasized the singular discovery of modern philosophy as inconclusiveness. Endlessness has been the guarantee of its vitality. Or rather it has been the pursuit of an end that could never be reached that has ensured its proliferation. Misconceptions have ever arisen from the conceit that we might yet be on the verge of grasping the goal of our search. The confusion has been of millennial scope, for it has rested on a fundamental misunderstanding of the very possibility of philosophy, of science, and of civilization. Attainment of the goal is fatal to the process of attainment itself. Now we are in a better position to appreciate why this must be so, for there is no goal external to the movement by which our whole existence is drawn. We cannot possess that which already possesses us so fully that it underpins all possibility of possession by us. But this also means that we can never lose that which we seek. Anxiety about the loss of existence, of the failure of the philosophical quest itself, need no longer deflect us into an illusory grasp at certitude. The burden of fashioning a cast-iron conclusion has been lifted. Life has been released into the openness that it must always rightfully claim.

Not even the conclusion of a project devoted to the problem of modernity can tempt us to pronounce on what cannot be pronounced upon because it first requires to be lived. By veering into prognoses and prognostications, we take the first step away from that responsibility of living. This is an insight that has been hard won through each of the three volumes of this study. It is an insight that defies the easy demand for the

461

ready-made, the tidy morsel of insight that can be conveniently packaged for distribution. What has been overlooked in all such discussions ever since Weber made the problematization of modernity a theme is that it has no answer as such. Neither the contradictions nor the crises of modernity constitute a problem, for they are the very horizon within which we exist. There is no stepping back to secure a vantage point of theoretical penetration. The puzzle waiting to be solved is none other than how we are going to live, for there is no imputation that can avoid the "so what?" question. Modernity is the ineliminable responsibility we face. To regard it as a topic for dissection is to shirk the moral obligation addressed to us. We cannot simultaneously hold at an objective distance what we have been called upon to accept as the burden of our own existence. There is no upbuilding discourse concerning modernity unless it includes the upbuilding of the discussants themselves.

This intuition has been a guiding thread from the very inception of my project. Dissatisfaction with the tone of sham superiority with which the issue of modernity had been discoursed has been an abiding intimation. Only now can its necessity be acknowledged in principle. There is no crisis other than the crisis, the judgment, under which each one of us stands, for modernity is not a condition apart from those who bear it inwardly as the inescapable choice between good and evil. It was those who thought that they could stand apart from that inexorability who gave the deepest evidence of the crisis, for a crisis does not consist simply of the breakdown of order, but of the failure of the restorative forces that ought to emerge in response. *After Ideology* was deliberately written to avoid furnishing one more brilliant diagnosis of the totalitarian upheaval of the modern world. The subtitle, *Recovering the Spiritual Foundations of Freedom,* underlines the existential imperative that informs the account – that is, that there is no adequate diagnosis of what went wrong that does not already begin to move in the direction of remediation. This was why the volume focused so selectively on those few figures who not only articulated the spiritual failure of modernity, but had followed the existential logic of such an undertaking to regain contact with the truth of order beyond the devastation. An abundance of critiques of the unreality of the ideological schemes of transformation have been available from the start. What has been missing is the deeper indwelling that is prepared to find its way through to the other side. The spell of revolutionary intoxication could be broken only by the encounter with the inner power of transfiguration. It is for this reason that there can be no adequate analysis of the totalitarian convulsion that engulfed our world, and still reverberates in the present, without the frank acknowledgment that it arose from the misdirection of spiritual longings that can be assuaged in no way other than their authentic inner fulfillment. Failure to acknowledge that holocausts are not primarily external phenomena, but first exist as a possibility within each of us, has been the principal reason we have still not been able to clarify the enormity of our recent modern past. No amount of historical documentation can substitute for the inward movement of repentance that alone anchors such an effort in reality. *After Ideology* was thus never about the future of the world from which ideological militancy had receded. It sought to remain as much as possible in the existential now of the struggle against murder that is the only point of luminosity for the analysis.

A similar imperative was required to understand the nonapocalyptic component of the modern world that had unfolded into the political form of liberal democracy. Through a series of pragmatic adjustments streaming from medieval Christendom, the liberal political tradition had come to define regimes of stability and decency that could ultimately defeat the worst totalitarian excesses. Yet the secret of their durability and success had eluded the finest commentators. Misled by the surface incoherence they presented, most observers had concluded that they were nothing more than a house of cards destined to fall before the totalitarian onslaughts of one stripe or another. Their inner staying power had eluded critics of the Right and the Left, while their defenders gave wildly improbable explanations of their source in contract, rights, or legality itself. Any serious account would, of course, have begun with the recognition that it is precisely fidelity to such principles that stands more in need of explanation than the principles themselves. The reason for this intellectual failure, explored in *The Growth of the Liberal Soul,* was that there could be no analysis of liberal democracy from outside of the convictions that underpin it. One could not absolve oneself from responsibility from the outcome of the analysis, as if one were equally capable of living in some alternative form not grounded in mutual respect for the dignity and rights of one another. No explanation was possible other than the explanation that constituted the very reality of liberal democracy itself. Nothing higher could be affirmed than the infinite worth of each human being and the imperative of building that recognition into the structure of regimes of self-government. Once that recognition emerges, the secret of the incredible stability of liberal polities begins to disclose itself – that is, that these are regimes that are not only rooted in mutual concern and respect, but recurrently call forth the interior movement by which such recognition is heightened and enlarged. They have no secret other than the existential dynamic by which the liberal soul is enlarged to fulfill its indispensable civic responsibility.

Such an inward movement is, of course, invisible to the critic who beholds only the flimsy externals of constitutions and institutions. Only when responsibility for their operation is borne within does their incredible power become manifest as a sacred duty to be fulfilled by none other than oneself. Perhaps not coincidentally the perspective of the critic is peculiarly susceptible to this blindness, for in prioritizing the declaration of what is wrong, one has automatically excused oneself from doing anything about it. Critique carries its own unnoticed fatality, since the issuance of judgments is both more satisfying and less arduous than the untidy struggle for remediation. This is, of course, why the extensive critiques of liberal atomistic nihilism have contributed so little to the task of reform. Their starting point often lies in such wildly utopian fantasies as that we could revert to traditional small-scale communities or that we could readily abandon the only viable public moral language of rights for an alternative nowhere on the horizon. By contrast, only those who have assumed responsibility for making liberal democracy work can speak with the requisite authority concerning its strengths and weaknesses. Pontificating from the sidelines, while it may be a fascinating and agreeable pastime, can never be confused with the actions of those whose own exertions are the means by which the game is sustained. Whatever may be lost in conceptualizing the overall pattern of the movements, it is hard to deny that the vantage point of the participant both requires and provides a vastly deeper access to the reality that is lived. It is this imperative of living that ultimately means that liberal democracy is, like the larger modern world of which it is a part, a reality that can be known only from within.

Modernity cannot in this sense be comprehended, for to do so would be to remove oneself from living it. This was the insight that Kierkegaard had most fully realized. He had nothing but disdain for endless discussions of the age that betokened nothing so much as the deadliness of an age that has ceased to live, for the sake of reflecting on itself. One could not do both. He had an unerring nose for the mendacity of earnest conversations about the crisis of the time and put his finger on the existential emptiness behind them. All such denunciations, he knew, spring from a determination not to acknowledge that the age and its crisis arise from the speaker's own unwillingness to respond to it. The crisis, insofar as there is one, is the obsession with crisis itself that turns aside from the possibility of action. The last form that the crisis assumes is an endless discussion of crisis. By action, in contrast, the preoccupation is broken, the perspective is enlarged to include the enlargement of the heart by which remediative grace streams into existence. Ultimately the reason the perspective of the participant provides deeper access to the reality of history is that it actually enlarges the reality from the frozen specimen that analysis has snatched from it. The metaphor of the game only imperfectly captures the situation, for the game is played repetitively within its assigned boundaries, while history carries within it the inexhaustible novelty that is the birth of the person itself. At this point metaphors fail us, for although persons are just what are needed if the game is to be played, each one represents the irreducible possibility of a new game. History is borne by persons because in every moment they exceed all of history. Modernity is itself only one such moment, and the possibility of knowing it lies in the presence of persons who have already gone beyond it. Existence has in every instance already overflowed the historical and social boundaries ostensibly assigned to contain it.

But how, then, are we to orient ourselves within existence if there are no fixed parameters? Is it not necessary to have at least a provisional account of modernity in order to exist within it? Here the crucial qualification is "provisional," for the philosophical revolution we have traversed has dissolved the fixities by which we used to stabilize the world in which we find ourselves. The result can be as bewildering as the philosophical formulations themselves. The prioritizing of practical reason we have recounted has yet to be unfolded in terms of its theoretical consequences. We are moving from the comfortable framework provided by a history of ideas approach to the more fluid conception of ideas as the interior dimensions of our own lives. Rather than comprehending history, we live within it. The breakdown of historical narratives that has been a theme since the eighteenth century and now seems to have been accomplished is not simply a function of the overwhelming empirical expansion. That is certainly a factor, as is the disappearance of any historical center of meaning from which a narrative might be constructed. Yet it would be a distortion to stress such negatives too heavily. We have seen that the lifting of the weight of historical distance has also meant the contemporaneity of all events in which persons are mutually present to one another. On reflection, we realize that it has always been the priority of persons over history that has constituted the very possibility of history. How is it possible, Kierkegaard asked, that an event eighteen hundred years ago can have any relevance to me today? His answer was, of course, that the advent of Christ, as the church has always insisted, was never in the past.

History is always now in the mutuality of persons who overleap the space of all narrative distance. This does not mean that the role of narratives must now be discarded, but that they must undergo an adjustment in light of the provisionality that must attach to them in the mutuality of persons whose inwardness ever carries them forward.

Even the value of historical explanations must come under revision once we have acknowledged that there is no such thing as "the age" that stands in need of an explanation. If the response we are called upon to make must always take precedence over any historical account, the strictly secondary nature of all explanations robs them of all reductive force. Persons are the irreducibles of history, always more than the sum total of factors that have gone into their composition. Chronology itself must be displaced once we acknowledge that it is persons who constitute the meaning of their existence by ever going beyond their accumulated background. The mutuality of meeting, the presence and nonpresence of persons, which makes historical conversation possible, upends all fixity of explanation by means of linear position. But this does not mean that no explanation is possible. It is only that no unidirectional account exhausts the meaning. Narratives, as Eric Voegelin eventually concluded in *Order and History*, although he never fully elaborated, must move backward and sideways as well as before and after, if we are to move within the richness in which we find ourselves. To understand the present in terms of the past, as the famous thesis on the Gnostic character of modernity suggests, is to follow only one direction. It is equally plausible to understand Gnosticism in relation to the modern evocation of an alternative to it, as precisely the overcoming of the horror of existence that Gnosticism had expressed. In the end, however, no amount of analytic refinement can explain the genesis of human existence in the freedom of persons who daily go beyond what is in their self-enactment and self-disclosure. The mystery forestalls all accounts, not because we have reached the boundary of ineffability, but because no account can finally be given of that within which we live. Unattainability in words is the seal of inwardness from which all accounts in words must flow.

Works Cited

The following sources are for the most part cited in the body of the text rather than in the notes. In general, I have used the available English translations, although I have also occasionally altered them for the sake of consistency of terminology. Where possible, I have identified sources by numbered sections that can be located in both the original and the translation. Sometimes a numbered section is preceded by a roman numeral to indicate the part from which it is taken (e.g., IV, § 3). Where the translations incorporate marginal pagination from the standard editions, I have simply used this as the page reference, although always with the volume number before the page number. For those writers, Levinas and Derrida, for whom no collected works yet exist, it has been necessary to cite both the original edition and the translation in that order. The only exception to this practice of referring either to a standard pagination or to corresponding pages in the original and the translation is in the chapter on Kierkegaard. There I have simply referenced the pages in the wonderful edition, *Kierkegaard's Writings*, edited by Howard and Edna Hong. It includes both the standard pagination of the first edition of Kierkegaard's *Samlede Værker* and collations to subsequent editions, as well as supplementary material from his papers and journals relevant to each volume.

Derrida

Acts of Religion. Edited and with an introduction by Gil Anidjar. New York: Routledge, 2002.

Adieu à Emmanuel Lévinas. Paris: Galilée, 1997.

Adieu to Emmanuel Levinas. Translated by Pascale-Anne Brault and Michael Naas. Stanford, CA: Stanford University Press, 1999.

Aporias: Dying – Awaiting (One Another at) the "Limits of Truth." Translated by Thomas Dutoit. Stanford, CA: Stanford University Press, 1993.

Apories. Paris: Galilée, 1996.

"Circonfession." In *Jacques Derrida.* By Jacques Derrida and Geoffrey Bennington. Paris: Seuil, 1991.

"Circumfession." In *Jacques Derrida.* Translated by Geoffrey Bennington. Chicago: University of Chicago Press, 1993.

De la grammatologie. Paris: Minuit, 1967.

De l'esprit. Heidegger et la question. Paris: Galilée, 1987.

Derrida and Negative Theology. Edited by Harold Coward and Toby Foshay. Albany: State University of New York Press, 1992.

Dissemination. Translated by Barbara Johnson. Chicago: University of Chicago Press, 1982.

La dissemination. Paris: Seuil, 1972.

Donner la mort. In L'éthique du don. Jacques Derrida et la pensée du don. Colloque de Royaumont: Métaillé, 1992.

Donner le temps. I. La fausse monnaie. Paris: Galilée, 1991.

D'un tone apocalyptique adopté naguère en philosophie. Paris: Galilée, 1983.

L'écriture et la différence. Paris: Seuil, 1967.

Éperons. Les style de Nietzsche. Paris: Champs-Flammarion, 1978.

Force de loi. Paris: Galilée, 1994.

The Gift of Death. Translated by David Wills. Chicago: University of Chicago Press, 1995.

Given Time: I. Counterfeit Money. Translated by Peggy Kamuf. Chicago: University of Chicago Press, 1992.

Glas. Paris: Galilée. 1974.

Glas. Translated by John P. Leavey, Jr., and Richard Rand. Lincoln: University of Nebraska Press, 1986.

"How to Avoid Speaking: Denials." Translated by Ken Frieden. In *Languages of the Unsayable: The Play of Negativity in Literature and Literary Theory.* Edited by Sanford Budick and Wofgang Iser. New York: Columbia University Press, 1989.

Marges de la philosophie. Paris: Minuit, 1972.

Margins of Philosophy. Translated by Alan Bass. Chicago: University of Chicago Press, 1982.

Of Grammatology. Translated by Gayatri Spivak. Baltimore, MD: Johns Hopkins University Press, 1978.

Of Spirit: Heidegger and the Question. Translated by Geoffrey Bennington and Rachael Bowlby. Chicago: University of Chicago Press, 1989.

On Cosmopolitanism and Forgiveness. Translated by Mark Dooley and Michael Hughes. New York: Routledge, 2001.

On the Name. Edited by Thomas Dutoit. Stanford, CA: Stanford University Press, 1995.

Politics of Friendship. Translated by George Collins. New York: Verso, 1997.

Politiques de l'amitié. Paris: Galilée, 1994.

Positions. Paris: Minuit, 1972.

Positions. Translated by Alan Bass. Chicago: University of Chicago Press, 1984.

Raising the Tone of Philosophy: Late Essays by Immanuel Kant, Transformative Critique by Jacques Derrida. Edited by Peter Fenves. Baltimore, MD: Johns Hopkins University Press, 1993.

Sauf le nom. Paris: Galilée, 1993.

Specters of Marx: The State of the Debt, the Work of Mourning, and the New International. Translated by Peggy Kamuf. London: Routledge, 1994.

Spectres de Marx. L'état de la dette, le travail du deuil, et la nouvelle Internationale. Paris: Galilée, 1993.

Speech and Phenomena. Translated by David Allison. Evanston, IL: Northwestern University Press, 1973.

Spurs: Of Nietzsche's Styles. Bilingual edition, translated by Barbara Harlow. Chicago: University of Chicago Press, 1979.

La voix et le phénomène. Introduction au problème du signe dans la phénoménologie de Husserl. Paris: PUF, 1967.

Writing and Difference. Translated by Alan Bass. London: Routledge, 1978.

Hegel

Early Theological Writings. Translated by T. M. Knox. Philadelphia: University of Pennsylvania Press, 1971.

Encyclopedia of the Philosophical Sciences, pt. I: *Logic*; pt. II: *Philosophy of Nature*; pt. III: *Philosophy of Spirit.* These are cited by their separately published volumes: *Hegel's "Logic."* Translated by William Wallace. Oxford: Oxford University Press, 1975; *Philosophy of Nature.* Translated by A. V. Miller. Oxford: Oxford University Press, 1970; *Philosophy of Mind.* Translated by A. V. Miller. Oxford: Oxford University Press, 1971.

Gesammelte Werke. Kritische Ausgabe. Deutsche Forschungsgemeinschaft und Rheinisch-westfälischen Akademie der Wissenschaften. Hamburg: Meiner, 1968–.

Hegel's "Philosophy of Right." Translated by H. B. Nisbet. Cambridge: Cambridge University Press, 1991.

Hegel's Political Writings. Translated by T. M. Knox. Oxford: Oxford University Press, 1964.

Hegel's "Science of Logic." Translated by A. V. Miller. London: Allen and Unwin, 1969. This is the so-called "Greater Logic."

Hegels theologische Jugendschriften. Edited by Hermann Nohl. Tübingen: Mohr, 1907.

Lectures on the History of Philosophy. 3 vols. Translated by K. S. Haldane and F. H. Simpson. London: Routledge & Kegan Paul, 1955, 1963.

Lectures on the Philosophy of World History: Introduction – Reason in History. Translated by H. B. Nisbet. Cambridge: Cambridge University Press, 1975.

Natural Law. Translated by T. M. Knox. Philadelphia: University of Pennsylvania Press, 1975.

"The Oldest Systematic Programme of German Idealism." In F. Hölderlin, *Sämtliche Werke, Grosse Stuttgarter Ausgabe*, vol. 4, pt. 1. Edited by Richard Samuel et al. Stuttgart: Kohlhammer, 1960, 297–99; also in Frederick Beiser, ed. and trans., *The Early Political Writings of the German Romantics.* Cambridge: Cambridge University Press, 1996, 3–5.

Phenomenology of Spirit. Translated by A. V. Miller. Oxford: Oxford University Press, 1977.

Philosophy of History. Translated by J. Sibree. New York: Dover, 1956.

Sämtliche Werke Jubiläumsausgabe in zwanzig Bänden. Edited by Hermann Glockner. Stuttgart: Frommann, 1961.

Schriften zur Politik und Rechtsphilosophie, 2nd ed. Edited by G. Lasson. Leipzig: Meiner, 1923.

"System of Ethical Life" and "First Philosophy of Spirit." Translated by H. S. Harris and W. Cerf. Albany: State University of New York Press, 1979.

Werke. Werkausgabe. 20 vols. Edited by Eva Moldenhauer and Karl Michael. Frankfurt: Suhrkamp, 1969–72.

Heidegger

Being and Time. Translated by John Macquarrie and Edward Robinson. New York: Harper, 1962.

Contributions to Philosophy (from Enowning). Translated by Parvis Emad and Kenneth Maly. Bloomington: Indiana University Press, 1999.

Discourse on Thinking. Translated by John M. Anderson and E. Hans Freund. New York: Harper, 1966.

The End of Philosophy. Translated by Joan Stambaugh. New York: Harper, 1973.

The Fundamental Concepts of Metaphysics: World, Finitude, Solitude. Translated by William McNeill and Nicholas Walker. Bloomington: Indiana University Press, 1995.

Hegel's Concept of Experience. Translated by J. Glenn Gray. New York: Harper, 1970.

Hegel's "Phenomenology of Spirit." Translated by Parvis Emad and Kenneth Maly. Bloomington: Indiana University Press, 1994.

Hölderlin's Hymn "The Ister." Translated by William McNeill and J. Davis. Bloomington: Indiana University Press, 1996.

Identity and Difference. Translated by Joan Stambaugh. New York: Harper, 1969.

Introduction to Metaphysics. Translated by Ralph Mannheim. New Haven, CT: Yale University Press, 1959.

Kant and the Problem of Metaphysics. Translated by Richard Taft. Bloomington: Indiana University Press, 1997.

Martin Heidegger: Gesamtausgabe. Frankfurt: Klostermann, 1974–.

Martin Heidegger and National Socialism: Questions and Answers. Edited by Gunther Neske and Emil Kettering. Translated by Lisa Harries. New York: Paragon, 1990. Contains "The Self Assertion of the German University" (rectoral address), "The Rectorate 1933/34: Facts and Thoughts," "Only a God Can Save Us" (the *Spiegel* interview), and "Martin Heidegger in Conversation" with Richard Wisser.

Nietzsche I: The Will to Power as Art. Edited and translated by David F. Krell. New York, Harper, 1979.

Nietzsche II: The Eternal Recurrence of the Same. Edited and translated by David F. Krell. New York: Harper, 1984.

Nietzsche III: The Will to Power as Knowledge and Metaphysics. Edited by David F. Krell and translated by Joan Stambaugh. New York: Harper, 1987.

Nietzsche IV: Nihilism. Edited by David F. Krell. Translated by Frank A. Capuzzi. New York: Harper, 1982.

Off the Beaten Track. Translated by Julian Young and Kenneth Hayes. Cambridge: Cambridge University Press, 2002.

On Time and Being. Translated by Joan Stambaugh. New York: Harper, 1972.

On the Way to Language. Translated by Peter D. Hertz. New York: Harper, 1971.

Pathmarks. Translated by William McNeill. Cambridge: Cambridge University Press, 1998.

Phenomenological Interpretation of Kant's "Critique of Pure Reason." Translated by Parvis Emad and Kenneth Maly. Bloomington: Indiana University Press, 1997.

Phenomenological Interpretations of Aristotle. Translated by Richard Rojcewicz. Bloomington: Indiana University Press, 2001.

Poetry, Language, Thought. Translated by Albert Hofstadter. New York: Harper, 1971.

The Principle of Reason. Translated by Reginald Lilly. Bloomington: Indiana University Press, 1991.

The Question of Being. Translated by William Kluback and Tean T. Wilde. New York: Twayne, 1958.

"The Question Concerning Technology," and Other Essays. Translated by William Lovitt. New York: Harper, 1977.

Schelling's Treatise on Human Freedom. Translated by Joan Stambaugh. Athens: Ohio University Press, 1985.

Supplements: From the Earliest Essays to "Being and Time" and Beyond. Edited by John van Buren. Albany: State University of New York Press, 2002.

What Is Called Thinking? Translated by Fred D. Wieck and J. Glenn Gray. New York: Harper, 1968.

What Is a Thing? Translated by W. B. Barton and Vera Deutsch. Chicago: Regnery, 1969.

Kant

Critique of the Power of Judgment. Translated by Paul Guyer and Eric Matthews. Cambridge: Cambridge University Press, 2000.

Critique of Practical Reason. Translated by Mary Gregor. Cambridge: Cambridge University Press, 1997.

Critique of Pure Reason. Translated by Norman Kemp Smith. London: Macmillan, 1933.

"Dreams of a Spirit-Seer" and Other Writings. Edited by Gregory Johnson and translated by Glenn Alexander Magee. West Chester, PA: Swedenborg Foundation, 2002.

Gesammelte Schriften. Ausgabe der königlich preussischen Akademie der Wissenschaften. Berlin: de Gruyter, 1902–.

Groundwork of the Metaphysics of Morals. Translated by Mary Gregor. Cambridge: Cambridge University Press, 1997.

Metaphysics of Morals. Translated by Mary Gregor. Cambridge: Cambridge University Press, 1996.

Political Writings. Edited by Hans Reiss and translated by H. B. Nisbet. New York: Cambridge University Press, 1970.

Practical Philosophy. Translated and edited by Mary Gregor. Introduction by Allen Wood. Cambridge: Cambridge University Press, 1996.

Prolegomena to Any Future Metaphysics That Will Be Able to Come Forward as Science. Translated by Gary Hatfield. Cambridge: Cambridge University Press, 1997.

"Religion Within the Boundaries of Mere Reason" and Other Writings. Translated by Allen Wood and George di Giovanni. Cambridge: Cambridge University Press, 1998.

Kierkegaard

Samlede Værker. Edited by A. B. Drachman, J. L. Heiberg, and H. O. Lange. Copenhagen: Gylendals, 1901–6. This is the edition from which the marginal pagination of all later editions is derived.

Søren Kierkegaars Skrifter, 4th ed. Edited by N. J. Cappelørn et al. Copenhagen: Gads, 1997–.

The following volumes are from *Kierkegaard's Writings,* under the general editorship of Howard and Edna Hong, published by Princeton University Press.

II: *The Concept of Irony, with Continual Reference to Socrates / Notes of Schelling's Berlin Lectures.* Edited and translated by Howard V. Hong and Edna H. Hong. 1992.

III: *Either/Or: Part I.* Edited and translated by Howard V. Hong and Edna H. Hong. 1988.

IV: *Either/Or: Part II.* Edited and translated by Howard V. Hong and Edna H. Hong. 1988.

V: *Eighteen Upbuilding Discourses.* Edited and translated by Howard V. Hong and Edna H. Hong. 1992.

VI: *Fear and Trembling / Repetition.* Edited and translated by Howard V. Hong and Edna H. Hong. 1983.

VII: *Philosophical Fragments, or a Fragment of Philosophy / Johannes Climacus, or De omnibus disputandum est: A Narrative.* Edited and translated by Edna H. Hong and Howard V. Hong. 1985.

VIII: *The Concept of Anxiety: A Simple Psychologically Orienting Deliberation on the Dogmatic Issue of Hereditary Sin.* Edited and translated by Reidar Thomte. 1981.

IX: *Prefaces: Writing Sampler.* Edited and translated, with an introduction and notes, by Todd W. Nichols. 1998.

XI: *Stages on Life's Way.* Edited and translated by Howard V. Hong and Edna H. Hong. 1988.

XII: *Concluding Unscientific Postscript to Philosophical Fragments,* vol. 1. Edited and translated by Howard V. Hong and Edna H. Hong. 1992.

XIII: *Concluding Unscientific Postscript to Philosophical Fragments,* vol. 2. Edited and translated by Howard V. Hong and Edna H. Hong. 1992.

XIV: *Two Ages: The Age of Revolution and the Present Age – A Literary Review.* Edited and translated by Edna H. Hong and Howard V. Hong. 1978.

XV: *Upbuilding Discourses in Various Spirits.* Edited and translated by Howard V. Hong and Edna H. Hong. 1993.

XVI: *Works of Love: Some Christian Deliberations in the Form of Discourses.* Edited and translated by Howard V. Hong and Edna H. Hong. 1998.

XIX: *The Sickness unto Death: A Christian Psychological Exposition for Upbuilding and Awakening.* Edited and translated by Edna H. Hong and Howard V. Hong. 1983.

XX: *Practice in Christianity.* Edited and translated by Howard V. Hong and Edna H. Hong. 1991.

XXI: *For Self-Examination / Judge For Yourself!* Edited and translated by Howard V. Hong and Edna H. Hong. 1991.

XXII: *The Point of View.* Edited and translated by Howard V. Hong and Edna H. Hong. 1998.

XXIV: *The Book on Adler.* Edited and translated by Howard V. Hong and Edna H. Hong. 1998.

Levinas

Autrement qu'être ou au-delà de l'essence. The Hague: Nijhoff, 1974.

Beyond the Verse: Talmudic Readings and Lectures. Translated by Gary D. Mole. London: Athlone Press, 1982.

Collected Philosophical Papers. Translated by Alphonso Lingis. Pittsburgh: Duquesne University Press, 1998.

De Dieu qui vient à l'idée, 2nd ed. Paris: Vrin, 1986.

De l'existence à l'existant, 2nd ed. Paris: Vrin, 1978.

Dieu, la mort et le temps. Paris: L'Herne, 1991.

Difficile liberté. Essais sur le judaïsme, 3rd ed. Paris: Michel, 1984.

Difficult Freedom: Essays on Judaism (1963–76). Translated by Seán Hand. Baltimore, MD: Johns Hopkins University Press, 1990.

Ethics and Infinity: Conversations with Philippe Nemo. Translated by Richard A. Cohen. Pittsburgh: Duquesne University Press, 1985.

Existence and Existents. Translated by Alphonso Lingis. Pittsburgh: Duquesne University Press, 2001.

God, Death, and Time. Translated by Bettina Bergo. Stanford, CA: Stanford University Press, 2000.

The Levinas Reader. Edited by Seán Hand. Oxford: Blackwell, 1989.

Of God Who Comes to Mind. Translated by Bettina Bergo. Stanford, CA: Stanford University Press, 1998.

Otherwise Than Being or Beyond Essence. Translated by Alphonso Lingis. The Hague: Nijhoff, 1981.

Le temps et l'autre. Paris: Quadrige/PUF, 2001.

Time and the Other. Translated by Richard Cohen. Pittsburgh: Duquesne University Press, 1987.

Totalité et Infini. Essai sur l'extériorité, 4th ed. The Hague: Nijhof, 1971.

Totality and Infinity. Translated by Alphonso Lingis. Pittsburgh: Duquesne University Press, 1987.

Nietzsche

The Anti-Christ: A Curse on Christianity. Translated by R. J. Hollingdale. Harmondsworth: Penguin, 1968.

Beyond Good and Evil. Translated by Walter Kaufmann. New York: Random House, 1966.

"The Birth of Tragedy" and Other Writings. Translated by Ronald Speirs. Cambridge: Cambridge University Press, 1999.

The Case of Wagner. Translated by Walter Kaufmann. New York: Random House, 1967.

Daybreak. Translated by R. J. Hollingdale. Cambridge: Cambridge University Press, 1982.

Ecce Homo. Translated by Walter Kaufmann. New York: Random House, 1969.

Friedrich Nietzsche: Sämtliche Werke, Kritische Studienausgage. Edited by Griorgio Colli and Mazzino Montinari. Berlin: de Gruyter, 1976–77.

The Gay Science. Translated by Josefine Nauckhoff. Cambridge: Cambridge University Press, 2001.

Human, All Too Human: A Book for Free Spirits. Translated by R. J. Hollingdale. Cambridge: Cambridge University Press, 1986.

Nietzsche Contra Wagner. Translated by Walter Kaufmann. In *The Portable Nietzsche.* New York: Viking, 1968.

On the Genealogy of Morals. Translated by Walter Kaufmann. New York: Random House, 1969.

Thus Spoke Zarathustra: A Book for None and All. Translated by Walter Kaufmann. New York: Penguin, 1978.

The Twilight of the Idols. Translated by R. J. Hollingdale. Harmondsworth: Penguin, 1978.

Untimely Meditations. Translated by R. J. Hollingdale. Cambridge: Cambridge University Press, 1983.

The Will to Power. Translated by Walter Kaufmann and R. J. Hollingdale. New York: Random House, 1968.

Writings from the Late Notebooks. Translated by Kate Sturge. Cambridge: Cambridge University Press, 2003.

Schelling

The Abyss of Freedom: Ages of the World. 1813 draft. Translated by Judith Norman. Ann Arbor: University of Michigan Press, 1997.

Ages of the World. 1815 draft. Translated by Jason Wirth. Albany: State University of New York Press, 2000.

The Ages of the World. 1815 draft. Translated by Frederick de Wolfe Bolman. New York: Columbia University Press, 1942.

Friedrich Wilhelm Joseph von Schellings sämmtliche Werke, pt. I, vols. 1–10; pt. II, vols. 1–4. Edited by Karl Schelling. Stuttgart: Cotta, 1856–61.

The Grounding of Positive Philosophy: The Berlin Lectures. Translated by Bruce Mathews. Albany: State University of New York Press, 2007.

Historical-Critical Introduction to the Philosophy of Mythology. Translated by Mason Richey and Markus Zisselsberger. Albany: State University of New York Press, 2007.

Idealism and the Endgame of Theory: Three Essays by F. W. J. Schelling. Translated by Thomas Pfau. Albany: State University of New York Press, 1966.

On the History of Modern Philosophy. Translated by Andrew Bowie. Cambridge: Cambridge University Press, 1994.

Philosophical Inquiries into the Nature of Human Freedom. Translated by James Gutmann. La Salle, IL: Open Court Press, 1989.

Schelling. *Philosophie der Offenbarung, 1841/42.* Edited by Manfred Frank. Frankfurt: Suhrkamp, 1977. The abbreviated edition of the lectures published by Paulus, without Schelling's permission, in 1843.

"Schelling's Aphorisms of 1805." Translated by Fritz Marti. *Idealistic Studies* 14 (1984): 237–56.

Schelling's Philosophy of Mythology and Revelation. Three of seven books translated and reduced by Victor C. Hayes. Armidale: Australian Association for the Study of Religions, 1995.

Schellings Werke: Nach der Originalausgabe in neuer Anordnung. Edited by Manfred Schröter. Munich: Beck, 1927–59.

System of Transcendental Idealism. Translated by Peter Heath. Charlottesville: University of Virginia Press, 1978.

Select Bibliography of Secondary Sources

The secondary literature on the thinkers covered in this study is so extensive that few bibliographies can claim to have done justice to the subject. Yet an author does owe a particular debt to those whose work has been instrumental in the formation of his own understanding. That obligation is here partially discharged in a list of secondary sources as they appear in the notes.

Allison, David, ed. *The New Nietzsche*. Cambridge, MA: MIT Press, 1985.

Allison, Henry. *Kant's Theory of Freedom*. Cambridge: Cambridge University Press, 1990.

    Kant's Transcendental Idealism, rev. ed. New Haven, CT: Yale University Press, 2004.

Ameriks, Karl. *Kant and the Fate of Autonomy: Problems in the Appropriation of the Critical Philosophy*. Cambridge: Cambridge University Press, 2000.

    ed. *The Cambridge Companion to German Idealism*. Cambridge: Cambridge University Press, 2000.

Arendt, Hannah. *The Origins of Totalitarianism*, new ed. New York: Harcourt Brace Jovanovich, 1973.

Arendt, Hannah, and Martin Heidegger. *Letters: 1925–75*. Edited by Ursula Ludz and translated by Andrew Shields. New York: Harcourt, 2004.

Avineri, Shlomo. *Hegel's Theory of the Modern State*. Cambridge: Cambridge University Press, 1972.

Bakhtin, Mikhail. *Problems of Dostoevsky's Poetics*. Translated by R. W. Rotsel. Ann Arbor, MI: Ardis, 1973.

Balthasar, Hans Urs von. *Die Apokalypse der deutschen Seele*. 3 vols. Salzburg: Pustet, 1937–39.

Barnett, Stuart, ed. *Hegel After Derrida*. London: Routledge, 1998.

Batnitzky, Leora. *Leo Strauss and Emmanuel Levinas: Philosophy and the Politics of Revelation*. Cambridge: Cambridge University Press, 2006.

Bauer, Ferdinand Christian. *Die Christiliche Gnosis*. Tübingen: Osiander, 1835.

Beach, Edward Allen. *The Potencies of God(s): Schelling's Philosophy of Mythology*. Albany: State University of New York Press, 1994.

Beardsworth, Richard. *Derrida and the Political*. London: Routledge, 1996.

Beiser, Frederick. *Enlightenment, Revolution, and Romanticism: The Genesis of Modern German Political Thought 1790–1800.* Cambridge, MA: Harvard University Press, 1992.

　　The Fate of Reason: German Philosophy from Kant to Fichte. Cambridge, MA: Harvard University Press, 1987.

　　German Idealism: The Struggle Against Subjectivism, 1781–1801. Cambridge, MA: Harvard University Press, 2002.

　　ed. *The Cambridge Companion to Hegel.* Cambridge: Cambridge University Press, 1993.

　　ed. and trans. *The Early Political Writings of the German Romantics.* Cambridge: Cambridge University Press, 1996.

Beistegui, Miguel de. *Thinking with Heidegger: Displacements.* Bloomington: Indiana University Press, 2003.

Bergo, Bettina. *Levinas Between Ethics and Politics: For the Beauty That Adorns the Earth.* Dordrecht: Kluwer, 1999.

Berkowitz, Peter. *Nietzsche: The Ethics of an Immoralist.* Cambridge, MA: Harvard University Press, 1995.

Blattner, William D. *Heidegger's Temporal Idealism.* Cambridge: Cambridge University Press, 1999.

Bloechl, Jeffrey. *Liturgy of the Neighbor: Emmanuel Levinas and the Religion of Responsibility.* Pittsburgh: Duquesne University Press, 2000.

Blumenberg, Hans. *The Legitimacy of the Modern Age.* Translated by Robert M. Wallace. Cambridge, MA: MIT Press, 1983.

Bowie, Andrew. *Aesthetics and Subjectivity: From Kant to Nietzsche,* 2nd rev. ed. Manchester: Manchester University Press, 2000.

　　Schelling and Modern European Philosophy. London: Routledge, 1993.

Brown, Robert. *The Later Philosophy of Schelling: The Influence of Böhme on the Works of 1809–15.* Lewisburg, PA: Bucknell University Press, 1977.

Budick, Sanford, and Wolfgang Iser, eds. *Languages of the Unsayable: The Play of Negativity in Literature and Literary Theory.* New York: Columbia University Press, 1989.

Burns, Gerald L. *Heidegger's Estrangements: Language, Truth, and Poetry in the Later Writings.* New Haven, CT: Yale University Press, 1989.

Caputo, John. *The Mystical Element in Heidegger's Thought.* Athens: Ohio University Press, 1978.

　　The Prayers and Tears of Jacques Derrida: Religion without Religion. Bloomington: University of Indiana Press, 1997.

Caputo, John, and Michael Scanlon, eds. *Augustine and Post-Modernism: "Confessions" and "Circumfession."* Bloomington: Indiana University Press, 2005.

Carlson, Thomas. *Indiscretion: Finitude and the Naming of God.* Chicago: University of Chicago Press, 1999.

Caygill, Howard. *Levinas and the Political.* London: Routledge, 2002.

Chalier, Catherine. *What Ought I to Do? Morality in Kant and Levinas.* Translated by Jane Marie Todd. Ithaca, NY: Cornell University Press, 2002.

Cohen, Richard A. *Ethics, Exegesis and Philosophy: Interpretation after Levinas.* Cambridge: Cambridge University Press, 2001.

Cooper, Barry. *The End of History: An Essay on Modern Hegelianism.* Toronto: University of Toronto Press, 1984.

Corey, Paul. "Speaking Immorality through the Mouth of a Moralist: The Irony of Nietzsche's *Zarathustra.*" Paper delivered at the American Political Science Association annual meeting, 2006.

Critchley, Simon. *The Ethics of Deconstruction: Derrida and Levinas,* 2nd ed. West Lafayette, IN: Purdue University Press, 1999.

Critchley, Simon, and Robert Bernasconi, eds. *The Cambridge Companion to Levinas.* Cambridge: Cambridge University Press, 2002.

Dahlstrom, Daniel. *Heidegger's Concept of Truth.* Cambridge: Cambridge University Press, 2001.

Dallmayr, Fred. *The Other Heidegger.* Ithaca, NY: Cornell University Press, 1993.

Davenport, John, and Anthony Rudd. *Kierkegaard After MacIntyre.* Chicago: Open Court, 2001.

Day, Jerry. *Voegelin, Schelling, and the Philosophy of Historical Existence.* Columbia: University of Missouri Press, 2003.

Denis, Lara. *Moral Self-Regard: Duties to Oneself in Kant's Moral Theory.* New York: Routledge, 2001.

Desmond, William. *Hegel's God: A Counterfeit Double.* Aldershot: Ashgate, 2003.

Dickey, Laurence. *Religion, Economics, and the Politics of Spirit, 1770–1807.* Cambridge: Cambridge University Press, 1987.

Dostoevsky, Fyodor. *Brothers Karamazov.* Translated by Constance Garnett. New York: Modern Library, 1950.

Dreyfus, Hubert, and Harrison Hall, eds. *Heidegger: A Critical Reader.* Oxford: Blackwell, 1992.

Dudley, Will. *Hegel, Nietzsche, and Philosophy: Thinking Freedom.* Cambridge: Cambridge University Press, 2002.

Dupré, Louis. *Passage to Modernity.* New Haven, CT: Yale University Press, 1993.

Evans, C. Stephen. *Kierkegaard's Ethics of Love: Divine Commands and Moral Obligations.* Oxford: Oxford University Press, 2004.

Farias, Victor. *Heidegger and Nazism.* Translated by Paul Burel and Gabriel R. Ricci. Philadelphia: Temple University Press, 1989.

Ferreira, M. Jamie. *Transforming Vision: Imagination and Will in Kierkegaardian Faith.* Oxford: Clarendon, 1991.

Fichte, Johann G. *Foundations of Natural Right.* Edited by Frederick Neuhouser and translated by Michael Bauer. Cambridge: Cambridge University Press, 2000; original, 1796–97.

Flikschuh, Katrin. *Kant and Modern Political Philosophy.* Cambridge: Cambridge University Press, 2000.

Frank, Manfred. *Eine Einführung in Schellings Philosophie.* Frankfurt: Suhrkamp, 1985.

What Is Neostructuralism? Translated by Sabine Wilke and Richard Gray. Minneapolis: University of Minnesota Press, 1989; original, 1983.

Fraser, Giles. *Redeeming Nietzsche: On the Piety of Unbelief.* London: Routledge, 2002.

Fried, Gregory. *Heidegger's Polemos: From Being to Politics.* New Haven, CT: Yale University Press, 2000.

Furtak, Rick Anthony. *Wisdom in Love: Kierkegaard and the Ancient Quest for Emotional Integrity*. Notre Dame, IN: University of Notre Dame Press, 2005.

Garff, Joakim. *Søren Kierkegaard: A Biography*. Translated by Bruce H. Kirmmse. Princeton, NJ: Princeton University Press, 2005.

Giles, James. *Kierkegaard and Freedom*. New York: Palgrave, 2000.

Gillespic, Michael. *Hegel, Heidegger, and the Ground of History*. Chicago: University of Chicago Press, 1984.

    Nihilism Before Nietzsche. Chicago: University of Chicago Press, 1995.

Gouwens, David J. *Kierkegaard as Religious Thinker*. Cambridge: Cambridge University Press, 1996.

Green, Ronald M. *Kierkegaard and Kant: The Hidden Debt*. Albany: State University of New York Press, 1992.

Guyer, Paul. *Kant and the Claims of Taste*, 2nd ed. Cambridge, MA: Harvard University Press, 1997.

    Kant and the Experience of Freedom. Cambridge: Cambridge University Press, 1993.

    Kant on Freedom, Law, and Happiness. Cambridge: Cambridge University Press, 2000.

    ed. *The Cambridge Companion to Kant and Modern Philosophy*. Cambridge: Cambridge University Press, 2006.

Habermas, Jürgen. *Das Asolute and die Geschichte: von der Zweispältigkeit in Schellings Denken*. Bonn: Bouvier, 1954.

    Post-Metaphysical Thinking. Translated by William Mark Hohengarten. Cambridge, MA: MIT Press, 1996.

Hannay, Alastair. *Kierkegaard: A Biography*. Cambridge: Cambridge University Press, 2001.

Hannay, Alastair, and Gordon D. Marino, eds. *The Cambridge Companion to Kierkegaard*. Cambridge: Cambridge University Press, 1998.

Harris, H. S. *Hegel's Development Toward the Sunlight: 1770–1801*. Oxford: Oxford University Press, 1972.

Hemming, Laurence Paul. *Heidegger's Atheism: The Refusal of a Theological Voice*. Notre Dame, IN: University of Notre Dame Press, 2002.

Hill, R. Kevin. *Nietzsche's Critiques: The Kantian Foundations of His Thought*. Oxford: Clarendon, 2003.

Holgrebe, Wolfram. *Prädikation und Genesis. Metaphysik also Fundamentalheuristik in Ausgang von Schellings 'Die Weltalter.'* Frankfurt: Suhrkamp, 1989.

Holloway, Christina. *Derrida: Deconstruction from Phenomenology to Ethics*. Oxford: Polity, 1998.

Horowitz, Asher, and Gad Horowitz, eds. *Difficult Justice: Commentaries on Levinas and Politics*. Toronto: University of Toronto Press, 2006.

Houlgate, Stephen. *Hegel, Nietzsche and the Criticism of Metaphysics*. Cambridge: Cambridge University Press, 1986.

    ed. *Hegel and the Philosophy of Nature*. Albany: State University of New York Press, 1998.

Howland, Jacob. *Kierkegaard and Socrates: A Study in Philosophy and Faith*. Cambridge: Cambridge University Press, 2006.

Kates, Joshua. *Essential History: Jacques Derrida and the Development of Deconstruction.* Evanston, IL: Northwestern University Press, 2005.

Jennings, Theodore W. *Reading Derrida / Thinking Paul: On Justice.* Stanford, CA: University of Stanford Press, 2006.

Kaufmann, Walter. *Nietzsche: Philosopher, Psychologist, Antichrist.* Princeton, NJ: Princeton University Press, 1974.

Kirmmse, Bruce. *Kierkegaard in Golden Age Denmark.* Bloomington: Indiana University Press, 1990.

Kojève, Alexandre. *Introduction to the Reading of Hegel.* Translated by James H. Nichols. New York: Basic, 1969.

Kolb, David. *The Critique of Pure Modernity: Hegel, Heidegger, and After.* Chicago: University of Chicago Press, 1986.

Kosch, Michelle. *Freedom and Reason in Kant, Schelling, and Kierkegaard.* Oxford: Clarendon, 2006.

Kuehn, Manfred. *Kant: A Biography.* Cambridge: Cambridge University Press, 2001.

Lacan, Jacques. *Écrits.* Paris: Seuil, 1971.

Lafont, Cristina. *Heidegger, Language, and World-Disclosure.* Translated by Graham Harman. Cambridge: Cambridge University Press, 2000.

Lampert, Laurence. *Nietzsche's Teaching: An Interpretation of "Thus Spoke Zarathustra."* New Haven, CT: Yale University Press, 1986.

Lauer, Quentin. *Hegel's Concept of God.* Albany: State University of New York Press, 1982.

Law, David R. *Kierkegaard as Negative Theologian.* Oxford: Clarendon, 1993.

Lawrence, Joseph P. "Schelling as Post-Hegelian and as Aristotelian," *International Philosophical Quarterly* 26 (1986): 315–30.

Leavey, John, and Gregory Ulmer. *Glassary.* Lincoln: University of Nebraska Press, 1986.

Lewis, Michael. *Heidegger and the Place of Ethics.* London: Continuum, 2005.

Lippitt, John. *Kierkegaard and "Fear and Trembling."* London: Routledge, 2003.

Llewelyn, John. *Emmanuel Levinas: The Genealogy of Ethics.* London: Routledge. 1995.

Löwith, Karl. *From Hegel to Nietzsche.* Translated by David Green. New York: Doubleday, 1967; German original, 1941.

MacIntyre, Alasdair. *After Virtue.* Notre Dame, IN: University of Notre Dame Press, 1984.

Magee, Glenn Alexander. *Hegel and the Hermetic Tradition.* Ithaca, NY: Cornell University Press, 2001.

Magnus, Bernd. *Nietzsche's Existential Imperative.* Bloomington: Indiana University Press, 1978.

Magnus, Bernd, and Kathleen M. Higgins, eds. *The Cambridge Companion to Nietzsche.* Cambridge: Cambridge University Press, 1996.

Malik, Habib C. *Receiving Søren Kierkegaard: The Early Impact and Transmission of His Thought.* Washington, D.C.: Catholic University of America Press, 1997.

Malka, Salamon. *Emmanuel Levinas: His Life and Legacy.* Translated by Michael Kiegel and Sonja M. Embree. Pittsburgh: Duquesne University Press, 2006.

Marion, Jean-Luc. *Being Given: Toward a Phenomenology of Givenness*. Translated by Jeffrey L. Kosky. Stanford, CA: Stanford University Press, 2002.

God Without Being. Translated by Thomas A. Carlson. Chicago: University Press, 1991; original, 1982.

Marrati, Paola. *Genesis and Trace: Derrida Reading Husserl and Heidegger*. Stanford, CA: Stanford University Press, 2005.

Matušík, Martin J., and Merold Westphal, eds. *Kierkegaard in Post/Modernity*. Bloomington: Indiana University Press, 1995.

May, Simon. *Nietzsche's Ethics and His War on "Morality."* Oxford: Clarendon, 1999.

McNeill, William. *The Time of Life: Heidegger and Ēthos*. Albany: State University of New York Press, 2006.

Milbank, John. *Being Reconciled: Ontology and Pardon*. London: Routledge, 2003.

Mouffe, Chantal, ed. *Deconstruction and Pragmatism*. London: Routledge, 1996.

Moyn, Samuel. *Origins of the Other: Emmanuel Levinas Between Revelation and Ethics*. Ithaca, NY: Cornell University Press, 2005.

Mulholland, Leslie. *Kant's System of Rights*. New York: Columbia University Press, 1990.

Naas, Michael. *Taking on the Tradition: Jacques Derrida and the Legacies of Deconstruction*. Stanford, CA: Stanford University Press, 2003.

New, Melvyn, ed., with Robert Bernasconi and Richard A. Cohen. *In Proximity: Emmanuel Levinas and the Eighteenth Century*. Lubbock: Texas Tech University Press, 2001.

Norman, Judith, and Alistair Welchman, eds. *The New Schelling*. London: Continuum, 2004.

Oakeshott, Michael. *"Rationalism in Politics" and Other Essays*, expanded ed. Indianapolis, IN: Liberty Fund, 1991.

Okrent, Mark. *Heidegger's Pragmatism: Understanding, Being, and the Critique of Metaphysics*. Ithaca, NY: Cornell University Press 1988.

O'Meara, Thomas. *Romantic Idealism and Roman Catholicism: Schelling and the Theologians*. Notre Dame, IN: University of Notre Dame Press, 1982.

O'Regan, Cyril. *Gnostic Return in Modernity*. Albany: State University of New York Press, 2001.

The Heterodox Hegel. Albany: State University of New York Press, 1994.

Ott, Hugo. *Martin Heidegger: A Political Life*. Translated by Allan Blunden. New York: Basic, 1994.

Pattison, George. *Kierkegaard's Upbuilding Discourses: Philosophy, Literature and Theology*. London: Routledge, 2002.

Pinkard, Terry. *German Philosophy 1760–1860: The Legacy of Idealism*. Cambridge: Cambridge University Press, 2002.

Hegel: A Biography. Cambridge: Cambridge University Press. 2000.

Pippin, Robert. *Hegel's Idealism: The Satisfactions of Self-Consciousness*. Cambridge: Cambridge University Press, 1989.

The Persistence of Subjectivity: On the Kantian Aftermath. Cambridge: Cambridge University Press, 2005.

Polt, Richard. *The Emergency of Being: On Heidegger's* "Contributions to Philosophy." Ithaca, NY: Cornell University Press, 2006.

Poole, Roger. *Kierkegaard: The Indirect Communication.* Charlottesville: University of Virginia Press, 1993.

Putnam, Hilary. *Realism and Reason: Philosophical Papers*, vol. 3. Cambridge: Cambridge University Press, 1983.

Rae, Murray A. *Kierkegaard's Vision of the Incarnation.* Oxford: Clarendon, 1997.

Rawls, John. "Kantian Constructivism in Moral Theory," *Collected Papers.* Edited by Samuel Freeman. Cambridge, MA: Harvard University Press, 1999, 303–58.

A Theory of Justice. Cambridge, MA: Harvard University Press, 1971.

Reginster, Bernard. *The Affirmation of Life: Nietzsche on Overcoming Nihilism.* Cambridge, MA: Harvard University Press, 2006.

Richardson, John. *Nietzsche's New Darwinism.* Oxford: Oxford University Press, 2004.

Nietzsche's System. Oxford: Oxford University Press, 1996.

Risser, James, ed. *Heidegger Toward the Turn: Essays on the Work of the 1930s.* Albany: State University of New York Press, 1999.

Rojcewicz, Richard. *The Gods and Technology: A Reading of Heidegger.* Albany: State University of New York Press, 2006.

Rudd, Anthony. *Kierkegaard and the Limits of the Ethical.* Oxford: Clarendon, 1993.

Safranski, Rüdiger. *Martin Heidegger: Between Good and Evil.* Translated by Ewald Osers. Cambridge, MA: Harvard University Press, 1998.

Nietzsche: A Philosophical Biography. Translated by Shelley Frisch. New York: Norton, 2002.

Schalow, Frank. *Heidegger and the Quest for the Sacred: From Thought to the Sanctuary of Faith.* Dordrecht: Kluwer, 2001.

Schneewind, Jerome. *The Invention of Autonomy: A History of Modern Moral Philosophy.* Cambridge: Cambridge University Press, 1998.

Schulz, Walter. *Die Vollendung des deutschen Idealismus in der Spätphilosophie Schellings.* Neske: Pfullingen, 1975.

Schürmann, Reiner. *Heidegger on Being and Acting: From Principles to Anarchy.* Translated by Christine-Marie Gros. Bloomington: Indiana University Press, 1987.

Scott, Charles E., et al., eds. *Companion to Heidegger's "Contributions of Philosophy."* Bloomington: Indiana University Press, 2001.

Sherman, Nancy. *Making a Necessity of Virtue: Aristotle and Kant on Virtue.* Cambridge: Cambridge University Press, 1997.

Sikka, Sonya. *Forms of Transcendence: Heidegger and Medieval Mystical Theology.* Albany: State University of New York Press, 1997.

Small, Robin. *Nietzsche and Rée: A Star Friendship.* Oxford: Clarendon, 2005.

Smith, Steven. *Hegel's Critique of Liberalism: Rights in Context.* Chicago: University of Chicago Press, 1989.

Snow, Dale E. *Schelling and the End of Idealism.* Albany: State University of New York Press, 1996.

Solomon, Robert, ed. *Nietzsche: A Collection of Critical Essays.* Notre Dame, IN: University of Notre Dame Press, 1980.

Starobinski, Jean. *Jean-Jacques Rousseau: Transparency and Obstruction.* Translated by Arthur Goldhammer. Chicago: University of Chicago Press, 1988.

Stenstad, Gail. *Transformations: Thinking After Heidegger.* Madison: University of Wisconsin Press, 2006.

Stewart, Jon. *Kierkegaard's Relation to Hegel Reconsidered.* Cambridge: Cambridge University Press, 2003.

Strong, Tracy. *Friedrich Nietzsche and the Politics of Transfiguration.* Berkeley: University of California Press, 1978.

Taylor, Charles. *Hegel.* Cambridge: Cambridge University Press, 1975.

Taylor, Mark C. *Kierkegaard's Pseudonymous Authorship: A Study of Time and the Self.* Princeton, NJ: Princeton University Press, 1975.

Thomas, Michael. *The Reception of Derrida: Translation and Transformation.* London: Palgrave, 2006.

Thomson, Alex. *Deconstruction and Democracy.* London: Continuum, 2005.

Thomson, Iain D. *Heidegger on Ontotheology: Technology and the Politics of Education.* Cambridge: Cambridge University Press, 2005.

Tillich, Paul. *The Construction of the History of Religion in Schelling's Positive Philosophy: Its Presuppositions and Principles.* Translated by Victor Nuovo. Lewisburg, PA: Bucknell University Press, 1974.

    Mysticism and Guilt Consciousness in Schelling's Philosophical Development. Translated by Victor Nuovo. Lewisburg, PA: Bucknell University Press, 1974.

Tilliette, Xavier. *Schelling. Une philosophie en devenir.* 2 vols. Paris: Vrin, 1970.

Timmons, Mark, ed. *Kant's Metaphysics of Morals: Interpretative Essays.* Oxford: Oxford University Press, 2002.

Tocqueville, Alexis de. *Democracy in America.* 2 vols. Translated by Henry Reeve. New York: Vintage, 1956–58.

Velkley, Richard. *Being After Rousseau: Philosophy and Culture in Question.* Chicago: University of Chicago Press, 2002.

    Freedom and the End of Reason: On the Moral Foundations of Kant's Critical Philosophy. Chicago: University of Chicago Press, 1989.

Viksker, Ruki. *The Inhuman Condition: Looking for Difference after Levinas and Heidegger.* Dordrecht: Kluwer, 2004.

Villa, Dana. *Arendt and Heidegger: The Fate of the Political.* Princeton, NJ: Princeton University Press, 1995.

Voegelin, Eric. *History of Political Ideas,* vol. 5: *Religion and the Rise of Modernity.* In *Collected Works,* vol. 23. Edited by James Wiser. Columbia: University of Missouri Press, 1998.

    The New Order and Last Orientation. In *Collected Works,* vol. 25. Edited by Jürgen Gebhardt and Thomas Hollweck. Columbia: University of Missouri Press, 1999.

    "*The New Science of Politics*" and "*Science, Politics, and Gnosticism,*" both in *Modernity Without Restraint.* In *Collected Works,* vol. 5. Edited by Manfred Henningsen. Columbia: University of Missouri Press, 2000.

    "Nietzsche and Pascal," *History of Political Ideas,* vol. 7: *The New Order and Last Orientation.* In *Collected Works,* vol. 25. Edited by Jürgen Gebhardt and Thomas Hollweck. Columbia: University of Missouri Press, 1999, 251–303.

    "On Hegel: A Study in Sorcery," *Published Essays.* In *Collected Works,* vol. 12. Edited by Ellis Sandoz. Baton Rouge: Louisiana State University Press, 1990, 213–55.

    "On the Theory of Consciousness," *Anamnesis.* In *Collected Works,* vol. 6. Translated by G. Niemeyer and M. J. Hanak. Edited by David Walsh. Columbia: University of Missouri Press, 2002.

Order and History, vol. 3: *Plato and Aristotle*. In *Collected Works*, vol. 16. Edited by Dante Germino. Columbia: University of Missouri Press, 2000.

"Quod Deus Dicitur," *Published Essays*: 1966–1985. In *Collected Works*, vol. 12. Edited by Ellis Sandoz. Baton Rouge: Louisiana State University Press, 1990, 376–94.

Walsh, David. *After Ideology: Recovering the Spiritual Foundations of Freedom*. San Francisco: Harper San Francisco, 1990.

"The Ambiguity of the Hegelian End of History." In *After History? Francis Fukuyama and His Critics*. Edited by Timothy Burns. Lanham, MD: Rowman and Littlefield, 1994, 171–96.

The Growth of the Liberal Soul. Columbia: University of Missouri Press, 1997.

"The Historical Dialectic of Spirit: Jacob Boehme's Influence on Hegel." In *History and System: Hegel's Philosophy of History*. Edited by Robert Perkins. Albany: State University of New York Press, 1984, 15–35.

The Mysticism of Innerworldly Fulfillment: A Study of Jacob Boehme. Gainesville: University Presses of Florida, 1983.

Wheeler, Samuel C. *Deconstruction as Analytic Philosophy*. Stanford, CA: Stanford University Press, 2000.

White, Alan. *Schelling: An Introduction to the System of Freedom*. New Haven, CT: Yale University Press, 1983.

Williams, Robert R. *Hegel's Ethics of Recognition*. Berkeley: University of California Press, 1997.

Wirth, Jason. *The Conspiracy of Life: Meditations on Schelling and His Time*. Albany: State University of New York Press, 2003.

ed. *Schelling Now: Contemporary Readings*. Bloomington: Indiana University Press, 2005.

Wolin, Richard. *Martin Heidegger and European Nihilism*. New York: Columbia University Press, 1995.

The Politics of Being: The Political Thought of Martin Heidegger. New York: Columbia University Press, 1990.

Wood, Allen. *Kant's Ethical Thought*. Cambridge: Cambridge University Press, 1999.

Kant's Moral Religion. Ithaca, NY: Cornell University Press, 1970.

Wood, David. *Thinking After Heidegger*. Cambridge: Polity, 2002.

ed. *Derrida: A Critical Reader*. Oxford: Blackwell, 1992.

Of Derrida, Heidegger, and Spirit. Evanston, IL: Northwestern University Press, 1993.

Wyschgorod. Edith. *Emmanuel Levinas: The Problem of Ethical Metaphysics*, 2nd ed. New York: Fordham University Press, 2000; original, 1974.

Young, Julian. *Heidegger's Philosophy of Art*. Cambridge: Cambridge University Press, 2000.

Nietzsche's Philosophy of Art. Cambridge: Cambridge University Press, 1992.

Zantwijk, Temilo van. *Pan-Personalismus. Schellings Hermeneutik der menschlichen Freiheit*. Stuttgart: Frommann-Holzboog, 2000.

Zimmerman, Michael. *Heidegger's Confrontation with Modernity: Technology, Politics, Art*. Bloomington: Indiana University Press, 1990.

Zuckert, Catherine. *Postmodern Platos: Nietzsche, Heidegger, Gadamer, Strauss, Derrida*. Chicago: University of Chicago Press, 1996.

Index